Manual o
of Evi

AUSTRALIA AND NEW ZEALAND
The Law Book Company Ltd.
Sydney : Melbourne : Perth

CANADA AND U.S.A.
The Carswell Company Ltd.
Agincourt, Ontario

INDIA
N. M. Tripathi Private Ltd.
Bombay
and
Eastern Law House Private Ltd.
Calcutta and Delhi
M.P.P. House
Bangalore

ISRAEL
Steimatzky's Agency Ltd.
Jerusalem : Tel Aviv : Haifa

MALAYSIA : SINGAPORE : BRUNEI
Malayan Law Journal (Pte.) Ltd.
Singapore and Kuala Lumpur

PAKISTAN
Pakistan Law House
Karachi

Elliott and Phipson Manual of the Law of Evidence

Twelfth Edition

by

D. W. ELLIOTT, LL.B.
Solicitor,
Professor of Law,
University of Newcastle-upon-Tyne

LONDON
SWEET & MAXWELL
1987

First Edition	(1908)	By S. L. Phipson.
Second Edition	(1914)	,, ,, ,,
Third Edition	(1921)	,, ,, ,,
Fourth Edition	(1928)	,, ,, ,,
Fifth Edition	(1935)	By Sir Roland Burrows, K.C.
Sixth Edition	(1943)	,, ,, ,, ,, ,,
Seventh Edition	(1950)	,, ,, ,, ,, ,,
Eighth Edition	(1959)	By D. W. Elliott.
Second Impression	(1962)	
Ninth Edition	(1966)	By D. W. Elliott.
Tenth Edition	(1972)	,, ,, ,,
Eleventh Edition	(1980)	,, ,, ,,
Second Impression	(1984)	
Twelfth Edition	(1987)	By D. W. Elliott.

Published in 1987 by
Sweet & Maxwell Limited of
11 New Fetter Lane, London.
Computerset by Burgess & Son (Abingdon) Limited.
Printed in Great Britain by
Adlard & Son Ltd. The Garden City Press,
Letchworth, Hertfordshire

British Library Cataloguing in Publication Data
Phipson, Sidney L.
 Elliott and Phipson manual of the law of
 evidence.—12th ed.
 1. Evidence (Law)—England
 I. Title II. Elliott, D.W. III. Phipson,
 Sidney L. Phipson and Elliott manual of
 the law of evidence
 344.207'6 KD7499

ISBN 0-421-33810-5
ISBN 0-421-33820-2 Pbk

All rights reserved.
No part of this publication may be
reproduced or transmitted, in any form
or by any means, electronic, mechanical, photocopying,
recording or otherwise, or stored in any retrieval
system of any nature without the written permission
of the copyright holder and the publisher, application
for which shall be made to the publisher

©
D. W. Elliott
1987

PREFACE

In the seven years since the last edition of this work, undoubtedly the most important event for any statement of the English law of evidence has been the passage into law of the Police and Criminal Evidence Act 1984. This necessitated revision of nearly every chapter of the book and a complete replacement of the chapter on confessions. Moreover judicial development of the subject has in the last few years been as fast moving as ever, so much so that in producing a book on the subject an author can do little more than provide a snapshot of the law as it was at some particular moment of time. The particular moment selected is July 31, 1986, and it is hoped that account has been taken of decisions and statutes appearing since that date. Opportunity has been taken of inserting at proof stage some important cases reported since then, among them *R. v. Hunt* on reverse onuses, *Goddard v. Nationwide Building Society* on professional privilege, *R. v. Spencer* on mandatory warnings on corroboration, *R. v. Cooke* on photofit evidence, and *R. v. Bailey* on *res gestae* statements.

My thanks are due to the publishers for making these last minute changes possible. My thanks also are due to Mrs. Pam Weston for making the whole thing possible, in spite of the author's inability either to type or to write legibly.

February 1987   D. W. Elliott

CONTENTS

	page
Preface	v
Table of Cases	xi
Table of Statutes	xxxix
Table of Rules of the Supreme Court	xlv
References and Abbreviations	xlvi

I PRELIMINARIES

1.	**Introduction**	3
	Nature of the Subject	3
	Arrangement of the Subject	6
	Definitions	8
2.	**Preliminary Matters**	14
	Basic Rules	14
	Functions of Judge and Jury	35

II BURDEN AND STANDARD OF PROOF

3.	**Burden of Proof**	53
	The Different Burdens	53
	Incidence of the Burdens	66
4.	**Standard of Proof**	71
	Criminal Cases	71
	Civil Cases	74
5.	**Presumptions**	77
	Presumptions of Law	78
	Presumptions of Fact	89

III THE TRIAL

6.	**The Course of the Trial**	95
	Hearing in Open Court	95
	Order of Proceedings	97

	Examination of Witnesses	100
	Evidence Given on Appeal	126
7.	**Witnesses**	129
	Competence and Compellability	129
	Public Interest Protection and Privilege	135

IV THE PROTECTION OF THE ACCUSED

8.	**Corroboration**	159
	The Nature of Corroboration	160
	Corroboration Required by Statute	165
	Common Law rules on Corroboration	166
9.	**The Right of Silence**	180
	The Present Position	180
	Proposals for Reform	189
10.	**Confessions**	192
	Admissibility at Common Law	192
	Admissibility under Police and Criminal Evidence Act 1984	195
11.	**Character of the Accused**	204
	Good Character	204
	Bad Character	205

V HEARSAY

12.	**Hearsay**	239
	The Hearsay Rule	239
	Scope of the Rule	242
	Exceptions to the Rule	255
	Principal Classes of Exceptions	256
13.	**Hearsay in Civil Cases**	258
	Exceptions Made by the Act	259
	Common Law Exceptions Preserved by the Act	271
14.	**Hearsay in Criminal Cases**	291

VI THE EFFECT OF PREVIOUS ACTS AND JUDGMENTS

15.	**Estoppel**	307

Contents ix

	Estoppels by Record	310
	Estoppels by Conduct	311
	Estoppels by Agreement	314
	Estoppels by Deed	315
16.	**Judgments**	317
	Res Judicata	317
	Judgments as Evidence	337

VII DOCUMENTARY EVIDENCE

17.	**Documentary Evidence**	343
	Proof of the Execution of Documents	343
	Proof of the Contents of Documents	347
	Extrinsic Evidence in Relation to Documents	351

APPENDICES

1.	Section 1 of the Criminal Evidence Act 1898	367
2.	Civil Evidence Act 1968	369
3.	Police and Criminal Evidence Act 1984, Parts VII and VIII, Schedule 3	390
4.	Extracts from the Code of Practice for the Detention, Treatment and Questioning of Persons by Police Officers	404
5.	Extracts from the Code of Practice for the Identification of Persons by Police Officers	410

Index 417

TABLE OF CASES

A.C.T. Construction Ltd. v. Customs and Excise	38
A.M. & S. Europe Ltd. v. Commission of the European Communities	144
Abbott v. Hendricks	358
—— v. Massie	363
Abrath v. N.E.Ry.	55
Adams, Re	297
—— v. Batley	151
Ahmed v. Brumfitt	107
Air Canada v. Secretary of State for Trade	140, 141
Airey, Re	345
Ajodha v. State	47, 196
Aldersey, Re	86
Alderson v. Clay	353
Alexander v. Rayson	98
Alfred Crompton Amusement Machines Ltd. v. Customs and Excise Commissioners (No. 2)	136
Allen v. Dundas	321, 322
—— v. Pink	354
Allgood v. Blake	360, 361, 362
Alli v. Alli	174, 175
Amalgamated Investment & Property Co. Ltd. v. Texas Commerce International Bank Ltd.	310
Amstrad Consumer Electronics plc v. British Phonograph Industry Ltd.	75
Anderson, ex p.	338
—— v. R.	24
—— v. Weston	346
Armory v. Delamirie	89
Armstrong v. Whitfield	321
Arthurs v. Att.-Gen. for Northern Ireland	168, 176
Asher v. Secretary of State for the Environment	334
Asiatic Petroleum Co. Ltd. v. Anglo-Persian Oil Co. Ltd.	137
Aslin v. Parkin	318
Atherton, Re	153
Atkinson v. U.S.A. Government	331
Att.-Gen. v. Bradlaugh	90
—— v. Briant	143
—— v. Hitchcock	119, 122
—— v. Horner (No. 2)	289
—— v. Lundin	348
—— v. Mulholland	149
Att.-Gen. for South Australia v. Brown	32
Att.-Gen.'s Reference (No. 3 of 1979)	102
—— (No. 4 of 1979)	275
Avon County Council v. Howlett	307
Baden's Deed Trusts, Re	117
Baker v. Campbell	144
Bailey v. Bailey	318, 334
Banbury Peerage	84

xi

Case	Page
Bandon v. Becher	320
Bank of Australasia v. Harding	319
Bank of Hindustan, China and Japan, Re	325
Bank of New Zealand v. Simpson	352
Barker v. Wilson	283
Barrell Enterprises, Re	126
Barry v. Banner	288
Bartlett v. Smith	47
Bastable v. Bastable and Sanders	76
Bate v. Kinsey	148
Battie-Wrightson, Re	348
Bayliss v. Att.-Gen.	362
Beare v. Garrod	118
Beatson v. Skene	137
Beckett v. Nurse	354
Beeches Workingmen's Club v. Scott	325
Beevis v. Dawson	99
Bell v. D.P.P. for Jamaica	334
—— v. Holmes	318
Benyon, Re	87
Berger v. Raymond Sun Ltd.	19
Berkeley Peerage	288
Bernard v. Bernard	324
Berry v. Berry	358
Berryman v. Wise	87
Bessela v. Stern	274
Biche v. Billingham	320
Biddle v. Bond	314
Bigsby v. Dickinson	100
Bills v. Roe	126
Bird v. Adams	275
—— v. Keep	282
Birkett v. James	334
Birtley District Co-operative Society Ltd. v. Windy Nook and District Industrial Co-operative Society	320
Blaise v. Blaise	116
Blewitt v. Tritton	347
Blyth v. Blyth	75, 76, 82
Boston v. Bagshaw	143
Bosvile v. Att.-Gen.	33
Bowker v. Williamson	346
Bowman v. Hodgson	344
—— v. Taylor	315
Boydell v. Drummond	353
Boyes, Re	357
—— v. Cook	360
Boyle v. Wiseman	152
Bracegirdle v. Oxley	36
Bradshaw v. Murphy	153
Bramblevale Ltd., Re	76
Brandao v. Barnett	34
Bratty v. Att.-Gen. for Northern Ireland	53, 64
Bretan v. Cope	349
Brewster v. Sewall	349

Table of Cases

Bridlington Relay Ltd. v. Yorkshire Electricity Board	33
Bright v. Bright	329
Bristol, etc., Co. v. Fiat Motors	356
Bristow v. Sequeville (1850)	22
British Steel Corporation v. Granada T.V.	142
British Thomson-Houston Co. Ltd. v. British Insulated and Helsby Cables Ltd.	281
Brocklebank v. Thompson	289
Brooks Wharf and Bulls Wharf v. Goodman Bros.	58
Brooks & Burtons Ltd. v. Secretary of State for the Environment	309
Brown v. Dean	126
—— v. Dyerson	29
Browne v. Dunn	117
Bruce v. Garden	274
Brunsden v. Humphrey	324
Brunton v. Dullens	363
Buccleuch (Duke) v. Metropolitan Board of Works	144
Buckingham v. Daily News Ltd.	26
Buckland v. Palmer	336
Buckley v. Law Society (No. 2)	139
Bullard v. R.	46, 65
Burnaby v. Baillie	33
Burns v. Lipman	30
Bushel's Case	36
Butler v. Board of Trade	146
Burmah Oil v. Bank of England	140
Burman v. Woods	323
Burnell v. British Transport Commission	148
Burr v. Ware U.D.C.	280
Busby v. Avgherino	56, 57
Butler v. Board of Trade	147, 150
Buttes Gas & Oil Co. v. Hammer (No. 3)	138
C. v. C. and C.	27
Cadney v. Minister of Pensions	75
Cafoor v. Colombo Income Tax Commissioners	323
Calcraft v. Guest	136, 146, 147
Calderbank v. Calderbank	276
Calloway, Re	77
Campbell v. Tameside M.B.C.	136
—— v. Wallsend Slipway	79, 88
Campbell Discount Co. v. Gall	358
Canadian and Dominion Sugar Co. Ltd. v. Canadian National Steamship Ltd.	308
Carl-Zeiss-Stiftung v. Rayner (No. 2)	319, 320, 324, 325, 326, 327
—— v. —— (No. 3)	318, 327
Carmarthen Ry. v. Manchester Ry.	354
Carpenter v. Buller	315
Castanho v. Brown & Root	334
Castle v. Cross	88, 247, 248
Castledon v. Turner	360
Castrique v. Imrie	321, 326
Catherine Maria, The	282
Cattermole v. Miller	252

Central London Property Trust v. High Trees House Ltd. ... 312
Chan Wei Keung v. R. ... 196, 197
Chandrasekera v. R. ... 253
Chantrey Martin & Co. v. Martin ... 149
Chaproniere v. Lambert ... 354
Chard v. Chard ... 79, 85
Charrington v. Wooder ... 352
Charter v. Charter ... 360
Chatterton v. Secretary of State for India ... 136, 137
Chattopadhyay v. Headmaster of Holloway School ... 19, 211
Chipchase v. Chipchase ... 85, 86
Christopher Brown Ltd. v. Genossenschaft Oesterreichischer ... 85
Church of Scientology v. Department of Health and Social Security ... 149, 150
Cia Barca de Panama v. George Wimpey ... 147
City and Westminster Properties v. Mudd ... 356
Clark (H.) (Doncaster) Ltd. v. Wilkinson ... 29, 281
Clarke v. Clarke ... 345
Clayton v. Hardwick Colliery Co. ... 33
Clifford v. Hunter ... 117
Closmadeuc v. Carrel ... 347
Clothier v. Chapman ... 288
Coffin v. U.S. ... 77
Cohen decd., Re ... 89
Collins v. Blantern ... 358
—— v. Carnegie ... 282
Combe v. Combe ... 313
Commissioners of Customs and Excise v. Harz ... 154
Comptroller of Customs v. Western Lectric Co. ... 251, 275
Concha v. Concha ... 321
Connelly v. D.P.P. ... 331
Conquer v. Boot ... 325
Constantine v. Imperial Smelting Corporation ... 58
Conway v. Rimmer ... 138, 139, 140, 150
Cook, Re ... 361
Cooke v. Loxley ... 314
—— v. McCann ... 17
Cooper v. Cooper (No. 2) ... 325
—— v. Rowlands ... 87, 88
Corke v. Corke & Corke ... 163
Cornish v. Searell ... 315
Cottingham v. Shrewsbury ... 325
Countess of Rutland's Case ... 353
Coward v. Motor Insurers' Bureau ... 297
Cowling v. Matbro ... 126
Cox v. Couveless ... 353
Cozens v. Brutus ... 38
Crabb v. Arun District Council ... 310, 313
Cracknell v. Smith ... 161, 162
Crease v. Barrett ... 288, 289
Credland v. Knowler ... 162
Crescent Farm (Sidcup) Ltd. v. Sterling Offices Ltd. ... 146, 147
Cropper v. Smith ... 310
Crossley v. Dixon ... 314
Cummings v. Heard ... 319

Table of Cases

Curry v. Walter	143
Cuthbertson v. Irving	314, 315
Cutts v. Head	276
D. v. National Society for the Prevention of Cruelty to Children	43, 135, 136, 137, 139, 140, 143, 144, 149, 150, 277
D. (Infants), Re	139, 150
D. & C. Builders Ltd. v. Rees	313
Daintry, Re	278
Daniels v. Carmel Exporters and Importers	325
Danziger v. Thompson	357
Davey v. Harrow Corporation	34
Davidson v. Cooper	346
Davies v. D.P.P.	169, 170, 171
—— v. Lowndes	285, 287
Davy, Re	287
Dawson v. Great Central Ry.	281
—— v. R.	72
D'Israeli v. Jowett	282
De Laselle v. Guildford	356
Deeley's Patent, Re	326
Dennis v. White	33
Devala Provident Gold Mining Co., Re	280
D.P.P. v. A. & B.C. Chewing Gum Ltd.	24, 25
—— v. Boardman	209, 210, 212, 213, 214, 215, 216, 217, 220
—— v. Hester	159, 160, 165, 166, 174, 175
—— v. Humphreys	308, 320, 326, 332
—— v. Jordan	24
—— v. Kilbourne	10, 16, 160, 161, 163, 165, 172, 176, 178, 208
—— v. Maxwell	228
—— v. Nasralla	331
—— v. Ping Lin	193, 200
—— v. Smith	46, 90
—— v. Stonehouse	37, 38, 46, 47
Disher v. Disher	98
Dobell v. Stevens	357
Doe v. Bray 1828	283
—— v. Fowler	345
Doe d. Bamford v. Barton	287
Doe d. Bristow v. Pegge	314
Doe d. Davy v. Haddon	319, 320
Doe d. Gilbert v. Ross	349
Doe d. Gord v. Needs	362
Doe d. Hiscocks v. Hiscocks	360, 362
Doe d. Jenkins v. Davies	287, 289
Doe d. Tatum v. Catomore	346
Doe d. Thompson v. Hodgson	350
Doe d. Winter v. Perratt	360
Doe d. Wright v. Tatham	253, 255
Doncaster v. Day	240
Douglas v. Forrest	326
Drinkwater v. Porter	289
Duchess of Kingston's Case	320
Duff Development Co. v. Government of Kelantan	34

Table of Cases

Duke of Marlborough, *Re*	356
Duncan *v.* Cammell, Laird & Co. Ltd.	137, 139
Dunn *v.* Aslet	122
—— *v.* Dunn	54, 63
Dunraven *v.* Llewellyn	288
Durham Fancy Goods Ltd. *v.* Michael Jackson (Fancy Goods) Ltd.	313
Dwyer *v.* Collins	350
Dyer *v.* Dyer	78
Eaglehill Ltd. *v.* Needham (Builders) Ltd.	89
Earl *v.* Hector Whaling Ltd.	74
Eastern Distributors Ltd. *v.* Goldring	311
Edgington *v.* Fitzmaurice	311
Edkins *v.* Knowles	39
Edison *v.* Holland	338
Edwards *v.* Brookes (Milk) Ltd.	279
Elliott *v.* Totnes Union	83
Ellis *v.* Allen	29
—— *v.* Jones	296
English Exporters Ltd. *v.* Eldonwall Ltd.	23
Enoch, *Re*	124
Epps *v.* Rothnie	357
Ettenfield *v.* Ettenfield	84
Evans *v.* Getting	284
—— *v.* Merthyr Tydfil U.D.C.	274
Ewer *v.* Ambrose	113
F. *v.* Chief Constable of Kent	196
Falcon *v.* Famous Players Film Co.	273
Falkiner *v.* Commissioner of Stamp Duties	360
Fender *v.* St. John-Mildmay	137
Fenner *v.* L. & S.E. Ry.	145
Ferguson *v.* R.	40, 46, 73
Fidelitas Shipping *v.* V/O Exportchleb	319
Field *v.* Commissioner for Rys. for New South Wales	278
—— *v.* Field	329
Flynn, *Re*	74
Folkes *v.* Chadd	21
Ford *v.* Lewis	270
Formby *v.* Formby	357
Forster's Settlement, *Re*	90
Fowke *v.* Berington	284
Fox *v.* General Medical Council	107
Frank Truman Export Ltd. *v.* M.P.C.	144
Fred. Drughorn Ltd. *v.* Rederiaktiebolaget Transatlantic	357
Freeman *v.* Cooke	311, 312
Frost *v.* Frost	328
Fuld, *in the Estate of, deceased*, (No. 3)	74
Fung Sun *v.* Chan Fui Hing	312
G. *v.* Coltart	332
—— *v.* G.	279, 329
Galler *v.* Galler	175
Garton *v.* Hunter	12

Table of Cases   xvii

Gaskin v. Liverpool C.C.	139
Gatland v. Metropolitan Police Commissioner	70
Gatty and Gatty v. Att.-Gen.	82
General Accident Fire & Life Assurance v. Tanter	148
General Medical Council v. Spackman	322
George Doland Ltd. v. Blackburn & Co.	148
Gibbons v. Skinner	88
Gillie v. Posho	104, 105
Gillson, Re	360
Gleeson v. Whippell	324, 327
Glendaroch, The	57
Glinsky v. MacIver	241
Goddard v. Grey	319
—— v. Nationwide B.S.	147
Goode and Bennian v. Harrison	312
Goodright d. Stevens v. Moss	285
Goody v. Odhams Press	339
Goold v. Evans	26, 27
Gorman v. Hand in Hand Insurance	56
Gorringe v. Mahlstedt	360
Goss v. Nugent	358
Gray v. Barr	322
Grazebrook v. Wallens	149, 278
Greasley v. Cooke	313
Great Atlantic Insurance v. Home Insurance	148
Great Western Ry. v. Willis	280
Green v. New River Co.	338
Greenough v. Eccles	113, 116
Greenwood v. Martins Bank (1932)	307
—— v. ——	311, 312
Greenwood v. Martins Bank (1933)	311, 312
Greer v. Kettle	315
Gregory v. Taverner	103
Grey v. Pearson	360
Griffiths v. Young	356
Grundt v. Great Boulder Proprietary Gold Mines Ltd.	314
Guaret v. Audouy	319
Guest v. Warren	325
H. v. Schering Chemicals Ltd.	265
Habib Bank Ltd. v. Habib Bank A.G. Zurich	310
Haines v. Guthrie	240, 286
Hall v. Ball	346
—— v. R.	183
Hammington v. Berker Sportcraft Ltd.	31, 32
Hannaford v. Hunn	319
Harding v. Hayes	24
—— v. Williams	283
Harmony Shipping Co. v. Davis	130, 146
Harrington v. North London Polytechnic	142
Harris v. D.P.P.	217
—— v. Harris	148
—— v. Tippett	119
—— v. Willis	318

Table of Cases

Case	Page
Harrison, Re	348
—— v. Turner	106, 276
—— v. Vallance	279
—— v. Wells	315
Haynes v. Doman	25
Heather v. P.E. Consulting Group	24, 34
Hehr v. C.P.M.	136
Heilbut Symonds and Co. v. Buckleton	356
Henderson v. Arthur	356
—— v. Henderson	323, 324, 325
Henley v. Henley	277
Hennessy v. Wright	137
Hess v. Labouchere	318
Hetherington v. Hetherington	84
Heyne v. Fischel	282
Higgins v. Dawson	362
Hill v. Baxter	53, 65
—— v. Clifford	319
—— v. Hill	82
Hinds v. Sparks	339
Hinton v. Trotter	184
Hoare v. Silverlock	33, 34
Hobbs v. Tinling	115
Hocking v. Ahlquist	12
Holdfast d. Anstey v. Dowsing	344
Holdsworth v. Dinsdale	278
Hollington v. Hewthorn	20, 326, 338, 339
Holloway v. McFeeters	255
Holmes v. Holmes	84
Home v. Bentinck	137
Home Office v. Harman	141
Hopgood v. Brown	311
Hornal v. Neuberger Products Ltd.	73, 75
Hosegood v. Hosegood	90
Howard v. Beall	284
—— v. Borneman	55
Hoystead v. Commissioner of Taxation	324
Hubbard v. Lees	287, 346
Hubbuck, Re	362
Humble v. Hunter	357
Humphries v. Humphries	309
Hunt v. Hort	362
Hunter v. Chief Constable of West Midlands	326, 332, 335
—— v. Mann	149
Huntington v. Attrill	319
Huntley v. Gaskell	318
Hutton v. Watling	354, 355
I.T.C. Film Distributors v. Video Exchange	147
Ibrahim v. R.	193, 199, 200
Indian Government v. Taylor	319
Industrial Properties v. A.E.I. Ltd.	315
Ingram v. Percival	31
Initial Services Ltd. v. Putterill	150

Table of Cases

Ireland v. Livingstone	312
—— v. U.K.	198
Irish Society v. Derry	283
Ivory, *Re*	321
Jackson, *Re*	86
James v. Biou	89
—— v. R.	161, 173
Janov v. Morris	334
Jayasena v. R.	61
Jebb, *Re*	361
Jeffrey v. Black	44, 45
Jenion, *Re*	287
Johnson v. Barnes	87
—— v. Lawson	286
—— v. Lindsay	280
Jones v. James	18
—— v. D.P.P.	222, 224, 225, 226
—— v. Jones	311, 313
—— v. Metcalf	252
—— v. National Coal Board	124
—— v. South Eastern and Chatham Ry.	163
Jordan v. Money	311, 312
Jos. Miller & Partners v. Whitworth St. Estates	364
Jos. Travers & Son v. Cooper	56
Joseph Constantine Steamship Line Ltd. v. Imperial Smelting Corporation Ltd.	54
Joy v. Phillips Mills & Co. Ltd.	17
Judd v. Minister of Pensions	75
Kajala v. Noble	12, 27, 248, 348
Keane v. Mount Vernon Colliery Co.	31
Keene v. Holland	309
Kell v. Charmer	363
Kellett v. Stockport	358
Kent v. Stamps	31
Kerr v. Kennedy	34
Key v. Key	360
Khawaja v. S.S. for Home Department	75
Kinch v. Walcott	318
Kirby Hall, The	21
Kirkstall Brewery Co. v. Furness Ry.	280
Kitchin, *Re*	279
Knight v. David	266
Knowles v. Knowles	84
Koenigsberg, *Re*	325
Kok Hoong v. Leong Cheong Kweng Mines Ltd.	309, 324
Koscot Interplanetary (U.K.) Ltd., *Re*	260, 266
Kurtz v. Spence	278
Kuruma v. R.	44
L. v. K.	78
La Roche v. Armstrong	276, 277
Ladd v. Marshall	126

Langley's Settlement Trusts, Re	319
Lau Pat Ngam v. R.	102
Lauderdale Peerage Case	82
Lazarus-Barlow v. Regent Estates Co. Ltd.	321
Lee v. L. & Y. Ry.	354
—— v. Pain	361
Lek v. Matthews	75
Lennox, ex p.	328
Leslie v. Sheill	309
Leung Kam Kwok v. R.	106
Lewis v. Lewis	89
Lindall v. Lindall	116
Line v. Taylor	26
Lister v. Scaife	296
Lloyd v. Mostyn	136, 147
—— v. Powell	297
Lockyer v. Ferryman	326
Long v. Miller	353
Lonrho v. Shell	140
Lord Ashburton v. Pape	147
Low v. Bouverie	311
Lowery v. R.	206
Ludlow v. M.P.C.	219, 220
Lustre Hosiery Ltd. v. York	275
Lyell v. Kennedy (1883)	149
—— v. —— (1889)	282
—— v. —— (No. 3) (1884)	148
MacDonald v. Longbottom	363
McGreevy v. D.P.P.	17, 73
McKenzie v. British Linen Bank	311
McLoughlin v. Gordons (Stockport) Ltd.	328
McQuaker v. Goddard	34, 35
McQueen v. G.W.R.	62
McShane v. Northumberland Chief Constable	178
McTaggart v. McTaggart	277
Mackley v. Nutting	314
Magnay v. Knight	353
Mahadervan v. Mahadervan	82
Makin v. Att.-Gen. for New South Wales	210, 214, 217
Malcolmson v. O'Dea	251
Malindi v. R.	224
Mancini v. D.P.P.	60, 65, 72
Manchester Brewery v. Coombes	254
Manley's Will Trusts (No. 2)	323
Marginson v. Blackburn Borough Council	325, 327
Marks v. Beyfus	143, 146
Maritime Electric Co. v. General Dairies Ltd.	307, 308
Marriott v. Hampton	323, 324
Marshall v. Ford	17
Maugham v. Hubbard	103
Maxwell v. D.P.P.	206, 222, 223, 234
Meath (Bishop) v. Winchester (Marquis)	345
Mechanical, etc. Inventions v. Austin	117

Table of Cases

Medawar v. Grand Hotel Co.	59
Mercantile Investment and General Trust Co. v. River Plate Trust	327
Mercer v. Denne	289, 346
—— v. Whall	97
Metropolitan Ry. v. Jackson	40
—— v. Wright	40
Miller v. Howe	252
—— v. Minister of Pensions	73
Mills v. Cooper	308, 323, 326
—— v. Oddy	350
Milne v. Leisler	110
Minet v. Morgan	147
Mirehouse v. Rennell	137
Mitchell v. Croydon	31
Mohammed-Holgate v. Duke	198
Mole v. Mole	276, 277
Monckton v. Tarr	82
Montgomery v. Russell	334
Mood Music Publishing Co. v. De Wolfe	19
Moore v. Registrar of Lambeth County Council	96
Moorhouse v. Lord	74
Moorgate Mercantile Co. Ltd. v. Twitchings	312
Morel Bros. v. Earl of Westmoreland	336
Morgan v. Griffiths	356
—— v. Lee	247
Moriarty v. London, Chatham and Dover Ry.	274
Morris v. Baron	358
—— v. Davies	84
—— v. Miller	83
—— v. Stratford-upon-Avon U.D.C.	271
Morrison Pollexfen & Blair v. Walton	58
Morrison, Rose and Partners v. Hillman	318
Mortimer v. M'Callan	349, 351
Moseley v. Davies	289
Moxon v. Minister of Pensions	31
Murdoch v. Taylor	117, 234, 235
Murphy v. Stone Wallwork	126
Murray v. Parker	357
Myatt v. Myatt and Parker	279
Myers v. D.P.P.	240, 241, 249, 250, 251, 255, 256, 282, 291, 298
National Society for the Prevention of Cruelty to Children v. Scottish National Society for the Prevention of Cruelty to Children	360, 361
National Westminster Bank v. Hart	315
Neilson v. Harford	38
—— v. Laugharne	136, 140, 145
—— v. Poole	360, 364
Nembhard v. R.	168, 178, 298, 299
Nevill v. Fine Art Insurance Co. Ltd.	38
New Brunswick Ry. Co. v. British & French Trust Corporation Ltd.	323, 324
New Windsor Corporation v. Mellor	289
New York v. Phillip's Heirs	75
New's Trustee v. Hunting	274, 279
Nicholas v. Penny	166

Table of Cases

Case	Page
Nicholls v. Parker	288
Nicholson v. Smith Marriott	352
Nimmo v. Alexander Cowan & Sons Ltd.	68, 69
Nippon Menkwa Kabushiki Kaisha v. Dawson's Bank Ltd.	308
Nishina Trading Co. v. Chiyoda	75
Nixon v. U.S.	140
Noble v. Ward	358
Noor Mohamed v. R.	217
Norfolk County Council v. Secretary of State for the Environment	312
Norman v. Matthews	96
North Cheshire Brewery v. Manchester Brewery	25
Norwich Pharmacal v. Customs and Excise	140, 142
Nouvion v. Freeman	318
Nye v. Niblett	33
O'Connell v. Adams	117
Oakes v. Uzzell	113
Oakland Metal Co. v. Benaim	307
Ofner, Re	361
Ogilvie v. West Australian Mortgage Corporation	307
Oliver v. Nautilus Steam Shipping Co. Ltd.	277
Oppenheim v. Hajie Mahomed	320
Outram v. Morewood	324
Ovens, In the goods of	344
Overbury, Re	83
Owen v. Chesters	247
—— v. Edmonds	103
—— v. Nichol	124
Pacol Ltd. v. Trade Lines Ltd.	313
Paddock v. Forrester	277
Pais v. Pais	277
Palin v. Ponting	345
Papendick v. Bridgwater	279
Parker v. Smith	65
Parry v. Boyle	26, 27
Parry-Jones v. Law Society	144
Patel v. Comptroller of Customs	251
Pattle v. Hornibrook	356
Payne v. Harrison	98, 99
Pearce v. Gardner	353
Penn v. Jack	99
Perrin v. Morgan	359, 360, 362
Perton, Re	287
Petrie v. Nuttall	338
Pheasant v. Pheasant	76
Phelan v. Black	125
Phené's Trusts, Re	85, 90
Phibbs, Re	345
Phosphate Sewage Co. v. Molleson	326
Pickard v. Sears	311
Pickup v. Thames & Mersey Marine Insurance Co.	89
Piermay Shipping Co. v. Chester	262
Piers v. Piers	74, 82

Table of Cases

Pilkington v. Gray	344
Pinner v. Everett	39
Pinney v. Hunt	348
Plant v. Taylor	287, 289
Pontifex v. Jolly	97
Pool v. Pool	277
Pople v. Evans	318, 327
Post Office v. Estuary Radio Ltd.	75
Poulton v. Adjustable Cover and Boiler Block Co.	318
Powell v. Phillips	90
Practice Direction (Submission of No Case)	97
Practice Note (1950)	350
—— (1975)	121
Prasad v. R.	197
Prenn v. Simmonds	364
Preston-Jones v. Preston-Jones	33, 73
Price v. Manning	114
—— v. Woodhouse	348
Priestman v. Thomas	325
Prince v. Samo	123
Prudential Assurance v. Edwards	85
Public Trustee v. Kenward	323
Purcell v. Macnamara	337
Purser v. Jackson	324, 325
Pye v. Butterfield	151
Pym v. Campbell	356, 357
R. v. Abadom	23, 249, 256
—— v. Abbott	99
—— v. Abraham (1848)	108
—— v. —— (1973)	65
—— v. Adams	182
—— v. Agbim	36, 73
—— v. Agricultural Land Tribunal	284
—— v. Aickles	350
—— v. Airey	196
—— v. Ali & Hassan	102
—— v. Allen	202
—— v. Anderson	24
—— v. Andover JJ., ex p. Rhodes	284
—— v. Antrim JJ.	31, 124, 130
—— v. Apicella	45
—— v. Askew	108
—— v. Assim	219
—— v. Austin	298
—— v. Badjam	46
—— v. Bailey (1924)	164, 165
—— v. —— (1987)	303
—— v. Baillie-Smith	241
—— v. Ball	208, 211, 214, 216
—— v. Barker	203
—— v. Barrell	219, 220
—— v. Barrington	213
—— v. Barton	146

Table of Cases

R. v. Bashir	120
—— v. Baskerville	161, 162, 172
—— v. Bass	102
—— v. Bastin	207
—— v. Bates	39
—— v. Bathurst	188
—— v. Beck	162, 171
—— v. Bedfordshire	288
—— v. Bedingfield	299, 301, 303
—— v. Bellamy	129
—— v. Bennett	65
—— v. Beresford	127
—— v. Berger	288
—— v. Bernadotti	298
—— v. Berry (1924)	186
—— v. —— (1986)	216
—— v. Berryman	201
—— v. Bexley JJ., *ex p.* King	96
—— v. Bickley	170
—— v. Biggin	228
—— v. Birchall	172
—— v. Bircham	236
—— v. Bishop	231
—— v. Blank	161
—— v. Blastland	254, 255
—— v. Bliss	288, 289
—— v. Blithing	296
—— v. Bodmin JJ.	95
—— v. Bogdal	220
—— v. Bond	211, 217
—— v. Booth	114
—— v. Box	143
—— v. Boyes	151, 152, 153
—— v. Bracewell	73, 206
—— v. Bradley	207
—— v. Braithwaite	233
—— v. Brigden	186
—— v. Britzman	229, 230, 232
—— v. Brittle	204
—— v. Broad	125
—— v. Brophy	197
—— v. Brown (1867)	122
—— v. —— (1911)	161
—— v. —— (1960)	230
—— v. Brown and Routh	188
—— v. Brown, Smith, Woods, Flanagan	213
—— v. Browne	125
—— v. Bruce	235
—— v. Bryant	204, 228
—— v. Burdett	62
—— v. Burgess	172
—— v. Burke	233
—— v. Burke & Kelly	110

Table of Cases

R. v. Busby	122
—— v. Butterwasser	205, 227, 236
—— v. Buttery and Macnamara	322
—— v. Calder	24
—— v. Callum	204
—— v. Camelleri	108
—— v. Campbell (1911)	48
—— v. —— (1956)	160
—— v. —— (1983)	129, 162, 173
—— v. Carr-Briant	67, 71, 74
—— v. Cavanagh	125
—— v. Chandler	182, 183
—— v. Chapman (1838)	125
—— v. —— (1969)	243
—— v. —— (1973)	162
—— v. Chard	24
—— v. Chatwood	275
—— v. Chauhan	164
—— v. Cheng	102
—— v. Chief Registrar of Friendly Societies	96
—— v. Ching	6, 73
—— v. Chitson	225
—— v. Christie	43, 110, 163, 164, 182, 183, 184
—— v. Clark	229
—— v. Clarke (1925)	333
—— v. —— (1977)	215
—— v. Clarkson's Tours Ltd.	38
—— v. Clayton-Wright	219
—— v. Clifton	178
—— v. Clynes	165
—— v. Cokar	225, 226
—— v. Collins	349
—— v. Coltress	223
—— v. Conde	300
—— v. Conti	131
—— v. Cook (1959)	231, 232
—— v. —— (1980)	251
—— v. —— (1986)	102, 248
—— v. Cooper (1969)	40
—— v. —— (1979)	185, 187
—— v. Coote	152
—— v. Corless	126
—— v. Cowper	300
—— v. Cox & Railton	146
—— v. Cramp	161
—— v. Cresswell	87
—— v. Crush	33
—— v. Culbertson	45
—— v. Cummings	109
—— v. Cunningham	100, 196
—— v. Curgerwen	86
—— v. Curry & Keeble	179
—— v. Cwmbran JJ., ex p. Pope	335
—— v. Dadson	283

Table of Cases

R. v. Dallas	127
—— v. Davies (No. 2) (1962)	21, 25
—— v. Davis	235
—— v. Day	100, 125
—— v. De Vere	205, 227
—— v. Deacon	333
—— v. Denley	122
—— v. Derby JJ., *ex p.* Brooks	334
—— v. Denbigh JJ.	95
—— v. Dodson	112
—— v. Donald and Donald	109
—— v. Donaldson	106, 107
—— v. Doolin	117
—— v. Doran	125
—— v. Dorking JJ., *ex p.* Harrington	330
—— v. Dossi	161
—— v. Dowley	164
—— v. Downer	280
—— v. Dunbar	67
—— v. Duncan	106, 107
—— v. Dunkley	224, 228
—— v. Dwyer & Ferguson	112
—— v. Dytche	19
—— v. Edwards (1975)	69, 70
—— v. —— (1983)	45, 71, 182
—— v. Eidinow	227
—— v. Ellis	227
—— v. Epping and Harlow JJ.	125
—— v. Epping & Ongar JJ.	196
—— v. Evans-Jones and Jenkins	67
—— v. Exall	108
—— v. Falconer-Atlee	98
—— v. Farndale	27
—— v. Fannon & Walsh	111
—— v. Feely	38
—— v. Fenlon	103, 117
—— v. Field and Others	31
—— v. Fisher (1910)	212
—— v. —— (1983)	45
—— v. Flynn (1957)	125
—— v. —— (1972)	117, 198
—— v. —— (1985)	73
—— v. Fordingbridge	345, 349
—— v. Foster	302
—— v. Fowden	112, 248
—— v. Fowkes	109, 246, 302
—— v. France	226
—— v. Frances	23
—— v. Francis	211
—— v. Fraser and Warren	114
—— v. Frost	100
—— v. Galbraith	98
—— v. Gallagher	189
—— v. Garbett	152

Table of Cases

R. v. Gargan	198
—— v. Gazard	143
—— v. Ghosh	38
—— v. Gibbs	186
—— v. —— (1887)	253, 302
—— v. Gibson (1983)	71
—— v. Gill	65
—— v. Gloster	300
—— v. Goddard and Goddard	165
—— v. Golder	115
—— v. Gowan	198
—— v. Graham	102
—— v. Gray	72
—— v. Greenwich	281
—— v. Grimer	112, 248
—— v. Grout	227
—— v. Gunewardene	123, 279
—— v. Gurney	27
—— v. Gwilliam	265, 291
—— v. Hadwen and Ingham	234
—— v. Hall	296
—— v. Hallett	143
—— v. Halpin	256, 282
—— v. Hamand	106
—— v. Hardy	104, 163, 273
—— v. Harris	124
—— v. Hart	117
—— v. Harward	220
—— v. Harvey (1858)	143
—— v. —— (1869)	22
—— v. Haslam	111
—— v. Hassan	186, 187
—— v. Hatton	235
—— v. Haworth	350
—— v. Hay	332
—— v. Hayes	129
—— v. Henry & Manning	164, 173
—— v. Hepworth and Fearnley	72, 89
—— v. Hewett	179
—— v. Hill	211
—— v. Hilton	116, 117
—— v. Hoare	184
—— v. Holmes (1871)	120
—— v. —— (1953)	25
—— v. Holy Trinity, Hull	353
—— v. Horsham JJ., ex p. Bukhari	45, 110
—— v. ——, ex p. Farquharson	97
—— v. ——, ex p. Reeves	335
—— v. Horwood	216
—— v. Houghton & Franciosy	202
—— v. Hubbard	298
—— v. Hudson	231
—— v. Hulbert	275
—— v. Hunjan	178

Table of Cases

R. v. Hunt	68, 69, 70
—— v. Hunter (1969)	110
—— v. —— (1985)	26
—— v. Hutchison	49
—— v. Hutchinson	100, 293
—— v. Inder	212, 213, 232
—— v. Inhabitants of Eriswell	240
—— v. Ireland	128
—— v. Jackson (1953)	161, 187, 188
—— v. —— (1973)	185
—— v. —— (1985)	196
—— v. James	127
—— v. Jameson	284
—— v. Jenkins (1869)	299
—— v. —— (1981)	167, 171
—— v. Johannsen	220
—— v. John	110
—— v. Johnson (1847)	300
—— v. —— (1961)	65
—— v. Jones (1923)	229
—— v. —— (1970)	34, 39, 79
—— v. Jones & Sullivan	265
—— v. Keane	178
—— v. Kelly	39
—— v. Kelsey	102, 252
—— v. Kilbourne	216, 218
—— v. King (1967)	216
—— v. —— (1983)	146, 171
—— v. Kinglake	147, 152
—— v. Knight	164
—— v. Knowlden	170
—— v. Korniak	45
—— v. Krausz	120
—— v. Kray	219
—— v. Kurasch	225
—— v. Kurshid	105
—— v. Lal Khan	166
—— v. Lamb	111, 112
—— v. Lanfear	24
—— v. Lattimore	127
—— v. Lawrence (1968)	126
—— v. —— (1977)	121
—— v. Lecky	183
—— v. Lee	236
—— v. Leverson	148
—— v. Lewes JJ.	136, 138, 139, 140, 143
—— v. Lewis (1969)	186, 187
—— v. —— (1973)	185, 186
—— v. —— (1982)	217
—— v. Lillyman	108, 124
—— v. Littleboy	184
—— v. Llanfaethly	350
—— v. Lobell	65
—— v. Longman and Richardson	206, 228

R. v. Loveridge	170, 171
—— v. Lovett	232, 234, 235
—— v. Lucas	162
—— v. Luffe	33
—— v. M'Naghten	66
—— v. McCormick	198
—— v. McDowell	125
—— v. McGarth	198
—— v. McGee	229, 232
—— v. McGlinchey	220
—— v. McGrath	197
—— v. McGregor	106, 276, 274
—— v. McGuire	297
—— v. McKay	105
—— v. MacKenny	24, 123
—— v. McLean	111, 252
—— v. Malik	207
—— v. Moloney	219
—— v. Mandry & Wooster	70
—— v. Mann	114, 183
—— v. Mansfield	98, 210
—— v. Maqsud Ali	27
—— v. Marlow JJ.	76
—— v. Marsh	211
—— v. Masih	24
—— v. Mason	23
—— v. Matthews	124
—— v. Maynard	112
—— v. Maywhort	154
—— v. Mead	298
—— v. Meecham	169
—— v. Melville	128
—— v. Mendy	122
—— v. Merry	127
—— v. Midwinter	172
—— v. Miller	206
—— v. Milligan	49
—— v. Mills	102
—— v. Mitchell	182
—— v. Moghal	29
—— v. Moore	73
—— v. Muir	250
—— v. Mullen	108
—— v. Mullins	162, 170
—— v. Murray	48, 197
—— v. Murtagh and Kennedy	72
—— v. Mustapha	218
—— v. Mutch	188
—— v. Myers	241
—— v. Nabarro	127
—— v. Nation	124
—— v. Naudeer	134
—— v. Neale	206
—— v. Nelson	229

Table of Cases

R. v. Nelson & McLeod	179
— v. Newcastle JJ., ex p. Hindle	65
— v. Newsome	107
— v. Newton	49
— v. Nixon	126
— v. Norcott	109
— v. Nottingham County JJ., ex p. Bostock	278
— v. Nottingham JJ.	333
— v. Nottingham City JJ., ex p. Lynn	153
— v. Novac	220
— v. Nowaz	350
— v. Nugent	125
— v. Nye	204
— v. O'Reilly	167, 172, 173
— v. O'Sullivan	22
— v. Oakwell	179
— v. Okorodu	111
— v. Olaleye	162
— v. Oliva (1960)	71
— v. —— (1965)	125
— v. Ollis	332
— v. Orpin	35
— v. Orrell	12
— v. Orton	284
— v. Osborne	108, 109
— v. Osbourne & Virtue	110, 111
— v. Ovenell	196, 197
— v. Owen	126
— v. Oyesiku	107
— v. Palin	205
— v. Palmer	224
— v. Paraskeva	122
— v. Parks	127
— v. Patel	249
— v. Patterson	67
— v. Paul	132, 134
— v. Payne (1950)	131
— v. —— (1963)	203
— v. —— (1972)	131
— v. Peach	167
— v. Pentonville Governors, ex p. Schneider	131
— v. Perry (1909)	298, 299
— v. Perry (1984)	207
— v. Pervez and Khan	333
— v. Pettigrew	247
— v. Phillips	122
— v. Pipe	131
— v. Pitt	113, 134
— v. Platt	202
— v. Powell (1985)	114
— v. —— (1986)	223, 233, 234
— v. Power	99
— v. Prager	193, 198, 202
— v. Prater	167, 170, 172

Table of Cases

R. v. Pratt	188
—— v. Preston	232
—— v. Priestley	198
—— v. Quinn	73
—— v. Rance	210, 213, 217, 218
—— v. Rankine	143
—— v. Rappolt	229
—— v. Ratcliffe	124
—— v. Redd	227
—— v. Redgrave	204
—— v. Redpath	163, 164
—— v. Regan	347
—— v. Rennie	200
—— v. Rhodes	131, 188, 211
—— v. Rice	118, 251
—— v. Richardson (1967)	131
—— v. —— (1968)	122, 227
—— v. —— (1971)	102
—— v. Riebold	333
—— v. Riley (1887)	120
—— v. —— (1896)	29
—— v. Rimmer	274
—— v. Rimmer & Beech	10, 39, 45, 204
—— v. Rivers	74
—— v. Roberts	87
—— v. Robinson (1953)	212
—— v. —— (1974)	331
—— v. Robson	348
—— v. Roberts	335
—— v. Rogers and Tarran	43
—— v. Rose	45
—— v. Rossborough	186
—— v. Rowson	118
—— v. Rouse	229
—— v. Rowton	204, 205, 224
—— v. Royce-Bentley	169
—— v. Rudd	132, 134
—— v. Ryan	184, 186
—— v. Samuel	227, 228
—— v. Sanders	173
—— v. Sanderson	125
—— v. Sang	43, 44, 45, 202, 203
—— v. Saunders	241
—— v. Scaife	299
—— v. Scarrott	210, 212, 218, 220, 221
—— v. Schama	73, 89, 108
—— v. Scott	152, 154
—— v. Seaman	217
—— v. Secretary of State, *ex p.* Lees	137
—— v. Secretary of State for the Environment, *ex p.* Hackney Borough Council	326
—— v. Senat	27
—— v. Shields and Patrick	127

xxxii Table of Cases

R. v. Shillingford	165
—— v. Shone	250, 256
—— v. Sidhu	170
—— v. Silverlock	22
—— v. Simmonds	102
—— v. Simons	274
—— v. Simpson	35
—— v. Skegness Magistrates' Court	141
—— v. Slender	212
—— v. Smallman	121
—— v. Slinger	71
—— v. Smith (1915)	208, 210
—— v. —— (1959)	200
—— v. —— (1985)	161, 183
—— v. Smith (Joan)	96
—— v. Smith (Percy)	248
—— v. Socialist Worker Printers, *ex p.* Att.-Gen.	97
—— v. Southampton JJ.	76
—— v. Sparrow (1962)	71
—— v. —— (1973)	37, 108, 132, 161, 187, 188, 189
—— v. Spencer	167, 168, 171
—— v. Spinks	300
—— v. Stafford and Luvaglio	127
—— v. Stainton	171
—— v. Stannard (1837)	204, 228
—— v. —— (1965)	234, 235
—— v. Statutory Visitors to St. Lawrence's Hospital, Caterham	149
—— v. Steane	90
—— v. Steel	254, 255
—— v. Sterk	125
—— v. Stevenson	348
—— v. Storey (1965)	107
—— v. —— (1968)	107
—— v. Straffen	211, 215, 216
—— v. Stubbs	152, 205
—— v. Sullivan (1923)	125
—— v. —— (1967)	184
—— v. —— (1971)	185
—— v. Summers	72
—— v. Sunair Holidays Ltd.	38
—— v. Sutton and Moore	40
—— v. Sweet–Escott	121
—— v. Tanner	229
—— v. Tate	182
—— v. Taylor (1924)	333
—— v. —— (1978)	182
—— v. Thomas (1959)	165
—— v. —— (1985)	115, 330
—— v. Thompson (1912)	118, 240
—— v. —— (1962)	143
—— v. —— (1975)	107
—— v. —— (1977)	113
—— v. —— (1982)	256, 296
—— v. Tilley	22

Table of Cases

R. v. Tirado	265
—— v. Tiverton JJ.	95
—— v. Tolson	248
—— v. Tomey	131
—— v. Tompkins	118, 147
—— v. Townsend	45
—— v. Tragen	165
—— v. Treacy	118, 197
—— v. Tregear	125
—— v. Tricoglus	212, 213
—— v. Trigg	172
—— v. Trump	45
—— v. Tune	185
—— v. Turnbull (1977)	177, 178, 179
—— v. —— (1984)	303
—— v. Turner (1910)	27
—— v. —— (1832)	337
—— v. —— (1944)	231
—— v. —— (1975)	10, 24
—— v. Turner and Shervill	131, 281
—— v. Tyson	178
—— v. Vandercomb and Abbott	331
—— v. Varley	235
—— v. Verelst	87
—— v. Vernon	170
—— v. Vickers	223, 232
—— v. Viola	120, 121
—— v. Virgo	103, 163
—— v. Voisin	189, 201
—— v. Wainwright	111
—— v. Wallwork	108, 125
—— v. Walshe	47
—— v. Walters	72, 73
—— v. Warickshall	201
—— v. Watson	122
—— v. Watson & Daniel	300
—— v. Watts (1980)	186
—— v. —— (1983)	223, 233, 234
—— v. Wayte	348
—— v. Weaver	205
—— v. Webb	34
—— v. West	162
—— v. Westfall	228
—— v. Weston-super-Mare JJ.	232
—— v. Westwell	102
—— v. Wheeler	124
—— v. Whickham	133, 188
—— v. White	115, 116
—— v. Whitaker	171
—— v. Whitehead	163
—— v. Wilbourne	109
—— v. Wiles	247
—— v. Willshire	90, 205
—— v. Wilson (1973)	213, 216

xxxiv Table of Cases

R. v. Windle	66
— v. Winfield	206, 227
— v. Winter	205
— v. Withecombe	88
— v. Wolverhampton Crown Court	320, 330
— v. Wood	27, 247, 248, 256
— v. Woodcock	298
— v. Yacoob	130
— v. Yousry	118
Rabin v. Gerson Berger Association	363
— v. Mendoza	277
Raffles v. Wichelhaus	363
Ramsay v. Margrett	89
— v. Watson	23
Ramsden v. Dyson	313
Randolph v. Tuck	325
Randle v. Blackburn	106, 276
Rank Film Distributors v. Video Information Centre	151
Raphael decd., Re	340
Rasool v. West Midlands Transport Executive	262, 263
Ratten v. R.	245, 301, 302, 303
Read v. Bishop of Lincoln	34, 284
Reynolds, Re	152
— v. Llanelly Tinplate Co.	31
Rice v. Connolly	180
— v. Howard	114
Richards v. Morgan	281
Richardson v. Peto	281
— v. Watson	360
Riddick v. Thames Board Mills	29, 141
Rigby v. Woodward	234
Rio Tinto Zinc Corporation v. Westinghouse Electric Corporation	153
River Wear Commissioners v. Adamson	359, 363
Robb v. Green	355
Robinson v. Williams	319
Rochefoucauld v. Boustead	357
Roddy v. Fitzgerald	360
Roe d. Trimlestown v. Kemmis	275
Rootkin v. Kent County Council	309
Roper v. Taylor's Central Garage	34
Rosedale Mouldings v. Sibley	43
Rosher, Re	34
Rossi, ex p.	88
Routledge v. Hislop	325
— v. McKay	346
Rowe v. Rowe	326, 328
Rowley v. L. and N.W. Ry.	284
Royal Bank of Australia, Re	280
Rumping v. D.P.P.	136, 274
Rutherford v. Richardson	279
S. v. McC. (1872)	274
— v. — (1972)	82, 84
S. & M. Carpets v. Cornhill Insurance Co.	75

Table of Cases

St. Edmundsbury Board of Finance *v*. Clark (No. 2)	364
Sakhuja *v*. Allan	39
St. George and St. Margaret, Westminster, *Inter the Parishes of*	84
Salsbury *v*. Woodland	27
Sambasivam *v*. Public Prosecutor	332
Sankey *v*. Whitlam	140
Sastry Velaider Aronegary *v*. Sembecutty Vaigalle	83
Savings & Investment Bank *v*. Gasco Investments B.V.	266
Saxby *v*. Fulton	30
Scarf *v*. Jardine	336
Scarfe *v*. Adams	360
Schneider *v*. Leigh	147
Schuler A.G. *v*. Wickman Ltd.	364
Science Research Council *v*. Nassé	137, 138, 141
Scott *v*. Baker	88
—— *v*. Scott	95, 96
Scrimaglio *v*. Thornett and Fehr	320
Secretary of State for Defence *v*. Guardian Newspapers	151
Secretary of State for Employment *v*. Globe Elastic Thread Co. Ltd.	309
Seldon *v*. Davidson	55, 97
Selvey *v*. D.P.P.	224, 228, 231, 232, 234
Senat *v*. Senat	103
Sergeant *v*. Nash, Field & Co.	315
Seyfang *v*. Searle & Co.	130
Sharratt *v*. Mountford	361
Sheddon *v*. Att.-Gen.	285, 287, 288
—— *v*. Patrick	320
Shields *v*. Boucher	286
Shore *v*. Wilson	360
Shrewsbury Peerage	286
Sidnell *v*. Wilson	75
Simm *v*. Simm	126
Simmons *v*. London Bank	279
Simms *v*. Moore	100
Skone *v*. Skone	126
Slaney *v*. Wade	287
Slatterie *v*. Pooley	273, 274, 348
Smalley, *Re*	361
Smith *v*. Birch	335
—— *v*. Blandy	276
—— *v*. Hawkins	180
—— *v*. Lister	289
—— *v*. Smith	278
Sneddon *v*. Stevenson	170
Snowden dec'd. *Re*	74
Soanes *v*. London and South Western Ry.	307
Society of Medical Officers of Health *v*. Hope	323, 325
Sodeman *v*. R.	74
South Staffs. Water Co. *v*. Sharman	89
Soward *v*. Leggatt (1836)	55
Sparks *v*. R.	42, 111, 240
Spiro *v*. Lintern	312
Spittle *v*. Spittle	110
Splents *v*. Lefevre	286

Table of Cases

Stafford v. D.P.P.	40
Starr v. Minister of Pensions	31
State of Penang v. Beng Hong Oon	314
Statue of Liberty, The	27, 247
Steeds v. Steeds	358
Steel v. Smith	56
Stevens v. Tillet	326
Stirland v. D.P.P.	206, 224, 231
Stobart v. Dryden	241, 251
Stollery, Re	282
Storey v. Storey	98
Stotesbury v. Turner	276
Strauss v. Sutro	352
Stupple v. Royal Exchange Insurance Co.	81, 339
Sturla v. Freccia	225, 282, 283, 286
Subramanian v. Public Prosecutor	243
Suffolk County Council v. Mason	204
Sugden v. Lord St. Leonards	255
Surujpaul v. R.	275
Sutton v. Sadler	61
Swain v. Gillet	166
Sweet v. Parsley	65
Swift v. Barrett	88
Swinnerton v. Stafford	346
T. v. T.	82, 84
Tak Ming Ltd. v. Yee Sang Co.	318
Tameshwar v. R.	26, 27
Taplin, Re	83
Taylor v. Chief Constable of Cheshire	248
—— v. Taylor (1967)	82
—— v. —— (1970)	81, 260, 266
—— v. Witham	297
Taylor Fashions Ltd. v. Liverpool Victoria Trustees Ltd.	310, 314
—— v. —— (1982)	310
Teper v. R.	246, 302
Theodoropoulas v. Theodoropoulas	277
Thoday v. Thoday	324, 325, 328
Thomas v. David	122
—— v. Jones	161
—— v. Secretary of State	148
Thompson v. R.	214
—— v. Thompson (1956)	86
—— v. —— (1957)	328, 329
—— v. Trevanion	302
Thoreburn v. Barnes	320
Thrasyvoulos Ioannou v. Papa Christoforos Demetriou	265, 282
Thynne v. Thynne	321, 327
Timmins v. Moreland Street Property Co.	353
Tingle Jacobs & Co. v. Kennedy	88
Tomlin v. Standard Telephones	278
Tomlinson v. Tomlinson	96
Toohey v. Metropolitan Police Commissioner	24, 48, 123, 130
Tool Metal Manufacturing Co. Ltd. v. Tungsten Electric Co. Ltd.	312

Table of Cases

Townsend v. Bishop	326
Treacy v. D.P.P.	330
Tremelbye v. Stekel	262
Triplex Safety Glass Co. Ltd. v. Lancegaye Safety Glass	152, 153
Tucker v. Oldbury U.D.C.	297
Tumath v. Tumath	326
Turner v. Forwood	358
Tutton v. Darke	284
Tweney v. Tweney	82
Tyrer v. U.K.	198
Urquhart v. Butterfield	29
Van Laun, Re	328
Vere-Wardale, Re	345
Vines v. Djordjevitch	57
Vocisano v. Vocisano	301
Vooght v. Winch	337
Vowles v. Young	286, 287
Wagstaffe v. Wilson	279
Wakefield v. Cooke	321
Wakelin v. L. & S.W. Ry.	55
Waldridge v. Kennison	278
Walker v. Wilsher	276, 278
Walker Property Investments v. Walker	356
Wallworth v. Balmer	27
Wallwork v. Rowland	33
Waltham Forest L.B.C. v. Mills	38
Ward v. Shell-Mex & B.P. Ltd.	144
Watcham v. Att.-Gen. of East Africa Protectorate	364
Waterhouse v. Barker	153, 284
Watkins, Re	85
Watt v. Thomas	40
Waugh v. British Railways Board	145
—— v. R.	188, 299
Webb v. Leadbetter	126
Weight v. Mackay	320, 330
Welch v. Nagy	309
Wentworth v. Lloyd	152
Western Fish Products v. Penwith District Council	309, 313
Westminster C.C. v. Croyalgrange Ltd.	67
Wetherall v. Harrison	32
Wheeler v. Le Marchant	145
Wiedemann v. Walpole	182, 274
Wilson, Re	86
Wharam v. Routledge	350
Whitelock v. Baker	286
Whitmore v. Lambert	314
Whittington v. Seale-Hayne	357
Wigglesworth v. Dallinson	355
Williams, Re	232, 363
—— v. Innes	279
—— v. Stern	358

xxxviii Table of Cases

Williams v. Summerfield 153, 284
Willmott v. Barber 314
Wilson v. Keating 316
—— v. Wilson 315
Wing v. Angrave 87
Wong Kam-Ming v. R. 196, 197
Wood v. Braddick 279
—— v. Luscombe 324
—— v. Mackinson 117
Woodhouse v. Hall 243
Woodhouse & Co. Ltd. v. Woodhouse 147, 148
Woodhouse A.C. Israel Cocoa Ltd. S.A. v. Nigerian Produce Marketing
    Co. Ltd. 312
Woods v. Wise 358
Wooley v. North London Ry. 145
Woolmington v. D.P.P. 60, 64, 66, 68
Woolway v. Rowe 278
Workington Harbour Board v. Trade Indemnity Co. 323, 325
Wright, Re 318
—— v. Doe d. Tatham 20, 253
Wyld v. Silver 289
Wynne v. Humberstone 148

Yanov v. Morris 318
Yat Tung v. Dao Hong Bank 323
Ymnos, The 260
Young v. H.M. Advocate 132
—— v. Queensland Trustees Ltd. (1956) 55
—— v. Rank 98
—— v. Schuler 357

TABLE OF STATUTES

1677	Statute of Frauds (29 Car. 2, c. 3)	309	1898	Criminal Evidence Act—*cont.* s. 1—*cont.*		
1837	Wills Act (7 Will. 4 & 1 Vict. c. 26)	357		(i)	224–226	
	s. 9	352		(ii)	226–234	
	s. 21	346		(iii)	234–236	
1843	Libel Act (6 & 7 Vict. c. 96)—		1911	Perjury Act (1 & 2 Geo. 5, c. 6)—		
	s. 6	66		s. 1(1)	121	
1861	Offences against the Person Act (24 & 25 Vict. c. 100)—			s. 13	166	
				Official Secrets Act (1 & 2 Geo. 5, c. 28)—		
	s. 57	86		s. 1(2)	207	
1865	Criminal Procedure Act (28 & 29 Vict. c. 18)	268		(3)	207	
	s. 3	113, 114, 116	1915	Indictments Act (5 & 6 Geo. 5, c. 90)—		
	s. 4	114, 121		s. 5(3)	218	
	s. 5	114, 121	1916	Larceny Act (6 & 7 Geo. 5, c. 50)—		
	s. 6	121		s. 43(2)	154	
	s. 7	344		Prevention of Corruption Act (6 & 7 Geo. 5, c. 64)—		
	s. 8	22				
1874	Infants Relief Act (37 & 38 Vict. c. 62)	309		s. 2	67	
1879	Bankers' Books Evidence Act (42 & 43 Vict. c. 11)	283	1920	Official Secrets Act (10 & 11 Geo. 5, c. 75)—		
	s. 6	130, 284		s. 6	180	
	s. 7	153		s. 8(2)	180	
1882	Bills of Exchange Act (45 & 46 Vict. c. 61)—			(4)	96	
	s. 30(2)	66	1925	Law of Property Act (15 & 16 Geo. 5, c. 20)	87	
1883	Explosive Substances Act (46 & 47 Vict. c. 1)—			s. 40	352	
	s. 4	66		s. 184	87	
1890	Partnership Act (53 & 54 Vict. c. 39)—			Administration of Estates Act (15 & 16 Geo. 5, c. 23)—		
	s. 15	279		s. 46	87	
1891	Stamp Act (54 & 55 Vict. c. 39)—			(3)	87	
	s. 14	346		Criminal Justice Act (15 & 16 Geo. 5, c. 86)—		
1897	Police (Property) Act (60 & 61 Vict. c. 30)	81		s. 13(3)	296	
1898	Criminal Evidence Act (61 & 62 Vict. c. 36)	205	1933	Children and Young Persons Act (23 & 24 Geo. 5, c. 12)—		
	s. 1	132, 221–236, **367–368**		s. 37	96	
	(a)	132, 133, 187		s. 38	130	
	(b)	132, 187		s. 39	96	
	(e)	153, 221, 222		s. 99	27	
	(f)	221–236				

xxxix

Year	Statute	Page
1936	Public Order Act (1 Edw. 8 & 1 Geo. 6, c. 6)	38
1938	Evidence Act (1 & 2 Geo. 6, c. 28)	258, 265
	s. 3	345
	s. 4	345
1946	Borrowing (Control and Guarantees) Act (9 & 10 Geo. 6, c. 58)—	
	Sched. 1, para. 2 (1)	154
1949	Representation of the People Act (12, 13 & 14 Geo., c. 68)—	
	s. 146 (5)	165
	s. 168 (5)	165
	National Parks and Access to the Countryside Act (12, 13 & 14 Geo. 6, c, 97)—	
	s. 32	284
1950	Arbitration Act (14 Geo. 6, c. 27)—	
	s. 23	320
1952	Diplomatic Immunities (Commonwealth Countries and Republic of Ireland) Act (15 & 16 Geo. 6 & 1 Eliz. 2, c. 18)—	
	s. 1	130
	Customs and Excise Act (15 & 16 Geo. 6 & 1 Eliz. 2, c. 44)—	
	s. 290 (1)	66
	Intestates' Estates Act (15 & 16 Geo. 6 & 1 Eliz. 2, c. 64)—	
	s. 1 (4)	87
1953	Prevention of Crime Act (1 & 2 Eliz. 2, c. 14)	35
1955	International Finance Corporation Act (3 & 4 Eliz. 2, c. 5)—	
	s. 3	130
	Food and Drugs Act (4 & 5 Eliz. 2, c. 16)—	
	s. 111	67
1956	Sexual Offences Act (4 & 5 Eliz. 2, c. 69)—	
	ss. 2–4	165
	s. 22	165
	s. 23	165
	s. 30 (2)	67
1957	Homicide Act (5 & 6 Eliz. 2, c. 11)—	
	s. 2 (2)	66
	Solicitors Act (5 & 6 Eliz. 2, c. 27)—	
	s. 17	283
	Dentists Act (5 & 6 Eliz. 2, c. 28)—	
	s. 25 (3)	340
	Cheques Act (5 & 6 Eliz. 2, c. 36)—	
	s. 3	88
	Affiliation Proceedings Act (5 & 6 Eliz. 2, c. 55)	319
1958	Crimes Act (Vic.)—	
	s. 62 (3)	174
1959	Obscene Publications Act (7 & 8 Eliz. 2, c. 66)—	
	s. 4	66
1963	Purchase Tax Act (c. 9)—	
	s. 24 (5)	180
	(6)	154, 180
	s. 33 (5)	180
	Children and Young Persons Act (c. 37)—	
	s. 28	128
1964	Criminal Procedure (Right of Reply) Act (c. 34)	97
	Diplomatic Privileges Act (c. 81)—	
	s. 2	130
	Sched. 1	130
	Criminal Procedure (Insanity) Act (c. 84)—	
	s. 6	66
1965	Criminal Evidence Act (c. 20)	291
	National Insurance Act (c. 51)—	
	s. 90	180
1966	Selective Employment Payments Act (c. 32)—	
	s. 64 (4)	154
1967	Road Safety Act (c. 30)—	
	s. 2 (1)	39
	Criminal Law Act (c. 58)—	
	s. 1	169
	s. 4	169

1967	Road Traffic Regulation Act (c. 76)—	
	s. 78A (2)	166
	Criminal Justice Act (c. 80)—	
	s. 8	90
	s. 9	295
	s. 10	29, 60, 66
	s. 11	185, 186, 293
	(2)	185
	(3)	185
	(5)	280
	(8)	186
1968	Criminal Appeal Act (c. 19)	331
	s. 2	40, 127, 167, 169, 187, 189
	(1)	40, 47, 71, 126, 128, 172, 205
	s. 7	127
	s. 23	127
	(1)	127
	(2)	127
	Firearms Act (c. 27)—	
	s. 211	207
	International Organisations Act (c. 48)	130
	Theft Act (c. 60)	38
	s. 9 (1) (a)	331
	(b)	331
	s. 25 (3)	9
	(4)	67
	s. 27 (3)	207
	s. 31 (1)	155
	Sched. 3, Pt. 1	154
	Civil Evidence Act (c. 64)	16, 23, 42, 114, 274, 284, 285, 291, 297, 350, **369–389**
	Pt. I	258, 259, 391
	s. 1	281, **369**
	(1)	239, 257, 271
	s. 2	99, 105, 114, 116, 118, 123, 256, 258–267, 269–270, 272–276, 278, 280, 281, 285, 287, 289, 290, 292, 293, **369–370**
	(1)	259, 260, 264
	(2)	261, 264
	(a)	262
	(3)	260
	s. 3	116, 259, 268–270, 272, **370**
	(b)	107
	(2)	103, 106

1968	Civil Evidence Act—*cont.*	
	s. 4	99, 123, 256, 258, 259, 264–267, 269–270, 272, 281, 289, 290, 292, 293, **370–371**
	(2)	265
	(3)	264, 266
	s. 5	99, 256, 258, 259, 267–270, 272, 292, 336, 370, **371–373**
	(2)	267, 268
	(3)	268
	(4)	268, 374
	(6)	267, 294
	s. 6	258, 259, **373–375**
	(1)	351
	(2)	287
	(3)	13, 269, 294
	(4)	163
	(5)	268
	s. 7	99, 270, **375**
	(1)	123
	s. 8	261, **375–377**
	(3)	256
	(a)	271
	(b)	271
	s. 9	257, 258, 271, **378–379**
	(1)	271
	(2)	271
	(c)–(d)	281
	(3)	285, 289
	(a)	272, 285
	(5)	258
	s. 10	**379–380**
	(1)	260
	s. 11	78, 81, 337, 338, **381–382**
	s. 12	328, 339, **382–383**
	(3)	340
	s. 13	338, 381, **383–384**
	s. 14	151, **384–385**
	(1) (a)	153
	s. 15	149, **385–386**
	s. 16	**386–387**
	s. 18	**387–388**
	(1)	258
	(5)	271
	s. 19	**388**
	s. 20	**388–389**
	s. 46 (3)	294
1969	Family Law Reform Act (c. 46)—	
	s. 23 (1)	181
	(2)	181
	s. 26	84

1971	Courts Act (c. 23)—	1974	Consumer Credit Act (c. 39)—
	s. 7 (2) 35		s. 165 (3) 154
	Misuse of Drugs Act (c. 38)—		Rehabilitation of Offenders Act (c. 53) 121
	s. 5 .... 69, 70		Pt. VII **393–399**
	(2) 69		s. 4 (1) 121
	Criminal Damage Act (c. 48)—		s. 7 121
	s. 9 155	1975	Finance Act (c. 7)—
1972	Road Traffic Act (c. 20)—		s. 22 (9) 87
	s. 7 (1) 181		Social Security Act (c. 14)—
	s. 99 207		s. 50 (3) 66
	s. 143 (3) 66	1976	Sexual Offences (Amendment) Act (c. 82)—
	s. 168 (2) 154		
	(3) 180		
	Civil Evidence Act (c. 30)—		s. 2 120
	s. 1 259		s. 4 97
	s. 2 (3) 145		s. 6 97
	s. 3 (1) 25		s. 7 (2) 120
	(2) 21	1977	Rent Act (c. 42) 309
	s. 4 (1) 22		Criminal Law Act (c. 45)—
	(2) 34, 47, 340		s. 7 (6)–(8) 66
	Finance Act (c. 41)—		s. 54 398
	s. 35 154	1978	Oaths Act (c. 19)—
	(2) 180		s. 1 129
	(3) 180		s. 3 129
	s. 38 (7) 180		s. 4 129
	Affiliation Proceedings (Amendment) Act (c. 49) 165		s. 5 129
			s. 6 129–
			Interpretation Act (c. 30)—
	s. 4 165		s. 7 88
	s. 8 165		Employment Protection (Consolidation) Act (c. 44)—
	Local Government Act (c. 70)—		
	s. 250 (2) 154		s. 133 (*b*) 149, 278
	Criminal Justice Act (c. 71)—		s. 134 (5) 149, 278
		1979	Wages Councils Act (c. 12)—
	s. 36 36		s. 1 221
1973	Matrimonial Causes Act (c. 18)—		s. 22 (3) 154
			Banking Act (c. 37)—
	s. 1 (1) 76		Sched. 6, para. 1 283
	(3) 328	1980	Magistrates' Courts Act (c. 43)—
	s. 4 329		
	s. 19 (3) 86		s. 2 96
	s. 45 321		s. 6 (2) 95
	(5) (*b*) 321		s. 69 97
	s. 48 (2) 96		(2) 96
	Powers of Criminal Courts Act (c. 62)—		(4) 96
			s. 101 .... 67, 69, 70
	s. 20 (5) 27		s. 102 .... 293, 296
1974	Legal Aid Act (c. 4)—		
	s. 22 154		

Table of Statutes

1980	Magistrates' Courts Act —cont.	
	s. 111	36
	Highways Act (c. 66)—	
	s. 35	284
1981	Contempt of Court Act (c. 49)—	
	s. 4 (1)	95
	(2)	96
	s. 10	142, 149, 150
	Supreme Court Act (c. 54)—	
	s. 42	334
	s. 72	151, 154
	Criminal Justice (Amendment) Act (c. 27)—	
	s. 1	96
1982	Civil Jurisdiction and Judgments Act (c. 27)—	
	s. 32	319
	s. 34	320
	s. 72	130, 131, 191
	Local Government (Miscellaneous Provisions) Act (c. 30)—	
	Sched. 3, para. 6	67
	para. 20	67
	Administration of Justice Act (c. 53)	191
	s. 20	357, 362
	s. 21	363
1984	Road Traffic Regulations Act (c. 27)—	
	s. 168 (3)	180
	Police and Criminal Evidence Act (c. 60)	7, 70, 105, 191, 195–203, 256, 291, 294, 350, **390–409**
	Pt. VII	**390–392**, 395
	s. 8	144, 151
	s. 9	144
	s. 11	151
	s. 18	144
	s. 19	144
	ss. 34–44	198
	ss. 41–44	202
	s. 56	202
	s. 58	202
	s. 66	199, 202, 293
	s. 67 (8)	199
	(10)	199
	(11)	199, 202

1984	Police and Criminal Evidence Act—cont.	
	s. 68	116, 123, 291, 292–295, 298, **390**
	(1) (a)	293
	(2)	201
	(3)	292
	s. 69	292, 293, 294, 295, **391**
	s. 70	**391**
	s. 71	**391**
	s. 72	**391–392**
	(1)	293
	(2)	293, 294
	s. 73	121, **392–393**
	s. 74	78, 338, **393**
	(1)	339
	(2)	339
	(3)	330
	s. 75	**393–394**
	s. 76	192, 299, **394–395**
	(1)	107, 195, 197, 300
	(2)	47, 152, 195, 196, 197, 199, 201
	(b)	199
	(3)	195
	(4)	201
	(5)	201
	s. 77	166, **396**
	s. 78	**396**
	(1)	43, 44, 196, 296
	(8)	198
	s. 79	100, **397**
	s. 80	**397–398**
	(1) (a)	133
	(b)	133
	(3)	134
	(a)	134
	(b)	134
	(c)	134
	(4)	133
	(6)	134
	(8)	134
	s. 82	107, **398–399**
	(1)	195, 197
	(3)	43, 117, 201, 202
	s. 118 (1)	293
	Sched. 3	292, 293, **399–403**
	para. 2	293
	para. 3	99, 294
	(b)	123, 294
	(c)	116
	para. 7	294
	para. 13	351
	para. 14 (a)	293

1984	Police and Criminal Evidence Act—*cont.*		1985	Insolvency Act (c. 65)—	
	Sched. 3—*cont.*			s. 68	154
	para. 14(*b*)	293		s. 119	321
	para. 15	293		s. 126	321
	Sched. 8, para. 8	295		s. 136	321
	para. 9	295		s. 137	154
1985	Prosecution of Offences Act (c. 23)—			s. 138(1)	66
	s. 24	334	1986	Agricultural Holdings Act (c. 5)	309

RULES OF THE SUPREME COURT

Ord. 24, r. 2	141	
r. 3	141	
r. 5	141	
r. 8	141	
r. 9	141	
r. 15	141	
Ord. 26	28	
r. 1	95	
Ord. 27—		
r. 1	29	
r. 2	28	
r. 8(1)	26	
Ord. 38	265, 269, 272	
r. 2	95	
r. 21	262	
r. 22	262	
r. 24	268	
r. 25	262	
r. 26	262	
(4)	262	
r. 27	262	
(4)	264	
Ord. 38—*cont.*		
r. 28	262, 271	
r. 29	256, 270	
(1)	264	
r. 30	270	
r. 31	270	
r. 32	263	
r. 34	259	
r. 38	145	
Ord. 39, r. 1	95	
r. 8	95	
Ord. 53	326	
Ord. 55, r. 7	40	
Ord. 59, r. 3	126	
r. 9	126	
r. 10	126	
r. 11	40	
(5)	347	
r. 12	126	
Ord. 73, r. 2	320	
Ord. 112, r. 6	40	

REFERENCES AND ABBREVIATIONS

Archbold	*Pleading, Evidence and Practice in Criminal Cases* (42nd ed. 1985)
Blackstone	*Commentaries* (1769)
C.L.J.	*Cambridge Law Journal*
C.L.R.C.	*Criminal Law Revision Committee, 11th Report: Evidence (General), Cmnd. 4991* (1972)
Crim. L.R.	*Criminal Law Review*
Cross	*Evidence* (6th ed. 1985)
Eggleston	*Evidence, Proof and Probability* (2nd ed. 1983)
Hale	*Pleas of the Crown* (1778 ed.)
Halsbury	*The Laws of England* (Hailsham ed. 1976)
Heydon	*Evidence: Cases and Materials* (2nd ed. 1984)
J.S.P.T.L.	*Journal of the Society of Public Teachers of Law*
L.Q.R.	*Law Quarterly Review*
M.L.R.	*Modern Law Review*
Phipson	*The Law of Evidence* (13th ed. 1982)
R.S.C.	*Rules of the Supreme Court*
Stephen	*Digest of the Law of Evidence* (10th ed. 1922)
Thayer	*A Preliminary Treatise on Evidence at the Common Law* (1898)
Wigmore	*A Treatise on the Anglo-American System of Evidence* (Chadbourn rev. 1979)
Williams: C.L.G.P.	*Criminal Law: The General Part* (2nd ed. 1961)
Williams: Textbook	*Textbook of Criminal Law* (2nd ed. 1983)

Part I

PRELIMINARIES

CHAPTER 1
INTRODUCTION

	Page
A. The Nature of the Subject	3
1. Evidence Generally	3
2. Judicial Evidence	4
B. Arrangement of the Subject	6
C. Definitions	8

CHAPTER 2
PRELIMINARY MATTERS

A. Basic Rules	14
1. What Facts may be Proved	14
2. How may Facts be Proved?	26
3. Facts which need not be Proved	27
B. Functions of Judge and Jury	35
1. Judicial Control of the Jury	37
2. Facts for the Judge	47

Chapter 1

INTRODUCTION

A. The Nature of the Subject

1. Evidence Generally

Evidence is anything which tends to persuade an inquirer of the existence or non-existence of some fact or situation which he is inquiring about. It need not in fact persuade the inquirer; it is enough that it *tends* to persuade him. The inquirer may disbelieve it or prefer other contrary evidence which he finds more persuasive. But anything which, if accepted, would tend as a matter of logic to render it more probable than before that the inquired-about fact or situation exists or does not exist is evidence. If A, on arrival at a station, is told by B, a person already there, that a particular train has not yet departed, A may disbelieve B. Nevertheless, B's statement is evidence, because if he believed it A could deduce that the train had not yet departed.

Evidence might give the inquirer the wrong answer, without ceasing to be evidence. If B lies in his teeth when he tells A that the train has not gone, B's statement is still evidence; A is entitled to deduce from it that the train has not gone. That he does not choose to do so makes no difference. Likewise A may accept the fact that the platform is still full of people as indicating that the train has not yet gone, so the presence of those people is evidence. A's logical deduction may be wrong; the bystanders may be as deluded as he is; but since he can logically deduce from the presence of the crowd the fact that the train has still to go, the presence of the crowd is evidence on the question he is engaged with. Evidence may offer an answer which is rejected, or one which, although accepted, is wrong; but if logically it offers an answer at all, it is evidence. It is only if no-one can reasonably draw an inference at all from the material about the existence of the fact inquired about that that material is not evidence of the fact.

Sometimes we use the word "evidence" in a loose, figurative, way, as if one says: "I deduce that it is dinnertime from the evidence of my stomach," and it is common to say, "I believe the evidence of my own eyes." But evidence is more accurately used of some external thing, something other than the direct perception of the inquirer, which makes up for the lack of direct perception by tending to persuade him of a fact or situation which he has *not* directly perceived. We all act on evidence, in this proper sense of the word, every day. There are no rules imposed on us from outside telling us what evidence we can act on in ordering our own affairs. We may be as capricious or illogical as we wish in making our private decisions. If I am thinking of investing my own money in some undertaking, I can form my own estimation of that undertaking's solvency, I can act on the most untrustworthy evidence imaginable. It is my own money I am risking. I can refuse to eat at a certain restaurant because I have been told, through several unreliable intermediaries, that the kitchen is swarming with cockroaches. Neither the disappointed restaurateur nor anyone else can complain to me about the way I have arrived at my decision. So it is throughout all the affairs of my life. The only exceptions are those few cases where the law requires me to act reasonably or on reasonable grounds. For example, if I dismiss an employee for misconduct, the law might condemn the dismissal as unfair if my decision was reached on wholly unreliable evidence.

2. Judicial Evidence

But when we come to judicial evidence, we are at once in a thicket of rules. If, in the course of settling a dispute, a court has to make up its mind on facts (as it usually has to do), it is not allowed to accept just any evidence of those facts. It must observe a large number of rules about this, which rules make up the law of evidence; and if these rules are broken, the court's decision may be challenged on just that ground. Even if the evidence listened to was quite cogent, and the view of the facts arrived at by the court very probably the true one, if the court acted on wrong evidence, or without rightful evidence, its decision is in principle impeachable.

Many of the rules of evidence are rules of exclusion: *this* kind of evidence cannot be taken account of; *this* kind of evidence is not, without more, evidence of this fact; *this* class of persons cannot testify in this sort of case, and so on. The reason for these exclusionary rules is historical. Until quite recently in our history the only judges of fact were jurors (or lay justices of the peace). Completely without experience in evaluating witnesses or evidence, they were assumed to be prone to overvalue certain types of misleadingly attractive evidence, which a trained person would handle with caution. The common law compensated—indeed, over-compensated—for the jurors' innocence by putting them in blinkers and not allowing them to hear the suspect evidence at all. It insisted on doing this even if there was no other acceptable evidence at all, which amounted to throwing the baby out with the bath water. No doubt the jury was prevented from overvaluing what it was not allowed to hear, but a lover of justice would regard that as scant compensation if a just claim or defence was defeated solely because there was no evidence which was acceptable under the common law's artificial and rigid rules.

The rigidity of those rules is exposed nowhere more clearly than by the fact that on the whole they are not relaxed if the arbiter of fact is not a jury but a professional judge. Where trial is by judge alone, the reason for many of the common law rules disappears. He is certainly capable of giving due weight and no more than due weight to each piece of evidence. His long training and experience will have taught him how to do it. But usually he is treated by the law in exactly the same way as an untrained juror; what the latter cannot listen to, he cannot listen to. This is all the more remarkable when it is remembered that today the once ubiquitous jury is just about obsolete in wide areas of the law. It is hardly ever seen in civil cases, and the overwhelming proportion of crimes, even indictable crimes, is now tried summarily, *i.e.* by magistrates who, if they are lay magistrates, may not indeed have much formal legal training, but at least have day-to-day experience of evaluating evidence partially to compensate for that lack.[1] Clearly the law ought to have been changed to take account of the virtual disappearance of the jury, but to a large extent it remains as it was in the jury's hey-day. The law's operation can only be described as baneful. It excludes evidence which is logically probative, and that must make it more difficult for the court to do what it is supposed to be doing, which is getting at the truth.

Of course it must be admitted that the court is trying to "get at the truth" only in a very limited sense. "What is Truth? said jesting Pilate, and would not stay for an answer." No mortal man can hope to get at the truth of any occurrence completely and

---

[1] Nor, perhaps, is the modern jury quite such a party of yokels as tradition would have them. "Perhaps it is not irrelevant in the year 1976 for the Court to take judicial notice of the fact that one of the popular forms of entertainment nowadays on television is a series of reconstructed trials which have a striking degree of realism. Most jurors nowadays know something about the burden and standard of proof before they ever get into the jury box"; *per* Lawton L.J., in *R. v. Ching* (1976) 63 Cr.App.R. 7 at p. 9.

utterly, and a court is not even claiming to do that. It is not conducting a scientific investigation. It can only examine that aspect of an incident which the parties ask it to look at and which is relevant to the legal issues raised by the litigation. It can only use the evidence which the parties put before it. It must make up its mind *now*; even if the matter being investigated, although now lying partly in shadow, is likely to be fully illuminated by future events, the court cannot wait for them. And it must make up its mind one way or the other, even if a scientific inquirer would throw up his hands and cry, "We just don't know." On the other hand, a philosopher made uneasy by the shallowness of the excavation may comfort himself by the thought that the court does not declare what it has unearthed to be the truth for ever and for all purposes. Its findings usually bind only those who asked it to dig, *i.e* the parties. Other persons with an interest in the matter may later try to persuade another court that the "truth" was otherwise.

Still, that the inquiry is limited in scope and superficial in depth is no good reason why the law of evidence should actively contribute to those shortcomings. On the contrary, the shortcomings make it all the more important that the tribunal should not be plagued by the superfluous illogicalities which are, on the whole, all that the law of evidence can contribute. The law is unattractive not only in excluding logically probative evidence, but also in being very complicated, thus obliging a judge to bemuse a jury by inflicting on them tortuous and unintelligible explanations. The need for reform, mostly consisting in drawing the law of evidence's teeth one by one, has become widely recognised in this century, and a fair amount of progress has been made in the last few decades. It may be that the movement for reform has temporarily run out of steam, but however that may be, let no-one think that any amount of reform will ever allow courts to "get at the truth" in any complete sense.

B. Arrangement of the Subject

It is necessary to say something about the arrangement of this work. Doubts about how the subject ought to be arranged seem to afflict writers on evidence more than other legal authors. No two books on evidence are arranged in the same way; and some authors, the present one not excluded, have been known to alter arrangements in successive editions. Part of the difficulty stems from the fact that in theory, but no longer in reality, the law is the same for civil and criminal cases. In former times this was largely true in reality, and most of the law consisted of exceptions to one great exclusionary rule, the hearsay rule. A natural arrangement then was to state the rule, to follow with a detailed exposition of the exceptions to the rule, and to round off with certain isolated topics which were not connected with the rule.

But now civil and criminal evidence have drifted apart, although there is still some overlap. In civil cases, the jury has all but disappeared and the hearsay rule has all but been abolished by statute. But on the criminal side, the jury still plays an important part, and the hearsay rule and its exceptions continue to flourish. There are many more rules on the criminal side and, as they mostly cannot be waived, they remain active there. This all suggests that a book should have two parts—civil evidence and criminal evidence, but there is still a sizeable portion of overlap and there will always be problems which affect both sides equally.

Moreover, if we ask, why has evidence largely withered on the vine in civil cases, when it is still flourishing exuberantly on the criminal side, the answer is, because of the presence of the accused person in a criminal trial and the consequent need to protect his special position, which is unlike that of any other litigant. For much of our history, the practical and procedural difficulties under which an accused person laboured meant that to a considerable extent the scales were loaded against him, and many of the rules were developed by the judges as a necessary counterbalance in his favour. Now that most of the difficulties have disappeared, it is arguable that he is less in need of special protection. In 1972, the Criminal Law Revision Committee proposed a substantial dismantling of the apparatus of protection, particularly with regard to the accused's "right of silence."[2] However, their Report[3] got a rough handling from public opinion, and was pigeonholed for over a decade. Some of its less controversial suggestions were implemented by the Police and Criminal Evidence Act 1984, but its more radical proposals for making the position of an accused person much more like that of a litigant in a civil action look unlikely to be acted upon in the foreseeable future. So the apparatus of protection is still there and, realistically speaking, is what the modern law of evidence is chiefly about.

Recognition of this reality demands that topics germane to the

---

[2] As to this, see *post*, Chap. 9.
[3] Criminal Law Revision Committee, 11th Report: Evidence (General), Cmnd. 4991 (1972) (hereinafter referred to as "C.L.R.C.").

protection of the accused be accorded a prominence they were not given in traditional tables of contents.[4] But although such a plan may succeed in reflecting more perfectly than some others the living as opposed to the moribund part of the law, it will not achieve what seems as far away as ever it was, namely, a tidy exposition of the whole subject.[5] Among the various factors which make loose ends and repetitions inevitable is the fact that some of most of the topics found under the rubric "Protection of the Accused" have a continuing, usually minor, relevance in civil proceedings. For example, one very important topic in criminal evidence is confessions. But confessions are one type of admission, and admissions form one exception to the hearsay rule which is still active in civil proceedings. Most of the cases on who can make admissions, what force admissions have and so on, are civil cases. Yet the current importance of and activity in the topic is largely found on the criminal side, because of the need to protect the accused from improperly obtained confessions.

Some areas of the law of evidence are today moribund, although technically not dead. Prominent among these are those exceptions to the hearsay rule which, although once nominally applicable to both civil and criminal cases, were in practice found on the civil side only. They were abolished as to civil cases in 1968. They would have been abolished as to criminal cases if the Criminal Law Revision Committee's Report of 1972 had been fully implemented. Since it has not been fully implemented, they are theoretically applicable in criminal cases although never in fact found there. It seems a waste of time and space to treat of these (*e.g.* various declarations by deceased persons), and they get only the briefest of mentions. Further accounts may be found in other works.

C. Definitions

The exposition of the law of evidence suffers from a vitiated and incoherent vocabulary of key terms. Terms are used in different senses, and there are places of overlap in that more than one term can be used for one concept. A comprehensive and water-tight set of definitions is therefore an elaborate affair which is often not only daunting to the student but also in some sense counter productive. One is usually in little doubt as to what is meant by

---

[4] The arrangement adopted in this work owes much to the example of Heydon, *Evidence: Cases and Materials* (2nd ed., 1984).
[5] In particular, that curse of evidence books, the ever-present swarm of footnote cross-references, seems impossible to avoid however one proceeds.

Definitions

some judicial utterance, *unless* one remembers some hard-learned glossary, when ambiguities at once creep in. A failure to master the vocabulary at the outset, while it might seem fainthearted, appears to have something to be said for it in practical terms. We may compromise by defining only a few terms and in a fairly rough and ready way,[6] sufficient to make what follows comprehensible, but not sufficient to satisfy all purists and not to be taken literally and rigidly when considering every reported judgment. Perhaps it is true that sloppy language has made sloppy law in places,[7] but the damage has long since been done and nothing will be gained, at any rate for the student, by a belated adherence to a comprehensive and logical scheme of terms.

Proof is the establishment of the existence or non-existence of some fact to the satisfaction of the tribunal charged with the duty of trying fact (*i.e.* if there is a jury, the jury is the tribunal of fact; if the trial is by judge alone or before magistrates, he or they is or are the tribunal of fact). The commonest means of proof is evidence,[8] although there are others, namely, formal admissions, judicial notice and presumptions.[9]

Evidence in a legal context,[10] is used in at least two senses. First, evidence is the means of proof, *how* things are proved although as seen above, it is not the only means. The commonest form which evidence takes is the testimony of witnesses, oral or written, but it may also take the form of the production of things, including documents (real evidence).[11] The term "evidence" is also applied to *facts* which are allowed to be proved (*i.e.* are admissible) because *relevant*. A fact is said to be "evidence" of a second fact if the law allows the first fact to be proved in order to establish the

---

[6] None but the bold should, on a first reading, tackle the footnotes, for they often contain dismaying qualifications of the definitions in the text.
[7] See Thayer, § 511, cited Wigmore, para. 2, p. 8.
[8] "Evidence becomes proof when the jury accept it as being sufficient for proof" Williams *Textbook*, p. 53. Proof may also be evidence, see *e.g.* The Theft Act 1968, s.25(3) (*post*, p. 67) which provides that proof that a man had with him certain articles shall be evidence that he had them with him for certain purposes. Moreover, the word "proof" is also applied to a written statement made by a prospective witness indicating to the lawyer who is hoping to call him the evidence that he is able to give (see *post*, Chap. 6, on Examination of Witnesses).
[9] See *post*, Chap. 2.
[10] The *nature* of evidence generally is discussed *ante*, pp. 3, 4.
[11] For real evidence, see *post*, p. 26.

second fact.[12] Thus the possession of goods which have been recently stolen is "evidence" of guilty knowledge.[13] This means that in order to prove guilty knowledge (a fact in issue in a prosecution for handling stolen goods) it is permitted to prove possession of recently stolen goods.

Admissibility. Said of evidence in its first sense above, admissibility means that the court is not precluded from receiving it by some rule of law: *e.g.* evidence may be inadmissible because it is hearsay. Said of a fact, admissibility means that the law allows it to be proved. It is only allowed to be proved if it is either in issue or has some degree of relevance to the facts in issue.

A fact in issue is one which is directly in contention between the parties, *i.e.* one which the plaintiff (or prosecutor) must establish to win his case, or which the defendant must establish to succeed in some defence which is open to him.

Relevance is the relationship between one fact and another wherein, according to the rules of logic and the common experience of men, the existence of the one renders probable the existence or non-existence of the other. A fact which is not actually in issue but is in this relationship with a fact in issue is a relevant fact. Relevance is not a legal concept, being rather one of logic and common sense, but the law insists on its presence, by ruling that all irrelevant facts are inadmissible. However this does not mean that all relevant facts are admissible,[14] for there are many rules excluding evidence of relevant facts on some ground or other.[15]

---

[12] Such is often called "circumstantial evidence," but this is not the only meaning of the that term; see *post*, p. 11.
[13] Note that it is not conclusive evidence, but guilty knowledge *may* be inferred from possession, so possession is *evidence* of guilty knowledge. See *post*, p. 89.
[14] "Opinions from knowledgeable persons about a man's personality and mental make-up play a part in many human judgments. In our judgment, the psychiatrist's opinion was relevant. Relevance, however, does not result in evidence being admissible; it is a condition precedent to admissibility": *per* Lawton L.J., in *R. v. Turner* [1975] Q.B. 834 at p. 841.
[15] Which is why, although relevance and admissibility are often used interchangeably, it makes for clarity if they are kept separate: see *per* Lord Simon of Glaisdale in *D.P.P. v. Kilbourne* [1973] A.C. 729 at p. 754. But they are not always kept separate. See, *e.g. R. v. Rimmer & Beech* [1983] Crim.L.R. 250 where, speaking of medical evidence which is only marginally relevant, the Court of Appeal said that it was the judge's duty to ensure that the only evidence allowed was that which was not only admissible but also relevant. On marginal relevance, see *post*, p. 17.

Definitions

Direct evidence is contrasted with circumstantial evidence. Direct evidence consists either of the testimony of a witness who perceived the fact to be proved or the production of a document or thing which constitutes the fact to be proved. Circumstantial evidence of a fact to be proved is the testimony of a witness who perceived, not the fact to be proved, but another fact from which the existence or non-existence of the fact can be deduced, or the production of a document or thing from which the fact to be proved can be deduced.[16] The fact to be proved can be either a fact in issue or a fact relevant to the issue. Suppose a fact in issue is whether A used a certain knife. A fact relevant to this fact in issue is whether A had the knife in his possession, for if we find he had it in his possession, we may go on and find he used it. If T says that he saw A use the knife he is giving direct evidence of a fact in issue. If T says he saw the knife in A's hand, he is giving direct evidence of a relevant fact (possession), but only circumstantial evidence of A's using the knife. If T says he saw the knife among A's belongings, he is giving circumstantial evidence of A's possession of the knife (a relevant fact) and circumstantial evidence of A's using the knife (a fact in issue). Of course, all witnesses necessarily give direct evidence of whatever it was they perceived, and here T is giving direct evidence of the position of the knife, from which we may deduce A's possession of it, and thus A's use of it.

Circumstantial evidence is also used, not in contrast to direct, *i.e.* not in describing the quality of the testimony given, but as a description of the facts proved, if they are not directly in issue, but only logically related to a fact in issue.[17] Relevant facts constitute circumstantial evidence, *e.g.* "Possession of recently stolen goods is circumstantial evidence of guilty knowledge."

Original evidence is contrasted with hearsay evidence. Original evidence is the evidence of a witness who deposes to facts of his own knowledge.[18] If his information is derived from other persons and he himself has no personal knowledge of the facts to which he deposes then his evidence is said to be hearsay.[19] The general

---

[16] See further on this, *post*, p. 16.
[17] See, *ante*, p. 10.
[18] Some writers use, instead of the word "original," the word "direct" in contrast to "hearsay." The possibility of confusion with "direct" as opposed to "circumstantial" (see above) ought to be obvious. One might wish to say of a particular piece of evidence (a narration by A of B's statement about a fact in issue) that it is both direct and hearsay, which will be productive of much puzzlement in one used to using "direct" and "hearsay" as opposites.
[19] For a more exact discussion of hearsay, see *post*, Chap. 12.

rule, at any rate in criminal cases, is that hearsay evidence is not admissible. The person who saw or heard or otherwise perceived the fact must be produced and not someone to whom he gave or wrote an account of what happened. There are numerous exceptions where hearsay evidence is allowed, and it must also be borne in mind that it does not always follow, if A is giving evidence of what B said, that A is giving hearsay evidence. The fact of B's saying the words might be a fact in issue, as if B is being sued for slander, and if so A is giving original evidence of that fact. It is only when the object of A's testimony is to persuade the court that some fact is as B said it was that A's evidence is hearsay.

Oral and documentary evidence. Oral evidence consists of statements in court by witnesses. Documentary evidence consists of documents produced for inspection by the court. The distinction is dictated by the fact that special rules govern the proof of contents of documents, as to which, see Chapter 17.

Best and inferior evidence. Inferior evidence is that which suggests that better evidence might be available, *e.g.* a copy of a document which suggests that somewhere the original exists, or a description of an object by a witness when the object could be produced for inspection. The so-called best evidence rule precluded the production of inferior evidence if the best could be produced. The rule, once thought to be fundamental, has declined greatly in importance, and now applies exclusively to documents and copies of documents[20] (where the terms usually used are "primary" and "secondary" evidence). It does not now prevent the description of an object when the object could be produced,[21] nor, apparently, the production of a copy film or tape recording where the original could be produced[22].

These divisions of evidence are different ways of dividing up the same entity, evidence. How an item is placed inside one classification has no necessary consequences for how it is placed in another classification.[23] Thus an item of documentary evidence

---

[20] *Garton v. Hunter* [1969] 2 Q.B. 37, *per* Lord Denning M.R. at p. 44. On this see *post*, Chap. 17.
[21] *Hocking v. Ahlquist* [1944] K.B. 120 at pp. 123, 124; *R. v. Orrell* [1972] R.T.R. 14.
[22] *Kajala v. Noble* (1982) 75 Cr.App.R. 149.
[23] Cheese may be Cheddar, Cheshire or Brie. Cheese may also be fresh, stale or mouldy. To describe one hunk as Cheddar is not to say whether it is fresh, stale or mouldy; condemning another hunk as stale does not identify it as Cheddar, Cheshire or Brie.

Definitions

may be testimonial, hearsay and circumstantial. An item of oral evidence may be direct and original and even real.[24]

Admissibility of evidence must be distinguished from weight of evidence. Admissibility refers to whether a piece of evidence is permitted to be given. Weight refers to the evidence's cogency, *i.e.* the degree of persuasiveness it exhibits. As will be seen, questions of admissibility are for the judge, but deciding what weight to give to evidence if it is admitted is for the jury.[25] If it is said that an objection to certain evidence "goes to weight not to admissibility" (*e.g.* the fact that the absent maker of a statement now proved in court had a motive to misrepresent the facts[26]), what is meant is that the objection does not require the judge to prevent the evidence being given, but does require to be borne in mind by the jury in deciding how persuasive the evidence is. Occasionally the judge has to form a view of the weight of evidence before he can rule on its admissibility (*e.g.* similar fact evidence[27]), and in every trial, he has to decide whether the plaintiff or prosecutor has adduced sufficient evidence, *i.e.* evidence weighty enough to justify a finding in that party's favour, before he allows the jury to consider whether the evidence convinces them.[28]

Weight must be distinguished from credibility. Evidence is credible if it is worthy of belief, *e.g.* if it comes from a trustworthy source. It does not follow that it is entitled to much weight. If it is circumstantial evidence and its logical connection with a fact in issue is tenuous, we may consider that it is certainly true but that it does not persuade us of the existence of the fact in issue. Like weight, credibility of evidence is for the jury to assess. An objection to a piece of evidence might be as to its credibility, but not as to its admissibility or weight. Thus the fact that the witness giving the evidence is a convicted perjurer many times over does not prevent the jury from hearing his evidence (*i.e.* does not make it inadmissible); nor does it affect the degree to which the evidence persuades the jury of the existence of the fact in issue if the evidence is believed; but it does (or ought to) make the jury pause before accepting the evidence as true.

---

[24] It being in issue whether A speaks educated English, A enters the witness box and speaks. For real evidence, see *post*, p. 26.
[25] See *post*, p. 37.
[26] *cf.* The Civil Evidence Act 1968, s.6(3); *post*, p. 269.
[27] *Post*, Chap. 11. Moreover, exceptionally, *relevance* depends on weight. Sometimes evidence is only relevant as corroboration, and whether any evidence is corroborative depends, *inter alia*, on what weight the jury attaches to it. See, *post*, Chap. 8.
[28] On sufficiency of evidence, see *post*, p. 39.

Chapter 2

PRELIMINARY MATTERS

A. Basic Rules

The principal questions for which answers may be sought in the law of evidence are as follows:

(1) What facts are in principle provable in any particular judicial proceedings? For present purposes, we may call these *admissible* facts.
(2) Which admissible facts *need* not be proved?
(3) Which admissible facts *may* not be proved?
(4) By what means, by which party to the proceedings, and to what standard are admissible facts to be proved?

Some of these questions are deferred until later in this book. Thus the exclusion of facts which are prima facie admissible may be by reason of, *e.g.* public policy (Chap. 7) or estoppel (Chaps. 15, 16). Who must prove them and to what standard is treated of in Chapters 3–5 on burdens, standard of proof, and presumptions. We will also be engaged with the procedure before, at and after the trial at which the facts must be established: Chapter 6. We are presently considering what facts are admissible (*i.e.* what may be proved), how that is done, and when admissible facts need not be proved, but some parts of these topics need expanded treatment, and so must also be deferred for full discussion in later chapters.

1. What Facts may be Proved

The only facts which may ordinarily be proved in judicial proceedings are facts in issue, facts relevant to the issue, and collateral facts, *i.e.* those which affect the admissibility of evidence.

(a) Facts in issue
   These are the facts which a plaintiff (or prosecutor) must prove in order to win, or which a defendant must prove in order to succeed in some defence which is open to him. It is not the law of evidence's business to say what those facts are in any particular

case. They are determined by the substantive law or by the pleadings. Thus in an action in tort, it is the law of tort which prescribes the elements of the tort; these the plaintiff must prove if he is to win. The law of tort will also say what defences are available in an action on the particular tort involved, *e.g.* self-defence in the tort of trespass to the person. In addition to the substantive law, the pleadings determine the facts in issue, especially in civil proceedings. The pleadings are the formal assertions and formal denials which are made before trial in order to narrow and focus the issue between the parties. Narrowing the issue necessarily cuts down the number of facts in issue. If A is suing B for the price of goods sold and delivered, B may in his defence admit the sale and delivery, but aver that the goods were defective for the purposes for which A knew he wanted them. A might reply, admitting the defects but denying that he knew the purposes B had in mind. It will be obvious that at the trial evidence aimed at showing that there was no delivery of the goods will be rejected, for delivery is no longer a fact in issue. Evidence tending to show that A made fraudulent misrepresentations to induce B to enter into the contract will also be rejected. B could have raised the issue of fraud in his defence, but he did not, so whether A was fraudulent or not is not a fact in issue.

Res gestae: What is called a "fact" may consist of a series of facts, or be the result of one or more facts, and so may be more conveniently called a transaction. If such transaction be in issue, all facts, whether they be acts or omissions or declarations, which either are part of the transaction, or accompany and explain it, are admissible, and are usually called the *res gestae*.[1] In testifying to the matters in issue, therefore, witnesses are required to state them, not in their barest possible form, but with reasonable fullness of such accompanying and explanatory detail and circumstance. If A is alleged to have threatened B, and T testifies that A said, "I'll murder you if you don't get out of my way," the jury will need to know the tone of voice used by A and the expression on his face, and the reaction of B, before it can evaluate the expression as either a threat or a mere jocular

---

[1] Sometimes it is the central transaction itself which is called the *res gestae*, when the constituent or accompanying facts are described as parts of the *res gestae*. Sometimes the accompanying and explanatory facts are categorised not as parts of the fact in issue (as in this work), but as facts relevant to the fact in issue (*e.g.* Cross, p. 24). Nothing turns on these different methods of exposition.

remark.[2] No particular discussion of this kind of evidence is needed except in one particular, namely that under the doctrine of *res gestae*, evidence may sometimes be given of statements which would normally be excluded by the hearsay rule. Consideration of this is postponed until Chapter 14, on hearsay in criminal cases.[3]

(b) Facts relevant to the issue

Suppose a fact in issue is whether A stabbed B. Clearly evidence of an eye-witness of the alleged stabbing (what is called direct evidence) would be admissible. But life does not usually arrange things so conveniently for those who have to try fact, and make up their minds on what happened. Stabbings often do not take place before eye-witnesses, and if eye-witnesses were insisted on, miscarriages of justice would be common. Usually, all that can be shown by direct evidence is some other fact which stands logically in such a relation to the main fact as to render it more likely or less likely that the main fact happened. Most people would accept as logically relevant the fact that A was seen outside B's bedroom with a blood-stained knife in his hand, or even that A had bought what newspapers call the "murder weapon" the day before, or that A had expressed hostility to B. It needs no deductive genius to appreciate that these facts have a bearing on the fact in issue, whether A stabbed B. What is relevant to the facts in issue is obviously a question of degree.

Evidence of relevant facts is called "circumstantial"[4] and sometimes tends to be slighted by unthinking persons, who murmur, "The evidence against him was only circumstantial." Circumstantial evidence does not deserve this slight, for it may be much more cogent than direct. An eye-witness might be mistaken or short-sighted or biased; but a confluence of many independently proved facts, *e.g.* as to motive, opportunity, malice, etc., may be too potent to resist.[5] Circumstances may lie, of course, but so may witnesses. Any evidence which convinces one of the facts

---

[2] But note that it is not for the witness T to make the evaluation. *His* opinion is irrelevant: see *post*, p. 20.
[3] Since the Civil Evidence Act 1968, when such expressions are admitted in civil cases they are admitted by virtue of the Act and not under any common law exception to the hearsay rule. *Post*, p. 258.
[4] See *ante*, p. 11.
[5] "[Circumstantial evidence] is evidence of facts from which, taken with all the other evidence, a reasonable inference is a fact directly in issue. It works by cumulatively, in geometrical progression, eliminating other possibilities.": *per* Lord Simon of Glaisdale in *D.P.P.* v. *Kilbourne* [1973] A.C. 729 at p. 758.

Basic Rules

in issue is better than any other evidence which leaves one unconvinced.[6]

It is pointless to multiply examples of circumstantial evidence, although some which are of reasonably frequent occurrence may be mentioned.[7] There is a well-recognised probability that certain conditions and relationships endure for some time, *e.g.* human life, marriage, sanity, opinions, title, partnership, domicile; so the existence of a condition at one time may often be shown by evidence that it existed before or after that time. The fact that a person habitually acted in a certain way is some evidence that he acted in that way on the occasion in question. In *Joy* v. *Phillips Mills & Co. Ltd.*,[8] a stable boy was found dying in a stable, having been apparently kicked by a horse. There was a halter in his hand, and in order to prove that he had contributed to his own death it was allowed to show that it was his habit to tease horses with a halter. In cases where it is necessary to decide whether a party's conduct was reasonable in the circumstances, *e.g.* questions involving negligence, evidence of what other persons in the same position did is admissible as affording a standard by which the party's conduct can be gauged.[9] If a party's knowledge is in issue, evidence that he had the means of knowledge is relevant. If a party's intention at a particular time has to be proved, his prior or subsequent declarations on the point may afford evidence of it for his opponent.[10] In a prosecution for a driving offence it has been held that the fact that the defendant has answered a summons issued in the name on a driving licence produced by the driver at the time is evidence that the defendant was the driver.[11]

What is relevant is obviously a question of degree. There are degrees of relevant fact, from the most direct and obvious which no reasonable person can avoid seeing, shading away to facts the relevance of which is hardly discernible. The law is obliged to exclude remotely relevant evidence for the rather obvious reason that the trial has to be kept within some bounds, and it is neither

---

[6] Certainly, in criminal cases, there is no rule that the jury need a special direction on standard of proof where the Crown's case depends on circumstantial evidence: *McGreevy* v. *D.P.P.* [1973] 1 W.L.R. 276. See *post*, p. 73.
[7] Some of these arise so frequently that they have been dignified by the term "presumptions of fact," as to which see *post*, p. 89.
[8] [1916] 1 K.B. 849.
[9] But if the question is what the party *did*, evidence of what others did on similar occasions is usually regarded as irrelevant, see *post*, p. 19.
[10] It will not usually be allowed as evidence for the party himself because of the rule that a party cannot make evidence for himself (the rule against self-serving statements). See *post*, p. 104.
[11] *Cooke* v. *McCann* [1974] R.T.R. 131; *Marshall* v. *Ford* (1908) 99 L.T. 796.

feasible to investigate an endless succession of essentially side issues, nor, indeed, fair to the other party. So some evidence of marginal relevance is excluded on the grounds that it is more trouble than it is worth, or seriously embarrasses or prejudices the other party, or confuses the jury. Apart from this general prohibition of any evidence which is too remote from the central issues (a question which the judge decides), there are certain matters, evidence of which, even its relevance is palpable, is usually excluded.[12]

(i) Character. The character of a party is occasionally a fact in issue, the obvious example being the character of the plaintiff in a defamation action. In such a case it is provable just like any other fact in issue. But we are here concerned with where evidence of character is proffered as circumstantial evidence of a fact in issue, where in effect it is sought to prove that a person did a certain act by evidence that his character or disposition is such that he would be likely to do the act, therefore probably did it. In the great bulk of cases, character is regarded as insufficiently relevant,[13] and if evidence of good character is rejected it will be on that ground. Evidence of bad character is additionally objectionable on the ground that its admission would harass and prejudice the party against whom it is offered by raking up the whole of his career, which he would not be prepared to defend without notice; so even if the evidence has some distinct relevance, it may be rejected on that score. This is especially so with evidence of bad character offered against a defendant in a criminal case, and only in very exceptional cases will such be allowed.[14]

The character of any witness is invariably regarded as relevant to his credit; but it has always been clear that if the parties were permitted to impose on the court a thorough investigation of witnesses' characters, the central issues would disappear from sight in a blizzard of charges and counter-charges. A party is therefore permitted *to ask questions* of any opposing witness about

---

[12] It is sometimes said that hearsay evidence is irrelevant, but this is a case of confusing "relevance" with "admissibility" (*ante*, p. 10). It is better to say that hearsay evidence is excluded however relevant it may be. The kinds of evidence discussed in the text are admitted if they are relevant enough, which is not the case with hearsay.

[13] See, *e.g. Jones* v. *James* (1868) 18 L.T. 243, where the plaintiff was allowed to call evidence of her character but only because it had been directly put in issue in the pleadings. In other cases, "the character of the parties to a civil suit affords in general such a weak and vague inference as to the truth of the points in issue between them, that it is not usual to admit evidence of this description" (*Phillips and Arnold on Evidence* (10th ed.), p. 502, cited *ibid.*).

[14] *Post*, Chap. 11.

Basic Rules

his character, but is not usually permitted *to call evidence* about the witness's character.[15]

(ii) Similar conduct on other occasions. If the purpose of proving this is to show that the party has a certain character or a particular propensity, the evidence will fall under the ban discussed above. Even if there is some other purpose involved, *e.g.* to show that an alleged accidental happening was not accidental by showing that it had happened frequently before, the courts are very chary of allowing the evidence in a criminal case because of unfairness to the accused.[16] In civil cases, the courts are not so reluctant, and will admit such evidence if it has a clear logical bearing on the matter in issue and is not oppressive or unfair to the party against whom it is offered.[17] In *Mood Music Publishing Co. v. De Wolfe*,[18] in an action for putting out a musical work in breach of copyright, the defence was coincidental similarity. The plaintiff was allowed to show that three other works similar to copyright works had been put out by the defendant. The unlikelihood of coincidence was very strong and the plaintiff had warned the defendant that he proposed to adduce this evidence.

(iii) Conduct of other persons. It is usually nothing to point, when seeking to show that A did an act, to give evidence of what B did.[19] No amount of evidence that other customers of the Dog and Duck order whisky chasers with their beer will serve to show that I did not order beer alone. It is different if A is in law responsible for B's acts or is identified with B[20]: here evidence of what B did is relevant evidence against A. And even when A and B are strangers, there are occasions where the relevance of what B is shown to have done cannot be denied, as where A is accused of murdering Q, and evidence is tendered that B murdered Q.[21] And, as we have seen,[22] if the standard of A's behaviour, compared

---

[15] See *post*, p. 118.
[16] See *post*, Chap. 11.
[17] *Mood Music Publishing Co. v. De Wolfe* [1976] Ch. 119. And see *Berger v. Raymond Sun Ltd.* [1984] 1 W.L.R. 625; *Chattopadhyay v. Headmaster of Holloway School* [1982] I.C.R. 132.
[18] *Supra.*
[19] The rejection of the evidence about B is occasionally justified by reference to an alleged fundamental rule enshrined in a fittingly sonorous maxim, *res inter alios acta alteri nocere non debet* (no-one should be prejudiced by a transaction between others); but for a convincing demonstration of the insubstantiality of the rule and the uselessness of the maxim, see Cross, (5th ed.), pp. 61–63.
[20] See *post*, p. 278.
[21] *R. v. Dytche* (1890) 17 Cox 39.
[22] *Ante*, p. 17.

with those in a similar position, is what is in issue, it must be relevant to show what these others have done in comparable situations. But sometimes, although the act of B has a high degree of logical persuasiveness, it is nevertheless rejected because it manifests an *opinion* of B about the facts in issue (see below). Thus if the question is whether A was sane during a certain period, evidence that his acquaintance B treated him as sane will be rejected, for the reasons given in the next section.[23]

(iv) Opinion. Opinion evidence has a special kind of irrelevance, arising from the legal position that it is the tribunal of fact, not anyone else, which is under a duty of reaching a conclusion on the issue between the parties. If the conclusion involves, as it often does, forming an opinion on the facts, evaluating them, drawing inferences from them, this is not the function of any other person, be he witness or not. If a witness, he must confine himself to stating the facts in his personal knowledge. Thus, if the question is whether A behaved negligently on a certain occasion, one who saw him act will say what he did; but the court or jury will decide whether, if that testimony is believed, what he did amounts to negligent behaviour. The opinion of an eye-witness, or indeed of any other person, even an earlier tribunal investigating the same incident, is strictly irrelevant.[24] The present court or jury is as capable of forming an opinion as the witness, and it is the present court or jury on whom the law casts the duty of doing so. However, there are some cases where the opinion of a witness is admissible, and it is necessary to deal with them in some detail.[25]

Ordinary witnesses. There are some matters which are commonly thought of as matters of direct perception but which are really matters of inference. For example, T says that A shot B. What he is really saying is that he saw A point a gun at B, heard a report and saw B fall. It is really a matter of inference that a bullet left the gun and entered B's body, but the inference is so straightforward that T is allowed to say "I saw A shoot B." Such a case is hardly describable as involving opinion at all; but there are other cases where the inference is less straightforward, more "visible," than that, but in which it would be impossible for the witness to confine himself to the observed facts and leave the inference to others. An example is testimony as to the speed of a vehicle.

---

[23] *Wright v. Doe d. Tatham* (1838) 5 Cl. & F. 670.
[24] *Hollington v. Hewthorn* [1943] K.B. 587. In some circumstances the conclusion of an earlier tribunal is relevant; see *post*, p. 338.
[25] On the whole subject, see Eggleston, Chap. 11.

Almost any testimony on this, whether apparently objective ("it was more than 30 m.p.h."), or openly evaluative ("it was very fast"), can only be a matter of opinion. Identification of a person or thing is almost always opinion evidence. The witness is in reality saying no more than that the person seen by him "resembles," *i.e.* was in the witness's opinion similar in features and build to, a person seen on another occasion. Handwriting is often identified by someone who says no more than that the disputed handwriting resembles in its general character the impression received from seeing other pieces of handwriting in the past. Often a witness is asked how old a person appeared to be, or whether he thought a person had taken drink.[26] In all these kinds of case the witness may well not be particularly skilled in evaluating the matter on which he forms his opinion. Nevertheless, his opinion is received because in the nature of things it is impossible to separate out the matters of perception on which it is formed, or because the opinion is a sensible compendious way of stating the matters perceived. ("I thought he had taken drink [because his speech was slurred and his gait was unsteady]"). So far as the latter reason is concerned, in civil cases it is declared by statute[27] that the witness's statement of opinion is evidence of the facts perceived by him, but at common law the rule is the same in criminal cases.

Opinions of experts. If the reason why opinion evidence is normally rejected is that the court or jury is just as capable of forming an opinion as the witness, it must be obvious that there are some cases where this is not true. Jurors are ordinary sensible persons, not polymaths, and where the matter at issue is a matter of "art or science," which requires long study or experience, they cannot form an opinion without the help of someone who *has* undergone long study or acquired the experience.[28] In such a case, the opinion of such an expert is admissible. The matters fit for expert evidence are very numerous, and include such things as causes of death, effects of poison or drugs, genuineness of works of art, literary or artistic merits of articles said to be obscene, value of objects or land, genuineness of handwriting, proper navigation of vessels[29] causes of traffic accidents, meaning of trade terms,

---

[26] *R. v. Davies (No. 2)* [1962] 1 W.L.R. 1111.
[27] Civil Evidence Act 1972, s.3(2).
[28] *Folkes v. Chadd* (1782) 3 Doug. 157.
[29] But in *The Kirby Hall* (1883) 8 P.D. 71 at p. 75, it was held that expert evidence on navigation was not admissible where the court is assisted by nautical assessors.

accepted principles of accountancy and foreign law. The judge decides whether the witness is suitably qualified to offer an opinion. He must be skilled in the branch of knowledge involved, but he need not have acquired the knowledge in the course of professional practice. In *R. v. Silverlock*[30] a solicitor who had been an amateur student of handwriting for 10 years was allowed to give an expert opinion on the similarity of two samples of handwriting.

The contrast between expert and non-expert opinion may be illustrated by the position on disputed handwriting. Suppose the question is whether the handwriting in a certain document is that of A. If the court does not have before it two documents, the one in dispute and another proved or admitted to be written by A, the court cannot make a comparison, and perforce has to rely on any witness who can say that he, having seen (or being shown) the disputed document is of opinion that it is similar to other writings he has seen which he knows to be by A. But if both disputed writing and an admitted sample are before the court, the opinion of a non-expert is no better than that of the court. Indeed in a jury trial, the jury ought not to be left to make a comparison without expert help.[31] *A fortiori*, the opinion of a non-expert will be rejected.[32]

Material on which an expert opinion may be founded. An expert witness is in effect asked to generalise from his experience of other similar occurrences in the past. Inevitably these other occurrences will not all have been personally witnessed by him. He will not have performed every experiment supporting the scientific laws he uses, or witnessed every sale of property on which he bases his opinion as to the value of the property at issue. He will have read about these occurrences or discussed them with his fellows in his particular discipline, as well as directly perceiving some transactions. This generalised mass amounts to his experience and it is that which forms the basis of his opinion. The fact that it is inevitably founded on hearsay (or even on double or multiple hearsay, for the authors of the learned

---

[30] [1894] 2 Q.B. 685. Because of doubts whether experts in foreign law would be qualified unless practitioners in that law (see *Bristow v. Sequeville* (1850) 19 L.J.Ex. 289), the Civil Evidence Act 1972, s.4(1) declares that in civil proceedings they may be qualified although not practitioners. The Act does not apply to criminal proceedings.
[31] *R. v. Tilley* [1961] 3 All E.R. 406; *R. v. O'Sullivan* [1969] 2 All E.R. 237.
[32] *R. v. Harvey* (1869) 9 Cox 546 at p. 548 (Blackburn J.). This is in spite of s.8, Criminal Procedure Act 1865, which appears on the face of it to make the opinion of any witness receivable on a question of disputed handwriting.

works he uses will not themselves have had personal knowledge of the transactions detailed in their works) is no objection.[33] And he may refresh his memory from these learned works in a way not permitted by the normal rules on refreshing memory.[34]

But generalising from a mass of earlier incidents is one thing, generalising from particular incidents is quite another.

> "It is one thing to say 'From my general experience of recent transactions comparable with this one, I think the proper rent should be £X'; it is another thing to say 'Because I have been told by someone else that the premises next door have an area of X square feet and were recently let on such and such terms, I say the rent for these premises should be £Z a year.' What he has been told about the premises next door may be inaccurate or misleading.... The other party to the litigation is entitled to have a witness whom he can cross-examine on oath as to the reliability of the facts deposed to."[35]

In *Ramsay* v. *Watson*,[36] the question was whether A had contracted lead poisoning while working for B. B called a doctor to say that he had examined A's 21 workmates who had worked in similar conditions. The doctor was not allowed to state what these 21 men had told him about their state of health. He was not applying his general experience to the question in issue, but giving hearsay evidence about the condition of directly comparable individuals.[37]

Still less may an expert found his opinion on the facts of the instant case if those facts are in issue. It is not for him, in giving an opinion, to accept one version of the disputed facts rather than the other. He must be asked hypothetical questions, *viz.* assuming that the facts were as one party contends, what is his opinion?, and of course in cross-examination can be asked what his opinion is on the assumption that the facts were as the other party contends.[38]

Matters not for experts. Certain matters are not for any expert,

---

[33] R. v. *Abadom* (1983) 76 Cr.App.R. 48.
[34] See *post*, p. 101.
[35] *English Exporters Ltd.* v. *Eldonwall Ltd.* [1973] Ch. 415, *per* Megarry J. at p. 421.
[36] (1961) 108 C.L.R. 642.
[37] Such hearsay evidence would now be admissible in an English civil case by virtue of the Civil Evidence Act 1968, as to which see *post*, Chap. 13.
[38] R. v. *Frances* (1849) 4 Cox 57; R. v. *Mason* (1911) 28 T.L.R. 120.

even if the witness commonly considers such matters in his calling. Obviously, matters of construction of documents[39] and matters of English law[40] are for the court and not for any witness. Moreover there are many matters of fact upon which a layman is as competent as any expert to form an opinion; for example, whether any matter is obscene,[41] and what would be the likely reaction of the accused on hearing of his girl-friend's infidelity.[42] "Jurors do not need psychiatrists to tell them how ordinary folk who are not suffering from any mental illness are likely to react to the stresses and strains of life."[43] It is different if the person is abnormal,[44] or perhaps a small child,[45] but with normal people,[46] neither their likely reaction to events nor their credibility as witnesses can be the subject of expert evidence—that would allow trial by psychiatrists to take the place of trial by jury and magistrates.[47]

The question also arises as to how far experts are competent to give an opinion on the ultimate question the court or jury has to decide. This is not the same question as to how *conclusive* is an expert opinion; *that* question is soon answered—it is never conclusive on any point,[48] although if the matter is one of art or science and the expert's opinion is unchallenged, it is a misdirection to invite the jury to disregard it and substitute their own judgment.[49] The present question is whether an expert can even be invited to give an opinion on the very question the court or jury has to decide. There is supposed to be a common law rule

---

[39] Phipson, 27–46; unless indeed the words are used in some non-legal technical sense. See *Harding* v. *Hayes* [1974] Crim.L.R. 713 on "the flowering and fruiting tops" in the statutory definition of cannabis.
[40] See, *e.g. Heather* v. *P-E Consulting Group* [1973] Ch. 189.
[41] *R.* v. *Calder* [1969] 1 Q.B. 151; *R.* v. *Anderson* [1972] 1 Q.B. 304, at p. 313.
[42] *R.* v. *Turner* (1975) 60 Cr.App.R. 80.
[43] *Ibid.* per Lawton L.J. at p. 83, approved in *D.P.P.* v. *Jordan* [1977] A.C. 699; see also *R.* v. *MacKenny* (1981) 76 Cr.App.R. 271.
[44] *Toohey* v. *M.P.C.* [1965] A.C. 595; *post*, p. 123.
[45] *D.P.P.* v. *A. & B.C. Chewing Gum Ltd.* [1968] 1 Q.B. 159; but see *R.* v. *Anderson*, *supra*.
[46] For a strict application of this rule, see *R.* v. *Masih* [1986] Crim.L.R. 395, where on a charge of rape, the defence was that D did not understand P to be objecting. D had an I.Q. of 72, on the boundary of dull-normal/subnormal. I.Q. 69 is subnormal. Held, applying *Turner*, *supra* and *Jordan*, *supra*, psychiatric evidence that he was of low intelligence was inadmissible.
[47] *R.* v. *Turner*, *supra*, at p. 83. And see *R.* v. *Chard* (1971) 56 Cr.App.R. 268, where it was said that no-one can claim to be an expert on the intent of a normal man.
[48] *R.* v. *Lanfear* [1968] 2 Q.B. 77.
[49] *Anderson* v. *R.* [1972] A.C. 100.

against this,[50] although it is now abrogated as to civil cases by the Civil Evidence Act 1972.[51] But in any event, it was never absolute. The issue might be, e.g. the value of some unique object, where the ultimate question is how much would a purchaser be prepared to pay, and there is no way in which an answer can be arrived at except by asking an expert.[52] What the rule really forbids is an opinion on the proper inference to be drawn from a heap of disputed facts, e.g. who was responsible for a collision. Even here, however, if the expert confines himself to admitted facts or to clearly stated hypotheses, he can be asked, e.g. whether the accused (who had pleaded insanity) knew right from wrong as required by the M'Naghten rules[53]; whether the accused was so drunk as not to have proper control of his car,[54] whether the matter was likely to deprave or corrupt small children,[55] whether the accused was suffering from diminished responsibility.[56] The question always is, about any matter however basic to the litigation, is the expert better equipped to give an opinion than the court or jury? If he is, his opinion may be sought, although, as mentioned above, it is not conclusive—indeed it will often be one of two conflicting expert opinions.

(c) Collateral facts

These are facts which affect the admissibility of evidence. Some kinds of evidence are not allowed unless some pre-condition is shown to exist. For example, what are called "dying declarations" are not admissible unless the declarant knew he was dying. His knowledge of impending death has no logical connection with the fact in issue which we are trying to establish, yet we are allowed to prove, indeed *required* to prove, that he knew he was dying if we are to use his statement about the fact in issue. As will be seen, it is the judge who decides whether collateral facts are established, as part of his general duty to rule on the admissibility of evidence.[57]

---

[50] *North Cheshire Brewery* v. *Manchester Brewery* [1899] A.C. 83; *Haynes* v. *Doman* [1899] 2 Ch. 13.
[51] s.3(1).
[52] See Eggleston, *op. cit.* p. 147.
[53] *R.* v. *Holmes* [1953] 1 W.L.R. 686.
[54] *R.* v. *Davies* [1962] 1 W.L.R. 1111.
[55] *D.P.P.* v. *A. & B.C. Chewing Gum Ltd.* [1968] 1 Q.B. 159.
[56] *Ibid.* p. 164, *per* Lord Parker C.J., suggesting that the advance of science is making this sort of question put to an expert more and more common.
[57] *Post*, p. 47.

2. How may Facts be Proved?

(a) Testimony

This is the chief method of establishing facts, and is oral evidence upon oath in open court by a competent witness who has personal knowledge of the fact he is deposing to.[58] This rules out unsworn evidence, out-of-court evidence, and the evidence of incompetent witnesses or of witnesses who have no personal knowledge of the fact deposed to (hearsay evidence). There are exceptions to all these exclusions, which will be dealt with later.

(b) Real evidence

This consists primarily of the inspection of objects, other than documents, produced for examination by the tribunal of fact. Thus a dog whose disposition is in issue may be produced so that the jury may form its own impression.[59] Non-portable objects and places may be viewed out of court by the tribunal of fact.[60] The real evidence of a view is as much evidence as the testimony of witnesses and, provided that the matter is not a technical one where the assistance of expert witnesses is required, the tribunal is entitled to prefer the impression gained from a view to the testimony of a witness.[61]

In this connection there is a difference between a mere inspection of an object or the *locus in quo*, and a demonstration or reconstruction staged by witnesses in the *locus in quo*. Both are a stage in the trial and the judge must be present to control what goes on.[62] Moreover both must take place before counsel's addresses, so that comment can be made on what was seen.[63] However, a demonstration by witnesses is more in the nature of testimonial evidence, and testimonial evidence must be given in the presence of judge and jury and both parties. It follows that a demonstration or reconstruction not in the presence of everyone concerned is irregular, and indeed a fatal defect.[64] This is not strictly true of a view properly so called, where the *locus in quo* is inspected without witnesses. Ideally this ought to be done with

---

[58] Which is not necessarily a fact in issue. The fact he is deposing to may be *relevant* to a fact in issue, *i.e.* be circumstantial evidence thereof. The witness need have no personal knowledge of the fact in issue, but he must have such knowledge of the fact he is deposing to.
[59] *Line* v. *Taylor* (1862) 3 F. & F. 731.
[60] R.S.C., Ord. 35, r.8(1).
[61] *Buckingham* v. *Daily News Ltd.* [1956] 2 Q.B. 534.
[62] *R.* v. *Hunter* [1985] 2 All E.R. 173.
[63] *Parry* v. *Boyle* [1986] Crim.L.R. 551.
[64] *Tameshwar* v. *R.* [1957] A.C. 476; *Goold* v. *Evans* [1951] 2 T.L.R. 1189.

all parties present, but it need not be, at any rate if parties and representatives are invited to attend.[65] Moreover, as will be seen, the layout of a *locus in quo* is a matter upon which the tribunal is entitled to act upon its own personal knowledge.[66] It does not seem necessary for this knowledge to be acquired before rather than during the proceedings, and it seems that members of the tribunal of fact can acquire it by private inspection during an adjournment. It has been said that there is nothing to stop any juror during an adjournment going off and looking at the scene of the events in question.[67]

Mechanical recordings of events or places, such as a photograph,[68] a trace of radar echoes,[69] a print-out of a computer's calculations[70] or a tape recording of sounds[71] are also admitted, subject to proper verification, and are probably a species of real evidence.[72]

Valuable inferences are often obtained from the demeanour of witnesses in giving evidence; comparisons may be made between a disputed and an admitted sample of the handwriting of some person, or between the features of a child and the person alleged to be his parent[73]; and statute allows the court in certain circumstances to estimate the age of a person before it from his personal appearance.[74] There is a common law power to do so in any case.[75]

3. Facts which need not be Proved

The court is sometimes able to treat as established (and so act upon) facts which have not been proved. One case is where a fact is presumed in a party's favour. Presumptions are dealt with in

---

[65] *Goold* v. *Evans, supra; Salsbury* v. *Woodland* [1970] 1 Q.B. 324; *Parry* v. *Boyle, supra.*
[66] *Post,* p. 30.
[67] Per Lord Denning in *Tameshwar* v. *R., supra,* p. 483–4. But it is certainly wrong to depute one juror to view the scene and then describe it to the others: *R.* v. *Gurney* [1976] Crim.L.R. 567.
[68] *Kajala* v. *Noble* (1982) 75 Cr.App.R. 149.
[69] *The Statue of Liberty* [1968] 1 W.L.R. 739.
[70] *R.* v. *Wood* (1982) 76 Cr.App.R. 23.
[71] *R.* v. *Maqsud Ali* [1966] 1 Q.B. 688; *R.* v. *Senat* (1968) 52 Cr.App.R. 282.
[72] *The Statue of Liberty, supra.*
[73] See *C.* v. *C and C* [1972] 1 W.L.R. 1335, where photographs of the persons concerned were compared.
[74] Children and Young Persons Act 1933, s.99; Powers of Criminal Courts Act 1973, s.20(5). See *R.* v. *Farndale* (1973) 58 Cr.App.R. 336.
[75] *R.* v. *Turner* [1910] 1 K.B. 346; *Wallworth* v. *Balmer* [1966] 1 W.L.R. 16.

28   *Preliminary Matters*

Chapter 5. Other cases are facts which are formally admitted and facts which are judicially noticed.

(a) Formal admissions

Formal admissions are those which are made expressly for a particular trial in order to save the other side the trouble and expense of proving matters about which there may be no real dispute. It should be apparent that for the particular trial involved a formal admission is normally conclusive; the party is not allowed at the trial to withdraw his admission or seek to explain it away or contradict it by other evidence. Equally obviously, such a formal admission only operates in the particular litigation in which it was made, and cannot be used on any other occasion against the party making it. In both these particulars, formal admissions differ from informal admissions, which are dealt with later,[76] and which must be sharply distinguished from the subject-matter of the present section. Informal admissions are merely an item of evidence against the party making them. They are by no means conclusive and may be explained away or rebutted by other evidence. As an item of evidence, they may be used against the party making them in any proceedings at all in which the party is involved.

In *civil cases*, formal admissions may be made in the following manner:

By the pleadings, e.g. if the defendant, in answer to an action for breach of contract, admits the contract and its breach, but pleads minority, fraud or other defence, the plaintiff need give no evidence of his own allegations, being relieved therefrom by his opponent's admissions.

In answer to a notice under R.S.C., Ord. 27. Such a notice calls on the party to whom it is addressed to admit any specific facts or documents mentioned in the notice. Since unreasonable failure to admit matters may make the party in default liable to pay the costs occasioned by proving them, such admissions are often made, thereby saving time and money. They are only available for the particular person giving, and the cause affected by, the notice, and may be amended or withdrawn on terms (r. 2).

In answer to interrogatories. Under the provisions of Order 26, a party may, with the leave of the court or a judge, deliver written interrogatories to the other party before the trial. These must be

---

[76] *Post*, Chap. 13.

answered by affidavit and the answers may be used at the trial against the party making them.[77]

In correspondence or at the trial. Letters written by a solicitor or barrister, in the scope of his authority to act on behalf of the client, may contain formal admissions which will bind his client and may entitle the other party to sign judgment.[78] At the trial the party himself or his solicitor or barrister may admit facts, and so preclude the giving of evidence on the matter.[79] However an admission made by counsel in interlocutory proceedings is comparable to admissions in answer to a notice to admit facts (*supra*), *i.e.* it may be subsequently withdrawn, on terms, provided the other party has not acted on the admission, when an estoppel would arise.[80]

In criminal cases, by section 10 of the Criminal Justice Act 1967, any fact of which oral evidence may be given in any criminal proceedings may be admitted for the purposes of those proceedings (and any appeal) by either the prosecutor[81] or defendant; and such admission shall be conclusive evidence in those proceedings, including a re-trial or appeal, of the fact admitted. The admission may be made in court or in writing, and may be withdrawn by leave of the court.

At common law, after conviction, a defendant may make admissions affecting his sentence. Apart from that, no formal admissions were allowed except by a plea of guilty which, however, only admits the charge, not the truth of the depositions.[82]

(b) Judicial notice

When a court takes judicial notice of a fact, it finds that it exists although no evidence of the fact has been given. There are many cases where this is enforced by the express provisions of a statute or by the settled practice of the courts. The reason for these instances is that the fact is easily demonstrable by reference to a readily available and authoritative source, and it would be pettifogging and time-wasting (and sometimes highly awkward) to insist on evidence of the fact. These instances involve such

---

[77] But they may not be used for any other purpose: *Riddick* v. *Thames Board Mills* [1977] Q.B. 88; *post*, p. 141.
[78] *Ellis* v. *Allen* [1914] 1 Ch. 94; see R.S.C., Ord. 27, r. 1.
[79] *Urquhart* v. *Butterfield* (1887) 37 Ch.D. 357.
[80] *H. Clark (Doncaster) Ltd.* v. *Wilkinson* [1965] Ch. 694.
[81] See *Brown* v. *Dyerson* [1969] 1 Q.B. 45 at p. 52; *R.* v. *Moghal* [1977] Crim.L.R. 373.
[82] *R.* v. *Riley* (1896) 18 Cox 285.

things as English law and the law of the European Economic Communities (but not other foreign law[83]), the divisions and procedure of English superior courts, the seals and signatures of various public officials and the judges of the superior courts. There is also a class of constitutional and political matters where the settled practice is to seek information from a secretary of state and to take his certificate as conclusive.[84]

One of the objects of judicial notice is to save time and expense by not having to prove things which are already known to the tribunal because they are matters of common knowledge. In pursuance of this object, a judge has a wide discretion and may notice much which he cannot be required to notice, sometimes refreshing his memory as described below. However at the outset it is necessary to distinguish matters of common knowledge from matters in the personal knowledge of the tribunal.

(i) Personal knowledge of the tribunal. Personal knowledge and experience plays a much larger part in trials at law than is sometimes appreciated. All judges and juries use their knowledge of common affairs in weighing the probabilities of an event happening or not happening given the facts proved by evidence, or of a proved event being or not being the result of certain other proved facts. There is no way in which they can avoid, or be prevented from, drawing on their personal experience in assessing probabilities.[85] If the result of a case depends upon what a motorist would expect on approaching an intersection at which another vehicle is waiting on a minor road, the tribunal of fact will apply its own experience to arrive at a common sense answer.[86] This is not so much finding facts as reasoning from them. If the matter is one of "art or science," the jury may be assisted by the opinion of an expert,[87] but in any event they are not using their own experience as a substitute for evidence.

The question raised in this section is, when *is* it permissible for the tribunal to use its own experience as a substitute for evidence? The answer in general terms is that a judge or juryman must not use his own particular knowledge of the matter in question. If he has material facts to impart, he must be sworn as witness and

---

[83] Unless the point is truly notorious in England, *e.g.* that roulette is legal in Monte Carlo: see *Saxby* v. *Fulton* [1909] 2 K.B. 208 at p. 211.
[84] For a full account, *see* Phipson, §§ 2.14, 2.15.
[85] See Eggleston, Chap. 11.
[86] Compare *Burns* v. *Lipman* (1975) 132 C.L.R. 157, discussed in Eggleston, *op. cit.* p. 144.
[87] See *ante*, p. 21.

Basic Rules

stand cross-examination.[88] Thus to take a clear cut example, the medical member of a social security appeal tribunal is not entitled to use his particular knowledge of the case not given in evidence.[89] But many cases are not clear cut, and the distinction between general knowledge which can be used and particular knowledge which cannot, while it may be easy to state, is difficult to apply to individual cases. Many of the cases where the point has been raised on appeal concern the use made by a judge, in assessing compensation for a partially disabled plaintiff, of his own knowledge of working conditions in the neighbourhood of the court, and there are conflicting authorities on the propriety of such use.[90] A dictum often cited as authority is one of Lord Buckmaster's,[91] to the effect that the use of knowledge of local industrial conditions is acceptable "if properly applied and within reasonable limits." The practical effect of this rather vague statement is usually to uphold on appeal a "moderate" estimate of the plaintiff's earning capacity in a neighbourhood even if not founded on evidence, but to upset a "surprising" estimate unless it *is* supported by evidence.[92] In other types of case where the use of personal knowledge has been forgiven, the decision is often explicable on the ground that the tribunal was using such as material on which to form an estimate of quality or reasonableness rather than as a substitute for evidence.[93] Certainly, if knowledge *is* general, and not particular, the fact that it is local and not common to all mankind seems to be no objection. In *Ingram* v. *Percival*[94] the use by magistrates of their knowledge of the extent of local tidal waters was upheld.

There is a kind of particular knowledge which consists of general experience of some particular field, *e.g.* medicine or architecture, rather than knowledge of the actual facts of the case—the sort of matter which ought to be the subject of expert

---

[88] Probably he must not then adjudicate on his own evidence; R. v. *Antrim JJ.* [1895] 2 Ir.R. 603; *Mitchell* v. *Croydon* (1914) 30 T.L.R. 526. On the whole subject, see Schiff (1963) 41 Can.B.R. 335.
[89] *Moxon* v. *Minister of Pensions* [1945] K.B. 490; *Starr* v. *Minister of Pensions* [1946] K.B. 345.
[90] See the authorities reviewed in *Reynolds* v. *Llanelly Tinplate Co.* [1948] 1 All E.R. 140. And *Hammington* v. *Berker Sportcraft Ltd.* [1980] I.C.R. 248.
[91] *Keane* v. *Mount Vernon Colliery Co.* [1933] A.C. 309 at p. 317.
[92] See *Reynolds* v. *Llanelly Tinplate Co., supra.*
[93] *e.g.* R. v. *Field and Others* (1895) 64 L.J.M.C. 158. Willes J. at p. 159, after remarking that one could not avoid using particular knowledge in the sort of case there involved, added "I might as well be asked to decide a question as to the sufficiency of an alpine rope without bringing my personal knowledge into play."
[94] [1960] 1 Q.B. 548. And see *Kent* v. *Stamps* [1982] R.T.R. 273.

evidence.[95] In this regard, a judge is treated differently from a magistrate. A medically qualified judge is expected to put this experience out of his mind when assessing the medical evidence.[96] But there is no way in which a non-lawyer could put on one side his own training or experience, and anyway magistrates are selected so as to cover a wide range of experience.[97] Consequently a medically-trained magistrate may use his training and experience to interpret the medical evidence, and may tell his fellow magistrates the way in which his specialised knowledge accords with the evidence. Of course he must confine himself to interpreting and evaluating the evidence given in open court. "He can explain evidence they have heard; he can give his own view as to how the case should go and how it should be decided; but he should not be giving evidence behind closed doors which is not available to the parties."[98] Presumably it is the same with a medically trained juror.

However, knowledge which is *not* particular but general may be used as a substitute for evidence. If a fact is known to all mankind, the judge may notice it and direct the jury to notice it without any evidence.

(ii) Cases when the judge acts without inquiry. There are many matters upon which it is an insult to the intelligence to require evidence, so notorious are they. That the month of September has only 30 days is an example. If such were in issue or relevant to the issue the judge would, without making any inquiries at all, direct the jury on the point and, if he did not, the jury are quite entitled to take notice themselves without any direction or evidence. No one could object if they did so; indeed if they did not, any verdict which disclosed their failure would be upset on appeal as perverse. It is, of course, pointless to multiply examples of facts so notorious that they are judicially noticed. The only difficulty with the doctrine is that its limits are necessarily indefinite. One can easily think of facts which are not so notorious as the number of days in September, and where there might be more than one view as to whether the fact is one of common knowledge. Some notoriety is exceptionally transient or confined to particular sectors of the population or to particular age groups. An example would be the

---

[95] See *ante*, p. 21.
[96] *Att.-Gen. for South Australia* v. *Brown* [1960] A.C. 432 at p. 449; *Wetherall* v. *Harrison* [1976] Q.B. 773.
[97] As indeed are members of Industrial Tribunals: see *Hammington* v. *Berker Sportcraft Ltd.* [1980] I.C.R. 248.
[98] *Wetherall* v. *Harrison, supra*, per Lord Widgery C.J. at p. 778. See also *Hammington* v. *Berker Sportcraft, supra*.

Basic Rules

identity of a famous television personality. As a rule, a judge will not notice such nine-day wonders, and will expose himself to popular reproach as a judicial ignoramus by requiring evidence on the point. By contrast, some past cases noticing what was supposed to be common knowledge excite bewilderment in a present-day reader. In *Hoare* v. *Silverlock*,[99] five judges held that the expression "her friends had realised the fable of the Frozen Snake" had a meaning too clear for argument or evidence.

The sort of notoriety which is clearly within the doctrine is a much more permanent and general notoriety. Examples are that the streets of London are crowded and dangerous,[1] that boys are naturally reckless,[2] that cats are ordinarily kept for domestic purposes,[3] that television is normally received in households for recreational rather than educational purposes,[4] that motorways have a thick white line separating the nearside lane from the hard shoulder,[5] and that it is impossible for a child to be born alive after a mere fortnight's gestation.[6] But the courts are on the whole very cautious in this field. If a fact is in issue, and is not admitted, then the mere probability that it happened, even a very strong probability, is not enough to dispense with evidence. Only if "no person can raise a question"[7] should judicial notice be taken. So although judicial notice has been taken of the length of normal gestation,[8] the majority of the House of Lords in *Preston-Jones* v. *Preston-Jones*[9] refused to take judicial notice of the fact that a 360-day period of gestation is impossible.[10]

(iii) Cases where the judge acts after inquiry. There are many cases in which one knows in a general way that a fact is a matter of common knowledge, although one does not know it oneself. For instance, many persons are incapable of memorising any historical dates other than that of the Battle of Hastings, and judges have

---

[99] (1848) 12 Q.B. 624.
[1] *Dennis* v. *White* [1916] 2 K.B. 1.
[2] *Clayton* v. *Hardwick Colliery Co.* (1916) 32 T.L.R. 159.
[3] *Nye* v. *Niblett* [1918] 1 K.B. 23.
[4] *Bridlington Relay Ltd.* v. *Yorkshire Electricity Board* [1965] Ch. 436.
[5] *Wallwork* v. *Rowland* [1972] 1 All E.R. 53.
[6] *R.* v. *Luffe* (1807) 8 East 193.
[7] *Ibid. per* Ellenborough C.J. at p. 207.
[8] *Bosvile* v. *Att.-Gen.* (1887) 12 P.D. 177 at p. 183; *Burnaby* v. *Baillie* (1889) 42 Ch.D. 282 at p. 296.
[9] [1951] A.C. 391.
[10] Compare *R.* v. *Crush* [1978] Crim.L.R. 357, where a judge refused to take notice that an event happening early on an autumn evening happened at least an hour after sunset; presumably it would have been different if the event happened at midnight in January.

no special exemption in this regard. If the date of the Battle of Bannockburn were in issue, a judge would do the same as anyone else, and take steps to inform himself, by consulting the appropriate works of reference. In any case, he may refresh his memory by consulting such works and listening to such experts as he thinks fit,[11] and if there is a conflict between them, it is he, not the jury, who settles it, since he is not hearing evidence, merely equipping himself to take judicial notice.[12]

The court does not normally notice facts proved in an earlier case,[13] but customs settled by earlier decisions are an exception[14] and the court has taken notice of the Home Secretary's approval of a particular breath test device, such having been proved in many previous cases.[15] Professional practice of conveyancers,[16] cartographers[17] and accountants[18] has also been noticed after consulting appropriate experts.

Judicial noting of facts of the kind discussed so far does not result in future courts being obliged to notice the same facts. Since no general legal significance is involved in a finding that a certain fact is notorious, a future tribunal must be free to find that that fact is no longer notorious. It is hard to believe that if today the meaning of a reference to the fable of the frozen snake needed to be elucidated, *Hoare v. Silverlock*,[19] would constitute any binding precedent. Moreover sometimes the reason for taking judicial notice appears to be to avoid embarrassing the Crown by taking divergent views on, *e.g.* foreign political questions. But the Crown's views may well change. In *Duff Development Co. v. Government of Kelantan*[20] the question arose as to whether the defendant was of sovereign status. The judge advised himself by reference to a certificate from the Colonial Secretary, which was held by the House of Lords to be conclusive of the matter. In any future case concerning the Government of Kelantan, *Duff's* case

---

[11] *Read v. Bishop of Lincoln* [1892] A.C. 644; *Kerr v. Kennedy* [1942] 1 K.B. 409; *R. v. Webb* [1964] 1 Q.B. 357; *Davey v. Harrow Corporation* [1958] 1 Q.B. 60 at p. 69.
[12] *McQuaker v. Goddard* [1940] 1 K.B. 687 at p. 700.
[13] *Roper v. Taylor's Central Garage* [1951] 2 T.L.R. 284.
[14] *Brandao v. Barnett* (1846) 12 Cl. & F. 787; And see the Civil Evidence Act 1972, s.4(2); where a point of foreign law has been found in citable form by an English superior court, on production of the finding, the law shall be taken as there found until the contrary is proved.
[15] *R. v. Jones* [1970] 1 W.L.R. 16.
[16] *Re Rosher* (1884) 26 Ch.D. 801.
[17] *Davey v. Harrow Corporation* [1958] 1 Q.B. 60.
[18] *Heather v. P.E. Consulting Group* [1973] 1 Ch. 189.
[19] (1848) 12 Q.B. 624, *ante*, p. 33.
[20] [1924] A.C. 797.

will constitute no precedent, and a fresh certificate will be sought from a secretary of state, from which it might appear that the Crown's view of the status of Kelantan has changed since 1924.

(iv) Legally binding judicial notice. There is another class of case of taking judicial notice which is more like declaring law than establishing a fact. The matter may not be one of common knowledge, or of any agreement between judicial authorities or knowledgeable persons, yet the necessity for a uniform approach by courts of law may be enough for the Court to take judicial notice of the matter. In *R. v. Simpson*,[21] the question was whether a flick knife was an offensive weapon for the purposes of the Prevention of Crime Act 1953, *i.e.* on whether such articles are made for the purpose of causing injury to the person. Although the views of authors and judicial utterances did not agree (indeed *because* they did not agree) the Divisional Court held that to avoid scope for unevenness in the administration of the law the fact that flick knives were made for the purpose of causing injury to the person should be judicially noted.[22] This is indistinguishable from ruling as a matter of law that flick knives are offensive weapons within the meaning of the Act, for two reasons. One is that the judge may direct the jury on the matter, whereas if it were a question of fact, it would have to be left to them, even if it was a question admitting of only one answer.[23] The other is that until this "decision" is overruled by a higher court it is binding on future courts.

B. Functions of Judge and Jury

The fact that traditionally both civil and criminal trials in this country have been trials by judge and jury has left deep and probably ineradicable marks on our law—the substantive law as well as the adjective law (*i.e.* procedural law) but particularly the latter. In the process of disposing of an issue submitted to a trial at law, these two separate parts of the tribunal exercise quite separate functions. Now that trial is usually before a judge alone, the two separate functions remain. The judge performs them both,[24] but he must take care to keep them separate. In the

[21] [1983] 3 All E.R. 789.
[22] See also *McQuaker v. Goddard* [1940] 1 K.B. 687.
[23] *Post*, p. 46.
[24] A special case is where a judge sits with lay justices *and* a jury under the Courts Act 1971, s.7(2). Some, but not all, of the judicial function is performed by the judge and justices together and on this the justices can outvote the judge. See *R. v. Orpin* [1975] Q.B. 2830.

discharge of the judge-function, he can be corrected on appeal; but in discharge of the jury-function he, like the jury, cannot easily be controlled by an appellate court.

Although the two parts of the tribunal are separate in function, the English system of trial has always been marked by a high degree of control by the judge of the jury. The judge is in control to a much greater extent than in, say, the United States. In England, the jury has customarily collected encomiums in political and after-dinner speeches, including some from judges speaking extra-judicially. But in reality judicial admiration is reserved not for the free-ranging uncontrolled institution found in the United States, but only for the severely limited English variety. In England, an unfettered jury has always excited judicial distrust because of its inconsistency, irresponsibility and uncontrollability on appeal. Inconsistency showed in jury awards for damages for personal injuries and still does in defamation awards. A jury, dispersing after verdict, does not have to live with the consequences or the implication for later cases of what they have done. There is absolutely no appeal from an acquittal by a jury in a criminal case[25]; and against other verdicts, successful appeal must always be difficult, if only because no reasons are given.[26] Nor may unrighteous, oath-disregarding jurors be disciplined personally.[27]

This independence, although often and perhaps rightly justified as a check against official tyranny, is clearly capable of developing into a tyranny nearly as oppressive and quite as arbitrary as any it prevents, unless the area of its operation is confined. And confined it has been, to one particular function, namely choosing between opposing witnesses and deciding whom to believe. Although *in form* the jury disposes of the whole matter by bringing in a general verdict one way or the other, it is not allowed to roam over the whole controversy and dispense what is sometimes called "palm-tree justice." The jury must take its law from the judge; irrelevant evidence he will either prevent it from hearing or instruct it to ignore. Thus he ensures that the jury

---

[25] But after an acquittal, the Att.-Gen. may refer a *point of law* arising in the case to the Court of Appeal for an opinion on it: Criminal Justice Act 1972, s.36. This does not affect the inviolability of a jury's verdict on the facts. It must also be noted that, by the Magistrates Courts Act 1980, s.111, on a dismissal of a charge by magistrates, the prosecutor may appeal by way of case stated on a point of law, which includes the ground that the finding on the facts is perverse: *Bracegirdle v. Oxley* [1947] 1 All E.R. 126.
[26] Nor, in the normal case, can the trial judge ask them for their reasons: see *R. v. Agbim* [1979] Crim.L.R. 171.
[27] *Bushel's case* (1670) Vaugh. 135.

at least answers the right question, and to some extent at least he can tell the jury what the right answer is. He is not expected to take a passive role. "The judge is more than a mere referee who takes no part in the trial save to intervene when a rule of procedure or evidence is broken. He and the jury try the case together, and it is his duty to give them the benefit of his knowledge of the law and to advise them in the light of his experience as to the significance of the evidence.[28]

There are certain matters which are solely for the judge. With others, although they are nominally for the jury, there is a substantial amount of judicial control. Put shortly, the division of functions sounds simple: matters of law are for the judge, matters of fact are for the jury. But this puts it too shortly,[29] because the jury is certainly not left in complete charge of a matter of fact. It is better to say: questions as to the production and admissibility of evidence are for the judge; questions as to its credibility and weight are for the jury, although there are exceptional cases where the law puts the deciding of facts solely on the judge. To expand further, the judge exercises general control of the orderliness of the proceedings, and decides questions of substantive law arising. He rules on the competence of proffered witnesses, and on the admissibility of evidence. The latter will involve him in taking a view of the relevance of the evidence[30] and if certain facts are conditions precedent of admissibility, it is for him to say whether they have been established. Subject to what is said below, the construction of words is for him. He decides whether to reject on discretion evidence which is legally admissible, and whether the evidence which is admitted on an issue is sufficient for it to be considered by the jury. It is his duty to comment on the evidence which has been given in his summing up, and to instruct the jury on what is their duty if they find the evidence on both sides evenly balanced[31] and on what degree of conviction evidence must carry for them before they can act on it.[32]

1. Judicial Control of the Jury

(a) Construction of words

What words were used on a particular occasion is for the jury to

---

[28] *Per* Lawton L.J. in *R.* v. *Sparrow* [1973] 1 W.L.R. 488.
[29] See *per* Lord Diplock in *D.P.P.* v. *Stonehouse* [1978] A.C. 55 at p. 69..
[30] *Ante*, p. 17.
[31] See *post*, Chap. 3.
[32] See *post*, Chap. 4.

settle as a matter of fact in the ordinary way. However, traditionally, the *meaning* of ordinary words, both spoken and written, was a question of law for the judge.[33] This may possibly still be the case for civil cases tried by a jury, but in criminal cases, so far as concerns ordinary words in a statute, the position nowadays is different. In *Cozens* v. *Brutus*,[34] a criminal case on the meaning of "insulting behaviour" in the Public Order Act 1936,[35] Lord Reid said, "The meaning of an ordinary word of the English language is not a question of law. The proper construction of a statute is a question of law." If the word is used in some unusual sense, or if there are more than one possible usual meaning, the judge indicates which meaning is to be taken. But if there is no question of a word being used in other than its ordinary meaning, the jury decides what the meaning is and thereby, *pace* Lord Reid, construes the statute. It has been held, for example, that "dishonestly" in the Theft Act 1968 is a word whose meaning is for the jury without assistance from the judge.[36] This appears to risk uncertainty in the application of the law, in that in identical cases, different juries could reach different conclusions on whether certain conduct was dishonest and within the Theft Act. However they are not completely in control, able to give the word *any* meaning they choose. They must not be perverse; they must not give it a meaning which no person acquainted with the ordinary use of language could give it. Perverse findings can be prevented or corrected to some extent as will be seen,[37] and although a perverse finding resulting in an acquittal cannot be upset, that was always the case with perverse acquittals, even in the days when the jury were supposed to take the meaning of a word from the judge.

Moreover, there is a class of word where the boundaries of acceptable meaning are settled, not by ordinary English usage, but by judicial decision.[38] An example is the expression "a person

---

[33] *Neilson* v. *Harford* (1841) 8 M. & W. 806, per Parke B. at p. 823. There were two specific exceptions to this rule, where the meaning was for the jury,*i.e.* in defamation cases: *Nevill* v. *Fine Art Insurance Co. Ltd.* [1897] A.C. 68, and in cases of false trade descriptions: *R.* v. *Sunair Holidays Ltd.* [1973] 1 W.L.R. 1105; *R.* v. *Clarkson's Tours Ltd.* (1972) 55 Cr.App.R. 28.

[34] [1973] A.C. 854 at p. 861.

[35] See also *D.P.P.* v. *Stonehouse* [1978] A.C. 55, where the meaning of an "imprecise" word in a common law definition of a crime, *i.e.* "proximity" in the crime of attempt, was held to be a jury matter.

[36] *R.* v. *Feely* [1973] Q.B. 530. See now *R.* v. *Ghosh* [1982] Q.B. 1053.

[37] *Post*, pp. 40, 41.

[38] In addition to the example discussed in the following text, see *Waltham Forest L.B.C.* v. *Mills* [1980] R.T.R. 201, on "pitching a stall," and *A.C.T. Construction Ltd.* v. *Customs & Excise* [1981] 1 W.L.R. 49 on "maintenance" of buildings.

driving" in section 2(1) of the Road Safety Act 1967. This has been the subject of a large number of cases, including two in the House of Lords, in which it is laid down that "a person driving" a vehicle is not as extensive as "the driver" of the vehicle, but does include someone whose vehicle is temporarily halted, e.g. at traffic lights or at the request of a policeman, even if he is not inside his vehicle.[39] It is difficult to describe a concept so heavily shot over by the judges as one of fact. However, inside the judicially set parameters,[40] it is for the jury to decide whether the accused was a "person driving."[41] The judge must leave it to them, although "there may be cases in which (he), with his knowledge of the authorities, may have to indicate to the jury that the argument is really all one way."[42] Moreover, control may be exercised by the technique of legally binding judicial notice referred to earlier in this chapter.[43]

(b) Sufficiency of evidence

Whether there is any *sufficient evidence* on an issue is a question of law for the judge.[44] He decides whether a party has adduced enough evidence on an issue for it to be said that, if the evidence is believed, it could reasonably be taken as establishing the fact that the party is seeking to establish. If there is no sufficient evidence, it is the judge's duty to withdraw the issue from the jury, *i.e.* to direct them that there is no acceptable evidence on that issue and that they must not find on that issue in favour of the party on whom is the burden of adducing evidence (the proponent[45]). If he does not do this, he will be corrected on

---

[39] *Pinner* v. *Everett* [1969] 1 W.L.R. 1266; *Sakhuja* v. *Allan* [1973] A.C. 152, and see the cases cited *ibid.* and in Wilkinson, *Road Traffic Offences* (8th ed.), pp. 184–192.
[40] Conveniently summarised by Griffiths J. in *Edkins* v. *Knowles* [1973] Q.B. 748 at p. 756.
[41] *R.* v. *Jones* [1970] 1 W.L.R. 211, at p. 215; *R.* v. *Bates* [1973] 1 W.L.R. 718 disapproving of *R.* v. *Kelly* [1970] 1 W.L.R. 1050.
[42] *R.* v. *Bates, supra, per* Lord Widgery C.J. at p. 722. Presumably he must do so only if the present fact situation exactly corresponds to one the subject of an earlier decision; it has been said that the jury are not bound by any of the illustrative examples of a "person driving" given in earlier judgments, even of the House of Lords: *per* Lord Salmon in *Sakhuja* v. *Allan, supra,* at p. 201.
[43] *Ante,* p. 35.
[44] This is different from his duty to exclude evidence which is not sufficiently relevant to be worth the time and trouble involved in listening to it: see, *e.g. R.* v. *Rimmer & Beech* [1983] Crim.L.R. 250. *Ante,* p. 17.
[45] The proponent is usually the plaintiff or prosecutor but not always: see Chap. 3 on burden of proof.

appeal[46]—the appeal court will reverse the jury's finding on that issue if they find in favour of the proponent—they *should* have been told that they could *not* find for him.[47] But if the judge rightly holds that there is sufficient evidence to go to the jury, then he leaves it to them to say whether the proponent has in fact convinced them on this issue. Thus in a negligence action the judge rules on whether the evidence adduced by the plaintiff is such that negligence by the defendant *can* be inferred. If he rules "yes" then the jury decide whether it ought so to be inferred.

In *Metropolitan Ry. v. Jackson*[48] a person sued for negligence because his thumb was crushed in a slammed railway carriage door. The jury found in his favour, but the railway won its appeal because, although there was evidence that it was negligent in allowing the carriage to be overcrowded, there was no evidence which could reasonably be taken as suggesting that the overcrowding was the cause of the plaintiff's thumb being crushed. The judge should have withdrawn the issue from the jury and directed a verdict for the defendant.

If there *is* sufficient evidence to go to the jury, the verdict of the jury will rarely be interfered with, in the absence of some misdirection by the judge. In a criminal case, as has been seen, there is no appeal from a jury's verdict of acquittal.[49] On an appeal from a conviction, the Court of Appeal must allow the appeal if they think that the verdict of the jury should be set aside on the ground that under all the circumstances of the case it is unsafe or unsatisfactory.[50] This by no means necessarily involves the court thinking that the verdict is perverse, merely that the general feel of the case leaves a lurking doubt in the court's mind.[51]

[46] Unless the appeal court considers, in a criminal case, that no miscarriage of justice, or in a civil case, that no substantial wrong or miscarriage of justice, has actually occurred: Criminal Appeal Act 1968, s.2(1) proviso; R.S.C., Ord. 55, r. 7; Ord. 59, r. 11; Ord. 112, r. 6.
[47] It hardly needs saying that this is not the only ground upon which a decision will be upset on appeal. Misdirection on substantive law or on the burden or standard of proof, misreception of evidence, defective procedure, are some examples of grounds for upsetting a decision.
[48] (1877) 3 App.Cas. 193.
[49] See *ante*, p. 36, n. 25.
[50] The Criminal Appeal Act 1968, s.2. The court's general duty to allow an appeal on various grounds is subject to the proviso mentioned in n. 46, *supra*, but if the ground is that the verdict is unsafe or unsatisfactory, it necessarily follows that the proviso cannot be applied. See *Ferguson v. R.* [1979] 1 All E.R. 877.
[51] *Stafford v. D.P.P.* [1974] A.C. 878, approving a dictum to this effect by Widgery L.J. in *R. v. Cooper* [1969] 1 Q.B. 267 at p. 271. Even the physical conditions under which the jury reached their verdict may be enough to make the verdict unsafe. See *R. v. Sutton and Moore* [1978] Crim.L.R. 442: "10.30 p.m. was not the time for juries to reach conclusions...."

But in a civil case, only if the verdict is *perverse, i.e.* such that no reasonable jury, applying their minds correctly to the evidence on both sides, would have reached, will the verdict be upset.[52] Where the judge sits without a jury, the position is different to some extent. The appellate court will not disturb questions which depend on the credibility of witnesses, for the judge saw the witnesses and observed their demeanour, and the printed transcript, which is all that is normally available to the appellate court, is no substitute for that. However, with questions which do not depend purely on credibility, but on inferences to be drawn from undisputed facts, there is a difference in attitude in the appellate court. Such a decision by judge alone will be upset if it appears to be affected by inconsistencies and inaccuracies or a failure to appreciate the weight or bearing of circumstances admitted or proved, or otherwise to have gone plainly wrong.[53] But a verdict of a jury, which cannot be subjected to the same degree of examination (no reasons being given) will only be disturbed if it can be described as perverse.

(c) Discretion to admit or reject evidence

A matter which is certainly within the sole responsibility of the judge is the exercising of any relevant discretion, particularly with regard to the admission or rejection of evidence. The extent of this particular discretion is discussed in this section.

As we have seen, the judge's duty includes ruling on whether any piece of evidence is relevant enough to be admitted. However, what is relevant is not necessarily admissible; it must also be allowed by the many rules of evidence, discussion of which occupies the bulk of this book. These rules are rules of law, for the judge to apply, and prima facie binding on him. The question arises, are they absolutely binding on him? If a piece of evidence is not allowed by the rules, may a judge nevertheless admit it on the grounds of convenience or of ensuring a just result? If an item *is* allowed by the rules, may he exclude it on similar grounds? In short, once he has decided that a rule applies, may he ignore it and admit or reject the proffered evidence in apparent breach of it?

If he has power to do this, he has a discretion in the strict sense

---

[52] *Metropolitan Ry.* v. *Wright* (1886) 11 App.Cas. 152 at p. 153.
[53] *Watt* v. *Thomas* [1947] A.C. 484 at p. 491.

of the word[54]; but it must be noted in this connection that there are many places in the law where, although a judge is bound by a rule if it applies, he has a measure of freedom in deciding whether it does apply.[55] For instance, in deciding on the persuasiveness of a Ministerial certificate claiming protection from disclosure of a matter on public interest grounds, his duty is to ask whether the litigant's private interest in disclosure is outweighed by the public interest in non-disclosure.[56] In deciding in a rape trial whether to admit or reject evidence of the complainant's sexual experience with third parties, he must ask himself whether exclusion is "unfair" to the defendant.[57] Both of these questions are necessarily rather subjective but once answered, the judge's duty to admit or reject becomes plain, and binding. Discretion is not used in this discussion to denote what is involved in this kind of situation. The word is used in its strict sense as denoting "a situation where instead of deciding a question by recourse to a fixed legal rule of decision, the judge is left with a choice and is able to decide on the merits of the case."[58]

In this sense of the word, the common law[59] gives the judge no discretion to admit that which the rules make inadmissible. In *Sparks* v. *R.*,[60] evidence which would strongly suggest the accused's innocence was hearsay evidence, not falling within any of the exceptional cases where hearsay evidence is allowed.[61] It was held by the Privy Council that it was inadmissible; hearsay evidence does not become admissible merely because to exclude it might risk an unmerited conviction.

As to exclusion of that which is legally admissible, there is a power, in the interests of fairness to witnesses, to disallow questions in cross-examination which the judge considers oppressive or offensive,[62] and there may be a power to protect confidentiality, if he thinks that disclosure would involve a

---

[54] See Pattenden, *The Judge, Discretion and the Criminal Trial* (1982).
[55] *Op. cit.* p. 4: "Discretion, in a third sense, arises where the judge is automatically obliged to act in a given way if the elements of a fixed rule are satisfied, but the rule contains a standard which requires a personal assessment of the circumstances."
[56] See *post*, p. 140.
[57] See *post*, p. 120.
[58] Pattenden, *op. cit.* p. 3.
[59] For a rare statutory exception, see the discretion to admit hearsay in civil cases although it does not comply with the conditions of the Civil Evidence Act 1968, *post*, p. 270.
[60] [1966] A.C. 964.
[61] See *post*, Chap. 12.
[62] *Post*, p. 117.

breach of confidence which would do more harm than good.[63] Further than that, it seems that there is no authority for an exclusionary discretion in civil cases.[64] "When it comes to the forensic crunch ... it must be law not discretion which is in command."[65] However in criminal cases, there is discretion to reject legally admissible crown evidence. Section 82(3) of the Police and Criminal Evidence Act confirms it so far as it existed in 1984, and section 78(1) purports to extend its area of operation.

At common law, there were two particular well-established discretions to exclude Crown evidence. The first is where the evidence may have been got perfectly fairly, but it has a prejudicial effect out of all proportion to its real worth. Putting it in will make the trial unfair, so the judge, whose duty it is to see that the trial is fair, can exclude it. The existence of this discretion is usually thought to have originated in a dictum of Lord Moulton in *R. v. Christie*,[66] a case concerning admission by equivocal response in the face of accusation.[67] The discretion was later held to apply to cases where the accused, having thrown away his immunity by attacking Crown witnesses, had made himself liable to having his criminal record cross-examined on and proved if he did not admit it[68]; and also to cases where the Crown sought to prove against the accused similar discreditable conduct on other occasions.[69] It has been said that the categories of such cases where the judge ensures a fair trial by excluding legally admissible evidence are not and never can be closed.[70] The second case where a discretion to exclude was well established concerned confessions, which are discussed in Chapter 10.

But further than this a judge had no discretion to exclude

---

[63] *Post*, p. 149.
[64] Even a body which is not bound by the strict rules of evidence, such as an industrial tribunal, has no discretion to reject evidence which is both admissible under those rules and probative: *Rosedale Mouldings v. Sibley* [1980] I.C.R. 816 (E.A.T.).
[65] *Per* Lord Simon in *D. v. N.S.P.C.C.* [1978] A.C. 171 at p. 239, said in a particular context but apparently of general application. *Post*, p. 149.
[66] [1914] A.C. 545 at p. 559.
[67] See *post*, p. 182.
[68] See *post*, p. 231.
[69] See *post*, p. 217. For reasons explained *post*, p. 218, the discretion is not likely to be exercised in this sort of case nowadays.
[70] *Per* Lord Salmon in *R. v. Sang* [1980] A.C. 402 at p. 445; see also Lord Scarman, *ibid.* pp. 452, 453. In *R. v. Rogers and Tarran* [1971] Crim.L.R. 413, evidence against A was excluded because it unfairly prejudiced a fellow accused B in the eyes of the jury.

Crown evidence. Evidence which was *not* unduly prejudicial and did *not* consist in a confession could not be excluded merely because the authorities had obtained it in some dubious, or underhand, or even downright illegal way. The judicial attitude in England has been that *how* evidence was got is no concern of the present Court. Illegally obtained evidence has never been *inadmissible* on that account. That was finally established in *Kuruma* v. *R.*,[71] and although in that case Lord Goddard C.J. said there was a discretion to exclude such, 14 years later that was denied in the case of *R.* v. *Sang*,[72] which concerned evidence got by an *agent provocateur*. The House of Lords confirmed the two particular discretions mentioned above, but denied that there was any general discretion to exclude Crown evidence.[73] Section 78(1) of the Police and Criminal Evidence Act 1984 is an attempt to reverse this and to confer a general discretion to exclude. It provides:

> "In any [criminal] proceedings the court may refuse to allow evidence on which the prosecution proposes to rely to be given if it appears to the court that, having regard to all the circumstances, including the circumstances in which the evidence was obtained, the admission of the evidence would have such an adverse effect on the fairness of the proceedings that the court ought not to admit it."

The reference to adverse effect on the fairness of the proceedings clearly covers the area of the former discretion about evidence the use of which will have an unduly prejudicial effect, but does not easily cover evidence where all that is wrong with it is the way it was obtained. Although the court is directed to have regard to the circumstances in which it was got, in practice those circumstances will not usually affect the fairness of the proceedings, in the sense of inhibiting a just result, and it was regularly so held.[74] Presumably Parliament envisaged that there must be *some* circumstances in which the way evidence was got will cause its admission to have such an adverse effect on the fairness of the proceedings that the court ought not to admit it, but such circumstances will not often be present. As to illegally obtained

---

[71] [1955] A.C. 197 (P.C.).
[72] [1980] A.C. 402.
[73] But if the conduct of the prosecution amounts to an abuse of process, any Court has an inherent power to prevent it. See, *post*, p. 333.
[74] See, *e.g. Jeffrey* v. *Black* [1978] Q.B. 490.

Functions of Judge and Jury 45

evidence, the occasions when the discretion can be used will be rare. Occasions when it is actually used in favour of the accused are likely to be rarer still. Before 1980, when R. v. *Sang* denied the existence of a general discretion, judges often referred to it but hardly ever used it. A simple irregularity in the obtaining of the evidence was not enough to cause the general discretion to be exercised,[75] or to invoke the specific discretion relating to prejudice at the trial.[76] Confessional evidence was, and is, a special case.[77] In any event examining magistrates have no discretion to reject any legally admissible evidence; they must admit all that is proffered and leave it to the court of trial to decide whether any is to be excluded on discretion.[78]

(d) Summing up

At a trial on indictment, it is the judge's duty, after the evidence has been given, and counsel have made their addresses, to sum up the case for the jury, and to deal with any points of difficulty which the jury may raise after they have started their deliberations.[79] The form the summing up takes depends on the nature of the case and the law involved, and thus is in principle for the judge. However, although it has been said that he, "is not concerned to write a chapter for a text book on the law of evidence. He guides the jury in their deliberations knowing full well the submissions which have already been made to them [by counsel],"[80] there are certain matters which he must not omit even if they have been the subject of correct submissions, *e.g.* the burden and standard of proof.[81]

In summing up, the judge is entitled to comment on the plausibility and credibility of the witnesses.[82] Sometimes he must be especially circumspect on this.[83] In any case at all, he must

[75] *Jeffrey* v. *Black, supra;* R. v. *Trump* (1979) 70 Cr.App.R. 300.
[76] R. v. *Apicella* (1985) 82 Cr.App.R. 295, (decided on the law before the Act).
[77] As to which, see *post*, p. 201.
[78] R. v. *Horsham JJ., ex p. Bukhari* (1982) 74 Cr.App.R. 291.
[79] Any communication with the jury must be in the presence of counsel for both sides: R. v. *Townsend* [1982] 1 All E.R. 509; R. v. *Rose* [1982] 2 All E.R. 536. On the other hand, discussions with counsel as to how their questions should be answered ought to be in the absence of the jury: R. v. *Rimmer & Beech* [1983] Crim.L.R. 250.
[80] R. v. *Korniak* (1982) 76 Cr.App.R. 145, *per* Eveleigh L.J. at p. 150.
[81] R. v. *Edwards* (1983) 77 Cr.App.R. 5. See *post*, Chap. 4, and also Chap. 8, on corroboration warnings, and warnings on identification evidence; and Chap. 14, on the admissibility of a confession only against the defendant who made it.
[82] He must not however suggest that police witnesses are especially reliable: R. v. *Culbertson* (1970) 54 Cr.App.R. 310; R. v. *Fisher* [1983] Crim.L.R. 486.
[83] See Chap. 9, *post*, on comment on the accused's silence.

make it clear that the matter of accepting or rejecting evidence is essentially for the jury themselves. He cannot in plain terms advise them to reject certain (relevant) evidence, or to prefer one account of a transaction to another. Nor may he dismiss evidence by the device of failing to mention it in his summing up.[84] But if there is only one answer which a jury doing its duty could find, the judge is allowed to indicate what the only answer is. Thus although it has been said that every man on trial for murder has the right to have the issue of manslaughter left to the jury if there is evidence on which such a verdict can be given,[85] it has also been held that if there is no such evidence, a judge is entitled to direct the jury: "You convict of murder or acquit."[86]

May he go further and direct a particular verdict? No one doubts that the judge in a criminal trial can direct an *acquittal*,[87] but it is passionately denied by some[88] that he can on any occasion whatever direct a conviction. The controversy is a shade artificial, for most of those who deny his right to *direct*, accept with equanimity his right in an appropriate case to *exhort* a conviction in terms so blunt and compelling as to amount to a direction in all but name.[89] There can be but few jurors saucy enough to resist something like the following, which on appeal was held to be fully justified on the evidence[90]: "There is a limit, is there not, members of the jury, to human credulity, and you may think that the accused man's unsupported assertion on this part of the case goes well past it, that the evidence was overwhelming, and he knew his car was carrying the officer up the road? The matter is one for you but if you arrived at the conclusion that, of course, he knew, it is one which I would regard as abundantly right. Indeed, on the evidence I do not see how you could properly arrive at any other conclusion. If that be so the defence of pure accident goes."

No doubt a judge who is minded to give a mandatory direction should always take care to make it a qualified direction—"if you

---

[84] See *R.* v. *Badjam* (1966) 50 Cr.App.R. 141, where the judge ignored the evidence of self-defence. On appeal, "it was a defence which, in the light of the evidence, might have been regarded as of tenuous worth, but it was a defence which the appellant was entitled to have left to the jury for their assessment": *per* Edmund Davies L.J. at p. 143.
[85] *Bullard* v. *R.* [1957] A.C. 635, *per* Lord Tucker at p. 644.
[86] *Ferguson* v. *R.* [1979] 1 All E.R. 877.
[87] Or in a civil trial, direct a verdict for either party.
[88] *e.g.* Lord Devlin in *Trial by Jury* (3rd imp., 1966), pp. 83 *et seq.* and App. II; and see *D.P.P.* v. *Stonehouse* [1978] A.C. 55 at pp. 80, 87.
[89] See Lord Salmon in *D.P.P.* v. *Stonehouse, supra* at p. 80.
[90] See *D.P.P.* v. *Smith* [1961] A.C. 290.

find this, *then* it is your duty to convict," but even an unqualified mandatory direction will, in an appropriate case, be forgiven by the appellate court, by the use of the proviso to section 2(1) of the Criminal Appeal Act 1968.[91]

2. Facts for the Judge

(a) Foreign law

Foreign, Colonial and Scottish, but probably not Irish, law is a matter for the judge, who listens to expert witnesses. It is a matter of fact, being proved by witnesses, or by the production of a report of any previous determination of the point in question by an English superior court,[92] but it is nevertheless for the judge. There is a presumption that foreign law is identical with English law, so if there is no acceptable evidence of any difference, the judge must hold that it is the same.

(b) Collateral facts

In many cases, evidence of a particular type is only admissible if certain other facts exist or do not exist, *e.g.* a "dying declaration" is only admissible if the utterer knew that he was dying; a confession is only admissible if it was not obtained in breach of the conditions in section 76(2) of the Police and Criminal Evidence Act 1984; a copy document may only be proved if the absence of the original is satisfactorily accounted for; evidence from any witness is only admissible if he is competent. It is for the judge, not the jury, to decide whether such conditions precedent exist.[93]

The enquiry conducted by the judge into facts affecting the admissibility of evidence is called the *voir dire*[94] (or trial within a trial). The witnesses as to those facts are examined by the parties

---

[91] Which provides that the Court of Appeal may, notwithstanding that they are of opinion that the point raised in the appeal might be decided in favour of the appellant, dismiss the appeal if they consider that no miscarriage of justice has actually occurred. See *D.P.P.* v. *Stonehouse, supra.*

[92] Civil Evidence Act 1972, s.4(2). See *ante*, p. 34. This is the production of presumptive evidence, not the refreshing of the judge's memory so that he can take judicial notice. It is only taken as settling the point until the contrary is proved.

[93] *Bartlett* v. *Smith* (1842) 11 M. & W. 483.

[94] Credibility or weight are not *voir dire* matters. If the question about a confession is whether it was ever made at all, or the question about identification evidence is whether it is satisfactory enough to be acted upon, these are not for the judge, not being on the *admissibility* of the evidence: see *Ajodha* v. *State* [1982] A.C. 204, *post*, p. 196; *R.* v. *Walshe* (1980) 74 Cr.App.R. 85.

or by the judge himself. If the enquiry is as to the competence of a witness to take the oath, it is held in the presence of the jury.[95] But if there is any danger of the jury hearing evidence which may be ruled inadmissible, as in cases of disputed confessions, the *voir dire* is held with the jury absent.

Although on the *voir dire*, the judge is not deciding any of the issues involved in the trial but merely ruling on evidence, it not infrequently happens that the evidence relevant to the question for him is also relevant to the question for the jury. In such a case, the evidence may be gone through twice, the second time before the jury. In *R. v. Murray*,[96] the Recorder listened to witnesses in the absence of the jury on the question of whether an alleged confession was voluntary, that being a precondition of its admissibility.[97] After he had ruled that it was voluntary, the trial proceeded and the confession was put in by the Crown. When the accused sought to prove to the jury that it was not voluntary, the Recorder refused to allow this because he had already decided the matter. On appeal, it was held that this was wrong. Although the accused was not entitled to dispute the confession's admissibility, he was entitled to dispute its weight, and the voluntariness or otherwise was relevant to its weight. Admissibility is for the judge, credibility and weight are for the jury, and both parts of the tribunal need to decide whether the confession is voluntary to perform their respective functions.[98]

(c) Facts bearing on punishment

In criminal trials, after conviction, the judge conducts a *voir dire* on the question of what is the appropriate sentence or treatment for the accused. He hears witnesses on the accused's antecedents, previous convictions, way of life, etc. He is not normally bound by the strict rules of evidence, unless the accused challenges or contradicts statements made by the Crown, in which case the judge should require proper proof, if necessary after an adjournment.[99] But he cannot take other offences into consideration, even if they are proved on oath at the *voir dire*, unless the accused admits them, for to do so would be to deprive the accused of his right to trial by jury in respect of those other offences. If the judge feels that he cannot adequately sentence the accused on the offence of which he has been convicted, he can give the

---
[95] *Toohey v. Metropolitan Police Commissioner* [1965] A.C. 595, *post*, p. 130.
[96] [1951] 1 K.B 391.
[97] For the present preconditions, see *post*, Chap. 10.
[98] *Ante*, p. 37.
[99] *R. v. Campbell* (1911) 6 Cr.App.R. 131.

prosecution leave either to prefer a voluntary bill charging the other offences or to amend the indictment.[1]

In sentencing on a plea of guilty, where there is a dispute about the details of the offence, *e.g.* how it was committed, the judge should either enter a plea of not guilty, so that a jury may determine the matter,[2] or hear evidence and decide the matter himself,[3] or accept the version most favourable to the accused.[4]

---

[1] *R. v. Hutchison* (1972) 56 Cr.App.R. 307.
[2] *i.e.* provided that the indictment can be framed in such a way that the jury's verdict will indicate a finding by them on the disputed matter.
[3] He should not empannel a jury to deal solely with the disputed matters: *R. v. Milligan* [1982] Crim.L.R. 317.
[4] *R. v. Newton* (1982) 77 Cr.App.R. 13. See also Thomas, "Establishing a Factual Basis for Sentencing" [1970] Crim.L.R. 80.

Part II

BURDEN AND STANDARD OF PROOF

Chapter 3
BURDEN OF PROOF

	Page
A. The Different Burdens	53
1. The Persuasive Burden	54
2. The Evidential Burden	61
B. The Incidence of the Burdens	65
1. The General Rule	65
2. Insanity	66
3. Formal Admissions	66
4. Express Statutory Reversals of the Normal Rule	66
5. Implied Statutory Reversals	68

Chapter 4
STANDARD OF PROOF

A. Criminal Cases	71
B. Civil Cases	74

Chapter 5
PRESUMPTIONS

A. Presumptions of Law	78
1. General Considerations	79
2. Some Important Presumptions	82
B. Presumptions of Fact	89

Chapter 3

BURDEN OF PROOF

In every litigation, there are occasions in the proceedings on which the question will arise as to which of the parties has the burden of proof on a given issue, and the answer to the question may well dictate the result of the proceedings. Most of the difficulties in expounding this subject arise from the fact that the expression "burden of proof" has more than one meaning. Judges not infrequently fail to make clear in which sense they are using the term (by omitting to prefix the expression with identifying adjectives or adjectival phrases), and although writers on the subject do use identifying adjectives, there seems to be little agreement on which adjectives should be used or even on how many meanings the expression "burden of proof" has. But it is clear that there are two principal kinds of burden of proof which must be kept distinct.

A. The Different Burdens

On every issue, there is an obligation on one party to convince the tribunal of fact (whether by preponderance of evidence or beyond reasonable doubt[1]) of the truth of some proposition of fact which is in issue and which is vital to his case. This obligation will be called "the persuasive burden"[2]; and the party on whom it is cast will be referred to as the proponent; the other party will be referred to as the opponent. Failure to discharge this burden is failure in the whole or some part of the litigation. The stage in the proceedings when the incidence of this burden is seen as vital is when all the evidence on both sides has been given, because it then becomes the duty of the judge to instruct the tribunal of fact as to what their verdict should be if they remain in doubt on the issues.

But there is also an obligation to adduce sufficient evidence on

---

[1] *Post*, Chap. 4.
[2] See Glanville Williams, *Criminal Law, the General Part*, Chap. 23. Other terms used are "burden of proof on the pleadings" (Phipson, 12th ed., Chap. 4); "legal burden" (Cross, Chap. III; Lord Denning (1945) 61 L.Q.R. 379): "the risk of non-persuasion" (Wigmore, § 2485); or sometimes, the unqualified expression "burden of proof": see *Hill* v. *Baxter* [1958] 1 Q.B. 277 at p. 284; *Bratty* v. *Att.-Gen. for Northern Ireland* [1963] A.C. 386 at pp. 407, 414.

53

a particular fact to justify a finding on the fact in favour of the party who is under the obligation, which will be referred to as the evidential burden. The stages at which this obligation has to be considered are, (i) at the outset, to answer the question of who should begin, and produce his evidence first, and (ii) at the close of that party's evidence, to answer the question of whether enough has been shown by him to require the other party to produce evidence in reply.

Failure to discharge the evidential burden means that the judge will rule that there is insufficient evidence on the issue to justify consideration by the jury. If the party who suffers this misfortune of failing to "pass the judge" is also under the persuasive burden (*i.e.* is the proponent) on the issue, he must inevitably fail on the issue, because there is no chance of his discharging the persuasive burden (*i.e.* persuading the jury of his allegations) if the judge refuses to let the evidence go to the jury. On the other hand, successfully passing the judge does not mean that he must win. Although the judge will have ruled that his evidence is sufficient to go to the jury, that body remains to be convinced and they might not be, perhaps because they do not believe his witnesses or refuse to draw the required inferences from the evidence. Such a proponent, who labours under two burdens, must see his evidence surmount two hurdles—it must pass the judge *and* convince the jury.

It follows that if it is not the proponent but the opponent who is under the evidential burden, failure to discharge it does *not* mean that he will inevitably lose on the issue. The persuasive burden remains on the proponent and has still to be discharged, which it might not be,[3] although, as will be seen, the very fact of the opponent's failure with the evidential burden will increase the likelihood of the proponent's succeeding.

1. The Persuasive Burden

The general rule is that he who asserts must prove, whether the allegation be an affirmative or a negative one, and not he who denies. "It is an ancient rule founded on considerations of good sense, and it should not be departed from without strong reasons."[4]

The effect of this general rule is that the obligation of satisfying the court on an issue rests upon the party (plaintiff, prosecutor or

---

[3] See the passage quoted from *Dunn* v. *Dunn, post,* p. 63.
[4] *Joseph Constantine Steamship Line Ltd.* v. *Imperial Smelting Corporation Ltd.* [1942] A.C. 154 at p. 174.

defendant) who, in substance, asserts the affirmative of the issue; that is to say, where a given allegation, whether affirmative or negative, forms an essential factor of a party's case, the proof of such an allegation rests on him. Thus, if the defendant has sold a horse with a warranty of soundness, and the plaintiff sues him for breach of the warranty, it is for the plaintiff to prove the horse unsound, and not for the defendant, at the outset, to prove it sound.

In deciding which of the parties asserts the affirmative, the substance, rather than the grammatical construction, of the pleadings is the decisive factor. If a landlord-plaintiff claims that the tenant-defendant did not repair the premises, and the latter asserts that he did well and sufficiently repair, it is the plaintiff's allegation which is in substance positive, although cast in negative terms. His allegation could as well be phrased that the defendant allowed the premises to fall into disrepair; in substance he is saying that the defendant broke his covenant, and it is for him, the plaintiff, to prove it.[5] Moreover, by the substantive law a negative averment may be an essential part of a party's case, so that he must prove it to make out his case. For instance, one of the essentials of the tort of malicious prosecution is that the defendant had no reasonable and probable cause for the prosecution, so that he who alleges that the tort has been committed (*i.e.* the plaintiff) must prove the absence of reasonable and probable cause, although this requires him to prove a negative.[6]

However, in most civil actions, the burden of the issues is divided, each party having one or more cast upon him. Certainly if the defendant responds to a claim, not by merely denying its existence, but by raising a defence to it, the burden of proving all the elements of the defence will be on him. Thus, in an action by A against B to recover a loan, to which the defence is a denial of the loan, and in the alternative that it has been discharged, the onus of proving the debt is on A and its discharge on B.[7] And in negligence, the onus of proving the negligence is upon the plaintiff, but if the defendant pleads contributory negligence, the onus of proving it is upon him.[8]

Exceptions and provisos. The party who relies on an exception (or

---

[5] *Soward* v. *Leggatt* (1836) 7 C. & P. 613; see also *Howard* v. *Borneman* [1972] 1 W.L.R. 863.
[6] *Abrath* v. *N.E. Ry.* (1883) 11 Q.B.D. 440.
[7] *Young* v. *Queensland Trustees Ltd.* (1956) 99 C.L.R. 560, and see *Seldon* v. *Davidson* [1968] 1 W.L.R. 1083.
[8] *Wakelin* v. *L. & S.W. Ry.* (1886) 12 App.Cas. 41.

proviso) to some general rule imposing liability has the burden of proving that the exception applies to the case. An exception must be distinguished from a negative precondition of the general rule founding a claim. If A charges B with some liability, he must prove all the preconditions of liability, including any negative ones. Thus, as we have seen, one of the essentials of the tort of malicious prosecution is that there was an absence of reasonable and probable cause for the prosecution. A, the plaintiff, who says that B committed this tort, must prove this element along with all the others. But if the law says in effect that in some exceptional case where all the conditions of liability are present, a defendant is not liable, then if B alleges that he is within that exceptional case, it is for B to prove it, it is not for A to disprove.[9] It is the same with a *defence* allowed by the law. If B is to rely on that defence, he must raise and prove all the elements of it, including negative ones. But if the law, in describing the defence, allows some exceptional cases when the defence is not to be available, B does not have to prove that no such exceptional case applies. If A avers that B is disabled from relying on the defence because it is within one of the exceptional cases, he (A) must prove it.

If the cause of action arises under statute, it is a question of interpretation whether the qualification on a claim or defence is a precondition or an exception. The actual arrangement of the statutory wording used to be crucial; there used to be a technical distinction between an "exception in the enacting clause," which was always construed as a precondition, and a "separate proviso" which was always construed as an exception, rather than a precondition.[10] Thus if a statute imposed liability for trespass on anyone other than a constable, the plaintiff must show (1) that the defendant trespassed and (2) was not a constable. But if the statute imposed liability on anyone trespassing, but then went on to say that a constable was not to be liable, the plaintiff need not aver or prove that the defendant was not a constable. It was for the defendant to raise the proviso if he wished and to prove that he was a constable. In *Busby* v. *Avgherino*, a statute imposed a tithe at a rate of 2s.9d. in the pound, but in a later clause provided

---

[9] In the language of pleading, if the defence is a traverse of an allegation comprised in the general averments in the statement of claim, the plaintiff must prove the disputed matter; but if the defendant's plea is in confession and avoidance *i.e.* if the defendant admits the averments in the statement of claim, but alleges further facts which excuse him, he must prove these further facts, see, *e.g. per* Palles C.B. in *Gorman* v. *Hand in Hand Insurance* (1877) L.R. 11 C.P. 224 at p. 230.

[10] Abbott J. in *Steel* v. *Smith* (1817) 1 B. & Ald. 94 at p. 99.

that where a tithe at a less rate was customarily paid at the date of the statute, the tithe-payer should continue to pay at that less rate. It was held that the burden was on those who alleged the customary less rate because "it is a particular exception out of the general charging provision made for all cases where no such customary rate exists."[11]

But in recent times the distinction has become less technical, and although the language is still important in deciding what is the substance of the claim and the substance of the available defence, it is the substance which is decisive, not the order of the statutory words. "In whatever form the enactment is cast, if it expresses an exculpation, justification, excuse, ground of defeasance or exclusion which assumes the existence of the general or primary grounds from which the liability or right arises but denies the right or liability in a special case by reason of additional or special facts, then it is evident that such an enactment supplies considerations of substance for placing the burden of proof on the party seeking to rely on the additional or special matters."[12] This was said in a case where statute allowed a person injured in a motor accident by a hit and run driver to obtain judgment against a nominal defendant, and then continued: "Provided that no such judgment may be obtained unless such person as soon as possible after he knew that the identity of the motor car could not be established gave to the Minister notice of intention to make the claim." Although the qualification on a plaintiff's right was expressed as a proviso and therefore looked at first sight to be an exception to be dealt with by the defendant, the High Court of Australia noted that *every* plaintiff had to give notice and concluded that the legislature did not mean the necessity for giving notice to be exceptional. The court therefore held the section meant to impose a condition precedent to the cause of action, and accordingly the burden of proof was on the plaintiff.

A similar rule applies to written contracts. In the absence of an express reference to the burden of proof, the essential intentions of the parties must be gathered from the words they have used, *i.e.* it is a question of construction as to what is a negative precondition of a claim or defence and what is an exception. In *The Glendaroch*,[13] A agreed with B for the carriage of B's goods by sea. The contract provided that A was not to be liable for loss caused by the perils of the sea, provided that his servants were

[11] [1928] A.C. 290, *per* Lord Sumner at p. 293.
[12] *Vines* v. *Djordjevitch* (1955) 91 C.L.R. 512, *per* Dixon C.J. at p. 519.
[13] [1894] P. 226 at p. 231.

not negligent. On the goods being lost at sea, B sued A for non-delivery. It was held that B must prove non-delivery (*i.e.* the breach of contract complained of); A, to escape liability, must prove that the loss was due to the perils of the sea; while the burden of showing that the exception relied on by A did not apply because his servants were negligent, was on the party who relied on the exception to the exception, *i.e.* B.

But where a claim or defence arises under a common law or equitable doctrine, we are in a difficulty. There is no authoritative form of words defining the doctrine; its effect will be variously stated in different books and judgments. In discovering what is a negative precondition and what an exception, construction cannot be resorted to, for there is nothing to construe. Thus, the law about frustration of charterparties is that a shipowner is excused from making his ship available to the charterer if it is destroyed without fault by him. Does this mean that destruction of the ship excuses the shipowner except where it is caused by his own fault? If so, the plaintiff charterer must prove fault in the shipowner to win. Or does it mean that a "faultless" destruction lets out the shipowner? If so, the defendant shipowner must prove a faultless destruction to escape. If a ship is lost with no evidence as to how it happened, the answer given by the law is going to be decisive of the action.

In *Constantine* v. *Imperial Smelting Corporation*,[14] the House of Lords decided this particular one by holding that the "without fault" factor was a true exception. So where A chartered B's ship, which was not delivered because it was sunk, A failed because no one could say if fault in B was involved. This result is dictated, not by construction, but by public policy and the balance of convenience. Because it is often difficult to say how ships lost at sea *were* lost, it is felt to be fairer to allow the contract to be frustrated in the absence of positive evidence of fault. Instead of allocating the burden by construing a rule, the words of the rule are formulated to take account of what is felt to be a fair allocation of the burden.[15] What will be held to be fair will vary with the subject-matter of any particular doctrine. So although a bailee of goods is not liable if the goods are lost without fault by him, the onus is on him to prove "no fault."[16] In short, except possibly in a case of first impression, there is no general rule and the matter is

---

[14] [1942] A.C. 154.
[15] See Stone, "The Burden of Proof and the Judicial Process" (1944) 60 L.Q.R. 262.
[16] *Brooks Wharf and Bulls Wharf* v. *Goodman Bros.* [1937] 1 K.B. 534. And see dictum of Lord Loreburn in *Morrison Pollexfen & Blair* v. *Walton* (1907) unreported, quoted in *Jos. Travers & Sons* v. *Cooper* [1915] 1 K.B. 73 at p. 90: "I cannot think it

The Different Burdens

governed by precedents in the particular branch of the law involved.

The rule that the burden of proving exceptions to liability is on the defendant applies also to criminal cases, but to a more limited extent. Its application to criminal cases is therefore reserved for discussion later.[17]

The incidence of the persuasive burden of proof is fixed as a matter of law at the beginning of the trial, either by the substantive law or by the pleadings, which show whether any particular allegation is admitted or denied, *e.g.* define the facts in issue. So, for instance, it is the substantive law which casts upon the plaintiff in an action for malicious prosecution the burden of proving various allegations, including the negative one referred to above; whereas if a defendant is under the burden of proving contributory negligence, it is the pleadings which have brought this about. He could have merely rested upon a denial of the negligence alleged by the plaintiff; but in his defence he raised a separate positive issue (contributory negligence) which he must now prove.

Since the persuasive burden is only discharged if the tribunal of fact is satisfied of the truth of the proponent's allegations, and since no-one knows if it is satisfied until it gives a verdict one way or another at the end of the day, it follows that it is inappropriate and misleading to speak of the persuasive burden shifting from one party to another. A situation where it is difficult to avoid reference to shifting is where there is more than one issue in a case, and the burden on one issue is on the plaintiff, while the burden on the other is on the defendant. Only if the plaintiff discharges his does the defendant have to discharge his. Thus if A sues B for negligence and B pleads contributory negligence, the burden of proving contributory negligence is on B, but only if A succeeds in establishing negligence. If A fails to do this he loses anyway. Consequently, it is sometimes said that by discharging his burden on the first issue, A shifts the burden to B.[18] However B's burden is on a completely different issue. In respect of any one issue, it remains true that the burden never shifts. This "burden" which might be said to shift, but which is not really *one* burden at

---

is good law that in such circumstances [the bailee] should be permitted to saddle upon the parties who have not broken their contract the duty of explaining how things went wrong."

[17] *Post*, p. 67.
[18] *e.g. Medawar* v. *Grand Hotel Co.* [1891] 2 Q.B. 11 at p. 23.

all, is sometimes called the "ultimate" burden—the burden on the ultimate issue in a case involving more than one issue.[19]

The persuasive burden of proof is not invariably on the party who is substantially asserting the positive. The placing of the burden can be affected by the operation of presumptions. With a rebuttable presumption of law,[20] once certain facts (called the basic facts) are proved or admitted, a further fact (the presumed fact) is taken as proved, unless the opponent rebuts the presumption with evidence of his own. Some presumptions require, for rebuttal, the opponent to *disprove* the presumed fact.[21] Where this is the case, the persuasive burden on the issue is on the opponent, and if the basic facts have been admitted in the pleadings, it is on him from the outset. If the basic facts are not admitted and have to be proved, the persuasive burden is at the outset on the proponent. Only if he proves those facts (and that of course will not be known until the end of the day) does the opponent come under a persuasive burden of disproving the presumed fact. This is best regarded as an instance of separate issues with separate burdens, of the sort explained in the previous paragraph. To succeed, the proponent must prove the basic facts, if they are in issue; if he does, the opponent is under the burden of disproving a different fact now in issue, *i.e.* the presumed fact.[22]

In criminal cases, the burden of proving the guilt of the accused beyond reasonable doubt is on the prosecution and remains there throughout the trial. A plea of "not guilty" puts in issue every material averment in the indictment, other than those formally admitted under section 10 of the Criminal Justice Act 1967[23]; and these averments, whether positive or negative, must all be made good by the prosecution. There are no pleadings in which the defendant raises separate issues and so assumes persuasive burdens; indeed there are no separate issues (subject to some exceptions to be mentioned later); only the one issue of whether the accused is guilty as charged. The requirement that he who asserts must prove is reinforced by the presumption that the accused is innocent, and if upon the whole of the evidence there remains some reasonable doubt, the prosecution has not discharged its burden and the jury must acquit.[24]

This was first laid down in clear terms by the House of Lords in

---

[19] Lord Denning (1945) 61 L.Q.R. 379.
[20] *Post*, Chap. 5.
[21] See, *post*, p. 80.
[22] See Hoffman, *South African Law of Evidence*, p. 348.
[23] See *ante*, p. 29.
[24] *Woolmington* v. *D.P.P.* [1935] A.C. 462; *Mancini* v. *D.P.P.* [1942] A.C. 1.

Woolmington v. *D.P.P.*[25] Woolmington was charged with murdering his wife, who lived apart from him. His defence was that in order to persuade her to return to him, he had threatened to shoot himself; and in the course of the resultant argument the gun went off accidentally and she was shot. The jury were directed that once the Crown had satisfied them that the woman died at the accused's hands, then he had to show some alleviating circumstance, such as provocation or accident. This was held to be a misdirection, Lord Sankey L.C. saying: "Throughout the web of the English Criminal Law one golden thread is always to be seen, that it is the duty of the prosecution to prove the prisoner's guilt, subject . . . to the defence of insanity and subject also to any statutory exception. . . . No matter what the charge or where the trial, the principle that the prosecution must prove the guilt of the prisoner is part of the common law of England and no attempt to whittle it down can be entertained."

Even if the Crown produces compulsive evidence on the unlawful conscious act of the prisoner which, in the absence of any further facts constituting such a defence as accident, provocation, etc., is said to amount to the crime charged, this does not mean that the Crown has discharged its burden, so that a burden of proving some defence attaches to the accused. The judge cannot direct that, in the absence of proof of an excusing fact by the accused, the jury must convict; he cannot say that if the accused fails to satisfy them of the facts constituting his defence, he has not discharged his burden and must fail, *i.e.* be convicted. There is no burden for him to discharge; it is the prosecution who must fail if there remain any reasonable doubt in the matter at all.[26]

2. The Evidential Burden

When a party A produces so much evidence of a fact in issue that, if the evidence is believed, any reasonable man could infer that the fact exists, he is said to have produced prima facie evidence of the fact in issue. If the burden of making out a case rests on A, he has not thereby discharged it,[27] because, as we saw, that burden is

---

[25] [1935] A.C. 462.
[26] *Woolmington* v. *D.P.P., supra*; see also the cases mentioned in n. 40, *post*, p. 65. In this connection English law was altered in *Woolmington's* case. Before that case, the law was that with regard to certain defences (*e.g.* self-defence) a persuasive burden lay on the accused. Certain colonial codifications of the existing common law are based on this position and are not affected by the later decision as to English law in *Woolmington's* case: see *Jayasena* v. *R.* [1970] A.C. 618.
[27] See *Sutton* v. *Sadler* (1857) 3 C.B.(N.S.) 87.

never discharged until the court finds in his favour at the close of the trial, and it might not so find, perhaps because it disbelieves his witnesses. A has, however, discharged the evidential burden—the burden of adducing evidence on a particular fact. He has at least avoided the misfortune of having his case withdrawn from the jury by the judge, and conversely he has reached a position where, if no contrary evidence is adduced by his opponent B, that failure will of itself increase the likelihood of the court's finding in favour of A on that fact. It must be noted that this is only true if A *has* made out a prima facie case. If he has not, he cannot hope to have his prima facie case made for him by B's failure to call evidence, because unless and until there is a prima facie case to meet, the stage at which any explanation by B is called for has not yet arrived. But prima facie evidence can be rendered conclusive by a failure to meet it. As it is put in an oft-quoted dictum,

> "No person is to be required to explain or contradict, until enough has been proved to warrant a reasonable and just conclusion against him, in the absence of explanation or contradiction; but when such proof has been given, and the nature of the case is such as to admit of explanation or contradiction, if the conclusion to which the proof tends be untrue, and the accused offers no explanation or contradiction, can human reason do otherwise than adopt the conclusion to which the proof tends?": Abbott C.J. in *R. v. Burdett*.[28]

This observation applies to civil and criminal cases alike,[29] but in criminal cases is subject to special rules about an accused person's failure to testify *personally*. The judge may, but counsel for the Crown may not, comment on this failure.[30]

It is not only the adduction of prima facie evidence by the proponent which relieves him of the evidential burden in respect of facts in issue. The same effect may result from the operation of a presumption.[31]

In whatever way A discharges the evidential burden, this never makes a verdict in A's favour inevitable in the absence of

---

[28] (1820) 4 B. & Ald. 95 at p. 161.
[29] See *McQueen* v. *G.W.R.* (1875) L.R. 10 Q.B. 569 at p. 574, *per* Cockburn C.J.
[30] See *post*, Chap. 9.
[31] *Post*, p. 80.

The Different Burdens

response by B. B is not bound as a matter of law to lose on the issue if he fails to take up the challenge; but obviously he runs a risk of a finding against him. Because he is likely to lose on the issue if he adduces no evidence, and because if he does lose he will not be able to complain that there was insufficient evidence for a finding against him, it is said that the burden of adducing evidence on the point is now on him.

The interaction of the persuasive and evidential burdens may be seen from the following passage from the judgment of Denning L.J. in *Dunn* v. *Dunn*,[32] which was concerned with a husband's petition for divorce on the grounds of desertion:

> "In this case the legal[33] burden throughout was on the petitioner to prove that his wife deserted him, without cause. In order to discharge that burden the petitioner relied on the fact that he asked her to join him and she refused. That is a fact from which the court might have inferred that she had deserted him without cause, but it was not bound to do so. Once he proved the fact of refusal she might seek to rebut the inference of desertion by proving that she had just cause for her refusal; and, indeed, it is usually wise for her to do so. But there is no legal burden on her to that effect. Even if she did not affirmatively prove just cause the court had still, at the end of the case, to ask itself: has the legal burden been discharged?"

It has been seen that the discharge of the evidential burden by one side puts the other side under a similar burden or, as it is often put, "passes" the burden to him. However, it is important not to envisage a trial as a sort of tennis match[34] with evidential burdens passing to and fro over the net. In a single issue case there are only two occasions when the judge has to rule on the evidential burden. One is at the outset in deciding who must start, *i.e.* who must lose if no evidence is adduced by either side. It is normally although not invariably the party under the persuasive burden (the proponent) who is under an evidential burden and must therefore start. The second occasion is at the conclusion of the proponent's evidence, when a submission is made that no case to answer has been made out. The judge will rule, either that the proponent has not made out a case, in which event he will at

---

[32] [1949] P. 98 at p. 103.
[33] *i.e.* persuasive.
[34] See Hoffman, *South African Law of Evidence*, p. 353.

once give judgment for the opponent. Or he will rule that there is a case to answer (*i.e.* the proponent has discharged his evidential burden) in which event the opponent is faced with the desirability (not the necessity) of adducing evidence. If he does adduce prima facie evidence, this is not an occasion for a further ruling by the judge; there is no casting of the evidential burden back to the proponent. The tribunal proceeds to decision, and here and only here is the incidence of the *persuasive* burden important, for if the evidence leaves the tribunal of fact undecided, the proponent must lose. Each side (normally) gets one turn only,[35] and although to a spectator in the courtroom the fortunes of the two sides may swing to and fro, as evidence is produced which appears[36] to be convincing or which appears to be demolished, these swings have no legal significance. Only when the judge has to rule on who begins and on the sufficiency of that party's evidence when it is completed, and only when he directs the tribunal of fact on what to do if the whole of the evidence leaves them in doubt, do questions of burden become legally significant, and therefore fit to ground an appeal to a higher court.

The position in criminal cases is similar, except that the very high standard of proof required of the prosecution[37] necessarily means that any burden resting on the defence is lighter than that under which a defendant in a civil case may find himself. Although the persuasive burden remains on the prosecution throughout, it may discharge its evidential burden by adducing prima facie evidence of the offence charged. When that has happened the accused, like a defendant in a civil case, is under the risk of an adverse verdict on sufficient evidence, and although he may decide merely to await the outcome, which might not be adverse after all, he will be wise to call evidence. But any reasonable doubt at the end of the day will mean that the Crown has not discharged its persuasive burden; and therefore all the accused needs to aim at is the raising of such reasonable doubt by his evidence, which may well be enough for this limited purpose even if it is a long way short of *prima facie* evidence.[38]

Except in the special cases mentioned in the next section, the defence never comes under a persuasive burden to prove a defence. There are no separate issues of the sort found in civil

---

[35] For the exceptional cases where rebutting evidence is allowed, see *post*, p. 99.
[36] *i.e.* appears to the spectator; but of course it is not the spectator but the tribunal of fact who have the only say.
[37] On this, see *post*, p. 71.
[38] *Woolmington* v. *D.P.P.* [1935] A.C. 462; *Bratty* v. *Att.-Gen. for Northern Ireland* [1963] A.C. 386, *per* Lord Morris at p. 416.

cases—only the single issue of guilt. Nevertheless, "Woolmington's case did not decide anything so irrational as that the prosecution must call evidence to prove the absence of any mistaken belief in the existence of facts which, if true, would make the act innocent."[39] It is not up to the Crown to adduce evidence about (or for the judge to mention in his charge to the jury) some excusing factor which is more than a simple denial of the elements of the crime charged unless it is properly raised by the defence.[40] If the defence wishes to have that excusing factor dealt with, it must raise it by evidence,[41] and not by mere assertion by defence counsel.[42] The defendant must "lay a foundation"[43] for his defence.[44] If he does, the Crown must negative it.[45] Even if he does not produce evidence or is wholly disbelieved, D is still entitled to be acquitted if there remains any doubt on any part of the case. But since there is obviously less chance that doubt will remain, he may be described as under an evidential burden.

B. THE INCIDENCE OF THE BURDENS

1. The General Rule

We have already collected the general rule. In the absence of some relevant presumption, the persuasive burden is normally on the plaintiff in civil cases; *i.e.* unless all the issues putting the burden on him have been formally conceded by the defendant. In criminal cases, the persuasive burden is on the Crown. The evidential burden is borne at the outset by him who has the

---

[39] *Per* Lord Diplock, in *Sweet* v. *Parsley* [1970] A.C. 132 at p. 172.
[40] *Mancini* v. *D.P.P.* [1942] A.C. 1 (provocation); *R.* v. *Lobell* [1957] 1 Q.B. 547 (self defence); *R.* v. *Gill* [1963] 1 W.L.R. 983; *Bratty* v. *Att.-Gen. for Northern Ireland, supra* (non-insane automatism); *R.* v. *Johnson* [1961] 3 All E.R. 969 (alibi); *R.* v. *Newcastle JJ., ex p. Hindle* [1984] 1 All E.R. 770 (consumption of alcohol after driving and before breath test); *R.* v. *Bennett* (1979) 68 Cr.App.R. 168 (impossibility on a conspiracy charge).
[41] Either from defence witnesses or elicited from crown witnesses in cross-examination: *Bullard* v. *R.* [1957] A.C. 635.
[42] *Parker* v. *Smith* [1974] R.T.R. 500. See also *Hill* v. *Baxter* [1958] 1 Q.B. 277.
[43] *Bratty* v. *Att.-Gen. for Northern Ireland, supra, per* Lord Denning at p. 413.
[44] Some of the "defences" comprehended in this principle (alibi, non-insane automatism) seem to be no more than mere denials of the Crown case; nevertheless the better view is that D must lay a foundation for them. See the relevant cases in n. 40, *supra*.
[45] The judge must not give the impression that the matter is a separate issue on which D bears a persuasive burden: see *R.* v. *Abraham* [1973] 3 All E.R. 694 at p. 696.

persuasive burden, because unless he produces prima facie evidence of his assertions, the case will never get to the jury. The judge will withdraw it. However, there are exceptional cases where an accused, or defendant in a civil case, has a burden cast on him by the law. Only the position of an accused in this situation needs special consideration.[46]

2. Insanity

As the opinion of Lord Sankey in *Woolmington* v. *D.P.P.*[47] makes clear, the defence of insanity is in a special case. It is not strictly a defence, but rather a quite separate issue, in which the persuasive burden is on the accused.[48] "The jurors ought to be told in all cases that every man is presumed to be sane . . . until the contrary is proved to their satisfaction."[49] Although the burden is not as heavy as that resting on the prosecution as to other issues,[50] it remains on the accused throughout the trial, and the judge may rule that he has not discharged it if, in the judge's view, there is not sufficient evidence to justify a finding of insanity.[51]

3. Formal Admissions

It is possible for the defence in a criminal case to make formal admissions under section 10 of the Criminal Justice Act 1967.[52] It seems that the prosecution is under no burden with regard to facts so admitted.

4. Express Statutory Reversals of the Normal Rule

In his statement of the "golden thread" principle in *Woolmington* v. *D.P.P.*[53] Lord Sankey admitted that the principle was "subject to any statutory exception." Sometimes a statute provides expressly that the burden of proving a particular fact shall be upon the accused,[54] or that on proof of certain facts, certain other

---

[46] For instances of the reversal of burden in civil cases, see the Bills of Exchange Act 1882, s.30(2) and the Social Security Act 1975, s.50(3).
[47] [1935] A.C. 462; *ante*, p. 61.
[48] Unless, indeed, the Crown raises the issue under the Criminal Procedure (Insanity) Act 1964, s.6.
[49] *R.* v. *M'Naghten* (1843) 10 Cl. & F. 200 at p. 210.   [50] See *post*, p. 70.
[51] *R.* v. *Windle* [1952] 2 Q.B. 826, *per* Goddard L.C.J. at p. 831.
[52] See *ante*, p. 29.   [53] *Ante*, p. 61.
[54] *e.g.* Libel Act 1843, s.6; Explosive Substances Act 1883, s.4; Customs and Excise Act 1952, s.290(1); Homicide Act 1957, s.2(2); Obscene Publications Act 1959, s.4; Road Traffic Act 1972, s.143(3); Criminal Law Act 1977, s.7(6)–(8); Insolvency Act 1985, s.138(1).

facts shall be deemed to have happened unless the contrary is proved by him.[55] Much depends on the precise statutory wording involved but it seems clear that if the accused is required to "prove" anything, he is put under a persuasive burden, and if the jury are in doubt about the matter, he must fail. It is not sufficient that his evidence raises a reasonable doubt in the minds of the jury; he must persuade the jury that his story is more probably true than false. Thus, on a charge under the Prevention of Corruption Act 1906, a gift to an official is deemed to have been given and received corruptly unless the contrary is proved.[56] In such a case, if the jury, after hearing the accused's evidence, are in any doubt as to whether the gift was a corrupt one, it is their duty to convict.[57]

It is different if the statute says that something shall be *evidence* against the accused, *e.g.* Theft Act 1968, s.25(4). This, after making it an offence for a person, not at his place of abode, to have with him an article for use in connection with any burglary, theft or cheat, goes on in subsection 3 to provide that proof that he had with him an article made or adapted for use in committing burglary, theft or cheat *shall be evidence that* he had it with him for such use. This is the same as saying that proving that he had such an article with him establishes a prima facie case on the issue of his intent; and the burden thus cast on him is not of disproving intent, but the evidential burden only, *i.e.* the risk that if he adduces no evidence in reply he may be convicted.

Most statutes talk of "proof," putting a persuasive burden on the accused. One statutory provision in this field which is of very wide application is found in Magistrates Courts Act 1980, s.101. This applies only to summary trial (including summary trial for an indictable offence), but subject to that is as wide as could be. Where a defendant to an information or complaint relies for his defence on any exception, exemption, proviso, excuse or qualification, whether or not it accompanies the description of the offence[58] or matter of complaint in the enactment creating the

---

[55] *e.g.* Prevention of Corruption Act 1916, s.2; Food and Drugs Act 1955, s.111; Sexual Offences Act 1956, s.30(2).
[56] Prevention of Corruption Act 1916, s.2.
[57] *R.* v. *Evans-Jones and Jenkins* (1923) 17 Cr.App.R. 121; *R.* v. *Carr-Briant* [1943] 1 K.B. 607; and see *R.* v. *Dunbar* [1958] 1 Q.B. 1; *R.* v. *Patterson* [1962] 2 Q.B. 429.
[58] The section does not apply if the exception is not to the *offence*, but to a prohibition which it is not always an offence to break: *Westminster C.C.* v. *Croyalgrange Ltd.* [1986] 2 All E.R. 353 (H.L.). D was charged, under para. 20, Sched. 3, of the Local Government (Miscellaneous Provisions) Act 1982, with permitting the use of premises as a sex establishment without a licence. Para. 6 prohibited such use without a licence, except where the user was so using on a

offence or on which the complaint is founded, the burden of proving the exception, exemption, proviso, excuse or qualification shall be on him; and this notwithstanding that the information or complaint contains an allegation negativing the exception, exemption, proviso, excuse or qualification.

The question to be answered here is whether the "excusing" words are an integral part of the definition of the offence, or some "let out" for one who otherwise satisfies the definition of the offence. The statutory words *can* settle this; *e.g.* such words as "except" or "provided always" will be held to put the burden of proving the exception or proviso on to the defence; but where the statutory language is not clear, the substance rather than the form of the enactment is what is important, and that construction which best achieves the result in substance sought by the draftsman will be the one adopted.[59] Just as in civil cases the arrangement of the statutory words is no longer crucial, so in statutes leading to summary trials.[60]

5. Implied Statutory Reversals

It was thought by some that when in *Woolmington's* case Lord Sankey made his "golden thread" principle "subject to any statutory exceptions," he was thinking of express statutory reversals of the normal rule of the sort just discussed, where the legislature has expressly put the burden of proving certain facts on the accused. The corollary of this view was that unless an enactment did reverse the usual rule expressly, *Woolmington's* case applied and the persuasive burden on all issues remained on the Crown. But it was held in *R. v. Hunt*[61] that this is not so. There are cases where it is held that the legislature has, not expressly but impliedly, put the burden on an issue on to the accused. The difficulty lies in determining upon whom Parliament intended to place the burden when the statute has not expressly so provided[62].

---

certain date and had since applied for a licence. D knew that X was using without a licence, but it was not shewn that he knew that X was not an existing user who had applied for a licence. It was held that the burden of proving that D knew this was on the prosecution.

[59] See *Nimmo v. Alexander Cowan & Sons Ltd.* [1968] A.C. 107.

[60] *Ante*, p. 57. The position is now substantially the same in trials on indictment: see *R. v. Hunt* [1987] 1 All E.R. 1 (H.L.) (*post*, p. 69), adopting the sense of the majority speeches in *Nimmo's case.*

[61] [1987] 1 All E.R. 1 (H.L.)   [62] *Ibid*, per Lord Griffiths at p. 10.

The Incidence of the Burdens

For a long time, the reversal of the usual rule only occurred with regard to a negative averment peculiarly within the knowledge of the accused, or when the excusing proviso was separate from the words creating the defence. But in *R. v. Edwards*,[63] it was said by Lawton L.J. that the principle was rather that reversal of onus depended on whether the enactment was considered to "prohibit the doing of an act save in specified circumstances or by persons of specified classes or with specific qualifications or with the licence or permission of specified authorities." However it was decided in *R. v. Hunt*[64] that this principle, although a helpful approach to the question of construction, was by no means exhaustive, and the burden of proof could be held to be intended to be on the accused although the *Edwards* principle was not involved. The question is one of construction of the particular statute. Just as with the application of Magistrates Courts Act 1980, s.101,[65] the Court is not restricted to the form of wording of the statutory provisions, but is entitled to have regard to matters of policy.[66] The fact that leaving the burden with the Crown will seriously hamper prosecutions is an indication that Parliament intended that the defence should bear the burden,[67] as is the fact that in the nature of things the defence can easily discharge it.[68] On the other hand, the fact that offence is a serious one of strict liability would make it right to resolve ambiguity in favour of the defendant.[69]

In *R. v. Hunt*, D was charged with unlawful possession of a controlled drug, namely morphine, contrary to section 5(2) of the Misuse of Drugs Act 1971. The Act gave power to the Secretary of State by regulations to expect from section 5 such controlled drugs as he specified, and power to make it lawful for such persons as he specified to possess controlled drugs which it would otherwise be unlawful for them to possess. Regulation 4 excepted from section 5 powder containing not more than 0.2 per cent. morphine; other regulations excepted possession of a controlled drug by certain persons, *e.g.* doctors. An analyst's certificate was put in stating that the powder possessed by D contained morphine, but not stating the percentage. It was held that D had no case to answer. A distinction was made between Regulation 4, and the others which excepted possession by doctors etc.

---

[63] [1975] Q.B. 29 (C.A.)
[64] *Supra, per* Lord Griffiths at p. 11, Lord Ackner at p. 19.
[65] See, ante p. 68 and *Nimmo v. Alexander Cowen & Sons Ltd.* [1968] A.C. 107.
[66] [1987] 1 All E.R. 1, *per* Lord Ackner at p. 17.
[67] *Ibid., per* Lord Griffiths at p. 13, Lord Ackner at p. 17.
[68] *Per* Lord Griffiths at p. 11.
[69] *Per* Lord Griffiths at p. 13.

No doubt in prosecutions involving those other regulations, the *Edwards* principle would apply, and the burden of proving that he came within an exception would be on the defendant. But Regulation 4 made it entirely lawful for anyone to possess a powder containing not more than 0.2 per cent. morphine. It amended the definition of the offence in section 5 to exclude possession of this powder. It was for the prosecution show that D possessed a drug comprehended in the offence; not for D to show that the drug he possessed was not such a drug. The House of Lords rejected the claim that this construction would hamper prosecutions.

As to the kind of burden which construction might place on the accused, although it has been argued that it should be an evidential one,[70] it is settled that it is a persuasive burden, and the accused is not entitled to succeed unless he proves the matter on the balance of probabilities.[71] It is as though the statute has said "he must prove" the relevant fact, although it has not in terms done so. Whatever method is used by Parliament to make an exception to the usual rule, whether by express words or by necessary implication, it can't make any difference to the quality or status of such an exception.[72] Moreover, since many offences are triable "either way," and since it is accepted that if such a one is tried summarily section 101 of the Magistrates Courts Act 1980 will place a persuasive burden on the defence,[73] it would be a remarkable anomaly if, as to the self-same offence, trial in a Crown Court were to subject the defence to an evidential burden merely.[74]

The limitations on the scope of the doctrine of implied statutory reversals of the usual rule as to the incidence of the burden of proof must be noted. The doctrine being one of statutory interpretation, it has no application to common law defences and excuses, which remain under the golden rule. The accused does not come under the burden of proving facts alleged to be a defence merely because those facts, if true, could easily be proved by him.[75] Of course, the jury may well think that his failure to offer that evidence strengthens any prima facie case made out by the Crown[76]; but that risk is no more than an evidential burden.[77]

---

[70] C.L.R.C., Cmnd. 4991, paras. 137–142, clause 8, Draft Bill.
[71] [1987] 1 All E.R. 1 at pp. 11, 19.   [72] *Ibid., per* Lord Ackner at p. 15.
[73] *Gatland* v. *Metropolitan Police Commissioner* [1968] 2 Q.B. 279.
[74] [1987] 1 All E.R. 1, *per* Lord Ackner at p. 19.
[75] *R.* v. *Mandry & Wooster* [1973] 1 W.L.R. 1232.
[76] See *R.* v. *Burdett, ante*, p. 62.   [77] *Ante*, p. 75.

CHAPTER 4

STANDARD OF PROOF

We have seen that one party to legal proceedings must persuade the tribunal of fact of the truth of some proposition of fact which is in issue and which is vital to his case, or else fail in the whole or some part of the litigation. It should be obvious that this means that he must adduce more persuasive evidence on the point than his opponent does, for if the evidence adduced on both sides is equally persuasive, so that the person charged with the duty of coming to a decision on the facts is in doubt as to which evidence to prefer, it cannot be said that this person has been convinced by the party upon whom the burden lies. The question now arises: By how much must the weight of evidence adduced by the person under the burden of proof exceed the weight of that adduced by his opponent? There are no precise rules regulating this subject, but it can be said that different standards are adopted in civil and criminal cases[1]; and that sometimes the civil standard is adopted in a criminal case, and vice versa.

A. CRIMINAL CASES

It is a serious irregularity for the judge to fail to direct the jury on the standard of proof required of the prosecution.[2] It used to be thought that such a failure was so fundamental a defect that an appeal must inevitably be allowed.[3] The Court of Appeal seems to have abandoned this strict view,[4] and the appeal will be dismissed under the Proviso to section 2(1) of the Criminal Appeal Act 1968,[5] if the jury would undoubtedly have convicted anyway had a proper direction been given.[6]

As to what is required of the prosecution, it must establish the guilt of the accused beyond all reasonable doubt. It is sometimes

[1] *R. v. Carr-Briant* [1943] K.B. 607.
[2] *R. v. Edwards* (1983) 77 Cr.App.R. 5.
[3] *R. v. Oliva* (1960) 46 Cr.App.R. 241.
[4] *R. v. Slinger* (1961) 46 Cr.App.R. 244; *R. v. Sparrow* (1962) 46 App.R. 288; *R. v. Edwards, supra.*
[5] *Ante*, p. 47.
[6] *R. v. Edwards, supra.* But it depends on the circumstances. Where the jury expressed themselves as being in difficulty over the matter, an appeal was allowed because the judge, who had already given a proper direction, did not repeat it: *R. v. Gibson* (1983) 77 Cr.App.R. 15.

said that this is because of the presumption of innocence, which works in favour of the accused and has to be rebutted decisively. This is merely another way of stating the same rule and does not explain why we have such a rule anyway. Since most persons who face trial are guilty, common sense would say that if there is doubt it should be resolved in favour of the State.[7] Stephen[8] suggested that it is because the State is so much stronger than the individual that it can afford to be generous. Others, such as Cross,[9] while arguing that it is right that the standard of proof required of the Crown should be a heavy one, refuse to erect the principle into a sacred cow, and insist that it should not allow a man to rest on silence and brazen out his trial, when common sense would suggest that if he is innocent, he will speak. The so-called right of silence will be dealt with later.[10]

"Beyond all reasonable doubt" is the time-honoured expression, and it has always proved difficult to find other words to express what it means. Various judges have tried it (indeed, every judge must try it if asked point-blank by the foreman of the jury), but "attempts to substitute other expressions... have never prospered."[11] During a short period when English judges were forbidden to use "beyond all reasonable doubt,"[12] so many unmeritorious appeals succeeded on the ground that the standard of proof had been wrongly described to the jury that the ban was soon withdrawn[13] and the traditional expression re-asserted itself.[14] Of course the standard required is greater than a mere preponderance of probability; if the extent of the jury's impression of the case is that the accused is probably guilty, they must acquit him.[15] On the other hand, "beyond reasonable doubt" does not mean beyond a shadow of a doubt. "The law would fail to protect the community if it admitted fanciful possibilities to

---

[7] See Cross, "The Right to Silence and the Presumption of Innocence—Sacred Cows or Safeguards of Liberty?" (1970) 11 J.S.P.T.L. 66.
[8] *History of the Criminal Law*, Vol.1, p. 354.
[9] *Op. cit.*
[10] *Post*, Chap. 9.
[11] *Dawson v. R.* (1961) 106 C.L.R. 1, per Dixon C.J. at p. 18.
[12] *i.e.* after *R. v. Summers* (1952) 36 Cr.App.R. 14.
[13] *R. v. Hepworth and Fearnley* [1955] 2 Q.B. 600 at p. 603; *R. v. Murtagh and Kennedy* (1955) 39 Cr.App.R. 72.
[14] In *R. v. Walters* [1969] 2 A.C. 26, the trial judge found himself reduced to saying, *inter alia*, "A reasonable doubt is a reasonable doubt. It says what it means." The Privy Council, in approving the general sense of his direction, deprecated any particular form of words. Nevertheless in *R. v. Gray* (1973) 58 Cr.App.R. 177 (C.A.), the omission of a particular adjective from a direction which otherwise followed that in *R. v. Walters* made that direction faulty.
[15] *Mancini v. D.P.P.* [1942] A.C. 1 at p. 11.

deflect the course of justice."[16] There is a distinction between scientific proof and legal proof. Many hypotheses may be unable to be disproved scientifically while being highly unlikely.[17]

The judge should stick to the time-honoured expression and avoid searching for substitutes,[18] but if the jury actively seek his guidance, then no particular formula is insisted on, provided the sense of his explanation is that the jury must be completely satisfied or feel sure of his guilt.[19] It is best left to each judge to find the words most suited to explain to the particular jury he is directing.[20] The required degree of conviction in the jury's minds is proportional to the seriousness of the charge,[21] for although they will not lightly convict a man of even a trivial charge, they are, or ought to be, even more reluctant to do so in a serious case. "What is a reasonable doubt . . . varies in practice according to the nature of the case and the punishment which may be awarded."[22] It need hardly be added that this degree of conviction must still be attained even if the accused offers no evidence to be weighed against that of the Crown.[23]

What the jury as a body have to be satisfied of is the accused's guilt of the crime charged. There is no necessity for all the jurors to be satisfied as to any particular piece of evidence, provided they are unanimous (or in the case of a majority verdict, the majority are unanimous) that the prosecution has proved the charge.[24]

As far as the accused is concerned, it follows from the fact that the jury must be satisfied of his guilt beyond reasonable doubt that in the normal case he is entitled to succeed if his evidence

---

[16] Denning J. in *Miller v. Minister of Pensions* [1947] 2 All E.R. 372 at p. 373 (a useful discussion of the differences between the civil and criminal standards).
[17] *R. v. Bracewell* (1979) 68 Cr.App.R. 44.
[18] *R. v. Ching* (1976) 63 Cr.App.R. 7 at p. 10; *Ferguson v. R.* [1979] 1 W.L.R. 94 at p. 99.
[19] *R. v. Walters, supra*. No special direction is called for even if the Crown's case largely rests on circumstantial evidence: *McGreevey v. D.P.P.* [1973] 1 W.L.R. 276.
[20] *R. v. Ching, supra*. On the other hand, it has been said to be wise to stick to "you must be satisfied so as to feel sure": *R. v. Quinn* [1983] Crim.L.R. 475, where the omission of a reference to feeling sure was enough to allow the appeal.
[21] Kenny, *Outlines of Criminal Law* (1962), p. 501, approved in *Hornal v. Neuberger Products Ltd.* [1957] 1 Q.B. 247 at pp. 262, 263.
[22] *Preston-Jones v. Preston-Jones* [1951] A.C. 391, *per* Lord Oaksey at p. 409.
[23] *R. v. Schama* (1914) 84 L.J.K.B. 396.
[24] *R. v. Agbim* [1979] Crim.L.R. 171; *R. v. Flynn* (1985) 82 Cr.App.R. 319; *R. v. Moore* [1986] Crim.L.R. 552. For discussion of the rule, see Eggleston, pp. 121–122, and for criticism of its implications, see Smith, [1986] Crim.L.R. 240.

does no more than raise a doubt in the jury's minds.[25] Occasionally, however, the onus of proof on a particular issue is cast upon the accused either by the common law[26] or by statute.[27] In either case, it is settled that the burden on the accused is not as heavy as that which the Crown bears on the general issue, and the standard of proof required of him is the same as that required of a plaintiff in civil cases. This means that he is entitled to succeed if he persuades the jury that on the particular issue his evidence is more probably true than false,[28] and it is grounds for appeal if the judge omits to instruct the jury that the criminal standard of proof does not apply.[29]

B. CIVIL CASES

The general rule is that the party upon whom the persuasive burden of proof[30] rests (*i.e.* usually the plaintiff) is entitled to a verdict if his evidence establishes a preponderance of probability in his favour, *i.e.* if he persuades the tribunal of fact that his version of the facts is more probable than that of his opponent.

Occasionally however a party in a civil case is faced with a presumption which casts on him a higher standard. For example, in cases where domicile is in issue, the intention to abandon a domicile of origin must be clearly and unequivocally proved,[31] and the acquisition of a domicile of choice is a serious matter not to be lightly inferred from slight indications or casual words.[32] This higher standard may be as high as the criminal standard. Thus, he who seeks to show that parties who went through an apparently regular marriage ceremony were not validly married thereby may be required to prove invalidity beyond reasonable doubt[33] and a similar standard is required of him who asserts that a written agreement does not accurately express the joint intention of the parties thereto.[34] And sometimes statute places a

---

[25] For cases where he must "lay a foundation,' see *ante*, p. 65.
[26] *i.e* where the defence of insanity is raised; ante, p. 66.
[27] See *ante*, p. 67.
[28] *R. v. Carr-Briant* [1943] K.B. 607; *Sodeman v. R.* [1936] 2 All E.R. 1138.
[29] *R. v. Rivers* [1974] R.T.R. 31.
[30] *Ante*, p. 54.
[31] *Moorhouse v. Lord* (1863) 10 H.L.C. 272 at p. 286; *In the Estate of Fuld deceased, (No. 3)* [1968] P. 675 at p. 685.
[32] *In the estate of Fuld deceased (No. 3), supra*; *Re Flynn* [1968] 1 W.L.R. 103.
[33] *Piers v. Piers* (1849) 2 H.L.C. 331, *post*, p. 82.
[34] *Earl v. Hector Whaling Ltd.* [1961] 1 Lloyd's Rep. 459 at pp. 468, 470. Not however for establishing a secret trust, at any rate if no fraud is alleged: *Re Snowden dec'd* [1979] Ch. 528.

Civil Cases 75

party under a burden as heavy as the one normally on the prosecution in a criminal case.[35] Conversely, where a party is required to establish some fact in an interlocutory application, e.g. for leave to commence proceedings, the full civil standard may not be required and it will be sufficient if he produces prima facie evidence of the fact.[36]

Moreover, "in English law, the citizen is regarded as being a free man of good repute."[37] This means that a party who alleges against anyone, be he party or stranger, conduct which amounts to fraud or a crime or a matrimonial offence, is required to prove it in a satisfactory manner, according to how serious is the misconduct alleged.[38] It used to be thought that there was a rule that the criminal standard of proof beyond reasonable doubt is required for any allegation of fraud or crime.[39] However this is no longer the case. The standard is the civil one of preponderance of probabilities,[40] but what is "probable" depends upon the heinousness of what is alleged. "The very elements of gravity become a part of the whole range of circumstances which have to be weighed in the scale when deciding as to the balance of probabilities."[41] If the fact alleged, although nominally criminal, has no or little element of moral turpitude, the bare balance of probabilities will suffice.[42] However, "in proportion as the offence is grave, so ought the proof to be clear."[43] Thus if "theft" is alleged, especially if the person against whom the allegation is made is not one of the parties to the action and so not able to defend himself, the court will require to be satisfied that it is safe to find such proved.[44] And of course if the result of a finding will

---

[35] *Judd* v. *Minister of Pensions* [1966] 2 Q.B. 580; cf. *Cadney* v. *Minister of Pensions* [1966] 1 W.L.R. 80.
[36] *Sidnell* v. *Wilson* [1966] 2 Q.B. 67.
[37] *Hornal* v. *Neuberger Products Ltd.* [1957] 1 Q.B. 247, per Morris L.J. at p. 266.
[38] However, if a litigant seeks a declaration that what he is doing is lawful, the burden is on him to satisfy the Court that he is entitled to the relief he seeks, and the presumption of innocence is entirely beside the point: *Amstrad Consumer Electronics PLC* v. *British Phonograph Industry Ltd.* [1986] F.S.R. 159 (C.A.).
[39] *New York* v. *Phillips' Heirs* [1939] 3 All E.R. 952 at p. 954.
[40] *Lek* v. *Matthews* (1927) 27 Ll.L.R. 141; *Hornal* v. *Neuberger Products* [1957] 1 Q.B. 247 at pp. 262, 263.
[41] *Hornal* v. *Neuberger Products*, supra, per Morris L.J. at p. 266.
[42] *Post Office* v. *Estuary Radio Ltd.* [1968] 2 Q.B. 740.
[43] *Blyth* v. *Blyth* [1966] A.C. 643, per Lord Denning at p. 669.
[44] *Nishina Trading Co.* v. *Chiyoda* [1969] 2 Q.B. 449, and see *Khawaja* v. *S.S. for Home Department* [1984] A.C. 74 (H.L.) (allegation that immigrant got permission to land by fraud); *S. & M. Carpets* v. *Cornhill Insurance Co.* [1981] 1 Lloyds Rep. 667 (C.A.) (allegation that the insured burned down his own premises).

directly result in coercive sanctions being applied against the person concerned, as in civil contempt of court, the full criminal standard of proof applies.[45]

There used to be a rule that matrimonial offences had to be proved to the criminal standard of proof. The rule, as a rigid rule, was abrogated in 1966 by *Blyth* v. *Blyth*.[46] Thereafter the presumption referred to above that a person is of good repute was capable of requiring matrimonial offences to be proved by more than the bare balance of probabilities.[47] However the replacement of the idea of the matrimonial offence by the doctrine of irretrievable breakdown of marriage[48] makes it unlikely that anything other than the bare civil standard will ever be insisted on in matrimonial proceedings.[49]

---

[45] *Re Bramblevale Ltd.* [1970] Ch. 128. This principle does not apply to proceedings to forfeit a recognizance to keep the peace: *R.* v. *Marlow JJ.* [1984] Q.B. 381; or a surety's bail recognizance: *R.* v. *Southampton JJ.* [1975] 2 All E.R. 1073.
[46] *Supra.*
[47] *Bastable* v. *Bastable and Sanders* [1968] 1 W.L.R. 1684.
[48] See, Matrimonial Causes Act 1973, s.1(1).
[49] *Pheasant* v. *Pheasant* [1972] Fam. 202 at p. 208.

CHAPTER 5

PRESUMPTIONS

It has been seen that the incidence of the burden of proof, in both senses of that term, may be affected by the operation of presumptions.[1] This operation being usually to establish a fact without any or any complete proof, it follows that a party who is under a burden of proving a fact may be relieved of this necessity without offering any or complete proof if a presumption works in his favour.

A presumption may be defined as a conclusion which may or must be drawn in the absence of contrary evidence. Sometimes the presumption only arises if some basic fact is first proved; sometimes it arises in all cases without proof of any particular fact. It is as well to distinguish these two types of presumption at the outset.

There are cases where the law says that something shall be presumed until the contrary is proved. No basic fact is needed to activate the presumption which applies in every case. Every person accused of crime is presumed to be innocent until the contrary is proved[2]; his sanity is also presumed.[3] One cannot quarrel with the describing of these rules as presumptions, but they could with equal correctness and less confusion[4] be put in terms of burden of proof. What they really say is, the burden in criminal cases is on the Crown, except as to insanity where (when the defence raises the matter) it is on the defence. The term presumption in this chapter is applied to a rule which says that *on proof of certain basic facts*, certain other facts may or must be taken as proved in the absence of contrary evidence.

At this preliminary stage it is also necessary to dispose of certain cases where it is said that a conclusion *must* be drawn from a given premiss and no rebutting evidence is allowed. These

---

[1] *Ante*, pp. 60, 62.
[2] The presumption also applies where a person is accused of crime, *e.g.* fraud, in a civil case. See *ante*, p. 75.
[3] See *ante*, p. 66. The presumption also operates in civil cases. See, *e.g. Re Calloway* [1956] Ch. 559.
[4] *i.e.* confusion with other types of presumption which on one occasion led, erroneously, to the presumption of innocence being regarded as something different from the burden of proving guilt beyond reasonable doubt, namely as an item of evidence about which the jury ought to have been reminded: *Coffin* v. *U.S.*, 156 U.S. 432 (1895).

are usually described as irrebuttable presumptions of law (or *praesumptiones juris et de jure*); in reality they are not presumptions at all, and have no place in the law of evidence, being rather substantive rules of law. Examples of these so-called presumptions are that a child under 10 is incapable of committing any crime, and that a boy under 14 is incapable of committing any crime involving sexual intercourse including rape[5], propositions which could as effectively be framed in language which used none of the terminology of the law of evidence.

Presumptions, in the sense in which the term is used in this chapter, are only activated by proof of some prescribed basic fact or facts. In some cases, upon such proof the law prescribes what other facts shall be inferred in the absence of further evidence. In others, upon such proof the law *allows* but does not *require* other facts to be inferred in the absence of further evidence. The first class of cases are called presumptions of law[6] (*praesumptiones juris sed non de jure*), the second, presumptions of fact (*praesumptiones hominis*, or *facti*). With the first class, the conclusion from the proved basic facts is drawn by the judge, who will direct the jury accordingly; whereas with presumptions of fact the conclusion is drawn, if at all, by the jury.

A. Presumptions of Law

These are presumptions where on proof of certain basic facts certain prescribed conclusions must as a matter of law be drawn in the absence of rebutting evidence. Thus if it is shown that A pays for property which is conveyed to B, it is presumed that A did not mean to make a gift of the property to B, so that B holds the property as trustee for A.[7] Again, in any proceedings, if it is shown that A has earlier been convicted of a criminal offence, it is presumed that he committed that offence.[8] The court cannot avoid drawing the indicated conclusion in the absence of rebutting evidence.

There are a large number of these presumptions scattered throughout the law, so large that most of them can only be

---

[5] That this is a rule of criminal law, rather than a rule of evidence, is shown by the fact that in affiliation proceedings an underage boy may be adjudged to be the father of a child: *L.* v. *K.* [1984] 1 All E.R. 961.

[6] Or, more fully, rebuttable presumptions of law, if there is a need to distinguish them from the so-called irrebuttable presumptions of law mentioned above.

[7] *Dyer* v. *Dyer* (1788) 2 Cox Eq.Cas. 92 at p. 93.

[8] Evidence Act 1968, s.11: Police and Criminal Evidence Civil 1984, s.74: *post*, p. 338.

usefully discussed in connection with the area of law which they inhabit. To take for example the presumption of resulting trust referred to above, the delineation of its precise scope and effect, and what evidence is needed to rebut it, is a task more fitly undertaken by books on equity[9] than by those on evidence.

So heterogeneous are presumptions of law that little can usefully be said of them as a class. However, before dealing with a few presumptions of wide application, two matters of general interest may be dwelt on briefly.

1. General Considerations

(a) The reason for presumptions

It may be asked, why is it that the law insists that in the absence of rebutting evidence the indicated conclusion must be drawn? It is not, as may be thought, that logic compels it, so that failure to find the presumed fact can be impeached as a perverse verdict. Although there is almost invariably a logical connection between basic fact and presumed fact, in the case of most presumptions it is by no means intellectually compelling. As has been pointed out,[10] seven years' proved absence of a person is hardly more compelling a reason for presuming him dead than an absence of six years and 11 months, yet the law compels a finding of death in the first case but not in the latter.[11] Again, in the case of some presumptions, such logical power as the basic fact might have if unchallenged may be reduced to vanishing point by evidence to the contrary, yet if the contrary evidence does not reach the standard required for rebutting the presumption, it does not rebut it and the indicated conclusion must still be drawn. The explanation of these and similar cases is that the law, for some reason of public policy which has not necessarily anything to do with logic, artificially inflates the logical value of the basic fact. The public policies involved in the various presumptions, which may be founded on convenience, or seemliness, or the sanctity of the marriage bed, vary in strength, and so prescribe different standards for evidence in rebuttal. What is required may be prima

---

[9] *e.g.* Snell's *Equity*, (28th ed.), pp. 179, 185.
[10] See Sachs J. in *Chard* v. *Chard* [1956] P. 259 at p. 272; *post*, p. 85.
[11] But for another view, see *Campbell* v. *Wallsend Slipway* [1978] I.C.R. 1015 *per* Eveleigh J. at p. 1025; "Presumptions of Law have developed over the years after the courts have seen the cogency of certain inferential evidence from established facts, until a point is reached where those established facts can be relied upon to give rise to an inference." This, with respect, sounds more like an explanation of certain aspects of Judicial Notice: see *R.* v. *Jones* [1970] 1 W.L.R. 16, *ante*, p. 34.

facie evidence, or proof on the balance of probabilities, or proof beyond reasonable doubt, or some intermediate standard, depending upon what presumption is sought to be rebutted.

It is possible to classify presumptions according to the standard of rebutting evidence they require. Some merely require *evidence* to the contrary of the presumed fact, not *proof* of the contrary; in other words, they do not affect in any way the persuasive burden of proof on the issue.[12] Once prima facie evidence of the basic facts has been given by the proponent, the opponent comes under an evidential burden. If he discharges it by adducing sufficient evidence to "pass the judge," *i.e.* fit to be left to the jury,[13] the presumption no longer applies and the matter is settled by reference to the persuasive burden. Examples are the presumption of regularity and the presumption of death.[14] This type has been termed "evidential presumptions of law."[15] Other presumptions require the opponent to prove the contrary of the indicated conclusion, either on the balance of probabilities or beyond reasonable doubt, so that it can be said that on the issue of whether the presumed fact exists, the persuasive burden is on the opponent. Examples are the presumption of formal validity of marriage, and legitimacy.[16] Such have been termed "persuasive presumptions of law."[17] This classification into evidential and persuasive presumptions is hardly worth making however; partly because inside each so-called class, particular presumptions have special rules about the weight to be looked for in the rebutting evidence, and partly because in criminal proceedings no presumption working in favour of the Crown can affect the Crown's duty of proving every part of its case beyond reasonable doubt. No presumption, even a persuasive one, can increase in any way the most that any accused ever needs to do, which is to raise a reasonable doubt.[18] The accused effectively rebuts any presumptions, even the presumption of legitimacy at common law[19] which required proof beyond reasonable doubt to rebut it normally, by

---

[12] See *ante*, p. 54.
[13] *Ante*, p. 62.
[14] See *post*, pp. 87, 85, respectively.
[15] Glanville Williams, C.L.G.P. pp. 877 *et seq.*
[16] See *post*, pp. 82 and 83, respectively.
[17] Glanville Williams, *op. cit.*
[18] Unless indeed it is the presumption of sanity, which is a special case, or unless it embodies one of the express statutory reversals of burden, *e.g.* the presumption in a corruption case that a gift was given corruptly unless the contrary is proved. See *ante*, pp. 66 and 67, respectively.
[19] The standard necessary to rebut this presumption in civil proceedings has now been lowered by statute; see *post*, p. 84.

adducing evidence which raises a doubt in the jury's mind. Suppose P is charged with incest with Q who is alleged to be his daughter and his defence is that although Q was born to P's wife during wedlock she was the child of the lodger R. It is clear that to succeed P does not have to prove that Q was not his daughter beyond all reasonable doubt or even on the balance of probabilities.

(b) The function of the basic fact

The second general question, which arises as to those presumptions which require proof to the contrary, is whether, in weighing rebutting evidence and deciding whether it has come up to the standard required by the law for the particular presumption involved, any weight is to be given to the proved basic fact which activated the presumption? Is its function *merely* to activate the presumption and thus place the burden on the opponent, or is it to be weighed in the scales alongside the evidence proffered in rebuttal? In *Stupple* v. *Royal Insurance Co.*[20] the question received a divided answer. A sued B for the return of money seized from him by the police and awarded to B by magistrates' order under the Police (Property) Act 1897. B pleaded that the money was his, stolen by A. To prove that A stole the money, B relied on A's conviction for theft of the money, which conviction raised a statutory presumption that A did steal it.[21] A replied by attacking certain of the evidence given at the criminal trial and by producing fresh evidence of an alibi. The trial judge disbelieved the alibi evidence, but held that the attack on the Crown evidence given at the criminal trial, while not proving his innocence, raised a reasonable doubt about his guilt. In the Court of Appeal, Lord Denning M.R. held that the doubt was not enough to diminish the considerable probative force of a conviction coming after a lengthy trial, a unanimous verdict of a jury, and confirmation on appeal.[22] Winn and Buckley L.JJ. held that evidence aimed at reducing the probative force of the conviction was beside the point. The conviction had no probative force. The question for the civil court was not, how weighty is this conviction? but, has A discharged the onus of proving his innocence cast on him by the fact of the conviction? It is suggested that this latter view is right and has a general application to presumptions. Apart from disproving the presumed fact, the opponent can only rebut a

---
[20] [1971] 1 Q.B. 50.
[21] Civil Evidence Act 1968, s.11; *post*, p. 338.
[22] And see *Taylor* v. *Taylor* [1970] 1 W.L.R. 1148, *per* Davies L.J.

presumption by proving that the basic fact did not happen or exist, not by proving that the basic fact did not have as much probative force as usual. The converse follows: the proponent, having proved the basic fact, is entitled to rely on the presumption, not on the presumption *and* any probative value which the basic fact may possess.[23]

2. Some Important Presumptions

(a) Marriage

There are really two quite different presumptions of marriage. The first is that evidence of a marriage ceremony raises a presumption that the parties thereto were thereby validly married, *i.e.* that the ceremony was the proper one required by the law, and that the parties each had the necessary capacity to contract marriage. In *Piers* v. *Piers*,[24] there was a marriage in a private house. This needs a special licence, but although no evidence was adduced that any special licence had been obtained, the marriage was presumed valid. This case concerned formal validity, but it is quite established that the rule applies also to essential validity (*i.e.* capacity of the parties). Usually the ceremony is followed by cohabitation, but the latter is not necessary to raise the presumption, certainly if the circumstances are such that cohabitation would not be expected, *e.g.* a death-bed marriage.[25]

Rebutting this presumption, in civil cases, requires proof of invalidity beyond reasonable doubt,[26] at any rate where formal validity is concerned. As to essential validity, it may be that a lesser standard is required, and that *some* evidence of incapacity, by which one means prima facie evidence, will suffice to rebut,[27] but the cases are not clear.[28] In criminal cases, however, especially

---

[23] See the remarks of Lord Reid in *S.* v. *McC.* [1972] A.C. 24 at p. 41, *post*, p. 84, n. 42, and *T.* v. *T.* [1971] 1 W.L.R. 429.
[24] (1849) 2 H.L.C. 331.
[25] *Lauderdale Peerage Case* (1885) 10 App.Cas. 692; *Hill* v. *Hill* [1959] 1 W.L.R. 127.
[26] *Piers* v. *Piers* (1849) 2 H.L.C. 331; *Mahadervan* v. *Mahadervan* [1964] P. 233 at p. 246. This standard may however not be as high since the House of Lords decision in *Blyth* v. *Blyth* [1966] A.C. 643, *ante*, p. 76.
[27] *Tweney* v. *Tweney* [1946] P. 180.
[28] It appears that a prior marriage apparently valid and not shown to have ended is sufficient evidence to rebut the presumption of the present marriage's validity (*Gatty and Gatty* v. *Att.-Gen.* [1951] P. 444), but if the prior marriage is of doubtful validity, the presumption that the present marriage is valid is left unimpaired (*Taylor* v. *Taylor* [1967] P. 25). But see *Monckton* v. *Tarr* (1930) 23 B.W.C.C. 504.

Presumptions of Law

in bigamy prosecutions, where the Crown is alleging a valid first marriage, it seems clear that the accused need do no more than raise doubts as to the validity, essential or formal, of the earlier marriage. He has, after all, the presumption of innocence on his side.

The second presumption of marriage arises out of cohabitation. If a man and woman live together openly as man and wife, the law will presume that at some stage they went through a valid marriage, *i.e.* that they are not living in a state of concubinage.[29] This is a strong presumption, only to be rebutted by evidence of the most cogent kind. Thus in *Re Taplin*,[30] a man lived with a woman for 19 years. The birth certificates of their children referred to a marriage in Victoria. That state required registration of a marriage for it to be valid, but no registration of any marriage could be found. It was nevertheless presumed that the parties were validly married.

The presumption operates even if the parties are still alive and are giving evidence (usually they are long since dead). In *Elliott* v. *Totnes Union*,[31] a man resisted a claim for maintenance for his children on the ground that he never married their deceased mother. Still, the presumption was applied against him in the face of his evidence, which was disbelieved.

Although strong, this presumption does not work in the face of the presumption of innocence. In a bigamy prosecution, the Crown cannot use it to prove the earlier valid marriage. It must bring evidence of an apparently valid ceremony, and then it may rely on the earlier presumption of marriage dealt with above.[32] The same may be said of the petitioner in a divorce suit who cannot rely on any presumption arising out of cohabitation; but is able to rely on the presumption based on an apparently valid ceremony.

(b) Legitimacy

It is presumed that a child, proved to have been born during lawful wedlock or during the period of gestation after its termination by death or divorce, is legitimate.[33] The presumption applies although the husband and wife are living apart at the

---

[29] *Sastry Velaider Aronegary* v. *Sembecutty Vaigalle* (1881) 6 App.Cas. 364.
[30] [1937] 3 All E.R. 105.
[31] (1892) 57 J.P. 151.
[32] *Morris* v. *Miller* (1767) 4 Burr. 2057.
[33] Even if the mother has married another man by the date of birth, the former husband is still presumed to be the lawful father: *Re Overbury* [1955] Ch. 122.

material time,[34] and even if proceedings for divorce have commenced,[35] but not if there is in force a judicial separation[36] or magistrates' separation order,[37] where the presumption is that the parties obeyed the order of the court and did not cohabit, so that the child is illegitimate.[38]

At common law the presumption could only be displaced by "strong, distinct, satisfactory and conclusive"[39] evidence that no sexual intercourse took place between the husband and wife at any time when, by such intercourse the husband could by the laws of nature, be the father of such child.[40] The reason for this was the undesirability of holding that a child was illegitimate except on the clearest possible evidence. Nevertheless, some judges chafed at the rule,[41] and now by section 26 of the Family Law Reform Act 1969, any presumption of legitimacy or illegitimacy may in civil proceedings be rebutted on the balance of probabilities. The section does not purport to alter the scope or operation of this presumption, merely the weight of evidence needed to rebut it. Thus if a child is born in wedlock, evidence that the wife had relations with another man at the relevant time will not of itself rebut the presumption, because it does not follow that the husband did not also have relations with her. But any evidence showing that the husband was not the father, such as blood group evidence, evidence of the use of contraceptives by the husband, the physical appearance of the child, or even the conduct of the parties, in accepting or rejecting the child, is in principle capable of reaching the standard of probability now required. "Even weak evidence against legitimacy must prevail if there is not other evidence to counterbalance it. The presumption will only come in at that stage in the very rare case of the evidence being so evenly balanced that the court is unable to reach a decision on it."[42]

---

[34] *Ettenfield* v. *Ettenfield* [1940] P. 96.
[35] *Knowles* v. *Knowles* [1962] P. 161, where the presumption was applied to the period between decree nisi and decree absolute.
[36] *Inter the Parishes of St. George and St. Margaret, Westminster* (1706) 1 Salk. 123.
[37] *Hetherington* v. *Hetherington* (1887) 12 P.D. 112.
[38] *St. George and St. Margaret, supra*.
[39] *Per* Lord Lyndhurst, *Morris* v. *Davies* (1837) 5 Cl. & F. 163 at p. 265.
[40] *Banbury Peerage* (1811) 1 Sim. & St. 153.
[41] *e.g.* Ormrod J. in *Holmes* v. *Holmes* [1966] 1 W.L.R. 187 at p. 188. "I know that it is a sad thing to bastardise a child, but there are graver wrongs."
[42] *Per* Lord Reid, *S.* v. *McC.* [1972] A.C. 24 at p. 41; and see *T.* v. *T.* [1971] 1 W.L.R. 429. But in view of the wording of s.26, Family Law Reform Act 1969, the evidence of illegitimacy must at least be strong enough to make illegitimacy more probable than legitimacy.

(c) Death

Where as regards A there is no acceptable evidence that he was alive at some time during a continuous period of seven years or more, then if it can be proved, first, that there are persons who would be likely to have heard of him during that period, secondly, that those persons have not heard of him, and thirdly, that all due inquiries have been made appropriate to the circumstances, A will be presumed to have died at some time within that period.[43] On this statement of the principles involved, the following points may be noted. First, the fact that there must be someone who would be likely to hear of A means that, *e.g.* a deserted wife whose husband emigrates will not often be able to rely on the fact that *she* heard nothing for seven years.[44] Secondly, "hearing" of A means becoming possessed of apparently reliable information that he is alive; apparently unreliable information does not affect the issue one way or another.[45] Thirdly, there is some authority for saying that due inquiries are an *alternative* to the first requirement of someone likely to hear of A. The presumption has been acted on where there have been relatives likely to hear, but no inquiries prosecuted.[46]

It must be noted that the presumption is only as to the fact of death, not as to the time of death, so that if it has to be established that A was alive or dead on a particular day during the seven-year period, that fact will have to be proved by evidence, aided by any presumption of fact which the jury may see fit to act on.[47] The presumption of death does not oblige the court to presume that death occurred at any time during the seven years, nor is there any presumption of law that life continued for any part of the seven-year period.[48] Strictly, according to the leading case on the subject—*Re Phené's Trusts*—the presumption only operates to establish that if at the date of an action in which the death is called in question, seven years or more have elapsed without news, A is dead at that date, *i.e.* the date of the action. Accordingly, it is impossible to use this presumption to prove that A was dead in, say 1950, even if he has not been heard of since 1943. This inconvenience has caused the strict rule to be departed

---

[43] *Chard v. Chard* [1956] P. 259, *per* Sachs J. at p. 272.
[44] See *Chard v. Chard, supra.* But on decrees of death and dissolution of marriage, see *post*, p. 86.
[45] *Prudential Assurance v. Edwards* (1877) 2 App.Cas. 487.
[46] *Doe d. France v. Andrews* (1850) 15 Q.B. 756; *Chipchase v. Chipchase* [1939] P. 391; *Re Watkins* [1953] 1 W.L.R. 1323.
[47] See *post*, p. 90 for the presumption of continuance.
[48] *Re Phené's Trusts* (1870) L.R. 5 Ch.App. 139.

from in some cases to allow presumption of death at *any* given date if seven years' absence before that is shown.[49]

There is no presumption that a person not heard of for seven years died childless or unmarried[50]; nor is there any presumption that one who *has* been heard of less than seven years ago is still alive.[51]

There are three statutory provisions in this field which should be noted.

Matrimonial Causes Act 1973, section 19(3). This provides that, in petitions for a decree of presumption of death and dissolution of marriage, the facts that (i) for a period of seven years or upwards the other party to the marriage has been continuously absent from the petitioner and (ii) the petitioner has no reason to believe that the other party has been living within that time, shall be evidence that he or she is dead until the contrary is proved. The burden thus placed on a petitioner is lighter in at least three respects than with the common law presumption of death discussed above. No inquiries are called for; the fact that the petitioner would be unlikely to hear of the *de cujus* is immaterial; and in deciding whether the petitioner has no reason to believe in the *de cujus's* continued existence, only events taking place inside the last seven years are relevant.[52] This means that the age and state of health of the *de cujus* and other circumstances existing at the beginning of the period are ignored. Thus if a husband, 21 years old and in good health, deserts his wife and goes abroad, exactly seven years later the wife may present a petition, although there is every reason to suppose that the husband was alive at some time during the last seven years.

Proviso to Offences against the Person Act 1861, section 57. A person is not guilty of bigamy if, when marrying a second time, the former spouse was continually absent for seven years last past; and was not known by the accused to have been living during that time.[53] This is more than a mere presumption since it secures an acquittal even if there is conclusive evidence that the

---

[49] See *e.g. Chipchase* v. *Chipchase* [1939] P. 391.
[50] *Re Jackson* [1907] 2 Ch. 354.
[51] *Re Aldersey* [1905] 2 Ch. 181; *Re Wilson* [1964] 1 W.L.R. 214. But for the presumption of continuance of life, which may help, see *post*, p. 90.
[52] *Thompson* v. *Thompson* [1956] P. 414, *per* Sachs J. at p. 425.
[53] Although this is in a proviso to s.57, it has been held that if evidence is given of seven years absence, the Crown has the persuasive burden of proving that the defendant *had* heard of his spouse during that period: *R.* v. *Curgerwen* (1865) L.R. 1 C.C.R. 1.

former spouse was alive at the relevant time, as, *e.g.* if he or she actually gives evidence at the trial.

Law of Property Act 1925, *section* 184. Where two or more persons have died in circumstances rendering it uncertain which of them survived the other or others, there is no common law presumption which would resolve this uncertainty.[54] However, for all purposes affecting title to property there is a presumption imposed by section 184 that the persons died in order of age, the eldest dying first.[55]

(d) Regularity

(i) Omnia praesumuntur rite esse acta: this presumption is chiefly applied to judicial and official appointments and acts.[56] Such are presumed to be regular until evidence is adduced to the contrary. Although the presumption is rebutted by quite slight evidence of irregularity, it is nevertheless extremely useful in that it removes the necessity for much quite formal evidence, and disposes of frivolous submissions of no case to answer and frivolous appeals on the ground that the proponent's case was not properly proved.

Thus, peace officers, justices of the peace and constables, acting as such, are presumed to be validly appointed.[57] The fact that a person presides over even an inferior tribunal carries a prima facie presumption that he was duly appointed,[58] but there appears to be no presumption that an inferior tribunal had jurisdiction in any particular matter.[59] Constant performance of divine service in a chapel raises a presumption of its consecration[60]; constant exercise of undisputed rights of pasturage leads the court to presume that they were validly granted.[61] Where statute authorises or requires any document to be served by post then, unless the contrary

---

[54] *Wing* v. *Angrave* (1860) 8 H.L.C. 183; *Re Benyon* [1901] P. 141.
[55] There is an exception in the case of an intestate and his or her spouse dying in circumstances which could normally attract s.184 of the Law of Property Act 1925. In such a case Administration of Estates Act 1925, s.46 shall have effect as if the spouse had not survived the intestate: *ibid.* s.46(3), as amended by Intestates' Estates Act 1952, s.1(4). See also Finance Act 1975, s.22(9).
[56] But see also the presumptions relating to the execution of documents, *post*, p. 345.
[57] *Berryman* v. *Wise* (1791) 4 T.R. 366; *Cooper* v. *Rowlands* [1972] Crim.L.R. 53.
[58] *R.* v. *Verelst* (1813) 3 Camp. 433; *R.* v. *Roberts* (1878) 14 Cox. 101.
[59] *Christopher Brown Ltd.* v. *Genossenschaft Oesterreichischer* [1954] 1 Q.B. 8, per Devlin J. at p. 13.
[60] *R.* v. *Cresswell* (1873) 1 Q.B.D. 446.
[61] *Johnson* v. *Barnes* (1873) L.R. 8 C.P. 527.

intention appears, the service is deemed to be effected by properly addressing, pre-paying and posting a letter containing the document and, unless the contrary is proved, to have been effected at the time at which the letter would be delivered in the ordinary course of post.[62] An unindorsed cheque which appears to have been paid by the banker on whom it is drawn is evidence of the receipt by the payee of the sum payable by the cheque.[63]

The maxim applies to criminal cases but to an uncertain extent, there being many conflicting cases. It has been said that the maxim will not be used to establish an ingredient of an offence,[64] at any rate if the matter is challenged at the trial. If it is not challenged at the trial then on appeal the defence may be taken to have admitted the regularity of the matter involved.[65] But if the maxim is applied, mere challenge is not enough; some evidence to the contrary there must be,[66] and in many cases the maxim *has* been applied even where the effect of so doing is to establish an ingredient of the offence.[67] It seems impossible to state any coherent principle which would allow a court to presume that a man in police officer's uniform who administered a breath test was validly appointed as such,[68] but not that the breathalyser he used was officially approved by the minister[69]; or would allow a court to presume that the road a local authority placed speed limit signs on was an officially designated road[70] but not that the signs themselves were of the officially approved size, colour and type.[71]

(ii) Other cases. There is a presumption that mechanical instruments which are usually in order (such as traffic lights[72] or a "Lion" intoximeter[73]) were in order when they were used. And if certain business transactions need to be done in a certain order to be effective, and there is no acceptable evidence that they were

---

[62] Interpretation Act 1978, s.7. Return of the letter marked "Undelivered" rebuts the presumption: *Ex p. Rossi* [1956] 1 Q.B. 682.
[63] Cheques Act 1957, s.3.
[64] *Scott* v. *Baker* [1961] 1 Q.B. 659, approved and followed by the Court of Appeal in *R.* v. *Withecombe* [1969] 1 W.L.R. 84.
[65] *Scott* v. *Baker, supra,* at p. 673.
[66] *Campbell* v. *Wallsend Slipway* [1978] I.C.R. 1015 at p. 1025.
[67] *Gibbons* v. *Skinner* [1951] 2 K.B. 379; *Cooper* v. *Rowlands* [1972] Crim.L.R. 53; *Campbell* v. *Wallsend Slipway, supra.*
[68] *Cooper* v. *Rowlands, supra.*
[69] *Scott* v. *Baker, supra; R.* v. *Withecombe, supra.*
[70] *Gibbons* v. *Skinner, supra.*
[71] *Swift* v. *Barrett* (1940) 163 L.T. 154.
[72] *Tingle Jacobs & Co.* v. *Kennedy* [1964] 1 W.L.R. 638 n.
[73] *Castle* v. *Cross* [1985] R.T.R. 62.

done in the wrong order, they are presumed to have been done in the right order.[74]

(e) Possession

In cases where it is doubtful which of several occupiers or *de facto* possessors is in legal possession, it is a presumption of law that the one with the legal title is the legal possessor.[75] There is a similar presumption that chattels found on land belong to the person with legal possession of the land.[76]

B. Presumptions of Fact

These are merely frequently recurring examples of circumstantial evidence. Where one fact stands in such a relation to a second, that as a matter of logic, the second fact can be deduced from the existence of the first, the first fact is said to be circumstantial evidence of the second.[77] Some of these fact-situations occur over and over again, resulting in a tendency to list them in books and to describe them as presumptions of fact. Examples are: the possession of stolen goods is evidence of guilty knowledge[78]; the loss of a ship shortly after putting to sea is evidence that it was unseaworthy on leaving harbour[79]; the destruction or concealing by a party of evidence is evidence that such evidence was unfavourable to him.[80]

What these propositions mean is that the tribunal (the jury, if there is one) may, not must, draw the indicated inferences. If it does no one can say that it has acted without evidence. If it does not, normally no one can quarrel with that failure. However, it all depends upon the circumstances, and sometimes the inference is so persuasive that for the tribunal not to draw it would indicate perverseness, so that an appellate court could interfere.[81]

Conversely, sometimes no inference can be drawn from a proved fact, although that proved fact is admissible as circumstantial evidence of a second fact. This is where it is the *combination* of one proved fact with other proved facts which has probative value. For example to show that A knew where the

[74] *Eaglehill Ltd. v. Needham (Builders) Ltd.* [1973] A.C. 992.
[75] *Ramsay v. Margrett* [1894] 2 Q.B. 18; *Re Cohen decd.* [1953] Ch. 88.
[76] *South Staffs. Water Co. v. Sharman* [1896] 2 Q.B. 44; *Re Cohen decd., supra.*
[77] See *ante,* p. 17.
[78] *R. v. Schama* (1914) 84 L.J.K.B. 396; *R. v. Hepworth & Fearnley* [1955] 2 Q.B. 600.
[79] *Pickup v. Thames & Mersey Marine Insurance Co.* (1878) 3 Q.B.D. 594.
[80] *Lewis v. Lewis* (1680) Cas. temp. Finch 471; *James v. Biou* (1826) 2 Sim. & St. 600; *Armory v. Delamirie* (1722) 1 Strange 505.
[81] *Pickup v. Thames & Mersey Marine Insurance Co., supra,* per Brett L.J. at p. 600.

stolen money was kept does not normally render it even marginally more likely that A stole the money, and a conviction on this evidence alone certainly could not be supported.[82] But if we add evidence of other facts, *e.g.* presence at the right time, possession of a pick-lock, destitute appearance before and affluent appearance after the theft, etc., it is the *combination* of facts which has persuasive force.[83] So although it may be said that all presumptions of fact are examples of circumstantial evidence, this is not to say that an item of circumstantial evidence necessarily has any persuasive force at all. It is where one item of circumstantial evidence almost always suggests an inference, more or less strong, about another fact that we can say we have a presumption of fact.[84]

The presumption that a legally normal person intends the natural consequences of his acts needs special mention. There is no doubt that normally this is a mere presumption of fact; and there is normally no compulsion for the jury to infer that the actor had such an intention.[85] As a result of *D.P.P.* v. *Smith*,[86] which was thought to elevate the presumption to one of law in murder cases, section 8 of the Criminal Justice Act 1967 was enacted to confirm that in all criminal cases the presumption is one of fact only.

Another commonly-met-with presumption of fact is the presumption of continuance. Any proved state of affairs may be presumed to have continued for some time. Thus, in *Att.-Gen.* v. *Bradlaugh*,[87] it was held that the fact that B had no belief in God in 1880 was strong evidence that he had no such belief in 1884. And if a man is proved to have been alive on a certain date, it may well be inferred that he was alive on a slightly[88] or even considerably later date,[89] depending upon his state of health and mode of life. The strength of the presumption will obviously fluctuate widely in accordance with the length of time between the proved fact and that sought to be inferred, and with all the other circumstances of the case. If continuance of life is concerned, the

---

[82] A failure to observe the Highway Code may, by statute, be relied on as circumstantial evidence establishing liability for a traffic accident, but on its own it is not strong enough to call for any reply by the opposing party: *Powell* v. *Phillips* [1972] 3 All E.R. 864.
[83] See *ante*, p. 17.
[84] See Eggleston, p. 108.
[85] *Per* Denning L.J. in *Hosegood* v. *Hosegood* (1950) 66 (Pt. 1) T.L.R. 735 at 738; *R.* v. *Steane* [1947] K.B. 997; Williams, G.L.G.P., para. 291.
[86] [1961] A.C. 290.
[87] (1885) 14 Q.B.D. 667.
[88] *Re Phené's Trusts* (1870) L.R. 5 Ch.App. 139.
[89] *R.* v. *Willshire* (1881) 6 Q.B.D. 366; *Re Forster's Settlement* [1942] Ch. 199.

presumption may eventually be negatived by the *legal* presumption of death.[90]

[90] *Ante,* p. 85.

Part III

THE TRIAL

CHAPTER 6
THE COURSE OF THE TRIAL

	Page
A. Hearing in Open Court	95
B. Order of Proceedings	97
C. Examination of Witnesses	100
1. Examination-in-chief	100
2. Cross-examination	116
3. Re-examination	123
4. Examination by Judge and Jury	124
D. Evidence given on Appeal	126
1. Civil Cases	126
2. Criminal Cases	127

CHAPTER 7
WITNESSES

A. Competence and Compellability	129
1. Competence	129
2. Compellability	133
B. Public Interest Protection and Privilege	135
1. Public Interest Protection	137
2. Privilege	144

Chapter 6

THE COURSE OF THE TRIAL

A. Hearing in Open Court

It is a fundamental rule that the whole hearing must take place in open court.[1] This involves three things: evidence must be given only at the hearing, by witnesses who are examined in public[2]; anyone has the right to be present[3] and anyone may publish fair, accurate and contemporaneous reports of what went on.[4] There are exceptions to all these rules.

In civil cases there are various provisions in the rules which allow evidence to be given before trial, by affidavit,[5] or before an examiner appointed by the court,[6] or in response to interrogatories, *i.e.* written questions served on a witness by the opposing party.[7] In criminal cases, magistrates may commit the accused for trial on written statements, and without considering the contents of the statements unless the accused is unrepresented or his counsel submits that there is an insufficient case for committal.[8] At trial on indictment, these written statements, and any others in proper form and not objected to by the opposite side, may be admitted.[9]

The public are not allowed in hearings where the court is exercising a parental or administrative function rather than a contentious one, such as on questions affecting mental patients, wards of court or adoption of children.[10] Although by statute evidence of sexual incapacity in a nullity suit is normally heard *in*

---

[1] *Scott* v. *Scott* [1913] A.C. 417; *R* v. *Bodmin JJ.* [1947] K.B. 321.
[2] See *R.* v. *Tiverton JJ.* [1981] R.T.R 280.
[3] It is no necessary objection that the members of the public admitted are few, or that individuals are kept out or ejected. It is for the judge or justices to decide on the adequacy of the facilities and the behaviour of individual spectators: *R.* v. *Denbigh JJ.* [1974] Q.B. 759.
[4] Contempt of Court Act 1981, s.4(1).
[5] Ord. 38, r. 2.
[6] Ord. 39, rr. 1, 8.
[7] Ord. 26, r. 1.
[8] Magistrates Courts Act 1980, s.6(2).
[9] See *post*, p. 295.
[10] *Scott* v. *Scott, supra.*

camera,[11] in general the mere fact that the evidence will be unsavoury, or that the parties have agreed to have the trial *in camera*, is no ground for excluding the public.[12] However it is otherwise if the presence of the public would make the administration of justice impracticable, *e.g.* where the litigation concerns a secret process or communication,[13] or if the interests of the State would be prejudiced.[14] No-one, other than those involved and press representatives, has a right to be present at hearings of domestic cases before magistrates,[15] or of certain criminal offences against children.[16] As to witnesses, there is in civil cases no rule that they must remain out of court until they give evidence. The judge may ask a witness to withdraw while other evidence is being given, but he cannot make him go, nor can he refuse to hear his evidence if he insists on remaining.[17] Magistrates have a discretion in this matter,[18] but in trials on indictment the universal practice is to make all witnesses on each side remain out of court until called.[19]

It is forbidden to publish written or broadcast reports of the evidence given at committal proceedings, or anything other than formalities such as names, charges and decision, until the accused is discharged or, if sent for trial, is disposed of by the court of trial. The accused may apply to have these restrictions lifted, in which case the magistrates must lift, unless one or more of several co-defendants objects, when they have a discretion.[20] Moreover, any court or tribunal, where it appears necessary for avoiding a substantial risk of prejudice to the proceedings before it or other pending or imminent proceedings, may order the postponement of any report of the whole or part of the proceedings for such period as the court thinks necessary for the purpose.[21] Magistrates are not prevented from making such an order by the fact that there has been an application to lift the restrictions imposed by

[11] Matrimonial Causes Act 1973, s.48(2); and see, Magistrates Courts Act 1980, s.69(4).
[12] *Scott* v. *Scott, supra.*
[13] *Ibid.*; *R.* v. *Chief Registrar of Friendly Societies* [1984] Q.B. 227.
[14] *Norman* v. *Matthews* (1916) 32 T.L.R. 369; Official Secrets Act 1920, s.8(4).
[15] Magistrates Courts Act 1980, s.69(2).
[16] Children and Young Persons Act 1933, s.37; see also s.39 (as amended) which prohibits the publication of the names of children concerned in criminal cases.
[17] *Moore* v. *Registrar of Lambeth C.C.* [1969] 1 W.L.R. 141.
[18] *Tomlinson* v. *Tomlinson* [1980] 1 All E.R. 593; *R.* v. *Bexley JJ., ex p. King* [1980] R.T.R. 49.
[19] *R.* v. *Smith (Joan)* [1968] 1 W.L.R. 636.
[20] Magistrates Courts Act 1980, s.2 (as amended by the Criminal Justice (Amendment) Act 1981, s.1).
[21] Contempt of Court Act 1981, s.4(2).

section 69 of the 1980 Act.[22] There are restrictions on publishing the names and addresses of complainants and defendants in rape cases,[23] and where the disclosure of the name and address might endanger the witness or the proper administration of justice, the judge has power to allow the details to be written down and to order that they be not disclosed.[24]

B. Order of Proceedings

In civil cases the plaintiff begins, if the evidential burden[25] on at least one issue[26] (including the amount of damages)[27] is on him. In criminal cases, the Crown begins, unless the defendant is making some plea in bar, *i.e.* some argument that he cannot be tried, *e.g. autrefois acquit*.[28] The party beginning addresses the court on what is involved, then calls his witnesses. He examines them in chief, they are then cross-examined by the defendant, and the plaintiff re-examines them. He then closes his case, and it is the defendant's turn. If he calls no witnesses, the plaintiff or prosecutor makes his closing speech, and then the defendant has the last word. If the defendant does call evidence, the plaintiff has the last word in civil cases; the defendant addresses the court at the close of his case, and the plaintiff then speaks. But in criminal cases, by statute the defendant always has the last word.[29]

At the close of the plaintiff's or prosecutor's case, the defendant may submit that there is no case for him to answer, *i.e.* no sufficient evidence of what the plaintiff or Crown is alleging. In considering this submission, the judge must be careful not to usurp the jury's function.[30] If the evidence taken at its highest is such that no jury, properly directed, could properly convict, he should stop the case. But evaluating the worth of witnesses is for the jury, so if the strength or weakness of the Crown's case

---

[22] *R.* v. *Horsham J.J., ex p. Farquharson* [1982] Q.B. 762.
[23] Sexual Offences (Amendment) Act 1976, ss.4,6.
[24] *R.* v. *Socialist Worker Printers, ex p. Att.-Gen.* [1975] Q.B. 637.
[25] As to this, see *ante*, p. 61.
[26] *Pontifex* v. *Jolly* (1839) 9 C. & P. 202; see also *Seldon* v. *Davidson* [1968] 1 W.L.R. 1083.
[27] *Mercer* v. *Whall* (1845) 5 Q.B. 447.
[28] Archbold, §§ 4–67 *et seq.*
[29] Criminal Procedure (Right of Reply) Act 1964; Magistrates Courts Rules 1981, rr. 13, 14.
[30] In magistrates' courts, since the magistrates are also the tribunal of fact, they may consider the *reliability* of the prosecutor's evidence in deciding whether there is no case: see *Practice Direction (Submission of No Case)* [1962] 1 W.L.R. 227.

depends on the view taken of the witnesses' reliability, he should allow the matter to be tried by the jury. If an ensuing conviction is unsafe or unsatisfactory, that will be grounds for quashing it on appeal, but the judge should not have regard to that factor in ruling on a submission of no case.[31]

If the judge accepts the submission, he gives judgment for the defendant. If he does not accept it, what happens then depends upon what kind of proceedings are involved.

In civil cases without a jury, the judge must put the defendant to his election before ruling on his submission of no case.[32] He must ask the defendant to declare formally that he intends to call no evidence. If the judge rules against the defendant, he has lost his chance, and judgment is normally given against him. The reason why he is put to this rather invidious election is that, in this type of proceedings, the Court of Appeal, if it thinks that the judge was wrong in ruling that there was no case, can dispose of the whole case completely by considering all the evidence on both sides. But if one side's evidence was not in, the Court of Appeal could not do this and would have to send the case for re-trial with consequent delay and expense.[33] It is important then, that the defendant must have indicated that the whole of the evidence *is* in, by saying that he has none to call.

In civil cases with a jury, however, the Court of Appeal cannot deal with the case completely anyway; if the judge's ruling was wrong, a re-trial before another jury is inevitable anyway. So there is no need for all the evidence to be in before the judge rules; and he therefore has a discretion whether to put the defendant to his election.[34] Magistrates, in a civil case, have a similar discretion.[35]

In criminal cases,[36] the judge cannot put the defendant to his election. If he rules against the defendant, the trial proceeds.[37]

---

[31] *R. v. Galbraith* [1981] 2 All. E.R. 1060 (not following *R. v. Mansfield* [1977] 1 W.L.R. 1102).

[32] *Alexander v. Rayson* [1936] 1 K.B. 169; *Storey v. Storey* [1961] P. 63.

[33] See *Young v. Rank* [1950] 2 K.B. 510 at p. 515.

[34] *Ibid.*, Note that where the Court of Appeal thinks that the judge was wrong in letting the trial go on, it will nevertheless consider, in deciding whether to allow the appeal, the whole of the evidence, including that given after the erroneous rejection of a "no case" submission: *Payne v. Harrison* [1961] 2 Q.B. 403.

[35] And if they decide that there is a case to answer, but the defendant calls no evidence, he must be allowed an opportunity to address them again on the facts: *Disher v. Disher* [1965] P. 31.

[36] In which the submissions of no case must always be made in the absence of the jury: *R. v. Falconer-Atlee* (1973) 58 Cr.App.R. 345 at p. 354.

[37] On appeal against the ruling there is a somewhat analogous rule to that in *Payne*

Normally, the party beginning must call all his evidence at the first instance. He is not entitled to call prima facie evidence, and then, after waiting to see what his adversary can prove, call further evidence to confirm his prima facie evidence. This rule must be borne in mind in connection with the evidential burden of proof. It has been said that the evidential burden may shift from one party to the other and then back again.[38] This does not necessarily mean that the party beginning has a second chance to adduce evidence in support of his case; he must normally anticipate his adversary's evidence when he is opening his case.

However, in certain circumstances, he may be allowed to call rebutting evidence, which, as the name suggests, is evidence directed solely towards nullifying or qualifying his opponent's evidence in some way, and not merely to confirming his own case.

The circumstances in which rebutting evidence may be called are as follows:

(1) The party beginning may call witnesses to say that they would not believe certain of the opponent's witnesses on oath, and, in exceptional cases, to contradict the answers of opposing witnesses in cross-examination as to credit.[39] This includes calling evidence under section 7 of the Civil Evidence Act 1968[40] as to the credibility of the maker of a statement put in under sections 2, 4 or 5 of the Act, and, similarly, in criminal cases calling evidence under Schedule 3, paragraph 3 of the Police and Criminal Evidence Act.[41]

(2) With the leave of the judge, he may call evidence in answer to that of the other party adduced in support of an issue the proof of which lay on the latter.[42] In summary proceedings he has the right to call evidence in reply.[43]

---

v. *Harrison, supra,* n. 34, *R.* v. *Power* [1919] 1 K.B. 572; except where the evidence against the accused after rejection of "no case" is given by or on behalf of a co-accused. On this, see *R.* v. *Abbott* [1955] 2 Q.B. 497. See also J. C. Wood, 77 L.Q.R. 491.
[38] See *ante,* p. 63.
[39] *Post,* p. 121 *et seq.*
[40] *Post,* p. 270.
[41] *Post,* p. 294.
[42] *Penn* v. *Jack* (1866) L.R.2. Eq.314; *Beevis* v. *Dawson* [1957] 1 Q.B. 195.
[43] Magistrates' Courts Rules 1981, rr. 13, 14.

(3) Where the party beginning has been taken by surprise, *e.g.* where the opposing party should have put questions in cross-examination of the former's witnesses, indicating that he meant to contradict them, but did not.[44] In criminal cases, the conditions under which the crown could call evidence under this head used to be very strict. The matter had to be one which arose *"ex improviso* which no human ingenuity could foresee,"[45] but in recent times the rule has been somewhat relaxed. It will still prevent a prosecutor from attempting to repair a sloppily prepared case with evidence after his case has been closed,[46] but it has been said that the *ex improviso* principle has to be applied with a recognition that the prosecution is expected to react reasonably to what might be suggested as pre-trial warnings of evidence likely to be given and to suggestions put in cross-examination of prosecution witnesses. They are not expected to take notice of fanciful and unreal possibilities.[47]

C. Examination of Witnesses

1. Examination-in-chief

This is the examination of a witness by the party calling him,[48] and its object is to elicit from the witness facts within his personal knowledge which assist the case of the party calling him. Examination-in-chief, (which is sometimes called direct examination), must be contrasted with the more hostile questioning by the opposite side called cross-examination. In many ways, cross-examination is a more effective way of penetrating the stubbornness or stupidity of some witnesses, but the general rule is that this weapon is reserved for one's opponent, and one may not cross-examine one's own witness, however much one would like to do so.

As will be seen,[49] one can sometimes and to some extent discredit one's own witness. But in general, the rule is that in examination-in-chief, a witness's evidence is confined to his

---

[44] *Bigsby* v. *Dickinson* (1876) 4 Ch.D. 24.
[45] *Per* Tindal C.J. in *R.* v. *Frost* (1840) 4 St.Tr.NS. 85, at p. 386.
[46] See *R.* v. *Day* [1940] 1 All E.R. 402.
[47] *R.* v. *Hutchinson* (1985) 82 Cr.App.R. 51. See, however, *R.* v. *Cunningham* [1985] Crim.L.R. 374.
[48] In a magistrates' court, if the prosecutor is not represented, the magistrates' clerk may conduct the examination for him: *Simms* v. *Moore* [1970] 2 Q.B. 327. In all criminal cases, the accused, if he gives evidence, must normally do so before his other witnesses: Police and Criminal Evidence Act 1984, s.79.
[49] *Post*, p. 112.

spontaneous answers in court. This rules out leading questions, prepared answers, and out-of-court previous statements confirming what the witness now says in court. We must look at these matters a little more closely.

(a) Leading questions

Almost invariably, the examiner will know in a general way what this witness is going to say—the witness will earlier have signed a statement, called his "proof," of what he can depose to, and it will be on the basis of this proof that counsel will have decided to call him. Nevertheless, the witness must tell his own story in court. This means that he must not be asked leading questions. A leading question is one which suggests the answer. So one must not ask, "Did you see John Smith at the scene of the crime?" but rather "Did you see anyone?" and "Whom did you see?" A question which admits a simple "Yes" or "No" as an answer is usually a leading one, but not always. It usually depends upon whether the question is as to a matter seriously in dispute. Thus "Did you see anyone?" is usually all right, because it is not usually in dispute whether the witness saw anyone or not; but "Did you see John Smith?" is usually objectionable. In civil cases, leading questions are admissible by consent, and in the absence of objection, the other side is taken to consent. In any proceedings, in the interest of time-saving, questions as to matters introductory and formal are usually leading—"You are Tom Jones, you live at Blackacre and you are a tallow chandler by trade?" Moreover some witnesses, through stupidity or nervousness, never get to the point unless they are led, so some leading, in order to get "near" the crux of their evidence is necessary. But when the crux is reached, the leading must stop. So if he is expected to testify that John Smith struck Brown in Gas Street on the 13th, he might fail to respond to questions such as "Where were you on the 13th?" and in the end have to be asked, "Were you in Gas Street on the 13th?" But we cannot go further and ask "Did you see John Smith there?" if that is disputed. Essentially, the principle is that a witness must not be prompted on matters in dispute.

(b) Refreshing memory[50]

It should be obvious that the witness is not allowed to read from his "proof" or any other document prepared for the purposes of litigation. That would destroy all spontaneity. But he

---

[50] See Newark and Samuels, "Refreshing Memory" [1978] Crim.L.R. 408.

is allowed to "refresh his memory"[51] from a document, tape recording,[52] or photofit picture[52a] made by him contemporaneously with the facts. The document noting the facts may be made by someone else at the witness's behest, provided the witness verifies it contemporaneously. This is usually done by the witness reading what has been written, but it has been held that verification can be by him listening to the writer reading back what he has written.[53] "Contemporaneously" is a somewhat misleading term in this context, nowadays meaning no more than at a time when the facts were still fresh in the witness's mind.[54] The matter is one of degree, to be decided by the judge, and a fair amount of latitude is allowed.[55] The note used in the box need not be the first note made, provided the first note was contemporaneous and the later note used is a true copy of it[56] or, if the later note supplements the first note, the supplementing was done from memory while the events were still fresh in the witness's mind.[57] The fact that two witnesses produce identical notes, having collaborated in recording an accurate account, is no objection.[58]

The conditions stated above only apply to documents used to refresh memory in the witness box. In a case where 18 months elapsed between the making of the proof and the trial, it was held that there was no objection to the witness refreshing his memory from it before entering the court room, although the proof was not contemporaneous and was made for the purpose of litigation.[59] Yet if that witness had tried to refresh his memory *in* the box, he would have been prevented.[60] The line is drawn the moment he enters the box. It may be thought odd that the law forbids the open, fair, use of the document in open court, but allows the secret, perhaps unfair, use of it beforehand out of view of the court. Perhaps a reason is to be found in the impossibility of controlling what witnesses do before entering the courtroom.

---

[51] *i.e.* he looks at the document and then gives evidence. He does not read the document aloud as his evidence.
[52] *R. v. Mills* [1962] 1 W.L.R. 1152; *R. v. Ali & Hassan* [1966] 1 Q.B. 688.
[52a] *R. v. Cook* (1986) *The Times*, December 10.
[53] *R. v. Kelsey* (1981) 74 Cr.App.R. 435.
[54] *Att.-Gen.'s Reference, No. 3 of 1979* (1979) 69 Cr.App.R. 411.
[55] *R. v. Simmonds* (1967) 51 Cr.App.R. 316.
[56] *R. v. Cheng* (1976) 63 Cr.App.R. 20.
[57] *Att-Gen.'s Reference, No. 3 of 1979, supra.*   [58] *R. v. Bass* [1953] 1 Q.B. 680.
[59] *R. v. Richardson* [1971] 2 Q.B. 484, approving *Lau Pak Ngam v. R.* [1966] Crim.L.R. 443 (P.C.). And see *R. v. Westwell* (1976) 62 Cr.App.R. 251.
[60] *R. v. Graham* [1973] Crim.L.R. 628. However, it has been said that since *R. v. Richardson, supra,* allows a witness to look at a proof *before* he enters the box, "to forbid him to look at it in the witness box would be a triumph of legalism over common sense": *R. v. Cheng, supra. Sed quaere.*

As to refreshing memory in the box, independent recollection is not essential: the witness may say quite frankly that he does not now recollect the event in question, but if he recorded it thus, it must have happened thus.[61] Non-recollection *may* affect the weight of his oral evidence, but in many cases, *e.g.* concerning a routine transaction among many similar, it will not even do that. However it is the witness's testimony which is the evidence, not the note, at any rate at the outset. The opposing party may inspect the document and cross-examine the witness on it,[62] without giving the document any evidential status at all, provided he sticks to the parts of the document which the witness used to refresh his memory.[63] However if he cross-examines on other parts, the party who called the witness can insist on the document being made evidence and, if there is a jury, being shown to the jury.[64] But, in criminal cases, it is only "evidence" to a very limited extent. It may be used by the jury as supporting the credit of the witness, but it is no evidence of the truth of its contents.[65] In *R. v. Virgo*,[66] a diary used by H, a crown witness, having been used to refresh his memory, was extensively cross-examined on by the defence, and shown to the jury. The conviction was quashed because the judge referred to it as the most important evidence in the case, when he should have emphasized that its only value was to bolster the credit of H. In civil cases, once the document becomes evidence because cross-examined on beyond the parts used to refresh memory, it is evidence of any fact stated therein of which direct oral evidence by the witness would be admissible.[67]

(c) Previous consistent statements

Sometimes a party will wish to show, either by the witness himself or by some other witness, that the present witness on some earlier occasion made a statement to the same effect as his present evidence.

---

[61] *Maughan v. Hubbard* (1828) 8 B. & C. 14.
[62] Even if the document was only used before the witness came into court: *Owen v. Edmonds* (1983) 77 Cr.App.R. 191 (D.C.).
[63] *Senat v. Senat* [1965] P. 172: *R. v. Fenlon* (1980) 71 Cr.App.R. 207. This is different from the normal rule on calling for the opponent's documents, as to which see *post* p. 350.
[64] *Gregory v. Taverner* (1833) 6 C. & P. 280.
[65] On this confusing, and essentially meaningless, distinction between using material as evidence, and using it for some other, more limited, purpose, see *post*, pp. 106–108.
[66] (1978) 67 Cr.App.R. 323.
[67] Civil Evidence Act 1968, s.3(2).

(i) *General rule.* Generally this is not allowed. There is a rule, sometimes called the rule against self-serving statements, or the rule against narrative, which prohibits a witness from saying that he made a statement in similar vein on an earlier occasion, or narrating the terms of his earlier statement, or producing a document containing the earlier statement; nor may another person who heard the earlier statement give an account of it. So far as the latter case is concerned, the evidence of the second person is hearsay in its strictest sense, if tendered as proof of what is narrated in the statement, because he is tendering the assertion of someone other than himself to prove facts of which he has no direct knowledge.[68] The usual objections to hearsay will require the rejection of that evidence. But if hearsay is defined more widely, as it usually is, as any assertion other than one made by a person while giving oral evidence, the hearsay rule will equally prevent a person tendering what he himself said on an earlier occasion as evidence of the facts narrated. However the objection to this sort of evidence has a different *rationale* from the hearsay rule in its strict sense. The objection to hearsay in its strict sense is essentially the absence of opportunity to test the statement by cross-examination.[69] That weakness is not present in the case of a witness describing in the box an earlier statement by himself, because he *can* be cross-examined on it. However, there are other objections and they are strong enough to exclude all self-serving statements, whether narrated by the maker or someone else, even if such are *not* tendered as proof of what is narrated, but for some more limited purpose, such as supporting his credit by showing consistency. These objections are, first, the ease with which such statements can be manufactured. As one judge said, if such were allowed, every person who expected to be a witness could go about making statements supporting the evidence which he was intending to give.[70] The second objection is that a previous statement usually adds nothing to the force of the present evidence. There is a popular fallacy about this—in every day life people tend to back up their present statement by saying that they have said it before—but it *is* a fallacy, and one to which the common law has always been very much alive.

In *Gillie* v. *Posho*,[71] the question was whether B had agreed to

---

[68] See *post*, pp. 239 *et seq*.
[69] *Post* p. 240.
[70] Eyre C.J. in *R.* v. *Hardy* (1794) 24 How.St.Tr. 199 at pp. 1093–1094. It is for this reason that self-serving statements, even when exceptionally they are allowed, can never amount to corroboration. See *post*, p. 163.
[71] [1939] 2 All E.R. 196.

Examination of Witnesses

buy A's farm before A published a misleading advertisement about the farm. A swore that B had done so, and produced a letter by himself to his own solicitor, dated before the advertisement, telling the solicitor that B had agreed to buy the farm. The Privy Council held that this letter should not have been admitted. This is a rather mechanical application of the rule, because the risk of fabrication by A was minimal[72]; but the rule is valuable because often the evidence it rejects is in reality quite worthless. For example, in *R. v. Kurshid*,[73] K was at a police station suspected of burglary. When he realised that he was going to be held until an identity parade could be arranged, he had a word with his solicitor and then made a full confession, after which he was released on bail. At trial, he claimed the confession was false, and offered to call his solicitor to testify that he (K) had told him he was going to make a false confession in order to get bail. This was rejected as obviously self-serving.[74]

There are at common law certain exceptional cases where self-serving statements are allowed.[75] However the common law now only applies in criminal cases, because the position in civil cases has been radically altered by section 2 of the Civil Evidence Act 1968.[76] This section, which has almost destroyed the hearsay rule in civil cases, allows any statement made by a witness to be admitted, as evidence of the facts in it, subject to the leave of the court.[77] There is however no corresponding provision in the Police and Criminal Evidence Act,[78] and in criminal cases a previous consistent statement is permitted only in the following exceptional cases. In most of these cases, the permission is, in theory at least, not in breach of the hearsay rule because, again in theory, the statement is no evidence of the truth of the facts in it, but only of the witness's consistency or of his reaction to accusation. In practice, there seems every reason to suppose that

---

[72] In a civil case today, the letter would be admissible with the leave of the court. See following text.

[73] [1984] Crim.L.R. 288 (C.A.).

[74] It has been held in New Zealand that the fact that the self-serving statement was made under the influence of so called "truth drugs" still does not make it admissible: *R. v. McKay* [1967] N.Z.L.R. 139 (applying *Gillie* v. *Posho*). A similar attitude has been taken by some American courts as to statements produced in a polygraph (lie-detector) test; see Elliott, "Lie Detector Evidence: Lessons from the American Experience," in Campbell & Waller (eds.) *Well and Truly Tried* (1982) pp. 100, 129.

[75] For a very full account of these, see R.N. Gooderson, "Previous Consistent Statements" [1968] C.L.J. 64.

[76] See *post*, Chap. 13.

[77] See also s.3(1)(*b*), on rebutting afterthought: *post* p. 107.

[78] Although one was proposed: C.L.R.C. para. 239, Draft Bill, Clauses 31, 32.

if the statement is believed by the jury, it is taken as evidence of the facts in it.

(ii) *Document used to refresh memory.* This, as has been seen,[79] becomes "evidence" if cross-examined on as to other parts of the document, but only to the limited extent of showing consistency in the witness.[80]

(iii) *Whole statement.* Where a party proves a statement against his opponent as an admission by the latter, the whole of that statement becomes admissible, including those parts which are favourable to the maker.[81] The favourable parts are evidence in favour of the maker although they are consistent with his present testimony. However they are only usable to qualify or affect the incriminatory parts. It was laid down in *R. v. Donaldson,*[82] that they are not evidence of the truth of what is narrated in them, but only go to help the tribunal of fact to decide whether the whole statement is in the nature of an admission or not. This distinction is probably beyond the comprehension of jurors and it may be guessed that it is ignored by them, *i.e.* if they believe the favourable parts, they take them as evidence of what is narrated in them.[83] But, according to *R. v. Donaldson* it is the judge's duty to impress the distinction upon them. However in a later case, *R. v. Duncan,*[84] it was said, "Judges should not be obliged to give meaningless or unintelligible directions to juries." In that case D, accused of murder, had made a "mixed" statement, admitting the killing but (so it was said) suggesting provocation. It was held to be wrong for the judge to rule that there was no evidence of provocation and to withdraw that issue from the jury. On dealing with any mixed statement, he should point out that the exculpatory parts had less weight than the inculpatory parts, but should tell the jury that, in deciding where the truth lay, they should consider the whole statement.[85] This gets near to telling

---

[79] *Ante,* p. 103.
[80] This exception still applies in civil cases, where if the document becomes evidence, it is evidence for all purposes: Civil Evidence Act, 1968 s.3(2).
[81] *Rundle v. Blackburn* (1813) 5 Taunt. 245: *Harrison v. Turner* (1847) 10 Q.B. 482; *R. v. MacGregor* [1968] 1 Q.B. 237.
[82] (1976) 64 Cr.App.R. 59, *per* James L.J. at p. 65. And see *Leung Kam Kwok v. R.* (1984) 81 Cr.App.R. 83 (P.C.).
[83] See Elliott and Wakefield, "Exculpatory Statements by Accused Persons" [1979] Crim.L.R. 428 at p. 434, where it is suggested that this rule as to the limited use to which the favourable statement can be put should, and could easily, be allowed to fall into disuse.
[84] (1981) 73 Cr.App.R. 359 at p. 364.
[85] See also *R. v. Hamand* (1985) 82 Cr.App.R.65.

the jury that the whole statement is evidence of the facts in it, which is what the Criminal Law Revision Committee proposed.[86] However that suggestion was not adopted in the Police and Criminal Evidence Act 1984, and although by section 82 a confession includes any statement wholly or partly adverse to the person who made it, section 76(1) provides that, subject to conditions[87] it may be given in evidence *against him*. Thus the evidential status of the self-serving parts is once again doubtful, as is the correctness of *R. v. Duncan*.

(iv) *Rebutting afterthought*. The mere fact that a witness's testimony is attacked in cross-examination does not allow him to show that he made an earlier statement consistent with his present testimony in order to re-establish his credit.[88] But if the suggestion made against him is that his account of the facts is a recent invention, he may rebut this suggestion by testifying that he made an earlier consistent statement.[89] Strictly speaking, at common law, the earlier statement merely confirms the witness's credit and is no evidence of the facts narrated. In the nature of things, this is an unimportant distinction, since *ex hypothesi*, the statement is in the same terms as the witness's testimony, which *is* evidence. The Civil Evidence Act 1968 abolishes the distinction as to civil cases.[90]

(v) *Statements made on accusation or discovery of incriminating articles*. Analogous to the rebutting afterthought exception is the rule that exculpatory statements made by the accused on being arrested[91] or perhaps on being taxed with the offence[92] may be admitted, not as evidence of the truth of the facts stated but as "evidence that the defendant made the statement and of his reaction[93] which is part of the general picture which the jury have to consider, but it is not evidence of the facts stated."[94] Of this it has

[86] C.L.R.C., Clause 2(4) Draft Bill.
[87] See *post* Chap. 10.
[88] But see *per* Diplock L.J. in *Ahmed v. Brumfitt* (1967) 112 S.J. 32.
[89] See *Fox v. General Medical Council* [1960] 1 W.L.R. 1017 (P.C.) and the authorities there cited; *R. v. Oyesiku* (1972) 56 Cr.App.R. 240.
[90] s.3(1)(*b*).
[91] *R. v. Storey* (1968) 52 Cr.App.R. 334: *R. v. Thompson* [1975] Crim.L.R. 34.
[92] See Gooderson *op. cit* pp. 67–70: as to *incriminatory* statements in such a situation, see *post*, Chap. 10.
[93] If the statement is no sense a spontaneous re-action, but a carefully prepared document made on legal advice, it is not admissible on the principle discussed in the text: *R. v. Newsome* (1980) 71 Cr.App.R.325.
[94] *R. v. Donaldson* (1976) 64 Cr.App.R. 59 at p. 65. Since the statement is not evidence, it cannot be used as a foundation of a submission of "no case": *R. v. Storey* (1965) Cr.App.R. 334.

been said, "Many lawyers find difficulty in grasping this principle of the law of evidence. What juries make of it must be a matter of surmise, but the probabilities are that they make very little."[95] No doubt if the jury believe the statement they will take it as evidence of the fact narrated, whatever the judge says.[96]

If the accused is found in possession of recently stolen goods, in the absence of an innocent explanation which the jury think might be true, the jury may conclude that he is a thief or a handler, *i.e.* may conclude that he knew they were stolen goods.[97] It follows therefore that any explanation he does give is admissible in evidence for him.[98] Apparently it is the same if the theft is merely incidental to some other charge,[99] *e.g.* murder, where the victim's belongings were found in the possession of the accused soon after the killing.[1]

(vi) *Complaints.* In cases of rape, indecent assault and similar offences on females (and of indecent assault on and gross indecency with young males[2]) the fact that the person assaulted made a complaint, shortly after the occurrence, of the matters charged against the accused, together with particulars of the complaint, is admissible as evidence in chief for the prosecution, not to prove the truth of the matters stated, nor as corroboration of the facts but (i) as evidence of the consistency of the complainant's conduct with her testimony, and (ii) where consent is in issue, to negative consent.[3] Conversely the fact that no complaint was made is evidence for the accused tending to show the inconsistency or insincerity of the complainant.[4] If consent is not in issue, the terms of the complaint are admissible only to show the consistency of the complainant's conduct with her testimony. It follows, therefore, that if the complainant does not give evidence, *e.g.* because she is too young, the terms of the complaint are inadmissible for this purpose.[5]

It does not matter that the complaint was made in the absence

---

[95] *Per* Lawton L.J., in *R. v. Sparrow* [1973] 1 W.L.R. 488 at p. 492.
[96] See Elliott & Wakefield, *op. cit.* p. 435.
[97] *R. v. Schama* (1914) L.J.K.B. 396.
[98] *R. v. Abraham* (1848) 3 Cox 430; Gooderson, *op. cit.* 70–73.
[99] *R. v. Exall* (1866) 4 F. & F. 922 at p. 925.
[1] *R. v. Muller* (1865) 4 F. & F. 383n, at p. 924n.
[2] *R. v. Camelleri* [1922] 2 K.B. 122.
[3] *R. v. Lillyman* [1896] 2 Q.B. 167; *R. v. Osborne* [1905] 1 K.B. 551.
[4] *R. v. Osborne, supra,* at p. 559. As to a complaint in terms *inconsistent* with her present testimony, the defence may use it to depreciate the latter under a wider general doctrine applying to all witnesses (see *post,* p. 114), but it is still no evidence of the facts narrated. See *R. v. Askew* [1981] Crim.L.R. 398.
[5] *R. v. Wallwork* (1958) 42 Cr.App.R. 153.

of the accused; nor at such an interval as not to form part of the *res gestae* (as to which, see below); nor that the complainant is so young that disproof of her consent is not necessary.[6] It must however have been voluntary and not in reply to leading or suggestive questions, although it is no objection that the statement was elicited by such a question as "Why are you crying?"[7] Moreover, it must be made by the complainant at the first opportunity which reasonably offers.[8] It is for the judge to decide whether evidence of the complaint is admissible.[9]

This exception to the general rule that a witness's credit cannot be supported this way is an anomalous survival from ancient times, resting on no distinct principle and carrying obvious dangers of concocted evidence being acted on as proof of disputed facts. Although it is axiomatic that the terms of the complaint are no evidence of the facts narrated, and cannot amount to corroboration, the fact remains that the repetition by another witness of the details of an alleged sexual offence is potentially prejudicial to the defendant, even though the judge stresses, as he ought, the limited use that can properly be given to the complaint. The fact that the jury may take it into account at all risks their using it as evidence of the facts, or at least as confirming the complainant's evidence. It is all very well to say that shewing consistency is one thing, corroboration is quite another, but the nature of the distinction is not obvious.

(vii) *Res gestae statements*. *Res gestae* means the transaction, and there is a doctrine that all events and utterances which are actually part of the transaction being deposed to are admissible, because to cut out anything would be to falsify the account of what went on. This doctrine is dealt with later[10]; here it is enough to say that sometimes part of the transaction might be utterances by the witness in the same sense as his oral evidence. For example, in *R. v. Fowkes*[11] F was charged with the murder of X by shooting him through a window. A and B were sitting in the room with X, when a face appeared at the window and the fatal shot

---

[6] *R. v. Osborne, supra.*
[7] *Ibid., R. v. Norcott* [1917] 1 K.B. 347 at p. 349.
[8] *R. v. Osborne, supra; R. v. Cummings* [1948] 1 All E.R. 511. The mere fact that it is not the first complaint is not sufficient to exclude it: *R. v. Wilbourne* (1917) 12 Cr.App.R. 280.
[9] *R. v. Cummings, supra.*
[10] *Post*, Chap. 14.
[11] [1856] *The Times*, March 8, cited Stephen, § 3. See also *R. v. Donald and Donald* [1986] Crim.L.R. 535.

was fired. Both A and B were allowed to depose that immediately before the shot was fired, A shouted "There's F."[12]

(viii) *Previous identification of a person.* If a witness identifies the accused in court as being the person he saw in the incident in question, he is permitted to say that he identified him on an earlier occasion,[13] *e.g.* at an identification parade.[14] The usual reason for rejecting an earlier consistent statement—that it adds nothing to the weight of the present testimony—does not apply here. Without this confirming evidence, an in-court identification is worth little, so little that an identification in court which is not confirmed this way is frowned on,[15] although it may be allowed in exceptional circumstances.[16] Even if the witness, having identified the accused in court, omits to testify to his earlier identification, any person who witnessed it can testify to it.[17] If the witness fails to identify the accused in court, he can testify that he identified someone earlier, and any person who saw or heard that identification can say who was identified.[18]

In the first two of these cases, the evidence of the earlier identification is proffered merely to confirm the witness's (W's) present testimony, and not as evidence of the truth of what is conveyed by the identification, *i.e.* that D was the person involved in the crime. In the third case, where W fails to identify D in court, and can only say that he made an identification of someone earlier, it is hard to see, when another person (P) testifies that W identified D, what this is confirming. Strictly it is only confirmatory of the fact that W made *an* identification, which will not usually be in issue. It is not confirming W's statement in court that D was the person he identified, because W gave no such testimony. The evidence of P looks like hearsay.[19]

---

[12] Compare and contrast *Milne* v. *Leisler* (1862) 7 H. & N. 786; *Spittle* v. *Spittle* [1965] 3 All E.R. 451.

[13] See Gooderson, *op. cit.* 74–81; D.F. Libling, "Evidence of Past Identification" [1977] Crim.L.R. 268.

[14] *R.* v. *Christie* [1914] A.C. 545 (H.L.).

[15] See the Attorney-General's guidelines for prosecutors: *Hansard*, May 27, 1976, Vol. 912. Col. 115: *Archbold* § 1348.

[16] Where, *e.g.* the accused refused to take part in an identification parade: *R.* v. *John* [1973] Crim.L.R. 113, or was of such unusual appearance that it was impracticable to assemble a fair parade: *R.* v. *Hunter* [1969] Crim.L.R. 262. Examining magistrates however have no right to reject a dock identification not preceded by a parade; if it is prejudicial it is for the judge at the trial to rule it out on discretion: *R.* v. *Horsham JJ, ex p. Bukhari* (1982) 74 Cr.App.R. 291.

[17] *R.* v. *Christie, supra,* Lord Moulton dissenting.

[18] *R.* v. *Burke & Kelly* (1847) 2 Cox 295; *R.* v. *Osbourne & Virtue* [1973] Q.B. 678.

[19] See *post*, Chap. 12.

Identification of accused persons gives rise to numerous problems and is subject to special safeguards.[20] Perhaps as a result, although it was said in 1964[21] that there is no rule which permits the giving of hearsay evidence merely because it relates to identity, in identification of persons[22] there appears to have developed an exception to the hearsay rule. In *R. v. Osbourne & Virtue*,[23] the Court of Appeal extended the third case mentioned above[24] to cover a case where W could *neither* identify D in court *nor* remember an earlier occasion on which she had identified him. P, who witnessed the earlier identification, was allowed to testify that on that occasion W identified D. Since W gave no useful evidence at all, it is as if she never gave evidence at all, and P's evidence looks to be the purest hearsay. The justification for allowing him to testify was said to be that identification parades are for the protection of the suspect and what happens at those parades is highly relevant to the establishment of the truth.[25]

Can a witness give evidence that before trial he identified the accused from photographs shown to him by the police?[26] Although it has been said that the principles are the same as for other pre-trial identifications,[27] the better view is that this kind of evidence ought not to be led by the prosecution, because of the inevitable prejudice to the accused in allowing the jury to know that his picture appears in the police's "Rogues Gallery."[28] Even if no reference is made at the trial, the use of photographs before trial is usually improper, because it must detract from the value of any subsequent "live" identification. The witness may well "identify" the person whose photograph he has seen, rather than the man he glimpsed, perhaps fleetingly, at the scene of the crime.[29] When, at the early stages of an investigation, the police do not know for whom to look, it is not improper for them to show photographs to a witness in order to obtain a lead,[30] but the

[20] See *post*, pp. 175 *et seq*.
[21] *Sparks* v. *R.* [1964] A.C. 964, *per* Lord Morris at p. 981.
[22] As opposed to things: see *R.* v. *McLean* (1968) 52 Cr.App.R. 80.
[23] [1973] Q.B. 678.
[24] Without however considering the hearsay objection.
[25] *Per* Lawton L.J. at p. 690. And see *R.* v. *Okorodu* [1982] Crim.L.R. 747 (Crown Ct.).
[26] See D. F. Libling, "The Use of Photographs for the Purpose of Identification" [1978] Crim.L.R. 343.
[27] *R.* v. *Fannon & Walsh* (1922) 22 S.R. (N.S.W.) 427 at p. 430; Gooderson, *op. cit.* 74.
[28] *R.* v. *Wainwright* (1927) 19 Cr.App.R. 52, at p. 54; *R.* v. *Lamb* (1980) 71 Cr.App.R. 195.
[29] *R.* v. *Haslam* (1925) 19 Cr.App.R. 59 at p. 60.
[30] See Appendix 5: Code of Practice on Identification of Suspects, Annex C.

prosecution ought to tell the defence what has been done, so that the defence can raise the matter at the trial,[31] and the jury ought to be warned of the danger of acting on that witness's subsequent "live" identification either in court or at an identity parade.[32]

There is no objection to using photographs automatically taken of the culprit engaged in the crime and inviting the jury to make their own comparison with the person in the dock.[33] Moreover, a witness who knows the accused may testify that the photograph is of him,[34] but, by analogy with the "Rogues Gallery" principle mentioned above, this should not be done by a witness whose acquaintance with the accused comes from an earlier criminal occasion. The defence would not be able to test his identification by cross-examination without embarrassment and prejudice to the accused.[35]

(d) Discrediting one's own witness

At common law one is not allowed to impeach one's own witness. Having called a witness as a witness of truth, a party is not allowed to try to shake his evidence or to cast aspersions on his truthfulness or credibility, in the way in which an opposing party would try to do in cross-examination.[36] In cross-examination, a party may ask leading questions. He may go into whether the witness was really in a position to know. He may ask the witness about previous inconsistent statements, he may drag up earlier discreditable conduct (including his previous convictions) in order to impeach his creditworthiness. He may ask questions in order to show that the witness is biased. He may call evidence to show that a witness ought not to be believed on his oath. None of these things can a party do with his own witness who disappoints, who fails to come up to proof, who proves the wrong things or does not prove the right things, in short who turns out to be a liability rather than an asset.

Such witnesses are called adverse, but in that class there are two sub-classes which must be kept sharply differentiated. One who merely fails to prove what the party hoped for or proves the contrary of what the party hoped for is called an unfavourable

---

[31] R. v. *Lamb, supra.*
[32] R. v. *Dwyer & Ferguson* (1924) 18 Cr.App.R. 145 at p. 148; R. v. *Maynard* (1979) 67 Cr.App.R. 309.
[33] R. v. *Dodson* [1984] 1 W.L.R. 971.
[34] R. v. *Fowden* [1982] Crim.L.R. 588; R. v. *Grimer* [1982] Crim.L.R. 674.
[35] R. v. *Fowden, supra.* For the position on photofits, see *post,* p. 102.
[36] See *post,* p. 116.

Examination of Witnesses

witness. He must be contrasted with a hostile witness, who is one who shows clearly that he is not desirous of telling the truth at the instance of the party calling him.

At common law an unfavourable witness cannot be cross-examined,[37] *i.e.* he cannot be subjected to the attacks just mentioned. The only way in which the party calling him can repair his fortunes is to call other witnesses to testify to the contrary of the unfavourable witness, and to hope that the jury will believe them, rather than him. In *Ewer v. Ambrose*[38] it was necessary for the defendant to prove that a certain partnership existed. He called A who swore that it did not exist. It was held that the defendant could contradict A by the evidence of other witnesses, for, as Littledale J. said, it would be very hard if a party had four witnesses to a fact and happened to call the first one who disappointed him. If he were not allowed to contradict him, he would be deprived of his other three witnesses, and all because he happened to call A first. But the court went on to affirm that the defendant could not impeach A, *e.g.* could not call evidence to the effect that A was not to be believed on oath.

If a witness is (in the opinion of the judge) not merely unfavourable but actually hostile[39] to the party calling him he may give the party leave to cross-examine him[40] except that he cannot actually attack his character by asking about earlier bad character or convictions, or calling witnesses to say he is liar. There was some doubt about whether at common law the party could prove against the witness his previous inconsistent statements, and the Criminal Procedure Act 1865, s.3, was passed in order to clear this up. The section is confusingly worded, but it was decided in *Greenough v. Eccles*[41] that the effect of the section (which applies to civil as well as criminal proceedings) was that a

---

[37] Where a party is required by law to call a particular witness, such as the attesting witness to a will, such witness is regarded as a witness of the court rather than of the party calling him, so the party can cross-examine him if he proves unfavourable: *Oakes v. Uzzell* [1932] P. 19.

[38] (1825) 3 B. & C. 746. The case was confirmed by the Criminal Procedure Act 1865, s.3. The Act applies to civil as well as to criminal proceedings.

[39] Standing mute of malice can amount to hostility: *R. v. Thompson* (1977) 64 Cr.App.R. 96.

[40] The fact that the witness was non-compellable for the party calling him does not prevent him from being ruled hostile and then cross-examined, but the witness must, before he takes the oath, be reminded of his right to elect not to give evidence: *R. v. Pitt* [1983] Q.B. 25.

[41] (1859) 28 L.J.C.P. 160, considering an identical provision in an earlier Act.

hostile witness could, but an unfavourable witness could not, have his previous inconsistent statements proved against him.[42]

So the position before the Civil Evidence Act 1968 was that with hostile witnesses, previous inconsistent statements, and conflicting testimony of other witnesses might be used; with unfavourable witnesses, conflicting testimony might be used; and with neither type of witness could the party calling him launch a general attack on his bad character. This is still the position in criminal proceedings, but in civil proceedings, *all* previous statements by *any* witness are allowed in by section 2 of the 1968 Act, subject to conditions.[43]

As to what is hostility, this is up to the judge,[44] but merely failing to come up to proof, failing to give the expected evidence, is not hostility.[45] Nor is it enough that the witness's sympathies would be expected to be with the other side. So if the Crown calls the accused's son or brother or mistress, or if the plaintiff calls the defendant,[46] without some indication of actual hostility, the witness must not be treated as hostile. If that indication does not emerge until after the examination-in-chief, the application to treat him as hostile may be made in re-examination.[47] Even if the judge does rule the witness hostile and permit the party calling him to cross-examine him, he still has a discretion whether or not to allow the proving of previous inconsistent statements against him.[48]

(e) Previous inconsistent statements

We have seen that with a hostile witness, the judge can allow his previous inconsistent statements to be proved against him. Moreover, with an opposing witness being cross-examined, the cross-examining party has an automatic right to prove such statements.[49] The question now arises, if such previous statements are proved, what is the evidential value of them? Are they

---

[42] Before proof is allowed, the earlier statement must be put to the hostile witness and he must be asked whether or not he made it: Criminal Procedure Act 1865, s.5.

[43] As to this, see *post* p. 259.

[44] *Rice* v. *Howard* (1886) 16 Q.B.D. 681.

[45] But see *per* Lord Goddard C.J. in *R.* v. *Fraser and Warren* (1956) 40 Cr.App.R. 160.

[46] *Price* v. *Manning* (1889) 42 Ch.D. 372.

[47] *R.* v. *Powell* [1985] Crim.L.R. 592. If hostility emerges at committal proceedings, the prosecution may defer making application until the trial: *R.* v. *Mann* (1972) 56 Cr.App.R. 750.

[48] Criminal Procedure Act 1865, s.3; *R.* v. *Booth* (1981) 74 Cr.App.R. 123.

[49] Criminal Procedure Act 1865, s.4.

evidence in their own right, or is their effect limited to demolishing the witness's contrary evidence in court? If W, who is ruled hostile, says that P was not present on some occasion, and if it is proved that on an earlier occasion, W said that P *was* present, is there now some evidence that P was present? First, if this earlier statement is put to W in cross-examination and he admits it is true, clearly it *is* evidence of the fact stated. Second, even if he does not admit its truth, if W is a party, the earlier statement may be used by his opponent as an admission.[50] But in all other cases, the position at common law is that the statement is not independent evidence, but at most merely demolishes the contrary statement made by W in the box. It is for the jury, not the judge, to say whether it has this effect,[51] but if that is its effect, it is its only effect. "If by cross-examination as to credit you prove that a man's oath cannot be relied on and he has sworn that he did not go to Rome on May 1, you do not, therefore, prove that he did go to Rome on May 1; there is simply no evidence on the point."[52]

This is still the position in criminal cases. Thus in *R. v. White*[53] W was charged with riot. Various Crown witnesses testified that W was not implicated in the riot. The Crown was given leave to treat them as hostile, and proved that they had previously told the police that W was implicated. The judge told the jury that they could choose between what the witnesses said now and what they had earlier said to the police. The jury, evidently preferring the earlier statements, convicted, but the conviction was quashed. A jury is quite entitled to disbelieve the witnesses when they now say W was not implicated, and it is their previous inconsistent statements which will persuade the jury to disbelieve them; but it is not entitled to believe and act on the previous statements that he *was* implicated. There is just no admissible evidence that he was implicated. The reason for this is that the earlier statements to the police are hearsay evidence and so inadmissible as evidence of the facts in them.[54]

Acting on the previous statement for one purpose but disregarding it for another may be child's play for a lawyer but is a difficult intellectual feat for laymen, including jurors. The aim of reformers has been to end these mental gymnastics by providing that once a piece of information is properly before the court it is

[50] On Admissions, see *post*, Chap. 13.
[51] *R. v. Thomas* [1985] Crim.L.R. 445.
[52] *Hobbs v. Tinling* [1929] 2 K.B.1, *per* Scrutton L.J. at p. 29.
[53] (1922) 12 Cr.App.R. 60. See also *R. v. Golder* [1960] 3 All E.R. 457, which reviews the authorities.
[54] On hearsay, see *post*, Chap. 12.

taken into account for all purposes. In the present connection, this aim has been achieved for civil cases by section 3 of the Civil Evidence Act 1968. This provides that where a previous contradictory statement is used this way it shall be evidence of any fact stated therein of which direct oral evidence by the witness would be admissible. Thus, in a civil case, if W is ruled hostile and says that P was not present, then according to section 3 of the 1865 Act, he may with leave of the judge be contradicted by proving his previous statement that P was there. Section 3 of the 1968 Act allows this statement to be used as evidence that P was present. Moreover, section 2 of the 1968 Act, a much more general section which makes most out-of-court statements admissible in civil cases, allows the use of previous statements of any sort by any witness, subject to conditions, chief of which is the leave of the court. This means that the previous inconsistent statements of a merely unfavourable witness are not only admissible, but evidence of the facts in them.

For criminal cases, a provision similar to section 3 of the 1968 Act was proposed,[55] but it was not enacted in the Police and Criminal Evidence Act 1984.[56] The position remains governed by the Criminal Procedure Act 1865, as interpreted in *Greenough* v. *Eccles* and by *R.* v. *White*. No previous statements, other than the admissions of a party, are ever evidence of the facts in them.

2. Cross-examination

This is the hostile questioning of the witnesses called by another party. When a witness has been intentionally called and sworn by any party,[57] any other party has the right, if the examination-in-chief has been either waived or closed, to cross-examine him.[58] It is not necessary that the evidence-in-chief should be *against* the cross-examining party.[59] The principle appears to be that any witness, other than in the exceptional cases mentioned in the next

---

[55] C.L.R.C.'s Draft Bill, cl. 33.
[56] Where documentary evidence is admitted under s.68, evidence tending to prove that the maker of the statement in the document made an inconsistent statement is admissible, but *only* for the purpose of showing that he has contradicted himself: Sched. 3, para. 3(*c*).
[57] Or if, on an originating summons, his affidavit has been read to the court; *Lindall* v. *Lindall* [1967] 1 W.L.R. 143.
[58] Failure to allow it is a substantial miscarriage of justice: see *Blaise* v. *Blaise* [1969] P. 54.
[59] *R.* v. *Hilton* [1972] 1 Q.B. 421.

Examination of Witnesses 117

paragraph, may be cross-examined by any party who did not call him.[60]

But a witness called merely to produce a document, or to be identified, cannot be cross-examined; nor can one who has been called by mistake and whose examination has not substantially begun.[61] And, if a witness die, or become permanently incapacitated, before cross-examination, his evidence will be admissible, though its weight may be impaired.[62] A witness called by the judge or recalled by the judge after he has given evidence can only be cross-examined by leave of the judge.

(a) Objects and scope

"Cross-examination is a powerful and valuable weapon for the purposes of testing the veracity of a witness and the accuracy and completeness of his story. It is entrusted to the hands of counsel in the confidence that it will be used with discretion, and with due regard to the assistance to be rendered by it to the court, not forgetting at the same time the burden that is imposed on the witness." It must display a due "measure of courtesy to the witness which is by no means inconsistent with a skilful, yet powerful, cross-examination."[63]

Cross-examination is not confined to matters proved in chief, but may embrace all facts which are in issue or relevant, as well as those which, though otherwise irrelevant, tend to impeach credit. Leading questions may also be put, but the witness must not be misled by false assumptions or actual misstatements,[64] and the judge has a discretion to disallow any question which he considers to be improper or oppressive.[65] Failure to cross-examine a witness will generally amount to an acceptance of his version of a transaction.[66] The cross-examination of accused persons is subject to special rules.[67]

---

[60] *Murdoch v. Taylor* [1965] A.C. 574 at p. 584; *Re Baden's Deed Trusts* [1967] i W.L.R. 1457; *R. v. Hilton supra*; *Cross*, p. 278.
[61] *Clifford v. Hunter* (1827) 3 C. & P. 16; *Wood v. Mackinson* (1840) 2 M. & R. 273.
[62] *R. v. Doolin* (1832) Jebb C.C. 123.
[63] Per Hanworth M.R., cited with approval by Sankey L.C., in *Mechanical, etc. Inventions v. Austin* [1935] A.C. 346 at p. 359.
[64] See the rules as to cross-examination approved by the Bar Council in 1981: Archbold, App.C; Phipson, § 33–71.
[65] *R. v. Flynn* [1972] Crim.L.R. 438. This discretion is preserved as to criminal cases by Police & Criminal Evidence Act 1984, s.82(3).
[66] *Browne v. Dunn* (1869) 6 R. 67; *R. v. Hart* (1932) 23 Cr.App.R. 202; *R. v. Fenlon* (1980) 71 Cr.App.R. 307. But it is not an absolute rule, see *O'Connell v. Adams* [1973] Crim.L.R. 113. If the party failing to cross-examine on the point later calls contradictory evidence, his opponent will have the right to call rebutting evidence. See *ante*, p. 100.
[67] See *post*, pp. 221–236.

There are two objects of cross-examination, namely, to elicit evidence which is favourable to the questioner's case, and to cast doubt on the witness's evidence-in-chief. These are two quite separate objects, and, as far as the first is concerned, the normal rules of evidence apply just as in examination-in-chief. Just as a witness is not (normally) allowed to give hearsay evidence-in-chief, so he is not to be invited to give it in cross-examination.[68] Just as the Crown could not ask its own witness about an inadmissible confession made by the accused, neither can it cross-examine the accused or his witnesses about it.[69] "It is a complete mistake to think that a document which is otherwise inadmissible can be made admissible evidence simply because it is put to the accused person in cross-examination."[70]

But with the object of impeaching the witness's credibility, relevance and hearsay are largely ignored. Questions may be put to him in order to elicit his means of knowledge, opportunities of observation, reasons for recollection or belief, and any special circumstances affecting his ability to speak to the particular case; to expose the errors, omissions, inconsistencies or improbabilities in his story; as well as to prove his character, antecedents, associations and mode of life. This power to range far afield is subject to two things. One is the discretion of the judge to exclude any questions which he considers improper or offensive. The other is the rule that on these matters not actually in issue (which are usually called collateral matters) the witness's answer must be accepted as final.

(b) Finality on collateral matters

Although *questions* as to credit are not limited to matters relevant to the issues, the bringing of evidence is so limited, and

---

[68] R. v. *Thompson* [1912] 3 K.B. 19; *Beare* v. *Garrod* (1915) 85 L.J.K.B. 717. But in civil cases, the hearsay evidence will usually be admissible anyway under the Civil Evidence Act 1968, s.2 (see *post*, p. 259). The judge might therefore allow the matter to be proved by the hearsay answers of the witness being cross-examined.
[69] R. v. *Treacy* [1944] 2 All E.R. 229. But it may be used as a *basis* of cross-examination, *i.e.* without revealing to the jury the existence of the confession, counsel may found his questions on material in the confession: see R. v. *Rice* [1963] 1 Q.B. 857. He must not "flourish" the confession in the sight of the jury while doing so. R. v. *Yousry* (1914) 11 Cr.App.R. 13. See also R. v. *Tompkins* (1978) 62 Cr.App.R. 181. And if the inadmissible confession is relevant to the defence of a co-accused, he may cross-examine on it; R. v. *Rowson* [1986] Q.B. 174.
[70] R. v. *Treacy, supra*, at p. 236.

the cross-examining party cannot usually introduce evidence of matters not relevant to the issues merely in order to contradict a witness's answers on credit.[71] The trial would never end if such collateral issues had to be thrashed out, and the central issue between the parties would be buried beneath a mountain of irrelevancies. There are some exceptions to the rule of finality, where a witness can be contradicted on collateral matters, as to which see below; but it is important to note that the rule itself applies only to collateral matters. Matters actually in issue may be pursued to the bitter end. Whether a matter is relevant or collateral is not always easy to tell. The test is usually said to be, could the cross-examining party introduce evidence on the matter if the witness had never given evidence at all?[72] If yes, it is relevant to the issue; if no, it is collateral, admissible only to discredit the witness being cross-examined, and so impossible to be pursued further, unless one of the exceptions mentioned in the next section applies.

This test usually, but not invariably, yields satisfactory results. If a bystander witness to a road accident is known to have been sacked for dishonesty, that has an obvious relevance to his credit as a witness. Equally obviously, the opposing party could not call as part of his case about the accident evidence that it took place in sight of someone who had recently been sacked for dishonesty. That is as irrelevant as anything could be, and the rule that the party can ask the witness about his sacking but not prove it is clearly both just and convenient. But it is neither so just nor so convenient if contradicting an important witness would strongly indicate that the whole of his evidence is untrue. Merely showing an incentive or propensity to lie, or even that the witness *has* lied by denying the matter put to him on his credit, is not shewing anything which could be shewn as part of the cross-examining party's case, and therefore falls foul of the traditional test. However, the rule is not without exceptions, and in many cases the untruth may spring from the witness's partiality, or life-long habit of lying, or from medical incapacity. In such cases, the evidence in contradiction is allowed under one of the exceptions to the rule of finality (see next section).

Some of the clearest examples of the distinction between relevant and collateral matters occur in cases of rape and indecent assault. If the defence is that the complainant consented, she may be asked in cross-examination (i) about her previous connection

---

[71] *Harris* v. *Tippett* (1811) 2 Camp. 637.
[72] See *per* Pollock C.B. in *Att.-Gen.* v. *Hitchcock* (1847) 1 Exch. 91 at p. 99.

with the accused,[73] and (ii) her previous connection with other men. If she denies such, (i) may be rebutted by evidence but (ii) may not.[74] This is because her previous sexual relationships with the accused have a bearing on the question of whether she consented on the occasion in question, but her relationships with other men can have no bearing on this question. At most they affect her credit as a witness, and in many cases they can only do that on one or other of the now discredited views that because a person is sexually experienced, she is likely to have consented to intercourse on any particular occasion, or is unlikely to tell the truth on oath.

Because these views are discredited, and because of the distress caused to complainants by having their sexual history explored in open court, this particular instance of cross-examination as to credit and evidence of collateral matters has been affected by statute. Section 2 of the Sexual Offences (Amendment) Act 1976 prohibits in prosecutions for a rape offence[75] questions or evidence on the sexual experience of a complainant with third parties, unless the judge thinks that that prohibition is unfair to the defendant, when he must give leave. The judge can of course only give leave if the evidence or questions would be admissible at common law. His task is an awkward one[76] because the accused can only adduce evidence on the matter at common law if it goes to the issue of consent, and if it does, the demand of a fair trial would suggest that he must always be given leave. Moreover, questioning purely as to credit does not always rely for its effectiveness on the discredited opinions. As a result of *R. v. Viola*,[77] it seems that if the sexual experience with others is actually relevant to the issues, leave should almost always be given. If it is only relevant to credit (when no *evidence* would be allowed at common law anyway) leave to ask about it in cross-examination may be given if the expected answers would tend to show strongly that the complainant is not telling the truth about the particular occasion in question. But leave will not be given as to questions which are designed to form the basis of the unspoken

---

[73] *R. v. Riley* (1887) 18 Q.B.D. 481.
[74] *R. v. Holmes* (1871) 12 Cox 137. She may also be asked, and contradicted by evidence if she denies, whether she is a prostitute or widely promiscuous and in the habit of having intercourse with first acquaintances: *R. v. Bashir* [1969] 1 W.L.R. 1303; *R. v. Krausz* (1973) 57 Cr.App.R. 466.
[75] *i.e.* rape, attempted rape, aiding, abetting, counselling or procuring rape or attempted rape: s.7(2).
[76] See Elliott, "Rape Complainants' Sexual Experience with Third Parties" [1984] Crim.L.R. 4.
[77] (1982) 75 Cr.App.R. 125 (C.A.).

comment, "Well, there you are, members of the jury, that is the sort of girl she is."[78]

(c) Cases where answers on collateral matters are not final

We have seen[79] that previous inconsistent statements may be proved against an opposing or hostile witness who does not admit their truth. Since by sections 4 and 5 of the Criminal Procedure Act 1865, these must be "relative to the subject matter of the indictment or proceeding," they are perhaps not cases of collateral matters being proved.[80] The following, however, are clearly exceptions to the rule of finality.

(i) *Previous convictions*. It may obviously be relevant to a witness's credit that he has been convicted of an offence, especially if the offence is perjury or some other fraudulent crime. It by no means follows that it is always so relevant.[81] However, section 6 of the Criminal Procedure Act 1865 allows any witness in *any* proceedings, to be asked whether he has been convicted of *any* offence and if he does not admit it, to have the conviction proved against him. The reason why contradiction is allowed is that the truth is so easy to establish—one simply puts in a certificate of conviction signed by the proper court officer.[82] However this is all subject to special rules about witnesses who are accused persons, which will be dealt with later[83] and also to the provisions of Rehabilitation of Offenders Act 1974, as to "spent" convictions. In civil proceedings, cross-examination on such is prohibited by section 4(1). Criminal proceedings are excepted by section 7, but the general intention of Parliament should be given effect to by counsel not referring to a spent conviction if it can reasonably be avoided, and never without first obtaining the leave of the judge.[84]

---

[78] *Per* May J. in *R. v. Lawrence* [1977] Crim.L.R. 492, approved in *R. v. Viola*.
[79] *Ante*, p. 114.
[80] But see Cross, p. 284.
[81] In *R. v. Sweet-Escott* (1971) 55 Cr.App.R. 316, a trial for perjury, Lawton J. held that certain old convictions which the accused, as a witness in an earlier proceeding, had denied in a cross-examination as to credit could not possibly have affected his credit in the eyes of the tribunal, so that the false denial was not "material" within the meaning of the Perjury Act 1911, s.1(1).
[82] Criminal Procedure Act 1865, s.6, as to civil cases. As to criminal cases, see Police and Criminal Evidence Act 1984, s.73.
[83] *Post*, Chap. 11.
[84] *Practice Note* [1975] 2 All E.R. 1072. Failing to ask for leave is not a ground for upsetting a conviction if the judge gives a strong direction to leave the spent conviction out of account: *R. v. Smallman* [1982] Crim.L.R. 175; and anyway leave should be given in an appropriate case, *e.g.* where in a case of assault, there was a head-on collision between the evidence of the accused and the

(ii) *Bias or partiality.* The fact that a witness is biased against one of the parties is obviously relevant to his credit. One would not, however, think that the bias of a witness was material to the issues but merely collateral.[85] However the matter is felt to be too important to the tribunal of fact not to be pursued fully. "A witness may be asked how he stands affected towards one of the parties; and if his relation towards them is such as to prejudice his mind, and fill him with sentiments of revenge or other feelings of a similar kind, and if he denies the fact, evidence may be given to show the state of his mind and feelings."[86] A witness is biased or partial if he is prepared to go to the length of cheating to further one side's cause, such as accepting[87] or offering to take a bribe,[88] "schooling" witnesses,[89] threatening the other party's witnesses,[90] or while duly remaining outside court while opposing witnesses are giving evidence, using a "spy" in court to report to him what they said.[91] A witness may also be contradicted if he denies being in such a relationship with a party that bias or partiality, either for or against him, might reasonably be expected.[92]

(iii) *Reputation for untruthfulness.* Independent evidence may be given that an adversary's (but not a party's own) witness bears such a general reputation for untruthfulness that he is unworthy of credit upon his oath. In theory, it seems that such evidence should relate to general reputation only, and not express the mere opinion of the impeaching witness, but in practice the question may be shortened thus: "From your knowledge of the witness, would you believe him on his oath?"[93] The impeaching witness is not allowed in his examination-in-chief, to give reasons for this opinion, although he may be cross-examined as to such reasons.[94]

---

complainant, both outwardly respectable but with the complainant having a spent conviction for theft: *R.* v. *Paraskeva* (1982) 76 Cr.App.R. 162.
[85] See Geoffrey Lane L.J. in *R.* v. *Mendy* (1976) 64 Cr.App.R. 4.
[86] *Att.-Gen.* v. *Hitchcock*, (1847) 1 Exch. 91 at p. 99.
[87] *Ibid.*
[88] *R.* v. *Denley* [1970] Crim.L.R. 583, but not *being offered* a bribe: *Att.-Gen.* v. *Hitchcock, supra.*
[89] See *R.* v. *Phillips* (1936) 26 Cr.App.R. 17, where the witnesses were children "schooled" by their mother.
[90] *R.* v. *Busby* (1982) 75 Cr.App.R. 79.
[91] *R.* v. *Mendy, supra.*
[92] *Dunn* v. *Aslet* (1838) 2 Moo. & R. 122; *Thomas* v. *David* (1836) 7 C. & P. 350.
[93] *R.* v. *Watson* (1817) 2 Stark. 116 at p. 152; *R.* v. *Brown* (1867) L.R. 1 C.C.R. 70.
[94] *R.* v. *Richardson* [1969] 1 Q.B. 299.

Examination of Witnesses

(iv) *Unsoundness of mind or other disability.* Expert evidence is allowed of a witness's incapability of giving a true or reliable account by reason of unsoundness of mind, or other disability, *e.g.* short-sightedness.[95] However with a witness who is capable of giving reliable evidence, it is not allowed to call psychiatric evidence to indicate that he might well not be doing so on the present occasion.[96] That is for the jury, suitably warned, to decide.[97]

(v) *Police and Criminal Evidence Act 1984, Sched. 3, para. 3(b).* In criminal cases, where a document containing a hearsay statement is admitted under section 68,[98] the credibility of the maker of the statement may be impeached, with the leave of the court, by the admission of evidence of collateral matters, *i.e.* matters which, if he had appeared as a witness, could have been put to him in cross-examination, but of which evidence could not have been adduced. Normally the maker will be unavailable as a witness, and this provision to some extent compensates for the opposing party's inability to cross-examine him. However there is no similar relaxation of the rule of finality in analogous situations in civil cases where hearsay statements are proved by virtue of section 2 and section 4 of the Civil Evidence Act 1968.[99]

3. Re-examination

Whenever there has been cross-examination, even upon inadmissible matters, the right to re-examine exists. Re-examination in general follows the same rules as examination-in-chief. It must, however, be confined to an explanation of matters arising in cross-examination, and no new facts may be introduced without the leave of the judge. Thus, where parts of a conversation had been elicited on cross-examination, distinct matters, though occurring in the same conversation, were rejected on re-examination.[1] This rule usually prevents a party from introducing inadmissible evidence on the pretext of dealing with matters

---

[95] *Toohey* v. *Metropolitan Police Commissioner* [1965] A.C. 595 at p. 608. This rule used to be part of, and subject to the conditions of, the rule about Reputation for Untruthfulness: *R.* v. *Gunewardene* [1951] 2 K.B. 600, overruled in *Toohey* v. *M.P.C., supra.*
[96] *R.* v. *MacKenny* (1981) 76 Cr.App.R. 271 (C.A.).
[97] On the scope of expert evidence see, *ante*, p. 23.
[98] See, *post*, p. 291.
[99] Civil Evidence Act 1968, s.7(1) Proviso, which sticks exactly to the finality rule. *Post*, p. 270.
[1] *Prince* v. *Samo* (1838) 7 A. & E. 627.

raised by the cross-examination, but cases may still arise in which the result of cross-examination is to let in in re-examination matters which could not be raised in examination-in-chief.[2]

4. Examination by Judge and Jury

A judge may put all such questions to a witness as the interests of justice require, and may base such questions not only on matters arising in the case, but on his own local or scientific knowledge.[3] So, to a limited extent, may the jury. But neither judge nor jury may ask inadmissible questions,[4] nor may the judge interpolate into an examination-in-chief or cross-examination questions so frequent as to diminish the effectiveness of the examination.[5]

> "The judge's part ... is to hearken to the evidence, only himself asking questions of witnesses when it is necessary to clear up any point that has been overlooked or left obscure; to see that the advocates behave themselves seemly and keep to the rules laid down by law; to exclude irrelevancies and discourage repetition; to make sure by wise intervention that he follows the points that the advocates are making and can assess their worth; and at the end to make up his mind where the truth lies. If he goes beyond this, he drops the mantle of a judge and assumes the robe of an advocate; and the change does not become him well."[6]

As to the judge's powers to call witnesses, "in civil cases the dispute is between the parties, and the judge keeps the ring, and the parties need not call hostile witnesses, but in criminal cases, the prosecution is bound to call all the material witnesses before the court, even though they may give inconsistent accounts, in order that the whole of the facts may be before the jury."[7] From this it will appear that in civil cases the judge has no right to call a witness[8] or to have regard to documents not in evidence[9] except

---

[2] See Cross, p. 285; *R. v. Nation* [1954] S.A.S.R. 189.
[3] *R. v. Antrim JJ.* [1895] 2 Ir.R. 603.
[4] *R. v. Ratcliffe* (1919) 14 Cr.App.R. 85; *R. v. Lillyman* [1896] 2 Q.B. 167.
[5] *Jones v. National Coal Board* [1957] 2 Q.B. 55; *R. v. Matthews* (1983) 78 Cr.App.R. 23.
[6] *Jones v. National Coal Board, supra, per* Denning L.J. at p. 64.
[7] *R. v. Harris* [1927] 2 K.B. 587, *per* Lord Hewart C.J. at p. 590; but see *R. v. Wheeler* [1967] 1 W.L.R. 1531.
[8] *Re Enoch* [1910] 1 K.B. 327.
[9] *Owen v. Nichol* [1948] 1 All E.R. 707.

with the consent of all parties.[10] In criminal cases, however, the judge may call any witness himself, especially if the jury desire it.[11] Indeed, it is the Crown's duty to secure the attendance of all witnesses who gave evidence at committal proceedings and whose names are on the back of the indictment; and to call them, unless in its discretion it thinks that the interests of justice would not be advanced by the calling of a particular witness.[12] If the Crown's decision not to call a witness appears to be dictated by oblique motives, the court has the ultimate sanction of calling the witness itself.[13]

On the late calling of witnesses, it has been said, "A little regularity about the conduct of criminal proceedings and trial on indictment is not unbecoming."[14] Witnesses for the Crown should not normally be called after the Crown's case has closed unless an unexpected point has arisen which could not have been foreseen[15]; and witnesses for the defence should not normally be called after the summing up has begun. But the rules are not a straitjacket and can be relaxed in a proper case. Thus the Crown has been allowed to call witnesses during the defence case, although their evidence was not in rebuttal.[16] The defence has been allowed to give evidence after the beginning of the summing up.[17] And although a judge sitting with a jury is not allowed to recall a witness once the defence case has closed,[18] a recorder sitting without a jury is entitled to recall a witness to refresh his memory on some point on which his note is unclear.[19] Once the summing up has been concluded, however, no further evidence

---

[10] *Re Enoch, supra.*
[11] *R. v. Chapman* (1838) 8 C. & P. 558; *R. v. Wallwork* (1958) 42 Cr.App.R. 153.
[12] *R. v. Oliva* [1965] 1 W.L.R. 1028; *R. v. Tregear* [1967] 2 Q.B. 574; *R. v. Sterk* [1972] Crim.L.R. 391; *R. v. Nugent* [1977] 1 W.L.R. 789. If the Crown is unable to secure the attendance of a witness, the judge has a discretion to allow the trial to proceed in his absence: *R. v. Cavanagh* [1972] 1 W.L.R. 676.
[13] *R. v. Oliva, supra.* This rule does not apply to committal proceedings it being entirely up to the prosecutor how he makes out a prima facie case. *R. v. Epping and Harlow JJ.* [1973] Q.B. 433. As to the judge's power to refuse to allow the Crown to offer no evidence at all, see *R. v. Broad* (1979) 68 Cr.App.R. 281.
[14] *Per* Cassels J. in *R. v. Browne* (1943) 29 Cr.App.R. 106 at p. 111.
[15] *R. v. Harris, supra; R. v. Day* (1940) 27 Cr.App.R. 168; *R. v. Browne, supra; R. v. Flynn* (1957) 42 Cr.App.R. 15. The position is the same with a witness called at the request of the jury to deal with a point made in the defence evidence. *R. v. McDowell* [1984] Crim.L.R. 486. On evidence in rebuttal, see *ante*, p. 99.
[16] *R. v. Doran* (1972) 56 Cr.App.R. 429.
[17] *R. v. Sanderson* (1953) 37 Cr.App.R. 32.
[18] *R. v. Sullivan* [1923] 1 K.B. 47.
[19] *Phelan v. Black* [1972] 1 W.L.R.

can be given by any witness[20] nor may real evidence be viewed out of court at this stage.[21]

D. Evidence given on Appeal

1. Civil Cases

On appeal, the court acts upon the evidence taken at the hearing.[22] There is a power in the Court of Appeal to hear further evidence,[23] but "when a litigant has obtained a judgment in a court of justice, be it a county court or one of the High Courts, he is by law entitled not to be deprived of that judgment without very solid grounds."[24] Moreover, "evidence not called at the trial is necessarily regarded with caution. It may be prompted or coloured by a knowledge of what has happened in the court below."[25] For these reasons the power to hear fresh evidence will only be invoked if the evidence could not have been obtained with reasonable diligence for use at the trial, would probably have had an important influence on the result of the trial, and is such as is presumably to be believed.[26] When the Court of Appeal does admit such evidence it does not usually decide the issue on this fresh evidence; it sends the case for a retrial.[27]

---

[20] R. v. Owen [1952] 2 Q.B. 362; R. v. Wilson (1957) 41 Cr.App.R. 226; Webb v. Leadbetter [1966] 1 W.L.R. 245. But if the fresh evidence was given at the request of the defence, an appeal may be dismissed under the proviso to s.2(1) of the Criminal Appeal Act 1968; R. v. Nixon [1968] 1 W.L.R. 577; compare R. v. Corless (1972) 56 Cr.App.R. 341.

[21] R. v. Lawrence [1968] 1 W.L.R. 341; R. v. Nixon, supra. For real evidence, see ante, p. 26.

[22] Ord. 59, r. 3; r. 9; r. 12.

[23] Ord. 59, r. 10. But a High Court judge does not have power to set aside the order of another High Court judge on the ground of fresh evidence. Re Barrell Enterprises [1973] 1 W.L.R. 19.

[24] Brown v. Dean [1910] A.C. 373, per Lord Loreburn at p. 374.

[25] Supreme Court Practice 1976, note to Ord. 59, r. 10; approved in Cowling v. Matbro [1969] 1 W.L.R. 598.

[26] Brown v. Dean, supra; Ladd v. Marshall [1954] 1 W.L.R. 1489; Skone v. Skone [1971] 1 W.L.R. 812 (H.L.): The same principles are applied by the Divisional Court in deciding whether to remit a case to a fresh bench of magistrates for a rehearing: Simm v. Simm [1968] 1 W.L.R. 125.

[27] Bills v. Roe [1968] 1 W.L.R. 925. As to the principles to be followed when the evidence is of facts which happened since the hearing in the court below, see Murphy v. Stone Wallwork [1969] 1 W.L.R. 1023.

2. Criminal Cases

Section 23 of the Criminal Appeal Act 1968 allows the Court of Appeal, on an appeal, to consider evidence which was not given at the trial. The court has, under section 2, power to allow the appeal and quash the conviction; but if the appeal is allowed only on the grounds of fresh evidence, then by section 7, the court may order a new trial. As to the hearing of fresh evidence, the court has a discretion in any case under section 23(1). However, it is provided by section 23(2) that unless the evidence appears not to afford any ground for allowing the appeal the court should hear it if (a) it appears to be credible[28] and would have been admissible at the trial,[29] and (b) there is a reasonable explanation for the failure to adduce it at the trial.[30] If the conditions mentioned in section 23(2) are present, the court is under a duty to receive the fresh evidence. "Nevertheless, public mischief would ensue and legal process could become infinitely prolonged were it the case that evidence produced at any time will generally be admitted by the court when verdicts are being reviewed."[31] Therefore the court, in considering whether to allow fresh evidence, bears in mind whether the proposed evidence would make the jury's verdict unsafe or unsatisfactory, and unless it would, refuses the application.[32]

However the conditions attaching to the court's *duty* under section 23(2) to admit fresh evidence do not apply to the court's *discretion* under section 23(1). If the court thinks it necessary or expedient, it may receive the evidence even if, for example, the proposed evidence could have been called at the trial.[33] But the court will always bear in mind the warnings quoted above from *R. v. Stafford and Luvaglio*[34]; and moreover will not usually be moved by change in the circumstances occurring after conviction;

---

[28] *i.e.* well capable of belief: *R. v. Parks* [1961] 1 W.L.R. 1484; *R. v. Beresford* (1971) 56 Cr.App.R. 143.

[29] See *R. v. Dallas* [1971] Crim.L.R. 90; *R. v. Lattimore* (1975) 62 Cr.App.R. 53 at p. 56.

[30] See *R. v. James* [1971] Crim.L.R. 477. An appellant is not debarred by the condition merely because he failed to apply for reporting restrictions to be lifted at the committal proceedings although it is due to that failure that the fresh evidence was not discovered in due time: *R. v. Nabarro* [1972] Crim.L.R. 497.

[31] *R. v. Stafford and Luvaglio* [1968] 3 All E.R. 752n, *per* Edmund Davies J. at p. 753. And see *R. v. Shields and Patrick* [1977] Crim.L.R. 281 where the Court deprecated an increasing tendency to treat the trial by jury as a preliminary skirmish rather than a trial.

[32] *Ibid.* and see *R. v. Beresford, supra*.

[33] *R. v. Merry* (1970) 54 Cr.App.R. 274.

[34] *R. v. Lattimore* (1975) 62 Cr.App.R. 53 at p. 56.

responding to such is for the Home Secretary, not the Court of Appeal.[35]

It must be borne in mind that the court's jurisdiction is subject to the proviso to section 2(1) of the Act, under which the court may dismiss any appeal if it thinks no miscarriage of justice has actually occurred, even if the point raised by the applicant is decided in his favour.

---

[35] *R.* v. *Melville* (1975) 62 Cr.App.R. 100 at p. 105; but see *R.* v. *Ireland* [1985] Crim.L.R. 367.

CHAPTER 7

WITNESSES

This chapter deals with who may and who must give evidence if called upon, and with when a witness may refuse to answer a particular question or produce a particular document.

A. Competence and Compellability

Subject to the exceptions mentioned below, every person is competent to give evidence, and compellable also. He may have a privilege which allows him to refuse to answer some particular question or to produce some particular document, but he must turn up and offer himself as a witness or run the risk of being committed for contempt. Privilege is dealt with in the next section of this chapter. This section deals with the exceptions to the general rule of competence and compellability.

1. Competence

(a) Miscellaneous cases of incompetence

The normal rule is that all evidence must be given on oath. Alternatives in the form of affirmation are allowed by statute,[1] but the normal rule remains that one who is not able to understand the obligation to speak the truth cannot give evidence. Ability to take the oath used also to require a belief in God, or an awareness of some kind of divine sanction for failure to tell the truth, but nowadays it is enough if the witness "has sufficient appreciation of the solemnity of the occasion, and the added responsibility to tell the truth which is involved in taking an oath, over and above the duty to tell the truth which is an ordinary duty of normal social conduct."[2] This was said in the case of a witness who was a child of tender years,[3] but the principle has been adopted in the case of an adult witness of limited mental capacity.[4]

In all cases, where competence is in doubt, the judge decides

---
[1] Oaths Act 1978, ss.5, 6. As to the form of oath or affirmation, see *ibid.* ss.1, 3 and 4; Children and Young Persons Act 1963, s.28.
[2] *R. v. Hayes* (1977) 64 Cr.App.R. 194, *per* Bridge L.J. at p. 196.
[3] See also *R. v. Campbell* [1983] Crim.L.R. 174.
[4] *R. v. Bellamy* (1985) 82 Cr.App.R. 222. For limited mental capacity affecting credibility rather than competence, see *ante*, p. 123.

the question after examining the witness, and any other witness as to his or her capacity, on *voir dire*. In a case of a child or a person of limited mental capacity, the examination ought to be in the presence of the jury, so that if he declares the witness competent, the jury will have heard material upon which to assess the witness's credibility.[5]

There is only one principal exception,[6] confined to criminal cases, where evidence not on oath may be given. Section 38 of the Children and Young Persons Act 1933 allows a child of tender age to give unsworn evidence in a criminal case, if the judge decides that he does not understand the oath but is sufficiently intelligent and understands the duty of telling the truth. This test seems virtually indistinguishable from the present day test of competence to give sworn evidence (see above). This does not mean that there is no practical difference involved between the sworn and unsworn evidence of such a child, because if the judge allows him to give unsworn evidence, the statute requires such evidence to be corroborated by some other, sworn, evidence.[7]

Until 1982, the accused was entitled to make an unsworn statement from the dock. This right was abolished by the Criminal Justice Act 1982, s.72, but an unrepresented accused may still address the court to the extent that his counsel could were he represented, and if he is convicted, he may make a statement in mitigation without being sworn.

Apart from incompetence dictated by the need for evidence to be given on oath, there are one or two other miscellaneous examples of incompetence[8]; or non-compellability[9]; but the

---

[5] *Toohey* v. *Metropolitan Police Commissioner* [1965] A.C. 595. But where the incompetence alleged was that the witness was the accused's spouse, the proper procedure was said to be to hold the enquiry in the absence of the jury: *R.* v. *Yacoob* (1981) 72 Cr.App.R. 313.

[6] Others are the Sovereign, a witness called merely to produce a document, and counsel explaining a case in which he acted as such. See Phipson, § 31–43.

[7] See *post*, p. 166.

[8] Judge, magistrates and jury in the case they are trying: see *R.* v. *Antrim J.J.* [1895] 2 Ir.R. 603.

[9] The Sovereign, foreign sovereigns, ambassadors and their suites, the staff of U.N.O. and other international organisations; Diplomatic Privileges Act 1964, s.2, Sched. 1; Diplomatic Immunities (Commonwealth Countries and Republic of Ireland) Act 1952, s.1; International Finance Corporation Act 1955, s.3; International Organisations Act 1968. A banker is not compellable to produce his books in any proceedings to which he is not a party: Bankers' Books Evidence Act 1879, s.6. See *post*, p. 283. An expert with no knowledge of the facts cannot be compelled to attend and give his opinion: *Seyfang* v. *Searle & Co.* [1973] Q.B. 148; *aliter* an expert who has examined exhibits and formed an opinion on them; *Harmony Shipping Co.* v. *Davis* [1979] 3 All E.R. 177 (C.A.).

important exceptions to the general rule of competence and compellability are found in criminal cases and revolve around the accused, his co-accused, and their spouses.

(b) The accused and his co-accused

(i) *As witnesses for the Crown*: At common law,[10] which is unaffected by any statutory provision, the accused and any person jointly tried with him[11] are incompetent as witnesses for the prosecution. Little need be said about the incompetency of the accused. As to a co-accused, he is one who is being jointly tried when the question of admitting his evidence arises.[12] It follows that he *is* competent if that position no longer obtains, if, *e.g.* proceedings against him have been dropped, or if he is being tried separately, or has already been acquitted,[13] or has pleaded guilty.[14] In the latter case, the judge ought to pass sentence at once, before the proposed witness gives evidence against the accused, so that he has nothing to hope for by colouring his evidence.[15] Even if he still has something to lose if he does not give evidence satisfactory to the Crown, this does not make him incompetent, nor is it "irregular" to call him[16]; though if the inducement operating on him is very powerful, the judge has a discretion to refuse to allow him to be called.[17] In any case, if the witness was an accomplice, a warning to the jury about the danger of acting on his uncorroborated evidence will have to be given.[18]

(ii) *As witnesses for the defence*: At common law an accused was not allowed to give evidence at all. The only concession which in later times crept in was that he could make an oral statement, without oath and without cross-examination, from the dock. This privilege was abolished in 1982.[19]

---

[10] R. v. *Rhodes* [1899] 1 Q.B. 77, 80.
[11] R. v. *Payne* (1872) L.R. 1 C.C.R. 349; R. v. *Richardson* (1967) 51 Cr.App.R. 381. See Gooderson, "The Evidence of Co-Prisoners" (1953) 11 C.L.J. 279.
[12] R. v. *Payne*, *supra*.
[13] See R. v. *Conti* (1973) 58 Cr.App.R. 387.
[14] R. v. *Tomey* (1909) 2 Cr.App.R. 329.
[15] R. v. *Payne* [1950] 1 All E.R. 102.
[16] R. v. *Turner, Shervill* (1975) 61 Cr.App.R. 67, disapproving of expressions to the contrary in R. v. *Pipe* (1967) 51 Cr.App.R. 17; R. v. *Pentonville Governors, ex. p. Schneider* (1981) 73 Cr.App.R. 200.
[17] R. v. *Turner, Shervill, supra*, where the fact that the witness might lose police protection for himself and his family if he did not give evidence satisfactory to the Crown was held to be not enough to prevent him being called.
[18] See *post*, Chap. 8.
[19] Criminal Justice Act 1982, s.72.

At length, the Criminal Evidence Act 1898, s.1 (see Appendix 1), made him a competent witness on his own behalf. This privilege is hedged about by restrictions and qualifications which will be dealt with later.[20] Here it is sufficient to say that if he does decide to give evidence, then as far as his co-accused is concerned, he becomes just like any other witness. Anything he says in favour of the co-accused, either in examination-in-chief or in cross-examination, enures for the benefit of that co-accused. But the other side of the coin is that anything the accused-witness says against his co-accused is evidence against him.[21] He may, by giving evidence against his co-accused, forfeit certain immunities of his own, but that is another story.[22]

It emerges from this, and indeed is specifically stated by the Act, section 1, that an accused is a competent witness for a co-accused. No accused is compellable,[23] but if accused A agrees, accused B can call him as a witness. Usually if A gives evidence for B, it is in the course of giving evidence for himself, but it is theoretically possible for A to act as a witness solely for B, and not for himself. But once he goes into the box, he can be cross-examined on his own defence anyway, so if he has much to hide he will be advised to stay away from the witness box.

Although no accused is compellable, and the Act purports only to give him a privilege which he may exercise or not as he sees fit, in practice most accused persons find it expedient to go into the box, even though they would rather remain in the dock. This is because, although the Act[24] prohibits Crown counsel from commenting on his failure to give evidence, the judge is not so prohibited, and in fact most judges do point out to the jury that in weighing the accused's defence they may take into account the fact that the accused has not seen fit to support it on oath and present himself for cross-examination. This is usually highly prejudicial to his chances of acquittal.[25] Moreover, counsel for a

---

[20] *Post*, Chap. 11.
[21] *R. v. Rudd* (1948) 32 Cr.App.R. 138 (examination-in-chief); *R. v. Paul* [1920] 2 K.B. 183 (cross-examination). *R. v. Paul*, in so far as it allowed a cross-examination of one accused which was solely directed at implicating the other accused, has been criticised as being inconsistent with the spirit of the rule that a co-accused is not competent for the Crown: *Young v. H.M. Advocate*, 1932 S.C.(J.) 63; and see Cross, p. 196.
[22] *Post*, Chap. 11.
[23] Criminal Evidence Act 1898, s.1, proviso (*a*).
[24] *Ibid*. proviso (*b*).
[25] As to the limits on the judge's freedom to comment, see *R. v. Sparrow* [1973] 1 W.L.R. 488, *post*, p. 189.

co-accused cannot be precluded from commenting on the accused's failure to testify.[26]

(c) The accused's spouse[27]

(i) *For the Crown*. Subject to some exceptions, at common law an accused's spouse was incompetent to give evidence for the prosecution. Now, however, by the Police and Criminal Evidence Act 1984, s.80(1)(*a*), a spouse is competent to give evidence for the prosecution in any criminal proceedings. The only exception is where husband and wife are jointly charged with an offence: section 80(4). In such a case she is incompetent for the Crown unless she is not, or is no longer, liable to be convicted of that offence at the trial as a result of pleading guilty or for any other reason. Thus if H and W are jointly charged with theft, if W pleads guilty, or if her trial is put back, she is competent for the Crown, but not otherwise. If H and W are charged with different offences, *e.g.* H with theft and W with handling, the exception in section 80(4) does not apply because they are not jointly charged with an offence: however they are each in the position of an accused and are incompetent on that account anyway.[28]

(ii) *For the defence*. In any criminal proceedings a spouse is competent to give evidence on behalf of the accused or any person jointly charged with the accused: section 80(1)(*b*). This remains the case even if the spouse is also charged in the same proceedings.[29]

2. Compellability

The general rule is that anyone who is competent to give evidence is also compellable.[30] However an accused person and his spouse are exceptional in this regard. The accused's position is expressly stated to be one of competence only.[31] A spouse is compellable for her husband: section 80(2), except where she is jointly charged with an offence. Subject to the same exception she is, by section

---

[26] R. v. *Whickham* (1971) 55 Cr.App.R. 199.
[27] For convenience, the spouse will be referred to as female, but, *mutatis mutandis*, the position is the same in respect of a husband's evidence at his wife's trial.
[28] See *ante*, p. 131.
[29] The exception in s.80(4) applies to competence under s.80(1)(*a*), but not to competence under s.80(1)(*b*).
[30] For miscellaneous cases of non-compellability, see *ante*, p. 130, n. 9.
[31] Criminal Evidence Act 1898, s.1, proviso (*a*). For the *practical* reasons why an accused finds it expedient to give evidence, see *ante*, p. 132.

80(3), compellable for the prosecution or for a co-accused if and only if:

> "(a) the offence charged involves an assault on, or injury or a threat of injury to, the wife or husband of the accused or a person who was at the material time under the age of 16; or
> (b) the offence charged is a sexual offence alleged to have been committed in respect of a person who was at the material time under that age; or
> (c) the offence charged consists of attempting or conspiring to commit, or of aiding, abetting, counselling, procuring or inciting the commission of, an offence falling within paragraph (a) or (b)."

For the purposes of section 80(3), the age of any person at the material time shall be deemed to be or to have been that which it appears to the court to be or to have been his age at that time: section 80(6). Neither in cases of assault or injury under section 80(3)(a), nor in cases of a sexual offence under section 80(3)(b) does the young person have to be a relation of the accused or living in the same household. Moreover, section 80(3)(a), which speaks of an offence which "involves" an assault or an injury or a threat of injury to the spouse or a person under 16, apparently covers accidental injury, *e.g.* reckless driving resulting in injury to either of those persons, in which case the spouse would be compellable for the prosecution or a co-accused.

If a spouse does elect to give evidence, her incompetence for the Crown does not prevent her evidence in chief[32] or in cross-examination[33] being used against either accused or co-accused. She becomes like any other witness, but if *competent* only, she must be told before she starts that she is non-compellable.[34]

The fact that the spouse is competent or compellable does not of course mean that she must be called, and if she is not, that fact cannot be made the subject of any comment by the prosecution: section 80(8). Neither the judge nor counsel for a co-accused are prohibited from commenting, and indeed if comment is wrongly made by the Crown, it is the judge's duty to counteract that by comment of his own, even if he privately feels the Crown's comment was justified, in the sense that it corresponds with what he might have said himself.[35]

---

[32] R. v. *Rudd*, (1948) 32 Cr.App.R. 138. See *ante*, p. 132, n. 21.
[33] R. v. *Paul* [1920] 2 K.B. 183.
[34] R. v. *Pitt* [1983] Q.B. 25.
[35] R. v. *Naudeer* [1984] 3 All E.R. 1036.

B. Public Interest Protection and Privilege

Because a witness is competent and compellable to give evidence, it does not follow that he will be obliged or indeed allowed to answer questions about some particular matter or to produce some particular document. He may be prevented from giving, or excused from giving, evidence on some relevant matter because some public interest, which is regarded as outweighing the need for all available evidence to be disclosed, is better served by non-disclosure.

The public interest in having all relevant evidence made available to a court when it is disposing of an issue is obvious. But it is not paramount, and it has always been recognised that under our law relevant evidence may nevertheless be inadmissible. Thus some evidence, *e.g.* hearsay evidence,[36] and evidence of criminal propensity in an accused person,[37] has an element of untrustworthiness or undue prejudice which outweighs its utility.[38] Again, the need for advocates to be fully briefed requires that what their clients say to them in the course of briefing should be protected.[39] The public interest in encouraging parties to settle their quarrels without recourse to litigation requires that admissions made by them while trying to reach a settlement should not be proved against them.[40] These are cases of the general public interest in the administration of justice being allowed to outweigh the interests of parties to a particular action,[41] but other public interests may be similarly decisive. The public interest in the detection of crime, or in the due working of the organs of government, or in the maintenance of national security may all require the non-disclosure of certain matters. This non-disclosure may well work injustice to a litigant by depriving him of vital evidence, but he has no redress. This makes it all the more important that the countervailing public interest which robs him of a rightful verdict is indeed a weighty one. Thwarting him (and the public interest in full disclouse of *all* relevant evidence) requires a convincing demonstration of an even higher public interest.[42] Thus it is settled that the mere fact that information has

---

[36] *Post,* Chap. 12.
[37] *Post,* Chap. 11.
[38] See the speech of Lord Simon of Glaisdale in *D.* v. *National Society for the Prevention of Cruelty to Children* [1978] A.C. 171 at p. 231.
[39] *Post,* p. 144.
[40] *Post,* p. 276.
[41] Lord Simon, *op. cit.* p. 232.
[42] See Lord Edmund-Davies in *D.* v. *N.S.P.C.C., supra,* p. 242; and Lord Hailsham, *ibid.* p. 223.

been communicated by one person to another in confidence is not enough.[43] Although the enforced betrayal of confidences may be unpleasing to an ethical person, confidentiality on its own gets no protection from the law of evidence[44]; there must be in addition some other public interest in non-disclosure.

Some of the cases where evidence is excluded are not usually thought of as involving public interest and are usually dealt with elsewhere, as they are in this book.[45] "But in reality they constitute a spectrum, refractions of the single light of a public interest which may outshine that of the desirability that all relevant evidence should be adduced in a court of law."[46] Some cases are, however, traditionally dealt with under the rubric "public interest and privilege"; and "public interest" is usually distinguished from "privilege." It is a convenience for them to be given distinct treatment, because matters subsumed under "public interest" are those where, *e.g.* the safety or well-being of the State is directly affected, whereas "privilege" covers matters which *directly* affect only the particular litigant or witness, *e.g.* the privilege as to legal advisers or the privilege against self-crimination.[47] This difference means that, with the former class, the claim for exclusion of evidence cannot be waived by the party or witness,[48] and no secondary evidence of the excluded matter is allowed[49]; whereas with the latter class, the person entitled to the privilege may waive it, and even if he does not, his opponent is allowed to prove the matter by other witnesses.[50] But although these differences justify separate treatment, it is a mistake to think of them as watertight, non-extensible doctrines. The whole

---

[43] *Alfred Crompton Amusement Machines Ltd.* v. *Customs and Excise Commissioners (No. 2)* [1974] A.C. 405, pp. 433–434; *D.* v. *N.S.P.C.C., supra,* pp. 218, 237, 246.
[44] "After all, an attempt to bribe is generally made confidentially": *per* Lord Simon, *ibid.* p. 238.
[45] Chaps. 11–14.
[46] Lord Simon, *op. cit.* p. 233.
[47] See Lord Simon, *op. cit.* p. 234.
[48] *R.* v. *Lewes JJ.* [1973] A.C. 388. It is perhaps an open question whether waiver is possible by or for the supplier of the confidential information. Lord Cross, *obiter* in *Alfred Crompton Amusement Machines Ltd.* v. *Customs & Excise (No. 2)* [1974] A.C. 405, at p. 434, said that there may be waiver in such a case: see also Lord Denning M.R. in *Neilson* v. *Laugharne* [1981] 1 Q.B. 736 at p. 747, and in *Campbell* v. *Tameside M.B.C.* [1982] Q.B. 1065 at p. 1073; but Lord Cross's dictum was not followed by Lawton L.J. in *Hehir* v. *C.P.M.* [1982] 1 W.L.R. 715; and Brightman L.J., *ibid.*, reserved his position on the point. The ratio of *Hehir* is that the Crown cannot waive the protection in order to cross-examine the maker of the protected statement.
[49] *Chatterton* v. *Secretary of State for India* [1895] 2 Q.B. 189.
[50] *Lloyd* v. *Mostyn* (1842) 10 M. & W. 478 at p. 481; *Calcraft* v. *Guest* [1898] 1 Q.B. 759; *Rumping* v. *D.P.P.* [1964] A.C. 814.

subject rests on public interest, and sufficiently important interests are identified in the light of public policy, which, although it must always be handled cautiously by judges, is capable of development.[51] Indeed the matters subsumed under "public interest" in this book have developed so much in recent years that it is no longer appropriate to give them their former rubric of "state privilege."[52]

1. Public Interest Protection

(a) National security and public functions

It has always been recognised that the safety of the State and the due working of the public service outweigh the interests of any particular litigant, and if these public interests are or may be threatened by the disclosure of any particular matter or the production of any particular document, such will not be disclosed or produced. It makes no difference in principle whether the official department claiming non-disclosure is or is not a party to the litigation.

There are many illustrations concerning national security. Examples are, communications between the governor of a colony and the Secretary of State,[53] a report of a military court to the commander-in-chief as to the conduct of an officer[54]; confidential reports upon which the Home Secretary made a detention order under regulation 18B of the Defence of the Realm Regulations 1939[55]; documents relating to the details of the construction of a submarine[56]; and government plans relating to the conduct of a military campaign in the First World War.[57] Although foreign state privilege as such is unknown to English law, there is a recognised public interest arising out of comity, protecting confidential documents to or from a foreign sovereign or

---

[51] *Mirehouse* v. *Rennell* (1833) 1 Cl. & F. 527 at p. 546; *Fender* v. *St. John-Mildmay* [1938] A.C. 1 at p. 38; *D.* v. *N.S.P.C.C.* [1978] A.C. 171 at p. 235.
[52] But Lord Scarman in *Science Research Council* v. *Nassé* [1980] A.C. 1028 at p. 1087, regretted the passing of the term "Crown privilege," which at least served to indicate the very restricted area of the protection and confined it to the realm of public affairs only.
[53] *Hennessy* v. *Wright* (1888) 21 Q.B.D. 509; *Chatterton* v. *Secretary of State for India*, supra.
[54] *Home* v. *Bentinck* (1820) 2 Brod. & B. 130; *Beatson* v. *Skene* (1860) 5 H. & N. 838.
[55] *R.* v. *Secretary of State, ex p. Lees* [1941] 1 K.B. 72.
[56] *Duncan* v. *Cammell, Laird & Co. Ltd.* [1942] A.C. 624.
[57] *Asiatic Petroleum Co. Ltd.* v. *Anglo-Persian Oil Co. Ltd.* [1916] 1 K.B. 822.

concerning the interests of a foreign state in connection with a territorial dispute.[58]

The due working of the public service is a more controversial matter. It is often claimed that this requires the utmost candour in officials in their interdepartmental communications, in their advice to Ministers, and in reports to them from agents and members of the public. This candour will be inhibited, and the public service will suffer, it is said, unless the persons making such communications can be absolutely assured of complete secrecy at all times. On this ground protection may be claimed for a document which is harmless enough in itself, but which belongs to a class all of which must be protected, if the public interest is not to suffer. For example, in *Conway v. Rimmer*,[59] a case of malicious prosecution brought by a probationary police constable against his superintendent, the plaintiff wished to see routine reports on his progress made between his superiors. No doubt, the disclosure of this trifling matter would not cause the utter ruination of the police service, but it was objected that unless all internal memoranda were protected, the efficiency of the police service would inevitably decline. This "inhibition of candour" argument used to be accepted uncritically by the Courts. However, it was rejected in *Conway v. Rimmer*, which dealt it a blow from which it has never recovered,[60] at any rate so far as concerns reports made by officials under a duty to do so. As Lord Reid pointed out,[61] no doubt they will continue to do their duty, even if there is a remote chance of their memoranda seeing the light of day at some time in the future. But with voluntary reports by the public it is different, and the inhibition of candour argument is still accepted. The reason is of course that members of the public may well not bother to report, unless assured of secrecy. In *R. v. Lewes JJ.*,[62] protection was given on this ground to reports by individuals to the Gaming Board on the question of the suitability of applicants for a gaming licence.

The protection used to cover organs of central government only, but it has become recognised in recent years that it is the *public function* in which there is a public interest in protecting, not just the civil service or military authorities; and this public function may sometimes be entrusted to a non-government

---

[58] *Buttes Gas & Oil Co. v. Hammer (No. 3)* [1981] Q.B. 223 (C.A.).
[59] [1968] A.C. 910.
[60] See Lord Salmon in *Science Research Council v. Nassé* [1980] A.C. 1028 at p. 1070.
[61] [1968] A.C. at p. 952.
[62] [1973] A.C. 388. See also *D. v. N.S.P.C.C.* [1978] A.C. 171.

Public Interest Protection and Privilege 139

functionary. It ought to make no difference in this matter of protection *who* exercises the function; the question is, is the function a public one?[63] Thus the Gaming Board was allowed to claim in *R.* v. *Lewes JJ.*,[64] a local authority in respect of case records of boarded-out foster children in *Re D (Infants)*,[65] and the Cheshire Police Force in *Conway* v. *Rimmer*.[66] In *D.* v. *N.S.P.C.C.*,[67] the N.S.P.C.C., a private society, was exercising a function which it shares with other, public, bodies, that of enforcing the legislation protecting children from cruelty. A complaint by a member of the public to it was held to be protected from disclosure.[68]

Although the claim may be made by such non-governmental persons, if the matter comes within the sphere of some Minister of the Crown it will be appropriate if objection is taken by the Attorney-General on his behalf, supported by the Minister's certificate as to why he thinks that disclosure would be prejudicial to the public interest. This has the advantage that the court will have the assistance of a carefully considered and authoritative opinion at an appropriately high level.[69] But it is not true, as was once thought[70] that a ministerial certificate in proper form is binding on the court.

That view was rejected by the House of Lords in *Conway* v. *Rimmer*,[71] and it is now clear that the Court must decide whether the prejudice likely to the public interest is such as to outweigh the injustice done to the individual litigant if production is withheld. Moreover the Court has the power to inspect the documents privately in order to make up its mind on the matter, and indeed it will be rare for a Court to be able properly to come to a conclusion without inspection.[72] The view was expressed in *Conway* v. *Rimmer* that documents in certain exalted spheres, such as Cabinet minutes, reports from ambassadors, communications between Ministers, or between Ministers and their advisors, on the formulation or exercise of high Government policy, would

---

[63] Lord Simon in *D.* v. *N.S.P.C.C.* [1978] A.C. 236.
[64] [1973] A.C. 388.
[65] [1970] 1 W.L.R. 599; see also *Gaskin* v. *Liverpool C.C.* [1980] 1 W.L.R. 1549.
[66] [1968] A.C. 910.
[67] *Supra.*
[68] Similarly with a complaint to the Law Society causing it to invoke its statutory power to intervene in the practice of a solicitor by reason of suspicion of his dishonesty: *Buckley* v. *Law Society* (No. 2) [1984] 3 All E.R. 313.
[69] *R.* v. *Lewes JJ., supra,* at p. 406.
[70] *Duncan* v. *Cammell Laird* [1942] A.C. 624.
[71] [1968] A.C. 910.
[72] But for a case where a judge was held right to protect documents without inspecting them, see *Gaskin* v. *Liverpool C.C.* [1980] 1 W.L.R. 1549.

never be disclosed until they became of merely historical interest; but that case, although in many respects the foundation of the present law, is not the last word on the subject, and from later House of Lords cases it appears that even documents in these classes are not assured of automatic protection, or immunity from being weighed in the balance.[73] However, if disclosure is ordered, the Crown must always have an opportunity of appealing before disclosure is actually made.[74]

The factors which ought to be weighed in the balance include not only the fact that the matters sought to be disclosed relate to high Government policy (*i.e.* the factor which used to be thought to be enough to confer automatic immunity); but also the relative importance of disclosure in the context of the whole case of the party seeking disclosure[75]; the availability of the information from other sources[76]; the likelihood of reports from informants drying up if they are not assured of complete confidentiality[77]; the fact that non-disclosure would in practice involve protecting wrong-doers[78]; the fact that the purposes of a statutory or Government enquiry will be frustrated if protection is not granted.[79] It is difficult and probably undesirable to compile a complete list of such factors.

This weighing of competing factors for and against disclosure means that the adjudication on a claim for protection is virtually indistinguishable from the exercise of a discretion.[80] A possible source of confusion here is that many of the reported cases in this area concern the discretionary remedy of Discovery, as to which see below. Discovery rests on a different discretion, which however often turns on the same kinds of factor as are involved in the process of weighing public interest against private right.

Discovery. A party hoping to make use at the trial of documents not in his own possession will almost invariably need to see them before trial. If they are in the possession of his opponent the

---

[73] *Burmah Oil* v. *Bank of England* [1980] A.C. 1090; *Air Canada* v. *Sec. of State for Trade* [1983] 2 A.C. 394. Two overseas cases have proved influential on this point: *Nixon* v. *U.S.* 418 U.S. 683 (1975), *Sankey* v. *Whitlam* (1978) 53 A.L.J.R. 11.
[74] *Conway* v. *Rimmer, supra; Burmah Oil* v. *Bank of England, supra.*
[75] *Burmah Oil* v. *Bank of England, supra.*
[76] *Air Canada* v. *Sec. of State for Trade, supra.*
[77] *R.* v. *Lewes JJ.* [1973] A.C. 388; *D.* v. *N.S.P.C.C.* [1978] A.C. 171.
[78] *Norwich Pharmacal* v. *Customs & Excise* [1974] A.C. 133.
[79] *Neilson* v. *Laugharne* [1981] 1 Q.B. 736; *Lonrho* v. *Shell* [1980] 1 W.L.R. 627.
[80] Although it is not strictly the exercise of a discretion (see *ante,* p. 42), it is often referred to as such.

procedure of Discovery will normally ensure this. Order 24, r. 2[81] provides that in most actions begun by writ the parties must make discovery by exchanging lists of documents relative to the proceedings which are or have been in their possession custody or power, and (r. 9) must state a time when and place where the listed documents may be inspected and copied. A party may claim privilege for any of his documents (r. 5), and the whole procedure is subject to any rule of law which authorises or requires the withholding of any document on the ground that disclosure would be injurious to the public interest (r. 15). If no privilege or public interest immunity is involved, a party who fails to make discovery may be ordered to do so, (r. 3), but not necessarily, because the Court must refuse to make such an order if and in so far as it is of opinion that discovery is not necessary either for disposing fairly of the cause or matter[82] or for saving costs (r. 8).[83]

This means that if there is no "legal" protection from production at the trial, there may still be an "equitable" protection from discovery before trial. In *Science Research Council v. Nassé*,[84] N was complaining of discrimination by his employer in not promoting him. He sought discovery of confidential reports on the other candidates, including the successful one. This was resisted on the ground that such reports were confidential; but it was held that there was no public interest protection for the reports. However it was also held that the Industrial Tribunal had a discretion about whether to order discovery of them. This should never be exercised on the sole ground of confidentiality, but the Tribunal should inspect them and ask itself, is it necessary for disposing fairly of the litigation? and is it possible to get the necessary information while limiting the damage caused by the disclosure by blanking out the names or irrelevant parts?

If the person who has the documents is not a party to the action, then discovery cannot be ordered in the action, and if he is

---

[81] For the position in the County Court, see C.C.R. Ord. 14; There is no Discovery in criminal cases: *R. v. Skegness Magistrates' Court* [1985] R.T.R. 49.

[82] This means assisting the case of the party seeking disclosure; it is not sufficient that disclosure may assist the Court at arriving at the truth: *Air Canada v. Secretary of State for Trade* [1983] A.C. 394.

[83] A party who obtains disclosure of documents by discovery may make no use of them except for the purposes of the action: *Riddick v. Thames Board Mills* [1977] Q.B. 881 (C.A.), even if they become in a sense public property by being read out in open court: *Home Office v. Harman* [1983] 1 A.C. 280 (H.L.).

[84] [1980] A.C. 1028.

a "mere witness," nothing can be done about inspecting his documents before trial. All that can be done, if he is not disposed to co-operate, is to subpoena him to produce them at the trial. The Attorney-General can apply to have the subpoena set aside on the ground that the documents are protected.[85] But a person is not a "mere witness" if he was implicated, even innocently, in the activities of a wrongdoer which have harmed the plaintiff. In such case, he can be required to give such information as will assist the plaintiff in his action against the wrongdoer, and to that end the plaintiff may bring an independent action for discovery against him; *Norwich Pharmacal* v. *Customs & Excise*.[86] The relief sought in this procedure, which is founded on the old Bill of Discovery in Chancery, is also discretionary. In *British Steel Corporation* v. *Granada T.V.*,[87] B sought an order compelling G to disclose the name of the person who had, in apparent breach of confidence, supplied G with confidential documents belonging to B. G objected that it had promised the informant that his identity would remain secret, and that there was a public interest protecting journalists' sources. The House of Lords held that journalists had no immunity based on public interest and, applying the *Norwich Pharmacal* principle, held that G owed a duty to help B by disclosing the wrongdoer's name. However, there undoubtedly is a public interest in protecting journalists' sources, even if it did not then[88] confer "legal" immunity, and it was only after that public interest had been weighed against, and found to be outweighed by, the public interest in preserving confidentiality in large organisations that the judge's order for discovery was upheld.

(b) Information for the detection of crime

It is in the public interest that informers about crime should not be deterred from making statements to the police by fear of reprisals from the persons they name or their friends and associates. It is therefore a strict rule that in public prosecutions, and in civil proceedings arising therefrom, witnesses will not be allowed to disclose the channels through which came the

---

[85] See, *e.g. R.* v. *Lewes JJ.* [1973] A.C. 910.
[86] [1974] A.C. 133. For the position of the servants or agents of a defendant, see *Harrington* v. *North London Polytechnic* [1984] 3 All E.R. 666.
[87] [1981] A.C. 1096.
[88] But see now, Contempt of Court Act 1981, s.10; *post*, p. 150.

information which led to the prosecution.[89] The rule has been held to prevent the identification of premises used for surveillance purposes or the owners or occupiers of such premises.[90] The exception to the rule is any case where the judge considers that such disclosure is necessary to show the innocence of the accused, for "then one public policy is in conflict with another public policy, and that which says that an innocent man is not to be condemned when his innocence can be proved, is the policy that must prevail."[91] Save in the exceptional case, the matter is not one of discretion and the judge must prevent the disclosure.[92] A witness may not be asked if he himself supplied the information to the authorities.[93]

This rule protecting police informers has been extended by analogy to persons supplying information to other agencies relying on volunteered statements by members of the public. In *R. v. Lewes JJ.*[94] it was held by some members of the House of Lords to cover communications to the Gaming Board on the suitability of an applicant for a gaming licence, and in *D. v. N.S.P.C.C.*[95] some speeches in the House extended the principle to cover persons who informed the N.S.P.C.C. of possible cases of cruelty to children. In both cases, however, the majority of the speeches went on grounds of the proper functioning of the public service.[96]

(c) Judicial disclosures

Judges of the superior courts cannot be compelled to testify to matters which arose before them in their judicial capacity[97]; nor can barristers be compelled to disclose matters which were stated by them while conducting a case.[98] Jurors may not testify as to what passed between them in the discharge of their duties.[99]

---

[89] *Att.-Gen. v. Briant* (1846) 15 M. & W. 169; *Marks v. Beyfus* (1890) 25 Q.B.D. 494.
[90] *R. v. Rankine* [1986] 2 All E.R. 566; *R. v. Hallett* [1986] Crim.L.R. 462.
[91] *Per* Lord Esher, in *Marks v. Beyfus, supra,* at p. 498.
[92] *Marks v. Beyfus, supra.*
[93] *Att.-Gen. v. Briant, supra.*
[94] [1973] A.C. 388 at pp. 401, 408.
[95] [1978] A.C. 171 at pp. 218, 241.
[96] *Ante,* p. 138.
[97] *R. v. Gazard* (1838) 8 C. & P. 595; but perhaps county court judges have no such immunity; see *R. v. Harvey* (1858) 8 Cox 99 at p. 103.
[98] *Curry v. Walter* (1796) 1 Esp. 456.
[99] *R. v. Thompson* [1962] 1 All E.R. 505; and see *R. v. Box* [1964] 1 Q.B. 430; *Boston v. Bagshaw* [1966] 1 W.L.R. 1135; "It would be destructive of all trials by jury ... there would be no end to it"; *per* Harman L.J. at p. 1137.

Arbitrators may be compelled to testify as to what passed before them at the arbitration, but not as to their reasons for making the award.[1]

2. Privilege

(a) Professional confidences

A client (whether party or stranger) cannot be compelled, and a legal adviser (whether barrister, solicitor, or the clerk or intermediate agent of either) will not be allowed, without the consent of his client, to disclose communications, or to produce documents passing between them in professional confidence.[2] This privilege probably only protects communications or documents from being disclosed in judicial proceedings, not, *e.g.* from production to an investigating inspector acting under statutory powers.[3] This restrictive view is not nowadays widely taken in the Commonwealth, where the privilege has been held to protect from an otherwise valid search warrant,[4] on the view that the privilege "is essential for the orderly and dignified conduct of individual affairs in a social atmosphere which is being poisoned by official and unofficial eaves-dropping and other invasions of privacy."[5]

The reasons for the privilege in its traditional restricted form have been variously expressed, but we may take as a typical expression the words of Lord Simon in *D.* v. *N.S.P.C.C.*[6]

"To promote justice the adversary procedure involves advocacy of contrary contentions by representatives with

---

[1] *Buccleuch (Duke)* v. *Metropolitan Board of Works* (1872) L.R. 5 H.L. 418; and see *Ward* v. *Shell-Mex & B.P. Ltd.* [1952] 1 K.B. 280.
[2] A similar privilege attaches to documents passing between lawyer and client on an investigation by the Commission of the European Communities to decide whether the E.E.C. Treaty rules on competition have been infringed: *A.M. & S. Europe Ltd.* v. *Commission of the European Communities* [1983] Q.B. 878 (C.J.E.C.).
[3] *Parry-Jones* v. *Law Society* [1968] 1 All E.R. 177, especially *per* Diplock L.J. at p. 179. And see *Frank Truman Export Ltd.* v. *M.P.C.* [1977] Q.B. 952. But by statute, "items subject to legal privilege" cannot be included in a search warrant or seized by the police: Police and Criminal Evidence Act 1984, ss.8, 9, 18, 19.
[4] *Baker* v. *Campbell* (1983) 49 A.L.R. 385 (H.C. of Australia); and see the New Zealand, Canadian and U.S. authorities there cited.
[5] *Per* Murphy J., 49 A.L.R. 385 at p. 411.
[6] *D.* v. *N.S.P.C.C.* [1978] A.C. 171 at p. 231.

special gifts and training... This process would be undermined if the trained advisers were compelled to divulge weaknesses of their cases arising from what they have been told by their lay clients. Indeed, the adversary system, involving professional assistance, could hardly begin to work effectively unless the lay client could be sure that his confidences would be respected. And a legal representative with only a partial knowledge of his case would be like a champion going into battle unconscious of a gap in his armour."

Lord Simon goes on to point out most potential disputes are settled or obviated without recourse to a fight in court, which is in the public interest. "Thus similar considerations apply whenever a citizen seeks professional guidance from a legal adviser, whether with a view to undertaking or avoiding litigation, whether in arranging his affairs in or out of court."

Moreover communications between the legal adviser and third parties are similarly privileged, but only if litigation, or advice on a contentious matter, is contemplated.[7] Where litigation is pending, communications between solicitor and prospective witnesses are privileged,[8] as are reports by experts enabling the adviser to decide whether and how a claim should be pursued or resisted.[9] But where a client is, for instance, merely contemplating a loan on the security of property, reports by surveyors to the legal adviser as to the value of the property are not privileged, since no dispute or litigation is envisaged.[10] Even if litigation is envisaged, the dominant purpose of the communication with a third party must be the giving or getting of legal advice. If another purpose is dominant or equally important, *e.g.* the purpose of conducting a statutory enquiry,[11] or preventing the repetition of an accident,[12] there is no professional privilege.[13] In *Waugh* v. *British Railways Board*,[14] the House of Lords took the point that

[7] *Wheeler* v. *Le Marchant* (1881) 17 Ch.D. 675.
[8] *Fenner* v. *L. & S.E. Ry.* (1872) L.R. 7 Q.B. 767 at p. 771.
[9] *Wooley* v. *North London Ry.* (1869) L.R. 4 C.P. 602. But by R.S.C., Ord. 38, r. 38, disclosure of expert's reports may be ordered notwithstanding privilege. See Civil Evidence Act 1972, s.2(3).
[10] *Wheeler* v. *Le Marchant, supra.*
[11] *Neilson* v. *Laugharne* [1981] 1 Q.B. 736.
[12] *Waugh* v. *British Railways Board* [1980] A.C. 521.
[13] These purposes may, however, mean that the communication, although not professionally privileged, is entitled to public interest protection: *Neilson* v. *Laugharne, supra.* See *ante,* p. 137.
[14] *Supra.*

although the public interest in the administration of justice requires that the preparation of a party's case for trial should be confidential, that same public interest also (inconsistently) requires that all available evidence should be disclosed. The "dominant purpose" test serves as an intermediate line allowing each requirement scope in its proper sphere.[15]

Although privilege may attach to communications between a lawyer and an expert, it does not cover the objects, *e.g.* samples of handwriting, sent to him for his opinion, nor, since no party has a property in a witness, to his opinion.[16] If a party seeks an opinion from an expert and, because it is not favourable to him, does not use it, his opponent can subpoena the expert to testify as to his opinion,[17] and to produce the materials on which he bases that opinion.[18]

Communications in furtherance of a fraud or crime are not privileged, even though the solicitor was ignorant of the fraud,[19] for otherwise a man intending to commit a crime might safely take legal advice for the purpose of enabling him to do so with impunity.[20] It is different with bona fide advice from the lawyer advising his client that by his conduct he is risking prosecution; that is not "in furtherance of" fraud or crime and will be privileged.[21]

As usual, the public interest in avoiding the conviction of an innocent man when his innocence can be proved is paramount,[22] and it has been held, in a trial of a solicitor's managing clerk for misappropriating the funds of his principal's clients, that no privilege could be claimed in respect of documents passing between the solicitor (a Crown witness) and those clients.[23]

It has been said of matters protected by this privilege that "once privileged, always privileged."[24] This means that as regards communications made during the existence of a lawyer and client relationship, the privilege continues after the latter's termination, and in all subsequent proceedings; but it can only be claimed by

---

[15] See Lord Simon at p. 537.
[16] *Harmony Shipping Co.* v. *Davies* [1979] 3 All E.R. 177 (C.A.).
[17] However, an unwilling expert who knows nothing of the facts will not be compelled to give his opinion: *Seyfang* v. *Searle* [1973] Q.B. 148.
[18] *R.* v. *King* [1983] 1 W.L.R. 411.
[19] *R.* v. *Cox & Railton* (1884) 14 Q.B.D. 153.
[20] *Ibid. per* Stephen J. at p. 165.
[21] *Butler* v. *Board of Trade* [1971] Ch. 680; and see *Crescent Farm (Sidcup) Ltd.* v. *Sterling Offices Ltd.* [1972] Ch. 553.
[22] Compare *Marks* v. *Beyfus* (1890) 25 Q.B.D. 494, *ante*, p. 143.
[23] *R.* v. *Barton* [1973] 1 W.L.R. 115 (Caulfield J.).
[24] *Per* Lindley M.R., in *Calcraft* v. *Guest* [1898] 1 Q.B. 759 at p. 761.

the original client and his successors in title to the subject-matter of the communications.[25]

Since the privilege is personal and belongs to the client, it cannot be claimed by other persons, *e.g.* witnesses in the original client's action.[26] And it follows that if the client is a mere witness in an action, neither of the parties can claim the privilege, or have any grounds for complaint if the client/witness waives the privilege or is wrongly obliged to answer despite the privilege.[27]

The privilege is lost if the information or document comes to the ears or possession of the other party. That party may use it, even if he obtained it wrongfully.[28] But, if he obtained it wrongfully, it seems he can be restrained by injunction from using it in any way, which means he cannot use it as evidence.[29] If A's papers are stolen by the other party B, then if A does not find out until the hearing at which B attempts to make use of them, there is nothing A can do to prevent him.[30] But if A finds out before the hearing, as if, *e.g.* B in his defence pleads matters in the papers, A can apply for an injunction and/or to have the pleading struck out. This relief is discretionary, but it is no answer to A's claim for it for B to aver that he intends to use the material as evidence.[31] If it is granted, B will not be able to use the material.

Where several persons have a common interest in property, an opinion having regard to that property, paid for out of common fund, is the common property of those persons, so that if they afterwards join issue with each other, one cannot claim privilege for the opinion against the others.[33] But if the parties are already at odds when one of them obtains the opinion, that one can claim privilege as against the others.[34] Thus if a trustee takes advice for

---

[25] *Minet v. Morgan* (1873) L.R. 8 Ch.App. 361; *Calcraft v. Guest, supra.* A successor in title includes one who is prospectively interested, *e.g.* deciding whether to purchase the property: *Crescent Farm (Sidcup) Ltd. v. Sterling Offices, supra.*

[26] *Schneider v. Leigh* [1955] 2 Q.B. 195.

[27] *R. v. Kinglake* (1870) 22 L.T. 335, a case on the privilege against self-crimination, as to which see *post*, p. 151.

[28] *Lloyd v. Mostyn* (1842) 10 M. & W. 478 at p. 481; *Calcraft v. Guest* [1898] 1 Q.B. 759; *R. v. Tompkins* (1978) 62 Cr.App.R. 181.

[29] *Lord Ashburton v. Pape* [1913] 2 Ch. 469; *Goddard v. Nationwide B.S.* [1986] 3 All E.R. 264 (C.A.).

[30] However in *I.T.C. Film Distributors v. Video Exchange* [1982] Ch. 431, Warner J. refused to allow a party who got possession of his opponent's documents by a trick practised in the courtroom to make any use of them. "I must balance the public interest in the truth emerging against the public interest that litigants should be able to bring their documents to court without fear that they may be filched and then used in evidence" (at p. 440).

[31-32] *Goddard v. Nationwide B.S., supra.*

[33] *Cia Barca de Panama v. George Wimpey* [1980] 1 Lloyds Rep. 598.

[34] *Woodhouse & Co. Ltd. v. Woodhouse* (1914) 30 T.L.R. 559.

the purpose of defending the trust property against strangers, he cannot claim privilege therefor in subsequent litigation with a beneficiary,[35] but it is otherwise if he obtains the advice for the purpose of resisting the claim of the beneficiary.[36] And if two clients jointly retain a solicitor, who advises one of them on a matter not covered by the joint retainer, that one can claim privilege for that advice as against the other[37]; but advice given to one about their joint concerns is not privileged as against the other. As against third parties, any of the joint interested parties can claim privilege.[38] Thus if A writes a book and B publishes it, and they take advice about a possibly defamatory statement in it, and exchange documents and opinions, if either is sued by a third party, he can claim privilege for all the material.[39]

Since the privilege is that of the client, it is the client, not the legal adviser, who can waive it. The waiver may be express, or implied from, *e.g.* the client examining the solicitor as to the privileged matter.[40] Waiver of part of a document extends to all of it. A party cannot pick and choose between passages in the document.[41] The principle is one of fairness, under which the opponent and the Court must be able to see that a false impression of the document's purport is not being given by disclosing parts only of it.[42] However waiver of one document does not extend to documents dealing with different topics merely because they are referred to in the waived document.[43] Waiver of privilege relating to a conversation before litigation was contemplated does not result in waiver of protected documents brought into existence for the purpose of litigation.[44]

(b) Communications with other than lawyers

The claim to privilege does not rest on the sanctity of confidences, but on the impossibility of administering justice

---

[35] *Wynne v. Humberstone* (1858) 27 Beav. 421.
[36] *Woodhouse & Co. Ltd. v. Woodhouse, supra; Thomas v. Secretary of State* (1870) 18 W.R. 312.
[37] *Harris v. Harris* [1931] P. 10.
[38] *Buttes Gas & Oil Co. v. Hammer (No. 3)* [1981] Q.B. 223 (C.A.).
[39] See Lord Denning M.R., [1981] Q.B. at p. 243.
[40] *Bate v. Kinsey* (1834) 1 C.M. & R. 38; *R. v. Leverson* (1868) 11 Cox 152; *Burnell v. British Transport Commission* [1956] 1 Q.B. 187; *George Doland Ltd. v. Blackburn & Co.* [1972] 1 W.L.R. 1338.
[41] *Great Atlantic Insurance v. Home Insurance* [1981] 1 W.L.R. 529 (C.A.).
[42] *Ibid: Lyell v. Kennedy (No. 3)* (1884) 27 Ch.D. 1; *Burnell v. British Transport Commission, supra.*
[43] *General Accident Fire & Life Assurance v. Tanter* [1984] 1 W.L.R. 100.
[44] *George Doland Ltd. v. Blackburn & Co., supra.*

unless there is full and frank disclosure between litigants and their legal advisers.[45] Consequently, it is settled that the only professional confidences covered by privilege are those between client and legal adviser.[46] Confidential communications with other than legal advisers, *e.g.* with priests, doctors, agents, bankers, accountants, "conciliators," or friends, are not protected.[47] However, the witness may refuse to give evidence or produce a document until he is ordered to do so by the court[48]; and the court may take into account the confidential nature of a document by making the order on terms that the party seeking its discovery makes no use of the document except for the purposes of the present litigation.[49] It is a moot point whether the court has a discretion to refuse to order the giving of evidence or the production of a document if it considers that by reason of the breach of confidence involved more harm than good would result from compelling a disclosure or punishing a refusal. There are expressions to the effect that the policy of the law has been "to limit to a minimum the categories of privileges which a person has an absolute right to claim, but to accord to the judge a wide discretion to permit a witness ... to refuse to disclose information where disclosure would be a breach of some ethical or social value and non-disclosure would be unlikely to result in serious injustice in the particular case in which it is claimed."[50] But the existence of this discretion was strongly denied in *D. v. N.S.P.C.C.* in the House of Lords. Lord Simon approved the use of the judge's moral persuasion of either the questioner or the relevant witness as may seem appropriate. But the exercise of a formal

---

[45] *Lyell v. Kennedy* (1883) 9 App.Cas., per Lord Blackburn at p. 86; *D v. N.S.P.C.C.* [1978] A.C. 171, at p. 231; *ante* p. 144.
[46] *Att.-Gen. v. Mulholland* [1967] Q.B. 477; C.L.R.C., para. 272; *D. v. N.S.P.C.C. supra, per* Lord Edmund-Davies at p. 244.
[47] But by statute, communications with patent agents in connection with patent proceedings are equated with communications with legal advisers: Civil Evidence Act 1968, s.15. And see, Employment Protection (Consolidation) Act 1978, ss.133(6), 134(5) and *Grazebrook v. Wallens* [1973] 2 All E.R. 868, as to communications with conciliation officers in employment cases. As to journalists and their sources, see, Contempt of Court Act 1981, s.10, *post*, p. 150.
[48] *R. v. Statutory Visitors to St. Lawrence's Hospital, Caterham* [1953] 1 W.L.R. 1158.
[49] *Chantrey Martin & Co. v. Martin* [1953] 2 Q.B. 286; *Church of Scientology v. Department of Health and Social Security* [1979] 1 W.L.R. 723.
[50] Law Reform Committee, 16th Report (Privilege in Civil Proceedings) 1967, Cmnd. 3472, para. 1; approved by Lord Hailsham (with whom Lord Kilbrandon agreed) in *D. v. N.S.P.C.C., supra*, at p. 227. See also Donovan L.J., in *Att.-Gen. v. Mulholland, supra*, at p. 492, Lord Denning M.R. in *D. v. N.S.P.C.C.* [1978] A.C. 171 at p. 190 (C.A.), and Lord Widgery C.J. in *Hunter v. Mann* (1974) 59 Cr.App.R. 37 at p. 41.

discretion is something different.⁵¹ He has no such discretion.⁵² "If it comes to the crunch ... it must be law, not discretion, which is in command."⁵³ The question of the existence of what sometimes is called an "equity of confidentiality," protectable by discretion, is thus an open one, but certainly such an "equity," if it does exist, cannot be resorted to if it would hamper a public prosecution for a serious crime.⁵⁴

It must be borne in mind however that the evidence of non-lawyer confidants may be protected by public policy, *e.g.* the proper functioning of the public service,⁵⁵ or by some other doctrine of evidence, *e.g.* "without prejudice" statements,⁵⁶ or the rule that answers to interrogatories cannot be used for any purposes except to dispose fairly of the litigation in which they are elicited.⁵⁷

Journalists. It was settled in *British Steel Corporation* v. *Granada T.V.*⁵⁸ that at common law journalists have no privilege to protect their sources, even if such persons had been promised that their communications would be kept secret. The common law went no further than allowing them to refuse to answer interrogatories about their sources in a defamation action⁵⁹; this rule had no application to answering questions at the trial.⁶⁰ However, now section 10 of the Contempt of Court Act 1981, provides that no court may require a person to disclose, nor is any person guilty of

---

⁵¹ [1978] A.C. 239.
⁵² *Ibid.* p. 245, *per* Lord Edmund-Davies.
⁵³ *Ibid.* p. 239, *per* Lord Simon, who points out that the duty to weigh conflicting public interests, which the court undoubtedly has as a result of *Conway* v. *Rimmer* [1968] A.C. 910, is confined to considering the persuasiveness or otherwise of a ministerial certificate in "public interest" cases (see *ante,* p. 140) and has no application to privilege.
⁵⁴ *Butler* v. *Board of Trade* [1971] Ch. 680.
⁵⁵ See, *e.g. Re D. (Infants)* [1970] 1 W.L.R. 599, *ante,* p. 138.
⁵⁶ These are indeed sometimes described as protected by privilege: see Cross, p. 408, and Lord Simon in *D.* v. *N.S.P.C.C., supra,* at p. 232. However, since the statements sought to be excluded are always in the nature of admissions, it seems better to treat the subject under "Admissions," *post,* Chap. 13.
⁵⁷ *Church of Scientology* v. *Department of Health and Social Security* [1979] 1 W.L.R. 723.
⁵⁸ [1981] A.C. 1096 (H.L.).
⁵⁹ Since 1945, this privilege has extended to all defendants in defamation actions, not just journalists: see Order 82, r. 6.
⁶⁰ A journalist also has a right not to hand back to the owner documents communicated to him by a servant of the owner if they disclose "iniquity" by the latter: *Initial Services Ltd.* v. *Putterill* [1968] 1 Q.B. 396, but this is not an evidential privilege.

contempt of court for refusing to disclose, the source of information contained in a publication, addressed to the public or a section of it, for which he is responsible, unless it is established to the satisfaction of the court that disclosure is necessary, in the interests of justice or national security or for the prevention of disorder or crime.[61]

The section applies if disclosure *might* reveal the source, and is not precluded by the fact that the owner of property is seeking its return; delivery up should not be ordered if that might reveal the source of information, unless one of the exceptions applies, and the interests of justice referred to is the administration of justice in the course of legal proceedings, not the concept of justice in the abstract.[62]

(c) **Incriminating questions**

No witness in civil or criminal proceedings, is compellable to answer any question if the answer would tend to expose him (or his spouse) to any criminal charge or penalty.[63] The privilege also enables him to refuse to produce documents or things at or before trial or to answer interrogatories.[64] As to "penalty," which refers to common informers and is virtually obsolete, the privilege was developed by equity, and survived the Judicature Act.[65] As to crime, the privilege is an old common law one springing out of the unpopularity of the Star Chamber; and sustained ever since then by the view that it is unfair to put a man in a position whereby he must either answer correctly and go to gaol for what

---

[61] By the Police and Criminal Evidence Act 1984, ss.8, 11, "journalistic material" can be ordered to be produced to the police only by a circuit judge under the special procedure in Sched. 1.
[62] *Secretary of State for Defence* v. *Guardian Newspapers* [1985] A.C. 339 (H.L.).
[63] *R.* v. *Boyes* (1861) 1 B. & S. 311. See now, Civil Evidence Act 1968, s.14. The privilege also extended to exposure to forfeiture: *Pye* v. *Butterfield* (1864) 34 L.J.Q.B. 17, but this extension has been abolished as to civil cases (the only kind where it is likely to arise) by s.16.
[64] It thus applies to Anton Piller orders: *Rank Film Distributors* v. *Video Information Centre* [1982] A.C. 380 (H.L.). Since these are much used in piracy proceedings in connection with intellectual property, and since production will almost invariably disclose a conspiracy to defraud, the effect of the privilege was to end the usefulness of Anton Piller orders. As a result, s.72 of the Supreme Court Act 1981 was enacted to remove the privilege in infringement or passing off actions relating to intellectual property, although a limited immunity is granted in return: see *post*, p. 154.
[65] *Adams* v. *Batley* (1887) 18 Q.B.D. 625.

emerges, answer incorrectly and go to gaol for perjury, or refuse to answer and go to gaol for contempt of court.[66] The privilege allows him to refuse to answer; and it is well established that if he is wrongly forced to answer, his answers cannot be used against him in subsequent proceedings.[67] But, since the privilege is personal to the witness, if he is wrongly obliged to answer, no one else can complain.[68]

The privilege is a privilege not to answer, not a right to insist on the question not being put. The witness must listen to the question and then claim the privilege.[69] If he does so, no adverse inference may be drawn from that fact.[70] If he does not claim privilege, his answer is admissible both then and in later criminal proceedings against him.[71] This is so even if it is ignorance of his rights which causes him to neglect to claim; there is no general duty in the judge to warn him,[72] although nowadays it is usual for a caution to be given.[73]

Obviously, it cannot be left entirely to him to say that he is in danger, even if he appears bona fide and otherwise perfectly candid. The judge must be satisfied that there is a real and not imaginary possibility of a prosecution following an admission; but if such a possibility does exist, then the witness ought to be given a large amount of latitude in deciding which questions tend to put him in a position of danger.[74] In *R. v. Boyes*[75] a witness refused to answer on the ground of privilege. He was then handed a pardon under the Great Seal, but took the objection that under the Act of Settlement, a pardon is no bar to proceedings

---

[66] For arguments for and against the privilege, see Heydon pp. 139–144.
[67] The expressed reason is that they count as an involuntary confession and therefore are unlikely to be true: *R. v. Garbett* (1847) 1 Den. 236; but the real reason is the need to uphold the privilege: see *R. v. Scott* (1856) D. & B. 47 at p. 59. The rule is therefore unlikely to have been affected by the substitution of a new test for the admissibility of confessions by the Police & Criminal Evidence Act, s.76(2), as to which, see *post*, Chap. 10.
[68] *R. v. Kinglake* (1870) 22 L.T. 335; *quaere*, whether it is different if he is wrongly allowed to refuse to answer, for in that case a party might be said to have been deprived of admissible evidence.
[69] *Boyle v. Wiseman* (1855) 10 Ex. 647.
[70] *Wentworth v. Lloyd* (1864) 10 H.L.C. 539, (H.L.).
[71] *R. v. Coote* (1873) L.R. 4 P.C. 599.
[72] *Ibid.*
[73] See *R. v. Stubbs* [1982] 1 W.L.R. 509.
[74] *R. v. Boyes, supra; Re Reynolds* (1882) 20 Ch.D. 294; *Triplex Safety Glass Co. Ltd. v. Lancegaye Safety Glass* [1939] 2 K.B. 395.
[75] (1861) 1 B. & S. 311.

by way of impeachment in Parliament. These are theoretically open in the case of any offence, even the most trivial, but the Court of Queen's Bench *in banc* took the view that the contingency was so remote that it should be ignored; and no privilege allowed.

If the witness *cannot* be prosecuted for the offence revealed, if, *e.g.* he has already been convicted or acquitted, or if the time for proceedings has expired, the protection ceases.[76] But the fact that his wrongdoing is already known to the authorities, who already have some evidence against him, does not prevent him from claiming privilege, for his answers might authenticate and confirm that evidence and so increase his exposure to prosecution.[77] The fact that the witness's master may be prosecuted for what is revealed does not allow the master to require the servant to refuse to answer.[78]

In civil proceedings, there is no protection as to crimes cognisable by foreign law[79]; it may be the same in criminal proceedings.[80] The privilege does not extend to an incriminating public document in the custody of a witness.[81] The defendant in a criminal case cannot object to an application to produce bankers' books for inspection[82] on the grounds that the books may incriminate him.[83] However the procedure must not be used for the purposes of a "fishing expedition"; there must already be evidence of the commission of an offence before an order can be granted.[84]

If an accused in a criminal trial elects to give evidence, the privilege does not apply to questions tending to criminate him as to the offence wherewith he is charged,[85] for the obvious reason

---

[76] *R. v. Boyes, supra.*
[77] *Triplex Safety Glass Co. Ltd.* v. *Lancegaye Safety Glass Ltd., supra; Rio Tinto Zinc Corporation* v. *Westinghouse Electric Corporation* [1978] A.C. 547.
[78] *R.T.Z.* v. *Westinghouse, supra,* per Lord Diplock at p. 637.
[79] Civil Evidence Act 1968, s.14(1)(*a*): but a breach of EEC law cognisable by English courts is protectable: *Rio Tinto Zinc* v. *Westinghouse, supra.*
[80] *Re Atherton* [1912] 2 K.B. 251 at p. 254.
[81] *Bradshaw* v. *Murphy* (1836) 7 C. & P. 612.
[82] Under Bankers' Books Evidence Act 1879, s.7. See post, p. 283.
[83] *Williams* v. *Summerfield* [1972] 2 Q.B. 512. In a *civil* case however, the Act is applied on the principles governing Discovery (ante, p. 141), which do allow objection on the ground of self-crimination: *Waterhouse* v. *Barker* [1924] 2 K.B. 759.
[84] *Williams* v. *Summerfield, supra; R.* v. *Nottingham City JJ., ex p. Lynn* (1984) 79 Cr.App.R. 238.
[85] Criminal Evidence Act 1898, s.1, proviso (*e*).

that privilege would make him virtually immune from cross-examination. He may not however be asked questions tending to show that he is guilty of other crimes.[86]

Sometimes statute provides that answers may be extracted from a person by compulsory examination.[87] Since these answers may well be incriminating and fit to be used against him in a subsequent prosecution, the question arises as whether he may claim privilege in the examination. The general rule is that, if the statute is silent on this point, he must answer, and his answers can be used against him subsequently.[88] By imposing the duty to answer and saying nothing about the privilege, Parliament has impliedly abolished the privilege. If the statute does give the person being examined any protection in this matter, it is not usually by giving a privilege not to answer,[89] but rather by granting him some immunity in respect of what emerges from his answers. It is usually regarded as more important to get at the truth in the compulsory examination than to prosecute for any wrongdoing revealed thereby.[90] The statute may afford him a complete immunity from prosecution for anything first revealed in his answers,[91] but more usually the approach is to provide that his answers cannot be proved against him in a subsequent prosecution, except for perjury in respect of the answers.[92] This is not by any means a complete protection, since for that future prosecution the authorities may well be able to use his admissions to unearth independent evidence on the same matter, and in any event the defence will be embarrassed by the knowledge that what he is now denying has been admitted by him on a former occasion. An example of this latter approach may be found in the provision that in proceedings for the recovery or the administration of property, the execution of a trust, or for an account of any property or dealings with property, a witness may not refuse to answer any question on the ground that to do so might

---

[86] *Ibid.* proviso (f). For the important exceptions to this proviso, see *post*, pp. 221–236.
[87] *e.g.* Insolvency Act 1985, ss.68, 137; Purchase Tax Act 1963, s.24(6); Finance Act 1972, s.35; Road Traffic Act 1972, s.168(2); Local Government Act 1972, s.250(2).
[88] *R.* v. *Scott* (1856) D. & B. 47; *Commissioners of Customs and Excise* v. *Harz* [1967] 1 A.C. 760, *per* Lord Reid, at p. 816.
[89] But see, Borrowing (Control and Guarantees) Act 1946, Sched., para. 2(1); Wages Councils Act 1979, s.22(3); Selective Employment Payments Act 1966, s.64(4); Consumer Credit Act 1974, s.165(3).
[90] See *per* Sellers J. in *R.* v. *Maywhort* [1955] 1 W.L.R. 848 at 853.
[91] *e.g.* Larceny Act 1916, s.43(2), repealed by the Theft Act 1968, Sched. 3, Pt. 1.
[92] *e.g.* Legal Aid Act 1974, s.22; Supreme Court Act 1981, s.72.

incriminate him or his spouse of any offence under Theft Act 1968, or Criminal Damage Act 1971; but the witness's answers are not admissible against him in subsequent proceedings for an offence under those Acts, or, unless they married after the answer was given, against his spouse.[93]

---

[93] Theft Act 1968, s.31(1); Criminal Damage Act 1971, s.9.

Part IV

THE PROTECTION OF THE ACCUSED

CHAPTER 8
CORROBORATION

A. The Nature of Corroboration	160
B. Corroboration Required by Statute	165
C. Common Law Rules on Corroboration	166
1. Accomplices	169
2. Sexual Offences	172
3. Sworn Evidence of Children	174
4. Matrimonial Offences	174
5. Identification Evidence	175

CHAPTER 9
THE RIGHT OF SILENCE

A. The Present Position	180
1. Silence out of Court	180
2. Silence in Court	187
B. Proposals for Reform	189

Chapter 10
CONFESSIONS

A. Admissibility at Common Law	192
B. Admissibility under Police and Criminal Evidence Act	195
1. Conditions of Admissibility	195
2. Discretion to Exclude Confessions	201

Chapter 11
CHARACTER OF THE ACCUSED

A. Good Character	204
B. Bad Character	205
1. Character in Issue	205
2. Miscellaneous Cases	206
3. Similar Fact Evidence	207
4. Proviso (f) to Section 1 of the Criminal Evidence Act 1898	221

Chapter 8

CORROBORATION

Corroborative evidence is that which confirms or supports other evidence of the same fact. It must be said at the outset that as a general rule such confirmation or support is not necessary. Unlike some civil law systems, English law never required a plurality of witnesses. A court is quite entitled to act on the uncorroborated evidence of one witness, even in the face of more than one witness to the contrary. The only criterion is credibility and if a tribunal believes A, and disbelieves P, Q and R on the other side, its finding cannot be challenged merely on the ground that there was only one witness as to the fact found, nor on the ground that there were fewer witnesses for the fact than against the fact. Of course, a verdict may be upset if it is perverse, *i.e.* such as no reasonable jury could reach on the evidence before them.[1] But perversity is one thing, a mere counting of witnesses' heads is quite another, and English law has never indulged in the latter practice. There are however some exceptional cases where corroboration is either necessary or desirable; they nearly all relate to the Crown's case against the accused in a criminal trial. "The accumulated experience of courts of law, reflecting accepted general knowledge of the ways of the world, has shown that there are many circumstances and situations in which it is unwise to found settled conclusions on the testimony of one person alone. The reasons for this are diverse. There are some suggestions which can readily be made but which are only with more difficulty rebutted. There may in some cases be motives of self-interest; or of self-exculpation; or of vindictiveness. In some situations the straight line of truth is diverted by the influences of emotion or of hysteria or of alarm or of remorse. Sometimes it may be that owing to immaturity or perhaps to lively imaginative gifts there is no true appreciation of the gulf that separates truth from falsehood. It must, therefore, be sound policy to have rules of law or of practice which are designed to avert the peril that findings of guilt may be insecurely based."[2]

This rationale, persuasive as it may at first appear, is not

---

[1] See *ante*, p. 41.
[2] *D.P.P.* v. *Hester* [1973] A.C. 296, *per* Lord Morris at p. 309.

nowadays without its critics.[3] Even if the courts' accumulated experience does make necessary a policy designed to avert the peril referred to, it by no means follows that that policy should be embodied in rules putting witnesses into classes where corroboration is necessary or desirable. Such a policy assumes that every witness in one of the classes is unreliable, even if the circumstances of a particular case, and the demeanour and background of a particular witness, indicate a high degree of reliability. "The desirable rule should be that if a particular [witness] is challenged on the basis of being a liar or deluded, the jury should be directed to use caution in view of that challenge before acting on the [witness's] testimony."[4] That is not the rule in the classes of case discussed in this chapter. Moreover, these classes are somewhat arbitrarily chosen, and some are riddled with inconsistencies[5]; and instead of a simple need to handle the suspect evidence with caution, which is usually all that justice requires, the law looks for corroboration, a technical concept the absence of which may cause a "technical" acquittal, or allowing of an appeal, which is undeserved on the merits.

A. The Nature of Corroboration

Corroboration is any evidence which confirms a witness's statement and is extraneous to that witness. It has been said that the word "corroboration" has no special technical meaning.[6] This is no doubt true in so far as the kinds of evidence which are in principle capable of being corroboration are almost infinitely various, making it impossible, and undesirable, to try to impose artificial limits.[7] Nevertheless there are some requirements which are always present, for instance, the extraneousness mentioned above, and some which are present in some cases, for instance,

---

[3] See, *e.g.* Dennis *"Corroboration Requirements Reconsidered,"* [1984] Crim.L.R. 316
[4] *Op.cit*, p. 331.
[5] *e.g.* accomplices, *post*, p. 169.
[6] D.P.P. v. *Hester, supra*; D.P.P. v. *Kilbourne* [1973] A.C. 729; in particular, there is no difference, as was once thought (see R. v. *Campbell* [1956] 2 Q.B. 432 at p. 438) between corroborative evidence properly so-called and evidence which helps the jury to determine whether some other evidence is true: *D.P.P. v. Kilbourne, supra*, per Lord Reid at p. 752.
[7] Where statute exceptionally requires corroboration and defines what is required, it does not do so in any consistent way: compare the various forms mentioned at p. 165, *post*.

the rule that evidence of an accomplice cannot consist in the evidence of a fellow accomplice.[8]

Clearly, corroboration can consist in the evidence of a second witness. Perhaps this is the commonest case, but it is not the only case, and in the few places where the law requires corroboration, or thinks it desirable, it does not usually specify this on any other form. Any independent testimony will do, provided it confirms in some material particular the evidence standing in need of corroboration, and if the identity of the defendant is in issue, implicates him.[9] Thus corroboration may be found in a document or thing, such as bloodstains on clothes, or the injuries suffered by a rape victim. It may also be found in the actions or statements of the defendant himself. His conduct on previous occasions, although not usually provable, may be proved in some cases,[10] and if it is proved may amount to corroboration of the case against him.[11] An admission out of court will suffice, and so will silence if that silence can amount to an admission, as it sometimes can.[12] Although admissions in the course of giving evidence which appear to confirm the Crown witness's account are well capable of being corroboration,[13] mere failure to give evidence can never amount to corroboration.[14] Although the jury "very properly could and very probably would"[15] take that failure into account, and although the judge may comment on it in terms more or less strong,[16] he must not say it can be corroboration.[17]

The concoction of a false story, *e.g.* telling the police that he was not with the complainant on the occasion in question, may, if shewn to be false, be taken as confirming the complainant's

---

[8] *Post*, p. 172.
[9] R. v. *Baskerville* [1916] 2 K.B. 658 at p. 667; *Thomas* v. *Jones* [1921] 1 K.B. 22 at p. 32; *James* v. *R.* (1971) 55 Cr.App.R. 229.
[10] *Post*, p. 207.
[11] *D.P.P.* v. *Kilbourne* [1973] A.C. 729.
[12] *Post*, Chap. 9, and particularly R. v. *Cramp* (1880) 14 Cox 390. For a case where failure to supply a forensic specimen on request was held to be capable of being corroboration, see R. v. *Smith* [1985] Crim.L.R. 590.
[13] R. v. *Jackson* [1953] 1 W.L.R. 591. See also *Cracknell* v. *Smith, supra;* R. v. *Blank* [1972] Crim.L.R. 176.
[14] R. v. *Brown* (1911) 6 Cr.App.R. 147; R. v. *Dossi* (1981) 13 Cr.App.R. 162.
[15] *Per* Lord Goddard C.J. in R. v. *Jackson, supra.*
[16] See R. v. *Sparrow* [1973] 1 W.L.R. 488, *post*, p. 188.
[17] This illogicality led the C.L.R.C. to propose that failure to testify should be capable of being corroboration: para. 111. They also proposed that failure to mention a defence when interrogated by the police should, in certain circumstances, be capable of being corroboration of the evidence against him: para. 40.

account of what went on.[18] However before a lie is capable of being corroboration it must comply with the guidelines laid down in R. v. Lucas,[19-20] namely, it must be deliberate, it must relate to a material issue, it must proceed from a realisation of guilt[21] and a fear of the truth, and, most importantly, it must be clearly shown to be a lie by evidence other than that of the witness to be corroborated, i.e. by an admission or by evidence from an independent witness. The reason for this last point is, of course, that if one found corroboration in the fact that one preferred the evidence of the witness needing corroboration to the accused's evidence, the requirement of corroboration would be meaningless. There must be something extra to justify that preference. Lies in the accused's testimony in court are in the same position with respect to these guidelines as lies by him out of court.[22]

The corroboration, whatever it consists of, need not be on the very point to which the witness speaks. If that were so, the witness's testimony would be unnecessary. It is anything which points to guilt in the accused. If D is charged with conspiracy to murder, and witness A says that D was at the meeting at which the conspiracy was hatched, A is capable of being corroborated by B, who testifies that D did one of the acts in pursuance of the alleged conspiracy, e.g. lured the victim to the place where the murder was to take place. The fact that B says nothing about the meeting does not matter.[23]

But although the corroboration need not relate directly to the witness's evidence, it must implicate the accused, if his involvement is in issue. As was said in R. v. Baskerville,[24] it must not only confirm the commission of a crime, but also that the accused committed it. In R. v. Campbell,[25] the charge was indecent assault on a girl of nine. The defendant denied being involved. There was medical evidence of the state of her body. The judge said that this

---

[18] Credland v. Knowler (1951) 51 Cr.App.R. 48. The concoction of a false story in his interest by a third party cannot be corroboration, unless it is shown that the defendant incited him to do so: Cracknell v. Smith [1960] 1 W.L.R. 1239.

[19-20] [1981] Q.B. 720.

[21] i.e. of the offence for which corroboration is needed. A lie is not corroboration if it proceeds from a desire to avoid conviction of another offence: R. v. West (1984) 79 Cr.App.R. 45.

[22] Ibid. explaining statements apparently to the contrary in R. v. Chapman [1973] Q.B. 774.

[23] R. v. Mullins (1848) 3 Cox 517, 531; R. v. Beck (1982) 74 Cr.App.R. 221 at p. 230.

[24] [1916] 2 K.B. 658, 667. But it seems that evidence implicating the principal offender is corroboration against a secondary party, although it does not implicate him; R. v. Olaleye (1986) 82 Cr.App.R. 337. Sed quaere; see [1986] Crim.L.R. 459.

[25] [1983] Crim.L.R. 174; 147 J.P. 392 (C.A.).

The Nature of Corroboration 163

could corroborate as to the assault, *and as to D committing it*. This was held to be wrong, and the conviction was quashed.

Moreover, it must be *independent* testimony; no corroboration is afforded by mere re-iteration by the same witness. Although in ordinary life one is often influenced by the fact that the maker of a doubted statement has made it many times, it would be too dangerous for the law to adopt this attitude.[26] A liar could corroborate his lies merely by repeating them. Self-serving statements never corroborate a witness's evidence,[27] for otherwise "every man, if he was in difficulty . . . would make declarations for himself."[28] "In order that evidence may amount to corroboration, it must be extraneous to the witness to be corroborated."[29] Self-serving statements are sometimes admissible, *e.g.* to rebut afterthought,[30] or to show consistency, especially in a complainant in a sexual case.[31] But shewing consistency is one thing, corroboration is another, and in sexual cases, where corroboration is looked for, it is a misdirection to tell the jury that they may find such in the fact that the victim complained to a third party soon after the alleged offence,[32] or apparently to say or imply that the fact, although not corroboration, is the next best thing.[33] Valuable though this evidence may be,[34] it is not extraneous to the witness whose evidence is sought to be confirmed.

Although complaints cannot be corroboration because not extraneous to the complainant, it has never been doubted that the condition of her clothes or body is so capable, because it *is* extraneous to her. Her distressed condition, observed by a third party, seems to be half-way between these two positions. In *R.* v. *Redpath*,[35] a bystander saw a little girl emerge from a moor in an extremely distressed condition, just after D emerged from the

---

[26] Lord Reid in *D.P.P.* v. *Kilbourne, supra*, at p. 750.
[27] *Jones* v. *South Eastern and Chatham Ry.* (1918) 87 L.J.K.B. 775; *Corke* v. *Corke & Cooke* [1958] P. 93.
[28] *R.* v. *Hardy* (1794) How.St.Tr. 199, *per* Eyre C.J.
[29] *R.* v. *Whitehead* [1929] 1 K.B. 99, *per* Lord Hewart C.J. at p. 102; and see, the Civil Evidence Act 1968, s.6(4), which provides that a statement rendered admissible by the Act shall not be treated as corroboration of the evidence given by the maker of the statement.
[30] *Ante*, p. 107.
[31] *Ante*, p. 108.
[32] *R.* v. *Christie* [1914] A.C. 545; *R.* v. *Whitehead, supra*.
[33] *R.* v. *Virgo* (1978) 67 Cr.App.R. 323 at p. 331. This was not a "sexual complaint" case, but a case where, an accomplice witness having refreshed his memory from a contemporaneous diary, it became evidence by being cross-examined on.
[34] Although the implication of *R.* v. *Virgo, supra*, is that if it is not corroboration it is of very little value. *Sed quaere.*
[35] (1962) 46 Cr.App.R. 319.

same place himself. It was held that in the special circumstances of that case, the bystander's evidence could corroborate her story of being molested by D. In *R.* v. *Knight*,[36] Lord Parker C.J., who had given the leading judgment in *R.* v. *Redpath*, stressed that it was a very special case, and deprecated what he saw as a tendency after *R.* v. *Redpath* to leave to the jury almost every case where the complainant was seen in a distressed condition. More recently, however, the Court of Appeal appears to have been ignoring lack of extraneousness in this class of case, if the evidence is of sufficient weight.[37]

It was once thought that evidence which itself needed corroboration was incapable of corroborating anything. In other words, there could not be mutual corroboration. It was thought to be a circular (and therefore false) argument to say that evidence A could be corroborated by evidence B, although evidence B needed corroboration and could only be corroborated by evidence A. As was said by Lord Hewart C.J. in *R.* v. *Bailey*[38]: "It is so easy to derive from a series of unsatisfactory accusations, if there are enough of them, an accusation which at least appears satisfactory. It is so easy to collect from a mass of ingredients not one of which is sufficient, a totality which will appear to contain what is missing." But it is now recognised that there is no *general* rule forbidding corroboration to be found in evidence which itself stands in need of corroboration.[39] Such evidence is not without some force and may be enough to amount to corroboration, if there is no likelihood of collusion between the two witnesses involved.[40] But it must be borne in mind that evidence which is disbelieved cannot be turned into effective evidence by the presence of corroboration,[41] nor has such evidence any force as corroborative evidence[42]; and to that extent the dictum of Lord

---

[36] [1966] 1 W.L.R. 230.
[37] *R.* v. *Henry & Manning* (1968) 53 Cr.App.R. 150 at p. 153; *R.* v. *Chauhan* (1981) 73 Cr.App.R. 232; *R.* v. *Dowley* [1983] Crim.L.R. 168. *Sed quaere*; complaints themselves may be weighty, but that does not make them corroboration: see *R.* v. *Christie, supra.*
[38] [1924] 2 K.B. 300 at p. 305.
[39] *D.P.P.* v. *Hester, supra D.P.P.* v. *Kilbourne, supra.*
[40] But as to accomplices in one crime, see *post*, p. 172, and as to the special position of the unsworn evidence of children, *post*, p. 166.
[41] *Per* Lord Hailsham, in *D.P.P.* v. *Kilbourne, supra*, at p. 746. "In the present case, M's evidence (count 3) was corroborated. But it was not credible and the conviction founded on it was rightly quashed."
[42] *Ibid.*

Hewart in *R. v. Bailey*[43] may be accepted as expressing a useful warning.

Judge and jury have separate functions as to corroboration. The judge may, and sometimes must,[44] indicate the need for or desirability of corroboration, and he may tell the jury that a particular piece of evidence can or cannot in law amount to corroboration.[45] If he is wrong on this, he may be reversed on appeal[46]; but he will also be reversed if he invades the jury's province and tells them that a particular piece of evidence *is* corroboration. That is for them to decide.[47] If he refers to the subject at all, he must explain what corroboration is,[48] tailoring his remarks to the particular circumstances. He should avoid a general disquisition on the law, which can only bemuse a party of laymen.[49]

B. Corroboration Required by Statute

In a few cases, all statutory, corroboration is positively required by law. If in his view there is nothing which is capable of being corroboration in the evidence against the accused, the judge should stop the case and direct an acquittal. If there *is* material which is capable of being corroboration, he must warn the jury in clear terms that unless the corroboration required by the statute is found by them to be present they cannot convict.[50]

Corroboration is required of the mother's evidence of paternity in affiliation proceedings[51]; and in prosecutions for procuration of women or girls[52] or for personation at elections[53] or for perjury

---

[43] *Supra.*
[44] See *infra,* p. 166.
[45] *R. v. Goddard and Goddard* [1962] 1 W.L.R. 1282.
[46] *R. v. Thomas* (1959) 43 Cr.App.R. 210.
[47] *R. v. Tragen* [1956] Crim.L.R. 332.
[48] *R. v. Clynes* [1960] 44 Cr.App.R. 158.
[49] *D.P.P. v. Hester* [1973] A.C. 296, *per* Lord Diplock at p. 327; *D.P.P. v. Kilbourne* [1973] A.C. 729, *per* Lord Hailsham at p. 741.
[50] *R. v. Shillingford* (1968) 52 Cr.App.R. 188.
[51] Affiliation Proceedings Act 1957, ss.4,8, as amended by the Affiliation Proceedings (Amendment) Act 1972, "If the evidence of the mother is corroborated in some material particular by other evidence to the Court's satisfaction, the court may adjudge the defendant to be the putative father."
[52] Sexual Offences Act 1956, ss.2–4, 22, 23. No conviction . . . "unless the witness is corroborated in some material particular by evidence implicating the accused."
[53] Representation of the People Act, 1949, s.146(5), which requires two or more credible witnesses; and see, R.O.P.A., 1983, s.168(5).

and kindred offences.[54] A person is not to be convicted of speeding solely on the opinion of one witness that he was driving at a speed in excess of the speed limit.[55] And in no case may an accused against whom the unsworn evidence of a child[56] is offered be convicted, unless such is corroborated by "some other material evidence in support thereof implicating him."[57] "Some other evidence" means evidence other than unsworn evidence, so in this case corroboration cannot be found in the unsworn evidence of another child,[58] although, as we have seen, in any other case, unsworn evidence is perfectly capable of amounting to corroboration.[59]

Although it is not a case where corroboration as such is actually insisted on, mention must be made of confessions by handicapped persons. It is sometimes suggested that no accused should ever be convicted upon his confession alone, uncorroborated by other evidence, but this has not found favour.[60] However, Section 77 of Police and Criminal Evidence Act 1984 provides that where on a trial on indictment the case against the accused depends wholly or substantially on a confession by him, *and* he is mentally handicapped, *and* the confession was not made in the presence of an independent person, then the court shall warn the jury that there is a special need for caution before convicting him and shall explain that the need arises because of those three factors. There is similar provision for summary trial. An independent person is someone not employed for or engaged on police purposes. The section in no way cuts down the judge's right and duty to direct the jury on any matter on which he thinks it appropriate to do so.

C. COMMON LAW RULES ON CORROBORATION

Apart from the statutory cases just mentioned, in no case at all is corroboration positively required. Equally, in no case at all is a

---

[54] Perjury Act 1911, s.13; no conviction solely on the evidence of one witness as to the falsity of any statement alleged to be false.
[55] Road Traffic Regulation Act 1967, s.78A(2); but see *Nicholas* v. *Penny* [1950] 2 K.B. 466; *Swain* v. *Gillet* [1974] R.T.R. 446.
[56] See, *ante*, p. 130.
[57] Children and Young Persons Act 1933, s.38(1). If there is no corroboration, a conviction will be quashed if the judge did not enquire into the child's competence before allowing him or her to give *sworn* evidence: *R.* v. *Lal Khan* (1981) 73 Cr.App.R. 190.
[58] *D.P.P.* v. *Hester* [1973] A.C. 296.
[59] *Ibid.* and see *ante*, p. 164.
[60] See Royal Commission on Criminal Procedure Report, Cmnd. 8092 (1981), § 4.74.

judge precluded from warning the jury that it is unsafe to act on certain evidence unless it is corroborated. He has a general discretion to comment generally on the evidence and the reliability of the witnesses. An accused person cannot complain if a judge comments thus on evidence given in his favour.[61]

There are certain cases where judges regularly take account of the danger of acting on uncorroborated evidence. As a matter of practice a judge warns a jury of this danger, and if there is no jury, the tribunal warns itself. In the first three of the classes mentioned below, in which experience has shown that it can be unsafe to found convictions on the uncorroborated evidence of certain witnesses, the practice has hardened into a rule of law, in that a warning in suitable terms must be given, and if it is not, a conviction is liable to be upset on appeal. But if a warning is given, then since corroboration is not positively required, a conviction on uncorroborated evidence will never be upset on that ground alone. In the fifth case (identification evidence) neither corroboration nor a warning of the need for corroboration as such, is required, but the law has developed guidelines for minimising the danger in accepting such evidence.

In three classes of case, namely where the crown case rests on the evidence of accomplices, or on the evidence of the complainant of a sexual assault, or on the sworn evidence of children, it is incumbent upon the judge to give what is often called the "full" warning on the dangers of acting on uncorroborated evidence. This "full" warning became very technical, in particular in that unless the judge actually used the word "dangerous" or "unsafe" to describe the undesirability of accepting uncorroborated evidence, the conviction was liable to be quashed on appeal.[62] However it is now clear that the obligation does not involve some legalistic ritual. Rather must the good sense of the matter be expounded with clarity and in the setting of the particular case.[63] Where there is no corroboration, the jury should be warned of the danger and should have the nature of the danger explained, *i.e.* why the type of evidence involved is suspect. The jury are also told that they are entitled to convict if they feel sure that the uncorroborated witness is telling the truth. If there is evidence

---

[61] R. v. *Peach* [1974] Crim.L.R. 245.

[62] Although the appeal was often dismissed under the Proviso to s.2 Criminal Appeal Act 1968, if no miscarriage of justice had occurred: see R. v. *O'Reilly* [1967] 2 Q.B. 272; R. v. *Prater* [1960] 2 Q.B. 464; R. v. *Jenkins* (1981) 72 Cr.App.R. 354.

[63] R. v. *Spencer* [1986] 2 All E.R. 928 at p. 937 (H.L.).

which is capable of providing corroboration, the judge should identify such evidence and explain that it is up to the jury to decide whether to treat it as corroboration. Where appropriate, he should warn them against treating as potential corroborative evidence that which may appear to them to be such, but which in law cannot be, *e.g.* evidence of a recent complaint in a sexual case.[64] A particularly careful direction is needed as to lies by the accused,[65] or as to observed distress in the complainant;[66] and the judge must direct that accomplices in the same incident cannot corroborate each other.[67] But no particular formula is insisted on.[68]

Partly as a result of the full warning having become excessively technical and elaborate, the courts have been reluctant to add to or extend in any way the categories where such a warning is mandatory. In *Arthurs v. Att.-Gen. for Northern Ireland*,[69] there was a determined attempt to include identification evidence in the categories;[70] in *Nembhard v. R*,[71] dying declarations; in *R. v. Spencer*,[72] the evidence of patients in a secure hospital at the trial of nurses accused of assaulting them. All failed. Attempts to widen the existing category of accomplices have been equally unsuccessful: see below. In *R. v. Spencer*,[73] the House of Lords, in addition to making the full warning less technical, has held that outside the three established categories, a simpler warning may be enough, in that the question of whether and in what terms to refer to potentially corroborative evidence is for the judge. However a full warning is required in the following classes of case which, according to Lord Ackner[74] are all cases where the inherent unreliability of a witness in the class may well not be apparent to the jury. In other cases, since the potential unreliability of the witness is obvious, the judge has a larger measure of freedom in deciding whether and how to warn the jury on that unreliability.

---

[64] *Ante*, p. 163.
[65] *Ante*, p. 161.
[66] *Ante*, p. 163.
[67] *Post*, p. 172.
[68] *R. v. Spencer, supra* at p. 936.
[69] (1970) 55 Cr.App.R. 161 (H.L.).
[70] But as to identification evidence, the Court of Appeal has developed different safeguards, for which, see *post*, p. 175 (H.L.).
[71] [1982] 1 All E.R. 183 (P.C.).
[72] [1986] 2 All E.R. 928 [H.L.].
[73] *Supra*.
[74] *Ibid*. p. 937.

1. Accomplices

Accomplices obviously may have a motive in playing down their own part in a crime and consequently exaggerating the part played by their fellows. Because it *is* obvious in most cases,[75] one would think that the question of assessing the credibility of such persons could in most cases be safely left to the jury, with such judicial help in exceptional cases as seems to the judge to be appropriate.[76] But according to the House of Lords decision in *Davies* v. *D.P.P.*,[77] it is a rule of law that the judge must warn the jury of the dangers of convicting on the uncorroborated evidence of an accomplice called by the prosecution. If he does not, any conviction will be quashed,[78] unless the Court of Appeal is able to apply the proviso to section 2 of the Criminal Appeal Act. The rule in *Davies* v. *D.P.P.* is somewhat rigid and technical, because Lord Simonds L.C. proceeded to give what purported to be an exhaustive list of who are accomplices for this purpose and was not disposed to extend it in any direction. According to him,[79] the following persons, if called as witnesses for the prosecution, are accomplices:

(1) Persons who are *participes criminis* in the actual crime charged, *i.e.* principal offenders, secondary parties, and persons impeding the arrest or prosecution of the principal in an arrestable offence[80];
(2) Handlers giving evidence at the trial of the thief;
(3) Parties to other crimes of which evidence is admitted under the "similar facts"doctrine.[81]

---

[75] Cf. Lord Ackner, *ibid.* "Accomplices may have hidden reasons for lying, and this possibility may ... not be apparent to a jury".
[76] That in substance has been achieved or proposed in Canada and the United States, see Dennis, *op.cit.* at p. 324; but for comments on Dennis's article, see Carter, [1985] Crim.L.R. 143. See also C.L.R.C. para. 185, which however envisaged that if help is needed, it should be in the form of the present full warning.
[77] [1954] A.C. 378.
[78] But the warning is not mandatory if that evidence is partly against, partly in favour of the accused: *R.* v. *Royce-Bentley* [1974] 1 W.L.R. 535 and, possibly, if it is wholly trivial: *R.* v. *Meecham* [1977] Crim.L.R. 350.
[79] [1954] A.C. 378 at p. 400.
[80] Lord Simonds used the terminology applicable to the law of felonies and misdemeanours then current, which has been recast by the Criminal Law Act 1967. See ss.1, 4.
[81] As to which, see *post*, p.207.

This list can be criticised as too restrictive,[82] because it plainly fails to cover many persons who might loosely be described as implicated in the transaction for which the accused is being tried, and therefore as having a motive to falsify the relative parts played by the accused and the witness. Thus the list does not include even a *particeps criminis* in the strict sense if he is not a Crown witness but a co-accused giving evidence against the accused.[83] Moreover, as to Crown witnesses, it does not include an *agent provocateur*,[84] in an affray, an opponent of the defendant,[85] or a thief giving evidence at the trial of the handler,[86] or a person taking part in the transaction at issue who has some defence which allows him to escape conviction of the principal crime. Thus in *Davies* v. *D.P.P.*[87], D. was charged with the murder of B. by stabbing him. D. was one of a gang of youths who attacked another gang among whom was B. L. was one of the attacking party, but since he did not know that D. had a knife, he (L.) had been acquitted of murder and convicted of common assault. It was held that he was not an accomplice of D. in the murder of B., and there was thus no need to warn the jury about the dangers of convicting D. on L.'s uncorroborated evidence. Yet L. could hardly be described as a disinterested witness.[88]

It will be appreciated from the discussion of *Davies* v. *D.P.P.* that the concept of accomplice in the present context is very much a matter of law. It is therefore for the judge to decide whether a witness is within the concept. If there is evidence that he may be an accomplice, he must leave the question of whether he is to the jury, coupled with the full warning for use if they find that he is an accomplice.[89] However, this is only where there is actual

---

[82] And in one particular as being too wide, by including persons impeding prosecution. Such persons will normally have an interest in establishing the innocence of the principal offender, not his guilt; "any testimony as to his guilt bears the stamp of truth as being against interest": see Heydon, p. 75.
[83] *R.* v. *Prater* [1960] 2 Q.B. 464; *R.* v. *Knowlden* (1981) 77 Cr.App.R. 94; *R.* v. *Loveridge* (1982) 76 Cr.App.R. 125.
[84] *R.* v. *Mullins* (1848) 3 Cox 526; *R.* v. *Bickley* (1909) 2 Cr.App.R. 53; *Sneddon* v. *Stevenson* [1967] 1 W.L.R. 1051.
[85] *R.* v. *Sidhu* (1976) 63 Cr.App.R. 209.
[86] *R.* v. *Vernon* [1962] Crim.L.R. 35.
[87] [1954] A.C. 378.
[88] The fact that a witness has already been dealt with does not make him distinterested. Presumably at *his* trial he gave his suspect account of what happened and in the nature of things he is likely to stick to it at the present trial.
[89] *R.* v. *Vernon*, [1962] Crim.L.R. 35.

evidence of complicity; that fact that he could possibly be implicated is not enough.[90]

If there is no evidence fit to leave to the jury that he was actually implicated in the accused's crime, he is not in Lord Simonds' list in *Davies v. D.P.P.*; and in spite of the restricted nature of that list, it will not be extended. Thus it is now settled that no full warning is ever needed about a co-accused giving evidence against his fellow.[91] It is also settled that persons with interests of their own to serve in giving false evidence are not to be treated as analagous to accomplices, unless there is actual evidence that they were implicated in the crime. In *R. v. Beck*,[92] the case was one of fraud where the defence strongly suggested in cross-examination of Crown witnesses that they had to lie to preserve an insurance claim not directly involved in the case. The judge did advise particular care and attention to their evidence, in view of the defence's attack on them. It was argued on appeal that this was not enough, but the appeal was dismissed. The Court of Appeal said that, without detracting from the obligation to advise caution where there is material to suggest that a witness's evidence may be tainted by an improper motive, it could not accept that there is any obligation to give the accomplice warning, with all that that entails, when there is no basis for suggesting that the witness is an actual participant in the crime.[93]

It will be noticed that this passage speaks of an *obligation* to advise caution. There is a duty to give a warning, but it is satisfied by a simpler one than the full warning, and may be in any terms which the judge thinks appropriate. In a normal case he is not free to decide to give no warning at all. But even a failure to give any warning at all will be forgiven if it is perfectly obvious to the jury that the witness has his own purpose to serve. In *R. v. Whitaker*,[94] D was charged with the murder of the four year old child of B, with whom he was living. The only evidence against D was that of B. No warning was given about B's evidence. D's appeal against conviction was dismissed, for the reason that the jury must have appreciated that either D or B killed the child and that they had to choose between their conflicting stories.

As to what is capable of amounting to corroboration, this has

---

[90] *R. v. Beck* (1982) 74 Cr.App.R. 221; *R. v. Stainton* [1983] Crim.L.R. 171 (disapproving of *R. v. Jenkins* (1981) 72 Cr.App.R. 354); *R. v. King* [1983] 1 W.L.R. 411.
[91] *R. v. Loveridge* (1982) 76 Cr.App.R. 125.
[92] *Supra*.
[93] At p. 228, approved in *R. v. Spencer* [1986] 2 All E.R. 928 at p. 936.
[94] (1976) 63 Cr.App.R. 193.

largely been dealt with.[95] But there is a special rule about accomplices, to the effect that one accomplice cannot corroborate another. This used to be thought to be a perfectly general rule,[96] but it has now been held that it only applies to "fellow"accomplices, *i.e.* to participants in the same incident, where there is a danger that they may have concocted a false story in order to throw the blame on to the accused. But the rule does not apply to accomplices concerned in different transactions, particularly accomplices in Class 3 of Lord Simonds's list, who may never even have heard of each other. "The real need is to warn the jury of a conspiracy to commit perjury,"[97] and with persons implicated in wholly separate incidents this possibility can normally be discounted. In *D.P.P.* v. *Kilbourne*,[98] K. was charged with offences against one group of boys in 1970 and against another group of boys in 1971.[99] It was held that the evidence of those in the first group could be corroborated by the evidence of those in the second group, and vice versa, since the boys in one group did not know boys in the other and therefore could not be concerned in a plot with them to fabricate evidence against the accused.

2. Sexual Offences

On a charge of any kind of sexual offence, the judge must warn the jury of the danger of convicting on the uncorroborated evidence of the victim. This is now a rule of law; the absence of any warning on corroboration is prima facie fatal to a conviction[1] (although the warning need not be in any set terms and need not include the word "corroboration"[2]). Moreover, the court will not usually apply the proviso to section 2(1) of the Criminal Appeal Act 1968, in such a case, but will quash the conviction.[3] The rule also applies to indecent assaults committed against adult males.[4] However, no warning on corroboration is apparently required in

---

[95] *Ante,* p. 160.
[96] It was usually expressed in general terms; see, *e.g. R.* v. *Baskerville* [1916] 2 K.B. 658 at p. 663; *R.* v. *Prater* [1960] 2 Q.B. 464 at p. 465.
[97] *Per* Lord Hailsham in *D.P.P.* v. *Kilbourne* [1973] A.C. 729 at p. 748.
[98] *Supra.*
[99] The offences were all tried together because the evidence relating to any one change was admissible to prove any of the others, under the similar facts doctrine, as to which see *post* p. 207.
[1] *R.* v. *Trigg* [1963] 1 W.L.R. 305 at p. 309; *R.* v. *Midwinter* (1971) 55 Cr.App.R. 523.
[2] *R.* v. *O'Reilly* [1967] 2 Q.B. 722.
[3] *R.* v. *Trigg, supra; R.* v. *Birchall* (1985) 82 Cr.App.R. 208.
[4] *R.* v. *Burgess* (1956) Cr.App.R. 144.

respect of the evidence of a witness, other than the complainant, who is deposing to a similar incident in order to rebut the defence of accident.[5] Thus, if A is accused of indecently assaulting B, and the Crown calls X to say that A assaulted her in very similar circumstances, a warning on corroboration must be given in respect of B's evidence, but not in respect of X's evidence.[6]

The corroboration need not be and usually is not the evidence of a third person who witnessed the act; more usually it is found in the state of the clothes or bodies of either or both parties.[7] But it must be remembered that if consent, or the identity of the assailant, is in issue, such corroborative evidence must confirm in some material particular that the act was without consent or that the accused was the man who committed the crime.[8] Moreover the distressed condition of the complainant cannot often and her complaints to third parties cannot ever amount to corroboration, because not extraneous to the witness.[9]

The danger which the warning is designed to minimise is said to be that of unjustified complaints. "Human experience has shown that in these courts girls and women do sometimes tell an entirely false story which is easy to fabricate but extremely difficult to refute."[10] There is not only the possibility of deliberate falsification, as with accomplice evidence, but also the possibility of delusions in the complainant; and it is necessary to counter an unreasoning sympathy in the jury for the victim, which may undervalue the defendant's denials. It has been said that it is "really dangerous" to convict on the evidence of the complainant alone.[11] Nevertheless the law's requirement of a warning in this class of case has come under widespread attack.[12] Not only does the law lump together all cases in the class[13] (the criticism which can be made about all general rules requiring warnings about corroboration[14]), but in sexual cases the rule appears to be founded on an outmoded and offensive appraisal of female

---

[5] See *post*, pp. 207 *et seq.*
[6] *R.* v. *Sanders* (1961) 46 Cr.App.R. 60.
[7] See *R.* v. *O'Reilly, supra.*
[8] *James* v. *R.* (1971) 55 Cr.App.R. 299 (P.C.), *per* Viscount Dilhorne at p. 302; *R.* v. *Campbell* [1983] Crim.L.R. 174; *R.* v. *R.* [1985] Crim.L.R. 736.
[9] See *ante*, p. 16.
[10] *Per* Salmon L.J. in *R.* v. *Henry & Manning* (1968) 53 Cr.App.R. 150 at p. 153.
[11] *Ibid.*
[12] See Temkin, "Towards a Modern Law of Rape" (1982) 45 M.L.R. 319 at p. 417; Dennis, *op.cit.* p. 326.
[13] In *R.* v. *Henry & Manning, supra,* the Court of Appeal refused to countenance the idea that in some kinds of sexual case the warning was not very important.
[14] *Ante*, p. 160.

psychology which judges that false complaints are inherently likely; and appears to take no account of those factors which in practice make for the likelihood that a complaint which is persisted in is true, namely, the indignity inflicted by official handling in the early stages and the distress suffered in the box if the complaint gets as far as a trial. Moreover the necessity of giving a full warning in every case, while it may avoid some unjust convictions, has a potentiality for allowing guilty defendants to escape conviction. Criticisms such as these have led some overseas jurisdictions to abolish all common law rules of law and practice on the subject.[15] In England, the most that has been proposed has been the substitution of a simplified warning on a "special need for caution."[16]

3. Sworn Evidence of Children

Unsworn evidence of children must, as we have seen, be corroborated by something other than unsworn testimony.[17] There is no such positive requirement with sworn evidence, but a rule of practice has developed with regard to children who are old enough to take the oath but so young that their comprehension of events and of questions put to them or their own powers of expression may be imperfect.[18] A warning ought to be given on the dangers of acting on the uncorroborated evidence of such children; but corroboration of their testimony may be found in the sworn or unsworn evidence of other children.[19]

4. Matrimonial Offences

A court, including a magistrates' court, should look for corroboration of the evidence of a complaining spouse who alleges a matrimonial offence.[20] In cases in which a sexual crime, or adultery with a willing partner, is alleged, then, by analogy with

---

[15] *e.g.* s.62(3) Crimes Act (Vic.) 1958, introduced by Crimes (Sexual Offences) Act 1980.
[16] C.L.R.C. 14th Report: Evidence (General) 1972, para. 188. This was adhered to in the Committee's Working Paper on Sexual Offences, 1980 para. 149, but nothing is said in their final report: 15th Report, Sexual Offences, 1984, apart from remarks in the Introduction apparently favouring the need for corroboration: para. 2.9.
[17] See *ante*, p. 166.
[18] *D.P.P. v. Hester* [1973] A.C. 296., *per* Lord Diplock at p. 325. And see Heydon, p. 84.
[19] *D.P.P. v. Hester, supra*; and see *ante*, p. 166.
[20] *Alli v. Alli* [1965] 3 All E.R. 480.

the rules for sexual offences and accomplices in crime, the uncorroborated evidence of the victim or partner must not be acted upon without the court expressly adverting to the dangers of acting on uncorroborated evidence.[21] In other classes of case, *e.g.* where "cruelty" is alleged, the absence of an express indication that the desirability of corroboration was borne in mind will not of itself be grounds for appeal.[22]

5. Identification Evidence

For present purposes this can be taken to mean evidence by a witness who did not previously know the accused,[23] but saw the incident at issue and the person involved in it, and now claims that he recognises the accused as being that person. He will usually have made some prior identification of the accused, as at an identification parade arranged by the police.[24] He will often be certain of his identification, and will become more certain the harder he is cross-examined, and yet will often be quite wrong. There is a great deal of experience indicating that identification evidence is often quite dangerous to rely on and yet is uncritically and naively relied on by juries, to the extent even of disbelieving quite strong alibi evidence to the contrary. There have been some notorious miscarriages of justice,[25] as well as some controlled experiments,[26] demonstrating the frailty of a class of evidence which is popularly regarded as strong.

It might be expected that "the accumulated experience of courts of law"[27] would have led to the development for identification evidence of a similar practice about warnings on the desirability of corroboration as has grown up for the evidence of accomplices and sexual complainants.[28] It is true that the cause for concern with identification evidence is not the same as with those classes of case, but the difference is one which suggests, not less, but more need for corroboration warnings for identification evidence.

---

[21] *Galler* v. *Galler* [1954] P. 183.   [22] *Alli* v. *Alli, supra.*
[23] The same problem can arise even if the witness did previously know the accused, but usually in a much less acute form.
[24] On previous identification, see, *ante*, p. 110.
[25] See Williams, "Evidence of Identification: The Devlin report" [1976] Crim.L.R. 407.
[26] For a remarkable example, see Williams *The Proof of Guilt* (3rd ed.), Chap. 5 especially p. 88, and for a general discussion of the difficulties, psychological and practical, making for error, see Heydon, pp. 101–104.
[27] Lord Morris's phrase describing the source of the present law on corroboration, in *D.P.P.* v. *Hester* [1973] A.C. 296 at p. 309, *ante*, p. 159.
[28] See *ante*, pp. 167–174.

With accomplice and sexual complainant evidence, the principal perceived danger is that of fabrication; with identification evidence the untrustworthy factors are incomplete or unskilled observation or recall by an honest witness. Partiality and consequent fabrication may be obvious, or may be shewn up in cross-examination; the failings of an honest identification witness are often neither obvious nor exposable in cross-examination. This consideration has led some even of those who are critical of the law's requirements about corroboration warnings in accomplice and sexual cases to advocate a requirement of actual corroboration in identification cases.[29] However the law has developed neither a requirement of actual corroboration nor even a requirement of a warning of the desirability of such.[30]

It has been laid down by the House of Lords,[31] that, even for cases where a conviction would depend wholly or substantially on visual identification of the accused, "it would be undesirable to seek to lay down as a rule of law that a warning in some specific form or in some partly defined terms must be given." The difficulty is that particular cases vary enormously; visual identification evidence, while in some cases it may be poor, in other cases can be the strongest of all evidence, about which any kind of expressed reservations by the judge would be wholly inappropriate.

Nevertheless public unease led to the setting up of the Devlin Committee, which reported in 1976.[32] The Committee recognised the dangerous nature of identification evidence, but refused to recommend that corroboration, or even a warning about its desirability, should be required. Since such evidence can be very strong, forbidding a conviction without corroboration or a warning could result in many quite unjustified acquittals. But the Committee proposed that legislation should require the judge in an appropriate case to give a direction that, save in exceptional circumstances, identification evidence alone should not be enough. He should then point out any exceptional circumstances of the case which might make it enough, such as that the witness was familiar with the accused. He ought also to deal with any

[29] *e.g.* Dennis, *op.cit.* p. 335.
[30] Although Lord Hailsham in *D.P.P.* v. *Kilbourne* [1973] A.C. 729 at p. 740, treated it as still open that, in some cases at least of disputed identity, a warning on the need for corroboration is necessary.
[31] *Arthurs* v. *Att.-Gen. for Northern Ireland* (1970) 55 Cr.App.R. 161, *per* Lord Morris at p. 170, speaking for a unanimous House.
[32] Report to the Secretary of State for the Home Department of the Departmental Committee on Evidence of Identification in Criminal Cases (1976), H.C. 338; discussed by Williams at [1976] Crim.L.R. 407.

Common Law Rules on Corroboration 177

additional evidence in the Crown's case which might make it safe to convict. This additional evidence need not be corroboration in the legal sense, a concept which the Committee thought was too technical and had no wish to see extended. Thus such evidence need not be extraneous, but may depend on the same witness, as where the witness gives evidence of some fact which fixed the accused's features in his mind.

The recommended legislation has not yet appeared, but in *R*. v. *Turnbull*[33] the Court of Appeal gave guidance, in general in accordance with the Devlin Committee's recommendations, but with a changed emphasis. The court refused to use the phrase "exceptional circumstances" to describe situations in which the risk of mistaken identification is reduced.[34] That would be likely to result in the build up of case law about what are and what are not exceptional cases. But the *quality* of the identification evidence is what matters, and there would be no guarantee that any list of exceptional cases would necessarily produce good quality evidence; the converse would be equally true. What is needed is a proper appraisal of the quality of the evidence in each case, and the guidelines laid down in *R*. v. *Turnbull* are designed to secure that appraisal. These guidelines can be summarised as follows:

1. Whenever the case against an accused depends wholly or substantially on one or more disputed identifications of the accused the judge should warn the jury of the special need for caution; and should mention the reason for the need for such a warning, *i.e.* in this area a mistaken witness can appear convincing. No particular form of words is required.

2. The judge should direct the jury to examine closely the circumstances in which the disputed identification came to be made. How long did the witness have the accused in sight? At what distance? In what light? What time elapsed between observation and subsequent identification to the police? Any material discrepancy between the description first given by the witness and the accused's actual appearance? And although recognition of a known person may be more reliable than identification of a stranger, the jury should be reminded that mistakes in recognition of close relatives and friends are sometimes made.[35]

3. All these matters go to the quality of the identification

---

[33] [1977] Q.B. 224.
[34] *Ibid. per* Lord Widgery C.J. at p. 321.
[35] [1977] Q.B. at p. 228.

evidence. If it is good, the jury can be left to assess its value, even if there is no other evidence in support, provided an adequate warning has been given.[36] To hold otherwise would not be in the interests of justice or of the maintenance of law and order.

4. But if, in the opinion of the judge, the identification evidence is of poor quality, he ought to withdraw the case from the jury, unless there is other evidence which goes to support the correctness of the observation. This need not be corroboration in the strict sense, *e.g.* a witness may testify that after he saw a man whom he identifies as the accused commit the crime, he saw that man run away into a certain house, which turned out to belong to the accused's father. The judge should point out evidence which can amount to support, and also that which cannot, *e.g.* the accused's failure to give evidence.[37]

A failure to follow these guidelines is likely to result in a conviction being quashed and will do if in the judgment of the Court of Appeal on all the evidence the verdict is either unsatisfactory or unsafe.[38]

The limits of the decision in *R. v. Turnbull* must be noted. Even where the *Turnbull* guidance is appropriate, it is "guidelines" that that case sets out; it does not change the law, nor impose an elaborate specification to be adopted religiously on every occasion.[39] "A summing up, if it is to be helpful to the jury, should be tailored to fit the facts of the particular case and not merely taken ready-made 'off the peg.'"[40] Moreover the guidelines are not anyway considered appropriate in every case of disputed identification, but only in what may be called "fleeting glimpse" cases.[41] The guidelines were held to be inapplicable in a case where, it being accepted that a man and a woman were in a car, the only

---

[36] If it appears to be good, the warning is still needed, because one needs to bear the warning in mind before concluding that the evidence's quality *is* good: *R. v. Tyson* [1985] Crim.L.R. 49.
[37] But such failure can be taken into account in assessing the quality of the identification evidence (*ibid.* p. 230), a distinction which was condemned as meaningless and confusing by Lord Reid in *D.P.P. v. Kilbourne* [1973] A.C. 729 at p. 752.
[38] [1977] Q.B. at p. 231. For convictions quashed on these grounds, see *R. v. Hunjan* (1978) 68 Cr.App.R. 99; *R. v. Keane* (1977) 65 Cr.App.R. 247.
[39] *McShane v. Northumbria Chief Constable* [1980] R.T.R. 406 (D.C.); *Nembhard v. R.* (1981) 74 Cr.App.R. 144 (P.C.).
[40] *Per* Sir Owen Woodhouse, in *Nembhard v. R., supra,* at p. 148. But a summing up, otherwise satisfactory, which omitted a reference to the "special need for caution" mentioned in the first guideline has been criticised on appeal: *R. v. Clifton* [1986] Crim.L.R. 399.
[41] See Grayson, "Identifying Turnbull" [1977] Crim.L.R. 509.

question was whether it was the man who had been driving[42]; and also in cases of melees, where police witnesses claimed to identify which of the participants were attacking them, rather than defending the police or themselves as claimed.[43] It is said that it is "the ghastly risk of fleeting encounters"[44] which the guidelines are designed to lessen. Cases of confusion, with many people milling about, seem to carry similar risks of misidentification, but the Court of Appeal is not disposed to apply to them the guidance in *R. v. Turnbull.*

---

[42] *R. v. Hewett* [1977] Crim.L.R. 554.
[43] *R. v. Oakwell* (1978) 66 Cr.App.R. 174; *R. v. Curry & Keeble* [1983] Crim.L.R. 737. See also *R. v. Nelson & McLeod*, The Times, November 18, 1983.
[44] *Per* Lord Widgery L.J. in *R. v. Oakwell, supra,* at p. 178.

Chapter 9

THE RIGHT OF SILENCE

A distinguishing feature of Anglo-American criminal procedure is that no person accused of any crime is under the smallest obligation to help the authorities by answering questions or making statements or supplying information. It is not an offence to refuse to answer a policeman or other official. A suspect is not interrogated by an examining magistrate as in some Continental systems, and at his trial, no-one can make him leave the dock and be a witness. The Crown is expected to prove its case without his help.

Some regard this immunity as the cornerstone of all our liberties. Others see it as a pestilential nuisance, of use to guilty men, and only to guilty men, in escaping their just deserts. The controversy, which is an old one, was brought to a head in 1972 by the 11th Report of the Criminal Law Revision Committee.[1] This contained proposals for curtailing the right in some respects, but the resulting public outcry caused the whole Report to be shelved. Although some less controversial parts of it were later enacted by the Police and Criminal Evidence Act 1984, the proposals relating to the right of silence are most unlikely to be adopted in the near future. The controversy will be looked at later,[2] after the present position has been described.

A. The Present Position

1. Silence out of Court

There are certain exceptional statutory cases,[3] but in general it is not an offence to fail to answer questions by anyone on any subject.[4] If a person does answer, voluntarily, and his answers are against him,[5] then subject to safeguards to be mentioned later,[6]

[1] Evidence (General), Cmnd. 4991.
[2] *Post*, p. 189.
[3] *e.g.* Official Secrets Act 1920, ss.6, 8(2); Purchase Tax Act 1963, ss.24(5)(6), 33(5); Finance Act 1972, ss.35(2)(3), 38(7); Road Traffic Act 1972, s.168(3); National Insurance Act 1965, s.90; Road Traffic Regulation Act 1984, s.112(4); see, *e.g. Smith* v. *Hawkins* [1972] 1 All E.R. 910.
[4] See *per* Lord Parker C.J. in *Rice* v. *Connolly* [1966] 2 Q.B. 414 at p. 419.
[5] As to answers in his favour, see *ante*, p. 107.
[6] *Post*, Chap. 10.

those answers can be used against him at any subsequent trial. But failing to answer, as such, cannot be put against him later on.[7]

(a) Silence in the face of accusation

Suppose, however, that a man's failure to answer is alleged to *be* an answer. If a man listens to a statement alleging certain conduct by him and then says "I agree," both the statement and the response are provable against him. Suppose he does not say "I agree" but his silence says it for him. There are circumstances where it is reasonable to deduce that his silence is equivalent to "I agree." Sometimes failing to answer in the face of an accusation is tantamount to an admission that the accusation is true. If a denial would be expected from a person falsely accused, and no denial comes, the inference may be drawn that he is acknowledging the truth of what has been said. If A comes upon B and B's wife, the latter with bruises on her face, and says "I see you've taken to wife-beating now," B's failure to utter may, as a matter of common-sense inference, be taken as an admission that A's comment is accepted. There are two dangers in drawing this common-sense inference. One is, it really does depend on the exact facts of the encounter between A and B as to whether *any* inference should be drawn from B's silence. One would not expect any reply from B if he were a civic dignitary in the act of performing some solemn public ceremony and A was a drunken spectator in the crowd. No answer being expected, no inference can be drawn from its absence. The second difficulty is that even when an answer would be expected and an inference can be drawn from silence, it does not follow that the "common-sense" inference that B is admitting the truth of what is said is the right one to draw. B's silence may be due to timidity, embarrassment, misunderstanding, mishearing, indignation rendering him speechless—even a consciousness of guilt, which might not be the "relevant" guilt. B realises that his wife has had a lot to put up with, he has beaten her in the past, although these particular bruises were caused by her falling downstairs. To say that by his silence he admits he caused these bruises by beating her, and to convict him of wife-battering on the strength of that admission, is a strong and risky thing to do. The question is, does English law do it? To the extent that it does do it, B's right to remain silent in the face of A's accusation is a snare and a delusion.

The rule is that if and only if a person's reaction can fairly be

---

[7] Except under particular statutes: see, *e.g.* Family Law Reform Act 1969, s.23(1)(2); Road Traffic Act 1972, s.7(1).

taken as an adoption of the statement made in his presence,[8] and if such adoption can fairly be taken as evidence of guilt,[9] is the statement evidence against him.[10] This means that if the circumstances are such that no reply could reasonably be expected, or that although a reply could be expected, there is some other probable explanation of his silence, the statement made in his presence is not evidence against him.[11] Indeed, strictly, that statement is never evidence of what it asserts; it is his reaction which is the evidence[12] and only if that reaction can be taken as an adoption of the statement is the statement admissible. If it cannot be so taken, the judge will tell the jury to put the statement out of their minds. Since the jury may well find that difficult or impossible, the accused may be prejudiced by what has been ruled to be inadmissible evidence. One would expect, therefore, that the rule would be that the Crown are not allowed to prove the statement until they have laid a foundation for its admissibility by persuading the judge, in the absence of the jury, that the accused's silence could reasonably be taken as an adoption of the statement. But there is no such rule; the most that can be said is that there is a rule of practice by which a judge will prevent the giving of evidence of a statement where its evidential value in all the circumstances is non-existent or so small as not to justify the prejudice involved in proving the statement.[13]

One obvious case where no positive reaction to a statement can be expected, and therefore the statement cannot be used is where the accused has been cautioned.[14] If he has been told that he need not reply, then he need not reply and no inference can be drawn

---

[8] R. v. *Christie* [1914] A.C. 545, *per* Lord Atkinson at p. 554. Failure to reply to a letter is less likely to be taken as an admission than failure to reply to a statement made in his presence, but in appropriate circumstances it may be: see *Wiedemann* v. *Walpole* [1891] 2 Q.B. 534. This idea must be handled with especial care in a criminal case: R. v. *Edwards* [1983] Crim.L.R. 539.

[9] R. v. *Chandler* [1976] 1 W.L.R. 585, *per* Lawton L.J. at p. 590.

[10] But in R. v. *Christie, supra*, Lord Reading at pp. 555–556 indicated that the statement could be admitted in order to prove the conduct and demeanour of the accused when hearing the statement as a relevant fact in the case, even if such conduct did not amount to an adoption of the statement. In such a case the statement would be no evidence of the truth of its contents, only evidence of the fact that the accused did *not* accept its truth, *i.e.* a self-serving statement, as to which see *ante*, p. 107.

[11] R. v. *Mitchell* (1892) 17 Cox 503; R. v. *Tate* [1908] 2 K.B. 680; R. v. *Adams* (1923) 17 Cr.App.R. 77.

[12] R. v. *Christie, supra*, at pp. 556, 560.

[13] *Ibid. per* Lord Atkinson at p. 555. See R. v. *Taylor* [1978] Crim.L.R. 92.

[14] For the terms of the present caution, see Appendix 4.

from his silence. This was laid down in clear terms in *R. v. Lecky*[15]; and it has also been held by the Privy Council that even if a man is not cautioned, still if a policeman is present, silence cannot amount to an admission. This was in *Hall v. R.*,[16] where it was said that a caution does not *give* a man the right to remain silent, it merely reminds him of a right he already has, and the fact that he has not been reminded of the right does not mean that he may not be exercising it.[17] But if at an interview with a policeman, the accused chooses to answer some questions and to remain silent on others, the whole series of questions may be proved,[18] and it has been held[19] that if he has his solicitor with him, so that the parties are on equal terms, the principle stated in *Hall v. R.* does not apply anyway.[20] Moreover, the right to refuse to co-operate with the police by supplying specimens is not analogous to the right to refuse to speak to the police. In an appropriate case, if an accused refuses to supply, *e.g.* hair samples, at the request of a policeman, adverse inferences may be drawn from that refusal.[21]

(b) Equivocal answer or denial

In principle it is the same if the accused's reaction is not to remain silent but to reply in an equivocal manner, or even to *deny* the statement. A denial will not usually be taken as an endorsement of what is said to him, but it may be, because there are denials *and* denials, and the manner and circumstances of a denial may be such as to cause it to be regarded rather as an acknowledgment of the truth of the statement or part of it. In *R. v. Christie*,[22] a little boy had been indecently assaulted. With his mother, he went up to Christie, touched him and said "That is the man," and described the assault. Christie said, "I am innocent." It was held by the House of Lords that this remark was capable of being an admission and was properly proved against him. But it was also said that the value of a denial was likely to be small, and as a matter of practice the denied statement ought not to be

---

[15] [1944] K.B. 80.
[16] [1971] 1 W.L.R. 298.
[17] *Ibid.* p. 301.
[18] *R. v. Mann* (1972) 56 Cr.App.R. 750.
[19] *R. v. Chandler* [1976] 1 W.L.R. 585.
[20] *Sed quaere*. The fact that the accused and policeman are on equal terms seems irrelevant to the question of whether the accused is consciously exercising his right to remain silent. The presence of the solicitor, if relevant, can only be to strengthen the inference that he is exercising that right.
[21] *R. v. Smith* [1985] Crim.L.R. 590.
[22] [1914] A.C. 545.

admitted in a criminal case, although there is no rule of law against such admission.

(c) Failure to mention a defence

If silence on accusation consists in a failure to mention a defence which is subsequently raised at the trial, that failure is provable in order to show that the defence is invented rather than genuine.[23] "A fishy story is all the worse for being stale."[24] In *R.* v. *Foster*,[25] F, accused of driving with excess alcohol in his blood, was arrested at his home. At his trial, he claimed that he had consumed two whiskies at home before the police arrived, and it was held that the judge was right in commenting on his failure to mention this at the time of his arrest. And if a man, when first taxed with a violent assault, denies any assault, that denial becomes distinctly relevant if at his trial he no longer denies assault but pleads self-defence.[26]

It is true that the judge must be circumspect in his comments in this kind of situation.[27] He may remark that it is unfortunate that he did not speak up earlier, for that would have allowed the police to follow matters up,[28] or that the jury could take the lateness of the explanation into account in assessing the weight they think the explanation ought to bear.[29] But "members of the jury, what would you have done if you were an innocent man?"[30] or "you might well think that if a man is innocent he would be anxious to answer questions"[31] goes too far. The cases draw a distinction between comment on the weight to be given to an explanation and any kind of suggestion that the lateness may be indicative of guilt,[32] a distinction which has been denounced as "gibberish," and "absurd enough to bring a blush to the most hardened academic face."[33] But, comment apart, the *evidence* of failure to advance defences promptly is admissible, and no one

---

[23] *R.* v. *Ryan* (1966) 50 Cr.App.R. 144 at p. 148.
[24] *Per* Napier J. in *Hinton* v. *Trotter* [1931] S.A.S.R. 123 at p. 127, quoted Heydon, p. 159.
[25] [1975] R.T.R. 553.
[26] Lord Moulton in *R.* v. *Christie* [1914] A.C. 545 at p. 560.
[27] See Gooderson, *Alibi* (1977), p. 60.
[28] *R.* v. *Littleboy* (1934) 24 Cr.App.R. 192.
[29] *R.* v. *Ryan, supra.*
[30] *R.* v. *Hoare* (1966) 50 Cr.App.R. 166.
[31] *R.* v. *Sullivan* (1967) 51 Cr.App.R. 102.
[32] *R.* v. *Littleboy, supra; R.* v. *Ryan, supra.*
[33] Cross [1973] Crim.L.R. 333.

can complain if the jury, unaided by judicial prompting, draw the common-sense conclusion.[34]

(d) Failure to mention alibi[35]

A late defence of alibi always ran the risk of coming to grief this way, but if the accused was prepared to run the risk, he could at common law unveil it at the very last moment. Any comment by the judge would have to be in the delicate terms outlined above,[36] and that might be a small price to pay for the benefit of not having his alibi witnesses, who might be of dubious character, investigated by the police before the trial. Now, however, section 11 of the Criminal Justice Act 1967 robs him of this particular tactical ambush.

This provides that on a trial on indictment the defendant shall not without leave adduce evidence in support of an alibi unless within seven days from the end of committal proceedings he gives notice to the prosecution of his intention to do so. At the committal proceedings he must be warned of this obligation.[37] The notice must give the name and address of the proposed alibi witness; if such is unknown to the defence, it must take all reasonable steps to discover them and forward such to the prosecution's solicitor if and when they are discovered.[38] The section applies where the only evidence of alibi proposed is that of the accused himself.[39]

The object of section 11 is not to prevent unmeritorious defences by curtailing the time in which the accused may concoct such. The object is to prevent the defence from surprising the prosecution by suddenly producing at the trial alibi witnesses whose bona fides the prosecution will not have had opportunity to check. Therefore, if the notice is given out of time, even by several weeks, the judge ought to allow the alibi evidence nonetheless, as long as the prosecution has had enough time to make its investigations. Rather than refuse the evidence, the judge should adjourn the trial in order to make enough time.[40]

---

[34] See *R.* v. *Tune* (1944) 29 Cr.App.R. 162, *per* Humphreys J.: "If nothing is said by way of comment by the presiding judge, no point can be raised."

[35] See Gooderson, *op. cit.* particularly Chap. IV.

[36] Assuming indeed that the judge did not follow the advice of Humphreys J. in *R.* v. *Tune*, *supra*, and eschew any kind of comment. See also *R.* v. *Lewis* (1973) 57 Cr.App.R. 860.

[37] Criminal Justice Act 1967, s.11(3); Magistrates' Court Rules 1981, r. 7(9).

[38] Criminal Justice Act 1967, s.11(2).

[39] *R.* v. *Jackson* [1973] Crim.L.R. 536, Cusack J. And see *R.* v. *Cooper* (1979) 69 Cr.App.R. 229 (C.A.).

[40] *R.* v. *Sullivan* [1971] 1 Q.B. 253; *R.* v. *Cooper*, *supra*.

When the trial does take place, no doubt the judge may make the usual guarded comment[41] on the accused's failure to unveil the alibi in due time.[42] However where the notice *was* given inside the statutory time, *any* comment by the judge on the accused's failure to mention the alibi at the earliest practicable time must be irregular, because the statute having imposed a time for giving notice, the accused is not to be criticised for failing to give notice earlier than Parliament has provided.[43] If, after giving notice, the accused fails to call alibi evidence, it seems that in most cases the Crown will be justified in putting in the alibi notice and the judge may comment on the failure.[44]

For the purposes of the section, "evidence in support of an alibi" means evidence tending to show that by reason of the presence of the defendant at a particular place at a particular time he was not, or was unlikely to have been, at the place where the offence is alleged to have been committed at the time of its alleged commission.[45] This means that the charge must be specific as to both place and time. Where an offence was charged as happening between July 29 and August 21 in the City of Cardiff, it was held that section 11 could not apply.[46] Moreover, even if the section is capable of applying, alibi evidence has a restricted meaning for present purposes. It must be evidence placing the accused elsewhere on the occasion in question. What is loosely called "alibi evidence" may be relevant because it places the accused's *vehicle* elsewhere,[47] or an alleged Crown eye-witness elsewhere[48]; but such is not "evidence in support of an alibi" within the meaning of the section. Nor is evidence which is confined to showing that the accused was not at the scene of the crime (but not placing him at any other particular place)[49]: nor yet is evidence placing him elsewhere but on some other occasion.[50] Such evidence is not subject to the restrictions of the section,

---

[41] *i.e.* as in *R. v. Ryan* (1966) 50 Cr.App.R. 144 at p. 148; *ante*, p. 184.
[42] After all, at the committal proceedings he will have been warned by the magistrate that if his defence is alibi he must give notice of it within seven days. *Supra*, note 37.
[43] *R. v. Lewis*, *supra*.
[44] *R. v. Brigden* [1973] Crim.L.R. 579; *R. v. Rossborough* (1985) 81 Cr.App.R. 139; but see *R. v. Watts* (1980) 71 Cr.App.R. 136 at p. 141.
[45] Criminal Justice Act 1967, s.11(8). See T. M. S. Tosswill, "The Definition of an Alibi Defence" [1978] Crim.L.R. 276.
[46] *R. v. Hassan* [1970] 1 Q.B. 423.
[47] Gooderson, *op. cit.* p. 163.
[48] *R. v. Berry* (1924) 18 Cr.App.R. 65; Gooderson, *op. cit.* p. 165.
[49] *R. v. Gibbs* [1974] Crim.L.R. 474 (Bodmin Crown Court).
[50] *R. v. Lewis* [1969] 2 Q.B. 1.

however significant that evidence may be to the issues in the case. Thus if the accused is charged with robbery which is alleged to have been committed on a Monday and part of the evidence against him is that he was seen on the Tuesday driving a van which contained the stolen goods, he may tender evidence of alibi relating to the Tuesday without giving notice under the section.[51]

If the judge wrongly prevents the accused from giving or calling alibi evidence, the Court of appeal will rarely dismiss his appeal under the proviso to section 2 of the Criminal Appeal Act 1968, on the ground that no miscarriage of justice has occurred.[52]

2. Silence in Court

As we have seen[53] the Criminal Evidence Act 1898 makes an accused person a competent witness for himself or any co-accused. The Act purports to give him a privilege which he can exercise or not as he thinks fit, and it is specifically provided that he shall not be called except upon his own application.[54] He is not competent to give evidence for the Crown and not compellable to give evidence for anyone else. He may choose to remain entirely silent.

The policy of the Act is apparently to give the accused a wholly free choice in the matter. Nevertheless, most accused persons find themselves reluctantly leaving the safety of the dock and entering the witness box, there to run the gauntlet of cross-examination by the Crown and any co-accuseds. In practice the privilege of giving evidence is one which it is usually very risky to forgo. "Everybody now knows that absence from the witness box requires a very considerable amount of explanation,"[55] and the accused who clings to the sanctuary of the dock must not be surprised to find that he has only made things worse for himself.[56] It is true that the framers of the Act, in pursuance of their policy of making the giving of evidence by the accused a right and not a duty, forbade the Crown from making any comment on the

---

[51] R. v. *Lewis, supra.*
[52] *Ibid.* per Lord Widgery C.J., at p. 6; R. v. *Hassan, supra;* but see R. v. *Cooper* (1979) 69 Cr.App.R. 229.
[53] *Ante,* p. 131.
[54] s.1, proviso (*a*).
[55] *Per* Lord Goddard C.J. in R. v. *Jackson* [1953] 1 W.L.R. 591 at p. 595.
[56] "In our experience of trials, juries seldom acquit persons who do not give evidence when there is a clear case for them to answer and they do not answer it": *per* in Lawton L.J. R. v. *Sparrow* [1973] 1 W.L.R. 488.

accused's failure to enter the box.[57] However, they omitted to prevent counsel for a co-accused from commenting, and it has been held that he cannot be prevented from making any comments he thinks fit,[58] even to the extent of putting into words what the jury are probably thinking anyway, namely, if the accused is innocent, as he claims, why has he not gone into the box to say so?[59]

Moreover, the age-old power of the judge to comment on the evidence in the case and the manner in which it was conducted was not expressly or impliedly cut down by the Act,[60] and although some judges never comment on the accused's failure to testify, others regularly do, as indeed in an appropriate case it can be said to be their duty.[61] How far a judge can go in such comments, which has been the subject of numerous decisions,[62] depends upon the particular case. But it can be said that, since failure to give evidence has no *evidential* value, he must never say or imply that the jury may find corroboration in such failure.[63] Moreover, since the Crown must prove its case, he must not bolster up a weak prosecution case by making comments about the accused's failure to give evidence.[64]

Subject to this, in most but not all cases, the judge ought to follow the guidance given by Lord Parker C.J. in *R. v. Bathurst*[65]:

"The accepted form of comment is to inform the jury that, of course, he is not bound to give evidence, that he can sit back and see if the prosecution have proved their case, and that while the jury have been deprived of the opportunity of hearing his story tested in cross-examination the one thing

---

[57] s.1, proviso (*b*); but crown counsel is not prevented from commenting that certain crown evidence was unchallenged: *R. v. Brown and Routh* [1983] Crim.L.R. 38.
[58] *R. v. Whickham* (1971) 55 Cr.App.R. 199.
[59] See Lawton L.J. in *R. v. Sparrow, supra*, at p. 493.
[60] *R. v. Rhodes* [1899] 1 Q.B. 177, *per* Lord Russell of Killowen at p. 83.
[61] "The object of a summing-up is to help the jury and in our experience a jury is not helped by a colourless reading out of the evidence as recorded by the judge in his note-book": *per* Lawton L.J. in *R. v. Sparrow, supra*.
[62] They are reviewed in *R. v. Sparrow, supra*.
[63] *R. v. Jackson* [1953] 1 W.L.R. 591; indeed, since the temptation to do just that is probably strong in an uninstructed jury, it may be that the judge ought to give an express warning on the point: see Heydon, p. 166.
[64] *R. v. Sparrow, supra*, at p. 495, *per* Lawton L.J. summarising the effect of *Waugh v. R.* [1950] A.C. 203.
[65] [1968] 2 Q.B. 107 at p. 108, adopted in *R. v. Pratt* [1971] Crim.L.R. 234; *R. v. Mutch* (1973) 57 Cr.App.R. 196.

they must not do is to assume that he is guilty because he has not gone into the witness box."

But it all depends on the facts; sometimes a stronger comment is called for,[66] and repeated comments are not necessarily unfair.[67] The one thing he must not do is to say or imply that a defence *cannot* succeed unless the accused gives evidence. In *R. v. Sparrow*, the accused was tried with one Skingle for the murder of a police officer. Skingle shot the officer, when Sparrow was with him on a criminal enterprise. Sparrow's defence was that he was not party to any joint plan to use loaded weapons, but he did not give evidence. In his charge to the jury, the judge said: "Is it not essential that he should go into the witness box and tell you that himself and be subject to cross-examination about it?" It was held by the Court of Appeal that although the case warranted a very strong comment, "is it not *essential*...?" went too far and overstepped the limits of justifiable comment.[68]

Equally subject to comment by the judge is the accused's failure to call potential witnesses. In commenting, the judge should adopt the general approach set out in *R. v. Sparrow*.[69]

B. Proposals for Reform

The right of silence has never gone unchallenged. Jeremy Bentham employed his usual brilliant sarcasm on one aspect of it, namely the prohibition of judicial interrogation of a suspect.[70] "If all criminals of every class had assembled, and framed a system after their own minds, is not this rule the very first which they would have established for their security? Innocence never takes advantage of it. Innocence claims the right of speaking, as guilt invokes the privilege of silence." The Criminal Law Revision Committee[71] quoted this with approval as applying strongly to the whole doctrine; and said that although criminal trials must be

---

[66] "In the judgment of this court, if the trial judge had not commented in strong terms on the appellant's absence from the witness box, he would have been failing in his duty": *R. v. Sparrow, supra*, at p. 495.
[67] *R. v. Voisin* [1918] 1 K.B. 531, *per* A. T. Lawrence J. at p. 536; *R. v. Sparrow, supra*, at p. 495.
[68] [1973] 1 W.L.R. 488; but the proviso to s.2 of the Criminal Appeal Act 1968 was applied.
[69] *R. v. Gallagher* [1974] 1 W.L.R. 1204.
[70] *Treatise on Evidence*, p. 241; but he was much less severe on that part of the doctrine which concerns failure to answer questions out of court: *Ibid.*
[71] Cmnd. 4991, (1972) para. 31.

fair they must be fair to both sides.[72] The system grew up at a time when an accused was much more at a disadvantage than nowadays; but now he is at less of a disadvantge and "there is now a large and increasing class of sophisticated professional criminals who are not only highly skilful in organising their crimes and in the steps they take to avoid detection, but are well aware of their legal rights and use every possible means to avoid conviction if caught. These include refusal to answer questions by the police and the elaborate manufacture of false evidence."[73] The Committee therefore proposed that where an accused, on being questioned by the police[74] about an offence, or on being charged with an offence, failed to mention any fact relied on by him at his trial which he could reasonably be expected to have mentioned, the court or jury may draw such inferences from his failure as seem proper; and the failure is to be capable of amounting to corroboration.[75]

The caution administered to a suspect being interrogated or charged by the police warned him that he need not say anything.[76] The Committee proposed to dispense with any caution *before* charge,[77] and alter the caution *at* charge so that it plainly warned him to speak then or risk having adverse inferences drawn against him.[78]

Further, as to failure to give evidence, it was proposed that once a prima facie case had been made against the accused, the court should formally call upon him to give evidence. If he then did not, or without good cause refused to answer any question, that was to give rise to such inferences as seemed proper, and could amount to corroboration.[79]

These were radical proposals,[80] and found few supporters.[81] Reasoned objections to them include: the fact that unmeritorious

---

[72] para. 27.
[73] para. 21.
[74] Or other persons charged with the duty of investigating offences. Accusations or questions by others, such as friends, victims or eyewitnesses, and the accused's reactions thereto, would continue to be dealt with under the common law: para. 34. Draft Bill, cl. 1(3).
[75] *Ibid.* cl. 1(1).
[76] See Appendix 80.
[77] cl. 1(5).
[78] § 44.
[79] cl. 5(1)(3).
[80] For general discussion of the proposals and their critics, see Zuckerman (1973) 36 M.L.R. 509, and Heydon, pp. 166–175.
[81] A notable supporter was Professor Cross: see, "The Evidence Report. Sense or Nonsense" [1973] Crim.L.R. 329; "The Right of Silence and the Presumption of Innocence" (1970) 11 J.S.P.T.L. 66.

acquittals by juries are not as common as the Committee seem to think; the absence of research by the Committee into, *e.g.* what proportion of suspects are the sort of hardened, tactically skilful criminals they refer to; the view that if the last century has seen ameliorations of the accused's position, it has also seen improvements in that of the authorities, *e.g.* the rise of an organised, professional police force, the rise of summary trial for serious offences. The balance of advantage has not swung decisively in favour of the accused, who still tends to be, typically, an ignorant suspicious, frightened, highly suggestible person. The general sense of those objecting to the proposals on the right of silence was that the proposals about police questioning were misconceived, unlike the proposals on silence in court, which had some merit. Those who reacted thus would no doubt support the compromise suggestions made by Wigmore.[82] Have a right of silence out of court, says he, to protect people from oppressive officials; but in court, the accused is adequately protected and ought to be required to speak up, once a prima facie case has been made out against him. However, in 1981 the Royal Commission on Criminal Procedure[83] differed from the Criminal Law Revision Committee and recommended no change in the law on silence both on interrogation and at the trial.[84] In the event, the Police and Criminal Evidence Act 1984 left that law untouched.

---

[82] § 2251.
[83] Report (1981), Cmnd. 8092, paras. 4.53, 4.66.
[84] Both Reports however recommended the abolition of the accused's right to make an unsworn statement from the dock, and that was effected by s.72, Administration of Justice Act 1982: see *ante*, p. 130.

Chapter 10

CONFESSIONS

What a person says about the facts in issue otherwise than in the witness box is in principle not admissible, being hearsay evidence.[1] But admissions by a party have always constituted an exception to the hearsay rule.[2] One kind of admission is a confession by an accused person, *i.e.* an admission by him about the facts charged against him. A confession has therefore been in principle provable against an accused person, as an exception to the hearsay rule. Indeed the majority of all convictions in criminal cases have always depended wholly or partly on the accused's confession. However, the Crown had to prove certain preconditions of admissibility, and if it failed to do so, the confession was inadmissible. If it succeeded, the confession was admissible, but the judge had a discretion to refuse to admit it. This general position still obtains today. However the common law about the preconditions of admissibility became very rigid and technical, and was for some years the subject of attempts to get it abolished or changed. In 1984, it was wholly replaced by the Police and Criminal Evidence Act, principally section 76.[3]

A. Admissibility at Common Law

A brief outline of the common law on this subject will be enough to demonstrate its unsatisfactory nature. The law excluded altogether any confession which the Crown could not show to be voluntary, which often meant that, with the loss of the principal item in the Crown's case, an acquittal was inevitable. The reason why such a confession was excluded was originally that it was thought to be unreliable, but by the twentieth century it became recognised that the real reason was to restrain the activities of the police in the questioning of suspects in custody. It was recognised that irregularities can occur in police stations and, moreover, that for many suspects the mere fact of being interrogated in custody puts them at a heavy psychological disadvantage, which may cause them to speak when they would rather remain silent. It

---
[1] *Post*, Chap. 12.
[2] *Post*, Chap. 13.
[3] See, generally, Mirfield, *Confessions* (1985).

does not of course follow that what is said is untrue; on the contrary it is very often both true and believable. But it may not be, and in any event, whether the suspect speaks the truth or not, he has an absolute right to remain silent, which he must not be robbed of.[4] It has often been said, however, that if all suspects insisted on this right, the system of criminal justice in this country (or indeed in any other country where the right exists) would break down entirely. Society is thus confronted with a dilemma. Confessions are needed to make the system work, but how confessions are obtained must be controlled if that society is to have any claim to be a civilized one.

The common law doctrine of involuntary confessions (sometimes called the doctrine of *Ibrahim* v. *R*.[5] after the leading modern authority) was supposed to hold the balance between the two competing claims of efficiency and fairness. However it did this in a rigid and illogical manner. "Involuntariness" was a narrow concept, which by no means covered all undesirable causes of a confession. It covered oppression, which was anything which tended to sap and had sapped the suspect's free will.[6] Although this concept was broad, it was also uncertain, being dependent in any particular case on the strength of mind of the individual suspect. What would be oppression for one person would not necessarily be so for another. It also covered certain inducements; a statement was inadmissible if obtained either by fear of prejudice or hope of advantage excited or held out by a person in authority.[7] This was not of uncertain scope as was oppression, but it was narrow and technical. It was laid down that the fact that the interrogator thought he was acting perfectly properly, and did not mean to make a forbidden inducement, was quite immaterial.[8] If, as a result of any remark made by him, the suspect got the impression that he had better make a statement, any resulting statement was involuntary.

On the other hand, the doctrine of *Ibrahim* v. *R*. did not cover anything else which might be thought undesirable, such as questioning a person who was drunk, drugged, exhausted, frightened. Such further factors, perhaps unfair, perhaps making for doubt about the confession's reliability, might cause the judge to exercise his discretion against the Crown and reject the statement, but that is all they were capable of; they could not

[4] On the right of silence, see *ante*, Chap. 9.
[5] [1914] A.C. 599.
[6] *R.* v. *Prager* (1972) 56 Cr.App.R. 1511.
[7] *Ibrahim* v. *R.*, *supra*, at p. 609.
[8] *D.P.P.* v. *Pin Ling* [1976] A.C. 574.

make the statement inadmissible in law. As to part of the ground covered by this discretion, namely questioning in police custody, the judges issued rules, called the Judges' Rules,[9] indicating how they would exercise the discretion. The Rules were the subject of complaints from all sides, the police complaining that exact compliance would grossly hamper their work, civil libertarians complaining that the rules were not binding and breaches of them were often forgiven by trial judges.

The doctrine of involuntary confessions was not only rigid and narrow; it was also illogical. Such malpractices by the authorities as it punished, it punished by robbing the prosecution of its evidence, thereby often causing its case to collapse. It would seem more appropriate to discipline the transgressor in some way, rather than to confer an unmerited prize on the defendant. Where a reliable confession is ruled out because technically involuntary, the "penalty" is suffered by the public, in having a possibly dangerous criminal released without punishment. However there are difficulties about penalizing the transgressing policeman personally rather than the prosecution. Unlike the prosecution, which has no "human rights," a policeman is entitled not to be disciplined except for a specific wrongdoing strictly proved against him. Apart from the inevitable difficulties of proving to a satisfactory standard the allegations against him, what a policeman is alleged to have done "wrong" is often not describable as an "offence" at all, *e.g.* speaking coldly to a timid and suggestible suspect, and it is both unjust and ludicrous to discipline him for such a thing. So although penalizing the prosecution by robbing it of its evidence may be illogical and weak as a deterrent, in practice it is the only way to oblige the authorities to treat a suspect properly.

In 1972, the C.L.R.C. made proposals which merely tidied up the existing law, by altering the nature of the forbidden inducements but retaining exclusion as the sanction where a confession was the result of such inducements or of oppression.[10] The Committee's Report had not been acted upon when in 1981, the Royal Commission on Criminal Procedure[11] much more radically proposed that inadmissibility should go altogether, except where torture or inhuman treatment was involved. In every other case the way in which a confession was obtained would not make it inadmissible but at most affect its weight.

---

[9] See Appendix A to Home Office Circular No. 89/1978.
[10] Cmnd. 4991, Draft Bill, cl. 2.
[11] Cmnd. 8092.

Admissibility at Common Law

Breaches of a proposed code of practice on the conditions in which interrogation was to take place would be enforced only by police discipline. These latter proposals did not find favour, but their appearance caused the C.L.R.C.'s less radical proposals to be looked at again, and these are the basis of what was enacted in the Police and Criminal Evidence Act 1984.

B. Admissibility under the Police and Criminal Evidence Act 1984

Section 76(1) provides that a confession made by an accused may be given in evidence against him so far as it is relevant and not excluded under subsection 2. "Confession" includes any statement wholly or partly adverse to a person who made it, whether made to a person in authority or not, and whether made in words or otherwise.[12] Thus a "mixed" statement, *i.e.* one partly favourable, partly unfavourable, is admissible, but only "against him."[13] The statement need not be made in words. A nod or gesture is included, if intended to be assertive. Conduct not intended to be assertive is thought not to be hearsay, but mere circumstantial evidence of whatever can be deduced from it.[14] If so it will be admissible without recourse to section 76(1) and will not need to satisfy section 76(2).

1. Conditions of Admissibility: section 76(2)

If, in any proceedings where the prosecution proposes to give in evidence a confession made by an accused person, it is represented to the Court (or if the Court of its own motion takes the point[15]) that the confession was or may have been obtained:

(a) by oppression of the person who made it, or
(b) in consequence of anything said or done which was likely, in the circumstances existing at the time, to render unreliable any confession which might be made by him in consequence thereof

the court shall not allow the confession to be given in evidence against him except in so far as the prosecution proves to the court

---

[12] s.82(1).
[13] On the evidential status of the favourable parts, see, *ante,* p. 106.
[14] See, *post,* p. 254.
[15] s.76(3).

beyond reasonable doubt that the confession (notwithstanding that it may be true) was not obtained as aforesaid.

These conditions apply only where the prosecution proposes to put in a confession, not where a co-accused wishes to do so. If A and B are jointly charged, and A, said to have been oppressed by the police, makes a statement saying that he (A) was solely to blame, B can prove this against A.[16]

(a) Voir Dire

It is for the Crown to show beyond reasonable doubt that the conditions in section 76(2) are satisfied. If the matter is raised, it is in the vast majority of trials on indictment[17] gone into on the *voir dire* (sometimes called the trial within a trial), in the absence of the jury.[18] However, the defence may, if it wishes, raise the matter in the course of the trial in the presence of the jury.[19] If it is raised in the course of the Crown's case, the defence is not, save where it is an exceptionally clear case of inadmissibility, entitled to a ruling at the end of the Crown case; in all ordinary cases the ruling should be given at the end of all the evidence.[20] If the issue is raised after the Crown has closed its case, the Crown should be allowed to call witnesses in rebuttal.[21] In any event, the matter remains to be decided by the judge, not by the jury.[22]

The judge hears witnesses as to the circumstances of the statement's making and rules one way or the other. The enquiry at this stage is not as to the statement's truth or reliability, but as to whether it is admissible.[23] Although "reliability" is relevant to admissibility, and although the truth of the statement might be thought to have a bearing on its reliability, the accused may not be asked directly whether the statement is true.[24] If the judge decides that it is inadmissible, when the trial proceeds it is not put

---

[16] Nor will the Court's general discretion to exclude evidence under s.78(1), *ante*, p. 44, be exercisable, because that discretion only applies to Crown evidence.

[17] In summary trials, *voir dire* is not appropriate. The magistrates hear and decide questions of admissibility along with all the other issues: *F. v. Chief Constable of Kent* [1982] Crim.L.R. 682. See also *R. v. Epping & Ongar JJ.* [1986] Crim.L.R. 555.

[18] *Ajodha v. State* [1982] A.C. 204 (P.C.). But if the only question is, not whether a statement complies with the conditions in s.76(2), but whether it was ever made at all, this is not a *voir dire* question, being purely for the jury: *ibid.*

[19] *Ajodha v. State, supra.* For the problems raised by "tactical" postponements, see Rowe, "The Voir Dire and the Jury" [1986] Crim.L.R. 226.

[20] *R. v. Jackson* [1985] Crim.L.R. 444.

[21] *R. v. Cunningham* [1985] Crim.L.R. 374.

[22] *R. v. Airey* [1985] Crim.L.R. 305.

[23] *Chan Wei Keung v. R.* [1967] 2 A.C. 160 (P.C.); *R. v. Ovenell* [1969] 1 Q.B. 17.

[24] *Wong Kam-Ming v. R.* [1980] A.C. 247 (P.C.).

in, or referred to, or cross-examined upon.[25] Nor may any other statements made by the accused at the *voir dire* in any way relevant to how the confession came to be made, whether said in chief[26] or extracted in cross-examination,[27] be proved or cross-examined on in the trial proper. This is because the accused has an absolute right to say what he will at the *voir dire*, without running the risk of having anything he says there used in any way against him at the trial.[28]

If the judge decides that the confession is admissible, it is put in, but the accused may fight over again before the jury the issue of how it came to be made, in order that they may decide what weight to give it.[29] The jury cannot disregard or be invited to disregard the confession. The jury might conclude, differently from the judge, that the confession was obtained by threats amounting to oppression; still it is their duty to weigh it and ask themselves, whether it is true.[30] The Crown may cross-examine the accused as to inconsistent statements made by him at the *voir dire*,[31] but may not lead evidence of other admissions made thereat.[32]

(b) Oppression

The Crown may be called upon to prove that there was no oppression of the person who made the confession or, if there was, that the confession was not obtained by it, *i.e.* there was no causal connection. The subsection does not speak of "oppression *by* the person *to* whom it was made," nor does it require the oppression to be intended. Oppression can be the result of negligent arrangements causing unsatisfactory conditions of custody, for which the interrogator had no responsibility.[33]

---

[25] *R. v. Treacy* [1944] 2 All E.R. 229; see, *ante*, p. 118; *Wong Kam-Ming, supra; R. v. Brophy* [1982] A.C. 476 (H.L.).
[26] *R. v. Brophy, supra.*
[27] *Wong Kam-Ming v. R., supra.*
[28] It may be that the ruling has not survived the 1984 Act. Any statement made by D at the *voir dire* adverse to his interest is itself a confession under s.82(1); such may be given in evidence against him by s.76(1), unless it is obtained by oppression or in circumstances rendering it likely to be unreliable: s.76(2), which conditions can hardly apply to a statement made in the face of the Court. However, D would be protectable on discretion, as to which see, *post*, p. 201.
[29] *R. v. Murray* [1951] 1 K.B. 291; *Chan Wei Keung v. R., supra: Prasad v. R.* [1981] 1 All E.R. 319 (P.C.).
[30] *R. v. Ovenell, supra.* And it is the judge's duty to point this out to them: *R. v. McCarthy* (1980) 70 Cr.App.R. 270.
[31] *Wong Kam-Ming v. R., supra.*
[32] *Ibid.*
[33] See *R. v. McGrath* [1980] N.I. 91 (C.A.).

Although oppression will often result in the confession being "unreliable," (as to which see below), it need not do so. Although in practice they often overlap, oppression and unreliability are separate concepts, both of which have to be shewn to be absent if the confession is to be admissible.

Oppression is not completely defined, no doubt inevitably. At common law it was described as anything which tends to sap and has sapped, the accused's free will.[34] Prolonged questioning, or holding in isolation or in poor, e.g. cold, conditions, might be held to amount to oppression. However, as so described, oppression was very subjective, depending on the toughness of the individual suspect. What would sap the free will of a timid, suggestible, first-timer would not necessarily have that effect on a hardened experienced criminal who, it has been said, must expect tough questioning.[35] To the extent that oppression is still undefined[36] it remains an uncertain concept. The most that can be said that a set-up, or techniques, designed or likely to break the resistance of person subjected to it or them will be held to be oppression, if such are unacceptable to the Courts.[37] But not practices which are accepted. For example, a policeman may conclude that he has a much better chance of "cracking" a suspect if he detains him for questioning, but that is allowed,[38] and so unlikely in itself to be held to be oppression.

Oppression now has some objective features, by reason of its partial definition in section 78(8). It "includes torture, inhuman or degrading treatment and the use or threat of violence (whether or not amounting to torture)." The wording is taken from the European Convention on Human Rights[39] and has yet to be considered by English courts.[40] The use of violence not amounting to torture is also covered, so perhaps a single slap in the face will

---

[34] R. v. Prager (1972) 56 Cr.App.R. 151 (C.A.) adopting the description given in R. v. Priestley (1965) 51 Cr.App.R. 1.
[35] R. v. Gowan [1982] Crim.L.R. 281. But even the hardest criminal can be oppressed, and in fact Gowan's confession was excluded for oppression.
[36] The undefined concept developed by the common law remains after the partial statutory definition in s.76(8) (as to which see following text), which is to be regarded as enlarging not restricting the meaning of oppression: see Mirfield, Confessions (1985), p. 107.
[37] See R. v. Gargan and R. v. Flynn, noted at [1972] 24 N.I.L.Q. 199.
[38] See, Police & Criminal Evidence Act 1984, ss.34–44, and Mohammed-Holgate v. Duke [1984] A.C. 437.
[39] Art. 3.
[40] See however R. v. McCormick [1977] N.I. 105; R. v. McGrath [1980] N.I. 91 (C.A.); Tyrer v. U.K. (1978) 2 E.H.R.R.1 (E.C.H.R.); Ireland v. U.K. (1978) 2 E.H.R.R.25 (E.C.H.R.).

automatically exclude a confession obtained as a result.[41] Oppression, whatever it consists of, does not have to affect the reliability of the confession, although no doubt it often will.

The manner in which a person in police custody is to be treated is laid down in great detail by the Code of Practice, issued under section 66 of the Police and Criminal Evidence Act 1984, for the Detention, Treatment and Questioning of Persons in Custody by Police Officers. Although breach of the provisions of the Code does not in itself render the person responsible liable to criminal or civil proceedings,[42] but only (usually) to disciplinary proceedings,[43] the provisions of the Code are admissible in evidence in any proceedings and any relevant provision is to be taken into account in determining any question before the Court.[44] Thus, on the question whether any treatment counts as oppression under section 76(2), the Court will have regard to, but will not be bound by, the provisions of the Code as to such things as length of questioning, breaks for rest and refreshment, *etc*.

(c) Unreliability

The confession must be shown to be not "in consequence of anything said or done which was likely, in the circumstances, existing at the time, to render unreliable any confession which might be made by him in consequence thereof."[45] This replaces the concept of involuntariness defined in *Ibrahim* v. *R*.[46] which ruled out any statement obtained either by fear of prejudice or hope of advantage excited or held out by a person in authority. On the words of the sub-section, the things done or said need not be by a person in authority, or by the person to whom the statement is made. Nor need they be designed to induce a statement, or otherwise irregular. The only question is, in view of what was said or done, does the judge feel that any statement resulting is likely to be unreliable? If A on remand learns from his lawyer that his employer has told A's wife that if he does not get bail soon his job will be terminated, clearly that is capable of rendering unreliable any confession that A may make thereafter. Usually, of course, the words will be those of the interrogator, and examples of what may make a confession inadmissible are

---

[41] It may be that the expression will be construed to mean only substantial application of force: see Cross, p. 549.
[42] s.67(10).
[43] s.67(8).
[44] s.67(11).
[45] s.76(2)(b).
[46] [1914] A.C. 599.

promises to charge with a less serious offence, or not to oppose bail, or to have other offences taken into consideration, if the suspect makes a statement, or a threat to prosecute a friend or relation if he does not make a statement.

The test in *Ibrahim* v. *R.*, as applied, had nothing to do with reliability[47]; any threats or inducements which caused a confession[48] automatically resulted in inadmissability. Now unreliability is required, so a wholly trivial inducement may well be ignored. But it is an "objective" not an actual unreliability which is required. The fact that *this* confession is reliable is beside the point. The question is, was what was said or done likely, in the circumstances existing at the time, to render unreliable any confession which might be made by the defendant in consequence thereof? According to the C.L.R.C., which devised this test,[49] the judge should imagine that he was present at the interrogation and heard the threat or inducement, and consider whether, at the point when such was made, any confession which the accused might make as a result of it would be likely to be unreliable. If, for example, the threat was to charge the suspect's wife jointly with him, the judge might think that a confession even of a serious offence would be likely to be unreliable. If there was a promise to release the accused on bail to visit a sick member of his family, the judge might think that this would be unlikely to render a confession of a serious offence unreliable but likely to do so in the case of a minor offence. Although the form and contents of a statement may be relevant to the question of how it came to be made and thus to reliability, the fact that the confession is confirmed in some way, or even admitted to be true is irrelevant, because the Crown must prove absence of oppression or anything likely to make for unreliability in the confession "notwithstanding that it may be true."

(d) Facts discovered in consequence of an inadmissible confession

Sometimes a confession mentions the whereabouts of, *e.g.* the goods allegedly stolen by D. The discovery of the goods in the place indicated confirms, as a matter of common sense, the truth of at least part of D's confession. This confirmation does not make

---

[47] See *D.P.P.* v. *Ping Lin* [1976] A.C. 574; but see *R.* v. *Rennie* [1982] 1 All E.R. 385.
[48] They did not "cause" a confession if their effect had been removed by the passage of time or change in the circumstances before the statement was made: *R.* v. *Smith* [1959] 2 Q.B. 35.
[49] Cmnd. 4991, para. 65.

any part of an otherwise inadmissible confession admissible,[50] since in the absence of proof of the conditions of admissibility in section 76(2), the Court cannot allow it to be proved. However there has never been a rule that the *evidence discovered* is inadmissible by reason of the bad confession which produced it.[51] This rule is confirmed by section 76(4) which provides that the fact that a confession is wholly or partly excluded under section 76(2) shall not affect the admissibility in evidence of any facts discovered as a result of the confession.[52] Sometimes the discovered evidence in itself incriminates D because of some obvious link with him, *e.g.* it is in his private safe or has his fingerprints on it. But in other cases, the evidence is only useful if it is linked to D by shewing that it was he who told the police where to look. This linking is forbidden by section 76(5)[53]; evidence that a fact was discovered as a result of a confession excluded by section 76(2) shall not be admissible unless evidence of how it was discovered is given by the defence. Thus if D suggests that it was A who led the police to the property, the Crown may reply by proving that it was D's statement which revealed its whereabouts.

Section 76(4) also provides that the fact that a confession is inadmissible does not affect the admissibility of so much of it as shews that D writes, speaks or expresses himself in a particular way, if that is relevant.[54] Thus if D's handwriting is in issue, his written confession, although inadmissible as a confession, *i.e.* as to the truth of the contents, is admissible on that issue. And if a witness testifies that the person involved in an incident used particular picturesque oaths, D's recorded statement containing the same oaths would be admissible to identify D as the person involved, although inadmissible as a confession.

2. Discretion to Exclude Confessions

There is no discretion to admit a confession which does not satisfy the conditions in section 68(2). It does not follow however that the judge has no discretion to reject a confession which does satisfy that subsection; and which is therefore legally admissible. Section 82(3) provides that nothing in this part of the Act shall

---

[50] The same rule existed at common law: see *R.* v. *Warickshall* (1783) 1 Leach. 263.
[51] *R.* v. *Warickshall, supra.*
[52] Such evidence may however be excluded on discretion: see *post,* p. 203.
[53] This was probably the rule at common law: *R.* v. *Warickshall, supra, R.* v. *Berryman.*
[54] See *R.* v. *Voisin* [1918] 1 K.B. 521.

prejudice any power of a court to exclude evidence (whether by preventing questions being put or otherwise) at its discretion.[55] There was a power at common law to exclude confessions on discretion, which was confirmed by the House of Lords in *R. v. Sang*[56] in the course of denying any *general* discretion to exclude Crown evidence,[57] and the power is preserved by section 82(3).

The judges issued rules of practice, called the Judges' Rules, detailing how suspects in custody were to be treated, and the Preamble to the Rules contained a warning that non-conformity might render statements liable to be excluded in subsequent proceedings, although in practice breaches were very often forgiven, the Rules being rules of practice only.[58] The Judges' Rules were replaced by the Code of Practice for Detention, Treatment and Questioning of Persons by Police Officers,[59] and section 67(11) provides that the provisions of the Code are admissible and to be taken into account in settling any question to which they are relevant. In addition, the Police and Criminal Evidence Act 1984 contains several protective provisions, such as the right not to be held without charge for more than the permitted period[60]; the right to have someone informed of the arrest without delay[61]; the right to private consultation with a solicitor.[62] These rights are not given any specific sanction but they are none of them entirely new, and on past practice failure by the authorities to accord them is likely to be taken into account in deciding whether to exclude a confession on discretion.[63]

However, breaches of the Code or of the protective provisions of the Act are not likely to prove decisive. Occasions for exercising the discretion in favour of the defence will be rare, because the circumstances which might be persuasive will often relate to the confessions' forced nature or to the unlikelihood of its being reliable; and unless these are disproved beyond reasonable doubt by the Crown, the confession is inadmissible anyway. If it is proved beyond doubt that a confession was not obtained by oppression or in consequence of anything said or done which was likely to render any confession unreliable, the

---

[55] See also s.78(1), considered, *ante*, p. 44.
[56] [1980] A.C. 402.
[57] See, *ante*, p. 44.
[58] *R. v. Prager* (1972) 56 Cr.App.R. 151.
[59] Issued under s.66, Police and Criminal Evidence Act 1984; see Appendix 4.
[60] ss.41–44.
[61] s.56.
[62] s.58.
[63] See *R. v. Houghton & Franciosy* (1978) 68 Cr.App.R. 197 [s.41]; *R. v. Platt* [1981] Crim.L.R. 622 [s.56]; *R. v. Allen* [1977] Crim.L.R. 163 [s.58].

Admissibility under Police and Criminal Evidence Act 1984

Court is hardly likely to exclude that confession. However, if a confession, or evidence tantamount to such[64], is got by a trick, where the Code and the protective provisions are not in point because the suspect is not being interrogated in custody, the discretion may be exercised in favour of exclusion, even though no oppression or unreliability is involved, *e.g.* where incriminating documents are tricked out of the suspect or his advisers.[65]

The discretion discussed above overlaps but is probably distinct from the discretion to exclude any kind of Crown evidence, as to which see *ante*, p. 44.

---

[64] Lord Diplock's phrase denoting evidence which, although not strictly a confession, is against the accused and made available by him to the authorities at some time after the alleged offence: see *R. v. Sang* [1980] A.C. 402 at p. 436.

[65] See *R. v. Barker* [1941] 2 K.B. 381; *R. v. Payne* [1963] 1 W.L.R. 637.

CHAPTER 11

CHARACTER OF THE ACCUSED

We have seen[1] that the character of a party to litigation is not usually relevant to any issue in the litigation. When it is irrelevant, it may not be proved. When, exceptionally, it is relevant, it may be proved. But this is subject to special rules when the party is the accused in a criminal case. This chapter deals with those rules.

A. GOOD CHARACTER

In criminal cases, the accused is allowed to prove his good character, either in chief or in cross-examination. Strictly, what must be deposed to is, not particular good acts by him, but his general reputation in the community.[2] In practice considerable latitude is allowed both to the accused himself and a character witness, *e.g.* in a sexual case, he is allowed to say that he is happily married, or to call his wife to say so.[3]

As to the relevance of evidence of good character, it is wrong to describe this as neutral,[4] or as being only for use if the rest of the evidence leaves the jury in doubt,[5] for if they are in doubt they must acquit anyway. Although the evidence is primarily relevant as to credibility, *i.e.* it makes his testimony more worthy of belief, this does not mean that if the accused gives no evidence, the character evidence can be described as having little part to play. It can have a more general significance[6]; it can induce the jury to say whether they think it likely that a person with such a character would have committed the offence.[7] It is up to the judge to decide whether to allow a defendant with a "spent" conviction to describe himself as of good character,[8] and he has the usual power to reject character evidence which, in his view, is insufficiently relevant.[9]

[1] *Ante*, Chap. 2.
[2] *R.* v. *Rowton* (1865) 24 L.J.M.C. 57; *R.* v. *Redgrave* (1981) 74 Cr.App.R. 10.
[3] See *R.* v. *Redgrave, supra.*
[4] *R.* v. *Callum* [1975] R.T.R. 415.
[5] *R.* v. *Brittle* [1965] 109 S.J. 1028.
[6] *R.* v. *Bryant* (1977) 67 Cr.App.R. 157 at 165.
[7] *R.* v. *Stannard* (1837) 7 C. & P. 673 at 675.
[8] *R.* v. *Nye* (1982) 75 Cr.App.R. 247.
[9] *R.* v. *Rimmer & Beech* [1983] Crim.L.R. 250.

B. BAD CHARACTER

The general rule is that although the defence may,[10] the prosecution may not,[11] before verdict,[12] adduce evidence of the accused's bad character.[13] However, there are many important exceptions to this, the most important being where the accused puts his character in issue.

1. Character in Issue

Whenever the accused seeks to establish his own good character,[14] either by cross-examination, or by his own or another's testimony, the prosecution may rebut it. Thus the accused's witnesses as to character may be cross-examined, although this is not usual except on specific material. Evidence may also be given both of the accused's general bad character (though this is rarely tendered) and of his previous conviction for crime. As far as evidence of bad character is concerned, it was decided in the leading case at common law, *R. v. Rowton*,[15] that it must be of his general reputation, not of particular facts, nor merely the opinion of the witness[16]; but it appears that it need not be confined to the particular trait under consideration—if the charge involves indecency towards females, and evidence of bad character is admissible, such may be directed towards showing that he is

---

[10] Occasionally an accused may adduce evidence of a previous conviction in his own defence, as where he pleads *autrefois convict*; or where, being charged with bigamously marrying C during the life of his wife B, he proves the invalidity of his marriage to B by showing that he had been convicted of bigamously marrying her. (See *R. v. Willshire* (1881) 6 Q.B.D. 366).

[11] The judge is under a similar ban, and it is grossly unfair for him to undermine the credit of the accused by questioning him on the contents of his legal aid application: *R. v. Winter* (1980) 74 Cr.App.R.16; *R. v. Stubbs* [1982] 1 W.L.R. 509.

[12] After a plea or verdict of guilty, evidence of previous convictions may be given in order to determine the appropriate mode or amount of punishment.

[13] If such evidence is inadvertently let in, the judge has a complete discretion to discharge the jury and begin the case again: *R. v. Weaver* [1968] 1 Q.B. 353; *R. v. Palin* [1969] 1 W.L.R. 1544. Nor must it be forgotten that in any case of improper reception of evidence, the Court of Appeal may nevertheless dismiss an appeal if no miscarriage of justice has occurred: Criminal Appeal Act 1968, s.2(1).

[14] Merely attacking the character of others is not putting his own character in issue: *R. v. Butterwasser* [1948] 1 K.B. 4 at p. 7; *R. v. De Vere* [1982] Q.B. 75; although by so doing he may forfeit his statutory immunity from cross-examination on his character, as to which see, *post*, p. 227.

[15] (1865) 10 Cox 25; but in the Criminal Evidence Act 1898 (see *post* pp. 221–236), the word is not used in this restricted sense.

[16] *R. v. Rowton, supra.*

dishonest with regard to the property of others.[17] "There is no such thing in our procedure as putting half a prisoner's character in issue and leaving out the other half."[18] It may be noted that once evidence of bad character is allowed, it is not confined merely to rebutting the earlier evidence of good character; it bears on the accused's credibility generally,[19] and indeed on the question of his guilt. In so far as the object of the earlier evidence of good character was to show that by reason of his good character, he was unlikely to have committed the offence, the object of rebutting evidence of bad character is to shew the contrary, *i.e.* that he *is* likely to have committed the offence.[20]

2. Miscellaneous Cases

If the bad character of an accused (D1) is relevant to the defence of a co-accused (D2), D2 may call evidence about it and cross-examine the witnesses of the Crown and of D1 about it.[21] In *R. v. Miller*,[22] D1 and D2 were charged with certain frauds. It was D2's case that he was not involved at all, and that at all material times, he was impersonated by D1 who made unauthorised use of D2's office. To support this defence, his counsel was allowed to ask a crown witness whether the frauds did not cease entirely during a period when D1 was serving a prison sentence. Devlin J. (as he then was) held that if the question really was necessary for D2's defence, he could not prevent it, nor the actual giving of evidence to the same effect. D2 should be careful not to cause unnecessary prejudice to D1, counsel should consult together, and the judge should be asked to rule beforehand on whether the proposed evidence or questions are relevant,[23] but if they are, the judge cannot prevent them.[24]

Evidence of bad character may be let in under the doctrine of

---

[17] *R. v. Winfield* (1939) 26 Cr.App.R. 139; see also *Stirland v. D.P.P.* [1944] A.C. 315.
[18] *Per* Humphreys J. in *Winfield, supra,* at p. 141.
[19] *R. v. Longman and Richardson* [1969] 1 Q.B. 299.
[20] *Maxwell* v. *D.P.P.* [1935] A.C. 309, *per* Lord Sankey L.C. at p. 315.
[21] He will however not necessarily be able to cross-examine D1 himself about it; that is subject to special rules, as to which, see *post,* p. 221.
[22] [1952] 2 All E.R. 667; see also *Lowery* v. *R.* [1974] A.C. 85 at p. 102 (P.C.); *R. v. Neale* (1977) 65 Cr.App.R. 304 at p. 307 (C.A.); *R. v. Bracewell* (1978) 68 Cr.App.R. 44 (C.A.).
[23] *R. v. Miller, supra; R. v. Bracewell, supra.*
[24] See cases in previous note, and *R. v. Neale, supra.* By this line of defence, D2 will forfeit his own immunity from cross-examination as to character, but that is a different matter as to which see, *post,* p. 234.

res gestae,[25] as, e.g. where on a charge of using threatening, abusive and insulting words with intent to stir up racial hatred, witnesses give evidence of a speech made by the accused, which reveals that he has been in prison.[26]

Occasionally statute allows proof of bad character before conviction, the most commonly resorted to being the Theft Act 1968, s.27(3).[27] This allows on a handling charge, evidence of possession of other goods stolen within the previous twelve months, or a conviction of theft or handling within the previous five years, for the purpose of proving guilty knowledge on the present occasion.[28] In a few cases, the offence charged can only be committed by a person who has previously been convicted. An example is the offence in section 99 of the Road Traffic Act 1972 of driving while disqualified, which necessarily involves proof that the defendant was on an earlier occasion disqualified on conviction of a motoring offence.[29]

3. Similar Fact Evidence

It is sometimes possible to prove facts which show that the accused has a bad character or previous convictions under what is often called the similar facts doctrine. The cases where this is allowed are all exceptional, because the general rule is to the contrary, *i.e.* that the Crown is *not* allowed to reveal in any way that the accused is of bad character until after conviction.

As we have seen,[30] a fact in issue may be proved by circumstantial rather than direct evidence, *i.e.* by facts which are relevant to the facts in issue. It is sometimes the case that the facts of one transaction are relevant to the facts of another, disputed, transaction. As a matter of logic, one may deduce the facts of the latter from the facts of the former, if they are sufficiently similar in some significant aspect. Provided the logical connection between the two transactions is pronounced enough to compensate for the inconvenience of having to investigate a transaction not actually in issue,[31] the law allows proof of one transaction by evidence of the other.

---

[25] *Post*, p. 300. See *R. v. Malik* [1968] 1 W.L.R. 353; *R. v. Bastin* [1971] Crim.L.R. 529.
[26] *R. v. Malik, supra.*
[27] See also, Official Secrets Acts 1911, s.1(2), s.1(3).
[28] For the limited scope of this provision, see *R. v. Bradley* (1979) 70 Cr.App.R. 200. See also, *R. v. Perry* [1984] Crim.L.R. 680.
[29] See also Firearms Act 1968, s.211.
[30] *Ante*, p. 16.
[31] *Ante*, p. 17.

This is a perfectly general doctrine of evidence, and no particularly acute problems arise, except when one tries to use it in a criminal case against the accused. Proving that the accused on another occasion did something similar to what he is now accused of doing may be relevant, but it will inevitably show him in a bad light. It will thus fall foul of a cardinal principle of English criminal procedure. However great a ruffian or scoundrel he is, he is to be presented to the jury as a man of hitherto unspotted virtue against whom nothing is known. The reason is that although, in deciding whether a man accused of, e.g. burglary, is guilty of that crime, it is undoubtedly of some use to know that he is a life-long burglar, the probative force of this knowledge is often quite slight and nothing like enough to justify the likely reaction in the jury, who may well take it as conclusive. It is to protect him from this prejudice that evidence of his bad character is rigorously excluded. Logic would admit the forbidden evidence, but the need to avoid prejudice prevails over logic.[32] In the normal case, "you cannot convict a man of one crime by proving that he has committed some other crime."[33]

But sometimes the claims of logic are so overwhelmingly strong that they cannot be denied this way, if we are to avoid blatantly unjust acquittals. Consider for example the facts of *R. v. Smith*.[34] Smith was charged with the murder of A, his bigamous wife, who was found dead in her bath with no one in the house but Smith, who benefited financially from her death. There was no compelling evidence that A did not die of natural causes; but the Crown was allowed to prove that, after A's death, B and C, with whom Smith had contracted bigamous marriages and from whose deaths he benefited, were found dead in their baths with no one in the house but Smith. It is of course just conceivable that Smith was the victim of a horrible double coincidence, but the alternative explanation, that they were all planned deaths for financial gain, is so overwhelmingly probable that to keep the jury in ignorance of these other deaths would be to invite the risk of a scandalously wrong acquittal.

The law therefore concedes that the relevance of evidence of similar transactions can sometimes be so strong that it outweighs the disadvantage of using it, namely the risk of prejudice in the jury's eyes. Where this is so, the similar fact evidence must be admitted despite the prejudice.

---

[32] See Lord Simon of Glaisdale in *D.P.P. v. Kilbourne* [1973] A.C. 729 at p. 757.
[33] Lord Loreburn L.C. in *R. v. Ball* [1911] A.C. 47 at p. 71.
[34] (1915) 11 Cr.App.R. 229.

(a) D.P.P. v. Boardman[35]

It is nowadays comparatively easy to state the principle on which it may be decided whether similar fact evidence should be admitted, although the question is always one of degree and thus often difficult to apply to a particular case. The principle was authoritatively laid down by the House of Lords in *D.P.P. v. Boardman*.[36] B, the headmaster of a language school, was charged with buggery with one pupil S, and inciting another pupil H to commit buggery with him. The charges were tried together, and because in both cases B proposed to play the passive part with the pupil playing the active part and because there were certain other features common to the two alleged incidents, it was held that the evidence of the incident with S was admissible to prove the incident with B, and vice versa. The governing principle was expressed in various ways in different speeches. Similar fact evidence, to be admitted, requires a strong degree of probative force.[37] Its relevance must be such that to exclude it would be an affront to common sense.[38] According to Lord Salmon, the probative force must arise because the evidence as to the similar facts and the fact in issue is so strikingly similar that common sense makes the similarity inexplicable on the basis of coincidence.[39]

The vivid nature of Lord Salmon's phrase, "striking similarity" posed a danger of its being adopted as a universal test, applicable in all cases. But his reference to "inexplicability on the basis of coincidence" shows that it was not so designed. In *Boardman's* case, the object of giving evidence of both incidents was to lead to the irresistable inference that the only explanation of the similar stories told by S and H was *either* a remarkable coincidence of a sort most unlikely to occur, *or* that their stories were true in all their details. (Of course, in such a case, the judge must be satisfied that there is no real chance that the witnesses to the separate incidents have put their heads together to concoct false evidence; if he is not so satisfied the similar fact evidence must be

---

[35] Valuable articles on the position since *Boardman's* case are Cross, "Fourth Time Lucky: Similar Fact Evidence in the House of Lords" [1975] Crim.L.R. 62; Hoffman, "Similar Facts after Boardman" (1975) 91 L.Q.R. 193; Allan, "Similar Fact Evidence and Disposition" (1985) 48 M.L.R. 253. See also Eggleston, Chap. 7.
[36] [1975] A.C. 421.
[37] *Ibid.* p. 444, *per* Lord Wilberforce.
[38] *Ibid.* p. 453 *per* Lord Hailsham.
[39] *Ibid.* p. 462.

rejected.[40]) This sort of inference, depending upon the inherent unlikelihood of coincidence, is often involved; see for example *R. v. Smith*.[41] But there are cases where it is not involved, *e.g.* where the purpose of the similar fact evidence is to show knowledge in the accused. If it is shewn that it was gained by him in the former transaction, it will usually be irresistable that it was possessed by him in the transaction in issue. In such a case, striking similarity in the two transactions is beside the point.[42]

In view of this, in later cases it has been pointed out that "striking similarity" is only a label, which can lead to error.[43] The general sense of the speeches in *Boardman* is that "positive probative value" is what is required for the admissibility of similar fact evidence.[44] "Positive probative value" is a less vivid phrase than "striking similarity," but it is of general application, whereas the latter phrase is not apt for all cases where similar fact evidence may legitimately be used. "Positive probative value" means a high degree of cogency. This is a matter for the judge to decide[45]; unless the evidence is in his view extremely cogent, he must exclude it.

(b) Examples of cases where similar fact evidence was admitted[46]

In *Makin v. Att.-Gen. for New South Wales*,[47] A was charged with the murder of B, an infant whom she had promised to adopt and maintain on receipt of a small premium from B's mother. B's body was found buried in A's garden in a condition which left the cause of death uncertain. Evidence was admitted that A had received other infants from their mothers on similar terms, who

---

[40] *Ibid. per* Lord Cross at p. 459, Lord Wilberforce at p. 444; *R. v. Scarrott* (1977) 65 Cr.App.R. 125 at p. 134. This objection to similar fact evidence is sometimes called "the group objection."

[41] *Ante*, p. 208.

[42] Which is why the expression "Similar Fact Evidence," although hallowed by long usage, is not very apt as a title of the doctrine at present being discussed.

[43] *R. v. Rance* (1975) 62 Cr.App.R. 118; *R. v. Scarrott* (1977) 65 Cr.App.R. 125; *R. v. Mansfield* [1978] 1 All E.R. 134.

[44] *R. v. Scarrott, supra*, at p. 129, *per* Scarman L.J.

[45] *D.P.P. v. Boardman, supra*, at p. 462, *per* Lord Salmon. Cogency, or weight of evidence, is normally a matter for the jury, but this is one case where admissibility depends on cogency. The judge, in deciding on admissibility, must form a view on the weight to be given to the evidence. Since often a conviction is a near certainty if he admits the evidence, this area offers a striking example of judicial control of the jury; he allows them to hear the evidence only if it is virtually conclusive.

[46] See also *R. v. Smith, ante*, p. 208.

[47] [1894] A.C. 57.

had afterwards disappeared, and that the bodies of unidentified infants were found buried in the gardens of other houses occupied by A.

In *R. v. Ball*,[48] a brother and sister were charged with incest within a particular period of time.[49] During that period they lived in the same house and occupied the same bed, but there was no direct evidence that they had sexual intercourse. Evidence was admitted that prior to the period in question they lived openly as man and wife, and that the sister had had a child by the brother.

In *R. v. Straffen*,[50] A was charged with murdering a little girl B. B was strangled for no apparent reason, she was not interfered with sexually, and no steps were taken to hide her body. Evidence was admitted that A had formerly killed other little girls, C and D, in the same way, for no apparent reason, and left the bodies unhidden.

(c) Common elements in the two transactions

An earlier discreditable transaction may sometimes be proved, not in order to rely on any similarity it may exhibit with the present disputed transaction, but in order to establish some disputed element in the Crown's case by showing an earlier situation,[51] involving the accused, which did contain that element. An obvious example is knowledge, either of the falsity of a representation,[52] or likely result of an act.[53] If the accused knew then, it must follow that he knows now. It is the same with any presumably enduring condition, *e.g.* the bogus nature of a business carried on by the accused,[54] or his sexual passion for a particular individual.[55] In a case of false accounting, where no prompt explanation of shortfalls was given by D, who claimed that that was impossible, the Crown was allowed to show that it was possible to make such reports by proving an earlier shortfall where D did make a prompt explanation, which was disbelieved.[56]

---

[48] [1911] A.C. 47.
[49] *i.e.* between the passing of the Act which made incest criminal and the date of their arrest.
[50] [1952] 2 Q.B. 911.
[51] Or, where appropriate, a later situation; see *R. v. Rhodes* [1899] 1 Q.B. 77. See also *Chattopadhyay v. Headmaster of Holloway School* [1982] I.C.R. 132.
[52] *R. v. Francis* (1874) L.R. 2 C.C.R. 128.
[53] *R. v. Bond* [1906] 2 K.B. 389.
[54] *R. v. Rhodes, supra*.
[55] *R. v. Ball* [1911] A.C. 47; *R. v. Marsh* (1949) 33 Cr.App.R. 185.
[56] *R. v. Hill* (1982) (C.A.), 1718/B1/81, Transcript, p. 7. See also [1982] Crim.L.R. 518, which, however, does not make this point clear.

In this sort of case, any similarity between the two transactions is purely incidental. No similarity, striking or otherwise, is needed to make irresistable the inference which the Crown asks the jury to draw, which rests on the continued existence of the element shewn to be present in the first transaction. However, if the alleged common element is not knowledge, or sexual passion for V, but propensity to commit crimes, or even propensity to commit crimes of the type charged, the inference is by no means irresistable, in the absence of a really striking similarity which gives rise to the different inference mentioned below. For example, there are many fraudulent persons in the world, and merely showing that D is *a* fraudulent person does not show strongly that he is *the* fraudulent person who committed the present crime.[57] It is sometimes permitted to prove present guilt by shewing criminal propensity from an earlier crime,[58] but not by the argument that "he had it then, therefore he has it now, therefore he is guilty."

(d) Where the unlikelihood of coincidence is relied on

Coincidences are inherently unlikely to occur, and the more remarkable the coincidence, the greater the unlikelihood. Similar fact evidence is often admitted because "if the jury are precluded by some rule of law from taking the view that something is a coincidence which is against all the probabilities, if the accused person is innocent, then it would seem to be a doctrine of law which prevents a jury from using what looks like ordinary commonsense."[59] Thus the necessary degree of cogency for similar fact evidence may be found in the fact that two similar transactions are similar in a highly specific way. A detailed method of committing a crime has been used again in all its details, leading to an almost irresistible conclusion that the similarity is not mere coincidence, but that the same man was involved with both. An example would be rape committed in a highly unusual way.[60] Mere repetition of an unspecifically detailed transaction is not enough, on its own[61]; but even a specific repetition is not enough, if the specific details are perfectly commonplace[62]; they will not raise any irresistible

---

[57] See *R. v. Fisher* [1910] 1 K.B. 149; *R. v. Slender* (1938) 26 Cr.App.R. 155 at p. 162.
[58] See, *post*, p. 214.
[59] Hallett J. in *R. v. Robinson* (1953) 37 Cr.App.R. 95 at p. 106.
[60] See *R. v. Tricoglus* (1976) 65 Cr.App.R. 16.
[61] *D.P.P. v. Boardman* [1975] A.C. 421, *ante*, p. 209; *R. v. Scarrott* (1977) 65 Cr.App.R. 125.
[62] *R. v. Scarrott, supra*, p. 130; *R. v. Inder* (1977) 67 Cr.App.R. 142.

inference that coincidence is not involved. If a shop was entered during the lunch hour while the shopkeeper was away at lunch and the intruder used a skeleton key on the front door, the Crown will not be allowed to prove that on some earlier occasion the accused had worked in this way precisely. This *modus operandi* is common enough among raiders of shop premises; all that the evidence will show is that the accused is given to raiding shops, not that he was responsible for this raid, which could be the work of any of his criminal competitors.[63] If A is accused of child abuse using well-worn tricks such as tempting children into his car by offers of sweets, it is not allowed to show that he has done this before.[64] If he is accused of raping a woman after offering her a lift in his Mini, one does not bring home this crime to him by proving that A had solicited other women in the same area in the same type of car.[65] There is nothing unique in the accused's proved behaviour on these earlier occasions.

Sometimes the unlikelihood of coincidence is a compelling reason for admitting similar fact evidence even though the *transactions* deposed to are not themselves so strikingly similar. What is relied on by the Crown may be the fact that several witnesses, independent of each other, give evidence in similar terms about different incidents. *Boardman* may be described as an example of this. If A and B say that D treated them in similar ways, even if they are not exactly similar, then, in the absence of conspiracy between the witnesses, the similarity of testimony becomes compelling. In *R. v. Barrington*,[66] D was charged with indecently assaulting three young girls, A, B & C, who had been engaged as baby-sitters. D said it was a put-up job and that nothing happened. The Crown was allowed to call a further three girls, X, Y and Z, who had not been assaulted. All six girls deposed that they had been engaged as baby-sitters, that D pretended to be Terry Nation, a well-known T.V. script writer, and that D showed them an album of indecent photographs. His conviction was upheld on appeal. Sometimes the mere identifying of D as present on separate similar occasions can be inexplicable on the basis of coincidence. "If Robinson is not a guilty man, he is a singularly unfortunate man. He is identified by

---

[63] *R. v. Brown, Smith, Woods, Flanagan* (1963) 47 Cr.App.R. 204.
[64] *R. v. Inder, supra.* But if the relevance of the evidence is to show knowledge in the accused, a commonplace similar transaction may be enough: see *R. v. Rance* (1975) 62 Cr.App.R. 118.
[65] *R. v. Tricoglus, supra;* and see *R. v. Wilson* (1973) 58 Cr.App.R. 169.
[66] [1981] 1 All E.R. 1132.

two different people ... in respect of two entirely different raids."[67]

(e) Use of similar fact evidence to prove criminal propensity

The leading case on the whole subject before *D.P.P. v. Boardman* was *Makin v. Att.-Gen. for New South Wales*.[68] In that case, in an oft-quoted passage, Lord Herschell L.C. summed up the whole law in two rules[69]:

> "It is undoubtedly not competent for the prosecution to adduce evidence tending to show that the accused has been guilty of criminal acts other than those covered by the indictment, for the purpose of leading to the conclusion that the accused is a person likely from his criminal conduct or character to have committed the offence for which he is being charged.
>
> On the other hand, the mere fact that the evidence adduced tends to show the commission of other crimes does not render it inadmissible if it be relevant to an issue before the jury, and it may be so relevant if it bears upon the question whether the acts alleged to constitute the crime charged in the indictment were designed or accidental, or to rebut a defence which would otherwise be open to the accused."

This statement of the law has been approved and adopted by many judges, including the Law Lords in *D.P.P. v. Boardman*. Indeed Lord Hailsham[70] paraphrased it by pointing out that what is forbidden by the first rule is a chain of reasoning. If the only purpose of admitting similar fact evidence is to support the reasoning that A is the sort of man who would commit this sort of crime and therefore he committed it, the evidence is not allowed. Only if there is some other relevant probative purpose in putting in the evidence is it allowed by the second rule, and then the judge must warn the jury to eschew the forbidden reasoning.

But although the judges have adopted and approved Lord Herschell's statement, they have not acted on it. Several cases, including House of Lords cases,[71] have approved the use of similar fact evidence to prove that the accused was the sort of

---

[67] The trial judge in *R. v. Robinson, supra.*
[68] [1894] A.C. 57; *ante*, p. 210.
[69] [1894] A.C. 57 at p. 65.
[70] [1975] A.C. 421 at p. 453.
[71] *e.g. R. v. Ball* [1911] A.C. 47; *Thompson v. R.* [1918] A.C. 221.

man likely to have committed a particular sort of crime and therefore he committed the crime charged. *R. v. Straffen*[72] is a vivid example. Moreover the ratio of *D.P.P. v. Boardman* says nothing to require or forbid any particular kind of relevance; all that it requires is a high *degree* of relevance. If it is of high enough relevance, it will be allowed; as Lord Cross of Chelsea said of *R. v. Straffen* in *Boardman's* case,[73] it would have been absurd of the law to prevent the evidence of the other murders being put before the jury, although it was simply evidence to show that Straffen was a man likely to commit a murder of that particular kind.

The real point underlying Lord Herschell's statement and the cases which purport to follow it is that evidence which merely shows a disposition to commit crime, or crimes of a particular type, will not usually be of a high enough degree of relevance because, unless it is a very unusual disposition, there will usually be plenty of other men with the same disposition. Proof that the accused is inclined to commit a burglary is no compelling proof that he committed the burglary charged against him; the world is full of burglariously inclined men. The same may be said of a man charged with a homosexual offence who is shown to be a homosexual[74]; or a man charged with child abuse who is shown to be a child abuser.[75] Without something else, something more particular, as for example proof that the homosexual offence charged was committed by a man wearing the ceremonial headdress of a Red Indian chief and the accused had earlier committed homosexual offences similarly attired,[76] there is nothing so strikingly, uniquely, similar as to be unexplainable as mere coincidence.

(f) Categories of allowable similar fact evidence

Since according to Lord Herschell's first rule, one kind of relevance, namely relevance by way of criminal propensity or disposition, was forbidden, what was needed for similar fact evidence to be admitted was some other kind of relevance. It was relevant and admissible according to Lord Herschell's second rule if it bore upon the question whether the acts charged were designed or accidental, or to rebut a defence which would otherwise be open. In the light of this second rule, there was a tendency to categorise the allowable reasons for using similar fact

---

[72] [1952] 2 Q.B. 11, *ante*, p. 211.
[73] [1975] A.C. 421 at p. 457.
[74] *D.P.P. v. Boardman, supra*, at pp. 441, 443, 455, 458, 461.
[75] *R. v. Clarke* (1977) 67 Cr.App.R. 398.
[76] Lord Hailsham [1975] A.C. 421 at p. 454.

evidence; showing system, rebutting accident, rebutting innocent association, showing knowledge, etc. These categories came to be highly technical[77]: and there was also a tendency to decide the whole question of admissibility according to whether the case did or did not come within one of the permitted categories. In *Boardman's* case, several speeches deprecated the making of categories as unnecessary and dangerous[78]; and indeed categorisation of types of permitted relevance is beside the point when the only question now is, not what *kind* of relevance does the evidence have? but what *degree* of relevance does it have? how cogent is it?

Most of the speeches in *D.P.P. v. Boardman* appear to contemplate that the cogency of the proferred evidence must be weighed without any reference to the "defence" (*e.g.* accident, innocent association) being run by the accused, or the state of the rest of the evidence.[79] But in practice, in asking whether the similar fact evidence is positively probative, so strong that to fail to take it into account would be an affront to common sense, it is impossible to ignore any likely defence or the state of the rest of the evidence.

If the only evidence that A had intercourse with B is that his disposition, shown by similar fact evidence, was to have intercourse with B, the similar fact evidence is clearly not cogent enough.[80] It cannot in any ordinary case[81] be strong enough to prove the Crown's whole case. But if it is shown or admitted that A slept in B's bed and the only remaining question is whether the opportunity of sexual intercourse was taken advantage of, similar fact evidence showing disposition to have intercourse with B is, as a matter of common sense, well capable of settling this residual question.[82] If the only substantial question is whether the accused knew well the character of what he was doing on the occasion in

---

[77] *e.g.* the much canvassed question of whether to show "system" one needed at least three instances (postulated by a dictum of Lord Reid in *R. v. Kilbourne* [1973] A.C. 729, at p. 751; left open in *R. v. Wilson* (1973) 58 Cr.App.R. 169; decided in the negative by the C.A. in *R. v. Boardman, supra*, at p. 428).

[78] Lord Morris at p. 439, Lord Wilberforce at p. 463, Lord Hailsham at p. 452, Lord Cross of Chelsea at p. 457.

[79] See, however, Lord Cross at p. 457.

[80] See *R. v. Horwood* [1970] 1 Q.B. 133.

[81] *R. v. Straffen, ante*, p. 211, can be described as a wholly extraordinary case.

[82] *R. v. Ball* [1911] A.C. 47; and see *R. v. King* [1967] 2 Q.B. 338. In *R. v. Berry* (1986) 83 Cr.App.R. 7 at p. 10. (C.A.), *R. v. Ball* was described as being of dubious authority. *Sed Quaere*.

question,[83] or what its results would be,[84] to show that he has done it before will often conclude the matter.

Thus similar fact evidence, whether directed to showing disposition or to showing something else, will be more likely to be strong enough in some classes of case than in other classes of case. There will continue to be the temptation to group the former classes into categories and to appeal to decisions before *Boardman's* case as authorities of those categories.[85] But the old decisions, even if very few of them can be said to be "wrong" in the light of *Boardman*, were nevertheless nearly always concerned with issues which are now quite beside the point. The only question nowadays is, is the similar fact evidence very cogent, so cogent as to render its exclusion an affront to common sense?

(g) Discretion to exclude[86]

In *Harris* v. *D.P.P.*,[87] Viscount Simon L.C. emphasised that as to similar fact evidence there is a discretion to exclude it, which is quite distinct from the question of its admissibility. In other words, if that evidence is technically admissible, the judge may still exclude it if he feels that the strict application of the technical rules would operate unfairly against the accused.[88] Two of the speeches in *D.P.P.* v. *Boardman* confirmed the separate existence of this discretion,[89] but the tenor of two others was that it was now fused in the decision on admissibility.[90]

This discretion was appropriate when it was possible to have automatic admissibility, as it was, perhaps, possible before the decision in *Boardman*, when admissibility tended to depend on the evidence falling within some permitted category of relevance. But since that decision, and the abolition of categories, it is hard to see that there is any room for a separate discretion to exclude. The decision on admissibility, *i.e.* on whether the evidence has sufficient cogency to outweigh its prejudicial nature, is essentially

---

[83] *R.* v. *Rance* (1975) 62 Cr.App.R. 118.
[84] *R.* v. *Bond* [1906] 2 K.B. 389.
[85] For a case where the temptation was perhaps not resisted, see *R.* v. *Seaman* (1978) 67 Cr.App.R. 234, where it seems that, in a borderline case, the similar fact evidence was admitted, on the authority of *Makin's* case, because it rebutted the defence of accident. And see *R.* v. *Lewis* (1982) 76 Cr.App.R. 33, criticised by Carter, "Forbidden Reasoning Remissible: Similar Fact Evidence a Decade after *Boardman*" (1985) 48 M.L.R. 29.
[86] See Allan, "Similar Fact Evidence and Disposition" (1985) 48 M.L.R. 253.
[87] [1952] A.C. 694 at p. 707.
[88] Founding on *Noor Mohamed* v. *R.* [1949] A.C. 182 at p. 192.
[89] Lords Hailsham and Salmon, at [1975] A.C. 421 at p. 453 and at p. 463.
[90] Lords Morris and Wilberforce, *ibid.* p. 431 and at p. 442.

one of discretion. It would be odd for a judge to hold that the similar fact evidence is so strikingly similar, or has such positive probative value, that its exclusion would be an affront to commonsense and then go on to reject it. However, as explained earlier[91] the judge's decision on admissibility is not strictly a discretion, and is therefore not immune to upset if the Court of Appeal thinks that it would have reached a different decision. If, on the other hand, the judge does decide that the evidence is admissible and then goes on to admit it on discretion, the discretion will not be upset unless the decision on admissibility is reversed.[92]

(h) Similar fact evidence as corroboration

Similar fact evidence, if admitted, is capable of amounting to corroboration of the Crown's case.[93] That does not mean that the judge must decide on the question of admissibility by asking whether the evidence is capable of amounting to corroboration. He must ask himself the usual question, whether it is strikingly similar or strongly probative, and only if it is may he admit it.[94] If he does admit it, it will as usual be for the jury to decide whether it does amount to corroboration.[95]

(i) Joinder of two or more offences

There is no rule that the similar transaction, which is alleged to be cogent proof of the commission of the crime charged, must itself not be in serious contention.[96] The judge must ask himself whether the similar fact evidence, if believed, is positively probative of the crime charged. If the answer is yes, he may admit it and leave it to the jury to decide whether the similar transaction did happen. In fact, very often the similar transaction is the subject of another charge in the indictment. Rule 9 of the Indictment Rules 1971 provides that charges for any offences may be joined in the same indictment if those charges are founded on the same facts, or form or are a part of a series of offences of the same or similar character. This is subject to the judge's discretion to sever the counts[97] (*i.e.* order separate trials of the charges) if of opinion that the accused may be prejudiced or embarrassed in his

---

[91] *Ante*, p. 41.
[92] See *R.* v. *Mustapha* (1976) 65 Cr.App.R. 26.
[93] *R.* v. *Kilbourne* [1973] A.C. 729.
[94] *R.* v. *Scarrott* (1977) 65 Cr.App.R. 125.
[95] See *ante*, p. 165.
[96] *R.* v. *Rance* (1975) 62 Cr.App.R. 118 at p. 122.
[97] Under the Indictments Act 1915, s.5(3).

Bad Character

defence or if for any other reason it is desirable to direct separate trials of one or more offences in the indictment.[98]

The Crown, by putting both charges in one indictment, will hope that the evidence showing crime 1 will assist in proving crime 2 and vice versa; and that the whole of the evidence heard together will be more cogent than if the crimes are tried separately and the evidence at each trial is confined to the offence charged at that trial. The defence will usually submit that the offences should be tried separately so as to avoid prejudice, and will ask the judge to exercise his discretion to sever the counts and order them to be separately tried.

It might be thought that the decision on whether to try the two counts together will inevitably depend on whether the evidence on one count is admissible on the other and vice versa. However, this is not so. If the judge decides that the evidence *is* cross-admissible, he will almost invariably allow joinder, if the statutory conditions in Rule 9 are present (as they almost inevitably will be), but the converse is not true. He does not necessarily sever if the evidence is *not* cross-admissible.

In *Ludlow* v. *M.P.C.*,[99] it was held that the rule permitting joinder is *not* restricted to cases where the evidence is cross-admissible. For the *rule* to apply, similarity can be quite superficial; all that is needed is some nexus which enables the offences to be described as a series. As to nexus, the cases set a low standard.[1] In *R.* v. *Kray*,[2] two murders were held to be properly tried together because they were both gangland killings ordered by gangleaders upholding their authority. In *Ludlow* v. *M.P.C.*,[3] an attempted larceny from public houses on August 20, and a robbery with violence in another public house in the same town on September 5, were held to form a series. In most of the cases, it was held or conceded that there was no cross-admissibility. However the fact that all the charges are of offences

---

[98] There is a similar, inherent, power in the Court to allow offences by two or more defendants to be tried together if they are in some way related. Both the circumstances where this may be done, and the considerations which might persuade a judge not to allow joint trial, are in most respects similar to the factors relevant under the statutory power of joinder and discretion to sever in respect of several charges against one defendant, which are discussed in the text following: see *R.* v. *Assim* [1966] 2 Q.B. 249; *R.* v. *Maloney* [1985] Crim.L.R. 49.
[99] [1971] A.C. 29 at pp. 41–42.
[1] In addition to the cases mentioned in the text, see *R.* v. *Clayton-Wright* [1948] 2 All E.R. 763; *R.* v. *Barrell* (1979) 69 Cr.App.R. 250.
[2] [1970] 1 Q.B. 125.
[3] *Supra*.

of dishonesty is not on its own enough.[4] As to *discretion to sever*, although cross-admissibility or lack of it is a factor, it is only one among several. The judge must take into account such considerations as the delay and expense involved in having separate trials, inconvenience to witnesses, the prejudice to the accused in having his conviction on count 1 published to the world before he stands trial on count 2.[5] These considerations may persuade the judge that joint trial is desirable although the evidence is not cross-admissible.

This position is far from ideal from the point of view of securing a fair trial. Prejudice is inevitable if the jury hear evidence on count 1 although it is irrelevant to count 2, and vice versa. The judge must of course warn them to put the evidence on count 1 out of their minds when considering count 2. But that will be difficult for them to do. In *D.P.P.* v. *Boardman*,[6] Lord Cross thought that it was asking too much of any jury to tell them to perform mental gymnastics of this sort. Several speeches in that case adverted to this difficulty, and opined that if the evidence is not cross-admissible, there ought to be separate trials.[7] However, these *dicta* are *obiter* and contrary to the House's decision in *Ludlow* v. *M.P.C.*[8] In *R.* v. *McGlinchey*,[9] it was said that the *dicta* are confined to the sort of circumstances found in *Boardman's* case, involving charges of a scandalous nature likely to arouse in a jury's mind hostile feelings against the defendant. In less scandalous cases, *e.g.* concerning offences involving firearms, or offences of handling and burglary, the *dicta* are not to be followed.

In any event, this decision on joinder or severance, which is taken at the outset of the trial on the basis of the depositions, is not a final decision on the admissibility of the evidence.[10] The judge may allow joint trials and yet still form the view as the evidence comes out that there is no striking similarity, so that the evidence on count 1 is not admissible to prove the offence in count 2. Alternatively, after ordering separate trials and proceeding on count 1 only, he may hold that the evidence on the

---

[4] *R.* v. *Harvard* (1981) 73 Cr.App.R. 168. See also *R.* v. *Bogdal* [1982] R.T.R. 3295.
[5] See *R.* v. *Barrell* (1979) 69 Cr.App.R. 250.
[6] [1975] A.C. 421 at p. 459.
[7] *Ibid.* pp. 442, 447, 459; and see *R.* v. *Novac* (1976) 65 Cr.App.R. 107 (C.A.).
[8] [1971] A.C. 29 at pp. 41–42.
[9] (1983) 78 Cr.App.R. 282 (C.A.).
[10] *R.* v. *Johannsen* (1977) 65 Cr.App.R. 107; *R.* v. *Scarrott* (1977) 65 Cr.App.R. 125.

postponed count 2 is admissible under the similar facts doctrine to prove the offence in count 1.[11]

4. Proviso (f) to section 1 of the Criminal Evidence Act 1898

(a) The proviso

Evidence as to the bad character of the accused may also be elicited under the operation of this proviso. The policy of the Act is to make the accused a competent but not a compellable witness for the defence.[12] It was recognised that it would not be appropriate to make him a witness like any other witness, and his position was differentiated from that of any ordinary witness, in two important respects. The first is that the privilege against self-incrimination[13] is expressly negatived by proviso (*e*) so far as concerns the charge for which the accused is being tried; it says that the accused "may be asked any question in cross-examination notwithstanding that it would tend to criminate him as to the offence charged." The second is that his credibility as a witness cannot be attacked in the ordinary way by cross-examination directed at showing that he has a bad character,[14] for this would be highly prejudicial in many cases and would largely stultify an Act the aim of which is to enlarge the rights of accused persons. This immunity, which is by no means an absolute one, is conferred by proviso (*f*) which reads as follows:

> "A person charged and called as a witness in pursuance of this Act shall not be asked, and if asked shall not be required to answer, any question tending to show that he has committed or been convicted of or been charged with any offence other than that wherewith he is then charged, or is of bad character, unless—
> (i) the proof that he has committed or been convicted of such other offence is admissible evidence to show that he is guilty of the offence wherewith he is then charged; or
> (ii) he has personally or by his advocate asked questions of the witnesses for the prosecution with a view to establish his own good character, or has given evidence of his good character, or the nature or conduct of the defence is such as to involve imputations on the

---

[11] R. v. *Scarrott, supra,* at p. 135.
[12] See *ante,* p. 132.
[13] See *ante,* p. 153.
[14] See *ante,* p. 118.

character of the prosecutor or the witnesses for the prosecution; or
(iii) he has given evidence against any other person charged in the same proceedings."[15]

It must first of all be noted that the permissive proviso (*e*) is subject to the prohibitive proviso (*f*). A question which would tend to criminate the accused is not allowed under (*e*) if it falls foul of (*f*) unless it is within one of the excepted cases mentioned in (*f*). The excepted cases, being mentioned specifically, are the only cases to which the prohibition in (*f*) is subject: *expressio unius, exclusio alterius*.[16]

"In section 1, proviso (*e*), it has been enacted that a witness may be cross-examined in respect of the offence charged, and cannot refuse to answer questions directly relevant to the offence on the ground that they tend to incriminate him: thus if he denies the offence, he may be cross-examined to refute the denial. These are matters directly relevant to the charge on which he is being tried. Proviso (*f*), however, is dealing with matters outside, and not directly relevant to, the particular offences charged."[17]

Questions as to these indirectly relevant matters, if they tend to show that he has committed or been convicted of or been charged with any other offence or is of bad character, can only be asked if one of the excepted cases applies, *and* if the question is relevant either under the "similar facts" doctrine[18] or as impeaching his credit as a witness.[19] The Act does not make permissible any question which would be excluded under the ordinary rules; it merely makes some questions impermissible which the ordinary rules would have permitted.[20]

In *Maxwell* v. *D.P.P.*,[21] M, at his trial for manslaughter, had forfeited his immunity by giving evidence of his own good character. In cross-examination, he was asked about an earlier acquittal on a similar charge. It was held that the question ought

---

[15] "In the same proceedings" was substituted by s.1 of the Criminal Evidence Act 1979 for "with the same offence" which appeared in the original wording of proviso (*f*) (iii).
[16] *Jones* v. *D.P.P.* [1962] A.C. 635, *per* Lord Simonds at p. 658, Lord Reid at p. 663.
[17] *Per* Viscount Sankey L.C. in *Maxwell* v. *D.P.P.* [1935] A.C. 309 at p. 318.
[18] *Ante*, p. 207.
[19] *Ante*, pp. 118 *et seq.*
[20] *Jones* v. *D.P.P.*, *supra*, *per* Lord Reid at p. 662.
[21] [1935] A.C. 309.

not to have been asked. In the circumstances of the case, the acquittal had no relevance to the issue of his guilt, and of course to show that a person has been *acquitted* does not impair his credit. The question was not only prejudicial, but irrelevant on either score.

However, a *conviction*[22] does impair an accused person's credibility, even if normally it is irrelevant to the issues. Because of its relevance to credibility, it is in principle admissible if the statutory immunity has been forfeited, in spite of its irrelevance to the issues; but it ought to follow that it is to be used by the jury only in deciding on the accused's credibility as a witness, not in helping them to decide whether he committed the offence with which he is charged. It is a misdirection to suggest that it has some relevance to the issues,[23] and indeed the accused is entitled to have the jury directed in the opposite sense, *i.e.* that it has *no* relevance to the issues. The difficulty here is that such a direction may not be understood, or may be disregarded, and the jury may well conclude from the fact that the accused has a criminal record that he is guilty on this occasion.[24] In other words, although forbidden to do so, they may reason directly from conviction to guilt. Because of this danger, the judge has in most cases a discretion to disallow the question if he thinks that the danger is particularly acute[25]; if for example the relevance of the conviction to credit is slight, and the likelihood of the jury using it as indicating guilt is large.[26] However it depends upon which of the exceptional cases forfeiting the immunity is involved—sometimes the jury *is* permitted to reason directly from conviction to guilt—and the matter will therefore be expanded when those cases are dealt with.[27]

(b) The prohibitive part of proviso (f)

The accused must not be asked any question tending to show that he has committed or been convicted of or been charged with

---

[22] Including a conviction of an offence committed subsequently to the offence charged. Such can be cross-examined on if the accused has forfeited his immunity: *R.* v. *Coltress* (1979) 68 Cr.App.R. 193.
[23] *R.* v. *Vickers* [1972] Crim.L.R. 101.
[24] On the dangers and difficulties inherent in this part of the law see Munday, "Stepping Beyond the Bounds of Credibility: The Application of Section 1(f)(b)(ii) Criminal Evidence Act 1898" [1986] Crim.L.R. 511.
[25] *Per* Viscount Sankey, in *Maxwell* v. *D.P.P., supra*, at p. 321.
[26] *R.* v. *Watts* [1983] 3 All E.R. 101. But see *R.* v. *Powell* [1986] 1 All E.R. 193, *post*, p. 234.
[27] *Post*, pp. 226, 228. See Elliott, "The Young Person's Guide to Similar Fact Evidence—II" [1982] Crim.L.R. 352 at p. 357.

any offence other than that wherewith he is then charged, or is of bad character.

Several points need emphasising. Thus although the proviso says that the accused "shall not be asked" certain questions, this prohibits only questions by the prosecution, or a co-accused; the accused's own counsel may ask the questions in examination-in-chief if it is thought necessary.[28] If the accused is wrongly asked the forbidden questions, the judge may allow the trial to proceed nonetheless, after warning the jury to put the questions, and answers if any, out of their minds.[29]

The prohibited questions are those "tending to show" certain prejudicial matters. On the one hand, "tending to show" includes "tending to suggest"—"A veiled suggestion of a previous offence may be just as damaging as a definite statement,"[30]—but on the other hand, a question cannot "tend to show" anything of which the jury is already well aware.[31] "Charged with an offence" means charged in court[32] and, as we have seen, a question directed to showing that the accused was charged and acquitted on some former occasion will usually be rejected as irrelevant,[33] even if one of the three excepted cases applies.

"Bad character": wherever "character" is used in the proviso is not apparently confined to the restricted meaning given to the word at common law in *R. v. Rowton*,[34] *i.e.* reputation. It includes also disposition.[35]

(c) The excepted cases

In four[36] exceptional cases, the prohibition in proviso (*f*) does not apply, and the accused may be asked the questions normally excluded, provided, it must be remembered, such questions are relevant.[37]

(i) *Where the proof that he has committed or been convicted of such other offences is admissible evidence to show that he is guilty of the*

---

[28] *Jones v. D.P.P.* [1962] A.C. 635 at p. 663.
[29] *R. v. Palmer* [1983] Crim.L.R. 252.
[30] *Per* Lord Reid, in *Jones v. D.P.P., supra,* at p. 663.
[31] *Jones v. D.P.P., supra, per* Lord Simonds, Reid and Morris.
[32] *Stirland v. D.P.P.* [1944] A.C. 315.
[33] *Maxwell v. D.P.P., supra.*
[34] (1865) 34 L.J.M.C. 57; *ante,* p. 205.
[35] *R. v. Dunkley* [1927] 1 K.B. 323 at p. 329; *Stirland v. D.P.P.* [1944] A.C. 315 at p. 324; *Jones v. D.P.P.* [1962] A.C. 635; *Malindi v. R.* [1967] A.C. 439; *Selvey v. D.P.P.* [1970] A.C. 304.
[36] Proviso (*f*) is expressed to be subject to three exceptions, but it will be seen that exception (ii) has two separate limbs.
[37] *Maxwell v. D.P.P., supra.*

offence wherewith he is then charged

What this means in general is that he may be asked questions which are relevant according to the "similar facts" doctrine.[38] There was formerly a tendency to ignore the strict words of exception (i) and to concentrate on Parliament's supposed general intention to admit any questions which might be relevant under that doctrine. So in earlier cases, questions were allowed as to previous non-criminal immorality,[39] which is not comprehended in the words "he has committed or been convicted of such other offence" in exception (i). More recently, however, the strict words of exception (i) have been considered, so that a previous *charge* alleged to be relevant has been held not sufficient to bring the exception into play.[40] Moreover the majority of the House of Lords in *Jones* v. *D.P.P.*[41] disapproved of the reasons for the earlier decisions, and held that the questions involved in those cases were only permissible because, since the Crown had already given evidence of the alleged immorality, the questions did not "tend to show" a bad character already revealed to the jury.[42] In this connection, it has to be remembered that the similar facts doctrine is something separate and distinct from proviso (*f*). The former specifies the circumstances when evidence of conduct by the accused on other occasions may be led by the Crown; the latter merely prohibits a certain line of cross-examination of the accused. A matter may therefore be admissible as part of the Crown's case, even if it appears to come under the embargo on cross-examination imposed by proviso (*f*). In such a case, according to *Jones* v. *D.P.P.*, if the Crown lead evidence of earlier disreputable conduct, the proviso cannot apply because the matter is already known to the jury.

Suppose A is charged with theft from dustbins, to which his defence is a claim of right, *i.e.* that he thought the articles had been abandoned. He has formerly been charged with theft arising out of similar circumstances, but has been acquitted, after raising a similar defence. He may not be asked about the former occasion, because although it is relevant to negative his claim of right, it is not "proof that he has committed or been convicted of [another] offence": proviso (*f*)(i).[43] But if evidence of such was permitted to be led as part of the Crown case, then questions

---

[38] *Ante*, pp. 207 *et seq.*
[39] R. v. *Chitson* [1909] 2 K.B. 945; R. v. *Kurasch* [1915] 2 K.B. 749.
[40] R. v. *Cokar* [1960] 2 Q.B. 207.
[41] [1962] A.C. 635; Lords Simonds, Reid and Morris of Borth-y-Gest.
[42] But see the speeches of Lords Denning and Devlin, dissenting on this point.
[43] R. v. *Cokar, supra; Jones* v. *D.P.P., supra.*

about the matter would be allowed because they do not "tend to show" any of the prohibited things in proviso (*f*): *Jones* v. *D.P.P.*[44]

If evidence of such was not led because the Crown sought permission under the Similar Facts doctrine, but was refused, obviously exception (i) does not apply and questions tending to show bad character cannot be asked. If the Crown did not seek such permission, it is in principle allowed to do so during the accused's cross-examination. But it ought to have done so as part of its case and then led the evidence,[45] so as to enable the defence to cross-examine the Crown witnesses as to the earlier conduct, and so as to give the accused notice of what he would face if he went into the witness box. The fact that it neglected to do so may cause the judge to refuse to allow the matter to be raised in cross-examination.[46] But if it does at this stage secure a ruling that evidence of earlier discreditable conduct is positively probative of the accused's guilt, then exception (i) comes into play, and it may cross-examine him about it, provided it is evidence "that he has committed or been convicted of other offences," not merely of earlier charges or non-criminal bad character.[47] The object of any cross-examination allowed under exception (i) is not merely to attack credit, but to prove guilt, and the accused is not entitled to a direction that the jury should use his answers solely for the former purpose.[48]

(ii) *Where he has personally or by his advocate asked questions of the witnesses for the prosecution with a view to establish his own good character, or has given evidence of his good character, or the nature and conduct of the defence is such as to involve imputations on the character of the prosecutor or the witnesses for the prosecution.*

The first limb of this exception applies where the accused has put his character in issue,[49] "character" meaning both reputation and disposition.[50] When character is put in issue, the Crown may call evidence of bad character. Whenever it has this right, it also has the statutory right, if he gives evidence, to ask him the forbidden questions in cross-examination. If the accused "throws his hat in the ring"[51] in the matter of character, clearly he cannot complain if he also loses the shield provided by proviso (*f*).

---

[44] [1962] A.C. 635.
[45] *Ibid., per* Lord Denning at p. 668.
[46] *R.* v. *France* (No. 1854/C/78) [1979] Crim.L.R. 48. See Transcript, p. 5D.
[47] Proviso (*f*)(i); *R.* v. *Cokar, supra*.
[48] *Ante*, p. 223.
[49] See *ante*, p. 205.
[50] See authorities cited in n. 35, *supra*.
[51] See *per* Lord Devlin in *Jones* v. *D.P.P.* [1962] A.C. 635 at p. 701.

Nevertheless, this exception is not intended to prevent the accused developing his defence, and consequently protestations of innocence or repudiation of guilt and the reasons for such protestation or repudiation do not amount to an assertion of good character.[52] However, if the reasons depend for their force upon the jury assuming that as an honest man he is unlikely to have committed the present offence, then they amount to evidence of good character, and cross-examination as to bad character is allowed. Thus, in *R. v. Samuel*[53] the accused, who was charged with larceny by finding, gave evidence that he had previously found goods and handed them over to the police. The inference urged to be drawn from this evidence was that he intended to hand over the goods in the present case, but it inevitably also invited the inference that he was an *honest* finder, and so amounted to evidence of good character.

However, blackening the character of others is not tantamount to saying that one's own character is good.[54] Nor is the exception brought into play by the mere volunteering of a statement as to the accused's character by a witness who was not asked about such.[55] On the other hand, it seems clear that "has given evidence of his good character" includes calling a witness to give evidence of his good character, even though the accused in his own evidence, makes no allusion to his character.[56]

Once character has been put in issue, the accused may be cross-examined on his character to affect his general credibility[57]; the questions need not be confined to the facet of his character claimed to be good.[58] But it does not follow that what emerges in his answers cannot be taken as relevant to guilt. No doubt if the bad character uncovered has no conceivable relevance to the issues, but only to his credit as a witness, *e.g.* in a prosecution for wounding or rape, a claim of truthfulness demolished by getting him to admit to an earlier conviction for perjury, the judge ought to warn the jury that the conviction has no relevance to the issues. But where the evidence of good character invites the inference

---

[52] *R. v. Ellis* [1910] 2 K.B. 746. An accused person must not be cross-examined so as to bring himself unwittingly within the statute: *R. v. Grout* (1909) 74 J.P. 30; *R. v. Eidinow* (1932) 23 Cr.App.R. 145.
[53] (1956) 40 Cr.App.R. 8.
[54] *R. v. Butterwasser* [1948] 1 K.B. 4; *R. v. De Vere* [1982] Q.B. 75; but if the attacked persons are the prosecutor or Crown witnesses, the second limb of the exception will be brought into play.
[55] *R. v. Redd* [1923] 1 K.B. 104.
[56] Cross, p. 362.
[57] *R. v. Richardson* (1968) 52 Cr.App.R. 317 at p. 331.
[58] *R. v. Winfield* (1939) 27 Cr.App.R. 139.

that the accused is on that account unlikely to have committed the offence, the discovered bad character will (and may legitimately) suggest that on the contrary he *is* likely to have committed the offence.[59] Since the evidence of good character goes to the issues, not merely to credit,[60] the evidence of bad character extracted in cross-examination of the accused also goes to the issues, and the accused is not entitled to have the jury warned to use it only as to his credit as a witness.[61]

As to the second limb of this exception (imputations on the character of the prosecution's witnesses) it must be noted that here "character" means more than reputation, and includes disposition, so that a suggestion made to a Crown witness that he had a grudge against the accused and is therefore giving false evidence, may bring the exception into operation.[62] Moreover, once the exception is brought into play, whatever is brought out by the cross-examination goes to the accused's credibility generally; it is not merely used to discount the accused's attacks on the Crown witnesses which activated this exception.[63] The words "the character of the prosecutor or the witnesses for the prosecution" have been construed literally, so that attacks on other persons, such as a police officer not called as a witness[64] or the deceased in a murder or manslaughter trial,[65] do not attract the exception.

As to what is meant by "the nature or conduct of the offence is such as to involve imputations", it must first be noted that the expression covers both where the imputations are to show the unreliability of the witness independently of the evidence given by him, and also where the casting of such imputations is necessary to enable the accused to establish his defence.[66] Thus in principle the exception may be activated both, *e.g.* where the accused says that the crime was committed, not by him, but by the witness, and where he says that the witness is lying about the accused's involvement or about his alleged confession.

As to this latter, whenever the accused denies what is deposed

---

[59] *D.P.P.* v. *Maxwell* [1935] A.C. 309, *per* Lord Sankey at p. 319.
[60] *R.* v. *Bryant* (1977) 67 Cr.App.R. 157 at p. 165; *R.* v. *Stannard* (1837) 7 C. & P. 673 at p. 675.
[61] But see Lord Goddard in *R.* v. *Samuel* (1956) 40 Cr.App.R. 8 at p. 12, who appears to say that "in theory" in every case the object is to show that he is an unreliable witness.
[62] *R.* v. *Dunkley* [1927] 1 K.B. 323; *Selvey* v. *D.P.P.* [1970] A.C. 304.
[63] *R.* v. *Longman and Richardson* [1969] 1 Q.B. 299.
[64] *R.* v. *Westfall* (1912) 7 Cr.App.R. 176.
[65] *R.* v. *Biggin* [1920] 1 K.B. 213.
[66] *Selvey* v. *D.P.P.* [1970] A.C. 304, *per* Viscount Dilhorne at p. 339.

to by a witness, he is at least tacitly saying that the witness is mistaken and, according to the circumstances, lying. The strict implication of this would be that an accused could seldom deny a charge, except by a bare plea of "Not Guilty," without exposing his past. Because of this difficulty, it was for long accepted that mere denials of the charge, even if expressed in emphatic language, should not be regarded as coming within proviso (*f*)(ii)(2). In *R. v. Rouse*[67] R commented on a Crown witness and his evidence: "That is a lie and he is a liar." It was held that this was not an imputation on the character of the witness, but merely a denial in forceful terms. However it seems that nowadays, as a result of the decision in *R. v. Britzman*,[68] this would count as an imputation, the fact that it is an emphatic denial being no more than a factor to be taken into account in deciding whether to protect the accused on discretion.

In some cases, the version of events put forward by the accused is not a mere emphatic denial of the witness's evidence, but a suggestion that the witness concocted his story, either alone or in conspiracy with another Crown witness, and as such is clearly an imputation on his or their character. A very common case is where police witnesses give evidence of a detailed confession by the accused, and in his evidence he denies making any confession. A practice grew up of studiously avoiding saying outright that there had been concoction and courteously suggesting that there had been some mistake, thereby leaving the suggestion of fabrication or conspiracy tacit rather than expressed. This was in the hope, sometimes fulfilled, that the judge would rule that, there being no actual imputations on the character of the crown witnesses, the exception did not come into play.[69] However, in *R. v. Britzman*,[70] the Court of Appeal laid down that if the reality of the situation, obvious to the jury, is that the defence is suggesting, not a mistake but, that the witnesses have made up their evidence, this is an imputation on character, notwithstanding the delicacy of the language used. In *R. v. Britzman*, B and H were charged with burglary. PC1 said that B made a statement confessing his part. PC2 said he overheard a shouting match between B and H, containing admissions. B in cross-examination, said that PC1 was mistaken. B's counsel, cross-examining PC2, suggested that the alleged shouting match did not take place. It

---

[67] [1904] 1 K.B. 104; but *cf. R. v. Rappolt* (1911) 6 Cr.App.R. 156.
[68] [1982] 1 All E.R. 369; see text following.
[69] See *R. v. Clark* [1955] 2 Q.B. 469; *R. v. Jones* (1923) 17 Cr.App.R. 117.
[70] *Supra*, following *R. v. Tanner* (1977) 66 Cr.App.R. 56, and *R. v. McGee* (1979) 70 Cr.App.R. 247, and disapproving of *R. v. Nelson* (1978) 68 Cr.App.R. 12.

was held on appeal that there was no room for doubt or misunderstanding between the participants in these events; it was clear what was being suggested, namely that the police witnesses had fabricated their evidence. Accordingly the exception came into play.

However, as will be seen,[71] when this exception is involved, the judge has a discretion to disallow questions as to criminal record. In *R.* v. *Britzman,* the Court of Appeal laid down guidelines for the exercise of the discretion in this sort of situation. First, it should be used if there is nothing more than a denial, however emphatic or offensively made, of an act or a short interview. It is different with a long course of conduct observed over a period or a long interview. Second, the judge should only allow cross-examination if he is sure that there is no possibility of mistake, misunderstanding or confusion. With wild allegations of the sort which are sometimes made from the witness box, he should make allowance for the strain of being in the box and the exaggerated use of language which sometimes results from such strain, a lack of education, or mental instability. Third, there is no need for the Crown to rely on proviso (*f*)(ii) if the evidence against the accused is overwhelming.[72] As has been pointed out,[73] the third guideline is strange; there is *less* injustice in dragging in the record of a man whose guilt is clear, than in doing so with a man whose guilt is in the balance, yet the Crown are only to do it in the latter case.

We have seen, on what *are* imputations, the difficulty that if mere denials of Crown evidence were held to be such, an accused could hardly defend himself without letting in his record. A similar dilemma arises with assertions which are much more than mere denials and clearly *are* imputations, but which are absolutely necessary if the accused is to develop his defence. If the accused is charged with wounding V, and his case is self-defence, in that V was attacking him,[74] this is an imputation on V's character, and if the section is strictly construed, it will seem that he cannot defend himself against the prosecution without exposing his criminal record, which exposure is usually fatal to his chances of acquittal. On this construction, the statute, the general object of which was to lighten an accused person's lot, cannot help operating unfairly with regard to an accused with a

---

[71] *Post,* p. 231.
[72] [1983] 1 All E.R. at pp. 373, 374.
[73] By Birch, [1983] Crim.L.R. 107.
[74] See *R.* v. *Brown* (1960) 44 Cr.App.R. 181.

criminal record. He cannot defend himself as fully as an accused without a record.

Recognition of this dilemma produced much divergence of authority. On the one side it was said that the accused is not to be regarded as depriving himself of the protection of the section, because the proper conduct of his defence necessitates the making of injurious reflections on the prosecutor or his witnesses.[75] So in a rape case, the accused may legitimately suggest that the prosecutrix consented, without exposing himself to cross-examination as to his character and convictions, even though the suggestion reflects gravely on her character.[76] However, the opposing view is that this approach involves reading into the statute the words "unnecessary" or "unjustifiable" before the word "imputations," and this, it was forcibly said in *R. v. Hudson*,[77] is an illegitimate way of construing the statute. Thus, if his defence is that a witness for the prosecution committed the crime, this is held to deprive the accused of the protection of this section,[78] although the proper conduct of his defence necessitates the making of injurious reflections on the prosecutor or his witnesses. The question was settled by the House of Lords in *Selvey* v. *D.P.P.*[79] It was laid down in that case that, with the sole exception of rape cases, wherever the accused makes imputations on the character of the prosecutor or his witnesses, even if such attacks are necessary for the proper conduct of his defence, proviso (*f*)(ii) applies, and he may be cross-examined on his record.[80] However, the Crown never gains a right to such cross-examination; the court has a discretion whether to allow it or not, and must consciously exercise it before allowing the cross-examination. It is a complete discretion and there is no rule that the discretion ought normally to be exercised in the accused's favour if the attacks were necessary to his defence, although that is a factor to be taken into account. The prosecution ought to indicate in advance that it is going to claim its rights under the exception[81] and if the cross-examination of a Crown witness is leading the defence into the danger of falling foul of the exception, the judge ought to warn the defendant, certainly if he

---

[75] *Per* Viscount Simon in *Stirland* v. *D.P.P.* [1944] A.C. 315 at p. 327.
[76] *R.* v. *Turner* [1944] K.B. 463.
[77] [1912] 2 K.B. 464, *per* Lord Alverstone C.J. at p. 468.
[78] *R.* v. *Hudson* [1912] 2 K.B. 464.
[79] [1970] A.C. 304.
[80] It is immaterial that it is not the purpose of the questions to cast doubt on the credibility of the Crown witness: *R.* v. *Bishop* [1975] Q.B. 274.
[81] *R.* v. *Cook* [1959] 2 Q.B. 340.

is unrepresented,[82] and perhaps even if he is represented by counsel,[83] although it has been said that there is no general duty to warn counsel that he is sailing near the wind.[84]

Thus the way out of the dilemma[85] adopted by the House of Lords in *Selvey* v. *D.P.P.*[86] is that of confirming the strict construction approach but relying on discretion to mitigate the harshness of that approach. The fact that the discretion is an unfettered one without guidelines[87] means that defence counsel will never know how far he can safely go in impeaching the Crown witness. For that reason at least, the solution cannot be accounted an ideal one, but on the present statutory wording it is difficult to see any better alternative.[88]

On the statutory wording, an accused who attacks Crown witnesses renders himself liable to the possibility of cross-examination as to record, not only by the Crown, but also by any co-accused. It is however a matter of discretion[89]; there is no automatic right in the co-accused, as there is under exception (iii).[90]

As to the use which may be made of the record revealed by cross-examination under this exception, there is no doubt that it is confined to assessing the accused's credibility as a witness.[91] The reason for the exception has always been taken to be that if the defendant asks the jury to disbelieve a Crown witness upon the ground that his reprehensible conduct makes him an unreliable witness, then the jury ought also to know the character of the person who makes that charge.[92] In other words, the *credit* of the Crown witnesses and the accused are openly in competition.

---

[82] An unrepresented defendant should have the position explained to him in the absence of the jury or magistrates: *R.* v. *Weston-super-Mare JJ.* [1968] 3 All E.R. 225n. In the latter case the prosecution should ask for an adjournment and then seek the help of the magistrates' clerk.
[83] *R.* v. *Cook, supra.*
[84] *R.* v. *McGee* (1979) 70 Cr.App.R. 247.
[85] On this dilemma, see Heydon, pp. 291–298; C.L.R.C. 11th Report, Evidence (General) 1972, Cmnd. 4991 paras. 114–132.
[86] *Supra.*
[87] Except in the limited circumstances covered by the guidelines laid down in *R.* v. *Britzman, ante,* p. 230.
[88] For a proposed legislative compromise, see Cmnd. 4991, *supra,* Draft Criminal Evidence Bill, Clause 6(4), which would allow the cross-examination only if the main purpose of the imputation was to raise an issue as to the credibility of the witness who is attacked.
[89] *R.* v. *Lovett* (1973) 57 Cr.App.R. 332.
[90] See *post,* p. 234.
[91] See *e.g. R.* v. *Cook* [1959] 2 Q.B. 340; *R.* v. *Inder* (1977) 67 Cr.App.R. 143; *R.* v. *Vickers* [1972] Crim.L.R. 101.
[92] *R.* v. *Preston* [1909] 1 K.B. 568 at p. 575.

Because the earlier misconduct of the accused is not positively probative of his guilt on this occasion (since the Crown, *ex hypothesi*, has not secured a ruling allowing it to prove it under the similar facts doctrine[93]), and because the jury will probably take it as being probative, it follows that the judge must warn them not to take the criminal record as having anything to say on the question of whether he committed the crime he is charged with. The accused is of course entitled to have such a direction given, for what it is worth, but since in many cases it will not be worth much, more important from his point of view would be a duty in the judge to disallow the questions altogether if, realistically, their only relevance is on the issue of guilt. A case which came near to laying such a duty on the judge was *R. v. Watts*.[94] In that case, W was charged with indecently assaulting a woman in an underpass. He deposed that a police witness had fabricated an alleged confession by him. The Crown were allowed to ask him about two earlier convictions of sexual offences against children. The judge gave the standard warning, but even so the Court of Appeal held that he should not have allowed the questions, and quashed the conviction. Lord Lane C.J. said[95]:

> "The direction was, of itself, sound in law, but in the circumstances of this case it would have been extremely difficult, if not practically impossible, for the jury to have done what the judge was suggesting. The prejudice which the appellant must have suffered in the eyes of the jury when it was disclosed that he had previous convictions for offences against young children could hardly have been greater. The probative value of the convictions, on the sole issue on which they were admissible, was, at best, slight. The previous offences did not involve dishonesty. Nor were they so similar to the offences which the jury were trying that they could have been admitted as evidence of similar facts on the issue of identity. In short, their prejudicial effect far outweighed their probative value."

However, since this decision[96] the pendulum has swung back in

---

[93] See, *ante*, pp. 207 *et seq*.
[94] [1983] 3 All E.R. 101.
[95] *Ibid.* p. 104.
[96] *R. v. Watts* was followed in *R. v. Braithwaite*, unreported, November 24, 1983, doubted in *R. v. Burke* [1984] Crim.L.R. 660, disapproved in *R. v. Powell* [1986] 1 All E.R. 193.

favour of allowing questions on and evidence about even similar offences of a most prejudicial kind, if there has been a deliberate attack on the credit of police witnesses rather than the mere development of a legitimate defence. In *R. v. Powell*,[97] D was charged with knowingly living off immoral earnings. His defence was that the prosecution evidence was a total fabrication and he also gave evidence of his own good character. The judge allowed the Crown to prove three earlier convictions of allowing his premises to be used for the purposes of prostitution, giving the usual warning that the evidence of the convictions went to credibility only. The Court of Appeal held that in view of the way the defence had been conducted, the course taken by the judge was right. The similarity of the previous offences to the present charge was not a factor.[98] The dangers of prejudice adumbrated in *R. v. Watts* remain, but according to *R. v. Powell* have to be risked by a defendant who attacks Crown witnesses. Indeed, as has been said,[99] the sort of evidence usually rigorously excluded by the requirements of the Similar Fact doctrine[1] may now, depending on the line taken by the defence, be freely admissible in cross-examination of the accused.

(iii) *Where he has given evidence against any other person charged in the same proceedings.*

The reason for this appears to be that if A gives evidence against a co-accused B, then as regards B, A ought to be in the same position as a Crown witness and so liable to cross-examination as to credit by B.[2] It is a departure from common principles of justice not to allow a witness who has given evidence against an accused to be cross-examined.[3] This means that the court has no discretion to disallow such cross-examination at the instance of B.[4] However B's counsel must always warn the judge that he proposes to claim his rights, so that the judge can satisfy himself that the case does truly fall within the exception[5] and that the proposed questions are relevant to credit.[6]

[97] [1986] 1 All E.R. 193.
[98] The Court of Appeal was persuaded by the failure of the House of Lords in *Selvey* v. *D.P.P.* [1970] A.C. 304, *ante*, p. 231, to comment adversely on the fact that Selvey's earlier convictions were for exactly the same offence as the one for which he was standing trial (buggery).
[99] Munday, *op. cit.*
[1] See *ante*, pp. 207 *et seq.*
[2] *R. v. Hadwen and Ingham* [1902] 1 K.B. 882; *R. v. Stannard* [1965] 2 Q.B. 1.
[3] *Rigby* v. *Woodward* [1957] 1 W.L.R. 250 *per* Lord Goddard C.J. at p. 253.
[4] *Murdoch* v. *Taylor* [1965] A.C. 574.
[5] *R. v. Lovett* (1973) 57 Cr.App.R. 332.
[6] *Murdoch* v. *Taylor, supra;* see *Maxwell* v. *D.P.P.* [1935] A.C. 309, *ante*, p. 222.

Moreover, although the statutory wording would appear to allow cross-examination of A not only by the attacked co-accused B, but also by the Crown and any other accused, cross-examination by anyone other than B is a matter of discretion only and not of right.[7]

An accused forfeits his immunity whenever he gives "evidence against any other person" charged in the same proceedings. That expression has received a wide interpretation. In *Murdoch* v. *Taylor*[8] it was said that "evidence against" a co-accused means evidence which supports the prosecution's case or undermines the defence of the co-accused; it is not necessary for the accused giving evidence to have any hostile intent against his co-accused. In *R.* v. *Davis*,[9] A and B were charged with theft of a certain article and it was clear that either A or B must have stolen it. A testified that he had *not* done so, but avoided saying that B *had* done so. It was held that this evidence, if believed, must undermine B's defence that *he* had not stolen the article. It has been said that a mere conflict of evidence between A and B will not necessarily mean that the one has given evidence against the other[10]; but much depends on the relevance of the conflict to the issue and to B's credibility.[11] If on balance A's evidence does more to undermine B's defence than to undermine the Crown's case, B will be entitled to cross-examine A as to his record.[12]

This state of the law means that in many cases A will find himself unable to give any evidence in his own defence without having his record disclosed. For example, suppose that A and B are charged with a joint robbery, and B admits he was there but says he acted under duress from A. Even if A confines himself to denying his involvement, this, if believed, will mean that B was there on his own and was not acting under any duress. A is therefore giving evidence against B and he may be asked by B about his record.[13] Yet the only thing A could say less than denying his presence would be nothing at all, and that would lead the jury to conclude that he couldn't deny his part. In this sort of case, an accused person with a criminal record must inevitably face the jury with his record exposed, which hardly squares with

---

[7] *Murdoch* v. *Taylor, supra; R.* v. *Lovett, supra.*
[8] *Supra,* at p. 592.
[9] (1975) 60 Cr.App.R. 157.
[10] *R.* v. *Stannard, supra; Murdoch* v. *Taylor, supra,* at p. 591.
[11] *R.* v. *Davis, supra,* at p. 160.
[12] *R.* v. *Hatton* (1977) 64 Cr.App.R. 88. Compare *R.* v. *Bruce* (1975) 61 Cr.App.R. 123.
[13] See *R.* v. *Varley* [1982] 2 All E.R. 519.

the general object of the Act of lightening an accused person's lot. Unfortunately the Courts precluded resort to the compromise employed in respect of proviso (*f*)(ii) when they decided that if proviso (*f*)(iii) is involved, the judge has no discretion to protect the accused from cross-examination on record.

(d) Limits of proviso (f)

Before leaving proviso (*f*), it is important to notice that the only penalty imposed on the accused if his case comes within any of the exceptions is a liability to be cross-examined as to his record and character, and this can only arise if he chooses to give evidence. If he does not, neither the Crown nor a co-accused may call him,[14] nor may his bad character or convictions be independently proved, unless he has set up his own good character, and attacking Crown witnesses is not setting up his own good character.

In *R. v. Lee*,[15] L cross-examined a Crown witness as to someone else's convictions. Although L then gave evidence, he could not be cross-examined as to his own convictions because proviso (*f*)(ii) second limb did not apply (the subject of his attacks not being Crown witnesses) and proviso (*f*)(ii) first limb was not involved either because attacking others is not setting up his own good character.

In *R. v. Butterwasser*,[16] B cross-examined Crown witnesses as to their convictions. This would attract proviso (*f*)(ii) second limb, but since he did not give evidence, he could not be cross-examined at all. Nor could evidence of his convictions be given because he had not, merely by attacking Crown witnesses, set up his own good character.

In *R. v. Bircham*,[17] B gave evidence but did not attack anyone. However, his counsel in his final address attempted to suggest that either a co-accused F or a Crown witness W was solely responsible. He was prevented from doing this, as being unfair to both F and W and an attempt to get the benefit of an attack on them without the corresponding risk of having his client's bad record exposed.

---

[14] Criminal Evidence Act 1898, s.1, proviso (*a*).
[15] (1976) 62 Cr.App.R. 33.
[16] [1948] 1 K.B. 4.
[17] [1972] Crim.L.R. 430.

Part V

HEARSAY

CHAPTER 12
HEARSAY

	Page
A. The Hearsay Rule	239
B. Scope of the Rule	242
1. The Purpose of Proving an Assertion	242
2. Assertions	244
3. Is There a Human Informant?	246
4. Non-Spoken Assertions	250
C. Exceptions to the Rule	255
D. Principal Classes of Exceptions	256

CHAPTER 13
HEARSAY IN CIVIL CASES

A. Exceptions made by the Act	259
1. Statements Admitted under Section 2	259
2. Statements Admitted under Section 4	264
3. Statements Admitted under Section 5	267
4. Statements made Evidence by Section 3	268
5. Provisions Supplementary to Sections 2–5	269
B. Common Law Exceptions Preserved by the Act	271
1. Admissions	272
2. Statements in Public or Official Documents	281
3. Works of Reference	284
4. Declarations as to Pedigree	285
5. Declarations as to Public Rights	288

Chapter 14
HEARSAY IN CRIMINAL CASES

1. Statements in Public Documents and Public Works 291
2. Statements in Documentary Records 291
3. Statements in Computers 294
4. Miscellaneous Statutory Provisions, and Evidence at a Previous Trial 295
5. Statements by Deceased Persons 296
6. Confessions 299
7. Statements admitted as Part of the Res Gestae 300
8. Spontaneous Statements about an Event by Participants or Observers 301

Chapter 12

HEARSAY

The rule against hearsay used to be described as the great leading rule underlying a large part of our law of evidence. As will be seen, the Civil Evidence Act 1968 has reduced the importance of the rule in civil cases almost to vanishing point and for a long time there have been a large number of more or less particular exceptions, both common law and statutory, applying in civil and criminal cases to make what is hearsay evidence admissible. At the present time, them, the rule is in many areas of the law almost completely buried under exceptions. Nevertheless it is still there and is still capable of operating even in civil cases. Its formulation and scope are therefore still important, and will be dealt with in this chapter. The exceptions will be treated later and nothing further will be said of them here, except that it must be borne in mind that whenever in this chapter evidence is said to be hearsay, it may be that it would nevertheless be admitted under some relevant exception.[1]

A. The Hearsay Rule

The hearsay rule is a common law rule and is variously stated by judges and authors. The formulation in Cross,[2] following closely that in the Civil Evidence Act 1968, s.1(1), is "An assertion other than one made by a person while giving oral evidence in the proceedings is inadmissible as evidence of the facts asserted." This formulation forbids the assertions of persons *other than the person giving oral evidence*, which might be called the hearsay rule in its strict sense. The formulation also forbids assertions made on some earlier occasion by the *person who is actually testifying* from being used as evidence of the facts asserted. This is more often called the rule against narrative, or against self-serving state-

---

[1] Some exceptions are so well established and so frequent in occurrence (*e.g.* confessions) that the point that hearsay is involved passes without mention. The argument if any will be about whether the conditions of the exception are satisfied. If so, the evidence will be admitted; if not, it will be rejected, without any mention of hearsay or the hearsay rule. Occasionally this silent assumption that hearsay is involved has its dangers: see *post*, p. 247.
[2] p. 38.

ments. It has a different rationale from the rule in its first strict sense, and is better kept distinct. It has been treated of in Chapter 6. This and the following chapters will be concerned with the rule in its strict sense, under which assertions of persons other than the witness are not receivable to prove the truth of what is asserted. Evidence of such is called hearsay evidence and except in the cases mentioned in the next two chapters, hearsay evidence is not admissible. Thus if it is sought to prove that C kicked his wife, it is not allowed to call A to testify that B said that C kicked his wife. B must himself appear and give evidence on the point.

Many reasons have been given for the exclusion of hearsay evidence. Among them, there are the objections that the original maker of the assertion was not on oath when he made it, and did not make it in the face of all the world, but in a privacy which might have emboldened him to say what he would not even hint at in public. However, these are not essential objections, because the fact that the assertion was made on oath in earlier court proceedings does not save it from the rule.[3] Another reason depends upon the obvious danger that something may be lost (or added) in the repetition of a statement by a person who did not make it; but again this is not an essential objection because the rule applies even if there is no such danger, *e.g.* if the original assertion about the events in question was in writing, and this writing is produced to the court. The essential objections are that there was no opportunity for the opposing party to test the assertion by cross-examining the maker, and, subsidiary to this, there was no opportunity for the court to observe the maker's demeanour when he made the assertion, which might have shewn his assertion to have been made in a jocular vein, or have thrown suspicion on his bona fides or knowledge.

Whatever the reasons for the rule against hearsay, the rule itself is highly technical,[4] and is capable of excluding very cogent and safe evidence. Moreover, as it applies equally to defence evidence in criminal cases,[5] it is apparently possible for it to lead to the conviction of the innocent. It should be noted that the fact that the maker of the statement cannot give evidence because he is dead is irrelevant, and does not make evidence of his statement

---

[3] *R.* v. *Inhabitants of Eriswell* (1790) 3 T.R. 707; *Haines* v. *Guthrie* (1884) 13 Q.B.D. 878. It is otherwise if the later proceedings are between the same parties: *Doncaster* v. *Day* (1810) 3 Taunt. 262, see *post*, p. 296.

[4] "I would say, absurdly technical"—*per* Lord Reid, in *Myers* v. *D.P.P.* [1965] A.C. 1001 at p. 1019.

[5] *R.* v. *Thomson* [1912] 3 K.B. 19; *Sparks* v. *R.* [1964] A.C. 964.

admissible.[6] Equally, the fact that the maker of the statement is unidentifiable or untraceable, and unimportant anyway because the probable truth of the statement depends not on the credit of the maker, but on the circumstances of the making, does not make the statement admissible, unless some common law or statutory exception to the hearsay rule is involved.[7] Indeed it makes no difference how relevant or credible the evidence is.

> "No matter how cogent particular evidence may seem to be, unless it comes within a class which is admissible it is excluded. Half a dozen witnesses may offer to prove that they heard two men of high character, who cannot now be found, discuss in detail the fact now in issue and agree on a credible account of it, but that evidence would not be admitted although it might be by far the best evidence available."[8]

The rule forbids not only evidence of what the statement was, but also evidence of what it was about or the effect of it.[9] What is objectionable if fully exposed does not become permissible if it is decently veiled.[10] Nor may evidence be given of what T did as a result of a conversation with A, if the only relevance of what T did is to raise an inference as to what A said.[11] Equally objectionable is evidence of how in conversation with the accused inadmissible statements by a third party were mentioned to him.[12] The rule forbids the use of hearsay evidence for *any* purpose. It used to be thought that it could in some circumstances be used either to confirm or contradict other evidence given to the court,[13] but this idea was exploded by the House of Lords in *Myers* v. *D.P.P.*[14] An out-of-court statement can only operate to confirm or deny other evidence if it is assumed to be *true*, and the hearsay rule prohibits the tendering of the statement as evidence of the truth of the facts stated.[15] Nor is there any discretion in the judge to admit

---

[6] *Stobart* v. *Dryden* (1836) 1 M. & W. 615.
[7] *Per* Lord Reid, in *Myers* v. *D.P.P., supra*, at p. 1023.
[8] Lord Reid, *ubi supra*.
[9] *R.* v. *Saunders* [1899] 1 Q.B. 490.
[10] *Glinsky* v. *MacIver* [1962] Q.B. 726 at p. 780, *per* Lord Devlin.
[11] Lord Devlin, *ubi supra*.
[12] *R.* v. *Baillie-Smith* (1977) 64 Cr.App.R. 76; unless indeed the object of the evidence is to explain the accused's reaction to the statements, which is said to be a confession. See, *ante*, p. 182.
[13] See *R.* v. *Myers* [1965] A.C. 1001 (C.A.), *per* Widgery J. at p. 1008.
[14] [1965] A.C. 1001.
[15] *Ibid., per* Lord Reid at p. 1023.

inadmissible hearsay evidence because it is trustworthy and justice requires its admission.[16]

In view of the hearsay rule's strictness and technicality, its refusal to yield to necessity, and its imperviousness to judicial discretion, it is fortunate for the interests of justice, both that there are many exceptions to it[17] and that its scope is not as wide as may at first appear.

B. Scope of the Rule

Assertions of persons other than the witness who is testifying are not receivable to prove the truth of what is asserted. In one respect, the scope of the rule is very wide, indeed all-embracing. In spite of the word "hearsay," the assertion need not be a spoken one narrated to the court by one who heard it. The hearsay rule applies equally to written assertions and to assertions by conduct. If A is not allowed to testify as to what B said about the facts in issue, then he is not allowed to testify as to what B wrote about these facts (or to produce to the Court B's written account); nor is he allowed to say that B by conduct asserted a fact in issue. For example, it being in issue in which direction a culprit fled from the scene of an incident, it is no more permissible for A to testify that B pointed out the direction than it is for him to testify that B said the man went up the street or into a certain door.

But wide as the possible operation of the hearsay rule is in this respect, it bites only on assertions of persons which are proffered as evidence of the truth of what is asserted. There must be an *assertion*, it must be by a *human being*, and the purpose of proving it must be to establish the *truth of what is asserted* before the hearsay rule is involved. It is convenient to treat the last of these conditions first.

1. The Purpose of Proving an Assertion

The rule does not prohibit *all* assertions made by persons other than the witness who is testifying, but only those tendered as proof of the truth of the facts stated. Thus:

---

[16] *Ubi supra.*

[17] But the number and haphazard nature of these exceptions make the law absurdly complicated. "A picture of the hearsay rule with its exceptions would resemble an old-fashioned crazy-quilt made of patches cut from a group of paintings by cubists, futurists and surrealists"—Morgan and Maguire, "Looking Backward and Forward at Evidence" (1937) 50 Harv.L.R. 909 at p. 921.

Scope of the Rule

"evidence of a statement made to a witness by [another] person ... may or may not be hearsay. It is hearsay and inadmissible when the object of the evidence is to establish the truth of what is contained in the statement. It is not hearsay and is admissible when it is proposed to establish by the evidence, not the truth of the statement, but the fact that it was made. The fact that the statement is made, quite apart from its truth, is frequently relevant in considering the mental state and conduct thereafter of the witness or of some other person in whose presence the statement was made."[18]

From this it will appear that in deciding whether evidence is admissible of what someone, other than the testifying witness, said or wrote, the test is the purpose for which the evidence is tendered. Thus A *is* allowed to say that B said C kicked his wife if the fact in issue is *whether B made this statement or not*, not whether the statement is true or not. This would be a fact in issue if the action was one of defamation brought by C against B, and A would be giving original evidence of a fact in issue. It is the making of the statement, not its truth, which is in issue. If a case occurred in which both the making and the truth of the statement were facts in issue, then A's evidence of what B said could be tendered in proof of the former fact, but the truth of the statements would still have to be proved by other evidence.

The cases where statements may constitute original evidence are multifarious, and include statements constituting motive, conveying notice, or showing knowledge or good or bad faith. If T testifies that A told him that he had seen B do a certain thing, T is giving original, not hearsay, evidence if the issue is not, what did B do? but what did A know? In *R. v. Chapman*[19] the question was whether a doctor did or did not object to a breath test administered to a hospital patient. A policeman was allowed to depose that he asked the doctor (who was not called as a witness) and the doctor did not object. It was not the *truth* of anything said by the doctor which was being proved, but only whether he *objected*, and that could be proved by anyone who witnessed his reaction. In *Woodhouse v. Hall*[20] it was necessary to prove that premises managed by D were a brothel. Policemen were allowed

---

[18] *Subramanian v. Public Prosecutor* [1956] 1 W.L.R. 965, *per* Mr. L. D. M. de Silva at p. 970. D, claiming duress, was held entitled to prove that certain terrorists had told him what they had done to other persons who had not co-operated with them, *in order to prove that he was frightened*.
[19] [1969] 2 Q.B. 436.
[20] (1980) 72 Cr.App.R. 39.

to repeat what the women in the house said to them as to what they were prepared to do for them in the way of indecent acts. The question was not, did the women do indecent acts?, but, did they make indecent offers?

2. Assertions

The word "assertion" is used in preference to "statement" to emphasize that the utterance must be intended to convey the message which the words used contain. Two things follow from this. The utterance must be intended to convey a message; and it is only the message *in the words* which the hearsay rule is concerned with, not any message to be *implied* from the bare fact of the words being spoken or written, even if that implication is intended by the utterer[21] (Assertions to be implied from *acts* raise special problems and will be dealt with later).

Any piece of conduct can be said to be a "statement" if it tells an observer anything, *i.e.* if some fact can be deduced by reasoning from it. That piece of conduct is then said to be circumstantial evidence of the fact. This applies to utterances just as much as to other facts. As we have seen they may be circumstantial evidence of a fact in issue. The utterance can, without stretching language too far, be described as a statement that the fact exists; but it need not be an *assertion* by the utterer that the fact exists. Suppose it is sought to prove that B is a native of France and the fact that B spoke fluent French is offered as circumstantial evidence of this. A testifies that B told him in fluent French that he had been robbed on a train. This testimony not only tells us that B had been robbed, but also that B was a fluent French speaker. Yet B was not asserting "I can speak French" and it would be inapt for A to say, "I know B can speak French *because he told me so*." It would be more correct for him to say, "I know he can speak French because I heard him doing it," just like, "I know he can ride a bicycle because I saw him doing it." The French-speaking, like the bicycle-riding, tells A something, but he is not giving oral evidence of an assertion as evidence of the facts

---

[21] The text following, it is submitted, represents what is implicit in the practice of the courts, but direct authority is hard to find. Moreover, on the application of the hearsay rule to words not intended to be assertive, and to implied assertions, there is room for more than one opinion, in view of influential *dicta* from which it seems to follow that the rule does cover them. The *dicta* were pronounced in connection with assertions implied from *conduct*, and will be considered later: *post*, p. 252.

asserted. The only assertion by B is that he had been robbed, and the evidence is not proffered to prove that fact.[22]

Does it make any difference that the *object* of B's utterance is not to complain about being robbed, but to induce A to think that he is a Frenchman? The answer must be, No. It is still true that A is not testifying "I know that B can speak French (and therefore is probably French) because he told me so." He is still testifying "I know B can speak French because I heard him doing it." The inference which the Court is invited to draw (that B is a Frenchman) does not depend on the truth of what was directly asserted by B, *i.e.* that he had been robbed; but on the fact that the French words were spoken. That the inference to be drawn is logically weak, or wrong, or designedly false, does not mean that the evidence is hearsay. Hearsay evidence is supposed to be unreliable, but unreliable evidence is not necessarily hearsay. If B were to leave a piece of C's property at the scene of a crime in order to give the impression that C committed it, the inference that C did commit it may be weak, depending on the circumstances, and is designedly false, but the evidence is not hearsay.

It may be asked why A should be allowed to proffer evidence of spoken French words as circumstantial evidence of B's being French, when he would not be allowed to testify to an express assertion in English by B that he could speak French or was a Frenchman? The answer is that to rule out implied assertions as hearsay would be to widen the ambit of the hearsay rule to an unacceptable extent. Implied assertions are often found associated with express assertions, and to forbid the evidence of implied assertions would be to cut down the use of circumstantial evidence in an almost limitless and arbitrary way. In particular it would reduce the importance of the rule that spoken or written words are facts like other facts. As was said by Lord Wilberforce in *R. v. Ratten*[23]: "A question of hearsay only arises when the *words* are relied on "testimonially,' *i.e.* as establishing some fact narrated *by the words*." In that case, a telephone operator testified that a woman rang from a certain number and said "get me the police," before the connection was broken. The words, "Get me the police" *implied* that the caller was frightened; and the Court

---

[22] But an assertion implied *in the words* is equally subject to the hearsay rule. "I was robbed on a train," necessarily implies "I travelled by train," and if it is sought to prove that B had travelled by train, A's evidence that B said "I was robbed on a train" would be hearsay. What is *not* hearsay is any statement implied from the *fact* of the utterance, *e.g.* "I can speak French," or "I am a Frenchman."
[23] [1972] A.C. 378 at p. 387: emphasis added.

was allowed to deduce from the operator's evidence that that fact existed.[24] If B says, "X is the case," there is an *implied* assertion, "I believe that X is the case." Yet, if the issue is what did B believe? it is commonplace to allow A's testimony of B's words.[25] Although it can be said that the Court is being asked to accept the truth of B's implied assertion "I believe X to be the case," that is no objection. It is only the express assertion "that X is the case" which the rule bites on.[26]

There are difficult borderline cases in connection with words of greeting, protest, or promise, where it is unclear whether or not there is any intention by the speaker to assert anything. If A overhears B say "Hallo X," is it hearsay for A to testify to B's words for the purpose of proving the presence of X? Not if the words are construed purely as words of greeting, rather than as an assertion that X is present. This will depend on the precise words used and the circumstances,[27] but on the bare words "Hallo X," there is a conflict of opinion as to how they are to be construed.[28] In actual cases, the problem is likely to be sidestepped by admitting evidence of them under some exception to the hearsay rule, *e.g.* as *res gestae*.[29-30]

3. Is there a Human Informant?

(a) "Information" from machines

We have seen that the principal objection to hearsay evidence is that it requires the Court, in informing itself about some transaction in issue, to act on the assertions of some fallible human being who is absent and unavailable for cross-examina-

---

[24] And to infer the further fact that she was being attacked by R, the only other person in the house at the time. For the admissibility of the defendant's testimony as evidence of this further fact, see *post*, p. 302.
[25] *Ante*, p. 243.
[26] See Guest, "The Scope of the Hearsay Rule" (1985) 101 L.Q.R. 385.
[27] See, *e.g.* R. v. *Fowkes* (1856) *The Times*, March 8, cited Stephen's Digest, § 3, and *Teper* v. R. [1952] A.C. 480.
[28] Compare Cross (5 ed.), p. 472 and (6 ed.), p. 671; and see Guest *op. cit.*, p. 392; Heydon, p. 314. The C.L.R.C. Cmnd. 4991, Draft Bill, clause 41(3) would make such an utterance assertive of any fact which the utterance implies, on the arguably wrong view that if it were not assertive it might be taken as *no evidence* of the fact sought to be proved, *i.e.* X's presence. But it could be taken as circumstantial evidence of the fact even if not assertive. A scream is not assertive, but things can be deduced from it. If the C.L.R.C.'s view were right, in the absence of some exception to the hearsay rule, such an utterance could never be admitted to prove X's presence. If it is construed as assertive it is rejected as hearsay; if it is not so construed, it is rejected as worthless.
[29-30] As in R. v. *Fowkes, supra.*

Scope of the Rule

tion. The hearsay rule is not involved if the source of the testifying witness's knowledge of the transaction is a non-human source, *e.g.* a machine, which never could be cross-examined.

That fact that a witness used a simple machine, such as a stopwatch, weighing machine or measuring tape, to gain the information about an event which he narrates to the Court, would not lead anyone to object that his evidence was on that account hearsay. The position is just the same, although not so readily recognisable as such,[31] where the machine is more complicated, and appears to be more of an independent source of the witness's information, than the simple artifacts just mentioned. There is still no human informant however, and hearsay is not involved if the witness describes what he learnt from the machine. If he produces in Court a written record made by the machine of its "conclusions," *e.g.* a print-out, he is not producing a written statement by any absent person. It is more in the nature of real evidence, where the Court inspects an object and draws conclusions from its condition.[32] Of course, the evidence dependent on a machine may be attacked on the ground that the machine was faulty, *e.g.* not properly calibrated, or wrongly used or sited, but that is a matter of weight, not inadmissibility dictated by the hearsay rule.[33]

In the *Statue of Liberty*,[34] radar traces were allowed to prove the position and movements of ships. In *Castle* v. *Cross*[35] a printout on an intoximeter machine was held admissible to prove that the machine did not get a sufficient sample of breath to enable an analysis to be made, as was the evidence of an operator, who knew how the machine worked, that a particular reaction by the machine indicated no sufficient sample. In *R.* v. *Wood*,[36] it was necessary to show that a batch of metal contained trace elements in certain proportions. Chemists testified that they had analysed samples of the metal, and fed the results into a computer which had been programmed to convert the results into percentages. The printout was held admissible to prove the percentages. The

---

[31] For erroneous cases where there was such a failure of recognition, see *R.* v. *Wiles* [1982] Crim.L.R. 669 (Crown Ct.); and *R.* v. *Pettigrew*, (1980) Cr.App.R. 39, commented on in *R.* v. *Wood* (1982) 76 Cr.App.R. 23.
[32] *R.* v. *Wood, supra;* see, *ante*, p. 27.
[33] It may be that the attack shows that evidence is entitled to no weight at all, causing it to be rejected as worthless. But it is not rejected *as hearsay*.
[34] [1968] 1 W.L.R. 739.
[35] [1985] R.T.R. 62. Moreover, in a case where no printout was supplied, the operator was held able to testify to what he saw on the visual display panel: *Owen* v. *Chesters* [1985] R.T.R. 191; *Morgan* v. *Lee* [1985] R.T.R. 409.
[36] (1982) 76 Cr.App.R. 23.

computer was being used as a calculator, a tool, and did not contribute its "own knowledge." By this is meant, the knowledge of another person about the events recorded. If the machine's memory function is used, the printout may fall foul of the hearsay rule,[37] e.g. if A fed his results into a computer which combined them with observations fed in by B, A's evidence of the combined results, or a printout of them, would be hearsay, and at common law,[38] B would need to appear and say what he had done. But a mere programmer or calibrator is different. The fact that the efficiency of the device is dependent on more than one person does not make any difference in kind. Virtually every device will involve persons such as the maker or calibrator; even a simple clock involves the person who set it to the right time in the first place.[39] The contribution of these persons is not about the events recorded; and if they are needed, it will be to demonstrate the machine's reliability, if that is attacked or obviously doubtful. However there is a presumption under which, in the absence of evidence to the contrary, the court will take it that a machine is in order at the relevant time.[40]

If a culprit is photographed automatically in the commission of an offence, the photographic record is admissible even if no live witness saw the event.[41] In *Kajala* v. *Noble*,[42] a B.B.C. News film of a disturbance was allowed although the cameraman who witnessed the event was not called. The fact that the film had been edited by some absent person was a matter which went only to weight.

A photograph has been admitted for identification purposes ever since *R.* v. *Tolson*,[42a] where it was said that such is only a visible representation of the image or impression made upon the mind of the witness by the sight of what it represents, and is therefore only another species of evidence which persons give of identity when they speak merely from memory. Normally a photograph is produced automatically by the camera. Different considerations would appear to apply if it is "composed" by a human agent on the instructions of the witness, as in a photofit. In a sense a photofit can be said to be the agent's account of what

[37] *Castle* v. *Cross, supra,* at p. 69.
[38] For the position of computers under statute, see *post,* pp. 267, 294.
[39] *R.* v. *Wood, supra,* at p. 27.
[40] *Castle* v. *Cross, supra.* For the presumption of regularity, see, *ante,* p. 87.
[41] *R.* v. *Fowden* [1982] Crim.L.R. 588; *R.* v. *Grimer* [1982] Crim.L.R. 674. See also *Taylor* v. *Chief Constable of Cheshire* [1987] 1 All E.R. 225.
[42] (1982) 75 Cr.App.R. 149.
[42a] (1864) F. & F. 103; *Per* Willis J. at p. 104; *R.* v. *Cook* (1986) *The Times* December 10 (C.A.); *R.* v. *Smith (Percy)* [1976] Crim.L.R. 511 (C.A.); *R.* v. *Cook, supra.;* see *ante,* pp. 103, 112.

was said to him by the witness, and looks like hearsay. However it has been held that the picture is composed *by the witness*—the agent is merely doing what the witness could do if he possessed the necessary skill. The law regards a photofit as another form of a camera at work, and as such it is not subject to the hearsay rule. The same applies to a sketch made by an artist on the instructions of the witness. Both photofit and sketch are in a class of evidence of their own to which neither the rule against hearsay nor the rule against previous consistent statements applies.

(b) "Negative" information

The fact that records are systematically compiled by A from the reports of B, and C, and others, does not exempt the records from the hearsay rule at common law.[43] To prove that an event happened, A is not entitled to say, or to produce his records to show, that B reported that it happened. Nor is the rule avoided by A relying *on the system* and testifying that the system he operates is such that the fact that a record of an event appears therein is strongly indicative of the event having happened. It may indeed be strongly indicative, but it is hearsay evidence because in the last analysis the Court is being invited to take as true what the absent B reported about the event.

This was laid down by the House of Lords in *Myers* v. *D.P.P.*[44] However the bounds of that decision, so far as it relates to permissible inferences from the state of systematic records, are still unsettled.[45] It appears not to be hearsay for the keeper of the records to testify to the *failure* of any of his agents to report an event, leading to the inference that it did *not* happen. No absent human mind is involved in a failure to report. To prove that an event did not happen, it is not necessary to call every possible "reporter" to testify that he had nothing to report. It is sufficient for the compiler of the records to testify that nothing was recorded as happening, so the event did not happen.

In *R.* v. *Patel*,[46] it was necessary to prove that Q was an illegal immigrant. It was held to be permissible for the person in charge nationally of the records to say that if Q had been legally admitted to this country, the Immigration Officer who did so would have recorded that fact, no record appeared, so Q must

---

[43] Under statute, many records are allowed as an exception to the rule: see *post*, Chaps. 13, 14.
[44] [1965] A.C. 1001. See, *post*, p. 250.
[45] *R.* v. *Abadom* (1983) 76 Cr.App.R. 48 at p. 51 (C.A.).
[46] (1981) 73 Cr.App.R. 117.

have entered illegally. In *R. v. Shone*,[47] it was necessary to prove that certain goods had been removed from L's stock without authorisation. L's stock clerk and parts manager produced their stock records,[48] which did not show that they had been disposed of; and they testified that this meant that the goods had not been sold or consumed internally, and therefore had been removed without authorisation. The admission of this evidence was upheld on appeal. Both of these cases required the records to be explained by someone in charge of them who had personal knowledge of what they meant. This requirement has been dispensed with in a case which depended not so much on the records of the system, but on the system itself, *i.e.* where A said that under the system, if an event happened, it would have been done by himself, or by B, who would inevitably have told him, and that he (A) had not done it and B had not told him that *he* had done it.[49]

4. Non-spoken Assertions

(a) Written statements

The fact that the assertion is in written form is in principle quite immaterial. If A is not allowed to say, "This is what B said about the event," then he is equally not allowed to say, "This is what B wrote about the event." The fact that the writer can neither be identified, nor expected to give useful evidence if he were found and called, makes no difference. This is shown by the leading case on hearsay, *Myers v. D.P.P.*,[50] where it was necessary to prove that a certain car with particular chassis and engine numbers had a particular number stamped into its cylinder block.

---

[47] (1982) 76 Cr.App.R. 72.

[48] The stock records were admissible under statute to prove the movement of the goods *into* the stock, but the statute did not cover the alleged movement *out of* the stock.

[49] *R. v. Muir* (1984) 79 Cr.App.R. 153. M. was charged with theft of a video recorder which he had hired. In order to prove that it had not been repossessed by the owner (as M. alleged), the owner's local manager was called to say that he had not repossessed it, and neither had head office, because if head office had repossessed it, he would inevitably have been told, and he wasn't told. When cross-examined as to how he could be sure that head office had not repossessed it, he said that he checked with them and was told that central records contained no entry to that effect. This looks like hearsay, but the Court of Appeal held that the way it had come out (*i.e.* in cross-examination), it was admissible. The local manager's evidence did not really depend on the records; he was in charge of the transaction, knew most about it, and was the best person to give relevant evidence. *Sed Quaere*.

[50] [1965] A.C. 1001.

Scope of the Rule

The Crown could not call the workman who had done this because it was not known who he was. However that man had made a record of the number he had stamped into the block on a card which followed the car along the production line; and the Crown in effect produced this card. It was held by the House of Lords that this was hearsay evidence, and as it was not at that time covered by any exception to the hearsay rule,[51] it was inadmissible.

Of course to be hearsay evidence the writing must have been intended to be assertive and must be relied on as an assertion, as the card in *Myer's* case was. But D's calling card engraved with his name and address is different. If D's name appeared on a passport found under an airline seat, that would be admissible circumstantial evidence that D travelled in that seat. The writer of the name in the passport is not making any express assertion as to whom the passport was issued: the name is part of the thing issued, not a record of the identity of the issuee.[52] When a person signs a document as an attesting witness his writing is not an assertion that he witnessed the execution of the document; but merely part of the document being proved.[53] It is different if a party produces a letter in which the attesting witness states that he did witness the execution, or that he altered the document after it was executed.[54] And ancient documents showing ownership of property, such as leases or licences, are receivable not as declarations by the lessor but as acts by him from which ownership and possession can be deduced.[55]

On the other hand, labels and markings on objects are usually hearsay evidence of the origin or ownership of them, because the label or marking is usually intended as assertive of origin or ownership and relied on as such by the witness speaking in court. In *Patel* v. *Comptroller of Customs*,[56] the words "Produce of Morocco" on bags of seed were held to be inadmissible to prove the country of origin. Similarly with a date stamped on a document to prove the time of its receipt.[57] However if the testifying witness does not rely on any assertion in the words in the marking, but on the general appearance of the object as

---

[51] Since 1965, records of this type have been allowed by statute: see *post*, p. 291.
[52] See *R.* v. *Rice* [1963] 1 Q.B. 857 (C.A.), where an airline ticket was admitted as evidence that R travelled on a particular flight.
[53] *Stobart* v. *Dryden* (1836) 1 M. & W. 615 at p. 624.
[54] *Ibid.*
[55] *Malcolmson* v. *O'Dea* (1836) 1 M. & W. 615.
[56] [1966] A.C. 356; and see *Comptroller of Customs* v. *Western Lectric* [1966] A.C. 367.
[57] *R.* v. *Cook* (1980) 71 Cr.App.R. 205.

indicating its origin, that ought to be accepted as circumstantial evidence of origin.[58] The colour or shape of an object is admissible for this purpose, and it ought to make no difference if the make-up of the object includes words, provided they are not relied on as an assertion. Iago cannot prove that a handkerchief he saw Cassio wiping his beard with belonged to Desdemona if his knowledge was gleaned solely from the presence of her initials on it. But if he can say that he recognised the handkerchief as belonging to her because he had seen it (or similar ones) in her possession, that is admissible even though part of the appearance which caused him to recognise it is a device which contains an assertion (*i.e.* her initials).[59]

The fact that the written statement is obviously reliable because the witness A wrote it at B's dictation immediately after the event which B witnessed makes no difference. If A produces the note, it is no more than if he reported what B said. Nor is A's account of what B said made admissible even if B gives evidence and swears that he gave a true account of what happened to A. The issue is not whether B gave A a true account of what happened; the issue is, what happened? and B, who has personal knowledge, must give the evidence. Suppose A and B witnessed a road accident and the number of the offending car has to be proved. A did not see the number, B did see it and dictated it to A who wrote it down. B may be prepared to swear that he dictated the number to A, but if he cannot remember the number, no one can give evidence of what the number was.[60] However, if B verified the note while the event was still fresh in his memory, it counts as B's note and he may use it to refresh his memory.[61] It has been held that this verification may consist in A reading back the note and B agreeing it without seeing it, on the ground that there is no magic in verification by seeing as opposed to verification by hearing.[62]

(b) Assertions implied from conduct

It is clear that the hearsay rule prohibits testimony of what an absent person did if the object is to prove the truth of what that

---

[58] This is perhaps the justification of *Miller* v. *Howe* [1969] 1 W.L.R. 1510 (D.C.), where a policeman was allowed to prove that a breathalizer was an "Alcotest 80" by deposing that he recognised the box it came in, which bore those words.
[59] *cf. Othello*, Act III, Scene 3.
[60] *R.* v. *McLean* (1968) 52 Cr.App.R. 80; *Jones* v. *Metcalf* [1967] 1 W.L.R. 1286; *Cattermole* v. *Miller* [1977] Crim.L.R. 553.
[61] *Ante*, p. 101.
[62] *R.* v. *Kelsey* (1982) 74 Cr.App.R. 213. *Sed Quaere*; the verification (which has to be proved to allow refreshing memory) depends upon hearsay, *i.e.* on B relying on the accuracy of what A said he had written.

person intended to assert by his act, *e.g.* if A testifies that on being asked where X had gone, B pointed to a certain doorway.[63] There appears to have developed an exception, of dubious force and uncertain extent, under which evidence of B's out-of-court identification of a person (*e.g.* by pointing to him at an identification parade) is not fully subject to the hearsay rule.[64] But this exception apart, the rule certainly prohibits narration of a designedly assertive act. As to an act not designedly assertive, the position ought to be the same as with spoken or written words not designedly assertive. It was suggested earlier[65] that it is only words intended to be assertive and relied on as such on which the hearsay rule bites. But it cannot be said with confidence that the rule does not prohibit evidence of a piece of non-assertive conduct tendered as proof of what can be implied from it. The doubts are due almost entirely to some famous *dicta* by Parke B. in *Wright d. Doe v. Tatham.*[66]

The sanity of a testator, M, being in issue, it was sought to prove that he was sane by letters written and sent to him by various persons, apparently on the basis that he was sane. This evidence was rejected on several grounds, including that it was not sufficiently relevant.[67] Parke B., in rejecting it as hearsay, put it that at best the sending of the letters was no better than the making of express assertions by the letterwriters that M was sane, which would clearly be hearsay if proved by someone else.

> "The conduct of the family or relations of a testator; taking the same precautions . . . as if he were a lunatic; his election . . . to some high and responsible office; the conduct of a physician who permitted a will to be executed by a sick testator; the conduct of a deceased captain on a question of seaworthiness, who, after examining every part of the vessel, embarked on it with his family; all these, when deliberately considered, are, with reference to the matter in issue in each case, mere instances of hearsay evidence, mere statements, not on oath but implied in or vouched by the actual conduct

---

[63] See *R. v. Gibson* (1887) 18 Q.B.D. 539; *Chandrasekera v. R.* [1937] A.C. 220.
[64] See, *ante*, p. 110.
[65] *Ante*, p. 244.
[66] (1837) 7 Ad. & El. 313.
[67] As Bosanquet J. pointed out, at p. 381, it did not at all follow that the writers believed M to be sane: "The treatment of deranged persons as rational is one mode of promoting their recovery."

of persons by whose acts the litigant parties are not to be bound."[68]

There is no direct and very little indirect[69] authority in this country as to whether this statement, which can be said to be obiter, represents the law. It is certainly supported by logic. If evidence of express assertions of the persons mentioned by Parke B. would be excluded, logic suggests strongly that evidence of their conduct from which it is sought to deduce assertions ought similarly to be rejected. However common-sense suggests a different answer. The person whose actions are reported is hardly likely to be playacting; certainly not in cases like that of the sea captain embarking on the ship he has examined. And if he were minded to falsify the truth, it would be so much easier for him to *say* that the facts are as they are not in reality, rather than go through an elaborate charade.[70] There is thus some guarantee of his sincerity to make up for the inability to cross-examine him. More importantly, if the hearsay rule bites on all unintended but implied assertions, its operation will be vastly extended, because, as has been said, "Every human action can be presented as an implied assertion of the actor's belief in the satisfaction of the conditions under which he would be prepared to perform it."[71] The learned editor of Cross submits that "it is better to accept the dictates of common sense, and to restrict the definition of implied hearsay to that implied by conduct intended to be assertive."[72]

The question is unlikely to arise for decision in England for two reasons. The first is that the assertion, express *or* implied, is frequently admissible anyway under some *exception* to the hearsay rule, *e.g.* as part of the *res gestae* if the assertion is contemporaneous with and bound up in the transaction being deposed to,[73] or as an admission, if the actor is a party to the proceedings (*e.g.* an accused in a criminal case), and the assertion is contrary to his interest.[74] The second reason is that conduct is

---

[68] At p. 388.
[69] See the discussion of writing not intended to be assertive, *ante*, p. 251, and *R.* v. *Steel* (1981) 73 Cr.App.R. 173 at p. 186; *R.* v. *Blastland* [1986] A.C. 41; *Manchester Brewery* v. *Coombes* (1900) 8 L.T. 347 at p. 349.
[70] "It would be elaborate kind of deception to induce others to infer that you had a particular state of mind from actions which appear not to be directly to the point of your deception":—Guest, *op. cit.* p. 403.
[71] Cross (6th ed.), p. 473.
[72] *Ibid.* Sir Rupert Cross, after some changes of mind, came to the same conclusion; (5th ed.), p. 472. But see Wigmore, § 267.
[73] *Post*, p. 300.
[74] *Post*, p. 272.

often equivocal, and evidence of it may well be rejected as not sufficiently relevant. The inference sought to be drawn from it will not be sufficiently strong.[75] For example, if at D's trial for an offence, evidence is tendered that soon after the offence, A was seen running away, in order to support the inference that A was impliedly acknowledging that he had committed it, that evidence is likely to be rejected as irrelevant because other, equally likely, explanations of A's flight can be conjectured.[76] In *R. v. Blastland*[77] there was an attempt to prove what A said for the sake of what could be implied therefrom. At B's trial for murder of a 12-year old boy, he sought to prove that A, very soon after the murder, had told various persons that a young boy had been murdered, the suggested inference being that A had committed the murder himself. The House of Lords upheld the trial judge's rejection of the evidence, on the ground that that inference was a matter of the purest speculation, and did not feel it necessary to pronounce on the hearsay point.[78]

C. Exceptions to the Rule

In former times the courts were ready to create new exceptions to the rule against hearsay and to extend established exceptions; and over the years scores of exceptions, some particular, some general, have been created by statute. No new common law exceptions have been created since 1876,[79] and since 1880[80] the courts have not been prepared to extend any existing exceptions. In 1964, in *Myers v. D.P.P.*,[81] the House of Lords confirmed that any further erosion of the rule must be as a result of Parliament adding to the list of statutory exceptions.[82] Moreover, the effect of that case is to deny that there is any residual exception covering facts which by their very nature can only be established in a court of law by hearsay evidence. The judge has no discretion to admit legally inadmissible evidence, no matter how cogent it may

---

[75] As in *Doe d. Wright v. Tatham*, itself.
[76] But in Australia, flight has been treated as hearsay: *Holloway v. McFeeters* (1956) 94 C.L.R. 470.
[77] [1986] A.C. 41.
[78] To the same effect is *R. v. Steel* (1981) 73 Cr.App.R. 173 at p. 186, where the Court of Appeal held that the fact that another man interviewed about the crime had told lies about his whereabouts was irrelevant to the issues in the case.
[79] *Sugden v. Lord St. Leonards* (1876) 1 P.D. 154.
[80] *Sturla v. Freccia* (1880) 5 App.Cas. 623; *post*, p. 283.
[81] [1965] A.C. 1001.
[82] A sample of these is given by Lord Morris of Borth-y-Gest in *Myers v. D.P.P., supra*, at p. 1029.

appear to be in the particular case. Unless it comes within a class which is established as admissible, it remains inadmissible.[83]

Nevertheless some courts have chafed at this freeze on common law development. Myers' case has been distinguished on more than one occasion.[84] The ambit of the hearsay rule seems to have been rolled back in the case of negative information.[85] At least one exception to the rule has been extended,[86] and some new exceptions seem to have emerged, *i.e.* under the refreshing memory doctrine[87] and under the law relating to previous identification of a person,[88] an out of court statement was allowed but not for the purpose of proving the truth of what was asserted in it; both doctrines seem to have been extended so as to allow it for that purpose, in apparent breach of the hearsay rule.

D. PRINCIPAL CLASSES OF EXCEPTIONS

In criminal cases, the common law has not been greatly affected by any general statutory relaxation, and the common law exceptions to the hearsay rule remain. These include Confessions, statements made in some circumstances by persons since deceased, statements in public documents and statements accompanying and explaining an act. They are dealt with in Chapter 14, along with a statutory exception for documentary records introduced by the Police and Criminal Evidence Act 1984. In addition there are a large number of particular statutory exceptions, too numerous to mention in a book of this character.[89]

In civil cases, the effect of the Civil Evidence Act 1968 is that, subject to conditions set out in the Act, the court must admit all first-hand hearsay and must admit documentary records even if the contents are second-hand hearsay. See Chapter 13. The all-embracing nature of this "exception" to the hearsay rule leaves

---

[83] *Per* Lord Reid in *Myers* v. *D.P.P., supra*, at p. 1024. This is subject to the court's discretion to admit a statement under ss.2, 4 and 5 of the Civil Evidence Act 1968, although it does not comply with the conditions of admissibility laid down by those sections; *ibid.* s.8(3); R.S.C., Ord. 38, r. 29; see *post*, p. 270.

[84] *R.* v. *Wood* (1982) 76 Cr.App.R. 23; *R.* v. *Shone* (1982) 76 Cr.App.R. 72; *R.* v. *Abadom* (1983) 76 Cr.App.R. 48 at p. 51.

[85] *Ante*, p. 249.

[86] As to public documents, *post* p. 282. See *R.* v. *Halpin* [1975] Q.B. 907 at p. 915. *Sed Quaere*, since that was the very exception which the House of Lords refused to extend in *Myers* v. *D.P.P.* For a *post-Myers* "clarification" of a common law exception, see *R.* v. *Thompson* [1982] Q.B. 647.

[87] *Ante*, p. 102.

[88] *Ante*, p. 110.

[89] For some examples, see *Myers* v. *D.P.P.* [1965] A.C. 1001 at p. 1029.

Principal Classes of Exceptions 257

little room for the operation of other classes of exceptions. Nevertheless some remain and are still capable of operating. Apart from many particular statutory exceptions, some common law classes of exceptions are taken over and preserved by the Act.[90] They are: informal admissions, *some* statements by deceased persons, and statements contained in public documents. Other common law exceptions are wholly abolished. Thus it can be said that all exceptions to the hearsay rule operating in civil cases are statutory; any such must be:

(1) an exception depending on some other enactment, which is unaffected by the Civil Evidence Act, or
(2) one of the general exceptions actually created by the Act, or
(3) one of the erstwhile common law exceptions taken over and preserved by the Act.

Section 1(1) of the Act sets up this position by providing "In any civil proceedings a statement other than one made by a person while giving oral evidence in those proceedings shall be admissible as evidence of any fact stated therein to the extent that it is so admissible by virtue of any provision of this Part of this Act or by virtue of any other statutory provision or by agreement of the parties, but not otherwise."

---

[90] Civil Evidence Act 1968, s.9. See *post*, pp. 271–290.

CHAPTER 13

HEARSAY IN CIVIL CASES

THE general effect of Part I of the Civil Evidence Act 1968[1] is to reduce the importance of the hearsay rule almost to vanishing point, in civil proceedings at county court level and above.[2] To be more precise, but still speaking generally, the effect of Part I is to make first-hand hearsay generally admissible as of right, and to do the same with certain types of documentary second-hand hearsay. It is also provided that where a statement is properly before the court it is admissible as evidence of the facts in it and not solely for some other purpose, such as casting doubt on some other evidence. This is to get rid of the artificial requirement that the judge or jury should take such a statement into account for some ulterior purpose, but should not take it into account as evidence.[3]

The Act "fixes" the law of hearsay in civil proceedings by confirming some common law exceptions to the hearsay rule, abolishing all others, and then establishing a general relaxation of the rule, subject to certain conditions, some of which are found in the Act and others in the court rules made under the Act. Section 1 declares that only under the Act, or other Acts, or by agreement, is hearsay evidence allowed in a civil case. Sections 2, 4 and 5 make general exceptions to the hearsay rule, subject to conditions, and section 9 preserves certain common law particular exceptions. If a case comes under one of these common law exceptions, the evidence is admissible subject only to any common law conditions which may attach to it; the statutory conditions affecting statements introduced under sections 2, 4 and 5 do not apply at all (section 9(5)). Any other common law exceptions are wholly abolished, as to civil cases. Section 6 gives directions for estimating the weight to be given to any evidence let in by sections 2, 4 and 5, and provides that such does not count

---

[1] See App. 2.
[2] This part of the Act does not yet apply to civil proceedings in Magistrates' Courts, which are in matters of hearsay governed by the common law and the Evidence Act 1938, which is of more limited scope than the Act of 1968; nor does it apply to criminal proceedings. It does however apply to civil proceedings before any tribunal applying strict rules of evidence, and to arbitrations: s.18(1).
[3] *Ante,* p. 106

as corroboration where corroboration is necessary or desirable.[4] Section 3 provides that where, under the pre-existing law, a witness's previous out-of-court statement is admissible in order to contradict him or to prove his consistency, that statement is admissible as evidence of the facts in it. Again the statutory conditions affecting statements introduced under sections 2, 4 and 6 do not apply.

It must be added that the whole of Part I of the 1968 Act (except in relation to statements in computers under section 5) has, with the necessary modifications, been extended to statements of opinion,[5] by section 1 of the Civil Evidence Act 1972.[6]

As a result of Part I of the 1968 Act (in this chapter referred to as "the Act"), exceptions to the hearsay rule in civil actions are now so numerous and broadly based that the rule has almost disappeared, and it hardly seems any longer appropriate to refer to the cases where hearsay evidence is admissible as exceptions. Nevertheless, they *will* be referred to as exceptions, if only as a reminder that the rule has not entirely disappeared and is still capable of operating in a civil case. It is necessary to deal separately with those exceptions actually made by the Act and with those common law exceptions which are preserved and taken over by the Act.

A. Exceptions made by the Act

1. Statements Admitted Under Section 2

Section 2(1) provides that in any civil proceeding a statement made, whether orally or in a document or otherwise, by any person, whether called as a witness in those proceedings or not, shall, subject to the section and to rules of court, be admissible as evidence of any fact stated therein of which direct oral evidence by him would be admissible.

It must be noted how extremely wide this provision is. If the person making the statement could have given direct oral evidence of any fact in the statement, then the statement can, prima facie, be put in as evidence of that fact. It is immaterial whether the maker of the statement does in fact give evidence himself: he does not have to be adverse, the statement need not be inconsistent with his oral evidence, but can be to the same

---

[4] *Ante*, Chap. 8
[5] As to when these are admissible at common law, see *ante*, pp. 20–25
[6] And see R.S.C., Ord. 38, r. 34.

effect. The statement need not be in writing, indeed need not be in words at all. By section 10(1), "statement" includes any representation of fact (or opinion) whether made in words or otherwise. The word "representation" appears to cover intended assertions only, and not statements implied from non-assertive conduct. It was suggested that the hearsay rule does not apply to these latter anyway.[7]

Apart from giving notice and sometimes obtaining the Court's consent, which matters will be discussed in the next section of the text, there are only two limits on this very wide provision. The first is that the fact stated must be one "of which direct oral evidence by [the maker] would be admissible." This means that if A is to give evidence of a statement by M, that statement must be one which would be unobjectionable if given in the box by M. If M were incompetent, or if his evidence were insufficiently relevant, or if in M's mouth it would be hearsay, because he had no direct knowledge of the facts,[8] A cannot prove the statement under section 2(1). This is to avoid the situation where otherwise objectionable evidence would be "mysteriously purified"[9] by the fact that it is hearsay in the mouth of the witness giving evidence (A).

The other limit is that the evidence tendered must normally be first-hand hearsay, not second-hand or double hearsay. Section 2(3) provides that if a statement was made otherwise than in a document, no evidence other than direct oral evidence by the person who made the statement or any person who heard or otherwise perceived it being made shall be admissible for the purpose of proving it. Thus if C states to B that a certain fact occurred, of which fact C would be able to give direct oral evidence, that statement may be proved by C, who made it, or by B, who heard it. But it may not be proved by A, who only knows of it because B told him of it. A proviso to section 2(3) is to the effect that if the earlier oral statement by C was made in legal proceedings, whether civil or criminal, then it may be proved in any manner authorised by the court.[10]

If the statement by C was made in a document, the restriction

---

[7] *Ante*, p. 254
[8] *Re Koscot Interplanetary (UK) Ltd.* [1972] 3 All E.R. 829, at p. 833; *The Ymnos* [1981] 1 Lloyd's Rep. 550. *Aliter* if the statement in M's mouth, although hearsay, would be admissible anyway, *e.g.* as an admission by a party's agent; *ibid.*
[9] See Phipson, § 17.03.
[10] The correct manner, at any rate as to statements given in evidence, is by the official shorthand writer's transcript: *Taylor* v. *Taylor* [1970] 1 W.L.R. 1148.

on double hearsay does not apply. This is apparently to allow for the case where A produces a letter about the facts written by C to B. However, A is not allowed to produce a letter written by B stating what C told him about the events; the statement by C is not made in a document, and the statement by B, which *is* made in a document, is not about a fact of which direct oral evidence by B would be admissible, because he has no personal knowledge of the fact. However if B wrote at the instance of C, who checked what he had written, it is arguable that the statement in the document is made by C, through the agency of B[11]; if so A could produce the document.[12]

The extreme width of the rule in section 2 means that it could be abused. The party calling C could have two bites at the cherry by calling C to prove that a fact happened and then calling B to prove that C told him that the fact happened. Or he could prevent his opponent from cross-examining C, by refraining from calling C, and contenting himself by calling B to give evidence of C's statement. A party's right to have a statement admitted under section 2 is therefore made subject to two sets of conditions; the conditions in section 2(2) and those in rules of court made under section 8 of the Act.

Although in principle, for statements to be admissible under the section, it does not matter whether the maker of the statement is called as a witness or not, the conditions in section 2(2) apply to a maker who is called, not to one who is not called. It is thus convenient to distinguish these two cases.

(a) Previous statements by witnesses

The conditions in section 2(2) regulate the proving of a statement where the party also calls or intends to call the maker. It is provided that the statement cannot be proved without leave of the court, which will presumably require to be satisfied that some good reason exists for the double bite at the cherry. Moreover, if the statement is allowed to be proved, it must normally be after the conclusion of the maker's evidence in chief. The court *may* allow evidence of the statement to be given by someone other than the maker before the maker himself gives evidence and it may allow the maker to narrate the statement in the course of his evidence where otherwise the intelligibility of the evidence would be affected.

---

[11] See C.L.R.C.'s 11th Report, Cmnd. 4991 (1972), paras. 254, 255.
[12] And if it were lost, he could, subject to the rules about secondary evidence, give oral evidence of its contents: see, *post*, p. 348.

Order 38 of the Rules of the Supreme Court provides for the giving of due notice to every opposing party by a party intending to prove a statement under section 2 (r. 21). The notice must have annexed a copy of the statement, if that is in a document. If the statement is not in a document, the notice must specify the time, place and circumstances of the statement's making, who made it and to whom, and what the substance of the statement is (r. 22). If it is alleged that one of the specified reasons for not calling any person named in the notice exists, the notice must indicate the reason (*ibid*). The specified reasons are that the person in question is dead, or beyond the seas, or unfit by reason of his bodily or mental condition to attend as a witness, or cannot with due diligence be identified or found, or cannot reasonably be expected to have any recollection of matters relevant to the accuracy or otherwise of the statement (r. 25). These reasons are distinct, so if the person in question is abroad, the fact that no due diligence has been exercised to find his address is irrelevant.[13]

Any opposing party may serve a counter-notice requiring the calling as a witness of any person named in the notice as the maker of the statement or the person to whom it was made. But if the notice indicates one of the specified reasons why such a person should not be called, the counter-notice must contend that on the contrary he ought to be called (r. 26). The question whether the person can or should be called as a witness may be determined before trial (r. 27), when the onus is on the proponent to show on the balance of probabilities that one of the specified reasons exists.[14] If the statement sought to be put in was made in evidence in previous civil or criminal proceedings, an opposing party has no right to serve a counter-notice (r. 26), but any party may apply to the court for directions as to the manner in which such statement should be proved (r. 28).[15]

If the opponent has served a counter-notice; and if either none of the specified reasons was alleged or any that were alleged have been successfully challenged, the proponent must call the maker of the statement if he wishes to use his evidence. If he does call him, then he will need leave of the court to put in the statement as well (s.2(2)(*a*). If he does not call the maker, he has no right to put in the statement (r. 26(4)), although the court, if it thinks it just, may allow him to do so. There is also a power in the court to

---

[13] *Rasool* v. *West Midlands Transport Executive* [1974] 3 All E.R. 638; *Piermay Shipping Co.* v. *Chester* [1978] 1 W.L.R. 411.
[14] *Ibid*.
[15] For an order made under rr. 28 and 29, see *Tremelbye* v. *Stekel* [1971] 1 W.L.R. 226.

penalise in costs an opponent who unnecessarily requires the attendance of the maker (r. 32).

The operation of these provisions is to see to it that normally evidence is given once only, by statement if one of the specified reasons exists *or* if the other side does not object, and by calling the maker if none of the reasons exist *and* the other side desires him to be called.

(b) Previous statements by non-witnesses

If the appropriate notice has been served on the opponent, and either that person has not served a counter-notice requiring the attendance of the maker, or if one of the specified reasons for not calling him exists, then the proponent has an absolute right to put in the statement without calling the maker. The court has no discretion to exclude the statement, even in a case where in practical terms it is both highly desirable and perfectly easy to have him attend.[16] If the maker of the statement was a witness to a conversation the exact terms of which are in dispute (so that cross-examination of the witness is important) and he lives at a known address in Paris (so that it would be an easy matter to call him), the court can neither require him to be called nor exclude his statement. However the weight to be attached to the statement is another matter,[17] and in a case like this where the proponent adopts a method of proof which precludes cross-examination on the statement, no doubt the court would pay little attention to it.[18]

The operation of the section 2 and rules together can best be understood by examples. In those which follow, P is the proponent, the party who wishes to prove a statement by virtue of section 2. M is the maker of the statement, who will not usually be called. Q is the person to whom the statement was made. O is any opposing party. P is alleging that goods supplied by O under a contract of sale were defective when supplied. M, a foreman employed by P, examined the goods and reported on their state by telephone to Q, a manager, also employed by P.

(i) P wishes to prove M's statement by the manager, Q, but does not intend to call M. M is not unavailable for any of the reasons mentioned in rule 25. P must serve a notice of his intention on O, which must indicate the circumstances of the statement's making, who made it (M), to whom it was made (Q) and its effect. If O

---

[16] *Rasool* v. *West Midlands Transport Executive* [1974] 3 All E.R. 638.
[17] See s.6(3), *post*, p. 269.
[18] *Rasool* v. *West Midlands Transport Executive, supra, per* Finer J. at p. 642.

takes no further action, M's statement may be proved by Q. O may however serve a counter-notice requiring M's attendance. If P does not comply and does not produce M, by rule 27(4) M's statement cannot be given in evidence, unless the court exercises its dispensing power under rule 29(1). If P does comply and does produce M, then he will need the leave of the court to give evidence of the statement and will often have to be content with the evidence given by M.

(ii) P wishes to prove M's statement by calling Q, does not intend to call M, and alleges that M cannot reasonably be expected to have any recollection of the fitness of the particular consignment of goods. (This is one of the "specified reasons.") P must serve a notice on O, which must contain a statement of his reason for saying that M should not be called. O is not allowed to serve a counter-notice requiring M's attendance, unless he contends that M should be called, *i.e.* denying P's allegation that M could have no independent recollection of the fact to be proved. Either party may ask that this issue should be determined before the trial. If it appears that O was acting unreasonably in requiring M's attendance, the court may punish O in costs. If the preliminary hearing holds that M cannot reasonably be expected to have any recollection of the fitness of this particular consignment of goods, his attendance must be dispensed with.

(iii) P wishes to call M and also wishes to prove M's statement by calling Q. In principle, section 2(1) allows him to do this (provided he has given notice of his desire to do so), but by subsection (2), he needs leave of the court to call Q to prove M's statement, and will have to adduce some good reason for thus giving one piece of evidence twice. Moreover, if he is given leave, he must normally call M first, and only after the close of M's examination-in-chief may he call Q to prove M's statement.

2. Statements Admitted under Section 4

The operation of section 2, as has been seen, is to allow, subject to conditions, first-hand hearsay evidence in respect of all kinds of statements, documentary and otherwise. Second-hand hearsay is forbidden, so far as concerns statements not in documents, by subsection (3). However, second-hand hearsay in certain records is admissible under section 4.

The section provides that in civil proceedings a statement contained in a document shall be admissible of any fact stated therein of which direct oral evidence would be admissible, if the document is, or forms part of, a record compiled by a person acting under a duty from information which was supplied by a person (whether acting under a duty or not) who had, or may reasonably be supposed to have had, personal knowledge of the matters dealt with in that information and which, if not supplied by that person to the compiler of the record directly, was supplied by him to the compiler of the record indirectly, through one or more intermediaries each acting under a duty. This provision replaces the somewhat similar but not identical provisions of the Evidence Act 1938.

Admissibility under section 4 is subject to similar conditions attending section 2, namely if the original supplier of the information is called as a witness, the statement in the document is not admissible without leave, and shall not normally be given before the conclusion of the examination-in-chief of the supplier (s.4(2)). Moreover the provisions in Order 38 as to the giving of notice and counter-notice and the other matters mentioned earlier[19] apply *mutatis mutandis* to statements sought to be admitted under section 4.

Record. This term is not defined, but cases on comparable provisions in the Evidence Act 1938[20] and the Criminal Evidence Act 1965 give it a somewhat restricted interpretation and they have been followed with respect to section 4 of the 1968 Act. The record has to be compiled from information supplied, and it is doubtful whether a mere file of letters is comprehended.[21] A record means "a history of events in some form which is not evanescent,"[22] but the fact that it covers a single transaction and is not intended to be kept for very long is not a fatal objection.[23] More important, it has been held that the contents must be an original or primary source of information. In *H.* v. *Schering Chemicals Ltd.*,[24] a plaintiff wished to show that his deformities were caused by the negligence of the defendants in making and marketing a certain drug. He attempted to adduce as evidence articles and letters in the medical press, but Bingham J. held that such were not "records," which term means what a historian would regard as original or primary sources, *i.e.* documents which either gave effect to a transaction or which contain a contemporaneous register of information supplied by those with direct

---

[19] *Ante*, p. 262.
[20] See *Thrasyvoulos Iannou* v. *Papa Christoforos Demetriou* [1952] A.C. 84.
[21] *R.* v. *Tirado* [1968] 1 W.L.R. 756.
[22] *R.* v. *Jones & Sullivan* [1978] 1 W.L.R. 195 at p. 199.
[23] *Ibid.* But see *R.* v. *Gwilliam* [1968] 1 W.L.R. 1839.
[24] [1983] 1 W.L.R. 143.

knowledge of the facts. The proffered items were digests or analyses of records, not the records themselves.[25]

Duty. The inherent condition of admissibility under section 4 is duty; duty in the compiler of the record and any intermediaries between the maker of the statement and the compiler, although it must be noted that the maker of the statement need not be acting under a duty. What is required of him is that he had or may reasonably be supposed to have had,[26] personal knowledge of the matters dealt with in the statement. Acting under a duty is widely defined by section 4(3) to include acting in the course of any trade, business, profession, or other occupation in which a person is engaged or employed or for the purpose of any paid or unpaid office held by him.[27]

However it must be recalled that the conditions imposed by section 4 only apply if it is sought to introduce the statement under that section. If it is sought to prove the statement by the evidence of one who heard the maker utter (*i.e.* by first-hand hearsay) the statement is admissible under section 2, whether or not, for example, anyone was acting under a duty in recording it.

In the following examples on the working of section 4, it will be assumed that due notice has been given and that no counter-notice has been given requiring the attendance of the maker of the statement or the compiler of the record.

(i) M, a storeman, orally reports to S, a foreman, that a certain consignment of goods delivered to him is defective. S notes this in his daybook and also orally reports the statement to T, the shop manager, who makes a written note of the complaint. M's statement may be proved by the production of S's book or by T's note; these need not be produced by S or T, but by someone else, Q. S is both a compiler and an intermediary.

(ii) M, a witness of a traffic accident, reports the facts to P, a policeman, who notes his statement in his notebook. The facts may be proved in civil proceedings by the production of P's book though neither M nor P gives evidence. It would be the same if P were not a policeman, but a newspaper reporter.

(iii) M, an umpire at a cricket match, signals to the scorer that a "wide" has been bowled. P, a newspaper reporter, notes this in

---

[25] Followed in *Savings & Investment Bank* v. *Gasco Investments BV* [1984] 1 All E.R. 296; the selective inclusion of only some items reported, and the adding of comments, were further reasons for rejection. See also *Re Koscot Interplanatory (U.K.) Ltd.* [1972] 3 All E.R. 829.
[26] See *Knight* v. *David* [1971] 1 W.L.R. 1671.
[27] Probably a judge's summing-up in an earlier case is a record compiled by a person acting under a duty: *Taylor* v. *Taylor* [1970] 1 W.L.R. 1148.

Exceptions Made by the Act

his book. The fact is not provable by the production of P's book, because although P was acting under a duty, M's statement, *i.e.* signal, was not made to him, but to the scorer. However, M's statement[28] may be proved by P, who actually saw it, under section 2 (and he may use his notebook to refresh his memory.[29]).

3. Statements Admitted under Section 5

At the present day, many statements, not only in business, but in numerous other sectors of human affairs, are produced mechanically by computer. As we have seen[30] such a mechanically produced statement does not always break the hearsay rule, but often it does and so is inadmissible at common law. However, by section 5 a statement produced by a computer is admissible provided that the conditions of section 5 and the rules are complied with. A computer is widely defined as any device for storing or processing information.[31]

The conditions are as in subsection 2, and are:

(i) that the document containing the statement was produced by the computer during a period over which the computer was used regularly to store or process information for the purposes of any activities regularly carried on over that period, whether for profit or not, by any body, whether corporate or not, or by any individual;

(ii) that over that period there was regularly supplied to the computer in the ordinary course of those activities information of the kind contained in the statement or of the kind from which the information so contained is derived;

(iii) that throughout the material part of that period the computer was operating properly or, if not, that any respect in which it was not operating properly or was out of operation during that part of that period was not such as to affect the production of the document or the accuracy of its contents; and

(iv) that the information contained in the statement reproduces or is derived from information supplied to the computer in the ordinary course of those activities.

A certificate purporting to be signed by a person occupying a responsible position in relation to the operation of the computer or the management of the activities which are recorded in it

---

[28] M's gesture is certainly a statement, because it is intended to be assertive: see p. 252, *ante*.
[29] See *ante*, p. 101.
[30] *Ante*, p. 246.
[31] s.5(6).

which identifies the document containing the statement and describes how it was produced, which gives particulars showing that the document was produced by a computer, or which deals with any matter mentioned in the conditions in subsection (2), shall be evidence of any matter stated in the certificate.[32] Wilful mis-statement in such a certificate is an offence.[33] If more than one computer is used in the production of the statement all the relevant computers count as one for the purposes of the Act.[34] Neither the supply of information to the computer nor the production of the statement needs any human intervention,[35] *i.e.* the automatic monitoring and recording of physical processes is covered.

The rules treat a statement produced by a computer broadly like any other statement; the persons occupying responsible positions in relation to the supply of information to and the operation of the computer are treated like the maker and compiler of a statement respectively. They are specified in the notice under the rules, and a counter-notice can require their attendance to give evidence, which attendance may be dispensed with for exactly the same reasons as are applicable to the makers of ordinary statements and the persons to whom such statements are made.[36]

4. Statements Made Evidence by Section 3

In Chapter 6 it was seen that under the Criminal Procedure Act 1865 (which applies also to civil proceedings) it is sometimes possible to prove a witness's previous inconsistent statement in order to shake his credit. It is also sometimes possible to prove a witness's previous *consistent* statement in order to rebut the suggestion that he has concocted his story after the occasion about which he is testifying.[37] Moreover, there is a doctrine that when an opponent cross-examines a witness upon a document used by the witness to refresh his memory, the party calling the witness may be entitled to have the whole document put in evidence.[38]

It was clear that in the first two cases, the previous statement of

---

[32] *Ibid.* subs. (4).
[33] s.6(5).
[34] s.5(3).
[35] *Ibid.* subs. (5).
[36] See r. 24.
[37] *Ante*, p. 107.
[38] *Ante*, p. 103.

the witness was not evidence of the matters stated therein, but only bore on the reliability of the witness[39]; and there was some doubt as to the evidential value of a document used for refreshing memory which was in under the doctrine mentioned above. Now, however, in civil cases, section 3 of the Civil Evidence Act declares that where a statement or document is proved under any of these three doctrines it is evidence of any fact stated therein of which direct oral evidence by the witness would be admissible.

It must be noted that section 3 does not contain conditions similar to those found in sections 2 and 4, nor, unlike them, does section 3 make admissibility subject to rules of court. This means that if, for example, the common law doctrine referred to above, which allows proof of a witness's previous consistent statements, applies, the party calling him may use the previous statements as evidence without leave and without having served any notice under Order 38. It is the same with a party attacking a witness by proving his previous *inconsistent* statements, except that if it is his own witness he is thus attacking, he will need the judge to have ruled the witness hostile and to have given him leave to cross-examine him.[40]

5. Provisions Supplementary to Sections 2-5

(a) Weight of evidence

The question of how much weight should be given to any piece of evidence is essentially one for the tribunal of fact.[41] Nevertheless, section 6(3) defines with great particularity the circumstances to which regard *shall* be had in estimating the weight, if any, to be attached to a statement admitted under section 2, 3, 4 or 5. After stating that *all* circumstances must be taken into account from which any inference can reasonably be drawn as to the accuracy or otherwise of the statement, the subsection goes on to single out for consideration circumstances bearing on the question whether the statement was made contemporaneously with the facts stated therein and on the question whether the maker of the statement, or the compiler of the record, or the supplier of information to or operator of a computer, had any incentive to conceal or misrepresent the facts.

---

[39] *Ante*, p. 103.
[40] *Ante*, p. 113.
[41] *Ante*, p. 37.

(b) Credibility of a maker not called at the trial

Had the maker of a statement been called as a witness, then like any other witness his credibility might have been attacked or supported in any of the ways mentioned in Chapter 6, and in particular by proof of inconsistent or consistent statements made by him on some other occasion. As we have seen, section 3 provides that statements admitted for these purposes are also evidence of the facts stated therein.

The scheme of section 7 is to allow exactly the same process to be applied to a maker who is *not* called as a witness. The same rules about attacking and supporting his credit, and about the finality of his answers, supposing he had denied a matter properly put to him,[42] are made to apply in the case of an absent maker of a statement. Inconsistent statements by the maker which are thus admitted to shake his credibility are also evidence of the facts stated therein.

However, the provisions of section 7 are made subject to rules of court, and it must be noted that rule 30 of Order 38 forbids any party who did not serve a counter-notice requiring the maker to attend from using section 7 to adduce evidence to impeach the maker. It is different if one of the specified reasons for not calling the maker exists (*i.e.* that he is dead, unfit, beyond the seas, etc.). This would prevent a party who could not deny the death, etc., from serving a counter-notice, but that is no reason why he should not be permitted to impeach the maker's credibility. However, a party who effectively consents to the non-attendance of the maker by not serving a counter-notice when he could do so has in effect waived his right to impeach the absent maker of the statement. Moreover the proving of an inconsistent statement is only allowed to a party who has given notice of his intention to do so, unless the court gives him leave (r. 31).

(c) Judicial discretion

There is a discretion to admit a statement under sections 2, 4 and 5 although the rules about notice and counter-notice have not been complied with (r. 29). It was held in *Ford* v. *Lewis*[43] that this discretion must be exercised judicially, and never in favour of a party who breaks the rules deliberately in order to surprise his opponent. The object of the rules and the discretion is not to enable one to construct a tactical minefield in which one may ambush one's opponent. On the other hand, the discretion ought

---

[42] See *ante*, p. 118.
[43] [1971] 1 W.L.R. 623.

to be used in a proper case. The Act ought not to be construed so that a party would have to serve notice in respect of every single witness, just in case events at the trial might require an application to put in a witness's statement. In the normal case where a witness is to be called, there will be no thought of putting in the statement as well. But if the witness's oral evidence unexpectedly turns out to be inconsistent and confused, the party calling him ought to be given a chance to repair matters by putting in an earlier statement which is clearer. In *Morris* v. *Stratford-upon-Avon U.D.C.*[44] the defendants' servant had run over the plaintiff. He was called, but the accident being five years ago, his evidence was unsatisfactory and confused. The Court of Appeal approved the judge's allowing the defendants to put in a written statement he had made to their insurers soon after the accident, which *was* clear, although no notice had been given. Of course the judge can, and perhaps should, grant an adjournment so that the other side is not taken by surprise.

There is no discretion under the Act allowing the court to refuse to admit hearsay evidence which complies with the Act and the rules.[45] There is one exception to this, with regard to a statement made before an earlier court; the present court may give directions as to whether, and if so on what, conditions the statement will be admitted.[46] Moreover, section 18(5) of the Act preserves the court's overriding discretion to exclude evidence as part of its inherent power to control its own proceedings. How far there is any such general discretion in civil proceedings was considered in Chapter 2.[47]

B. COMMON LAW EXCEPTIONS PRESERVED BY THE ACT

The general scheme of the Act is to make hearsay admissible in civil cases only under statute or by agreement between the parties. This would involve abolishing all common law exceptions to the hearsay rule. This was felt to be too sweeping and some are preserved by section 9. All other common law exceptions are abolished.[48]

Section 9 by subsections (1) and (2) preserves the existing law about admissions, published works in matters of a public nature,[49]

[44] [1973] 1 W.L.R. 1059.
[45] s.8(3)(*a*).
[46] R.S.C., Ord. 38, r. 28; s.8(3)(*b*).
[47] *Ante*, p. 42.
[48] s.1(1).
[49] *Post*, p. 284.

and public documents and records.[50] Where a statement comes under one of these three excepted cases, it is admissible subject only to whatever conditions the common law had attached to them. The conditions in sections 2, 3, 4 and 5 and order 38 do not apply at all.

Subsections (3) and (4) preserve the common law relating to statements establishing reputation or family tradition, which allowed such in some cases to establish good or bad character,[51] and in pedigree cases,[52] and as to public or general rights.[53] The statements admitted under these doctrines are often cases of remote or multiple hearsay; if so, they are admissible just as formerly. But other such statements are merely first- or second-hand hearsay and there is no reason why the conditions in sections 2 and 4 and the rules about notice and counter-notice should not apply to them. The Act therefore provides that such are admissible as at common law in so far as they are not capable of being admitted under sections 2 and 4.[54] If they are capable of being admitted under those sections, they must comply with the statutory conditions.

1. Admissions

Statements made out of court by a party in his own interest are inadmissible. They offend the hearsay rule, and there is no reason why the rule should be breached in order to allow them in, since there is no obvious guarantee that they will be trustworthy. Indeed, quite the reverse, since they are self-serving. The rule against self-serving statements will usually secure their rejection, quite apart from the hearsay rule.[55] If they were admissible, anyone could manufacture evidence for himself by telling his tale to several persons out of court and then calling those persons.

But it is different with statements made out of court by a party against his interest. People do not usually speak falsely against themselves, and there is a reasonable guarantee of the statement's

---

[50] *Post*, p. 281.
[51] *Ante*, p. 18.
[52] *Post*, p. 285.
[53] *Post*, p. 288.
[54] s.9(3)(*a*).
[55] For the rule against self-serving statements, and the exceptional cases where such are admitted for some limited purpose, see *ante*, p. 104.

truth in the mere fact that it was uttered at all.[56] No man would declare anything against himself unless it were true.[57] Although that cynical observation does not adequately explain all the cases (*e.g.* those where a statement was received as an admission although not known by the party making it to be against his interest[58]), the law admits statements, made out of court by a party or some person having an identity of interest with him, *which are against that party's interests,* for the purpose (it is now generally agreed) of proving the truth of the facts stated, *i.e.* as an exception to the hearsay rule. It calls such statements admissions.[59] The precise characteristics of them and of their effect are dealt with in this section. It must be borne in mind however that if a statement is not technically an admission, that does not necessarily mean that it cannot be admitted. It will usually be easily provable anyway under the provisions of sections 2 and 4 of the Act, which are on the whole more ample and accommodating than the common law on admissions. However the survival of the common law doctrine of admissions is important, in that a statement which is an admission is allowed in without complying with conditions imposed by sections 2 and 4 and order 38.[60] This may be a pronounced tactical advantage for the party putting it in, because he may be able to "surprise" his opponent at the trial, which he never could do if obliged to go through the statutory procedure of notice and counter-notice.

(a) Conditions of admissibility

An admission is a statement against interest by a party (or one

---

[56] The party against whom an admission is proved can hardly complain that he had no opportunity of cross-examining the maker of the statement, since he *is* the maker and can explain the statement by giving evidence himself. See Morgan, *Basic Problems of Evidence* (1972), p. 266.
[57] R. v. *Hardy* (1794) 24 How.St.Tr. 199, *per* Lord Eyre C.J. at pp. 1093–1094; *Slatterie* v. *Pooley* (1840) 6 M. & W. 664, *per* Parke B. at p. 669.
[58] *e.g. Falcon* v. *Famous Players Film Co.* [1926] 2 K.B. 474. Wigmore originally thought that the principle on which admissions are allowed to be proved is that they contradict a party's present assertions: (1st ed., 1904), § 1048; but later was persuaded otherwise: see (3rd ed., 1940), § 1048, where he concludes that, although they may well have the effect of contradicting and thereby depreciating the admitting party's present assertions, they also "have such testimonial value as belongs to any testimonial assertions in the circumstances; and the more notably they run counter to the natural bias or interest of the party when made, the more credible they become; this element adding to their probative value, but not being essential to their admissibility."
[59] Admissions in criminal cases are called confessions. Basically they are similar, but confessions have additional conditions for admissibility, which require them to be treated of separately. *Ante,* Chap. 10.
[60] *Ante,* p. 262.

identified with him[61]); the fact that someone else made a statement against his own interest is not usually provable against the party.[62] On the other hand, the statement may be made before proceedings were contemplated,[63] and need not be made with reference to the proceedings. Nor usually[64] need it be made to the other party. It can be made to anyone, *e.g.* the maker's wife,[65] or even to no one. The party may be overheard talking to himself[66] or may have proved against him statements made in a private memorandum, not intended to be shown to anyone.[67]

Admissions may be oral or in writing or by conduct. Where a party signs or recognizes or adopts or acts upon any document, it may be tendered against him as an admission and so as evidence of the truth of its contents.[68] The contents of a document may also be proved by his oral admission of them.[69] As to conduct, if a party goes about suborning false witnesses for a pending action, that may be taken as an admission that his case is a bad one.[70] In appropriate cases, the failure of a party to undergo a medical examination may be evidence against him.[71] Moreover, as we have seen,[72] his demeanour or silence in the face of statements made in his presence and hearing may amount to an adoption of these statements and thus an admission.[73] A plea by him in an earlier proceeding may be used as an admission in a later proceeding.[74]

---

[61] On privity, see *post*, p. 278.
[62] Statements by a deceased person against his interest were provable against a party by virtue of a separate exception to the hearsay rule. This exception has been abolished as to civil cases by the Civil Evidence Act 1968; it is still theoretically available in criminal cases. See *post*, p. 297.
[63] But where a party is sued in a representative capacity, the person he represents cannot be prejudiced by statements made by the party before he assumed that capacity: *New's Trustee* v. *Hunting* [1897] 1 Q.B. 607 at p. 611. See *post*, p. 279.
[64] A solicitor's admission, in order to bind his client, must have been made to the opposite party or his solicitor, because he has no authority to make any other kind of admission. See *post*, p. 280.
[65] *Rumping* v. *D.P.P.* [1964] A.C. 814. The wife cannot usually be compelled to give evidence of the statement, but that is another matter. See *ante*, p. 134.
[66] See *R.* v. *Simons* (1834) 6 C. & P. 540.
[67] *Bruce* v. *Garden* (1869) 17 W.R. 990.
[68] *Evans* v. *Merthyr Tydfil U.D.C.* [1899] 1 Ch. 241.
[69] *Slatterie* v. *Pooley* (1840) 6 M. & W. 664, in which case the normal rules about the proof of the contents of documents (see *post*, p. 347) do not apply.
[70] *Moriarty* v. *London, Chatham and Dover Rly.* (1870) L.R. 5 Q.B. 314.
[71] *S.* v. *McC.* [1872] A.C. 24, *per* Lord MacDermott at p. 46.
[72] *Ante*, p. 181.
[73] Compare and contrast *Bessela* v. *Stern* (1877) 2 C.P.D. 265 and *Wiedemann* v. *Walpole* [1891] 2 Q.B. 534.
[74] *R.* v. *Rimmer* [1972] 1 W.L.R. 268; *R.* v. *McGregor* [1968] 1 Q.B. 371.

Common Law Exceptions Preserved by the Act 275

If the admission is founded on hearsay, or consists merely in the declarant's opinion or belief, does that render the statement inadmissible? The matter has been the subject of debate, the background to the debate being the reason why admissions are allowed.[75] In civil cases, the classical, and probably still existing, position is that such a statement *is* admissible provided it appears that the party affirmed or acknowledged the existence of the fact.[76] However, it is likely to be of little or no weight.[77] But in criminal cases, it has been laid down that the primary rule is that an accused can only make a valid and admissible admission of a statement of fact of which he could give admissible evidence.[78] This would mean that even if the evidential value of an admission is high (*e.g.* the admitter had many and reliable sources for what he said), it would still be inadmissible against him if these sources were hearsay. It appears, however, that if the case is such that the accused would clearly know what he was talking about when he made the admission, it will be allowed in as evidence of its truth.[79] The cases are not all reconcilable. It has been said that, in those cases,

> "the courts seem to be groping their way towards some considered view as to what may or may not be regarded as sources of information of sufficient quality to make the accused's admission receivable.... And it is still possible that the courts may revert to the classical position and hold that admissions made without knowledge are admissible but possibly of little or no evidential weight."[80]

The value of *any* admission depends on the circumstances. Unlike formal admissions,[81] an informal admission of the type discussed in this section is by no means conclusive. It is only an item of evidence like any other, can be weak or strong like any

---

[75] *Ante*, p. 273, n. 58.
[76] See *Lustre Hosiery Ltd.* v. *York* (1935) 54 C.L.R. 134 at pp. 138, 143, and the authorities there reviewed particularly *Roe d. Trimlestown* v. *Kemmis* (1843) 9 C. & F. 749 at p. 780; Cross, p. 520.
[77] *Lustre Hosiery Ltd* v. *York, supra,* p. 143; *Comptroller of Customs* v. *Western Lectric Co.* [1966] A..C. 367 at p. 371.
[78] *Att.-Gen.'s Reference (No.4 of 1979)* [1981] 1 All E.R. 1193; *Surujpaul* v. *R.* [1958] 1 W.L.R. 1050; *R.* v. *Korniak* (1983) 76 Cr.App.R. 145; *R.* v. *Hulbert* (1979) 69 Cr.App.R. 243.
[79] *Bird* v. *Adams* [1972] Crim.L.R. 174; *R.* v. *Chatwood* [1980] 1 All E.R. 467.
[80] Scott, "Controlling the Reception in Evidence of Unreliable Confessions," [1981] Crim.L.R. 285 at p. 296. See also Phipson, § 19.18; Heydon, p. 329.
[81] *Ante*, p. 28.

other, and like any other can be explained, or diminished, or controverted, or indeed enhanced, by other evidence, including evidence of the circumstances of its making. Thus it may be shown by the party against whom it is tendered to be untrue,[82] or made under a mistake of law or fact, or uttered in ignorance, levity or an abnormal condition of mind. On the other hand, its weight increases with the deliberation of the speaker and the solemnity of the occasion.

The *"whole statement"* rule. The party against whom an admission is tendered is entitled to have so much of the whole of the statement, document or correspondence containing the admission as relates to the question in dispute put in evidence, even if some parts may be favourable to himself,[83] although less weight may be attached to the favourable parts.[84] In any event, it seems that the favourable parts are evidence of the facts stated only to the extent that they minimize or qualify the unfavourable parts.[85]

(b) Statements "without prejudice"

If the circumstances are such that the statement alleged to be an admission was made in the course of an attempt to settle a dispute either before an action is commenced or while an action is going on, the statement is not admissible in evidence at all. This is because it is the policy of the law that disputes should be amicably settled if possible, and it would be unwise to enter into negotiations if statements made during such negotiations were admissible in evidence at the trial in the event of the attempt to settle not being successful.[86] Accordingly, what is said or written in the course of negotiations which are entered into expressly or impliedly "without prejudice" cannot be given in evidence, even on a question of costs,[87] without the consent of the party who made the statement. Moreover negotiations carried on through a solicitor may not be entirely frank unless the solicitor feels secure

---

[82] Unless the admission amounts to an estoppel, as to which see *post*, Chap. 15.
[83] *Randle v. Blackburn* (1813) 5 Taunt. 245; *Harrison v. Turner* (1847) 10 Q.B. 482.
[84] *Smith v. Blandy* (1825) Ry. & M. 257; *R. v. McGregor* [1968] 1 Q.B. 371.
[85] On this, see further, *ante*, p. 106.
[86] *La Roche v. Armstrong* [1922] 1 K.B. 485, *per* Lush J. at p. 489; *Mole v. Mole* [1951] p. 21.
[87] *Walker v. Wiltshire* (1889) 23 Q.B.D. 335; *Stotesbury v. Turner* [1943] K.B. 370. But if the party expressly reserves the right to produce a "without prejudice" letter on the question of costs, he may do so, provided the claim is not a money claim, where the appropriate method of affecting costs by an offer of compromise is payment into court. *Cutts v. Head* [1984] Ch. 290; *Calderbank v. Calderbank* [1976] Fam. 93.

in his own personal position. Consequently an admission made by a solicitor in the course of negotiations on behalf of his client, *e.g.* an admission that the disputed property is in the solicitor's hands, cannot be used against him if the other side decide to sue the solicitor personally.[88]

If the negotiations are by letter, the words "without prejudice" may be placed at the head of one or more of the letters, in which case both previous and subsequent letters in the correspondence are covered by the privilege, even though they are not so headed.[89] But the fact that the negotiations are without prejudice may also be gathered from the circumstances,[90] so that letters may be inadmissible even though none of them is expressly headed "without prejudice"; as will oral statements made at[91] or documents prepared in pursuance of[92] an interview at which negotiations are conducted.

The doctrine applies to matrimonial disputes[93] and if the parties approach a conciliator, such as a clergyman, probation officer, marriage guidance counsellor[94] or indeed any other person,[95] or even if the approach is made *by* the conciliator,[96] statements made to him will normally be inadmissible without the consent of the party making them. The wishes of the conciliator himself in the matter are irrelevant.[97] Statements made between the parties themselves in the course of an attempted reconciliation may not be disclosed by a person who casually overheard them.[98] Whether the doctrine described above concerning conciliators applies generally to disputes outside the matrimonial field is doubtful, but statute has imposed a similar position with regard to conciliation officers appointed by the Advisory, Conciliation and

---

[88] *La Roche v. Armstrong* [1922] 1 K.B. 485.
[89] *Paddock v. Forrester* (1842) 3 M. & G. 903; *Oliver v. Nautilus Steam Shipping Co. Ltd.* [1903] 2 K.B. 639.
[90] *Oliver v. Nautilus Steam Shipping Co. Ltd., supra.*
[91] *Pool v. Pool* [1951] P. 470.
[92] *Rabin v. Mendoza* [1954] 1 W.L.R. 271.
[93] *McTaggart v. McTaggart* [1949] P. 94; *Theodoropoulas v. Theodoropoulas* [1964] P. 311; *D. v. N.S.P.C.C.* [1978] A.C. 171, at pp. 236–237, where, however, Lord Simon treats the matter as a distinct doctrine separate from the "without prejudice" doctrine.
[94] *Mole v. Mole* [1951] P. 210; *Pais v. Pais* [1971] P. 119.
[95] *Theodoropoulas v. Theodoropoulas, supra.*
[96] *Henley v. Henley* [1955] P. 202.
[97] *Pais v. Pais, supra.*
[98] *Theodoropoulas v. Theodoropoulas, supra.*

Arbitration Service to assist in disputes between employer and employee.[99]

In any case, there must be negotiations, and the statement must be made in a bona fide attempt at a compromise[1]; and the judge is entitled to look at the statement in order to decide whether these conditions are satisfied.[2] So the mere heading of a letter "without prejudice" will not save it from being admissible if it constitutes an act of bankruptcy[3] or contains a threat, if that threat is material to the present action.[4] Moreover, independent facts admitted during negotiations for a settlement are receivable,[5] as where an injured plaintiff being medically examined by the defendant's surgeon volunteered a statement as to how the accident happened.[6] An admission made by a party, without prejudice, but on a condition which he afterwards violates, is evidence against him,[7] and if an offer made without prejudice is accepted, then the offer and acceptance form a new agreement, and can be proved notwithstanding that they were made "without prejudice."[8]

(c) Admission by privies and other third parties

When is A, a party, affected by statements made against A's interest by B, who is not a party? The usual rule is that he is not affected, but various exceptions arise through privity. The expression "privity" is used to devote mutual or successive relationship to the same interest in property and therefore an admission by the privy as to that interest is admissible against the party. An obvious example is the privity between present owner and predecessor in title. Thus if A, the present owner of Blackacre, is suing D for trespass, a statement by a previous owner B, made while he was owner, that he had no right to enclose the land, is admissible against A.[9] In *Smith* v. *Smith*,[10] P

---

[99] Employment Protection (Consolidation) Act 1978, ss.133(6), 134(5). See *Grazebrook* v. *Wallens* [1973] 2 All E.R. 868.
[1] Statements are not "without prejudice" if the negotiations are between the parties on the one hand and a third party on the other hand with some object other than the settlement of the dispute between them: *R.* v. *Nottingham County JJ., ex p. Bostock* [1970] 1 W.L.R. 1117.
[2] *Re Daintry* [1893] 2 Q.B. 116, *per* Vaughan Williams J at p. 119.
[3] *Re Daintry, supra.*
[4] *Kurtz* v. *Spence* (1887) 58 L.T. 438.
[5] *Waldridge* v. *Kennison* (1794) 1 Esp. 143, *per* Lord Kenyon C.J.
[6] *Field* v. *Commissioner for Rys. for New South Wales* (1957) 99 C.L.R. 285.
[7] *Holdsworth* v. *Dinsdale* (1871) 19 Q.R. 798.
[8] *Walker* v. *Wilsher* (1889) 23 Q.B.D. 335 at p. 337; *Tomlin* v. *Standard Telephones* [1969] 1 W.L.R. 1378.
[9] *Woolway* v. *Rowe* (1834) 1 A. & E. 114.
[10] (1836) 3 Bing N.C. 29.

sued A, the executor of B, for a watch which he said B had given him. A statement by B that he had given the watch to P was held admissible against A. Of course if B was the owner of a limited interest in the property, nothing he said could ever bind the freehold owner, so an admission by B, a former tenant, that Blackacre did not enjoy a right over neighbouring land, cannot be used against A, the fee simple owner of Blackacre.[11]

There is a privity between trustee and beneficiary,[12] so statements against his interest by the beneficiary are provable against the trustee and, of course, against the beneficiary's successors. One joint owner can make admissions which affect the other or others.[13] However there is no such joint interest between principal and surety,[14] nor normally between co-defendants or co-accused or respondent and correspondent in divorce cases.[15]

In cases where there is no privity, a party may be affected by the statements of another if he has expressly or impliedly given that other the authority to make statements on his behalf. Where A refers P to B for an opinion or information about a matter in contention between them, P may prove B's statements against A.[16] But many cases arise where the authority is given not expressly but impliedly. If a principal authorises his agent to represent him in a transaction, he impliedly authorises him to make admissions in the course of that transaction.[17] One partner will be affected by statements made by another partner as to partnership affairs,[18] a bank will be affected by admissions by its manager as to its practice in making loans to customers,[19] any

[11] *Papendick* v. *Bridgwater* (1855) 5 E. & B. 166.
[12] *Harrison* v. *Vallance* (1822) 1 Bing. 45; *New's Trustee* v. *Hunting* [1897] 1 Q.B. 607 at p. 611.
[13] *Wood* v. *Braddick* (1808) 1 Taunt. 104.
[14] *Re Kitchin* (1881) 17 Ch.D. 668.
[15] *R.* v. *Gunewardene* [1951] 2 K.B. 600, at p. 610; *Rutherford* v. *Richardson* [1923] A.C. 1; *Myatt* v. *Myatt and Parker* [1962] 1 W.L.R. 570.
[16] *Williams* v. *Innes* (1808) 1 Camp. 364.
[17] But the agent's authority, express or implied, must be proved before the statement can be put in, because the latter's admissibility *depends* on the authority: *Wagstaffe* v. *Wilson* (1832) 4 B. & Ald. 339. If the only evidence that B is A's agent is in B's statement "I am on behalf of A admitting such and such," that statement is inadmissible: *G.* v. *G.* [1970] 2 Q.B. 643. However, it has been held that the circumstances in which such a statement is made may afford circumstantial evidence of the authority: *Edwards* v. *Brookes (Milk) Ltd.* [1963] 3 All E.R. 62 (D.C.) *Sed Quaere*.
[18] Partnership Act 1890, s.15.
[19] *Simmons* v. *London Bank* (1890) 62 L.T. 427.

company will be affected by admissions by its directors made in the course of business to outsiders.[20]

Implied authority arises where a reasonable third party would expect it, *i.e.* where it is usual in the sort of relationship involved. This means that in most cases a servant does not have implied authority to make admissions on behalf of his master, even as to acts which it is in the course of his employment to do.[21] An engine driver is employed to drive trains, not to describe to third parties how he drove a train on a particular occasion. It may be his duty to report to his master how he drove a train, but a statement made by a servant *to* his master is not, it seems, admissible in favour of a third party.[22] Of course there may be cases where it is usual and therefore within the implied authority of a servant to report to third parties, as in *Kirkstall Brewery Co.* v. *Furness Railway*,[23] when the railway was affected by a station master's report to the police of a theft on railway property. But usually the position is as in *Burr* v. *Ware U.D.C.*[24] where the admissions of a driver employed by a local authority made to an inquest about a fatal accident he was involved in were not admissible against the local authority. It will be remembered that there is no privity between joint defendants, so the driver's admissions are still not evidence against his employers even if the plaintiff makes the driver a co-defendant. But of course anything said by the driver in court on oath is evidence both for and against his employers, and indeed that fact means that under section 2 of the Civil Evidence Act, whether he gives evidence or not, any one who heard his out-of-court statement may prove it subject to the statutory conditions.

After litigation has commenced and while it is going on, solicitors in civil cases have implied authority to make formal or informal admissions to the other party.[25] In criminal cases, there is no implied authority in a solicitor to make any kind of admission, although he may be given express authority by his client.[26] Counsel's implied authority extends only to the particular

---

[20] *Re Royal Bank of Australia* (1852) 2 De G.M. & G. 522, at p. 533.
[21] *Johnson* v. *Lindsay* (1889) 53 J.P. 599; *Great Western Ry.* v. *Willis* (1863) 18 C.B.(N.S.) 748.
[22] *Re Devala Provident Gold Mining Co.* (1883) 22 Ch.D. 593.
[23] (1874) L.R. 9 Q.B. 468.
[24] [1939] 2 All E.R. 688.
[25] See Phipson, § 20–38.
[26] *R.* v. *Downer* (1880) 14 Cox 486. A notice of alibi purporting to be given on behalf of a defendant by his solicitor shall, unless the contrary is proved, be deemed to be given with the authority of the defendant; Criminal Justice Act 1967, s.11(5).

occasion for which he is briefed.[27] Even on such an occasion an admission by counsel may be withdrawn by his client (and if so withdrawn does not bind the client), unless it amounts to an estoppel or is part of a compromise or settlement.[28] Admissions by counsel in a criminal case have been held admissible against the client in a subsequent prosecution.[29]

A witness is not normally the agent of the party calling him, and his oral evidence in a former suit will not count in a later suit as an admission by that party, even though the party had called the witness with the object of proving the facts to which the witness deposed.[30] The rule is different with affidavits, however, and the use by a party of an affidavit made by some person other than himself does, in a later suit, constitute an admission that what the deponent said is true.[31] Pleadings in other actions are not evidence against a party as admissions, unless signed, sworn, or otherwise adopted by him, as in the case of divorce petitions.

2. Statements in Public or Official Documents

These, subject to various conditions and qualifications, are admitted as proof of the facts stated.[32] This exception to the hearsay rule survives the Civil Evidence Act 1968.[33] Where the exception applies, a statement may be admitted without reference to the conditions in section 2 or 4 of the Act or the rules made under the Act.[34] If the conditions of this common law doctrine do not apply (*e.g.* if a register is not technically a public register[35]), then in civil proceedings the document may well be admitted under section 2 or 4, subject to the statutory conditions.

(a) Registers

Official registers and records are admissible in proof of the facts recorded when (1) the book is one required by law to be kept for

---

[27] *Richardson* v. *Peto* (1840) 1 M. & G. 96; *R.* v. *Greenwich* (1885) 15 Q.B.D. 54; and see *Dawson* v. *Great Central Ry.* (1919) 88 L.J.K.B. 1177.
[28] *H. Clark (Doncaster) Ltd.* v. *Wilkinson* [1965] Ch. 694.
[29] *R.* v. *Turner and Shervill* (1975) 61 Cr.App.R. 67.
[30] *British Thomson-Houston Co. Ltd.* v. *British Insulated and Helsby Cables Ltd.* [1924] 2 Ch. 160.
[31] *Richards* v. *Morgan* (1863) 4 B. & S. 641.
[32] Public documents as a class are also subject to special rules as to the mode of proving their contents, as opposed to proving the facts stated therein. This is a topic which is dealt with separately, in Chap. 17, *post.*
[33] ss.1 and 9(2)(*c*)–(*d*).
[34] See *ante*, pp. 261–267.
[35] See *infra*.

public information or reference; and (2) the entry has been made promptly, and by the proper officer. Admissibility here depends on the *public duty* of the person who keeps the register to make such entries after satisfying himself of their truth[36]; and on the availability of the document for public inspection.[37] Moreover, it is not enough that the document *is* available for public inspection; it must have been brought into existence for that very purpose.[38] From this it follows that registers kept merely under private authority, or for private information, are inadmissible. "A public document is one made by a public officer for the purpose of the public making use of it and being able to refer to it."[39] It is for this reason that business records are not admissible as public documents, for they are not kept for the information of the public.[40] Colonial registers are receivable if kept by the law either of their own or of this country; and foreign registers if kept under public authority and recognised by the local tribunals.[41] Apart from registers of births, deaths and marriages, further examples are coastguards' books as to the state of the weather,[42] the logbook of one of the King's ships as to the time of sailing[43] and university books as to degrees conferred.[44]

In all cases, the entries must have been made by, or under the direction of, the person whose duty it is to make them at the

---

[36] For this reason, it has held that a death certificate is not receivable as to the cause of death mentioned therein on information supplied by a coroner, for the registrar is bound to record the information whatever his own view of the matter; *Bird* v. *Keep* [1918] 2 K.B. 692, explained in *Re Stollery* [1926] Ch. 184. However in *R.* v. *Halpin* [1975] Q.B. 907, the Court of Appeal took account of changing modern conditions in allowing a return in the Companies Register to prove that H. was a director of a certain company, although the Registrar of Companies had no personal knowledge of the fact, holding it sufficient that he had the duty to make the entry, while the duty to satisfy himself of the truth of the matters recorded was in someone else, *i.e.* the company officer who made the return.

[37] *Sturla* v. *Freccia* (1880) 5 App.Cas. 623 at p. 644.

[38] *Thrasyvoulos Ioannou* v. *Papa Christoforos Demetriou* [1952] A.C. 84.

[39] *Sturla* v. *Freccia* (1880) 5 App.Cas. 623 at p. 643; *Heyne* v. *Fischel* (1913) 110 L.T. 264; *Thrasyvoulos Ioannou* v. *Papa Christoforos Demetriou, supra.*

[40] *Myers* v. *D.P.P.* [1965] A.C. 1001, but such may be admissible in a criminal case under the Police & Criminal Evidence Act 1984; see, *post.* p. 291.

[41] *Lyell* v. *Kennedy* (1889) 14 App.Cas. 437. *cf.* Evidence (Colonial Statutes Act 1907; and see now, Evidence (Foreign, Dominion and Colonial Documents) Act 1933, as amended by the Foreign Service Act 1943, s.6 and Sched. This Act is brought into operation as to each particular country, dominion or colony by Order in Council.

[42] *The Catherina Maria* (1866) L.R. 1 A. & E. 53.

[43] *D'Israeli* v. *Jowett* (1795) 1 Esp. 427.

[44] *Collins* v. *Carnegie* (1834) 1 A. & E. 695.

Common Law Exceptions Preserved by the Act

time,[45] and promptly; thus an entry more than a year after the event has been rejected.[46] But originality is not strictly essential, for many old registers were mere periodical transcripts from current notes; and, generally speaking, trifling errors, erasures and irregularities affect weight and not admissibility, as does the fact that the entry operated in the interest of the officer or body keeping the register.[47] It should be noted that by statute various professional lists and registers are made sufficient evidence of a qualification or position, *e.g.* the Law List is prima facie evidence of the qualifications of the solicitors named therein, and the absence of a name, evidence of non-qualification.[48]

(b) Returns made under public authority on matters of public interest

Inquisitions, surveys, assessments and reports are admissible in proof of their contents if made under public authority, and in relation to matters in which the public are interested.[49]

There must be a judicial or quasi-judicial duty to inquire by a public officer,[50] and the matter inquired into must be of a public nature, or required to be ascertained for a public purpose.[51] Inquisitions, etc., made under public legal authority but for private purposes, *e.g.* judgments, are not public documents in this sense; their evidentiary value is dealt with elsewhere.[52]

(c) Bankers' books

By the Bankers' Books Evidence Act 1879, copies of entries in bankers' books[53] are receivable in all legal proceedings (for or against anyone[54]) as prima facie evidence of the entries, or of the matters, transactions and accounts therein recorded upon proof

---

[45] *Doe* v. *Bray* (1828) 8 B. & C. 813.
[46] *Ibid.*
[47] *Sturla* v. *Freccia* (1880) 5 App.Cas. 623.
[48] Solicitors Act 1957, s.17.
[49] *Sturla* v. *Freccia* (1880) 5 App.Cas. 623.
[50] The fact that the return operates in the interest of the officer making it only affects weight, not admissibility: *Irish Society* v. *Derry* (1846) 12 Cl. & F. 641.
[51] *Sturla* v. *Freccia* (1880) 5 App.Cas. 623.
[52] *Post,* p. 337.
[53] Since 1982, this term has been extended to cover ledgers, day-books, cash books, account books, and other records used in the ordinary business of the bank, whether the records are in written form or are kept on microfilm, magnetic tape or any other form of mechanical or electronic data retrieval mechanism; Banking Act 1979, Sched. 6, para. 1. *Cf. Barker* v. *Wilson* [1980] 2 All E.R. 81, *R.* v. *Dadson* (1983) 77 Cr.App.R. 9, on the previous position.
[54] Thus, entries in the defendant's bankers' books are evidence against the plaintiff, and vice versa (*Harding* v. *Williams* (1880) 14 Ch.D. 197).

that (1) the book was, at the time of entry, one of the ordinary books of the bank; (2) that it is in the custody or control of the bank, and (3) that the entry was made in the ordinary course of business. The Act allows the court to give leave to inspect and take copies of entries in bankers' books, for the purpose of legal proceedings. This power is exercised only with great caution.[55] It is not limited to the accounts of parties,[56] and may be applied to the account of one who is not compellable as a witness.[57]

It must be noted that a bank which is not a party is not compellable to produce its books if it is willing to present copies.[58]

3. Works of Reference[59]

Approved public and general histories are admissible to prove ancient facts of a public nature.[60] Published maps, generally offered for sale, are admissible to show the relative positions of towns and counties and other matters of general geographical notoriety.[61] Any map or history may constitute proof of a highway,[62] and a map made in pursuance of a statutory survey is conclusive evidence of footpaths and bridleways.[63] Private maps may be admissible either as declarations by deceased persons as to public rights,[64] or as an admission by the maker, if he is a party.[65] Dictionaries and other established works of reference may be used to prove (or to assist the court in taking judicial notice of[66]) the meaning of words and other facts of public concern.[67]

---

[55] *Waterhouse* v. *Barker* [1924] 2 K.B. 759; *Williams* v. *Summerfield* [1972] 2 Q.B. 512.
[56] *Howard* v. *Beall* (1889) 23 Q.B.D. 1.
[57] *R.* v. *Andover JJ., ex p. Rhodes* [1980] Crim.L.R. 644.
[58] Bankers' Books Evidence Act 1879, s.6; *ante*, p. 130.
[59] This exception to the hearsay rule also survives the Civil Evidence Act 1968.
[60] *Read* v. *Bishop of Lincoln* [1982] A.C. 644 at p. 653; *Evans* v. *Getting* (1834) 6 C. & P. 586 at p. 587n.; *Fowke* v. *Berington* [1914] 2 Ch. 308.
[61] *R.* v. *Orton* (1874), cited Stephen, art. 36; *R.* v. *Jameson* (1896) Official Rep. 91–95.
[62] Highways Act 1980, s.35.
[63] National Parks and Access to the Countryside Act 1949, s.32. See *Suffolk County Council* v. *Mason* [1979] 2 All E.R. 369 (H.L.).
[64] *Post*, p. 288.
[65] *Ante*, p. 274.
[66] *Ante*, p. 33.
[67] See, *e.g. Tutton* v. *Darke* (1860) 5 H. & N. 647 (Almanac to Book of Common Prayer); *Rowley* v. *L. and N.W. Ry.* (1873) L.R. 8 Ex. 221 (Carlisle Tables of life expectancy); *R.* v. *Agricultural Land Tribunal* [1955] 2 Q.B. 140 (Fowler's *Modern English Usage*).

4. Declarations as to Pedigree

At common law, declarations made by deceased relatives, *ante litem motam*, are admissible to prove matters of pedigree. The declarations may be as to particular facts, *e.g.* declarations by deceased parents of a child that they married after the birth, to prove its illegitimacy. But equally they may be as to something of which the declarant has no personal knowledge, but of which he knows as reputed or as a tradition in the family.[68] Provided this reputation or tradition does not clearly appear to have been derived from strangers, the declaration about it is receivable to prove the matter reputed or the subject of the family tradition.[69]

Since the Civil Evidence Act 1968, such a declaration may well be admisssible under sections 2 or 4.[70] It will be admissible under section 2 if the declaration is one on which the declarant could have given direct oral evidence, *e.g.* the statement by deceased parents that they married after the birth. Moreover, since by section 9(3), reputation is to be treated as a fact and not as a statement or multiplicity of statements dealing with the matter reputed, it follows that if A says that his deceased father told him that the family tradition was that a certain relative was illegitimate, then since the father could have given direct oral evidence of this "fact," section 2 will allow A, who heard the declaration, to give evidence of it.

The effect of section 9(3)(*a*) is to require that declarations as to pedigree be admitted under section 2 or 4, if that is possible, which means that the statutory conditions about notice must be observed. Only if those sections cannot render the declaration admissible is it admissible at common law, provided the conditions described below are present. This will be the case if double or multiple hearsay is involved. If A says that his deceased father told him that his grandfather had said that a relation was illegitimate, or that the grandfather had said that there was a family tradition to that effect, neither section 2 nor section 4 will allow the admission of this evidence, it being what the father told A that the grandfather had said, but section 9(3)(*a*) will allow it, provided it would be admissible at common law.[71] If it is allowed

---

[68] *Goodright d. Stevens* v. *Moss* (1777) 2 Cowp. 591.
[69] *Shedden* v. *Att.-Gen.* (1860) L.J.P.M. & A. 217; *Davies* v. *Lowndes* (1843) 6 M. & G. 417.
[70] *Ante*, pp. 259–264.
[71] It will depend upon how A's evidence is expressed. "I have heard my father tell of a family tradition..." will attract s.2 but, "My father told me he heard my grandfather tell of a family tradition..." will come under s.9(3).

under section 9(3)(*a*), the statutory conditions about notice and the rules made under section 8 do not apply.[72]

The reason for the common law exception to the hearsay rule is that questions of pedigree usually involve remote facts of family history known to but few, and incapable of direct proof.[73] And an additional reason for relaxing the strict rule against hearsay evidence in this class of case is that members of the family have the greatest interest in knowing and the best opportunities of obtaining knowledge of the connections of the family.[74] Moreover, in the absence of *lis mota*, there is usually no reason for the declarant to do other than tell the truth.[75]

Declarations are only admissible under this head when pedigree is directly in issue. "Pedigree" means the relationship by blood or marriage between two or more persons. Such a relationship is often in issue in proceedings relating to succession to property, claims to peerages, and legitimacy proceedings; proof of such relationship involves proof of such facts as births, deaths and marriages, the dates and places of such events, celibacy, issue or failure of issue, and such incidents of domestic history as occupation and residence as are necessary to identify them. Where the relationship is in issue all or any of the foregoing facts may be proved by the declarations of deceased relatives.[76] Sometimes, however, such facts as births, deaths, marriages, etc., are relevant to an issue other than the relationship between certain persons, *e.g.* in an action against the insurers on a life policy where the death of the insured and perhaps his age would be relevant. But in such a case the central issue is not one of relationship, so that declarations of deceased relatives will not be admitted under this head to prove death, age, etc.[77] In *Haines* v. *Guthrie*,[78] A sued B for goods sold, to which B pleaded infancy. Here, family relationship was not in issue, so B's age was not provable under this head.

Declarants must have been blood relations or their spouses, not relations in law,[79] nor friends or neighbours or even confidential servants living with the family.[80] And the relationship must be a legitimate one, so that declarations by a deceased illegitimate are

[72] s.9(5).
[73] *Sturla* v. *Freccia* (1880) L.R. 5 App.Cas. 623 at p. 641.
[74] *Vowles* v. *Young* (1806) 13 Ves. 140.
[75] *Whitelock* v. *Baker* (1807) 13 Ves. 514.
[76] *Shields* v. *Boucher* (1847) 1 De G. & Sm. 40.
[77] *Splents* v. *Lefevre* (1865) 11 L.T.(N.S.) 114.
[78] (1884) 13 Q.B.D. 818.
[79] *Shrewsbury Peerage* (1857) 7 H.L.C. 1 at p. 23.
[80] *Johnson* v. *Lawson* (1824) 2 Bing. 86.

Common Law Exceptions Preserved by the Act

wholly inadmissible,[81] though if confined to his own illegitimacy they may be evidence as admissions.[82] Statements by deceased putative parents as to the fact of illegitimate parentage may sometimes be admitted.[83]

The declaration need not refer to contemporaneous matters,[84] but must have been *ante litem motam*, *i.e.* before the commencement of any controversy in which the subject-matter of the declaration was disputed in an action or otherwise.[85] If made *ante litem motam*, a declaration may be admitted even if the maker is interested in the subject-matter,[86] that circumstance going merely to weight, but a declaration obviously made to subserve the declarant's interest will be rejected. In *Plant* v. *Taylor*,[87] the question was whether A's marriage to his second wife was valid, although his first wife was still alive at the time. It was sought to prove a statement by A (now deceased) to the effect that his marriage to his first wife was void, since she was already married to another man; but this was rejected, since "it was manifestly in many ways directly for his interest to make a declaration tending to disavow his first marriage."[88]

The declarations may be in the form of oral statements, family correspondence, recitals or descriptions in settlements and wills, entries in almanacs and prayer-books, or inscriptions on tombstones, coffin-plates, rings, portraits and the like, if proved to have been made by a deceased relation,[89] or publicly exhibited.[90] Because of the custom of using family bibles as a family register, entries therein are receivable without proof of identity, relationship, or (presumably) death.[91] If the maker of a statement in prayer-books, bibles, tombstones and the like may reasonably be supposed to have direct knowledge of the matters recorded, the statement may be admitted under section 2 of the Civil Evidence Act, 1968.[92]

---

[81] *Doe d. Bamford* v. *Barton* (1837) 2 M. & R. 28; *Doe d. Jenkins* v. *Davies* (1847) 10 Q.B. 314.
[82] *Re Perton* (1885) 53 L.T. 707 at p. 710.
[83] See *Re Jenion* [1952] Ch. 454; *Re Davy* [1935] P. 1.
[84] *Davies* v. *Lowndes*, (1843) 6 M. & G. 417.
[85] *Shedden* v. *Att.-Gen.*, (1860) 30 L.J.P.M. & A. 217.; *Re Davy* [1935] P. 1.
[86] *Doe d. Jenkins* v. *Davies* (1847) 10 Q.B. 314.
[87] (1861) 7 H. & N. 211.
[88] *Ibid. per* Channell B.
[89] *Vowles* v. *Young* (1806) 13 Ves.Jun. 140.
[90] *Slaney* v. *Wade* (1836) 1 M. & C. 338.
[91] *Hubbard* v. *Lees* (1886) L.R. 1 Ex. 255.
[92] See s.6(2).

5. Declarations as to Public or General Rights.

At common law, declarations by deceased persons of competent knowledge concerning the reputed existence of a public or general right are admissible as evidence of the existence of that right. The principal reason for this exception to the hearsay rule is that direct evidence is often unobtainable.

The right or interest involved must be of a pecuniary or proprietary nature.[93] *Public* rights are those common to all members of the public, *e.g.* rights of highway and ferry, or of fishery in tidal waters. So the question of whether a certain road is a public highway or not can be proved by declarations under this head.[94] *General rights* are those affecting any considerable section of the community, *e.g.* questions as to the boundaries of a county, town, parish or manor,[95] or the election of churchwardens of a parish.[96] But questions as to the boundaries of a *private* estate,[97] and the boundary between an admitted highway and a private estate[98] involve private rights only, and declarations by deceased persons on the subject are inadmissible.

In the case of *public rights*, everyone is competent as everyone is concerned; so that the absence of peculiar means of knowledge goes to weight rather than to admissibility. But in the case of *general rights*, only those persons who have some connection with the locality or some other interest in the matter are competent. So customs of a manor may be proved by the declarations of tenants of the manor, or even residents within the manor[99] and declarations of deceased surface owners are admissible to prove a custom of mining.[1]

The declaration must have been made *ante litem motam*, i.e. before the commencement of any controversy in which the right was disputed in an action or otherwise.[2] Provided it is made *ante litem motam*, the fact that the declarant has an interest in the subject-matter does not render it inadmissible—it will be admit-

---

[93] *R. v. Bedfordshire* (1855) 4 E. & B. 535.
[94] *R. v. Bliss* (1837) 7 A. & E. 550; *R. v. Berger* [1894] 1 A.B. 823.
[95] *Nicholls v. Parker* (1805) 14 East 331n.
[96] *Berry v. Banner* (1792) Peake 212.
[97] *Clothier v. Chapman* (1805) 14 East 331n.
[98] *R. v. Berger, supra.*
[99] *Dunraven v. Llewellyn* (1850) 15 Q.B. 791.
[1] *Crease v. Barrett* (1835) 1 C.M. & R. 919.
[2] *Berkeley Peerage* (1811) Camp. 401. The fact that the declarant does not know of the existence of the controversy does not make his statements admissible, *ibid.* and see *Sheddon v. Att.-Gen.* (1860) 30 L.J.P.M. & A. 217.

ted *quantum valeat*[3] but it will be rejected if made in direct support of a claim contemplated to be brought by the declarant, or otherwise obviously to subserve his own interest.[4]

The most artificial and technical limitation on this doctrine is that the declaration must relate to the reputed existence of the right, and not to particular facts which support or negative the existence of the right. So if the question be whether a road is public or private, declarations by deceased residents in the neighbourhood that it was public,[5] or private,[6] are admissible as reputation, but not declarations that the land in question was laid out in streets[7] or that the road had been repaired,[8] or that the boundary was marked by a tree.[9] In *Mercer v. Denne*,[10] the question was whether a custom had been validly enjoyed on a certain piece of land since time immemorial. The defendant sought to prove a declaration of a deceased person that the land in question had within legal memory been covered by the tides, but this was rejected as being merely concerned with a particular fact and not the right itself.

The declarations may have been made in the form of oral statements, depositions in former suits, old deeds and leases, private maps, if made by, or under the direction, or from the knowledge of, deceased persons of competent knowledge,[11] or used by such persons to define the general right and not merely particular matters,[12] and newspapers.[13]

As with pedigree matters,[14] section 9(3) of the Civil Evidence Act 1968 provides that declarations are only admissible as at common law if they are not capable of being rendered admissible under sections 2 or 4. Since reputation is a fact,[15] it follows that if

---

[3] *Moseley v. Davies* (1822) 11 Price 162; *Doe d. Jenkins v. Davies* (1847) 10 Q.B. 314.
[4] *Brocklebank v. Thompson* [1903] 2 Ch. 344 at p. 351; see also *Plant v. Taylor* (1861) 7 H. & N. 211, *ante*, p. 287.
[5] *Crease v. Barrett* (1835) 1 C.M. & R. 919.
[6] *Drinkwater v. Porter* (1835) 7 C. & P. 181.
[7] *Att.-Gen. v. Horner (No. 2)* [1913] 2 Ch. 140.
[8] *R. v. Bliss* (1837) 7 A. & E. 550.
[9] *Ibid.*
[10] [1905] 2 Ch. 538.
[11] *Smith v. Lister* (1895) 72 L.T. 20; *Mercer v. Denne, supra.* at p. 568; *Att.-Gen. v. Horner* [1913] 2 Ch. 140 at pp. 153–156. Maps may be admitted as public documents: see *ante*, p. 281.
[12] *Smith v. Lister, supra.*
[13] *Wyld v. Silver* [1963] Ch. 243; *New Windsor Corporation v. Mellor* [1974] 2 All E.R. 570 (affirmed in the Court of Appeal [1975] Ch. 380.)
[14] See, *ante*, p. 285.
[15] s.9(3).

the declaration about the reputed right, *i.e.* about the "fact," was heard by the testifying witness, or was in writing produced by the witness, it not only may be admitted under the Act, but cannot be admitted under the common law doctrine. The fact that the declarant is not dead, or spoke *post litem motam*, or was not qualified to speak on a general (as opposed to a public) right, cannot matter since the common law doctrine is not involved. However, if the declaration is as to a particular fact from which the existence of the right may be inferred, that may still be an objection. It depends upon whether the common law is that public or general rights cannot be proved this way by any evidence, direct or hearsay; or whether it is that they cannot be proved this way by hearsay. If the former, the law is not affected by the relaxation of the hearsay rule in the Act; if the latter, it is simply a restriction on the use of hearsay evidence which is no longer in point if section 2 or 4 is applicable. The point is moot.[16]

---

[16] See, Cross, p. 506.

Chapter 14

HEARSAY IN CRIMINAL CASES

Most of the common law exceptions to the hearsay rule in theory applied both to civil and criminal cases. The Civil Evidence Act 1968 abolished many of them for civil cases, but did not touch criminal cases. Although reform in many respects similar was proposed for criminal cases,[1] in the event the Police and Criminal Evidence Act 1984 introduced only very limited changes on hearsay evidence in those cases. It is therefore necessary for any book on evidence to mention certain common law exceptions to the hearsay rule which still theoretically apply in criminal cases. Since in practice they were only found in civil cases, where they are now forbidden, they merit only the briefest of mentions. Others get similarly summary treatment in this chapter because, since they apply still in civil cases, they were dealt with in the previous chapter.

In the following cases, hearsay evidence is admissible in a criminal case.

1. Statements in Public Documents and Public Works

These are admissible to exactly the same extent and subject to the same conditions as in civil cases, and were dealt with in the previous chapter.

2. Statements in Documentary Records

When the House of Lords, in *Myers* v. *D.P.P.*,[2] held that business records were not public records and were fully subject to the hearsay rule, Parliament replied with the Criminal Evidence Act 1965, making certain business records admissible in criminal proceedings, subject to certain conditions. The operation of the Act was narrow, being confined to records of business undertakings.[3] Between 1965 and 1984, there was, for criminal cases, nothing corresponding to the wide provision about records in

---

[1] C.L.R.C., paras. 235–248, and the Draft Bill.
[2] [1965] A.C. 1001, *ante*, p. 250.
[3] See, *e.g. R.* v. *Gwilliam* [1968] 1 W.L.R. 1839 (not records of government departments).

section 4 of the Civil Evidence Act 1968,[4] and nothing about computers. Now however the 1965 Act is wholly repealed, and replaced by sections 68 and 69 of the Police and Criminal Evidence Act 1984, which provide a hearsay rule exception for records, comparable in width to that under section 4 of the 1968 Act, and deal with statements in computers in a somewhat similar way to that in section 5 of the 1968 Act.[5] What criminal procedure still does not have, and it remains as an important difference between civil and criminal evidence, is anything comparable to the widest section in the 1968 Act, *i.e.* section 2, which allows all first-hand hearsay in civil cases.[6] Oral hearsay, indeed any hearsay apart from that in the sort of records covered by section 68 of the 1984 Act, is still not allowed in a criminal case, unless it comes within one of the other, particular, exceptions dealt with in this chapter.

Section 68[7] provides that a statement in a document shall be admissible as evidence of any fact stated therein of which direct oral evidence would be admissible if the document is or forms part of a record compiled by a person acting under a duty from information supplied by a person (whether acting under a duty or not) who had, or may reasonably be supposed to have had, personal knowledge of the matters dealt with, and one of the following conditions is satisfied: (a) The supplier is dead or unfit to attend as a witness, or is outside the U.K. and it is not reasonably practicable to secure his attendance, or cannot reasonably be expected to have any recollection of the matters dealt with; (b) that all reasonable steps have been taken to identify the supplier but he cannot be identified; and (3) that, his identity being known, all reasonable steps have been taken to find him but he cannot be found.

The section is subject to section 69, on computers, which means that if a statement is in a computer, it is not admissible unless it complies with the conditions in section 69 and Schedule 3. Section 68 does not prevent the admission of any evidence which would be admissible anyway[8] (*e.g.* as a confession). On the other hand, a statement which complies with the conditions of section 68 is not necessarily bound to be admitted, because the section

---

[4] See *ante*, p. 264.
[5] For the position of computers in criminal cases, see, *post*, p. 294; in civil cases, *ante*, p. 267.
[6] See, *ante*, p. 259.
[7] See Appendix 3.
[8] s.68(3).

does not prejudice the court's power to exclude evidence on discretion.[9]

As to preconditions of admissibility, section 68 and Schedule 3 in general follow the provisions applicable to documentary records admitted in civil cases under section 4 of the Civil Evidence Act 1968.[10] "Statement" and "Document" are made to have the same meanings as in that Act[11]; the statement must be "in a document,"[12] which is or is part of a record,[13] compiled directly by a person acting under a duty, or indirectly where each person through whom it was supplied was acting under a duty, and the compiler may himself be the supplier of the information.[14] Save in this last case, the supplier need not have been acting under a duty,[15] but he must have had, or be reasonably supposed to have had, personal knowledge of the matters dealt with. He must be unavailable to give evidence for one of the reasons stated. In deciding on admissibility, the court may draw any reasonable inference from the circumstances in which the statement was made or from any other circumstances, including the form and contents of the document,[16] which may be proved by a copy, even if the original is still in existence.[17]

Since the maker of the statement is unavailable, there is nothing corresponding to the notice procedure under sections 2 and 4 of the Civil Evidence Act.[18] The opposite party gets no opportunity to require his attendance. However, there are various safeguards. In particular, the danger of manufactured evidence is taken account of by paragraph 2 of Schedule 3, which provides that a statement in a proof of evidence (*i.e.* one made for the

---

[9] s.72(2).
[10] See *ante*, p. 264.
[11] s.72(1); s.118(1).
[12] *Ante*, p. 260.
[13] *Ante*, p. 265.
[14] Sched. 3, para. 1.
[15] s.68(1)(*a*).
[16] Sched. 3. para. 14(*a*).
[17] *Ibid.* para. 14(*b*).
[18] *Ante*, p. 262. However Sched. 3, para. 15 provides that rules of court may be made supplementing ss.68, 69, and the Schedule. There is no duty on the defence to disclose any part of its case in advance of trial, except alibi notices under s.11, Criminal Justice Act 1967, as to which see, *ante*, p. 185. As to disclosure by the Crown, in Crown Court proceedings, the defence will have access to written statements on committal under s.102, Magistrates' Courts Act 1980, and any "unused material" in the Crown's possession; *Practice Note* [1982] 1 All E.R. 734. In some areas, pre-trial reviews before a judge in chambers are being conducted on an experimental basis; as to the status of these, and the use which can be made of anything disclosed at them, see *R. v. Hutchinson* (1985) 82 Cr.App.R. 51.

purposes of the proceedings) is not to be given in evidence under section 68 without leave. Leave can only be given if the court is of opinion that such ought to be admitted in the interests of justice, having regard to the circumstances in which the leave is sought and in particular to the contents of the statement, and to any likelihood that the accused will be prejudiced by its admission in the absence of the supplier of the information. Thus any attempt to put in the proof of a witness who conveniently disappears just before the trial is likely to get short shrift, especially if it is the prosecution which wishes to make use of section 68. Moreover, in estimating the weight, if any, of any statement which is admitted, as in civil proceedings[19] the Court must have regard to all the circumstances, and in particular to whether the supplier gave his information contemporaneously and whether he had any incentive to conceal or misrepresent the facts.[20] And evidence aimed at impeaching the credibility of the maker, including his inconsistent statements, is admissible under Schedule 3, para. 3. However, unlike the position in civil cases,[21] the rule of finality, which prevents *evidence* on collateral matters affecting only credibility,[22] does not necessarily apply. Evidence of matters which could only be put in cross-examination may be allowed, with the leave of the court.[23] Finally the court's general power to exclude any evidence at its discretion remains unaffected by section 68.[24]

3. Statements in Computers

The Police and Criminal Evidence Act 1984 has provisions for the admission of statements in computers, which are similar to but rather simpler than the corresponding provisions in the Civil Evidence Act 1968.[25] The principal section is section 69, which in fact starts out by creating a presumption of inadmissibility. It provides that a statement in a document produced by a computer[26] shall not be admissible unless it is shown that there are no reasonable grounds for believing that the statement is inaccurate because of improper use of the computer and that at all material times the computer was operating properly, or if not that

---

[19] *Ante*, p. 269. *Cf.* s.6(3) of the 1968 Act.
[20] Sched. 3, para. 7.
[21] *Ante*, p. 270.
[22] *Ante*, p. 118.
[23] Schedule 3, para. 3(*b*).
[24] s.72(2).
[25] *Ante*, p. 267.
[26] This term is not defined: *cf.* Civil Evidence Act 1968, s.5(6).

any respect in which it was not operating properly or was out of operation was not such as to affect the production of the document or the accuracy of its contents, and that any relevant conditions specified in rules of court were satisfied. The rules may require the giving of information concerning the statement, although no rules have yet been made. All these preconditions may be proved by certificate, which is evidence of anything stated in it.[27] It is sufficient for the matters to be stated to the best of the knowledge and belief of the person making the certificate,[28] but the court may require oral evidence to be given of any of the matters in the certificate.[29]

Section 69 does not render a computer statement admissible. If it is admissible under an exception to the hearsay rule or as not being hearsay anyway,[30] it must still comply with section 69. If it is hearsay and not admissible without the assistance of section 68, it must also comply with the conditions of that section, *i.e.* it must be in a record compiled under a duty from information supplied by a person with personal knowledge who is unavailable for the reasons stated.[31]

As under section 68,[32] in deciding on admissibility, the court may draw any reasonable inference from the circumstances, form or content of the document, which may be proved by copy; in deciding on weight, it must take into account the sort of factors mentioned in connection with that section; and the court's usual power to exclude on discretion remains.

4. Miscellaneous Statutory Provisions, and Evidence at a Previous Trial

By section 9 of the Criminal Justice Act 1967, a written statement of a witness is admissible in criminal proceedings other than committal proceedings if made in proper form and not objected to by the opposite party. The statement must be signed by the maker and contain a declaration that he knows he makes it subject to penalties if it is knowingly or recklessly false, and it must be served on the opposite party, who has seven days in which to object. If he does object, the witness must be called; the procedure can in practice be used only for non-contentious evidence. If the

---

[27] Sched. 3, para. 8.
[28] *Ibid.*
[29] Sched. 3, para. 9.
[30] *Ante*, p. 247.
[31] *Ante*, p. 292.
[32] *Ante*, p. 293.

opposite party does not object, the statement may be admitted to the same extent and with the same effect as if the maker actually gave oral evidence.[33] However the statement is in no sense conclusive; non-objection by the opposite party does not amount to his accepting the evidence. He may contradict it by other evidence, but he should not use the section 9 procedure as a device to avoid the usual rule that if it is proposed to contradict a witness, the contradictory story must be put to the witness in cross-examination so that he can comment on it. If contradictory evidence *is* given by the opposite party, the party using the section 9 procedure may ask for, and the Court of its own motion may order, an adjournment so as to allow the maker of the contradicted statement to attend and give oral evidence.[34]

A written statement put in at committal under section 102 of the Magistrates' Courts Act 1980, or a deposition of evidence given at committal, may be admitted at the subsequent trial on indictment if the witness was made subject to a "conditional witness order." If the defence wished for the witness to attend, it would ask at committal for a "full witness order," or before the trial notify the prosecution that his attendance was required. Even if attendance has been requested in either of these two ways, the statement may be read at the trial if the witness is dead, or insane, too ill to travel or kept out of the way by the defence.[35] This is subject to the court's general discretion to exclude if to admit it would be unfair to the accused.[36]

Behind these and other particular statutory provisions, there is a common law rule that if the present proceedings are between the same parties, if the other party had opportunity to examine the witness, and if the witness is dead, kept away by the other party, or too ill to attend, the transcript of the witness's evidence at a previous trial may be read, subject to the court's discretion to disallow it as unfair.[37]

5. Statements by Deceased Persons

Although the fact that the maker of a statement is dead is at

---

[33] *Ellis* v. *Jones* [1973] 2 All E.R. 893.
[34] *Lister* v. *Scaife* [1983] 2 All E.R. 29.
[35] s.13(3), Criminal Justice Act 1925, as amended.
[36] s.78(1), Police & Criminal Evidence Act 1984, *ante*, p. 43: See also R. v. *Blithing* (1983) 77 Cr.App.R. 86.
[37] See R. v. *Hall* [1973] Q.B. 496; R. v. *Thompson* [1982] Q.B. 647, and the authorities reviewed in the latter case.

common law no reason of itself for admitting his statement, there are certain cases where exceptionally this is allowed.

(a) Declarations as to public or general rights or on matters of pedigree

These are virtually never found in criminal cases, and have been sufficiently dealt with in the previous chapter.

(b) Declarations against interest

Declarations made by deceased persons against their pecuniary or proprietary interest are admissible in criminal cases[38] in proof of the fact stated, because of the inherent unlikelihood of anyone making a false statement against his own interest,[39] *i.e.* for the same reason as admissions and confessions are admitted. So the declarant must know that the statement is against his interest[40]; the fact that on further examination the statement turns out not to be against interest is immaterial if it was prima facie against interest.[41]

(c) Declarations in the course of duty

Declarations made by deceased persons in the ordinary course of duty, contemporaneously with the facts stated, and without motive to misrepresent, are admissible in criminal proceedings in proof of their contents. The special circumstance which prima facie guarantees the truth of the statement is the fact of the mechanical and generally disinterested nature of entries made in the routine of duty and their constant liability, if false, to be detected, with the consequent risk of punishment or dismissal for the maker.[42] This guarantee is, of course, just as potent whether the declarant is alive or dead at the date of the action but, as with all the exceptions to the hearsay rule discussed in this section he must be positively shown to be dead. It is not sufficient that he is

---

[38] Confined to such by the operation of the Civil Evidence Act 1968, but in practice hardly ever found in criminal cases.

[39] *Per* Fletcher Moulton L.J., in *Tucker* v. *Oldbury U.D.C.* [1912] 2 K.B. 317, at p. 321. Even if the declarant has a motive to misstate the facts, the declaration may still be admissible, although not entitled to much weight: *Taylor* v. *Witham* (1876) 3 Ch.D. 605.

[40] *Tucker* v. *Oldbury U.D.C., supra; Lloyd* v. *Powell* [1913] 2 K.B. 130 at p. 137.

[41] *Taylor* v. *Witham, supra; Re Adams* [1922] P. 240; *Coward* v. *Motor Insurers' Bureau* [1963] 1 Q.B. 259.

[42] These considerations do not apply to an *opinion* of an "expert" servant, and such is not provable under this exception. His notes of observations, measurements *etc.* are however provable, and another expert can be called to give *his* opinion on those facts: *R.* v. *McGuire* (1985) 81 Cr.App.R. 323.

unidentifiable or untraceable.[43] The doctrine covers both oral and written statements. A written statement in a document which is or is part of a record made under a duty will usually be admissible under section 68 of the Police and Criminal Evidence Act 1984, if the declarant is unidentifiable or untraceable, even if he cannot be shewn to be dead.[44]

(d) Dying declarations as to homicide

In trials for murder or manslaughter,[45] the dying declaration of the victim, made under the sense of impending death, is admissible to prove the circumstances of the crime. The special circumstance which is supposed to guarantee the truth of the statement is the solemnity of the occasion, when the sense of impending death creates a sanction equal to the obligations of an oath.[46] If this is acceptable in modern times as a good enough reason for admitting hearsay, one might expect it to allow all declarations on any subject made on the point of death. However the exception is confined to proceedings for the murder or manslaughter of the victim, and to declarations about the cause of death, not collateral matters.[47]

Although a more modern statement of the *rationale* for this exception to the hearsay rule dwells on the importance of a person implicated in a killing being obliged to meet in court the dying accusation of the victim,[48] the conditions for admissibility rest squarely on the original *rationale*, *i.e.* that no-one would wish to die with a lie on his lips. It must be proved to the satisfaction of the judge that the deceased, at the time of the making of the declaration, was in imminent danger of death and had abandoned all hope of recovery. If these conditions occur, it is immaterial that he lingered for some time, even for as long as three weeks,[49] or that he subsequently entertained hope.[50] There must, however, have existed a "settled, hopeless expectation of death" not qualified by any prospect of recovery, however slight, and the weight of authority requires a belief, not, indeed, in an immediate death, but in an impending and imminent, as distinguished from a deferred, one.[51] And if death overtakes the deceased so rapidly

[43] *Myers* v. *D.P.P.* [1965] A.C. 1001.
[44] *Ante*, p. 291.
[45] And possibly causing death by reckless driving and complicity in a suicide.
[46] R. v. *Woodcock* (1789) 1 Leach 500.
[47] R. v. *Mead* (1824) 2 B. & C. 605.
[48] *Nembhard* v. *R.* [1982] 1 All E.R. 183 (P.C.) *per* Sir Owen Woodhouse at p. 185.
[49] R. v. *Bernadotti* (1869) 11 Cox 316.
[50] R. v. *Hubbard* (1881) 14 Cox 565.
[51] R. v. *Perry* [1909] 2 K.B. 697; R. v. *Austin* (1912) 8 Cr.App.R. 27.

that he has no time to reflect or know that he is dying, any statement by him as to the cause of death is inadmissible as a dying declaration. In *R. v. Bedingfield*,[52] a young woman rushed from a room with her throat cut from ear to ear. She cried out "Oh, dear Aunt, see what Harry has done for me," and fell dead at the aunt's feet. This was held not admissible, because there was no settled hopeless expectation of death. Even if the deceased lingers, the courts do not like accepting that he was in expectation of death, unless he indicates the fact. What is usually required is something like "Oh, Gert, I shall go; but keep this a secret."[53] But the deceased must have been careful to admit of no doubt on this score. In *R. v. Jenkins*,[54] a woman on her deathbed had her statement taken down by a magistrates' clerk. He concluded with the words "I make the above statement with the fear of death before me, and no hope of recovery." When this was read over to the woman, she desired the insertion of the words "at present" after the word "hope." This was enough to exclude her statement.

The judge must point out to the jury that the declaration was not cross-examined on by the defence.[55] However, provided he does this, and otherwise deals fairly with the evidential value of the declaration, a conviction may be supported even in the absence of any corroboration at all.[56]

Although it is usually the Crown which uses a dying declaration, it may be used by the defendant if favourable to him, as if the deceased says that someone else was his assailant, or as if he says that the defendant would not have struck him had he not provoked him.[57]

6. Confessions

These are a large and important class of exceptions, but they have already been extensively discussed. A confession is an admission by an accused person, and admissions were dealt with in the previous chapter.[58] Before a confession can be admitted it needs to comply with the conditions of section 76 of the Police and Criminal Evidence Act 1984[59]; even if it does comply, it may be

---

[52] (1879) 14 Cox 341.
[53] *R. v. Perry, supra.*
[54] (1869) L.R. 1 C.C.R. 187.
[55] *Waugh v. R.* [1950] A.C. 203 (P.C.).
[56] *Nembhard v. R., supra.*
[57] *R. v. Scaife* (1836) 1 M. & R. 551.
[58] Chap. 13.
[59] Chap. 10.

excluded in the court's discretion under section 82(3).[60] If it is admitted it is admissible only against its maker[61]; it cannot be used in any way against a co-accused. In *R. v. Watson & Daniel*,[62] A's conviction was quashed, because the judge indicated that, although the confession of a co-accused B was no evidence against A, it could be used by the jury in evaluating the truth of the complainant's evidence against A. This common law rule is confirmed by the words of section 76(1) of the Police & Criminal Evidence Act 1984, which provides that a confession made by an accused may be given in evidence *against him*.

7. Statements Admitted as Part of the Res Gestae

In the discussion of facts in issue[63] it was seen that what is loosely called a fact may in reality be a series of facts or the result of more than one fact, and so more conveniently described as a transaction. If that transaction be in issue, a witness is expected to testify to the whole of it, including facts and declarations which accompany or explain it. Many of the declarations thus admitted will be original evidence.[64] Thus if the condition of Q is in issue, T, a person who observed him, will not only be allowed to say that Q's face was green, but also that Q said he felt ill.[65] Groans and complaints are as much the signs of a sick man as a clammy brow and furred tongue.[66] But it is different if T says that Q told him that *he had been sick last week* or Q said he felt ill now *because of what R had given him to eat*.[67] These statements are not symptoms observed by T, but narrations to him by one who is not called as to past facts, and are therefore hearsay. Normally such will be rejected, but if the narration is so intimately bound up with an observed fact that it was truly part of it, it will be admitted as part of the *res gestae*. If T says that he was outside a room when he heard the sound of retching and Q's voice saying "Don't make me drink any more, R, it is making me sick," he is giving original evidence of the medicine's effect on R and hearsay evidence as to

---

[60] *Ante*, p. 201.
[61] see *R. v. Spinks* (1982) 74 Cr.App.R. 263.
[62] [1973] Crim.L.R. 627.
[63] *Ante*, Chap. 2.
[64] See *ante*, p. 243.
[65] *R. v. Cowper* (1699) 13 How.St.Tr. 1106; *R. v. Conde* (1868) 10 Cox 547; *R. v. Johnson* (1847) 2 C. & K. 354.
[66] More easily faked perhaps, but that is another matter, affecting the weight of the evidence, not the original character of the evidence.
[67] *R. v. Gloster* (1888) 16 Cox 471.

where it came from, but he will be allowed to give both pieces of evidence, in spite of the hearsay rule.[68]

This doctrine used to allow in statements about what went on in an event by participants and observers, but it now seems that such are admitted under a different principle, as to which, see next section.

8. Spontaneous Statements about an Event by Participants or Observers

In some cases, T may be allowed to testify as to what someone involved in or observing an event said at the time about what went on. The reason why these are allowed in breach of the hearsay rule has varied over the years. At one time, it was because the statement formed part of the *res gestae*, i.e. it was because the statement was so much a part of the transaction that to cut it out would falsify entirely what went on on the occasion in question. This reason produced the requirement of an extremely high degree of contemporaneity. In *R.* v. *Bedingfield*,[69] a woman rushed from a room with her throat cut and blurted out the fact that B had attacked her. This was rejected as an account of a transaction which was over and done with.

This is the reason which is suggested by the term *"res gestae."* But in *Ratten* v. *R.*,[70] Lord Wilberforce described the phrase as opaque or at least imprecise, covering situations insufficiently analysed in clear English terms, and refused to be mesmerised by the implications of the Latin words. According to him the real reason why the law admits such contemporaneous expressions by participants is not that they are a part of the transaction, but that they are spontaneous, *i.e.* forced out of the declarant by the excitement generated by the event. It is spontaneity which gives a guarantee that the declarant is speaking the truth, the possibility of concoction or fabrication being very remote.[71] That guarantee is wholly lacking when the declarant purports to give any account of what has happened, which account T now wishes to give to the

---

[68] See *per* Lord Coleridge C.J. in *R.* v. *Bedingfield* (1879) 14 Cox 341 at p. 342.
[69] (1879) 14 Cox 341, *ante*, p. 299.
[70] [1972] A.C. 378, (P.C.) at p. 388.
[71] *Ratten's* case was an Australian appeal to the Privy Council. In a later case however the High Court of Australia took the opportunity to reiterate that it is not sufficient that the statement is unlikely to be fabricated; it must, to be admissible, be an actual part of the *res* (the transaction): *Vocisano* v. *Vocisano* (1974) 130 C.L.R. 267, *per* Barwick C.J. at p. 273.

court, and there is no reason why the hearsay rule should be relaxed.[72]

Thus in *Thompson v. Trevanion*[73] a woman's utterance immediately after she had been struck was admitted because, according to Lord Holt C.J., it was before she had time to devise or contrive anything to her own advantage. And in *R. v. Foster*[74] A was run over in the road. B saw him fall, went up to him and A ejaculated the cause of the accident. B was allowed to testify as to this.[75] In *Ratten v. R.*[76] A was accused of murdering his wife by shooting her. He said it was an accident while cleaning his gun. The time of death was pin-pointed at very shortly before 1.20 p.m. A telephonist at the local exchange was allowed to testify that at about 1.15 p.m. a woman rang from A's address. She was sobbing hysterically, and asked for the police, after which the receiver was replaced. The jury was allowed to deduce from this that the caller was B, and that B was being threatened or attacked by A.

On the other side of the line is *R. v. Gibson*.[77] A was struck by a stone. At the trial of G for throwing the stone, A said that immediately after the incident, a woman (who could not be found) said to A, "The man who threw the stone went in there." pointing to G's door. It was held that this ought to have been rejected. It was in no sense a spontaneous exclamation by the woman, but a narration by her afterwards with the object of bringing the offender to justice.[78] Her evidence would be highly relevant if given by her in the box, but in the mouth of someone else, it was merely hearsay.

Of course, spontaneity equally demands a high degree of contemporaneity, but not exact contemporaneity. The elapsing of time between the event and the utterance is merely a matter to be taken account of in deciding whether the possibility of concoction may be disregarded. It is easier to ask, had the speaker become

[72] It will be recalled from an earlier discussion of *Ratten* (*ante*, p. 245) that the words reported by the witness were held not to be hearsay. However, the Privy Council, after so holding, went on to hold that even if they *were* hearsay, they were admissible. It will also be noted that they were actually part of the transaction; but that was not the reason relied on by the Privy Council for holding they were admissible; the reason was that they were spontaneous.
[73] (1693) Skin. 402.
[74] (1834) 6 C. & P. 325. And see *R. v. Fowkes* (1856) *The Times*, March 8, cited Stephen, para. 3; *ante*, p. 109.
[75] Both of these cases were frowned on in later times for allowing statements not sufficiently part of the transaction, but they must be regarded as rehabilitated now; indeed *Thompson v. Trevanion* was expressly approved in *Ratten v. R.*
[76] [1972] A.C. 378.
[77] (1887) 18 Q.B.D. 537.
[78] See *per* Lord Normand in *Teper v. R.* [1952] A.C. 480.

disengaged enough from the transaction as to be able to construct or adapt his account? than to ask, was the utterance no longer part of the transaction? That question is not only difficult (because defining a transaction is difficult) but also tends to give absurd answers, as in the rejection of the remark in *Bedingfield's* case.

In *R. v. Bailey*[79], the House of Lords confirmed *R. v. Ratten*, and made clear that the real question for the judge is whether the possibility of correction or distortion by the declarant can be disregarded. In deciding this, the elapsing of time, the alleged malice of the declarant towards the accused, the declarant's intoxication, and the fact that he named the defendant in response to a question are only factors to be taken into account. If the judge admits the declaration, he must leave to the jury the question of what exactly was said, and also the possibility that the statement could have been misreported by the witness who heard it.

This latter consideration goes to weight only; it does not affect admissibility. In *R. v. Turnbull*,[80] V, after being stabbed, staggered into a bar in a state of collapse, and a few minutes later was removed to hospital where he died. In response to questions in the bar and in the ambulance V, who had been drinking and had a strong Scots accent, was understood to name his assailant as the defendant. Evidence of what he said was admitted as being spontaneous, with no likelihood of concoction or distortion by him.

---

[79] (1987) *The Times*, 4th February (H.L.).
[80] (1984) 80 Cr.App.R. 104 (C.A.).

Part VI

THE EFFECT OF PREVIOUS ACTS AND JUDGMENTS

CHAPTER 15
ESTOPPEL

	Page
A. Estoppels by Record	310
B. Estoppels by Conduct	311
C. Estoppels by Agreement	314
D. Estoppels by Deed	315

CHAPTER 16
JUDGMENTS

A. Res Judicata	317
1. Final Judgment of a Competent Court	318
2. Estoppel Per Rem Judicatam	320
3. Merger	335
B. Judgments as Evidence	337
1. Between the Same Parties	337
2. Between Strangers	337

CHAPTER 15

ESTOPPEL

ESTOPPEL is a rule whereby a party is precluded by some previous act to which he was party or privy from asserting or denying a fact. It is a rule of exclusion, making evidence of a relevant fact inadmissible. Two simple examples drawn from widely different situations are provided by *Oakland Metal Co. v. Benaim*[1] and *Soanes v. London and South Western Railway*.[2] In *Benaim's* case, A and B had a dispute about a contract existing between them. In accordance with the contract, the matter was taken to arbitration and A appointed X as arbitrator. X having found for B, A now sought to have the award set aside by the court on the ground that X was not duly qualified as required by the contract. He was not allowed to prove X's incapacity, since by appointing him he had estopped himself from denying X's qualification.

In *Soanes's* case, a railway company allowed a man in the uniform of one of their porters to meet a passenger at the entrance to Waterloo Station, to take his bag and walk through the barrier on to a departure platform, and there to remain in charge of the bag. When sued by the passenger for the loss of the bag, the company was not allowed to prove (as was in fact the case) that the man was not a porter employed by them at the station.

Estoppel is sometimes said to be merely a rule of evidence,[3] since its effect is to render inadmissible, evidence which would otherwise be admissible. That view would seem to be supported by the examples given above, which are cases of estoppel by conduct. The party who is able to estop his opponent from proving a fact is entitled to whatever follows from the non-proving of the fact. His relief is not limited to whatever damage he suffered as a result of the representation which gave rise to the estoppel. In *Avon County Council v. Howlett*,[4] A paid B a sum of money as a result, he alleged, of a mistaken overpayment of wages. B suffered detriment by spending some of that sum in the

---

[1] [1953] 2 Q.B. 261.
[2] (1919) 120 L.T. 598.
[3] *e.g. per* Maugham L.C. in *Maritime Electric v. General Dairies* [1937] A.C. 610 at p. 620.
[4] [1983] 1 All E.R. 1073 (C.A.). See also *Greenwood v. Martins Bank* [1932] 1 K.B. 371 at p. 384; *Ogilvie v. West Australian Mortgage Corporation* [1896] A.C. 257 at p. 270.

belief that it was wages to which he was entitled. It was held that this detriment raised an estoppel in favour of B, as a result of which A was not allowed to show that *any part* of the sum paid was not due. The estoppel did not mean that B could recoup himself for his detriment; it meant that A could not prove what he needed to prove to get any of his money back, *i.e.* that it was an overpayment.

But it has also been said that estoppel is more accurately viewed as part of the substantive law.[5] This also has force, because sometimes the operation of estoppel is to remove entirely an issue between the parties to which the proffered evidence would be relevant.[6] Even here however the better view is that estoppel does not directly create or remove a cause of action. Rather it may assist a plaintiff in enforcing a cause of action by preventing a defendant from asserting some fact which would destroy the cause of action[7] or it may prevent a plaintiff from enforcing a cause of action by disabling him from asserting some fact which is the basis of his cause of action.[8] The problem of categorising estoppel is not entirely academic, since in a case with a foreign element, the choice of law to be applied in respect of the alleged estoppel will depend on whether the estoppel is classified as a rule of evidence or a rule of substantive law.[9]

Before considering the different classes of estoppel it is as well to note the saying that estoppels cannot override positive rules of law or make legal that which is illegal,[10] or, as it is sometimes put, estoppels cannot be set up in the face of a statute.[11] There is some dispute as to how far if at all this principle applies to estoppel by record,[12] but even as to other types of estoppel arising out of the acts of the parties, it is certainly not an absolute principle. There

---

[5] *e.g. per* Lord Wright in *Canadian and Dominion Sugar Co. Ltd.* v. *Canadian National Steamship Ltd.* [1947] A.C. 46 at p. 56.
[6] See *per* Diplock L.J. in *Mills* v. *Cooper* [1967] 2 Q.B. 459 at p. 469; Lord Hailsham in *D.P.P.* v. *Humphreys* [1977] A.C. 1 at p. 27. Issue Estoppel is dealt with, *post*, p. 324.
[7] See *per* Lord Russell of Killowen in *Nippon Menkwa Kabushiki Kaisha* v. *Dawson's Bank Ltd.* [1935] 51 Lloyd's L.R. 147 at p. 150.
[8] "To use the language of naval warfare, estoppel must always be either a mine-layer or a mine-sweeper: it can never be a capital unit": Spencer-Bower and Turner, *Estoppel by Rrepresentation* (3rd ed. 1977), p. 7.
[9] See Dicey & Morris, *The Conflict of Laws*, (10th ed., 1980) p. 1180.
[10] *Maritime Electric Co.* v. *General Dairies Ltd.* [1937] A.C. 610.
[11] More properly this should be expressed, "in the face of a positive rule of law" because the principle is capable of applying to common law rules: See Andrews, "Estoppels Against Statutes" (1966) 29 M.L.R 1, for a general discussion of the subject.
[12] See Andrews, *op. cit.* p. 8.

are some statutes, *e.g.* the Statute of Frauds,[13] the operation of which may be defeated by estoppel; but with others, for example, the Infants Relief Act,[14] the Rent Acts,[15] and the Agricultural Holdings Act,[16] a party cannot be estopped from asserting that the transaction at issue is within the relevant statute. The test appears to be that if the law involved represents a social policy which the court must give effect to in the interests of the public generally, the parties themselves cannot prevent the operation of the law by private arrangement, and what cannot be got by private arrangement cannot be achieved by one party appealing to the doctrine of estoppel.[17] Similarly, since parties cannot usually by agreement confer on a court or tribunal a jurisdiction which it does not possess, no estoppel can confer such a jurisdiction.[18]

Moreover, a public authority cannot be prevented from making a decision or exercising a discretion by estoppel.[19] In planning matters, it is the elected planning body which has power to grant permissions or to judge whether permission is needed, not its officers. Certain matters are expressly allowed to be delegated, and certain procedural requirements may be waived. But in all other cases, to allow the authority to be estopped by the act of its officer would be to deprive the public of the right to make representations to the planning authority,[20] and moreover would inhibit the officer from offering informal advice and help to applicants for fear of binding his authority.[21] On the other hand, it may be said that adherence to strict principle means that an applicant can never rely on what a planning officer says or writes, and must get every detail settled in a regular way by the full planning authority. Over-slavish adherence to principle can result in administrative wheels grinding to a halt.[22] There seems no escape from this dilemma.

Estoppels may arise (i) by record, (ii) by conduct, (iii) by agreement or (iv) by deed. These different classes of estoppel are justified on quite different grounds. The reasons for estoppels by

[13] *Humphries v. Humphries* [1910] 2 K.B. 531.
[14] *Leslie v. Sheill* [1914] 3 K.B. 607.
[15] *Welch v. Nagy* [1950] 1 K.B. 455.
[16] *Keen v. Holland* [1984] 1 All E.R. 75.
[17] *Kok Hoong v. Leong Cheong Kweng* [1964] A.C. 993, *per* Lord Ratcliffe at p. 1017.
[18] *Secretary of State for Employment v. Globe Elastic Thread Co. Ltd.* [1980] A.C. 506.
[19] See *Rootkin v. Kent C.C.* [1981] 1 W.L.R. 1186.
[20] *Western Fish Products v. Penwith D.C.* [1981] 2 All E.R. 204 (C.A.).
[21] *Per* Widgery L.J. in *Brooks & Burtons Ltd. v. Secretary of State for the Environment* (1976) 75 L.G.R. 285, at p. 296, cited with approval in *Western Fish Products v. Penwith D.C., supra*.
[22] See Spencer-Bower & Turner, *Estoppel by Representation* (3rd ed.), pp. 151–154.

record are found in the public policy that disputes must not be endlessly re-litigated and that a person who has succeeded once in a claim or defence should not be put to the trouble of making it again. Estoppels arising out of conduct are justified by the need to allow people safely to rely on representations upon which they have acted. Estoppels by agreement (and nowadays, probably, estoppels by deed) oblige the parties to a transaction to adhere to the agreed facts which form the basis of their transaction.

A. Estoppels by Record

These almost always arise from the judgment of a competent court.[23] It is convenient to deal with the effect of judgments along with their admissibility as evidence; the discussion of estoppels by record will therefore be postponed until Chapter 15.

As to other estoppels, it has been said:

> "When the parties to a transaction proceed on the basis of an underlying assumption (either of fact or of law, and whether due to misrepresentation or mistake, makes no difference), on which they have conducted the dealings between them, neither will be allowed to go back on that assumption when it would be unfair or unjust to allow him to do so."[24]

This is said to be the principle underlying the categories of estoppel discussed below, and in accordance with it, there is nowadays a tendency to deprecate the separate existence of these categories. It is said that in all cases the enquiry should adopt the broad approach of discovering whether there is unconscionability, rather than ascertaining whether the facts fit into one or other of the categories.[25] But it is doubtful whether the categories have entirely dissolved, or even whether they ought to, since "if one scraps distinctions developed over the centuries, and reverts to a broad principle of unconscionability, the results will be longer hearings with ever wider and deeper analyses of the facts."[26] The

---

[23] They may also arise from the grant of letters patent by the Crown: see *Cropper v. Smith* (1884) 26 Ch.D. 700.
[24] *Per* Lord Denning M.R. in *Amalgamated Investment & Property Co. Ltd. v. Texas Commerce International Bank Ltd.* [1982] Q.B. 84 at p. 122.
[25] *Taylor Fashions Ltd. v. Liverpool Victoria Trustees Co. Ltd.* [1982] 1 Q.B. 133 *n.* at p. 151, per Oliver J., adopted in *Amalgamated etc. v. Texas, supra*, at p. 104 (Goff J.); *Habib Bank Ltd. v. Habib Bank A.G. Zurich* [1981] 2 All E.R. 650. See also *Crabb v. Arun D.C.* [1976] Ch. 179 at p. 193.
[26] *Note* (1981) 97 L.Q.R. 513 at p. 515.

discussion will therefore be in terms of the traditional classification.

B. Estoppels by Conduct

1. Estoppel by Representation

Where one person has made a representation to another person in words, or by acts and conduct, or (being under a duty to the representee to speak or act) by silence or inaction, with the intention (actual or presumptive), and with the result, of inducing the representee on the faith of such representation to alter his position to his detriment, the representor, in any litigation which may afterwards take place between him and the representee, is estopped, as against the representee, from making any averment substantially at variance from his former representation.[27] If the subject-matter of the representation is property, a person who takes the property from the representor as volunteer (but probably not one who takes as purchaser) is also estopped as privy.[28]

The representation must relate to a matter of fact, not a matter of opinion or law,[29] and although it can be a statement of present intention to do something,[30] it cannot, under the doctrine presently being discussed, amount to a promise.[31]

The representation may be made by words or conduct,[32] but not normally by silence or inaction. However if A owes a duty to B to speak out or to do something in a certain eventuality, and he remains silent or inactive, B may infer from this that A is representing that the eventuality has not occurred or is not present.[33] It must be a legal duty,[34] as opposed to a mere moral duty, to speak or act, such as the duty which a customer owes to his banker to take care not to cause the banker to suffer loss through payment out of money in excess of his authority. If he becomes aware that his cheques are being forged, and says

---

[27] Spencer-Bower and Turner, *op. cit.* p. 4, approved in *Hopgood* v. *Brown* [1955] 1 W.L.R. 213, *per* Evershed M.R. at p. 223; see also *Greenwood* v. *Martins Bank* [1933] A.C. 51, *per* Lord Tomlin at p. 57.
[28] *Eastern Distributors Ltd.* v. *Goldring* [1957] 2 Q.B. 600, *per* Devlin J. at p. 607; *Jones* v. *Jones* [1977] 1 W.L.R. 438.
[29] *Low* v. *Bouverie* [1891] 3 Ch. 82.
[30] *Edgington* v. *Fitzmaurice* (1885) 25 Ch.D. 459.
[31] *Jordan* v. *Money* (1854) 5 H.L.C. 185.
[32] *Pickard* v. *Sears* (1837) 6 Ad. & El. 469.
[33] *Freeman* v. *Cooke* (1848) 2 Exch. 654 at p. 663.
[34] *McKenzie* v. *British Linen Bank* (1881) 6 App.Cas. 82 at p. 100.

nothing, he may be estopped from denying their genuineness as against his banker who has honoured them.[35] A party to a negotiation or transaction who has made a relevant representation to the other party is under a duty to modify that representation if it becomes untrue, *e.g.* if A has represented to B that C is his agent, he must, if that agency terminates, inform B of the fact.[36]

The representation must be unambiguous,[37] save in certain relationships, *e.g.* principal and agent, where the principal owes a duty to his agent to be explicit.[38] The representation must be such as to induce the other party to act upon it. It is not necessary for the representor to intend the representee to act; it is sufficient if it was reasonable for the representee to act,[39] and if it was, is it immaterial that the representor did not know that his representation was false.[40] The representee must show that he has acted on the representation to his detriment.[41]

2. Promissory Estoppel

As noted above, an estoppel by representation cannot arise out of a promise.[42] However, this is not true of promissory estoppel, a comparatively recent invention which differs in this and in other important respects from estoppel by representation. Where one party says or implies to the other that their existing legal relations shall be affected in some way, with the intent that the other should and the result that he does act upon the supposed change in their relations, the first party must accept those relations subject to the qualifications which he himself introduced.[43]

It is immaterial that the representation consists of a promise as to future conduct. There must be a pre-existing legal relationship between the parties, although it need not be a contractual

---

[35] *Greenwood* v. *Martins Bank* [1933] A.C. 51.
[36] *Goode and Bennian* v. *Harrison* (1821) 5 B. & Ald. 147.
[37] *Woodhouse A.C. Israel Cocoa Ltd. S.A.* v. *Nigerian Produce Marketing Co. Ltd.* [1972] A.C. 741; *Moorgate Mercantile Co. Ltd.* v. *Twitchings* [1977] A.C. 890.
[38] *Ireland* v. *Livingston* (1872) L.R. 5 H.L. 395.
[39] *Freeman* v. *Cooke* (1848) 2 Exch. 654 at p. 663.
[40] *Spiro* v. *Lintern* [1973] 1 W.L.R. 1002 at p. 1012.
[41] *Fung Sun* v. *Chan Fui Hing* [1951] A.C. 489; *United Overseas Bank* v. *Jiwani* [1976] 1 W.L.R. 964; *Norfolk County Council* v. *Secretary of State for the Environment* [1973] 1 W.L.R. 1400.
[42] *Jordan* v. *Money* (1854) 5 H.L.C. 185.
[43] *Central London Property Trust* v. *High Trees House Ltd.* [1947] K.B. 130; *Tool Metal Manufacturing Co. Ltd.* v. *Tungsten Electric Co. Ltd.* [1955] 2 All E.R. 657; Spencer-Bower & Turner, *op. cit.* Chap. XIV.

relationship.[44] The doctrine is probably suspensory only, in that the representor may, by giving reasonable notice, revert to his previous position.[45] On principle, it appears that the representee must have acted to his detriment on the faith of the representation[46]; if his acts are apparently done on the faith of the representation, it will be presumed that they were so done, *e.g.* remaining in a house *after* an assurance that one may do so rent-free will be presumed to have happened because of that assurance.[47]

It must be noted, however, that the representation does not operate as a contract unless it is duly supported by consideration. Thus, a gratuitous promise intended to be acted upon may prevent the promisor from taking any action which may be construed as going back on his promise, but that does not mean that the promisee can ask the court to enforce the promise against the promisor. The doctrine may be used as a shield but not as a sword.[48] Moreover, since promissory estoppel is an equitable notion, inequitable conduct by the representee may prevent him from invoking it.[49]

3. Proprietory Estoppel

An owner of property (A) who sees another person (B) innocently acting in a way which is inconsistent with his (A's) rights, may not "lie by," saying nothing, and then assert his rights when B has acted on the assumption that *he* was entitled.[50] The operation of this doctrine being to confer on B the interest in A's land which he was justified in thinking he had or was to get, it follows that it only applies if B acts supposing that he has or will acquire a right in or over A's land; it is not sufficient if he improves his own land on the supposition that A will give him some necessary permission.[51] B must be "innocent," *i.e.* unaware of the extent of A's rights, and it used to be held that A must be under no

---

[44] *Durham Fancy Goods Ltd.* v. *Michael Jackson (Fancy Goods) Ltd.* [1968] 2 Q.B. 839; *Combe* v. *Combe* [1951] 2 K.B. 215; *Pacol Ltd.* v. *Trade Lines Ltd.* [1982] 1 Lloyd's Rep. 456.
[45] Spencer-Bower & Turner, *op. cit.* § 355.
[46] *Ibid.* § 353.
[47] See *Greasley* v. *Cooke* [1980] 1 W.L.R. 1306.
[48] *Combe* v. *Combe, supra,* n. 44.
[49] *D. & C. Builders Ltd.* v. *Rees* [1966] 2 Q.B. 617.
[50] *Ramsden* v. *Dyson* (1866) L.R.I H.L. 129; *Crabb* v. *Arun D.C.* [1981] Ch. 179 (C.A.); *Jones* v. *Jones* [1977] 1 W.L.R. 438 (C.A.).
[51] *Western Fish Products Ltd.* v. *Penwith D.C.* [1981] 2 All E.R. 204 (C.A.).

misapprehension as to his own rights.[52] This may still be the case where there is mere acquiescence by A, but where there is active encouragement by A, it was held in *Taylor Fashions Ltd.* v. *Liverpool Victoria Trustees Ltd.*[53] that A's misapprehending the extent of his own rights does not in itself prevent him from being estopped; it is merely one of the factors in determining whether insistence on those rights would be unconscionable. In that case, A, thinking that a covenant by him to renew B's lease was valid, encouraged B to make improvements to the property leased. When the covenant turned out to be invalid, A was nevertheless held to be estopped from relying on its invalidity.

C. Estoppels by Agreement[54]

Where parties have agreed a statement of facts as the basis for the transaction between them, each will be estopped as against the other from questioning the truth of that statement of facts. It is not necessary that one party should mislead the other; in fact it is not necessary that either party should believe in the existence of the stated facts.[55] It is the taking of the stated facts as the foundation of their transaction which precludes either one of them from afterwards departing from that foundation.

The commonest example of this sort of estoppel is that between landlord and tenant, although it also arises between bailor and bailee,[56] and licensor and licensee.[57]

Whether or not the lease is by deed[58] neither landlord nor tenant is allowed to deny the landlord's title to the premises at the date of the lease,[59] *i.e.* his right to grant the lease. A tenant is allowed to dispute his present landlord's title by assignment from the person

---

[52] *Willmott* v. *Barber* 15 Ch.D. 96 (C.A.).

[53] [1981] 2 W.L.R. 576 *n* (Oliver J.).

[54] See Spencer-Bower and Turner *op. cit.* Chap. VIII, *Estoppel by Convention.*

[55] See *per* Dixon J. in *Grundt* v. *Great Boulder Proprietary Gold Mines Ltd.* (1938) 59 C.L.R. 620 at p. 636, cited in Spencer-Bower and Turner, *op. cit.* p. 160.

[56] *Biddle* v. *Bond* (1865) 6 B. & S. 225. But see Torts (Interference with Goods) Act 1977, s.8.

[57] *Crossley* v. *Dixon* (1863) 10 H.L.C. 293; *State of Penang* v. *Beng Hong Oon* [1972] A.C. 425 (P.C.).

[58] *Mackley* v. *Nutting* [1949] 2 K.B. 55, and see *Whitmore* v. *Lambert* [1955] 1 W.L.R. 495.

[59] *Doe d. Bristow* v. *Pegge* (1785) 1 T.R. 758n; *Cuthbertson* v. *Irving* (1859) 4 H. & N. 762; *Cooke* v. *Loxley* (1792) 5 T.R. 4. Denial by the tenant may allow the landlord to forfeit the lease: see Woodfall, *Landlord and Tenant*, (28th ed., 1978) para. 1.1881.

who let him into possession[60]; and he can say that his landlord's title to receive rent has, subsequently to the grant, come to an end.[61] That is not a denial of his landlord's right to grant him the lease. If the tenant is disturbed in his possession by title paramount, he is no longer estopped; but if he has enjoyed his lease until its natural determination without disturbance, he thereafter cannot deny his landlord's title if, *e.g.* he is sued by the landlord on a dilapidations clause.[62]

D. Estoppels by Deed

It has been argued[63] that nowadays these are merely a species of estoppel by agreement, *i.e.* where an assumed factual basis of a transaction cannot be departed from thereafter. Originally, it was the solemnity involved in the execution of a deed which produced the estoppel,[64] and it is only in more recent times that any agreement not under seal was allowed to have this effect.[65] Now that this is allowed,[66] estoppels by deed are perhaps redundant as a separate class, but tradition has secured them separate treatment in both the books and the cases.

Neither party, nor his privy, will be permitted to deny the truth of facts assented to in their deed. If on the true construction of the deed the statement is one which all parties to a deed have mutually agreed to admit as true, it is binding on all of them and their privies; but if it is intended to be that of one party only, the only persons estopped are that party and his privies.[67] But if there are grounds for rectifying the deed because of mistake, no estoppel can be founded on the unrectified deed,[68] and if there are grounds for rescission for fraud or misrepresentation, the party at fault cannot set up an estoppel in reliance on the deed.[69] A receipt for money contained in a deed does not create an estoppel, and

---

[60] *Cornish v. Searell* (1828) 8 B. & C. 471 at p. 475.
[61] *Sergeant v. Nash, Field & Co.* [1903] 2 K.B. 304; *National Westminster Bank v. Hart* [1983] Q.B. 773 (C.A.).
[62] *Cuthbertson v. Irving, supra*; *Industrial Properties v. A.E.I. Ltd.* [1977] Q.B. 580, overruling the earlier C.A. decision in *Harrison v. Wells* [1967] 1 Q.B. 263.
[63] In Spencer-Bower and Turner, *op. cit.* Chap. VIII.
[64] 2 Co.Litt. 352a; *Bowman v. Taylor* (1834) 2 A. & E. 278 at p. 291.
[65] Since *Carpenter v. Buller* (1841) 8 M. & W. 209.
[66] See previous section.
[67] *Greer v. Kettle* [1938] A.C. 156.
[68] *Wilson v. Wilson* [1969] 1 W.L.R. 1470.
[69] *Greer v. Kettle, supra,* per Lord Maugham at pp. 171–172.

proof may be offered that the payment was not in fact made. In the absence of such proof, however, the receipt is sufficient evidence that the payment was made.[70]

---

[70] *Wilson* v. *Keating* (1859) 27 Beav. 121; and see Law of Property Act 1925, ss.67, 68.

CHAPTER 16

JUDGMENTS

It not infrequently occurs that a matter in issue between parties to litigation has been the subject of earlier litigation which resulted in a judgment. The question arises as to what use a party to the present proceedings can make of the earlier judgment. Can he say that since the judgment shows that another court adjudged that a fact existed, that finding is conclusive in the present proceedings? Or, without going so far, can he say that the earlier adjudication at least is evidence of the fact's existence? Can his opponent reply that the opinion of the earlier court on the existence of the fact is only an opinion like any other, and like any other opinion is strictly irrelevant to the task of the present court?[1] The answers to these questions differ with the circumstances.

The binding force of judgments will be dealt with first. This topic is usually known as the doctrine of *res judicata*. As will be seen, judgments do not have binding force on all persons or on all issues; so, after an account has been given of *res judicata*, it will be necessary to consider how far a judgment which in the circumstances has *no* binding force, is *evidence* of the facts comprised in it.

A. Res Judicata[2]

According to the doctrine of *res judicata*, a final judgment of a competent court disposes once and for all of the matters decided, so that they cannot be raised again between the same parties or their privies. It is against public policy, and oppressive to the individual, to re-agitate disputes which have been litigated once and for all to a finish. These two ideas are expressed in the maxims *interest reipublicae ut sit finis litium*, and *nemo debet bis vexari pro una causa*.

The doctrine involves two things. One is that a party is forever precluded from *disputing* what was necessarily decided; he is said to be estopped *per rem judicatam*. The other is that a party who has recovered judgment is forever precluded from claiming on his original cause of action. That cause of action has disappeared,

---

[1] On opinion evidence generally, see *ante*, p. 20.
[2] See, generally, Spencer-Bowen and Turner, *Res Judicata* (2nd ed. 1969).

being merged in the judgment. *Transit in rem judicatam.* Merger produces the result that the successful party has his judgment, and only his judgment, to rely on.

1. Final Judgment of a Competent Court

Res judicata arises only out of a final judgment of a competent court. The word "final" is used in contradistinction to interlocutory—an interlocutory decree or judgment normally has no binding force.[3] A final judgment is one which purports finally to determine the rights of parties, and binds even although an appeal may be brought,[4] or, indeed, is actually pending,[5] or even though inquiries or accounts have to be taken to implement the judgment.[6] The fact that the judgment is given after the issue of the writ in a second action where *res judicata* is pleaded is apparently immaterial.[7]

A judgment signed by consent is binding as to that which was the subject of the consent,[8] although it may in some cases be impossible, by reason of the lack of full pleading or argument, to discover what precisely was the subject of the consent. A default judgment is in principle as binding as one obtained after a contest[9]; a party cannot avoid being bound by a judgment likely to go against him by the expedient of not fighting it. If an action does not proceed to judgment, as if the judge refuses to entertain it on the grounds that he has no jurisdiction,[10] or if it is dismissed for want of prosecution[11] or discontinued before the hearing,[12] there is no *res judicata*.[13]

---

[3] *Nouvion* v. *Freeman* (1889) 15 App.Cas. 1; *Re Wright* [1954] Ch. 347. But see *Carl-Zeiss-Stiftung* v. *Rayner (No. 3)* [1970] Ch. 506 *per* Buckley J. at p. 539.
[4] *Huntley* v. *Gaskell* [1905] 2 Ch. 656, *per* Cozens-Hardy L.J. at p. 667.
[5] *Harris* v. *Willis* (1855) 15 C.B. 710.
[6] *Poulton* v. *Adjustable Cover and Boiler Block Co.* [1908] 2 Ch. 430.
[7] *Bell* v. *Holmes* [1956] 1 W.L.R. 1359; *Morrison, Rose and Partners* v. *Hillman* [1961] 2 Q.B. 266.
[8] *Kinch* v. *Walcott* [1929] A.C. 482 at p. 493 (P.C.).
[9] *Aslin* v. *Parkin* (1758) 2 Burr. 665 at p. 668.
[10] *Tak Ming Ltd.* v. *Yee Sang Co.* [1973] 1 W.L.R. 300 (P.C.).
[11] But if the want of prosecution consists of wilful disobedience of a peremptory order of the court to proceed within a certain time, a second action will be dismissed as an abuse of process: *Janov* v. *Morris* [1981] 1 W.L.R. 1389. *Aliter* simple failure to proceed expeditiously: *Bailey* v. *Bailey* [1983] 1 W.L.R. 1129. For abuse of process, see *post*, p. 333.
[12] But to discontinue after receipt of the defence the plaintiff may need leave (R.S.C., Ord. 21, r. 3), and such leave will usually only be given on terms that no other action be brought on the same matter: *Hess* v. *Labouchere* (1898) 14 T.L.R. 350.
[13] *Pople* v. *Evans* [1969] 2 Ch. 255.

A court includes not only the regular superior courts of judicature but also inferior courts and tribunals, even domestic tribunals, provided they have jurisdiction either by the law or by the parties consenting to submit their affairs to adjudication by such tribunals.[14] Thus the principle of conclusiveness has been held to be applicable to decisions of courts-martial,[15] arbitrators[16] and domestic tribunals such as the General Medical Council.[17] In the present context, the awards of any such tribunal, however lowly, "are as conclusive and unimpeachable (unless and until set aside on any of the recognised grounds) as the decisions of any of the constituted courts of the realm."[18]

Foreign judgments. The judgments of foreign courts are in general just as binding,[19] but foreign penal judgments,[20] and judgments in aid of foreign revenue laws[21] are exceptions and have no force in this country. Moreover, by Civil Jurisdiction and Judgments Act 1982, s.32, an overseas judgment in proceedings brought in breach of an agreement not to litigate in the foreign court is not to be recognised in the U.K. unless (*inter alia*) the party against whom the judgment was given submitted to the jurisdiction of that court.[22] At common law, a foreign judgment does not work a merger,[23] *i.e.* the successful litigant is not precluded from choosing to sue in this country on his original cause of action rather than on

---

[14] *Doe* d. *Davy* v. *Haddon* (1783) 3 Doug.K.B. 310 at p. 312; *Cummings* v. *Heard* (1869) L.R. 4 Q.B. 669.
[15] *Hannaford* v. *Hunn* (1825) 2 C. & P. 148, *per* Lord Abbott C.J. at p. 155.
[16] *Guaret* v. *Audouy* (1893) 62 L.J.Q.B. 633; *Fidelitas Shipping* v. *V/O Exportchleb* [1966] 1 Q.B. 630.
[17] *Hill* v. *Clifford* [1907] 2 Ch. 236.
[18] Spencer-Bower and Turner, *op. cit.* p. 28. But by statute affiliation proceedings are an exception; see, Affiliation Proceedings Act 1957, and *Robinson* v. *Williams* [1965] 1 Q.B. 89.
[19] *Goddard* v. *Grey* (1870) L.R. 6 Q.B. 139 at p. 150: *Carl-Zeiss-Stiftung* v. *Rayner & Keeler* (No. 2) [1967] 1 A.C. 853.
[20] *Huntington* v. *Attrill* [1893] A.C. 150 (P.C.); *Re Langley's Settlement Trusts* [1962] Ch. 541.
[21] *Indian Government* v. *Taylor* [1955] A.C. 491.
[22] The section does not apply to certain judgments within the Foreign Judgments (Reciprocal Enforcement) Act 1933, or to judgments required to be registered under the Brussels Convention of 1968 on the enforcement of judgments in civil and commercial cases: s.32(4). As to the latter, the Convention provides that the fact that a judgment was given in defiance of an agreement on jurisdiction is no ground for refusing recognition. However the view of H.M.G. is that the Convention does not apply to the validity or effect of arbitration agreements, so unless the European Court of Justices decides otherwise, a judgment in an EEC State in defiance of an arbitration clause will come within s.32. See Morris, *The Conflict of Laws* (3rd ed.), p. 112.
[23] *Bank of Australasia* v. *Harding* (1850) 9 C.B. 661.

the judgment. Now, however, by section 34 of the 1982 Act, no proceedings may be brought by a person in this country on a cause of action in respect of which judgment has been given in his favour in proceedings between the same parties or their privies, unless the judgment is not enforceable or entitled to recognition here.

The binding force of a judgment cannot be impeached by showing that the decision producing it was wrong in law or on fact. However fraud avoids all judicial acts, and proof of fraud by one of the parties[24] or by the tribunal itself,[25] or of collusion between the parties (*i.e.* putting up a sham rather than a real contest),[26] robs a civil judgment of all force. However, in a criminal case, an acquittal obtained by fraud cannot be directly impeached[27]; the appropriate remedy for the Crown may be to prefer perjury charges. Moreover, an arbitration award alleged to have been obtained irregularly can only be impeached by a motion to set aside,[28] and it is usually said that this means that fraud cannot be taken account of in any other proceedings.[29]

2. Estoppel Per Rem Judicatam

A final judgment of a competent court works an estoppel, that is to say "any party or privy to such litigation, as against any other party or privy thereto, is estopped in any subsequent litigation from disputing or questioning such decisions on the merits."[30]

---

[24] *Duchess of Kingston's Case* (1776) 20 How.St.Tr. 355.
[25] *Doe* d. *Davy* v. *Haddon* (1783) 3 Doug.K.B. 310.
[26] *Duchess of Kingston's Case, supra* (argument of Wedderburn S.G., approved in *Bandon* v. *Becher* (1835) 3 Ch. & F. 479 at p. 510; *Sheddon* v. *Patrick* (1854) 1 MacQ. 535 at p. 608.
[27] See *D.P.P.* v. *Humphreys* [1977] A.C. 1, *per* Lord Salmon, at p. 47. But an acquittal by a Crown Court on appeal from a magistrates' court may be quashed leaving the conviction by the magistrates to stand: *R.* v. *Wolverhampton Crown Court* [1982] 3 All E.R. 702; *Weight* v. *MacKay* [1984] 2 All E.R. 673, (H.L.).
[28] Under the Arbitration Act 1950, s.23; R.S.C., Ord. 73, r. 2.
[29] Spencer-Bower and Turner, *op. cit.* p. 325; *Thoreburn* v. *Barnes* (1867) L.R. 2 C.P. 384; *Biche* v. *Billingham* [1894] 1 Q.B. 107; *Oppenheim* v. *Hajie Mahomed* [1922] 1 A.C. 482 (P.C.); *Scrimaglio* v. *Thornett and Fehr* (1924) 131 L.T. 174; *Birtley District Co-operative Society Ltd.* v. *Windy Nook and District Industrial Co-operative Society* [1969] 1 W.L.R. 142. However the cases involve irregularities or misconduct less than actual fraud, and it may be that fraud going to the root of the award and rendering it void is a defence to proceedings on the award: see, *per* Viscount Cave in *Oppenheim* v. *Hajie Mahomed, supra*, at p. 487.
[30] *Per* Lord Guest in *Carl-Zeiss-Stiftung (No. 2)* [1967] A.C. 853 at p. 933, adopting Spencer-Bower and Turner, *op. cit.* p. 9.

(a) The binding force of judgments

Before considering the effect of a judgment on parties or privies, it must be noted that all judgments are conclusive as against all persons as to existence of the state of things they actually effect. Thus if A is convicted of forgery, and it is in issue between P and Q whether A has been convicted of forgery, the record of the court which convicted A concludes that matter.[31] Not, be it noted, that A was guilty of forgery, or committed forgery, or that a document produced by him was a forgery, but that A was *convicted* of forgery. If that fact is relevant, it is concluded by the earlier judgment, even though neither P or Q were in any way concerned in the former proceedings.

Nothing other than the point actually settled has this universal force, but with judgments *in rem* that point is much wider than with judgments *in personam*. A judgment *in rem* is the judgment of a court of competent jurisdiction determining the status of a person or thing, or the disposition of a thing (as distinct from the particular interest in it of a party to the litigation).[32] Examples of such are decrees of a competent court dissolving or declaring void a marriage,[33] decrees of legitimacy under the Matrimonial Causes Act 1973, s.45,[34] grants of probate[35] or administration,[36] adjudication in bankruptcy,[37] a justice's order that a street is a highway,[38] judgments of a prize court or Admiralty court condemning a vessel as prize,[39] or in an action for necessaries.[40] However, judgments in actions for the detention of chattels or the recovery of land are not judgments *in rem* because they do not affect any rights in the subject-matter vested in third parties.

All other judgments are judgments *in personam*. Such judgments determine the rights of the parties to or in the subject-matter of dispute but do not affect the status of things or persons or affect any rights in the subject-matter vested in persons not parties to the action. The point actually binding on all persons is

---

[31] See further on this, *post*, p. 337.
[32] Halsbury, Vol. XVI, para. 1522, approved in *Lazarus-Barlow* v. *Regent Estates Co. Ltd.* [1949] 2 K.B. 465 at p. 475.
[33] *Thynne* v. *Thynne* [1955] P. 272 at p. 285 *et seq.*
[34] But such a decree is not to prejudice any person unless he or the person under whom he claims was made party to the proceedings: Matrimonial Causes Act 1973, s.45(5)(*b*).
[35] *Allen* v. *Dundas* (1789) 3 T.R. 125; *Concha* v. *Concha* (1886) 11 App.Cas. 541.
[36] *Re Ivory* (1878) 10 Ch.D. 372.
[37] Insolvency Act 1985, ss.119, 126, 132.
[38] *Wakefield* v. *Cooke* [1904] A.C. 31; *Armstrong* v. *Whitfield* [1974] Q.B. 16.
[39] *Castrique* v. *Imrie* (1870) L.R. 4 H.L. 414.
[40] *Ibid.*

thus quite narrow, *e.g.* that A recovered judgment against B, or that C was convicted of forgery. So after a decree of divorce (a judgment *in rem*) all persons are estopped from denying the divorced status of the parties; but after a successful action in debt by A against B, no status being involved, the world is not obliged to admit that A was rightfully owed the money, only that he recovered judgment against B.

Nor are third parties, whatever kind of judgment is involved, estopped from disputing the *grounds* upon which the judgment proceeded. If H obtains a decree of divorce against W on the grounds of her adultery with Q, the world must accept that W is a divorced person, but non-parties are not estopped from disputing her adultery with Q.[41] If in a probate action, A sets up T's will and a grant of probate is made, declaring that A is the executor, no person may deny that A is T's executor and has the right to deal with his assets. If C is sued by A for the recovery of an asset, he cannot object that A has no right to demand it because the will naming him as executor was forged. But if A is prosecuted for forging the will, the grant of probate does not estop the prosecutor from proving that the will was forged by A.[42] In *Gray v. Barr*[43] in an action between A's executor and B, it was necessary for B to show that A had intentionally shot and killed Q. A had been acquitted of both murder and manslaughter. It was held that this was no bar to B's showing that A had intentionally killed Q.

(b) Effect against parties and privies

Persons not involved in the earlier litigation are not bound further than described above, but the actual parties and their privies[44] may be estopped from denying not only the fact of the earlier judgment or the status established by it, but also the grounds upon which the judgment proceeded. The parties are said to be estopped *per rem judicatam*. There are two kinds of estoppel *per rem judicatam*.

(i) *Cause of action estoppel.* This prevents a party to an action from asserting or denying, as against the other party, the existence of a particular cause of action, the non-existence or the existence of

---

[41] *General Medical Council* v. *Spackman* [1943] A.C. 627 at p. 635.
[42] *Allen* v. *Dundas* (1789) 3 T.R. 125; *R.* v. *Buttery and Macnamara* (1818) R & R. 342.
[43] [1971] 2 Q.B. 554.
[44] See *post*, p. 327.

which has been determined by a court of competent jurisdiction in previous litigation between the same parties.[45]

In *Marriott v. Hampden*[46] A sued B for a debt. B said he had paid but had lost the receipt. The court gave judgment for A. Later B found the receipt and sued A for the return of the money; but it was held that the former judgment was conclusive that B owed A the amount of the debt. The fact that a party reagitating a question proposes to use different evidence will not prevent him from being estopped. In *Workington Harbour Board v. Trade Indemnity Co.*,[47] a party to a building contract thought that the contract gave him the right to sue for any defects certified by his engineer. He therefore sued on the certificate, but his action was dismissed on its being held that the certificate was not binding on the parties. He brought a fresh action, proposing to prove the defects by evidence, but it was held that he was estopped by the dismissal of his earlier action.

But the question must be the same question as was decided in the former proceedings, not merely a similar one.[48] Thus if the question between A and B is whether on a certain day A was a gypsy, an earlier finding as between A and B that A was not a gypsy does not settle the present matter.[49] If the question between landlord and protected tenant is whether the balance of hardship allows the making of an order for possession of the premises, the fact that an earlier decision as between the same parties held that no order should be made does not preclude an order now, because the relative hardship may be different now.[50] A decision on tax or rates for one year of assessment raises no estoppel for another year of assessment.[51]

A judgment binds as to matters which could have been raised in the proceedings. A party cannot later raise a claim or defence which was open to him in the previous proceedings. He is required to bring forward the whole of his case on the first occasion.[52] However this doctrine, often called the rule in

---

[45] *Thoday v. Thoday* [1964] P. 181, *per* Diplock L.J. at p. 197.
[46] (1797) 7 T.R. 269.
[47] [1938] 2 All E.R. 101.
[48] *New Brunswick Rly. v. British and French Trust Corporation* [1939] A.C. 1; *Re Manley's Will Trusts (No. 2)* [1976] 1 All E.R. 673.
[49] *Mills v. Cooper* [1967] 2 Q.B. 459.
[50] *Burman v. Woods* [1948] 1 K.B. 111.
[51] *Society of Medical Officers of Health v. Hope* [1960] A.C. 551; *Cafoor v. Colombo Income Tax Commissioners* [1961] A.C. 584 (P.C.).
[52] *Henderson v. Henderson* (1834) 3 Hare 100, *per* Wigram V-C. at p. 114; *Public Trustee v. Kenward* [1967] 1 W.L.R. 1062; *Yat Tung v. Dao Hong Bank* [1975] A.C. 581 (P.C.).

Henderson v. *Henderson*, does not apply to default judgments.[53] The first claim could be trifling and not worth fighting, and it is hard for a party to be put to the trouble of defending it on the off chance that some issue, which might or might not arise in some later proceedings which might or might not be brought, might be held to be concluded against him.[54] For the same reason, the rule does not fully apply in cases of issue estoppel.[55]

(ii) Issue Estoppel. In later litigation the cause of action between the parties may be different from that which was fought in earlier proceedings. Nevertheless a party is estopped from contending the contrary of any point of law or of fact which, having been distinctly put in issue, has been decided against him.[56] "There are many causes of action which can only be established by proving that two or more different conditions are fulfilled. Such causes of action involve as many separate issues between the parties as there are conditions to be fulfilled by the plaintiff in order to establish his cause of action; and there may be cases where the fulfilment of an identical condition is a requirement common to two or more different causes of action. If in litigation upon one such cause of action any of such separate issues as to whether a particular condition has been fulfilled is determined by a court of competent jurisdiction, either upon evidence or upon admission by a party to the litigation, neither party can, in subsequent litigation between one another upon any cause of action which depends upon the fulfilment of the identical condition, assert that the condition was fulfilled if the court has in the first litigation determined that it was not, or deny that it was fulfilled if the court in the first litigation determined that it was."[57] In this connection, "parties" can include co-defendants. If A and B are sued by X, and there is a conflict of interest between A and B which must be

---

[53] *New Brunswick Rly. Co.* v. *British & French Trust Corporation Ltd.* [1939] A.C. 1; *Kok Hoong* v. *Leong Cheong Kweng Mines Ltd.* [1964] A.C. 993 (P.C.).
[54] See *Carl-Zeiss-Stiftung* v. *Rayner & Keeler Ltd. (No. 2)* [1967] 1 A.C. 853, *per* Lord Reid at p. 917.
[55] See *post*, p. 325, Nor to arbitrations: only the matters actually in the terms of reference, not those which *could* have been in, work an estoppel: *Purser* v. *Jackson* [1977] Q.B. 167. And as to a failure to join a party who could be joined, see *Gleeson* v. *Whippell* [1977] 1 W.L.R. 512, *post*, p. 327.
[56] *Marriott* v. *Hampton* (1797) 7 T.R. 269; *Outram* v. *Morewood* (1803) 3 East 346; *Hoystead* v. *Commissioner of Taxation* [1926] A.C. 155; *aliter* if the point, although in issue, was not decided one way or the other; *Bernard* v. *Bernard* [1958] 1 W.L.R. 1275.
[57] *Thoday* v. *Thoday* [1964] P. 181, *per* Diplock L.J. at p. 198.

resolved to give X the relief he claims, a judgment resolving this conflict will raise an estoppel between A and B.[58]

Before issue estoppel operates, the issue must be the same in both proceedings, but of course it is not necessary that it should be the only point determined in either. The question of the identity of the issues, which is often one of great nicety, must be determined by the judge on reference to the pleadings in the former action, or if necessary, to the actual words, duly verified, of the judgment itself.[59] On the one hand, the issues may be the same, although the form of action[60] and the marshalling of the parties[61] may be different. On the other hand the issues may be distinct, though both relate to the same transaction or property.[62] The test usually suggested is to inquire whether the same evidence would support both issues.[63] However, even if the object of the two actions is quite different, if a given fact has been put in issue and decided between the parties, the fact cannot be relitigated by the parties or their privies.[64] And even if the evidence is different, if the facts alleged in the second action are merely different particulars of a breach of contract litigated in the first, the matter is *res judicata*.[65]

In two respects, issue estoppel differs from cause of action estoppel. The rule in *Henderson* v. *Henderson*,[66] prohibiting a party from raising a claim or defence which was open to him in

---

[58] *Cottingham* v. *Shrewsbury* (1843) 3 Hare 627, *per* Wigram V.-C. at p. 638.
[59] *Thoday* v. *Thoday* [1964] P. 181, at p. 188. If the earlier proceedings were in a foreign court, it may be so difficult to ascertain whether issues are identical that great care and common sense will be required; see *Carl-Zeiss-Stiftung* v. *Rayner (No. 2)* [1967] 1 A.C. 853.
[60] See *e.g. Routledge* v. *Hislop* (1860) 29 L.J.M.C. 90.
[61] See *e.g. Re Bank of Hindustan, China and Japan* (1873) 9 Ch.App. 1.
[62] See *e.g. Re Koenigsberg* [1949] Ch. 348; *Guest* v. *Warren* (1854) 9 Ex. 379; *Cooper* v. *Cooper (No. 2)* [1955] P. 168; *Society of Medical Officers of Health* v. *Hope* [1960] A.C. 551; *Beeches Workingmen's Club* v. *Scott* [1969] 1 W.L.R. 550; *Spens* v. *I.R.C.* [1970] 1 W.L.R. 1173. For the difficulties produced by the subtle distinctions found in the substantive law of negligence, contrast *Marginson* v. *Blackburn Borough Council* [1939] 2 K.B. 426; *Randolph* v. *Tuck* [1962] 1 Q.B. 175; and *Wood* v. *Luscombe* [1966] 1 Q.B. 169; and see Spencer-Bower and Turner, *op. cit.* Chap. IX.
[63] *e.g. per* Brett M.R., in *Brunsden* v. *Humphrey* (1884) 14 Q.B.D. 141 at p. 146.
[64] *Priestman* v. *Thomas* (1884) 9 P.D. 210.
[65] *Conquer* v. *Boot* [1928] 2 K.B. 336; *Daniels* v. *Carmel Exporters and Importers* [1953] 2 Q.B. 242. And see *Workington Harbour Board* v. *Trade Indemnity Co.* [1938] 2 All E.R. 101, *ante*, p. 323. And note that if a contract provides for "serial" arbitration as and when breaches appear, an earlier award does not prevent breaches appearing subsequently being the subject of a fresh arbitration: *Purser* v. *Jackson* [1977] Q.B. 167.
[66] *Ante*, p. 323.

previous proceedings, probably does not apply.[67] And with issue estoppel it is not true that a party can never contend to the contrary of what was settled in the earlier proceedings. There is a doctrine of excusable ignorance which may allow evidence in later litigation of newly discovered facts,[68] if the new evidence "entirely changes the aspect of the case."[69] Nor does the doctrine of issue estoppel apply in criminal proceedings[70] or, probably, to applications for judicial review under R.S.C., Ord. 53.[71]

(iii) Parties and Privies; Res judicata only applies if it is the same parties (or their privies) who are involved on the second occasion. If in an action between A and B, B's agent Q is held to have been negligent on a certain occasion, in a subsequent action between A and Q respecting the same occasion, Q is not estopped by the finding in the earlier suit.[72] Similarly a party to a civil case is never estopped by a finding against himself in an earlier prosecution; the parties are necessarily different, as in criminal trials the issue is between the Crown and the accused.[73] Moreover, the parties must appear in the same capacity. If A is T's executor, then as such he is identified with T and is estopped by anything which would have estopped T.[74] But he is also a man in his own right, and if he sues for himself, he is not estopped merely because issues he now raises were settled earlier between T and the defendant, or between T's executor and the defendant. T and T's executor are the same person, but A in his private capacity is another person.[75]

The present parties need not have occupied identical positions in the earlier litigation, *e.g.* plaintiff and defendant now need not have been plaintiff and defendant earlier. They could have been in the opposite positions; or even hostile co-defendants, with an issue decided between them. In *Marginson* v. *Blackburn Borough*

[67] *Carl-Zeiss-Stiftung* v. *Rayner & Keeler (No. 2)* [1967] 1 A.C. 853 at pp. 916, 947; *Rowe* v. *Rowe* [1980] Fam. 47. It certainly does not apply to matrimonial proceedings: *Tumath* v. *Tumath* [1970] p. 78 at p. 86; *Rowe* v. *Rowe, supra.*
[68] See *Stevens* v. *Tillet* (1870) L.R., 6 C.P. 147 at p. 170; *Lockyer* v. *Ferryman* (1877) 2 App.Cas. 519 at pp. 525, 527; *Mills* v. *Cooper* [1967] 2 Q.B. 459 at pp. 468–469.
[69] *Phosphate Sewage Co.* v. *Molleson* [1879] 4 App.Cas. 801 at p. 814; *Hunter* v. *Chief Constable of West Midlands* [1982] A.C. 529 at p. 545.
[70] *D.P.P.* v. *Humphrys* [1977] 1 A.C. 1; *post* p. 332.
[71] *R.* v. *Secretary of State for the Environment, ex p. Hackney B.C.* [1984] 1 All E.R. 956 (C.A.).
[72] *Townsend* v. *Bishop* [1939] 1 All E.R. 805.
[73] *Castrique* v. *Imrie* (1870) L.R. 4 H.L. 414 at p. 434; *Hollington* v. *Hewthorn* [1943] K.B. 587; see also *Hunter* v. *Chief Constable of West Midlands* [1982] A.C. 529.
[74] *Douglas* v. *Forrest* (1828) 4 Bing. 686.
[75] See also *Re Deeley's Patent* [1895] 1 Ch. 687.

Council,[76] M's car, driven by M's wife, collided with B's bus. M's wife was killed, M was injured, and a house belonging to P was damaged. P sued M and B for the negligence of their respective drivers, and judgment was given for P on the footing that the drivers were equally to blame. M later brought an action against B (i) for his own injuries and (ii) as executor of his wife in respect of her loss of expectation of life. On his own claim, he was estopped from disputing the 50–50 finding of blame; but as executor of his wife, he was not estopped from showing that B's driver was entirely to blame.

Wherever parties are estopped, so are their privies. Privity may arise in various ways[77]; in general it may be said that anyone who derives title from the party by an act or operation of law after the judgment in question is bound by the decision, as against either parties or their privies, the reason being *qui sentit commodum sentire debet et onus*. The alleged privy must be affected by the result of the earlier proceedings, but that fact alone is not enough; he must derive title from or share a common interest in the subject-matter with the party.[78] There is no privity between litigant and solicitor nor between principal and agent.[79] If B and C collaborate in committing what is alleged to be a tort against A, and A sues B and loses, he is not estopped as against C, although he could have sued C in the same action. To require a plaintiff to sue in one action every conceivable defendant would only result in cumbrous, protracted and expensive litigation.[80]

(iv) Matrimonial proceedings. As we have seen, a judgment *in rem* is binding on all persons as to the status actually affected.[81] Decrees in matrimonial proceedings which affect status, *e.g.* divorce, nullity, legitimacy or illegitimacy are the same in this regard as any other judgments *in rem*; no person can deny the status pronounced on.[82] As to the grounds upon which any decree, whether *in rem* or *in personam*, proceeded, *e.g.* adultery by

---

[76] [1939] 2 K.B. 426.
[77] *Ante*, p. 327.
[78] *Mercantile Investment and General Trust Co.* v. *River Plate Trust* [1894] 1 Ch. 578; *Carl-Zeiss-Stiftung* v. *Rayner (No. 2)* [1967] 1 A.C. 853 at pp. 937, 945; *Carl-Zeiss-Stiftung* v. *Rayner (No. 3)* [1970] Ch. 506.
[79] *Carl Zeiss (No. 3), supra*; *Pople* v. *Evans* [1969] 2 Ch. 255.
[80] *Gleeson* v. *Whippell* [1977] 1 W.L.R. 512, *per* Megarry V.-C. at p. 517.
[81] *Ante*, p. 321.
[82] *Thynne* v. *Thynne* [1955] P. 272 at p. 315.

one of the parties, none but the parties are bound,[83] but they are not bound in the same way as with other judgments.

In custody proceedings, probably *res judicata* has no place at all,[84] and findings in earlier proceedings between the spouses have no binding force, perhaps because the child at issue is, in substance if not in form, a party to the subsequent custody proceedings, at which his best interests are not to be defeated by any technical rule.[85] With other matrimonial proceedings, *res judicata* applies, but how it applies depends upon the type of enquiry the Court is engaged in. It has been said that the doctrine of estoppel is only applicable in the adversary system of legal procedure, *i.e.* where the court acts only on such evidence as the parties choose or are able to put before it. Where the court is required to follow the inquisitorial procedure, and may enquire into facts which the parties do not choose to prove, or would under the rules of the adversary system be prevented from proving, the common law concept of estoppel is inapplicable.[86]

The adversary system is the almost invariable system found in English courts, unlike those on the Continent, but there are a few occasions where something akin to an inquisitorial procedure is followed. The chief of these are certain types of matrimonial proceedings, where section 1(3) of the Matrimonial Causes Act 1973 provides that on a petition for divorce it shall be the duty of the court to inquire, so far as it reasonably can, into the facts alleged by the petitioner and into any facts alleged by the respondent. Because of this duty, the rules of estoppel *per rem judicatam* are modified in matrimonial proceedings. Here it is said that "estoppels bind the parties but do not bind the court,"[87] which means that in a situation where a party would normally be

---

[83] Although strangers are not *bound* by a finding of adultery or paternity in earlier proceedings, the finding raises a presumption that the fact occurred: s.12, Civil Evidence Act 1968, *post*, p. 339.

[84] See *Frost v. Frost* [1965] 1 W.L.R. 1221 (C.A.); *Rowe v. Rowe* [1980] Fam. 47.

[85] Phipson, § 28–55.

[86] *Thoday v. Thoday* [1964] P. 181, *per* Diplock L.J. at p. 197. But for another view, see *McLoughlin v. Gordons (Stockport) Ltd.* [1978] I.C.R. 952 at p. 966 (E.A.T.). According to Kilner Brown J., the matrimonial cases are explicable on the same footing as the taxation and rating cases (as to which, see *ante*, p. 323), *i.e.* a continuing situation which is not static, so that a second suit invariably involves slightly different issues.

[87] See *Thompson v. Thompson* [1957] P. 19 at pp. 29 *et seq*. This maxim also applies in bankruptcy proceedings—although the bankrupt may be estopped from raising the question of the genuineness of a debt which has been the subject of a judgment against him, the court may raise the question: *Ex p. Lennox* (1885) 16 Q.B.D. 315, *per* Esher M.R. at p. 323; and so may the trustee in bankruptcy, although he is a privy of the bankrupt: *Re Van Laun* [1907] 2 K.B. 23.

estopped from disputing a former finding against him, he has no *right* to reopen the matter; but the court, if it thinks the public interest demands it, may allow him to do so.[88] The following general rules were laid down by the Court of Appeal in *Thompson v. Thompson*[89]: (1) Where a matrimonial offence or fact relied on as proof that the marriage has broken down irretrievably has been established against a party in previous proceedings, that party has no right to reopen the matter in subsequent proceedings between the same parties, but the court may allow him to do so.[90] (2) However, if a charge has been unsuccessfully brought in previous proceedings, the party making the charge will hardly ever be allowed to make it again, for it is unfair that a person who has resisted one attack should be called upon to defend himself again.[91] (3) But where the previous unsuccessful charge was made before magistrates, the court *may* allow the unsuccessful party to return to the attack in the High Court, which will regard the magistrates' findings as evidence, but not as conclusive, on the issue.[92]

It must be noted that unless the common law doctrine of issue estoppel would have been involved if the case had been other than a matrimonial one, there is no question of the principles of *Thompson v. Thompson* applying, and the court will not be able to prevent the calling of evidence on a particular point. The issues must be identical in accordance with the normal rules before any question of estoppel can arise.

Finally, it must be remembered that in some other matrimonial proceedings, the adversary system obtains. In such a case the normal rule of estoppel applies,[93] provided that the issues are the same, and provided that the issues were clearly decided in the former proceedings.

---

[88] *Thompson v. Thompson, supra*.
[89] *Supra*.
[90] However, the party who successfully alleged the fact will, of course, be allowed to repeat the allegation in subsequent proceedings: *Bernard v. Bernard and Sutton* [1958] 1 W.L.R. 1275.
[91] *Thompson v. Thompson, supra; Bright v. Bright* [1954] P. 270.
[92] *Thompson v. Thompson, supra.* at p. 32. And see, Matrimonial Causes Act 1973, s.4, which provides that a person shall not be prevented from presenting a petition for divorce by reason only that the petitioner or respondent has earlier been granted a decree of judicial separation or a magistrates' separation order. The decree of judicial separation or magistrates' order may be treated as sufficient proof of the matrimonial offence charged, but the court cannot grant a decree without hearing evidence from the petitioner.
[93] *Field v. Field* [1964] P. 336; *G. v. G.* [1970] 3 All E.R. 844.

(v) *Criminal Proceedings.* Cause of action estoppel applies in criminal proceedings, under which neither Crown nor defendant may deny the issue of guilt or innocence decided in earlier proceedings. The accused cannot now assert his innocence when he has been convicted. If the Crown proves his previous conviction against him under proviso (*f*) of the Criminal Evidence Act 1898,[94] it seems he cannot attempt to prove his innocence of the offence the subject of the conviction.[95] However, if the earlier conviction is proved under the similar fact doctrine,[96] section 74(3) of the Police and Criminal Evidence Act 1984 provides that his guilt on that occasion is a matter of presumption only.

Nor may the Crown assert his guilt of an offence of which he has formerly been acquitted. The area covered by this proposition is mostly comprehended in the doctrine of *autrefois acquit*, under which a defendant may not be tried again for an offence of which he has previously been acquitted.[97] If he is arraigned again; he will raise a plea in a bar and the indictment will be quashed. This doctrine rests on the notion of double jeopardy, forbidding the subjecting of a person more than once to the peril of conviction and punishment for one offence. The rule against double jeopardy is apparently strong enough to prevent a second trial even if the circumstances are such that cause of action estoppel would not apply in a civil case, *e.g.* because the earlier judgment was obtained by fraud.[98] However the earlier occasion must be one of real, not nominal, jeopardy, a real risk or danger of punishment following conviction. Thus although the doctrine applies to foreign convictions,[99] if the foreign trial, conviction and sentence were in the defendant's absence, and he cannot be extradited or deported to the foreign jurisdiction, so that there is no chance of his ever serving his sentence, the foreign conviction will not prevent a trial here for the same offence.[1]

---

[94] *Ante*, p. 220.
[95] He would in any event run foul of the finality rule (*ante*, p. 118), since his guilt or innocence on that occasion is collateral to the present issues.
[96] *Ante*, p. 206.
[97] The whole subject of *autrefois*, and the court's power to stay proceedings as an abuse of the process of the court (*post*, p. 333) is the subject of comprehensive proposals in Law.Com.No. 143: Codification of the Criminal Law (1985), Clause 15 of Draft Code, which however does not greatly differ from the present law. See paras. 5.24–5.41.
[98] *R.* v. *Wolverhampton Crown Court* [1982] 3 All E.R. 702 at p. 704; *Weight* v. *MacKay* [1984] 2 All E.R. 673 (H.L.). But if the earlier proceedings were a nullity, that is not an occasion of jeopardy: *R.* v. *Dorking JJ., ex p. Harrington* [1984] A.C. 743 (H.L.).
[99] *Treacy* v. *D.P.P.* [1971] A.C. 537 at p. 562.
[1] *R.* v. *Thomas* [1985] Q.B. 604 (C.A.)..

The requirements of *autrefois acquit* are anyway quite strict. The defendant must be able to show that he has been acquitted on precisely the same offence arising out of the same facts, or of a substantially similar offence, or that he *could* in the earlier proceedings have been convicted of the offence with which he is now charged.[2] What is not sufficient is that the charge in the second proceedings arises out of the same incident or set of facts as the charge in the first proceedings,[3] nor is it sufficient that the accused could have been acquitted but was not, because the jury, having disagreed, were discharged from giving a verdict.[4]

So if A is charged with manslaughter, having been previously acquitted of murder in respect of the same incident, the plea of *autrefois acquit* is a good one because it was open to the jury at the first trial to return a verdict of manslaughter. Likewise, if A is charged with murder, having been previously acquitted of manslaughter in respect of the same incident, the plea in bar is good because murder and manslaughter are substantially similar crimes. "It is all one death."[5]

But if A is charged with theft of a horse's bridle, having been previously acquitted of stealing the horse on the same occasion, the plea is bad because theft of a bridle and theft of a horse are different offences.[6] And if A is charged with entering a building as a trespasser with intent to steal, contrary to the Theft Act 1968, s.9(1)(*a*), having been previously acquitted of entering that building as a trespasser contrary to the Theft Act 1968, s.9(1)(*b*), and stealing, the plea is bad, because the offences are essentially different.[7]

Autrefois acquit does not completely exhaust the effect of *res judicata* in a criminal case. Something akin to cause of action estoppel can operate even where the defendant is not being tried for an offence of which he has earlier been acquitted. "The effect of a verdict of acquittal . . . is not completely stated by saying that

---

[2] If he is retried under the Criminal Appeal Act 1968, the position is the reverse of that stated in the text. He may *not* be tried for a different offence, but only for the offence of which he was convicted at the former trial, or an offence of which he could have been convicted at the former trial, or an offence charged in an alternative count in respect of which the jury were discharged from giving a verdict; *ibid.* s.7(2).
[3] On the whole subject, see the speech of Lord Morris in *Connelly* v. *D.P.P.* [1964] A.C. 1254 at p. 1306; *Atkinson* v. *U.S.A. Government* [1971] A.C. 197 at p. 210.
[4] *D.P.P.* v. *Nasralla* [1967] 2 A.C. 238; *R.* v. *Robinson* (1974) 60 Cr.App.R. 108.
[5] Blackstone, Vol. IV, 329.
[6] Hale, Vol. II, 245.
[7] See *R.* v. *Vandercomb and Abbott* (1796) 2 Leach 708.

the person acquitted cannot be tried again for the same offence."[8] In a subsequent trial for a *different* offence the prosecution is precluded from in any way contending to the contrary of the earlier acquittal. Thus if a statement proved against the defendant on the subject of the present charge contains an admission of another charge on which he has been acquitted at an earlier trial, the jury must be told that the confession must be conclusively taken as untrue as to the other charge, which might cause them to give it less weight as to the present charge.[9] In *G. v. Coltart*,[10] on a charge of theft from X, it was sought to rebut D's defence that she meant to return the goods, by evidence that she had earlier taken goods from Y and had not returned them. D had been acquitted of theft from Y. It was held that the evidence was inadmissible, because it could only be relevant if it was supposed that she *had* stolen from Y. However, the mere fact that evidence tends to suggest that D is guilty of something of which he has been acquitted is not an objection, if its relevance does not depend on D's guilt on that occasion, *e.g.* if it is tendered to show that D, now accused of obtaining by a worthless cheque, knew his bank account was empty. His earlier acquittal on a similar charge does not need to be denied in order to find that knowledge.[11]

There could be no question of issue estoppel in *G. v. Coltart* because it could not be shewn that D's acquittal at the earlier trial had been specifically on the ground that she meant to return Y's goods. This is always a difficulty with an acquittal, or indeed a conviction, by a criminal court. A jury gives no reason for its verdict of not guilty, and magistrates give no reason for dismissing a charge. It was principally on account of this difficulty that it was decided by the House of Lords that there is no doctrine of issue estoppel in criminal cases.[12] Neither Crown nor accused can claim that a particular issue having been settled in an earlier prosecution it should not be disputed again. In *D.P.P. v. Humphrys*,[13] H had been tried for driving while uninsured on July 18, 1972. At his trial, H swore that he had not driven during the

[8] Per Lord McDermott in *Sambasivam v. Public Prosecutor* [1950] A.C. 458 at p. 479 (P.C.).
[9] *Sambasivam v. Public Prosecutor, supra; R. v. Hay* (1983) 77 Cr.App.R. 70 (C.A.).
[10] [1967] 1 Q.B. 432.
[11] *R. v. Ollis* [1900] 2 Q.B. 758, as explained by Salmon L.J. in *G. v. Coltart (supra)* at p. 440.
[12] *D.P.P. v. Humphrys* [1977] A.C.1. Nor is the doctrine available in civil cases with regard to issues said to have been decided in earlier criminal proceedings: *per* Lord Diplock in *Hunter v. Chief Constable of West Midlands* [1982] A.C. 529 at p. 541.
[13] *Supra.*

whole of 1972. P gave evidence that he saw H driving on July 18, 1982. H was acquitted. Later he was tried for perjury in respect of his evidence, and it was held that P could give evidence that H was driving on July 18, 1972.[14]

Such protection as an accused person enjoys from being needlessly tried more than once in respect of the same incident lies partly in rules of practice and, nowadays increasingly, in the court's power to prevent an abuse of process. As to rules of practice, all charges arising out of one incident may be[15] and ought to be[16] tried together. If that practice *is* followed, everything against him will be disposed of on one occasion, and on a second occasion, *autrefois* will protect him. If some charges are not disposed of on the first occasion because the judge orders that those charges should lie on the file, the Crown will need leave to proceed on them later.[17] If it is the defence which gets some charges put back, by making an application to sever,[18] obviously the defence has no cause for complaint if the Crown proceeds with the put-back charges later. But if it is the Crown which leaves some for later, by neglecting to bring all possible charges at one time, the Court has no general discretion to prevent the others from being proceeded with later.[19] It may however act if the bringing of the second prosecution amounts to abuse of process, as to which see below.

(vi) Abuse of process. Any superior Court, civil or criminal, has an inherent jurisdiction to dismiss or stay a proceeding on the ground that it is frivolous, vexatious or an abuse of the process of the Court. There is a statutory power in the High Court to ban a person from bringing any proceedings, civil, or criminal, or both,

---

[14] There are however occasions on which a criminal court might not allow the re-opening of an issue decided against the accused. See *R.* v. *Nottingham JJ.* [1981] Q.B. 38 (D.C.), where justices were held right, on a renewed application for bail, to confine the enquiry to any change in the circumstances, since they had at an earlier hearing found that D came within the statutory exceptions to the right to bail; and also *R.* v. *Pervez and Khan* [1980] Crim.L.R. 108 (C.A.), where a judge on *voir dire* ruled that confessions were admissible, and then ordered separate trials of two of the defendants. The trial of these two was before a different judge, and he was held right to refuse to allow the issue of the confessions' admissibility to be re-opened, although since a ruling on *voir dire* is not a final judgment, there could strictly be no estoppel.

[15] Indictments Rules 1971, r. 9.

[16] *R.* v. *Taylor* (1924) 18 Cr.App.R. 25; *R.* v. *Clarke* (1925) 18 Cr.App.R. 166.

[17] *D.P.P.* v. *Humphrys, supra, per* Lord Edmund-Davies at pp. 54, 55; and see *R.* v. *Riebold* [1967] 1 W.L.R. 674; *R.* v. *Deacon* [1973] 1 W.L.R. 1618.

[18] *Ante,* p. 219.

[19] *D.P.P.* v. *Humphrys, supra.*

on the grounds that he has habitually and persistently and without reasonable ground instituted proceedings.[20] The inherent power, unlike the statutory power, is only to prevent a particular proceeding but, subject to this, it is wider than the statutory power. It does not require persistence or absence of reasonable ground, and may be used, *e.g.* wherever there is an attempt to take unfair advantage of the rules of court,[21] or undue and prejudicial delay in bringing proceedings[22] or in prosecuting an action already started.[23]

More important for present purposes, this power may be used where the conditions for estoppel or *autrefois* are not exactly present, but a second proceeding is on the same cause of action,[24] or is sufficiently close to the earlier one for it to be said of the second that it is oppressive or is an attempt to mount a collateral attack on an earlier judgment which cannot be attacked directly. In *Asher* v. *Secretary of State for the Environment*,[25] the Secretary of State ordered an extraordinary audit of a local authority's affairs, as a result of which the District Auditor surcharged some councillors. They appealed to the High Court, attacking the amount of the surcharge, but not attacking the Secretary of State's order to hold the audit, or making him a party, as they could have done. On their appeals being dismissed, their subsequent action against him for a declaration that he had no power to order the audit was struck out as frivolous.[26]

In criminal proceedings, abuse of process looks like developing a more flexible and just underpinning of the doctrine of double jeopardy[27] than is provided by the limited doctrines of *autrefois acquit*, or estoppel, or than would have been provided by issue estoppel if that had been allowed in criminal proceedings.[28] If the second prosecution is about damage which could have been

---

[20] s.42, Supreme Court Act 1981, as amended by s.24, Prosecution of Offences Act 1985.
[21] *Castanho* v. *Brown & Root* [1981] A.C. 557 (H.L.).
[22] *Bell* v. *D.P.P. for Jamaica* [1985] A.C. 937 (P.C.); *R.* v. *Derby JJ. ex p. Brooks* [1984] Crim.L.R. 754 (D.C.).
[23] *Birkett* v. *James* [1978] A.C. 297 (H.L.).
[24] *e.g.* where the first action was dismissed for want of prosecution, it does not work an estoppel, but bringing a second action on the same cause may be an abuse: *Janov* v. *Morris* [1981] 1 W.L.R. 1389 (C.A.); *cf. Bailey* v. *Bailey* [1983] 1 W.L.R. 1129 (C.A.).
[25] [1974] Ch. 208.
[26] And see *Montgomery* v. *Russell* (1894) 11 T.L.R. 112.
[27] See *ante*, p. 330.
[28] See Pattenden, *The Power of the Courts to Stay a Criminal Prosecution* [1985] Crim.L.R. 175.

included in the first, it is likely to be stayed[29]; likewise if it might result in a decision contradicting the first decision on the same facts, thereby shaking public confidence in the Courts. In *R. v. Cwmbran JJ., ex p. Pope*,[30] D had been acquitted of driving a motor vehicle with excess alcohol in his blood, his defence being that he had not been driving it. A later prosecution for careless driving arising out of the same facts was stayed on this ground. Further, although a refusal by magistrates to commit for trial has no binding force, a prosecution was held not entitled to regard a first sloppily prepared attempt as a "trial run" and try again with a better prepared case.[31]

In *Hunter v. Chief Constable of West Midlands*,[32] an attempt was made to re-open an issue settled at criminal proceedings in later civil proceedings. That issue, in an earlier prosecution for murder, was whether confessions were voluntary in view of alleged assaults on the defendants by police officers. This question, after a lengthy investigation on *voir dire*, was decided against the defendants by the judge, who admitted the confessions, and by the jury who convicted after the evidence of the alleged mistreatment was gone into again before them. The defendants brought civil proceedings for assault against the police. In the Court of Appeal, it was held that the defendants were estopped, since they had had their claim fully investigated and rejected.[33] The House of Lords, however, upheld the striking out of the claim on the grounds that, this being an attempt to mount a collateral attack on an earlier final decision which could not be attacked directly, it was an abuse of process. This reason is not only more defensible on legal grounds than the estoppel found by the majority of the Court of Appeal, but may also be thought to be more appropriate for general use, as being more flexible and more turning on the merits of any particular case than the technical doctrine of *res judicata*.

3. Merger

The doctrine of *res judicata* not only estops a party from controverting as against the other party anything decided in

---

[29] *R. v. Roberts* [1979] Crim.L.R. 44; *Smith v. Birch* [1983] Crim.L.R. 193 (both Crown Cts.)
[30] (1979) 143 J.P.R. 638 (D.C.).
[31] *R. v. Horsham JJ. ex p. Reeves* (1980) 75 Cr.App.R. 236 (D.C.).
[32] [1982] A.C. 529.
[33] *Sed quaere*, since there was no identity of parties in the two proceedings. See *ante*, p. 326.

former proceedings; it also bars the successful party from claiming again on the original cause of action. This original cause of action is said to have merged in the judgment. *Transit in rem judicatam.* If he sues again, he will be met by the plea of judgment recovered, which is a good defence, even if the judgment remains unsatisfied. The question of identity of issues, identity of parties are the same as with estoppel *per rem judicatam*,[34] and the same requirements of final judgment of a competent court exist.

An example of merger which occasionally arises in practice is where A insures his car, with the first £50 of any damage to be borne by him. If the car is damaged by B, and A recovers judgment against him for £50, this prevents the insurers from recovering the balance of the damage from B. Their claim is A's claim and that has merged in the judgment for £50 which A obtained against B.[35]

If A has a claim against either B *or* C and he recovers judgment against B, this extinguishes his claim against C.[36] Even if he does not proceed to judgment against B, if A clearly elects to hold B liable, as by starting an action against him, he loses his right to claim against C.[37] Thus if Q contracts with a firm which, through no fault of his own, he thinks consists of A and B, whereas in fact it consists of B and C, Q may either sue the firm as it appeared to him (A and B) or the firm as it was (B and C) but not both; so if he sues B and C, even if he does not recover judgment, he will not be permitted to sue A on the same cause of action.[38] This is not strictly a case of merger, since there is no judgment; it is usually called election, but has the same effect as merger.

In criminal cases, the doctrine of merger appears in the plea in bar called *autrefois convict*. The Crown cannot proceed against a man for that for which he has already been convicted. The identity of the charges on the former and the present occasions is governed by the same rules as in *autrefois acquit*.[39]

---

[34] See *ante*, pp. 322 *et seq.*
[35] See *Buckland v. Palmer* [1984] 3 All E.R. 554 (C.A.). In this case, A's action did not actually proceed to judgment, but was stayed on payment of £50 by B. With no final judgment it was not a case of merger, but the insurers were prevented from pursuing a second claim in A's name for the balance as it was an abuse of process (see *ante* p. 333). Their proper course was to seek to revive the original stayed action.
[36] *Morel Bros. v. Earl of Westmoreland* [1904] A.C. 11.
[37] *Scarf v. Jardine* (1882) 7 App.Cas. 345, *per* Lord Blackburn at p. 361.
[38] *Scarf v. Jardine, supra.*
[39] *Ante,* p. 331.

B. Judgments as Evidence

In some cases a judgment which has no binding force in the present proceedings nevertheless has some evidential value, so that a party can point to the finding in the earlier proceedings as some evidence (albeit not conclusive[40]) that a fact exists. In other cases, the earlier judgment is entirely irrelevant to the present proceedings.

1. Between the same Parties

Normally, as we have seen,[41] if the same cause of action or issue is involved between the same parties, the earlier judgment is conclusive, and works an estoppel *per rem judicatam*. But in order for it to have this effect, the estoppel must be expressly pleaded. If it is not pleaded as such, the judgment becomes merely an item of evidence. In *Vooght v. Winch*,[42] V sued W for diverting water from a stream. W put in evidence a former judgment between V and W in W's favour on exactly the same cause of action, and claimed that this concluded the matter. It was held that W should have pleaded the estoppel and not merely put the judgment in evidence. As an item of evidence, it had some force; it tended to show that W was justified in diverting the water, but it might be disregarded in favour of other evidence.

2. Between Strangers

It must be remembered[43] that in any proceedings at all, a judgment is conclusive evidence of the fact that judgment was passed, its date, the court which pronounced it, the parties to the proceedings and anything else which appears on the record; but of nothing else. Thus, if it is necessary to prove that A committed a crime, A's conviction of that crime is conclusive proof that he was convicted, but not of thre fact that he committed that crime.[44] And if B sues C for malicious prosecution, B's acquittal proves that he was prosecuted and acquitted but not that B was innocent nor that the prosecution was malicious[45] or even initiated by C, since the prosecutor on the record will be the Crown.

---

[40] Occasionally, it *is* conclusive evidence; see *post*, p. 339.
[41] *Ante*, pp. 322 *et seq.*
[42] (1819) 2 B & Ald. 662.
[43] See *ante*, p. 321.
[44] *R. v. Turner* (1832) 1 Moo.C.C. 347. But see, Civil Evidence Act 1968, s.11, *infra*.
[45] *Purcell v. Macnamara* (1807) 9 East 157, *per* Ellenborough C.J. at p. 362.

Further than this, as to facts found and issues decided, no estoppel is involved between strangers. If the issue between P and Q is, not whether A was *convicted* of forgery, but whether he was *guilty* of forgery, the conviction of A for forgery is not conclusive. The question is, can Q, who says that A forged the document, rely on the fact that an earlier court saw fit to convict A of forgery as evidence? Granted he cannot say that the matter is concluded by the conviction, but he may wish to say that it is a fact from which it may reasonably be inferred that A forged on a particular occasion. Common sense would appear to suggest that Q can do so, but at common law, the usual rule was that the former judgment was not even prima facie evidence of the facts upon which it was based.[46] So if A sues a master B for damage done to A's horse by B's servant C and recovers judgment, in a later action by B against C to recover what he has had to pay A, the earlier judgment is conclusive that A recovered damages from B, but not even prima facie evidence that C injured the horse.[47]

This is usually called the rule in *Hollington* v. *Hewthorn*.[48] In that case, it was held that in a civil action for damages for negligence arising out of a road accident, the defendant's conviction for careless driving on the occasion in question was no evidence that he had been negligent; the judgment of the earlier court was treated as irrelevant. This rule offends against common sense,[49] and statutes have established several wide exceptions to it. Sections 11 and 13 of the Civil Evidence Act 1968[50] make earlier convictions admissible in later civil proceedings. Section 74 of the Police and Criminal Evidence Act 1984[51] does the same with later criminal proceedings. These provisions deal only with earlier convictions in U.K. courts or courts martial, and not with earlier civil judgments, which are, with two exceptions, still subject to the rule in *Hollington* v. *Hewthorn*.

Section 11 of the 1968 Act provides that in civil proceedings, where the fact that a person committed an offence is relevant to an issue in the proceedings, the fact that he has been convicted of that offence is evidence that he committed it, and he shall be taken to have committed it unless the contrary is proved.

---

[46] *Hollington* v. *Hewthorn* [1943] K.B. 587.
[47] See *Green* v. *New River Co.* (1792) 4 T.R. 598.
[48] [1943] K.B. 587.
[49] There were some limited exceptions to it. See *Petrie* v. *Nuttall* (1856) 11 Exch. 569; *Ex p. Anderson* (1885) 14 Q.B.D. 606; *Edison* v. *Holland* (1888) 6 R.P.C. 248. On impeaching a witness's credit, see *ante*, p. 121.
[50] See Appendix 2.
[51] See Appendix 3.

Judgments as Evidence

Subsections 74(1) and (2) of the 1984 Act do the same for criminal proceedings, but are limited to earlier convictions of persons other than the present defendant. However subsection 3 provides that where evidence is admissible of the fact that the accused has committed an offence, in so far as that evidence is relevant to any matter in issue for a reason other than a tendency to show in the accused a disposition to commit the kind of offence with which he is charged (*i.e.* under the similar facts doctrine[52]), if the accused is proved to have been convicted of the offence, he shall be taken to have committed that offence unless the contrary is proved.

These provisions establish a rebuttable presumption that the person convicted did commit the offence,[53] but section 13 of the 1968 Act goes further than this. It provides that in a defamation action in which the question whether a person did or did not commit an offence is relevant, proof that he stands convicted of that offence is conclusive proof that he committed it. The reason for this provision is that *Hollington* v. *Hewthorn's* effect was thought to be particularly undesirable in the case of libel actions brought by convicted criminals. If A, a convicted burglar, sued B for calling him a burglar, B could not use A's conviction to support his plea of justification. The issue would have to be tried again, perhaps many years after the event.[54] The possibilities thus opened up of convicted men using defamation actions to get their cases thrashed out again, or merely to get unmerited damages, caused the law to be changed. The present rule, it may be noted, is that as long as the conviction stands, it is *conclusive* proof that the person concerned committed the offence.

These provisions concern earlier convictions only. However section 12 of the 1968 Act provides that in civil proceedings (i) the fact that a person was found guilty of adultery in any matrimonial proceedings in the High Court and (ii) the fact that a person has been adjudged to be the father of a child in affiliation proceedings, is admissible in evidence for the purpose of proving that he committed the adultery or was the father of the child, and he must be taken to have committed the adultery or to be the father of the child unless the contrary is proved. Moreover if the later proceedings are disciplinary proceedings before the General

---

[52] See, *ante*, pp. 207–220.
[53] On rebutting the presumption, see *Stupple* v. *Royal Exchange Insurance Co.* [1971] Q.B. 50, *ante*, p. 81.
[54] *Hinds* v. *Sparks* [1964] Crim.L.R. 717; *Goody* v. *Odhams Press* [1967] 1 Q.B. 333. The conviction could however be used in mitigation of damages: *ibid.*

Medical Council, the earlier finding is conclusive.[55] In civil proceedings, a finding made or decision given on foreign law[56] by certain English courts or the Judicial Committee of the Privy Council is, if reported or recorded in citable form, admissible in evidence for the purpose of proving the point of foreign law, and that law shall be taken to be in accordance with that finding or decision unless the contrary is proved.[57]

In other respects the common law rule remains—the earlier judgment is not even prima facie evidence of a fact sought to be proved in later proceedings. The statutory exceptions mentioned above cover some civil judgments, being used in later civil proceedings, and convictions[58] used in later civil or criminal proceedings. Other civil judgments, and acquittals, and foreign judgments, are no evidence in any later proceedings.

---

[55] Civil Evidence Act 1968, s.12(3); Medical Act 1956, s.33(2); Dentists Act 1957, s.25(3).
[56] In English Courts, questions of foreign law are questions of fact, although decided by the judge. *Ante*, p. 47.
[57] Civil Evidence Act 1972, s.4(2).
[58] The fact that the conviction is being appealed against is in principle immaterial, but the civil action will usually be adjourned until the criminal appeal has been disposed of: *Re Raphael, decd.* [1973] 1 W.L.R. 998.

Part VII

DOCUMENTARY EVIDENCE

CHAPTER 17
DOCUMENTARY EVIDENCE

	Page
A. Proof of the Execution of Documents	343
1. Public and Judicial Documents	343
2. Private Documents	343
B. Proof of the Contents of Documents	347
1. Primary Evidence	347
2. Secondary Evidence	348
C. Extrinsic Evidence in Relation to Documents	351
1. The Use of Extrinsic Evidence as a Substitute for a Document	352
2. The Use of Extrinsic Evidence to vary or contradict a Document	354
3. The Use of Extrinsic Evidence to Interpret a Document	358

CHAPTER 17

DOCUMENTARY EVIDENCE

IF a party wishes to rely on a document, the court will often need to be assured that the document was made by the person who is alleged to have made it, *i.e.* proof of its execution will be required. The terms of the document will in most cases be relevant, *i.e.* proof of its contents will be required. The normal rule is this must be by production of the original document, although there are many exceptions. The meaning of the document, and to what or to whom it applies, will often be in issue, and this will raise the question of how far the court may use for this purpose any evidence other than the document itself (*i.e.* extrinsic evidence).

A. Proof of the Execution of Documents

1. Public and Judicial Documents

The execution of public and judicial documents will be more fully considered when dealing with their contents,[1] since in most of the statutes providing for their proof the two subjects are treated together. It will suffice here, therefore, to say that certain of such documents (*e.g.* Acts of Parliament), being judicially noticed are admissible without any authentication whatever; while others need no further authentication than that of appearing in a government *Gazette*, or "purporting" to be printed by the official printers, or "purporting" to be certified, stamped, sealed or signed by certain officers or departments—the effect being to render such documents prima facie admissible so far as their genuineness and validity go, and to throw upon the opponent the onus of impeaching them if he can.

2. Private Documents

When private documents are relevant, their execution, whether they are produced or not, if proof has not been dispensed with by formal admission,[2] may be proved as follows:

[1] *Post*, p. 351.
[2] *Ante*, p. 28.

(a) Handwriting and signature

The handwriting and signature of unattested documents, or of attested ones not legally requiring attestation, may be proved by the following methods, all of which are equally primary and equally admissible:

(i) the evidence of the writer; or
(ii) the evidence of a witness who saw the document signed; or
(iii) the evidence of a witness who has acquired a knowledge of the writing and gives his opinion on the matter[3]; or by
(iv) comparison of the document in dispute with others proved to be genuine; or by
(v) the admissions of the party against whom the document is tendered.

It is not necessary to call the attesting witness where the document, although in fact attested, is not required by law to be attested.[4]

Even where signature is required by statute and for solemn documents, a manual signing is not generally essential, any form in which a person affixes his name, with intent that it shall be treated as his signature, being sufficient, *e.g.* deeds or wills are valid if signed by mark, stamp or initials.

(b) Attestation

The rule which formerly applied to all documents required by law to be attested, now only is imperative in the case of a will or testamentary disposition. Such a document must (subject to the exceptions mentioned below) be proved by calling the attesting witness, even though the document itself be lost, cancelled or destroyed. If there are several such witnesses, one only need be called[5]; but the absence of all must be explained before other evidence can be received. Where, however, the witness denies the execution,[6] or refuses to testify[7] other evidence will be admissible. Where the attesting witness is dead, insane, beyond the jurisdiction, or cannot be found, secondary evidence of execution must be given by proof of his handwriting; or if (but only if) this is not

---

[3] *Ante*, p. 22.
[4] Criminal Procedure Act 1865, s.7. The Act applies to civil proceedings: *ibid.* s.1. As to lost documents, see *post*, pp. 345, 349.
[5] *Holdfast* d. *Anstey* v. *Dowsing* (1746) 2 Stra. 1253.
[6] *Bowman* v. *Hodgson* (1867) L.R. 1 P. & D. 362; *Pilkington* v. *Gray* [1899] A.C. 401.
[7] *In the Goods of Ovens* (1892) 29 L.R.Ir. 451.

obtainable, by presumptive or other evidence.[8] There is no rule that the evidence of a witness to the document is conclusive or exclusive of other evidence. If he gives evidence that the requirements of the law were not carried out, other evidence is admissible to show that, in spite of what he says, the will or deed was in fact duly executed.[9] When the document is lost and the names of the witnesses are unknown, the execution may be proved by the recollection of witnesses,[10] by admission or otherwise, *e.g.* by the parties having acted on the document,[11] as if there were no attesting witness. In the case of documents (other than wills and testamentary dispositions), required by law to be attested, proof of due execution may be given as if no attesting witness is alive.[12]

Generally, any competent witness may attest, *e.g.* marksmen,[13] minors when of years of discretion, and (though this is undesirable) wives or husbands may attest the signatures of each other. But the parties to a deed are not competent to attest it, nor may proxies attest their own appointment, and warrants of attorney can only be attested by solicitors. A blind person cannot be a witness to a will nor, presumably, to any other document.

(c) Ancient documents

Documents 20 years old,[14] produced from proper custody, and otherwise free from suspicion, are presumed to have been duly executed, and no evidence of execution need be given, though the witnesses attesting them be alive and in court.[15] The proper custody of a document means its deposit with a person and in a place where it might naturally and reasonably be expected to be found, if authentic, even though there be some other custody more strictly proper.[16] Thus, the proper custody of parish registers is with the incumbent or in the church, and not, unless explained, with the parish clerk[17]; and of family Bibles with a member of the

---

[8] *Clarke v. Clarke* (1879) 5 L.R.Ir. 47; *Palin v. Ponting* [1930] P. 185.
[9] *Re Vere-Wardale* [1949] P. 395.
[10] *Re Phibbs* [1917] P. 93.
[11] *R. v. Fordingbridge* (1858) 27 L.J.M.C. 290.
[12] Evidence Act 1938, s.3.
[13] *i.e.* persons who cannot write and who make a mark instead of signing.
[14] The period of 30 years was reduced to 20 years for civil and criminal proceedings by the Evidence Act 1938, s.4.
[15] But if the document purports to have been executed under a power of attorney, it must be shown that the attorney was duly authorised: *Re Airey* [1897] 1 Ch. 164.
[16] *Meath (Bishop) v. Winchester (Marquis)* (1836) 3 Bing.N.C. 183.
[17] *Doe v. Fowler* (1850) 14 Q.B. 700.

family[18] and that of an expired lease with the lessor or lessee.[19] On the other hand, an ancient grant, produced from the British Museum, and not from the custody of persons interested in the property, has been rejected.[20]

(d) Other presumptions relating to execution

A document is presumed to have been executed on the date it bears[21] and alterations in deeds are presumed to have been made before execution, while those in wills are presumed to have been made after execution.[22] Material alterations made after execution of a deed without the concurrence of the party to be charged make the whole deed void[23]; but alterations to a will made after execution are of no effect, unless they obliterate some of the original text, when they will effect a partial revocation.[24]

(e) Stamps

Except in criminal proceedings, no instrument requiring a stamp "shall be given in evidence, or be available for any purpose whatever," unless:

(i) it is duly stamped in accordance with the law in force at the time when it was first executed; or
(ii) if the instrument is one which may be legally stamped after its execution, unless on payment to the officer of the court of the unpaid duty, together with the penalty payable on stamping the same, and of a further sum of one pound.[25]

Stamp objections are taken by the court,[26] and cannot be waived by the parties.[27]

---

[18] *Hubbard* v. *Lees* (1866) L.R. 1 Ex. 255.
[19] *Hall* v. *Ball* (1841) 3 Man. & G. 242.
[20] *Swinnerton* v. *Stafford* (1810) 3 Taunt. 91; *Mercer* v. *Denne* [1904] 2 Ch. 534, at p. 545. But a local authority, a public library, museum or similar institution may be a proper place for custody of manorial documents (under the Manorial Documents Rules 1959, as amended in 1963 and 1967), or tithe apportionments, etc., under the Tithe Act 1936, s.36(2) as amended by the Local Government (Records) Act 1962, s.7(1).
[21] *Anderson* v. *Weston* (1840) 6 Bing.N.C. 296.
[22] *Doe* d. *Tatum* v. *Catomore* (1851) 16 Q.B. 745.
[23] *Davidson* v. *Cooper* (1844) 13 M. & W. 343.
[24] Wills Act 1837, s.21.
[25] Stamp Act 1891, s.14.
[26] *Ibid.* if the court of first instance overlooks the matter it is the duty of the Court of Appeal to take the objection: *Routledge* v. *McKay* [1954] 1 W.L.R. 615.
[27] *Bowker* v. *Williamson* (1888) 5 T.L.R. 382.

No new trial,[28] or appeal,[29] is allowed where the judge has ruled that a stamp is sufficient, or not required. But this ruling is not final when he decides that the instrument is inadmissible.[30]

Where a document requiring a stamp is lost, or not produced upon notice, it will, in the absence of evidence to the contrary, be presumed to have been duly stamped; but where it is shown to have been unstamped, it will be presumed to have so continued until the contrary is proved.[31]

B. Proof of the Contents of Documents

The contents of public or judicial documents may, in general, be proved either by primary or secondary evidence. The contents of private documents must, subject to certain exceptions[32] be proved by primary evidence.

1. Primary Evidence

Primary evidence of the contents of a document may be given in the following forms:

(a) Production of the original document

When an original document is produced it must, unless it has been admitted, or is a public document receivable on its mere production, be identified on oath as being what it purports to be. But it is not always easy to determine what is the original document for this purpose, for sometimes the same document may be primary evidence for one purpose, and secondary for another. Duplicate originals are each primary evidence; counterparts are primary against an executing, but secondary only against a non-executing party. The original of a telegram is, at any rate if tendered as evidence against the sender, the message handed in to the post-office, not the message delivered to the addressee.[33]

(b) Admissions

Admissions of the contents of a document made either orally, in writing, or by conduct, by a party, are primary evidence against

---

[28] Ord. 59, r. 11(5).
[29] *Blewitt* v. *Tritton* [1892] 2 Q.B. 327.
[30] *Ibid.*
[31] *Closmadeuc* v. *Carrel* (1856) 18 C.B. 36.
[32] *Post*, p. 349.
[33] *R.* v. *Regan* (1887) 16 Cox 203.

him, or those in privity with him, without notice to produce, or accounting for the absence of the original, such proof not being open to the same objections as is parol evidence from other sources; while the sworn testimony as to its contents of witnesses who are strangers is only secondary evidence.[34] So copies, though usually only secondary evidence, may become primary by having been delivered by a party to his opponent as correct, or otherwise dealt with by him as true.[35]

(c) Copies made under public authority

In a few cases copies of an original document made under public authority are receivable as primary evidence thereof. Thus if the question be what are the words of a will of a deceased person which has been admitted to probate, the probate (*i.e.* official copy) is primary and conclusive evidence, and the original will is not admissible at all on this question.[36] However, the probate does not supersede the original for all purposes, and on a question of construction, where, for instance, everything may turn on the position of the words on the paper, both the probate and the original may be consulted.[37] If the will is referred to merely as a declaration by a deceased person on some extraneous subject, *e.g.* pedigree,[38] then it seems that the original is primary and the probate secondary evidence.

2. Secondary Evidence

In the absence of statutory exceptions, or in civil cases when the documents may be the subject of an admission by the other party, the general rule is that documents must be produced.[39] A photostat of an original does not count as an original for this purpose.[40] On the other hand, this rule is nowadays confined to written documents in the strict sense and has no relevance to tapes and films.[41] Where the rule does apply, the absence of the original must be satisfactorily accounted for before secondary evidence of it is admitted.

---

[34] *Slatterie* v. *Pooley* (1840) 6 M. & W. 664.
[35] *Price* v. *Woodhouse* (1849) 3 Ex. 616.
[36] *Pinney* v. *Hunt* (1877) 6 Ch.D. 98.
[37] *Re Harrison* (1885) 30 Ch.D. 390; *Re Battie-Wrightson* [1920] 2 Ch. 330.
[38] *Ante*, p. 285.
[39] *Att.-Gen.* v. *Lundin* (1982) 75 Cr.App.R. 90 at p. 98.
[40] *R.* v. *Wayte* (1982) 76 Cr.App.R. 110; *Att.-Gen.* v. *Lundin, supra.*
[41] *Kajala* v. *Noble* (1982) 75 Cr.App.R. 149. Contra *R.* v. *Stevenson* [1971] 1 All E.R. 678; *R.* v. *Robson* [1972] 1 W.L.R. 651.

(a) Kinds of secondary evidence

Secondary evidence of the contents of documents may take various forms. With private documents, it may be the testimony of witnesses who have read them and can recollect their contents; or proof that the parties interested have acted in accordance with the tenor of the documents.[42] Or it may take the form of one of the many types of copies. Examined copies are those proved to have been checked line by line with the original. Certified copies are those signed and certified as true by the officer to whose custody the original is entrusted. Office copies are those issued by an officer of the court in which they are filed. Queen's Printer's Copies are used to prove the contents of private Acts of Parliament, Royal Proclamations, Treaties, Journals of either House of Parliament, Orders in Council and Statutory Instruments.

All forms of secondary evidence are equally admissible, subject to adverse comment where more satisfactory proof is withheld,[43] except that public or judicial documents or private documents when registered or enrolled cannot be proved by oral evidence.[44] The proper method of proving most private documents, when secondary evidence is allowed, is by examined copy. There is no objection to a copy of a copy, provided the second is shown to have been compared with the first, and the first with the original.[45]

(b) When secondary evidence is admissible

Secondary evidence of the contents of documents may, provided the originals themselves would be admissible, be given in the following cases:

1. When the original has been lost or destroyed; but execution, and (where lost) search, must first be proved independently.[46]

2. When its production is physically impossible or highly inconvenient, *e.g.* in the case of tombstones, inscriptions on walls and the like.[47]

3. When the original is in the possession of a stranger who refuses to produce it, and is privileged to withhold it and so not

---

[42] *R. v. Fordingbridge* (1858) 27 L.J.M.C. 290.
[43] *Doe d. Gilbert v. Ross* (1840) 7 M. & W. 102.
[44] *Bretan v. Cope* [1791] 1 Peake 43.
[45] *R. v. Collins* (1960) 44 Cr.App.R. 170.
[46] *Brewster v. Sewell* (1820) 3 B. & Ald. 296.
[47] *Mortimer v. M'Callan* (1840) 6 M. & W. 58.

compellable by law to produce it, for example when it is an incriminating document, or one which he holds as trustee, solicitor, or mortgagee for another,[48] or where he claims diplomatic immunity[49]; but not where he unlawfully refuses to produce it.[50]

4. When the original is in the possession of the adversary, who refuses to produce it either after Notice to Produce, or when such notice is excused.[51] The object of a notice to produce is to enable the adversary to have the document in court, and if he does not, to enable his opponent to give secondary evidence thereof, so as to exclude the argument that the latter has not taken all reasonable means to procure the original.[52] If the document is produced, the producing party can insist that it be put in evidence by his opponent; the latter is not allowed to inspect it and then decide whether to put it in.[53] On the other hand if the party called upon to produce a document fails to do so, so that secondary evidence of its contents is allowed, he cannot afterwards put in the original.[54]

Notice to produce is excused:

(i) when the document is itself a notice served on the adversary[55]; or
(ii) where from the nature of the case the adversary is bound to know that he is required to produce the original, *e.g.* in a prosecution for theft of a bill of exchange[56]; or
(iii) where the adversary has it in court[57]; or has himself admitted its loss.[58]

5. Where the contents are admissible under statute in breach of the hearsay rule. Where the Civil Evidence Act 1968 or the Police and Criminal Evidence Act 1984 allow documentary hearsay,[59] the document may be proved by production of the document or

---

[48] *Mills v. Oddy* (1834) 6 C. & P. 728.
[49] *R. v. Nowaz* [1976] 1 W.L.R. 830.
[50] *R. v. Llanfaethly* (1853) 23 L.J.M.C. 33.
[51] *Dwyer v. Collins* (1852) 7 Ex. 639.
[52] *Dwyer v. Collins, supra.*
[53] *Wharam v. Routledge* (1805) 5 Esp. 235.
[54] *Doe d. Thompson v. Hodgson* (1840) 12 A. & E. 135.
[55] See *Practice Note* [1950] 1 All E.R. 37.
[56] *R. v. Aickles* (1784) 1 Leach 294.
[57] *Dwyer v. Collins, supra.*
[58] *R. v. Haworth* (1830) 4 C. & P. 253.
[59] See *ante,* Chaps. 13, 14.

Proof of the Contents of Documents

of a copy authenticated in such manner as the court may approve.[60]

6. Where the original is a public or judicial document, or a private one required to be registered or enrolled.

Chiefly on the grounds that it would be illegal or highly inconvenient if original public documents were required to be produced in court, the rule is that such may be proved by copy.[61] Special provision is made for particular public documents by a host of statutes, too numerous to mention here. Some of these not only provide for the proving of the contents of a particular document by producing a copy but go on to make the statements in the copy admissible as statements, *i.e.* in breach of the hearsay rule.[62] This topic was dealt with in Chapter 13, and must be kept distinguished from the present topic, which is the proof of the *contents* of documents.

Various statutes allow certified copies to prove entries in public registers, corporation books, bankers' books and by-laws. Such a statute will often provide that a document purporting to be a certificate for use under that statute will be taken to be so. Office copies are the usual methods of proving judgments, orders and affidavits, and Queen's Printer's copies are the usual and proper method of proving proclamations, statutory rules and orders, regulations and parliamentary journals. It should be remembered that statutes of the realm and decisions of all English courts are not proved at all, being judicially noted.[63]

C. Extrinsic Evidence in Relation to Documents

Where the term "extrinsic evidence" is used in connection with documents it means any evidence, whether oral or documentary, other than the document concerned.[64] The general rule is that extrinsic evidence is not admissible to prove the terms of the transaction which the document purports to effect, or the meaning which the maker of the document meant to give to the words used in the document.

Another way of expressing the same idea is that a document is

---

[60] s.6(1), Civil Evidence Act 1968; Sched. 3, para. 13 Police & Criminal Evidence Act 1984.
[61] *Mortimer* v. *M'Callan* (1840) 6 M. & W. 58.
[62] See, *e.g.* bankers' books, *ante*, p. 283.
[63] *Ante*, p. 30.
[64] Such evidence is sometimes called "parol," which is a faintly misleading term in that it suggests that the class of evidence described is oral evidence only; however, as said above, the class includes evidence in *documents* other than the document being considered by the court.

usually conclusive evidence of the terms of the transaction it effects, and of the meaning to be given to the words used in the document. As regards the terms of the transaction, the document is not only conclusive but *exclusive*, in that even if a party does not challenge the evidence of the document as to the terms of the transaction, *i.e.* he does not purport to contradict or vary the document, nevertheless he is not allowed to adduce any evidence of the terms other than the document. The document is not only the strongest evidence of the terms of the transaction; it is the only permissible evidence thereof.

1. The Use of Extrinsic Evidence as a Substitute for a Document

(a) Normally forbidden

Once the parties to a transaction have embodied it in a written document, either by agreement or because the law requires it, then in general the writing becomes the exclusive record of the transaction, and no evidence may be given to prove the terms of the transaction, except the document itself, or secondary evidence of its contents where such is allowed.[65]

Certain kinds of extrinsic evidence must always be admissible. Thus, if the execution of a document is not admitted or its genuineness is in dispute, the parties must be at liberty to prove or disprove the execution or genuineness of the document, or to show that the transaction was not concluded.[66] Again, evidence is always admissible to identify the persons and things to which the document refers.[67] This section deals with the case where the document is not in dispute and no question of identity arises.

The reason for the rule is sometimes that the law has required that the transaction must be in writing to be of any force at all (as in the case of most wills[68]), sometimes that the law has provided that the transaction is unenforceable unless it is evidenced by writing (as in the case of contracts for the sale of an interest in land[69]), and sometimes that expediency demands that the

---

[65] See *ante*, p. 349.
[66] *Nicholson* v. *Smith Marriott* (1947) 177 L.T. 189; *Strauss* v. *Sutro* (1947) 177 L.T. 562.
[67] *Bank of New Zealand* v. *Simpson* [1900] A.C. 182 at p. 188; *Charrington* v. *Wooder* [1914] A.C. 71.
[68] Wills Act 1837, s.9.
[69] Law of Property Act 1925, s.40.

certainty of writing be preferred to the uncertain memories of witnesses.[70]

The effect of this rule is that as soon as it appears that the transaction of which he is speaking is embodied in a document, a witness will not be allowed to give evidence of the transaction. To ascertain the fact, the opponent may interpose during the witness's examination-in-chief, in which case, if the document is admitted or there and then established to the satisfaction of the judge, he will not be allowed to speak as to the terms of the transaction,[71] or the opponent may reserve the question until the witness's cross-examination, and if the document's existence is then admitted or proved, the witness's evidence on the matter comprised in the document is ignored. However, if the plaintiff manages to establish a prima facie case without disclosing the existence of the document, he is not prejudiced by the defendant's proving its existence, for the evidential burden will have been shifted, and if the latter rely on the document he must produce it (with the usual liability as to stamping) as part of his own case.[72]

(b) Exceptions to the rule

1. If what is to be proved is the *fact* of the transaction (*e.g.* the fact that X is a tenant in a certain parish,[73] or that a partnership existed between certain persons[74]), rather than the *terms* of the transaction, parol evidence is not excluded by the circumstances that the transaction is embodied in a document.

2. If it is sought to show that the transaction is contained in two or more documents, extrinsic evidence is allowed to show the connection between them, but only if one refers to the other or others, where, in accordance with the usual role, parol evidence is admitted to identify things or documents mentioned in the document.[75] If there is no apparent connection between the documents, *i.e.* no reference in one to the other, parol evidence that in fact they are connected is inadmissible.[76]

3. Where the law requires that *all* the terms of a contract be evidenced in writing, it is permissible to use parol evidence to

---

[70] *Countess of Rutland's Case* (1604) 5 Co.Rep.25B, 26B.
[71] *Cox v. Couveless* (1860) 2 F. & F. 139.
[72] *Magnay v. Knight* (1840) 1 Ex. 279.
[73] *R. v. Holy Trinity, Hull* (1827) 7 B. & C. 611.
[74] *Alderson v. Clay* (1816) 1 Stark. 405.
[75] *Long v. Miller* (1879) 4 C.P.D. 450; *Pearce v. Gardner* [1897] 1 Q.B. 688.
[76] *Boydell v. Drummond* (1809) 11 East 142; *Timmins v. Moreland Street Property Co.* [1958] Ch. 110.

show that there are terms other than those contained in a written memorandum, so that the memorandum does not comply with the requirements of the law.[77]

4. Sometimes, in cases where statute requires the terms of a contract to be contained in a memorandum in writing, the court will accept in lieu proof of part performance of the contract. In such cases, parol evidence of the contract is admissible.[78]

5. If the writing is not intended to form the transaction, but merely records it, or part of it, the existence of the writing does not exclude extrinsic evidence of the terms of the transaction. Sometimes the law requires that a memorandum shall record the transaction, or it will appear from the memorandum that the parties intended it to constitute the transaction in question[79]; but otherwise it is competent for a party to show by extrinsic evidence, *e.g.* whether payment made by cheque and acknowledged in writing was in fact made,[80] or that there were other terms in the transaction which were not recorded in the writing.[81]

2. The Use of Extrinsic Evidence to Vary or Contradict a Document

(a) Normally forbidden

When a transaction has been reduced into writing either by requirement of law, or agreement of the parties, extrinsic evidence is, in general, inadmissible to contradict, vary, add to or subtract from the terms of the document.[82] The reason may be said to be that when the parties have deliberately put their agreement into writing, it is presumed between themselves and their privies that they intended the writing to form a full and final statement of their intentions, and one which should be placed beyond the reach of future controversy, bad faith, or treacherous memory.[83]

But although this appears plain and absolute enough, the rule contains within it a rather obvious limitation; it only applies *if* the parties intended the document to express the whole position

---

[77] *Beckett v. Nurse* [1948] 1 K.B. 535; but see *Hutton v. Watling* [1948] Ch. 398.
[78] *Chaproniere v. Lambert* [1917] 2 Ch. 356.
[79] *Hutton v. Watling* [1948] Ch. 398.
[80] *Carmarthen Ry. v. Manchester Ry.* (1873) L.R. 8 C.P. 685; *Lee v. L. & Y. Ry.* (1871) L.R. 6 Ch.App. 527. A receipt is usually only an admission, like all admissions explainable, but it may give rise to an estoppel.
[81] *Allen v. Pink* (1838) 4 M. & W. 140.
[82] As already stated, this principle does not apply to questions such as what constitutes the writing, or what is its legal effect, or to a claim for rectification.
[83] *Hutton v. Watling* [1948] Ch. 398.

between them. If one party seeks to show that there were other terms, or that their agreement was subject to a condition precedent, or that the whole bargain between them comprised one agreement incorporated in the document *and* another by parol, he is not so much seeking to break the rule as to show that it does not apply; and he must be allowed to try to do that. Moreover, if the entire transaction *is* recorded in the document, evidence of anything else is irrelevant, and to be rejected on that account, quite apart from the rule now being discussed.

Nevertheless the rule has obvious utility, in that it prevents avoidable disputes, by *presuming* that a document, which appears to incorporate a whole transaction, does so.[84] After complicated negotiations, a party is entitled to feel assured that the production of the document settles the matter, and the rule presently being discussed prevents the other party from lightly re-opening the settled matters. But he is entitled to do so in the following cases which are either exceptions to the rule, or cases not comprehended in the rule.

(b) Exceptions

1. Omitted Terms. Where a contract, not required by law to be in writing, purports to be contained in a document which the court holds was not intended to express the whole agreement between the parties, proof may be given of any omitted term expressly or impliedly agreed between them before or at the same time, if it be not inconsistent with the documentary terms. In *Robb* v. *Green*[85] A proposed to engage B as manager in a letter purporting to specify "the exact terms of the hiring." The only terms set out related to B's salary and house rent. B accepted the offer by letter. A was allowed to prove a prior oral agreement by which B was not to solicit A's customers, since the document did not purport to contain the whole of the contract, and the added term did not contradict what was written.

Custom or usage is admissible to annex unexpressed terms, provided such are not inconsistent with the written ones.[86] In *Wigglesworth* v. *Dallinson*,[87] A let agricultural land to B. B alleged a local custom allowing a tenant to enter the land after the expiration of the lease to harvest the crops he had sown. This is

---

[84] *Hutton* v. *Watling, supra,* at p. 405.
[85] [1895] 2 Q.B. 315.
[86] As to terms agreed subsequently, see *post,* p. 358.
[87] (1779) 1 Doug.K.B. 201.

contrary to the general law of emblements, but not contrary to anything said in the lease, so B was allowed to prove the custom.

2. *Collateral agreements and warranties.* Moreover, although there exists a contract purporting to be fully expressed in writing, whether required by law to be so or not, proof may be given of a prior or contemporaneous oral agreement, or warranty, which forms part of the consideration for the main contract and is not inconsistent with the document.[88] The collateral contract must not be subsequent to the main contract, for it could not then form part of the consideration.[89]

It is always possible to prove a collateral condition that the document will not come into force as a contract until the condition is fulfilled,[90] and parol evidence may be used to show that an expressed condition has been fulfilled or waived.[91] In *Morgan* v. *Griffiths*[92] A granted a lease of land to B, reserving the sporting rights. It was held that B might prove a prior oral agreement by which A promised to keep down the rabbits if B would take the lease. And in *De Lassalle* v. *Guildford*[93] A leased a house to B, the lease not mentioning the drains. B instructed his wife not to hand over the counterpart executed by B unless A guaranteed that the drains were in good order. Parol evidence of A's assurance that the drains were in good order was admitted as not contradicting the terms of the lease. But in *Henderson* v. *Arthur*[94] A covenanted in a lease to pay rent quarterly in advance. Evidence that the lessor at the time agreed to allow A to pay in arrear was not admitted, as contradicting the terms of the lease.

3. *True nature of the transaction.* Where legal or equitable rules insist upon having regard to the true nature of the transaction, regardless of its apparent nature, extrinsic evidence of the true nature may be given, even though the transaction is one required by the law to be in writing and even though the extrinsic evidence contradicts the terms of the written transaction. Thus what is apparently a sale can be proved to be a mortgage,[95] and what is

---

[88] *Heilbut Symonds and Co.* v. *Buckleton* [1913] A.C. 30 at pp. 47–51.
[89] *Bristol, etc., Co.* v. *Fiat Motors* [1910] 2 K.B. 831 at p. 838; and see *Walker Property Investments* v. *Walker* (1947) 177 L.T. 204.
[90] *Pym* v. *Campbell* (1856) 6 E. & B. 370; *Pattle* v. *Hornibrook* [1897] 1 Ch. 25.
[91] *Griffiths* v. *Young* [1970] Ch. 675.
[92] (1871) L.R. 6 Ex. 70; and see *City and Westminster Properties* v. *Mudd* [1959] Ch. 129.
[93] [1901] 2 K.B. 215.
[94] [1907] 1 K.B. 10.
[95] *Re Duke of Marlborough* [1894] 2 Ch. 133.

apparently a beneficial gift in a will can be shown to be a secret trust.[96]

4. *Capacity of parties.* Where the capacity in which a person executes a document is unequivocal, he cannot show that he executed it in some capacity other than the stated one, but where his stated capacity is equivocal, he may show that he executed it as agent for an undisclosed principal.[97] Apparently the designations "charterer,"[98] "tenant"[99] and "landlord,"[1] are equivocal, whereas "owner"[2] and "occupier"[3] are not, since only one person can comply with the latter two descriptions, whereas the expression "tenant" for instance can be applied to a party to a lease whether he executed on behalf of himself or another.

5. *Invalid documents or transactions.* Extrinsic evidence is admissible to prove any matter which by the substantive law affects the validity of a document, or entitles a party to any relief in respect thereof, notwithstanding that such evidence tends in some cases to contradict the writing, *e.g.* conditional or defective execution, contractual incapacity, fraud, forgery, duress, undue influence, illegality of subject-matter, mistake.[4]

One of the remedies which a party may seek on the ground of mistake is rectification, *i.e.* altering the document to make it accurately reflect what was in fact agreed. But as to wills, the clear policy of the law expressed in the Wills Act 1837 has been that the only source of the testator's intentions is his will, and there was never any jurisdiction to rectify a will. Now, however, as to wills coming into force on or after January 1, 1983, there is a limited power to rectify so as to carry out the testator's misunderstood *instructions*, or to correct clerical errors.[5]

6. *Consideration.* Since absence of consideration invalidates a transaction not under seal, in such a case that absence may be shown by parol, notwithstanding the fact that the document

---

[96] *Rochefoucauld v. Boustead* [1897] 1 Ch. 196; *Re Boyes* (1884) 26 Ch.D. 531.
[97] *Fred. Drughorn Ltd. v. Rederiaktiebolaget Transatlantic* [1919] A.C. 203; *Young v. Schuler* (1883) 11 Q.B.D. 651.
[98] *Fred. Drughorn Ltd. v. Red. Transatlantic, supra.*
[99] *Danziger v. Thompson* [1944] K.B. 654.
[1] *Epps v. Rothnie* [1945] K.B. 562.
[2] *Humble v. Hunter* (1848) 12 Q.B. 310.
[3] *Formby v. Formby* (1910) 102 L.T. 116.
[4] *Pym v. Campbell* (1856) 6 E. & B. 370; *Dobell v. Stevens* (1825) 3 B. & C. 632; *Whittington v. Seale-Hayne* (1900) 82 L.T. 49; *Murray v. Parker* (1854) 19 Beav. 305.
[5] Administration of Justice Act 1982, s.20. See *post,* p. 362.

contains such words as "for value received,"[6] Similarly, evidence may be given of the legality or illegality of the consideration.[7] Normally, consideration is irrelevant in the case of a deed, but if it is relevant, and no consideration or merely nominal consideration is referred to therein, parol evidence may be admitted to show that the true consideration was a valuable one.[8] Where in a written hire-purchase agreement the consideration was expressed to be an amount which put the agreement outside the Hire-Purchase Acts, extrinsic evidence was allowed to show that the true consideration made those Acts applicable.[9]

7. *Subsequent modification or rescission of transaction.* Written contracts not required by law to be in writing may, at any time before breach, be modified or rescinded by parol.[10] A written contract required by law to be in writing may also be wholly rescinded by an oral agreement[11] (though the latter be unenforceable because not in writing), but cannot be partially abandoned or varied thereby.[12] If variation is thus attempted, the original contract will still be binding.[13] Contracts by deed could, at common law, neither be rescinded nor varied by parol.[14] Now, however, deeds, though they cannot technically be released, may be varied[15] or wholly discharged by parol agreement, if made for valuable consideration.[16]

3. The Use of Extrinsic Evidence to Interpret a Document

Once the terms of a document have been established in the ways mentioned in the previous section, the question may arise as to what the author of the document (the parties in the case of a contract or the testator in the case of a will) meant by the words used. In particular, the question will be, how far may extrinsic evidence be resorted to for the purpose of finding this meaning. It will be appreciated that the task of settling what a document means is not primarily for evidence at all. There are rules for the

[6] *Abbott* v. *Hendricks* (1840) 1 M. & G. 791.
[7] *Collins* v. *Blantern* (1767) 2 Wils.K.B. 341; *Woods* v. *Wise* [1955] 2 Q.B. 29.
[8] *Turner* v. *Forwood* [1951] 1 All E.R. 746.
[9] *Campbell Discount Co.* v. *Gall* [1961] 1 Q.B. 431.
[10] *Goss* v. *Nugent* (1833) 5 B. & Ad. 58 at p. 65.
[11] *Morris* v. *Baron* [1918] A.C. 1; *Noble* v. *Ward* (1867) L.R. 2 Ex. 135.
[12] *Goss* v. *Nugent, supra; Noble* v. *Ward, supra.*
[13] *Noble* v. *Ward, supra.*
[14] *Steeds* v. *Steeds* (1889) 22 Q.B.D. 537.
[15] *Williams* v. *Stern* (1879) 5 Q.B. 409; *Berry* v. *Berry* [1929] 2 K.B. 316; but see *Kellett* v. *Stockport* (1906) 70 J.P. 154.
[16] *Steeds* v. *Steeds, supra.*

interpretation of documents which will be resorted to, and which are found in books devoted to interpretation or construction. However, in the past, many of these rules have been stated as rendering wholly inadmissible any attempt to demonstrate by evidence what the maker intended; and those rules, and the exceptions thereto, have on that account traditionally been accorded an ample treatment in books on evidence.[17] But the modern view is that extrinsic evidence is almost always allowed (although it may not always prevail) and the rules which positively forbid evidence are very few in number, so perhaps a work on evidence may be allowed to treat the matter shortly, and refer the enquirer to the books on wills or contracts, where the rules of construction are to be found.

In one sense any court attempting to give effect to a document cannot possibly act without extrinsic evidence, because it will need to identify the person or thing which is the object or subject of it. A simple bequest of "my grandfather clock to my eldest son" could not be given effect to without evidence as to which clock was the one referred to and which person is the eldest son of the testator. If the meaning of the writer is plain, and the only question is whether this is the clock owned by the testator (or whether it is the one owned by his lodger), or whether this person is the eldest son (or whether he is an impostor) the question, which is not one of interpretation at all, is only capable of being settled by evidence.

The sort of case we are concerned with here is where the controversy is essentially over what the maker meant. There are two grandfather clocks belonging to him, and the question is, which did he mean? Or a claimant admits that he is not the eldest son of the testator but insists nevertheless that he is the person whom the testator meant to benefit. The problem then posed is how far may questions of meaning be resolved by appeal to any "evidence" other than the words themselves?

It is obvious that the court must begin its task by looking at the actual words used. If the entire question was, what do the *words* mean? that would usually be easily answered, for the court judicially notes the meaning of ordinary English words, and may refresh its memory from dictionaries.[18] But the question is not, what do the words mean? but what did the author mean when he used these words?[19] To answer that the court may take into

[17] See, *e.g.* Phipson, Chap. 39.
[18] See *ante*, pp. 34, 38.
[19] *Perrin* v. *Morgan* [1943] A.C. 399 at p. 406; *River Wear Commissioners* v. *Adamson* (1877) 2 App.Cas. 743 at p. 763.

account, not only the context of the document as a whole (avoiding a line by line interpretation)[20] but also, more importantly for present purposes, by putting itself in the position of the author ("sitting itself in his armchair"[21]) and hearing evidence of his age and education, his relations with persons and things mentioned in the document, the things he knew when he wrote the document.[22] It may be that what was ambiguous before this process was applied will then become plain. Moreover there are certain presumptions which operate in elucidating meaning. Thus it is presumed that ordinary words are used in their ordinary meaning,[23] that technical words are used in their technical meaning,[24] that accepted rules of English grammar apply,[25] that a description of an object or person which fits exactly a given object or person is meant to indicate that object or person.[26] However if a word has two or more ordinary meanings, or an ordinary meaning and a special meaning in the writer's particular walk of life, there is no presumption that any particular meaning was intended.[27]

It may be that ambiguity remains *because* no presumption applies (*e.g.* there are two or more ordinary meanings to the words used, for instance "my money"[28]), or *after* a presumption is applied (*e.g.* there are two persons who fit the description exactly). Where this is the case, the ambiguity may be resolved under the armchair principle, *i.e.* by extrinsic evidence showing the author's circumstances, knowledge, etc.[29]

But it is different where a presumption dictates a particular unambiguous answer, but a party alleges that that is not what the

---

[20] *Grey* v. *Pearson* (1857) 6 H.L.C. 61 at p. 99; *Key* v. *Key* (1853) 8 De G.M. & G. 73 at pp. 84–85.
[21] See James L.J. in *Boyes* v. *Cook* (1880) 14 Ch.D. 53 at p. 56.
[22] *Allgood* v. *Blake* (1873) L.R. 8 Ex. 160 at p. 162; *Doe d. Hiscocks* v. *Hiscocks* (1839) 5 M. & W. 363 at pp. 367–368; *Charter* v. *Charter* (1874) L.R. 7 H.L. 364, at p. 377. *River Wear Commissioners* v. *Adamson, supra*.
[23] *Shore* v. *Wilson* (1842) 9 Cl. & F. 355 at p. 565; *Gorringe* v. *Mahlstedt* [1907] A.C. 225 at p. 227.
[24] *Doe d. Winter* v. *Perratt* (1843) 6 M. & G. 314 at pp. 342–343; *Falkiner* v. *Commissioner of Stamp Duties* [1973] A.C. 565 at pp. 577–578.
[25] *Castledon* v. *Turner* (1745) 3 Atk. 257; *Roddy* v. *Fitzgerald* (1858) 6 H.L.C. 876.
[26] *N.S.P.C.C.* v. *Scottish N.S.P.C.C.* [1915] A.C. 207 at pp. 212, 216.
[27] *Perrin* v. *Morgan* [1943] A.C. 399, at pp. 406–408; *Richardson* v. *Watson* (1833) 4 B. & Ad. 787 at p. 799; *Re Gillson* [1949] Ch. 99.
[28] *Perrin* v. *Morgan, supra*.
[29] If a conveyance does not clearly define the land or interest transferred (*e.g.* because the annexed plan is too small to be of use), extrinsic evidence, such as the auction particulars, is admissible to make clear what was transferred; *Neilson* v. *Poole* (1969) 20 P. & C.R. 909; *Scarfe* v. *Adams* [1981] 1 All E.R. 843.

writer meant (*e.g.* a reference to "John Q. Smith," there is a person called John Q. Smith, but it is alleged that the writer intended another person called James Q. Smith). The party is still entitled to adduce extrinsic evidence to support his assertion (after all, the presumption that a correct description is properly applied *is* only a presumption)[30]; but the armchair principle is not enough to rebut the presumption. The evidence must show *either*:

(i) That the writer used words or names in an unusual or incorrect fashion (that he "used his own dictionary"). He is after all entitled to use words how he wishes or to call people by whatever names he chooses, provided it is clear that he did so.[31] So it would not be sufficient to show that he probably made a mistake and really intended to benefit James, because, *e.g.* he disliked John intensely[32]; it must be shown that he called James, John[33]; *or*

(ii) In a case where the application of the presumption (*e.g.* that he meant the person whom he accurately described), does not make sense,[34] that there is an inaccurate use of words or description which does make sense.[35] It may well be difficult to show either of these two things by extrinsic evidence, but since the party is entitled to try, it is wrong to say that extrinsic evidence is *inadmissible* for the purpose of rebutting these presumptions about meaning.

There were really only two positively prohibitive rules of evidence, and they were probably confined to wills, since the reasons for them were (a) the statutory rule that in all ordinary cases the intention of the testator must be found in his will and nowhere else, and (b) the absence of any jurisdiction to rectify a will. These rules were:

(i) The court could not make a will which the testator did not

---

[30] See *N.S.P.C.C.* v. *Scottish N.S.P.C.C., supra.*
[31] *Re Cook* [1948] Ch. 212 at p. 216. As between words and author "the question is, which is to be master, that's all" per Humpty Dumpty, in *Through the Looking Glass*, Ch. 6.
[32] See *Sherratt* v. *Mountford* (1873) L.R. 8 Ch.App. 928.
[33] See, *e.g. Lee* v. *Pain* (1845) 4 Hare 251. This will usually require evidence that he *habitually* called James, John; but evidence that he called James, John once on an *important* occasion has been held to suffice: *Re Ofner* [1909] 1 Ch. 60.
[34] "An absurdity or inconvenience so great as to convince the court that the words could not have been used in their proper signification": per Blackburn J., in *Allgood* v. *Blake* (1873) L.R. 8 Excheq. 160 at pp. 163–164; a "strong" or "complete" improbability, per Denning M.R. and Danckwerts L.J. respectively in *Re Jebb* [1966] Ch. 666 at pp. 672, 674.
[35] See *Re Smalley* [1929] 2 Ch. 112.

himself make.[36] Because of this, extrinsic evidence was rejected if it was aimed at giving a meaning to the words which they just could not bear,[37] or at filling in blanks in the will.[38] With wills coming into effect on or after January 1, 1983, the court can rectify a will so as to carry out the testator's intentions, if as written it fails to carry out those intentions in consequence of a clerical error[39] or a failure to understand his instructions, provided an application to do so is made within (usually) six months of grant of probate.[40] Apart from clerical slips and misunderstood instructions, the rule remains as formerly. Thus evidence that the testator's *instructions* failed to carry out his intentions, or that his instructions were not misunderstood but deliberately departed from by the draftsman, will still be rejected.

With contracts, although the court cannot make one for the parties, a party has always been able to show by extrinsic evidence that the written contract does not accurately express their complete agreement, so as to get the written contract rectified.[41]

(ii) Save in one case, the extrinsic evidence of the testator's intention had to be circumstantial. Direct evidence of that, *i.e.* of his declarations on the point, was inadmissible.[42] The exceptional case was equivocations, where the words of the will applied equally to two or more subjects or objects, *e.g.* "my son," when he had two sons.[43] To solve such an equivocation circumstantial or direct evidence of the testator's intention was admissible, but in all other cases where extrinsic evidence was allowed, it had to be circumstantial.

With a will taking effect on or after January 1, 1983, direct or circumstantial evidence may be admitted to assist in its interpretation, in so far as it is meaningless, or in so far as the language is ambiguous on the face of it or in the light of surrounding

---

[36] *Allgood* v. *Blake* (1873) L.R. 3 Exch. 160 at pp. 163–164; *Perrin* v. *Morgan* [1943] A.C. 399 at p. 420.

[37] *Higgins* v. *Dawson* [1902] A.C. 1; unless indeed it was sought to show that the testator had his own peculiar meanings of words, under the dictionary principle, *ante*, p. 361.

[38] *Bayliss* v. *Att.-Gen.* (1741) 2 Atk. 239; *Hunt* v. *Hort* (1791) 3 Br.C.C. 311.

[39] Including, probably, a "writing" slip by the testator himself in a homemade will: see *Re Williams* [1985] 1 All E.R. 964 at p. 969, or in his instructions to the draftsman.

[40] Administration of Justice Act 1982, s.20.

[41] *Ante*, p. 357.

[42] *Doe* d. *Hiscocks* v. *Hiscocks* (1839) 5 M. & W. 363.

[43] *Doe* d. *Gord* v. *Needs* (1836) 2 M. & W. 129; *Re Hubbuck* [1905] P. 129.

circumstances.[44] So far as concerns circumstantial evidence, the area where this may be used is not extended, for that could be used to explain any kind of ambiguity, and as to meaninglessness, circumstantial evidence was allowed to explain "coded" messages, meaningless on their face.[45] Complete blanks could not be elucidated by evidence, and no doubt that is still the case, because there is nothing to interpret. In contrast, the area where *direct* evidence, *i.e.* evidence of the testator's intention, may be used is greatly expanded from merely solving equivocations to resolving all the kinds of ambiguities on which circumstantial evidence could be employed. However, the evidence, direct or circumstantial, is admitted only to *assist in the will's interpretation.* If the possible meanings on the face of a will are X and Y (so that there is an ambiguity), and the declarations of the testator show that meaning Z was intended (which meaning the will's language cannot bear), the Court cannot declare Z to be the meaning.[46] If Z is what the testator wanted, the proper course is an attempt to get the will rectified under section 20.

Except for this statutory relaxation, the rule remains—direct evidence of a settlor's intentions (or his draftsman's intentions, which are treated as his[47]) is inadmissible to interpret the words used. With contracts, direct evidence of what a party intended is usually rejected for a quite different reason, *i.e.* that his subjective intention is irrelevant anyway. English contract law adopts the objective test of intention; it is not what a party actually intended which is important, it is what a reasonable person in the position of the other party would think he intended. But if this objective test itself produces ambiguity, as where a contract deals with a cargo of cotton arriving ex *Peerless* from Bombay, and there are two ships of that name loaded with cotton from Bombay,[48] extrinsic evidence, both circumstantial and direct, is allowed of what the parties both,[49] or each,[50] intended.

As to circumstantial evidence, contracts, like wills, do not exist in a vacuum, and have a background or context which may be given in evidence,[51] *e.g.* to identify the meaning of descriptive terms by reference to mutually known facts.[52] But a lot of the

[44] Administration of Justice Act 1982, s.21.
[45] *Kell* v. *Charmer* (1856) 23 Beav. 195; *Abbott* v. *Massie* (1796) 3 Ves. 148.
[46] *Re Williams* [1985] 1 All E.R. 964.
[47] *Rabin* v. *Gerson Berger Association* [1986] 1 All E.R. 374 (C.A.).
[48] See *Raffles* v. *Wichelhaus* (1864) 2 H. & C. 906.
[49] *Brunton* v. *Dullens* (1859) 1 F. & F. 450.
[50] *Raffles* v. *Wichelhaus, supra.*
[51] *River Wear Commissioners* v. *Adamson* (1877) 2 App.Cas. 743.
[52] *MacDonald* v. *Longbottom* (1859) 1 E. & E. 977.

background in contract cases is irrelevant; pre-contract negotiations because they *are* negotiations, where the parties' positions are changing constantly,[53] and post-contract behaviour[54] (unless it amounts to a new agreement or estoppel),[55] because it is wrong to deduce what a man is bound to do from evidence of what he in fact did; that would be to encourage men to be churlish and to abstain from doing anything other than what they were strictly bound to do.[56]

---

[53] *Prenn* v. *Simmonds* [1971] 1 W.L.R. 1381.
[54] *Schuler A.G.* v. *Wickman Ltd.* [1974] A.C. 235; *Jos. Miller & Partners* v. *Whitworth St. Estates* [1970] A.C. 583.
[55] *Ante*, p. 311.
[56] *St. Edmundsbury Board of Finance* v. *Clark (No. 2)* [1973] 3 All E.R. 902, per Megarry V.-C. at p. 915. In that case it was held that disputed parcels in a deed, or disputed boundaries, are different from matters of obligation, and can be settled by reference to how the parties behaved. See also *Watcham* v. *Att.-Gen. of East Africa Protectorate* [1919] A.C. 533; *Neilson* v. *Poole* (1969) 20 P. & C.R. 909 at p. 914.

APPENDICES

	Page
Appendix 1	
Section 1 of the Criminal Evidence Act 1898	367
Appendix 2	
Civil Evidence Act 1968	369
Appendix 3	
Police and Criminal Evidence Act 1984 Parts VII and VIII, Schedule 3	390
Appendix 4	
Extracts from Code of Practice for the Detention, Treatment and Questioning of Persons by Police Officers	404
Appendix 5	
Extracts from Code of Practice for the Identification of Persons by Police Officers	410

Appendix 1

SECTION 1 OF THE CRIMINAL EVIDENCE ACT 1898[1]

Every person charged with an offence shall be a competent witness for the defence at every stage of the proceedings, whether the person so charged is charged solely or jointly with any other person. Provided as follows:

  (a) A person so charged shall not be called as a witness in pursuance of this Act except upon his own application:

  (b) The failure of any person charged with an offence to give evidence shall not be made the subject of any comment by the prosecution:

  (e) A person charged and being a witness in pursuance of this Act may be asked any question in cross-examination notwithstanding that it would tend to criminate him as to the offence charged:

  (f) A person charged and called as a witness in pursuance of this Act shall not be asked, and if asked shall not be required to answer, any question tending to show that he has committed or been convicted of or been charged with any offence other than that wherewith he is then charged, or is of bad character, unless—

(i) the proof that he has committed or been convicted of such other offence is admissible evidence to show that he is guilty of the offence wherewith he is then charged; or
(ii) he has personally or by his advocate asked questions of the witnesses for the prosecution with a view to establish his own good character, or has given evidence of his good character, or the nature or conduct of the defence is such as to involve imputations on the character of the prosecutor or the witnesses for the prosecution; or
(iii) he has given evidence against any other person charged in the same proceedings.

---

[1] As amended by Criminal Evidence Act 1979, s.1; Criminal Justice Act 1982, Sched. 16; Police and Criminal Evidence Act 1984, Sched. 7. The main provisions of this section are dealt with in Chaps. 7 and 11, pp. 129 *et seq.* and pp. 221 *et seq.*.

(g) Every person called as a witness in pursuance of this Act shall, unless otherwise ordered by the Court, give his evidence from the witness box or other place from which the other witnesses give their evidence:

APPENDIX 2

CIVIL EVIDENCE ACT 1968

PART I—HEARSAY EVIDENCE[1]

Hearsay evidence to be admissible only by virtue of this Act and other statutory provisions, or by agreement

1.—(1) In any civil proceedings a statement other than one made by a person while giving oral evidence in those proceedings shall be admissible as evidence of any fact stated therein to the extent that it is so admissible by virtue of any provision of this Part of this Act or by virtue of any other statutory provision or by agreement of the parties, but not otherwise.

(2) In this section "statutory provision" means any provision contained in, or in an instrument made under, this or any other Act, including any Act passed after this Act.

Admissibility of out-of-court statements as evidence of facts stated

2.—(1) In any civil proceedings a statement made, whether orally or in a document or otherwise, by any person, whether called as a witness in those proceedings or not, shall, subject to this section and to rules of court, be admissible as evidence of any fact stated therein of which direct oral evidence by him would be admissible.

(2) Where in any civil proceedings a party desiring to give a statement in evidence by virtue of this section has called or intends to call as a witness in the proceedings the person by whom the statement was made, the statement—
- (a) shall not be given in evidence by virtue of this section on behalf of that party without the leave of the court; and
- (b) without prejudice to paragraph (a) above, shall not be given in evidence by virtue of this section on behalf of that party before the conclusion of the examination-in-chief of the person by whom it was made, except—
  - (i) where before that person is called the court allows evidence of the making of the statement to be given on behalf of that party by some other person; or
  - (ii) in so far as the court allows the person by whom the

---

[1] The main provisions of this Part are dealt with in Chap. 13, *ante*.

statement was made to narrate it in the course of his examination-in-chief on the ground that to prevent him from doing so would adversely affect the intelligibility of his evidence.

(3) Where in any civil proceedings a statement which was made otherwise than in a document is admissible by virtue of this section, no evidence other than direct oral evidence by the person who made the statement or any person who heard or otherwise perceived it being made shall be admissible for the purpose of proving it:

Provided that if the statement in question was made by a person while giving oral evidence in some other legal proceedings (whether civil or criminal), it may be proved in any manner authorised by the court.

Witness's previous statement, if proved, to be evidence of facts stated

3.—(1) Where in any civil proceedings—
- (a) a previous inconsistent or contradictory statement made by a person called as a witness in those proceedings is proved by virtue of section 3, 4 or 5 of the Criminal Procedure Act 1865; or
- (b) a previous statement made by a person called as aforesaid is proved for the purpose of rebutting a suggestion that his evidence has been fabricated,

that statement shall by virtue of this subsection be admissible as evidence of any fact stated therein of which direct oral evidence by him would be admissible.

(2) Nothing in this Act shall affect any of the rules of law relating to the circumstances in which, where a person called as a witness in any civil proceedings is cross-examined on a document used by him to refresh his memory, that document may be made evidence in those proceedings; and where a document or any part of a document is received in evidence in any such proceedings by virtue of any such rule of law, any statement made in that document or part by the person using the document to refresh his memory shall by virtue of this subsection be admissible as evidence of any fact stated therein of which direct oral evidence by him would be admissible.

Admissibility of certain records as evidence of facts stated

4.—(1) Without prejudice to section 5 of this Act, in any civil proceedings a statement contained in a document shall, subject to this section and to rules of court, be admissible as evidence of any fact stated therein of which direct oral evidence would be admissible, if the document is, or forms part of, a record compiled by a person acting under a duty from information which was supplied by a person (whether acting under a duty or not) who had, or may reasonably be supposed to have had, personal knowledge of the matters dealt with in that information and which, if not supplied by that person to the compiler of the record directly, was supplied by him to the compiler of the record indirectly through one or more intermediaries each acting under a duty.

(2) Where in any civil proceedings a party desiring to give a statement in evidence by virtue of this section has called or intends to call as a witness in the proceedings the person who originally supplied the information from which the record containing the statement was compiled, the statement—
- (*a*) shall not be given in evidence by virtue of this section on behalf of that party without the leave of the court; and
- (*b*) without prejudice to paragraph (*a*) above, shall not without the leave of the court be given in evidence by virtue of this section on behalf of that party before the conclusion of the examination-in-chief of the person who originally supplied the said information.

(3) Any reference in this section to a person acting under a duty includes a reference to a person acting in the course of any trade, business, profession or other occupation in which he is engaged or employed or for the purposes of any paid or unpaid office held by him.

Admissibility of statements produced by computers

5.—(1) In any civil proceedings a statement contained in a document produced by a computer shall, subject to rules of court, be admissible as evidence of any fact stated therein of which direct oral evidence would be admissible, if it is shown that the conditions mentioned in subsection (2) below are satisfied in relation to the statement and computer in question.

(2) The said conditions are—
- (*a*) that the document containing the statement was produced by the computer during a period over which the computer was used regularly to store or process information for the purposes of any activities regularly carried on over that period, whether for profit or not, by any body, whether corporate or not, or by any individual;
- (*b*) that over that period there was regularly supplied to the computer in the ordinary course of those activities

information of the kind contained in the statement or of the kind from which the information so contained is derived;
(c) that throughout the material part of that period the computer was operating properly or, if not, that any respect in which it was not operating properly or was out of operation during that part of that period was not such as to affect the production of the document or the accuracy of its contents; and
(d) that the information contained in the statement reproduces or is derived from information supplied to the computer in the ordinary course of those activities.

(3) Where over a period the function of storing or processing information for the purpose of any activities regularly carried on over that period as mentioned in subsection (2)(a) above was regularly performed by computers, whether—
(a) by a combination of computers operating over that period; or
(b) by different computers operating in succession over that period; or
(c) by different combinations of computers operating in succession over that period; or
(d) in any other manner involving the successive operation over that period, in whatever order, of one or more computers and one or more combinations of computers,

all the computers used for that purpose during that period shall be treated for the purpose of this Part of this Act as constituting a single computer; and references in this Part of this Act to a computer shall be construed accordingly.

(4) In any civil proceedings where it is desired to give a statement in evidence by virtue of this section, a certificate doing any of the following things, that is to say—
(a) identifying the document containing the statement and describing the manner in which it was produced;
(b) giving such particulars of any device involved in the production of that document as may be appropriate for the purpose of showing that the document was produced by a computer;
(c) dealing with any of the matters to which the conditions mentioned in subsection (2) above relate,

and purporting to be signed by a person occupying a responsible position in relation to the operation of the relevant device or the management of the relevant activities (whichever is appropriate) shall be evidence of any matter stated in the certificate; and for

the purposes of this subsection it shall be sufficient for a matter to be stated to the best of the knowledge and belief of the person stating it.
   (5) For the purposes of this Part of this Act—
   (*a*) information shall be taken to be supplied to a computer if it is supplied thereto in any appropriate form and whether it is so supplied directly or (with or without human intervention) by means of any appropriate equipment;
   (*b*) where, in the course of activities carried on by any individual or body, information is supplied with a view to its being stored or processed for the purposes of those activities by a computer operated otherwise than in the course of those activities, that information, if duly supplied to that computer, shall be taken to be supplied to it in the course of those activities;
   (*c*) a document shall be taken to have been produced by a computer whether it was produced by it directly or (with or without human intervention) by means of any appropriate equipment.
   (6) Subject to subsection (3) above, in this Part of this Act "computer" means any device for storing and processing information, and any reference to information being derived from other information is a reference to its being derived therefrom by calculation, comparison or any other process.

Provisions supplementary to ss.2 to 5

   6.—(1) Where in any civil proceedings a statement contained in a document is proposed to be given in evidence by virtue of section 2, 4 or 5 of this Act it may, subject to any rules of court, be proved by the production of that document or (whether or not that document is still in existence) by the production of a copy of that document, or of the material part thereof, authenticated in such a manner as the court may approve.
   (2) For the purpose of deciding whether or not a statement is admissible in evidence by virtue of section 2, 4 or 5 of this Act, the court may draw any reasonable inference from the circumstances in which the statement was made or otherwise came into being or from any other circumstances, including, in the case of a statement contained in a document, the form and contents of that document.
   (3) In estimating the weight, if any, to be attached to a statement admissible in evidence by virtue of section 2, 3, 4 or 5 of this Act regard shall be had to all the circumstances from which

any inference can reasonably be drawn as to the accuracy or otherwise of the statement and, in particular—
- (*a*) in the case of a statement falling within section 2(1) or 3(1) or (2) of this Act, to the question whether or not the statement was made contemporaneously with the occurrence or existence of the facts stated, and to the question whether or not the maker of the statement had any incentive to conceal or misrepresent the facts;
- (*b*) in the case of a statement falling within section 4(1) of this Act, to the question whether or not the person who originally supplied the information from which the record containing the statement was compiled did so contemporaneously with the occurrence or existence of the facts dealt with in that information, and to the question whether or not that person, or any person concerned with compiling or keeping the record containing the statement, had any incentive to conceal or misrepresent the facts; and
- (*c*) in the case of a statement falling within section 5(1) of this Act, to the question whether or not the information which the information contained in the statement reproduces or is derived from was supplied to the relevant computer, or recorded for the purpose of being supplied thereto, contemporaneously with the occurrence or existence of the facts dealt with in that information, and to the question whether or not any person concerned with the supply of information to that computer, or with the operation of that computer or any equipment by means of which the document containing the statement was produced by it, had any incentive to conceal or misrepresent the facts.

(4) For the purpose of any enactment or rule of law or practice requiring evidence to be corroborated or regulating the manner in which uncorroborated evidence is to be treated—
- (*a*) a statement which is admissible in evidence by virtue of section 2 or 3 of this Act shall not be capable of corroborating evidence given by the maker of the statement; and
- (*b*) a statement which is admissible in evidence by virtue of section 4 of this Act shall not be capable of corroborating evidence given by the person who originally supplied the information from which the record containing the statement was compiled.

(5) If any person in a certificate tendered in evidence in civil proceedings by virtue of section 5(4) of this Act wilfully makes a statement material in those proceedings which he knows to be

false or does not believe to be true, he shall be liable on conviction on indictment to imprisonment for a term not exceeding two years or a fine or both.

Admissibility of evidence as to credibility of maker, etc., of statement admitted under s.2 or 4

7.—(1) Subject to rules of court, where in any civil proceedings a statement made by a person who is not called as a witness in those proceedings is given in evidence by virtue of section 2 of this Act—
- (a) any evidence which, if that person had been so called, would be admissible for the purpose of destroying or supporting his credibility as a witness shall be admissible for that purpose in those proceedings; and
- (b) evidence tending to prove that, whether before or after he made that statement, that person made (whether orally or in a document or otherwise) another statement inconsistent therewith shall be admissible for the purpose of showing that that person has contradicted himself;

Provided that nothing in this subsection shall enable evidence to be given of any matter of which, if the person in question had been called as a witness and had denied that matter in cross-examination, evidence could not have been adduced by the cross-examining party.

(2) Subsection (1) above shall apply in relation to a statement given in evidence by virtue of section 4 of this Act as it applies in relation to a statement given in evidence by virtue of section 2 of this Act, except that references to the person who made the statement and to his making the statement shall be construed respectively as references to the person who originally supplied the information from which the record containing the statement was compiled and to his supplying that information.

(3) Section 3(1) of this Act shall apply to any statement proved by virtue of subsection (1)(b) above as it applies to a previous inconsistent or contradictory statement made by a person called as a witness which is proved as mentioned in paragraph (a) of the said section 3(1).

Rules of court

8.—(1) Provision shall be made by rules of court as to the procedure which, subject to any exceptions provided for in the rules, must be followed and the other conditions which, subject as aforesaid, must be fulfilled before a statement can be given in evidence in civil proceedings by virtue of section 2, 4 or 5 of this Act.

(2) Rules of court made in pursuance of subsection (1) above shall in particular, subject to such exceptions (if any) as may be provided for in the rules—
- (*a*) require a party to any civil proceedings who desires to give in evidence any such statement as is mentioned in that subsection to give to every other party to the proceedings such notice of his desire to do so and such particulars of or relating to the statement as may be specified in the rules, including particulars of such one or more of the persons connected with the making or recording of the statement or, in the case of a statement falling within section 5(1) of this Act, such one or more of the persons concerned as mentioned in section 6(3)(*c*) of this Act as the rules may in any case require; and
- (*b*) enable any party who receives such notice as aforesaid by counter-notice to require any person of whom particulars were given with the notice to be called as a witness in the proceedings unless that person is dead or beyond the seas, or unfit by reason of his bodily or mental condition to attend as a witness, or cannot with reasonable diligence be identified or found, or cannot reasonably be expected (having regard to the time which has elapsed since he was connected or concerned as aforesaid and to all the circumstances) to have any recollection of matters relevant to the accuracy or otherwise of the statement.

(3) Rules of court made in pursuance of subsection (1) above—
- (*a*) may confer on the court in any civil proceedings a discretion to allow a statement falling within section 2(1), 4(1) or 5(1) of this Act to be given in evidence notwithstanding that any requirement of the rules affecting the admissibility of that statement has not been complied with, but except in pursuance of paragraph (*b*) below shall not confer on the court a discretion to exclude such a statement where the requirements of the rules affecting its admissibility have been complied with;
- (*b*) may confer on the court power, where a party to any civil proceedings has given notice that he desires to give in evidence—
    (i) a statement falling within section 2(1) of this Act which was made by a person, whether orally or in a document, in the course of giving evidence in some other legal proceedings (whether civil or criminal); or

Appendix 2

　　(ii) a statement falling within section 4(1) of this Act which is contained in a record of any direct oral evidence given in some other legal proceedings (whether civil or criminal),

　　　to give directions on the application of any party to the proceedings as to whether, and if so on what conditions, the party desiring to give the statement in evidence will be permitted to do so and (where applicable) as to the manner in which that statement and any other evidence given in those other proceedings is to be proved; and

　(c) may make different provision for different circumstances, and in particular may make different provision with respect to statements falling within sections 2(1), 4(1) and 5(1) of this Act respectively;

and any discretion conferred on the court by rules of court made as aforesaid may be either a general discretion or a discretion exercisable only in such circumstances as may be specified in the rules.

(4) Rules of court may make provision for preventing a party to any civil proceedings (subject to any exceptions provided for in the rules) from adducing in relation to a person who is not called as a witness in those proceedings any evidence which could otherwise be adduced by him by virtue of section 7 of this Act unless that party has in pursuance of the rules given in respect of that person such a counter-notice as is mentioned in subsection (2)(b) above.

(5) In deciding for the purposes of any rules of court made in pursuance of this section whether or not a person is fit to attend as a witness, a court may act on a certificate purporting to be a certificate of a fully registered medical practitioner.

(6) Nothing in the foregoing provisions of this section shall prejudice the generality of section 99 of the Supreme Court of Judicature (Consolidation) Act 1925, section 102 of the County Courts Act 1959, section 15 of the Justices of the Peace Act 1949 or any other enactment conferring power to make rules of court; and nothing in section 101 of the Supreme Court of Judicature (Consolidation) Act 1925, section 102(2) of the County Courts Act 1959 or any other enactment restricting the matters with respect to which rules of court may be made shall prejudice the making of rules of court with respect to any matter mentioned in the foregoing provisions of this section or the operation of any rules of court made with respect to any such matter.

Admissibility of certain hearsay evidence formerly admissible at common law

9.—(1) In any civil proceedings a statement which, if this Part of this Act had not been passed, would by virtue of any rule of law mentioned in subsection (2) below have been admissible as evidence of any fact stated therein shall be admissible as evidence of that fact by virtue of this subsection.

(2) The rules of law referred to in subsection (1) above are the following, that is to say any rule of law—
- (*a*) whereby in any civil proceedings an admission adverse to a party to the proceedings, whether made by that party or by another person, may be given in evidence against that party for the purpose of proving any fact stated in the admission;
- (*b*) whereby in any civil proceedings published works dealing with matters of a public nature (for example, histories, scientific works, dictionaries and maps) are admissible as evidence of facts of a public nature stated therein;
- (*c*) whereby in any civil proceedings public documents (for example, public registers, and returns made under public authority with respect to matters of public interest) are admissible as evidence of facts stated therein; or
- (*d*) whereby in any civil proceedings records (for example, the records of certain courts, treaties, Crown grants, pardons and commissions) are admissible as evidence of facts stated therein.

In this subsection "admission" includes any representation of fact, whether made in words or otherwise.

(3) In any civil proceedings a statement which tends to establish reputation or family tradition with respect to any matter and which, if this Act had not been passed, would have been admissible in evidence by virtue of any rule of law mentioned in subsection (4) below—
- (*a*) shall be admissible in evidence by virtue of this paragraph in so far as it is not capable of being rendered admissible under section 2 or 4 of this Act; and
- (*b*) if given in evidence under this Part of this Act (whether by virtue of paragraph (*a*) above or otherwise) shall by virtue of this paragraph be admissible as evidence of the matter reputed or handed down;

and, without prejudice to paragraph (*b*) above, reputation shall for the purposes of this Part of this Act be treated as a fact and not as a statement or multiplicity of statements dealing with the matter reputed.

(4) The rules of law referred to in subsection (3) above are the following, that is to say any rule of law—
  (a) whereby in any civil proceedings evidence of a person's reputation is admissible for the purpose of establishing his good or bad character;
  (b) whereby in any civil proceedings involving a question of pedigree or in which the existence of a marriage is in issue evidence of reputation or family tradition is admissible for the purpose of proving or disproving pedigree or the existence of the marriage, as the case may be; or
  (c) whereby in any civil proceedings evidence of reputation or family tradition is admissible for the purpose of proving or disproving the existence of any public or general right or of identifying any person or thing.

(5) It is hereby declared that in so far as any statement is admissible in any civil proceedings by virtue of subsection (1) or (3)(a) above, it may be given in evidence in those proceedings notwithstanding anything in sections 2 to 7 of this Act or in any rules of court made in pursuance of section 8 of this Act.

(6) The words in which any rule of law mentioned in subsection (2) or (4) above is there described are intended only to identify the rule in question and shall not be construed as altering that rule in any way.

Interpretation of Part I, and application to arbitrations, etc.

10.—(1) In this Part of this Act—
  "computer" has the meaning assigned by section 5 of this Act;
  "document" includes, in addition to a document in writing—
    (a) any map, plan, graph or drawing;
    (b) any photograph;
    (c) any disc, tape, sound track or other device in which sounds or other data (not being visual images) are embodied so as to be capable (with or without the aid of some other equipment) of being reproduced therefrom; and
    (d) any film, negative, tape or other device in which one or more visual images are embodied so as to be capable (as aforesaid) of being reproduced therefrom;
  "film" includes a microfilm;
  "statement" includes any representation of fact, whether made in words or otherwise.

(2) In this Part of this Act any reference to a copy of a document includes—

(a) in the case of a document falling within paragraph (c) but not (d) of the definition of "document" in the foregoing subsection, a transcript of the sounds or other data embodied therein;
(b) in the case of a document falling within paragraph (d) but not (c) of that definition, a reproduction or still reproduction of the image or images embodied therein, whether enlarged or not;
(c) in the case of a document falling within both those paragraphs, such a transcript together with such a still reproduction; and
(d) in the case of a document not falling within the said paragraph (d) of which a visual image is embodied in a document falling within that paragraph, a reproduction of that image, whether enlarged or not,

and any reference to a copy of the material part of a document shall be construed accordingly.

(3) For the purposes of the application of this Part of this Act in relation to any such civil proceedings as are mentioned in section 18(1)(a) and (b) of this Act, any rules of court made for the purposes of this Act under section 99 of the Supreme Court of Judicature (Consolidation) Act 1925 shall (except in so far as their operation is excluded by agreement) apply, subject to such modifications as may be appropriate, in like manner as they apply in relation to civil proceedings in the High Court:

Provided that in the case of a reference under section 92 of the County Courts Act 1959 this subsection shall have effect as if for the references to the said section 99 and to civil proceedings in the High Court there were substituted respectively references to section 102 of the County Courts Act 1959 and to proceedings in a county court.

(4) If any question arises as to what are, for the purposes of any such civil proceedings as are mentioned in section 18(1)(a) or (b) of this Act, the appropriate modifications of any such rule of court as is mentioned in subsection (3) above, that question shall, in default of agreement, be determined by the tribunal or the arbitrator or umpire, as the case may be.

Part II

Miscellaneous and General

Convictions, etc. as evidence of civil proceedings[2]

Convictions as evidence in civil proceedings

11.—(1) In any civil proceedings the fact that a person has been convicted of an offence by or before any court in the United Kingdom or by a court-martial there or elsewhere shall (subject to subsection (3) below) be admissible in evidence for the purpose of proving, where to do so is relevant to any issue in those proceedings, that he committed that offence, whether he was so convicted upon a plea of guilty or otherwise and whether or not he is a party to the civil proceedings; but no conviction other than a subsisting one shall be admissible in evidence by virtue of this section.

(2) In any civil proceedings in which by virtue of this section a person is proved to have been convicted of an offence by or before any court in the United Kingdom or by a court-martial there or elsewhere—

(a) he shall be taken to have committed that offence unless the contrary is proved; and

(b) without prejudice to the reception of any other admissible evidence for the purpose of identifying the facts on which the conviction was based, the contents of any document which is admissible as evidence of the conviction, and the contents of the information, complaint, indictment or charge-sheet on which the person in question was convicted, shall be admissible in evidence for that purpose.

(3) Nothing in this section shall prejudice the operation of section 13 of this Act or any other enactment whereby a conviction or a finding of fact in any criminal proceedings is for the purposes of any other proceedings made conclusive evidence of any fact.

(4) Where in any civil proceedings the contents of any document are admissible in evidence by virtue of subsection (2) above, a copy of that document, or of the material part thereof, purporting to be certified or otherwise authenticated by or on behalf of the court or authority having custody of that document shall be admissible in evidence and shall be taken to be a true copy of that document or part unless the contrary is shown.

[2] See Chap. 16, *ante.*

(5) Nothing in any of the following enactments, that is to say—
- (*a*) section 12 of the Criminal Justice Act 1948 (under which a conviction leading to probation or discharge is to be disregarded except as therein mentioned);
- (*b*) section 9 of the Criminal Justice (Scotland) Act 1949 (which makes similar provision in respect of convictions on indictment in Scotland); and
- (*c*) section 8 of the Probation Act (Northern Ireland) 1950 (which corresponds to the said section 12) or any corresponding enactment of the Parliament of Northern Ireland for the time being in force,

shall affect the operation of this section; and for the purposes of this section any order made by a court of summary jurisdiction in Scotland under section 1 or section 2 of the said Act of 1949 shall be treated as a conviction.

(6) In this section "court-martial" means a court-martial constituted under the Army Act 1955, the Air Force Act 1955 or the Naval Discipline Act 1957 or a disciplinary court constituted under section 50 of the said Act of 1957, and in relation to a court-martial "conviction", as regards a court-martial constituted under either of the said Acts of 1955, means a finding of guilty which is, or falls to be treated as, a finding of the court duly confirmed and, as regards a court-martial or disciplinary court constituted under the said Act of 1957, means a finding of guilty which is, or falls to be treated, as the finding of the court, and "convicted" shall be construed accordingly.

Findings of adultery and paternity as evidence in civil proceedings

12.—(1) In any civil proceedings—
- (*a*) the fact that a person has been found guilty of adultery in any matrimonial proceedings; and
- (*b*) the fact that a person has been adjudged to be the father of a child in affiliation proceedings before any court in the United Kingdom,

shall (subject to subsection (3) below) be admissible in evidence for the purpose of proving, where to do so is relevant to any issue in those civil proceedings, that he committed the adultery to which the finding relates or, as the case may be, is (or was) the father of that child, whether or not he offered any defence to the allegation of adultery or paternity and whether or not he is a party to the civil proceedings; but no finding or adjudication other than a subsisting one shall be admissible in evidence by virtue of this section.

(2) In any civil proceedings in which by virtue of this section a person is proved to have been found guilty of adultery as mentioned in subsection (1)(*a*) above or to have been adjudged to be the father of a child as mentioned in subsection (1)(*b*) above—

(*a*) he shall be taken to have committed the adultery to which the finding relates or, as the case may be, to be (or have been) the father of that child, unless the contrary is proved; and

(*b*) without prejudice to the reception of any other admissible evidence for the purpose of identifying the facts on which the finding or adjudication was based, the contents of any document which was before the court, or which contains any pronouncement of the court, in the matrimonial or affiliation proceedings in question shall be admissible in evidence for that purpose.

(3) Nothing in this section shall prejudice the operation of any enactment whereby a finding of fact in any matrimonial or affiliation proceedings is for the purposes of any other proceedings made conclusive evidence of any fact.

(4) Subsection (4) of section 11 of this Act shall apply for the purposes of this section as if the reference to subsection (2) were a reference to subsection (2) of this section.

(5) In this section—

"matrimonial proceedings" means any matrimonial cause in the High Court or a county court in England and Wales or in the High Court in Northern Ireland, any consistorial action in Scotland or any appeal arising out of any such cause or action;

"affiliation proceedings" means, in relation to Scotland, any action of affiliation and aliment;

and in this subsection "consistorial action" does not include an action of aliment only between husband and wife raised in the Court of Session or an action of interim aliment raised in the sheriff court.

Conclusiveness of convictions for purposes of defamation actions

13.—(1) In an action for libel or slander in which the question whether a person did or did not commit a criminal offence is relevant to an issue arising in the action, proof that, at the time when that issue falls to be determined, that person stands convicted of that offence shall be conclusive evidence that he committed that offence; and his conviction thereof shall be admissible in evidence accordingly.

(2) In any such action as aforesaid in which by virtue of this section a person is proved to have been convicted of an offence, the contents of any document which is admissible as evidence of the conviction, and the contents of the information, complaint, indictment or charge-sheet on which that person was convicted, shall, without prejudice to the reception of any other admissible evidence for the purpose of identifying the facts on which the conviction was based, be admissible in evidence for the purpose of identifying those facts.

(3) For the purposes of this section a person shall be taken to stand convicted of an offence if but only if there subsists against him a conviction of that offence by or before a court in the United Kingdom or by a court-martial there or elsewhere.

(4) Subsections (4) to (6) of section 11 of this Act shall apply for the purposes of this section as they apply for the purposes of that section, but as if in the said subsection (4) the reference to subsection (2) were a reference to subsection (2) of this section.

(5) The foregoing provisions of this section shall apply for the purposes of any action begun after the passing of this Act, whenever the cause of action arose, but shall not apply for the purposes of any action begun before the passing of this Act or any appeal or other proceedings arising out of any such action.

Privilege[3]

Privilege against incrimination of self or spouse

14.—(1) The right of a person in any legal proceedings other than criminal proceedings to refuse to answer any question or produce any document or thing if to do so would tend to expose that person to proceedings for an offence or for the recovery of a penalty—
  (a) shall apply only as regards criminal offences under the law of any part of the United Kingdom and penalties provided for by such law; and
  (b) shall include a like right to refuse to answer any question or produce any document or thing if to do so would tend to expose the husband or wife of that person to proceedings for any such criminal offence or for the recovery of any such penalty.

(2) In so far as any existing enactment conferring (in whatever words) powers of inspection or investigation confers on a person (in whatever words) any right otherwise than in criminal

[3] See Chap. 7, *ante.*

proceedings to refuse to answer any question or give any evidence tending to incriminate that person, subsection (1) shall apply to that right as it applies to the right described in that subsection; and every such existing enactment shall be construed accordingly.

(3) In so far as any existing enactment provides (in whatever words) that in any proceedings other than criminal proceedings a person shall not be excused from answering any question or giving any evidence on the ground that to do so may incriminate that person, that enactment shall be construed as providing also that in such proceedings a person shall not be excused from answering any question or giving any evidence on the ground that to do so may incriminate the husband or wife of that person.

(4) Where any existing enactment (however worded) that—
- (a) confers powers of inspection or investigation; or
- (b) provides as mentioned in subsection (3) above,

further provides (in whatever words) that any answer or evidence given by a person shall not be admissible in evidence against that person in any proceedings or class of proceedings (however described, and whether criminal or not), that enactment shall be construed as providing also that any answer or evidence given by that person shall not be admissible in evidence against the husband or wife of that person in the proceedings or class of proceedings in question.

(5) In this section "existing enactment" means any enactment passed before this Act; and the references to giving evidence are references to giving evidence in any manner, whether by furnishing information, making discovery, producing documents or otherwise.

Privilege for certain communications relating to patent proceedings

15.—(1) This section applies to any communication made for the purpose of any pending or contemplated proceeding under the Patents Act 1949 before the comptroller or the Appeal Tribunal, being either—
- (a) a communication between the patent agent of a party to those proceedings and that party or any other person; or
- (b) a communication between a party to those proceedings and a person other than his patent agent made for the purpose of obtaining, or in response to a request for, information which that party is seeking for the purpose of submitting it to his patent agent.

For the purposes of this subsection a communication made by or to a person acting—
  (i) on behalf of a patent agent; or
  (ii) on behalf of a party to any pending or contemplated proceedings,
shall be treated as made by or to that patent agent or party, as the case may be.

(2) In any legal proceedings other than criminal proceedings a communication to which this section applies shall be privileged from disclosure in like manner as if the proceedings mentioned in the foregoing subsection had been proceedings before the High Court and the patent agent in question had been the solicitor of the party concerned.

(3) For the purposes of this section a communication made for the purpose of a pending or contemplated application for a patent or any other pending or contemplated proceedings under the Patents Act 1949 shall be treated as made for the purpose of contemplated proceedings under that Act before the comptroller or the Appeal Tribunal of every kind to which a proceeding of that description may give rise, whether or not any such proceedings are actually contemplated when the communication is made.

(4) In this section—
  "the comptroller" and "the Appeal Tribunal" have the same meanings as in the Patents Act 1949;
  "patent agent" means a person registered as a patent agent in the register of patent agents maintained pursuant to the Patents Act 1949 or a company lawfully practising as a patent agent in the United Kingdom or the Isle of Man; and
  "party," in relation to any contemplated proceedings, means a prospective party thereto.

Abolition of certain privileges

16.—(1) The following rules of law are hereby abrogated except in relation to criminal proceedings, that is to say—
  (a) the rule whereby, in any legal proceedings, a person cannot be compelled to answer any question or produce any document or thing if to do so would tend to expose him to a forfeiture; and
  (b) the rule whereby, in any legal proceedings, a person other than a party to the proceedings cannot be compelled to produce any deed or other document relating to his title to any land.

(2) The rule of law whereby, in any civil proceedings a party to

Appendix 2

the proceedings cannot be compelled to produce any document relating solely to his own case and in no way tending to impeach that case or support the case of any opposing party is hereby abrogated.

(3) Section 3 of the Evidence (Amendment) Act 1853 (which provides that a husband or wife shall not be compellable to disclose any communication made to him or her by his or her spouse during the marriage) shall cease to have effect except in relation to criminal proceedings.

(4) In section 43(1) of the Matrimonial Causes Act 1965 (under which the evidence of a husband or wife is admissible in any proceedings to prove that marital intercourse did or did not take place between them during any period but a husband or wife is not compellable in any proceedings to give evidence of the matters aforesaid), the words from "but a husband or wife" to the end of the subsection shall cease to have effect except in relation to criminal proceedings.

(5) A witness in any proceedings instituted in consequence of adultery, whether a party to the proceedings or not, shall not be excused from answering any question by reason that it tends to show that he or she has been guilty of adultery; and accordingly the proviso to section 3 of the Evidence Further Amendment Act 1869 and, in section 43(2) of the Matrimonial Causes Act 1965, the words from "but" to the end of the subsection shall cease to have effect.

Consequential amendments relating to privilege[4]

General interpretation and savings

18.—(1) In this Act "civil proceedings" includes, in addition to civil proceedings in any of the ordinary courts of law—
  (a) civil proceedings before any other tribunal, being proceedings in relation to which the strict rules of evidence apply; and
  (b) an arbitration or reference, whether under an enactment or not,

but does not include civil proceedings in relation to which the strict rules of evidence do not apply.

(2) In this Act—
  "court" does not include a court-martial, and in relation to an arbitration or reference, means the arbitrator or umpire and,

---

[4] Section 17, and the Sched. to which it refers, are omitted.

in relation to proceedings before a tribunal (not being one of the ordinary courts of law), means the tribunal;
"legal proceedings" includes an arbitration or reference, whether under an enactment or not;
and for the avoidance of doubt it is hereby declared that in this Act, and in any amendment made by this Act in any other enactment, references to a person's husband or wife do not include references to a person who is no longer married to that person.

(3) Any reference in this Act to any other enactment is a reference thereto as amended, and includes a reference thereto as applied, by or under any other enactment.

(4) Nothing in this Act shall prejudice the operation of any enactment which provides (in whatever words) that any answer or evidence given by a person in specified circumstances shall not be admissible in evidence against him or some other person in any proceedings or class of proceedings (however described).

In this subsection the reference to giving evidence is a reference to giving evidence in any manner, whether by furnishing information, making discovery, producing documents or otherwise.

(5) Nothing in this Act shall prejudice—
  (a) any power of a court, in any legal proceedings, to exclude evidence (whether by preventing questions from being put or otherwise) at its discretion; or
  (b) the operation of any agreement (whenever made) between the parties to any legal proceedings as to the evidence which is to be admissible (whether generally or for any particular purpose) in those proceedings.

(6) It is hereby declared that where, by reason of any defect of speech or hearing from which he is suffering, a person called as a witness in any legal proceedings gives his evidence in writing or by signs, that evidence is to be treated for the purposes of this Act as being given orally.

Northern Ireland

19.—No limitation on the powers of the Parliament of Northern Ireland imposed by the Government of Ireland Act 1920 shall apply so as to preclude that Parliament from enacting a provision corresponding to any provision of this Act.

Short title, repeals, extent and commencement

20.—(1) This Act may be cited as the Civil Evidence Act 1968.
(2) Sections 1, 2, 6(1) (except the words from " "Proceedings' "

Appendix 2 389

to "references") and 6(2)(*b*) of the Evidence Act 1938 are hereby repealed.

(3) This Act shall not extend to Scotland, or, except in so far as it enlarges the powers of the Parliament of Northern Ireland, to Northern Ireland.

(4) The following provisions of this Act, namely sections 13 to 19, this section (except subsection (2)) and the Schedule, shall come into force on the day this Act is passed, and the other provisions of this Act shall come into force on such day as the Lord Chancellor may by order made by statutory instrument appoint; and different days may be so appointed for different purposes of this Act or for the same purposes in relation to different courts or proceedings or otherwise in relation to different circumstances.

APPENDIX 3

POLICE AND CRIMINAL EVIDENCE ACT 1984

PART VII

DOCUMENTARY EVIDENCE IN CRIMINAL PROCEEDINGS[1]

Evidence from documentary records

68.—(1) Subject to section 69 below, a statement in a document shall be admissible in any proceedings as evidence of any fact stated therein of which direct oral evidence would be admissible if—
  (a) the document is or forms part of a record compiled by a person acting under a duty from information supplied by a person (whether acting under a duty or not) who had, or may reasonably be supposed to have had, personal knowledge of the matters dealt with in that information; and
  (b) any condition relating to the person who supplied the information which is specified in subsection (2) below is satisfied.
(2) The conditions mentioned in subsection (1)(b) above are—
  (a) that the person who supplied the information—
    (i) is dead or by reason of his bodily or mental condition unfit to attend as a witness;
    (ii) is outside the United Kingdom and it is not reasonably practicable to secure his attendance; or
    (iii) cannot reasonably be expected (having regard to the time which has elapsed since he supplied or acquired the information and to all the circumstances) to have any recollection of the matters dealt with in that information;
  (b) that all reasonable steps have been taken to identify the person who supplied the information but that he cannot be identified; and
  (c) that, the identity of the person who supplied the information being known, all reasonable steps have been taken to find him, but that he cannot be found.
(3) Nothing in this section shall prejudice the admissibility of any evidence that would be admissible apart from this section.

[1] See Chap. 14, *ante*.

Evidence from computer records

69.—(1) In any proceedings, a statement contained in a document produced by a computer shall not be admissible as evidence of any fact stated therein unless it is shown—
  (*a*) that there are no reasonable grounds for believing that the statement is inaccurate because of improper use of the computer;
  (*b*) that at all material times the computer was operating properly, or if not, that any respect in which it was not operating properly or was out of operation was not such as to affect the production of the document or the accuracy of its contents; and
  (*c*) that any relevant conditions specified in rules of court under subsection (2) below are satisfied.

(2) Provision may be made by rules of court requiring that in any proceedings where it is desired to give a statement in evidence by virtue of this section such information concerning the statement as may be required by the rules shall be provided in such form and at such time as may be so required.

Provisions supplementary to sections 68 and 69

70.—(1) Part I of Schedule 3 to this Act shall have effect for the purpose of supplementing section 68 above.

(2) Part II of that Schedule shall have effect for the purpose of supplementing section 69 above.

(3) Part III of that Schedule shall have effect for the purpose of supplementing both sections.

Microfilm copies

71. In any proceedings the contents of a document may (whether or not the document is still in existence) be proved by the production of an enlargement of a microfilm copy of that document or of the material part of it, authenticated in such manner as the court may approve.

Part VII—supplementary

72.—(1) In this Part of this Act—
  "copy" and "statement" have the same meanings as in Part I of the Civil Evidence Act 1968; and
  "proceedings" means criminal proceedings, including—
    (*a*) proceedings in the United Kingdom or elsewhere before a court martial constituted under the Army Act 1955 or the Air Force Act 1955

(b) proceedings in the United Kingdom or elsewhere before the Courts-Martial Appeal Court—
    (i) on an appeal from a court-martial so constituted or from a court-martial constituted under the Naval Discipline Act 1957; or
    (ii) on a reference under section 34 of the Courts-Martial (Appeals) Act 1968; and
(c) proceedings before a Standing Civilian Court.
(2) Nothing in this Part of this Act shall prejudice any power of any court to exclude evidence (whether by preventing questions from being put or otherwise) at its discretion.

PART VIII

EVIDENCE IN CRIMINAL PROCEEDINGS—GENERAL

Convictions and acquittals[2]

Proof of convictions and acquittals
73.—(1) Where in any proceedings the fact that a person has in the United Kingdom been convicted or acquitted of an offence otherwise than by a Service court is admissible in evidence, it may be proved by producing a certificate of conviction or, as the case may be, of acquittal relating to that offence, and proving that the person named in the certificate as having been convicted or acquitted of the offence is the person whose conviction or acquittal of the offence is to be proved.
(2) For the purposes of this section a certificate of conviction or of acquittal—
(a) shall, as regards a conviction or acquittal on indictment, consist of a certificate, signed by the clerk of the court where the conviction or acquittal took place, giving the substance and effect (omitting the formal parts) of the indictment and of the conviction or acquittal; and
(b) shall, as regards a conviction or acquittal on a summary trial, consist of a copy of the conviction or of the dismissal of the information, signed by the clerk of the court where the conviction or acquittal took place or by the clerk of the court, if any, to which a memorandum of the conviction or acquittal was sent;
and a document purporting to be a duly signed certificate of

---

[2] See Chap. 6, p. 121 and Chap. 16, p. 339, *ante*.

conviction or acquittal under this section shall be taken to be such a certificate unless the contrary is proved.

(3) References in this section to the clerk of a court include references to his deputy and to any other person having the custody of the court record.

(4) The method of proving a conviction or acquittal authorised by this section shall be in addition to and not to the exclusion of any other authorised manner of proving a conviction or acquittal.

Conviction as evidence of commission of offence

74.—(1) In any proceedings the fact that a person other than the accused has been convicted of an offence by or before any court in the United Kingdom or by a Service court outside the United Kingdom shall be admissible in evidence for the purpose of proving, where to do so is relevant to any issue in those proceedings, that that person committed that offence, whether or not any other evidence of his having committed that offence is given.

(2) In any proceedings in which by virtue of this section a person other than the accused is proved to have been convicted of an offence by or before any court in the United Kingdom or by a Service court outside the United Kingdom, he shall be taken to have committed that offence unless the contrary is proved.

(3) In any proceedings where evidence is admissible of the fact that the accused has committed an offence, in so far as that evidence is relevant to any matter in issue in the proceedings for a reason other than a tendency to show in the accused a disposition to commit the kind of offence with which he is charged, if the accused is proved to have been convicted of the offence—
  (a) by or before any court in the United Kingdom; or
  (b) by a Service court outside the United Kingdom,
he shall be taken to have committed that offence unless the contrary is proved.

(4) Nothing in this section shall prejudice—
  (a) the admissibility in evidence of any conviction which would be admissible apart from this section; or
  (b) the operation of any enactment whereby a conviction or a finding of fact in any proceedings is for the purposes of any other proceedings made conclusive evidence of any fact.

Provisions supplementary to section 74

75.—(1) Where evidence that a person has been convicted of an offence is admissible by virtue of section 74 above, then without

prejudice to the reception of any other admissible evidence for the purpose of identifying the facts on which the conviction was based—
  (a) the contents of any document which is admissible as evidence of the conviction; and
  (b) the contents of the information, complaint, indictment or charge-sheet on which the person in question was convicted,
shall be admissible in evidence for that purpose.

(2) Where in any proceedings the contents of any document are admissible in evidence by virtue of subsection (1) above, a copy of that document, or of the material part of it, purporting to be certified or otherwise authenticated by or on behalf of the court or authority have custody of that document shall be admissible in evidence and shall be taken to be a true copy of that document or part unless the contrary is shown.

(3) Nothing in any of the following—
  (a) section 13 of the Powers of Criminal Courts Act 1973 (under which a conviction leading to probation or discharge is to be disregarded except as mentioned in that section);
  (b) section 392 of the Criminal Procedure (Scotland) Act 1975 (which makes similar provision in respect of convictions on indictment in Scotland); and
  (c) section 8 of the Probation Act (Northern Ireland) 1950 (which corresponds to section 13 of the Powers of Criminal Courts Act 1973) or any legislation which is in force in Northern Ireland for the time being and corresponds to that section,
shall affect the operation of section 74 above; and for the purposes of that section any order made by a court of summary jurisdiction in Scotland under section 182 or section 183 of the said Act of 1975 shall be treated as a conviction.

(4) Nothing in section 74 above shall be construed as rendering admissible in any proceedings evidence of any conviction other than a subsisting one.

Confessions

Confessions[3]
76.—(1) In any proceedings a confession made by an accused person may be given in evidence against him in so far as it is

[3] See Chap. 10, *ante*.

relevant to any matter in issue in the proceedings and is not excluded by the court in pursuance of this section.

(2) If, in any proceedings where the prosecution proposes to give in evidence a confession made by an accused person, it is represented to the court that the confession was or may have been obtained—
- (*a*) by oppression of the person who made it; or
- (*b*) in consequence of anything said or done which was likely, in the circumstances existing at the time, to render unreliable any confession which might be made by him in consequence thereof,

the court shall not allow the confession to be given in evidence against him except in so far as the prosecution proves to the court beyond reasonable doubt that the confession (notwithstanding that it may be true) was not obtained as aforesaid.

(3) In any proceedings where the prosecution proposes to give in evidence a confession made by an accused person, the court may of its own motion require the prosecution, as a condition of allowing it to do so, to prove that the confession was not obtained as mentioned in subsection (2) above.

(4) The fact that a confession is wholly or partly excluded in pursuance of this section shall not affect the admissibility in evidence—
- (*a*) of any facts discovered as a result of the confession; or
- (*b*) where the confession is relevant as showing that the accused speaks, writes or expresses himself in a particular way, of so much of the confession as is necessary to show that he does so.

(5) Evidence that a fact to which this subsection applies was discovered as a result of a statement made by an accused person shall not be admissible unless evidence of how it was discovered is given by him or on his behalf.

(6) Subsection (5) above applies—
- (*a*) to any fact discovered as a result of a confession which is wholly excluded in pursuance of this section; and
- (*b*) to any fact discovered as a result of a confession which is partly so excluded, if that fact is discovered as a result of the excluded part of the confession.

(7) Nothing in Part VII of this Act shall prejudice the admissibility of a confession made by an accused person.

(8) In this section "oppression" includes torture, inhuman or degrading treatment, and the use or threat of violence (whether or not amounting to torture).

Confessions by mentally handicapped persons

77.—(1) Without prejudice to the general duty of the court at a trial on indictment to direct the jury on any matter on which it appears to the court appropriate to do so, where at such a trial—
- (a) the case against the accused depends wholly or substantially on a confession by him; and
- (b) the court is satisfied—
  - (i) that he is mentally handicapped; and
  - (ii) that the confession was not made in the presence of an independent person,

the court shall warn the jury that there is special need for caution before convicting the accused in reliance on the confession, and shall explain that the need arises because of the circumstances mentioned in paragraphs (a) and (b) above, but in doing so shall not be required to use any particular form of words.

(2) In any case where at the summary trial of a person for an offence it appears to the court that a warning under subsection (1) above would be required if the trial were on indictment, the court shall treat the case as one in which there is a special need for caution before convicting the accused on his confession.

(3) In this section—

"independent person" does not include a police officer or a person employed for, or engaged on police purposes;

"mentally handicapped", in relation to a person, means that he is in a state of arrested or incomplete development of mind which includes significant impairment of intelligence and social functioning; and

"police purposes" has the meaning assigned to it by section 64 of the Police Act 1964.

Miscellaneous

Exclusion of unfair evidence[4]

78.—(1) In any proceedings the court may refuse to allow evidence on which the prosecution proposes to rely to be given if it appears to the court that, having regard to all the circumstances, including the circumstances in which the evidence was obtained, the admission of the evidence would have such an adverse effect on the fairness of the proceedings that the court ought not to admit it.

(2) Nothing in this section shall prejudice any rule of law requiring a court to exclude evidence.

---

[4] See Chap. 2, pp. 43–45 *et seq., ante.*

Time for taking accused's evidence
79.—If at the trial of any person for an offence—
- (a) the defence intends to call two or more witnesses to the facts of the case; and
- (b) those witnesses include the accused,

the accused shall be called before the other witness or witnesses unless the court in its discretion otherwise directs.

Competence and compellability of accused's spouse[5]
80.—(1) In any proceedings the wife or husband of the accused shall be competent to give evidence—
- (a) subject to subsection (4) below, for the prosecution; and
- (b) on behalf of the accused or any person jointly charged with the accused.

(2) In any proceedings the wife or husband of the accused shall, subject to subsection (4) below, be compellable to give evidence on behalf of the accused.

(3) In any proceedings the wife or husband of the accused shall, subject to subsection (4) below, be compellable to give evidence for the prosecution or on behalf of any person jointly charged with the accused if and only if—
- (a) the offence charged involves an assault on, or injury or a threat of injury to, the wife or husband of the accused or a person who was at the material time under the age of sixteen; or
- (b) the offence charged is a sexual offence alleged to have been committed in respect of a person who was at the material time under that age; or
- (c) the offence charged consists of attempting or conspiring to commit, or of aiding, abetting, counselling, procuring or inciting the commission of, an offence falling within paragraph (a) or (b) above.

(4) Where a husband and wife are jointly charged with an offence neither spouse shall at the trial be competent or compellable by virtue of subsection (1)(a), (2) or (3) above to give evidence in respect of that offence unless that spouse is not, or is no longer, liable to be convicted of that offence at the trial as a result of pleading guilty or for any other reason.

(5) In any proceedings a person who has been but is no longer married to the accused shall be competent and compellable to give evidence as if that person and the accused had never been married.

---

[5] See Chap. 7, pp. 132, 133 *et seq., ante.*

(6) Where in any proceedings the age of any person at any time is material for the purposes of subsection (3) above, his age at the material time shall for the purposes of that provision be deemed to be or to have been that which appears to the court to be or to have been his age at that time.

(7) In subsection (3)(b) above "sexual offence" means an offence under the Sexual Offences Act 1956, the Indecency with Children Act 1960, the Sexual Offences Act 1967, section 54 of the Criminal Law Act 1977 or the Protection of Children Act 1978.

(8) The failure of the wife or husband of the accused to give evidence shall not be made the subject of any comment by the prosecution.

(9) Section 1(d) of the Criminal Evidence Act 1898 (communications between husband and wife) and section 43(1) of the Matrimonial Causes Act 1965 (evidence as to marital intercourse) shall cease to have effect.

Advance notice of expert evidence in Crown Court

81.—(1) Crown Court Rules may make provision for—
  (a) requiring any party to proceedings before the Court to disclose to the other party or parties any expert evidence which he proposes to adduce in the proceedings; and
  (b) prohibiting a party who fails to comply in respect of any evidence with any requirement imposed by virtue of paragraph (a) above from adducing that evidence without the leave of the court.

(2) Crown Court Rules made by virtue of this section may specify the kinds of expert evidence to which they apply and may exempt facts or matters of any description specified in the rules.

Part VIII—Supplementary

Part VIII—Interpretation

82.—(1) In this Part of this Act—
  "confession" includes any statement wholly or partly adverse to the person who made it, whether made to a person in authority or not and whether made in words or otherwise;
  "court-martial" means a court-martial constituted under the Army Act 1955, the Air Force Act 1955 or the Naval Discipline Act 1957 or a disciplinary court constituted under section 50 of the said Act of 1957;
  "proceedings" means criminal proceedings, including—
    (a) proceedings in the United Kingdom or elsewhere before

Appendix 3 399

a court-martial constituted under the Army Act 1955 or the Air Force Act 1955;

(*b*) proceedings in the United Kingdom or elsewhere before the Courts-Martial Appeal Court—

(i) on an appeal from a court-martial so constituted or from a court-martial constituted under the Naval Discipline Act 1957; or

(ii) on a reference under section 34 of the Courts-Martial (Appeals) Act 1968; and

(*c*) proceedings before a Standing Civilian Court; and "Service court" means a court-martial or a Standing Civilian Court.

(2) In this Part of this Act references to conviction before a Service court are references—

(*a*) as regards a court-martial constituted under the Army Act 1955 or the Air Force Act 1955, to a finding of guilty which is, or falls to be treated as, a finding of the court duly confirmed;

(*b*) as regards—
  (i) a court-martial; or
  (ii) a disciplinary court,

constituted under the Naval Discipline Act 1957, to a finding of guilty which is, or falls to be treated as, the finding of the court; and "convicted" shall be construed accordingly.

(3) Nothing in this Part of this Act shall prejudice any power of a court to exclude evidence (whether by preventing questions from being put or otherwise) at its discretion.

SCHEDULE 3[6]

PROVISIONS SUPPLEMENTARY TO SECTIONS 68 AND 69

PART I

PROVISIONS SUPPLEMENTARY TO SECTION 68

1. Section 68(1) above applies whether the information contained in the document was supplied directly or indirectly but, if it was supplied indirectly, only if each person through whom it was supplied was acting under a duty; and applies also where the person compiling the record is himself the person by whom the information is supplied.

[6] See *ante*, pp. 291–295.

2. Where—
   (a) a document setting out the evidence which a person could be expected to give as a witness has been prepared for the purpose of any pending or contemplated proceedings; and
   (b) it falls within subsection (1) of section 68 above,
a statement contained in it shall not be given in evidence by virtue of that section without the leave of the court, and the court shall not give leave unless it is of the opinion that the statement ought to be admitted in the interests of justice, having regard—
      (i) to the circumstances in which leave is sought and in particular to the contents of the statement; and
      (ii) to any likelihood that the accused will be prejudiced by its admission in the absence of the person who supplied the information on which it is based.
3. Where in any proceedings a statement based on information supplied by any person is given in evidence by virtue of section 68 above—
   (a) any evidence which, if that person had been called as a witness, would have been admissible as relevant to his credibility as a witness shall be admissible for that purpose in those proceedings;
   (b) evidence may, with the leave of the court, be given of any matter which, if that person had been called as a witness, could have been put to him in cross-examination as relevant to his credibility as a witness but of which evidence could not have been adduced by the cross-examining party; and
   (c) evidence tending to prove that that person has, whether before or after supplying the information, made a statement (whether oral or otherwise) which is inconsistent with that information shall be admissible for the purpose of showing that he has contradicted himself.
4. A statement which is admissible by virtue of section 68 above shall not be capable of corroborating evidence given by the person who supplied the information on which the statement is based.
5. In deciding for the purposes of section 68(2)(a)(i) above whether a person is unfit to attend as a witness the court may act on a certificate purporting to be signed by a registered medical practitioner.
6. Any reference in section 68 above or this Part of this Schedule to a person acting under a duty includes a reference to a person acting in the course of any trade, business, profession or

other occupation in which he is engaged or employed or for the purposes of any paid or unpaid office held by him.

7. In estimating the weight, if any, to be attached to a statement admissible in evidence by virtue of section 68 above regard shall be had to all the circumstances from which any inference can reasonably be drawn as to the accuracy or otherwise of the statement and, in particular—
   (*a*) to the question whether or not the person who supplied the information from which the record containing the statement was compiled did so contemporaneously with the occurrence or existence of the facts dealt with in that information; and
   (*b*) to the question whether or not that person, or any other person concerned with compiling or keeping the record containing the statement, had any incentive to conceal or misrepresent the facts.

Part II

Provisions Supplementary to Section 69

8. In any proceedings where it is desired to give a statement in evidence in accordance with section 69 above, a certificate—
   (*a*) identifying the document containing the statement and describing the manner in which it was produced;
   (*b*) giving such particulars of any device involved in the production of that document as may be appropriate for the purpose of showing that the document was produced by a computer;
   (*c*) dealing with any of the matters mentioned in subsection (1) of section 69 above; and
   (*d*) purporting to be signed by a person occupying a responsible position in relation to the operation of the computer,
shall be evidence of anything stated in it; and for the purposes of this paragraph it shall be sufficient for a matter to be stated to the best of the knowledge and belief of the person stating it.

9. Notwithstanding paragraph 8 above, a court may require oral evidence to be given of anything of which evidence could be given by a certificate under that paragraph.

10. Any person who in a certificate tendered under paragraph 8 above in a magistrates' court, the Crown Court or the Court of Appeal makes a statement which he knows to be false or does not believe to be true shall be guilty of an offence and liable—

(a) on conviction on indictment to imprisonment for a term not exceeding two years or to a fine or to both;
(b) on summary conviction to imprisonment for a term not exceeding six months or to a fine not exceeding the statutory maximum (as defined in section 74 of the Criminal Justice Act 1982) or to both.

11. In estimating the weight, if any, to be attached to a statement regard shall be had to all the circumstances from which any inference can reasonably be drawn as to the accuracy or otherwise of the statement and, in particular—
 (a) to the question whether or not the information which the information contained in the statement reproduces or is derived from was supplied to the relevant computer, or recorded for the purpose of being supplied to it, contemporaneously with the occurrence or existence of the facts dealt with in that information; and
 (b) to the question whether or not any person concerned with the supply of information to that computer, or with the operation of that computer or any equipment by means of which the document containing the statement was produced by it, had any incentive to conceal or misrepresent the facts.

12. For the purposes of paragraph 11 above information shall be taken to be supplied to a computer whether it is supplied directly or (with or without human intervention) by means of any appropriate equipment.

Part III

Provisions Supplementary to Sections 68 and 69

13. Where in any proceedings a statement contained in a document is admissible in evidence by virtue of section 68 above or in accordance with section 69 above it may be proved—
 (a) by the production of that document; or
 (b) (whether or not that document is still in existence) by the production of a copy of that document, or of the material part of it,
authenticated in such manner as the court may approve.

14. For the purpose of deciding whether or not a statement is so admissible the court may draw any reasonable inference—
 (a) from the circumstances in which the statement was made or otherwise came into being; or

(*b*) from any other circumstances, including the form and contents of the document in which the statement is contained.

15. Provision may be made by rules of court for supplementing the provisions of section 68 or 69 above or this Schedule.

APPENDIX 4

EXTRACTS FROM THE CODE OF PRACTICE FOR THE
DETENTION, TREATMENT AND QUESTIONING OF
PERSONS BY POLICE OFFICERS[1]

10 Cautions[2]

10.1 A person whom there are grounds to suspect of an offence must be cautioned before any questions about it (or further questions if it is his answers to previous questions that provide grounds for suspicion) are put to him for the purpose of obtaining evidence which may be given to a court in a prosecution. He therefore need not be cautioned if questions are put for other purposes, for example, to establish his identity, his ownership of, or responsibility for, any vehicle or the need to search him in the exercise of powers of stop and search.

10.2 When a person who is not under arrest is initially cautioned before or during an interview at a police station or other premises he must at the same time be told that he is not under arrest, is not obliged to remain with the officer but that if he does, may obtain legal advice if he wishes.

10.3 A person must be cautioned upon arrest for an offence unless:
  (a) it is impracticable to do so by reason of his condition or behaviour at the time; or
  (b) he has already been cautioned immediately prior to arrest in accordance with paragraph 10.1 above.

10.4 The caution shall be in the following terms:
  "You do not have to say anything unless you wish to do so, but what you say may be given in evidence."
Minor deviations do not constitute a breach of this requirement provided that the sense of the caution is preserved.

10.5 When there is a break in questioning under caution the interviewing officer must ensure that the person being questioned is aware that he remains under caution. If there is any doubt the caution should be given again in full when the interview resumes.

11 Interviews: general

11.1 No police officer may try to obtain answers to questions

---

[1] Issued under s.66, Police and Criminal Evidence Act, 1984. For the admissibility of the Code in evidence, see s.66(11), *ante*, pp. 199, 201.   [2] See *ante*, p. 182.

or to elicit a statement by the use of oppression, or shall indicate, except in answer to a direct question, what action will be taken on the part of the police if the person being interviewed answers questions, makes a statement or refuses to do either. If the person asks the officer directly what action will be taken in the event of his answering questions, making a statement or refusing to do either, then the officer may inform the person what action the police propose to take in that event provided that that action is itself proper and warranted.

11.2 As soon as a police officer who is making enquiries of any person about an offence believes that a prosecution should be brought against him and that there is sufficient evidence for it to succeed, he shall without delay cease to question him.

11.3 (a) An accurate record must be made of each interview with a person suspected of an offence, whether or not the interview takes place at a police station.

(b) If the interview takes place in the police station or other premises:
- (i) the record must state the place of the interview, the time it begins and ends, the time the record is made (if different), any breaks in the interview and the names of all those present; and must be made on the forms provided for this purpose or in the officer's pocket book or in accordance with the code of practice for the tape recording of police interviews with suspects;
- (ii) the record must be made during the course of the interview, unless in the investigating officer's view this would not be practicable or would interfere with the conduct of the interview, and must constitute either a verbatim record of what has been said or, failing this, an account of the interview which adequately and accurately summarises it.

12 Interviews in police stations

12.1 If a police officer wishes to interview, or conduct enquiries which require the presence of, a detained person the custody officer is responsible for deciding whether to deliver him into his custody.

12.2 In any period of 24 hours a detained person must be allowed a continuous period of at least 8 hours for rest, free from questioning, travel or any interruption arising out of the investigation concerned. This period should normally be at night. The period of rest may not be interrupted or delayed unless there are reasonable grounds for believing that it would:

(i) involve a risk of harm to persons or serious loss of, or damage to, property;
(ii) delay unnecessarily the person's release from custody; or
(iii) otherwise prejudice the outcome of the investigation.

If a person is arrested at a police station after going there voluntarily, the period of 24 hours runs from the time of arrival at the police station and not the time of his arrest.

12.3 A detained person may not be supplied with intoxicating liquor except on medical directions. No person who is unfit through drink or drugs to the extent that he is unable to appreciate the significance of questions put to him and his answers may be questioned about an alleged offence in that condition except in accordance with Annex C.

12.4 As far as practicable interviews shall take place in interview rooms which must be adequately heated, lit and ventilated.

12.5 Persons being questioned or making statements shall not be required to stand.

12.6 Before the commencement of an interview each interviewing officer shall identify himself and any other officers present by name and rank to the person being interviewed.

12.7 Breaks from interviewing shall be made at recognised meal times. Short breaks for refreshment shall also be provided at intervals of approximately two hours, subject to the interviewing officer's discretion to delay a break if there are reasonable grounds for believing that it would:
(i) involve a risk of harm to persons or serious loss of, or damage to, property;
(ii) delay unnecessarily the person's release from custody; or
(iii) otherwise prejudice the outcome of the investigation.

13 Persons at risk: juveniles, and those who are mentally ill or mentally handicapped

13.1 A juvenile or a person who is mentally ill or mentally handicapped, whether suspected or not, must not be interviewed or asked to provide or sign a written statement in the absence of the appropriate adult unless Annex C applies. If he is cautioned in accordance with section 10 above in the absence of the appropriate adult, the caution must be repeated in the adult's presence (unless the interview has by then already finished).

13.2 If, having been informed of the right to legal advice under paragraph 3.6 above, the appropriate adult considers that legal advice should be taken, then the provisions of section 6 of this code apply.

13.3 Juveniles may only be interviewed at their places of education in exceptional circumstances and then only where the principal or his nominee agrees and is present.

17 Charging of detained persons

17.1 When an officer considers that there is sufficient evidence to prosecute a detained person he should without delay bring him before the custody officer who shall then be responsible for considering whether or not he should be charged. Any resulting action should be taken in the presence of the appropriate adult if the person is a juvenile or mentally ill or mentally handicapped.

17.2 When a detained person is charged with or informed that he may be prosecuted for an offence he shall be cautioned in the terms of paragraph 10.4 above.

17.3 At the time a person is charged he shall be given written notice showing particulars of the offence with which he is charged and including the name of the officer in the case, his police station and the reference number for the case. So far as possible the particulars of the charge shall be stated in simple terms, but they shall also show the precise offence in law with which he is charged. The notice shall begin with the following words:

"You are charged with the offence(s) shown below. You do not have to say anything unless you wish to do so, but what you say may be given in evidence."

If the person is a juvenile or is mentally ill or mentally handicapped the notice shall be given to the appropriate adult.

17.4 If at any time after a person has been charged with or informed he may be prosecuted for an offence a police officer wishes to bring to the notice of that person any written statement made by another person or the content of an interview with another person, he shall hand to that person a true copy of any such written statement or bring to his attention the content of the interview record, but shall say or do nothing to invite any reply or comment save to caution him in the terms of paragraph 10.4 above. If the person cannot read then the officer may read it to him. If the person is a juvenile or mentally ill or mentally handicapped the copy shall also be given to, or the interview record brought to the attention of, the appropriate adult.

17.5 Questions relating to an offence may not be put to a person after he has been charged with that offence, or informed that he may be prosecuted for it, unless they are necessary for the purpose of preventing or minimising harm or loss to some other person or to the public or for clearing up an ambiguity in a previous answer or statement, or where it is in the interests of justice that the person should have put to him and have an opportunity to comment on information concerning the offence which has come to light since he was charged or informed that he might be prosecuted. Before any such questions are put he shall be cautioned in the terms of paragraph 10.4 above.

17.6 Where a juvenile is charged with an offence and the custody officer authorises his continuing detention he must try to make arrangements for the juvenile to be taken into the care of a local authority to be detained pending appearance in court unless he certifies that it is impracticable to do so in accordance with section 38(6) of the Police and Criminal Evidence Act 1984.

Annex C

Urgent Interviews

1 If, and only if, an officer of the rank of superintendent or above considers that delay will involve an immediate risk of harm to persons or serious loss of or serious damage to property:
   (a) a person heavily under the influence of drink or drugs may be interviewed in that state; or
   (b) an arrested juvenile or a person who is mentally ill or mentally handicapped may be interviewed in the absence of the appropriate adult; or
   (c) a person who has difficulty in understanding English or who has a hearing disability may be interviewed in the absence of an interpreter.

2 Questioning in these circumstances may not continue once sufficient information to avert the immediate risk has been obtained.

3 A record shall be made of the grounds for any decision to interview a person under paragraph 1 above.

Annex E

Summary of Provisions Relating to Mentally Ill and Mentally Handicapped Persons

1 If an officer has any suspicion or is told in good faith that a person of any age, whether or not in custody, may be mentally ill or mentally handicapped, or cannot understand the significance

of questions put to him or his replies, then he shall be treated as a mentally ill or mentally handicapped person.

2 In the case of a person who is mentally ill or mentally handicapped, "the appropriate adult' means:
  (a) a relative, guardian or some other person responsible for his care or custody;
  (b) someone who has experience of dealing with mentally ill or mentally handicapped persons but is not a police officer or employed by the police; or
  (c) failing either of the above, some other responsible adult who is not a police officer or employed by the police.

3 If the custody officer authorises the detention of a person who is mentally handicapped or is suffering from mental illness he must as soon as practicable inform the appropriate adult of the grounds for the person's detention and his whereabouts, and ask the adult to come to the police station to see the person. If the appropriate adult is already at the police station when information is given as required in paragraphs 3.1 to 3.3 the information must be given to the detained person in his presence. If the appropriate adult is not at the police station when the information is given then the information must be given to the detained person again in the presence of the appropriate adult once that person arrives.

4 If a person brought to a police station appears to be suffering from mental illness, or is incoherent other than through drunkenness alone, or if a detained person subsequently appears to be mentally ill, the custody officer must immediately call the police surgeon or, in urgent cases, send the person to hospital or call the nearest available medical practitioner.

5 A mentally ill or mentally handicapped person must not be interviewed or asked to provide or sign a written statement in the absence of the appropriate adult unless an officer of the rank of superintendent or above considers that delay will involve an immediate risk of harm to persons or serious loss of or serious damage to property. Questioning in these circumstances may not continue in the absence of the appropriate adult once sufficient information to avert the risk has been obtained. A record shall be made of the grounds for any decision to begin an interview in these circumstances.

APPENDIX 5

EXTRACTS FROM THE CODE OF PRACTICE FOR THE
IDENTIFICATION OF PERSONS BY POLICE OFFICERS[1]

2 Identification by witnesses[2]

2.1 In a case which involves disputed identification evidence a parade must be held if the suspect asks for one and it is practicable to hold one. A parade may also be held if the officer in charge of the investigation considers that it would be useful.

2.2 Arrangements for the parade and its conduct shall be the responsibility of an officer in uniform not below the rank of inspector who is not involved with the investigation ('the identification officer'). No officer involved with the investigation of the case against the suspect may take any part in the arrangements for, or the conduct of, the parade.

2.3 A parade need not be held if the identification officer considers that, whether by reason of the unusual appearance of the suspect or for some other reason, it would not be practicable to assemble sufficient people who resembled him to make a parade fair.

2.4 If a suspect refuses or, having agreed, fails to attend an identification parade or the holding of a parade is impracticable, arrangements must if practicable be made to allow the witness an opportunity of seeing him in a group of people. Such a group identification may also be arranged if the officer in charge of the investigation considers, whether because of fear on the part of the witness or for some other reason, that it is, in the circumstances, more satisfactory than a parade.

2.5 If neither a parade nor a group identification procedure is arranged, the suspect may be confronted by the witness. Such a confrontation does not require the suspect's consent, but may not take place unless neither a parade nor a group identification is practicable, whether because the suspect has withheld his consent to them or his co-operation, or for some other reason.

2.6 A witness must not be shown photographs or photofit, identikit or similar pictures for identification purposes if there is a

---

[1] Issued under s.66 Police and Criminal Evidence Act 1984.
[2] See *ante*, p. 111.

suspect already available to be asked to stand on a parade or participate in a group identification.

2.7 Before (a) a parade takes place or (b) a group identification is arranged, the identification officer shall explain to the suspect:
   (i) the purpose of the parade or group identification;
   (ii) the procedures for holding it (including his right to have a solicitor or friend present);
   (iii) where appropriate the special arrangements for juveniles;
   (iv) where appropriate the special arrangements for mentally ill and mentally handicapped persons;
   (v) the fact that he does not have to take part in either procedure and, if it is proposed to hold a group identification, his entitlement to a parade if this can practicably be arranged; and
   (vi) the fact that, if he does not consent to take part in a parade or other group identification, he may be confronted by a witness and his refusal may be given in evidence in any subsequent trial, where a witness might be given an opportunity of identifying him in court.

2.9 Any parade or other group identification must be carried out in accordance with Annex A.

2.10 Any confrontation must be carried out in accordance with Annex B.

2.11 A police officer may take a witness to a particular neighbourhood or place to observe the persons there to see whether he can identify the person whom he said he saw on the relevant occasion. Care should be taken however not to direct the witness's attention to any individual. Where the suspect is at a police station, the provisions of paragraphs 2.1 to 2.10 must apply.

2.12 If photographs or photofit, identikit or similar pictures are shown to a witness for identification purposes this must be done in accordance with Annex C.

Annex A

Identification Parades and Group Identifications

1 A suspect must be given a reasonable opportunity to have a solicitor or friend present, and the identification officer shall ask him to indicate on a second copy of the notice to suspect whether or not he so wishes.

2 A parade may take place either in a normal room or in one equipped with a screen permitting witnesses to see members of

the parade without being seen. The procedures for the composition and conduct of the parade are the same in both cases, subject to paragraph 7 below (except that a parade involving a screen may take place only when the suspect's solicitor, friend or appropriate adult is present or the parade is recorded on video).

7 Once the parade has been formed, everything afterwards in respect of it shall take place in the presence and hearing of the suspect and of any interpreter, solicitor, friend or appropriate adult who is present (unless the parade involves a screen, in which case everything said to or by any witness at the place where the parade is held must be said in the hearing and presence of the suspect's solicitor, friend or appropriate adult or be recorded on video).

8 The parade shall consist of at least eight persons (in addition to the suspect) who so far as possible resemble the suspect in age, height, general appearance and position in life. One suspect only shall be included in a parade unless there are two suspects of roughly similar appearance in which case they may be paraded together with at least twelve other persons. In no circumstances shall more than two suspects be included in one parade and where there are separate parades they shall be made up of different persons.

9 Where all members of a similar group are possible suspects, separate parades shall be held for each member of the group unless there are two suspects of similar appearance when they may appear on the same parade with at least twelve other members of the group who are not suspects. Where police officers in uniform form an identification parade, any numerals or other identifying badge shall be concealed.

10 When the suspect is brought to the place where the parade is to be held, he shall be asked by the identification officer whether he has any objection to the arrangements for the parade or to any of the other participants in it. The suspect may obtain advice from his solicitor or friend, if present, before the parade proceeds. Where practicable, steps shall be taken to remove the grounds for objection. Where it is not practicable to do so, the officer shall explain to the suspect why his objections cannot be met.

11 The suspect may select his own position in the line. Where there is more than one witness, the identification officer must tell the suspect, after each witness has left the room, that he can if he wishes change position in the line. Each position in the line must be clearly numbered, whether by means of a numeral laid on the floor in front of each parade member or by other means.

12 The identification officer is responsible for ensuring that, before they attend the parade, witnesses are not able to:
  (i) communicate with each other about the case or overhear a witness who has already seen the parade;
  (ii) see any member of the parade;
  (iii) on that occasion see or be reminded of any photograph or description of the suspect or to be given any other indication of his identity; or
  (iv) see the suspect either before (or after) the parade.

13 The officer conducting a witness to a parade must not discuss with him the composition of the parade, and in particular he must not disclose whether a previous witness has made any identification.

14 Witnesses shall be brought in one at a time. Immediately before the witness inspects the parade, the identification officer shall tell him that the person he saw may or may not be on the parade and if he cannot make a positive identification he should say so. The officer shall then ask him to walk along the parade at least twice, taking as much care and time as he wishes. When he has done so the officer shall ask him whether the person he saw in person on an earlier relevant occasion is on the parade.

15 The witness should make an identification by indicating the number of the person concerned.

16 If the witness makes an identification after the parade has ended the suspect and, if present, his solicitor, interpreter, or friend shall be informed. Where this occurs, consideration should be given to allowing the witness a second opportunity to identify the suspect.

17 If a witness wishes to hear any parade member speak, adopt any specified posture or see him move, the identification officer shall first ask whether he can identify any persons on the parade on the basis of appearance only. When the request is to hear members of the parade speak, the witness shall be reminded that the participants in the parade have been chosen on the basis of physical appearance only. Members of the parade may then be asked to comply with the witness's request to hear them speak, to see them move or to adopt any specified posture.

20 If a parade is held without a solicitor or a friend of the suspect being present, a colour photograph of the parade shall be taken unless any of the parade members object. A copy of the photograph shall be supplied on request to the suspect or his solicitor within a reasonable time.

Annex B

Confrontation by a Witness

1 The identification officer is responsible for the conduct of any confrontation of a suspect by a witness.

2 The suspect shall be confronted independently by each witness, who shall be asked "Is this the person?" Confrontation must take place in the presence of the suspect's solicitor, interpreter or friend, where he has one, unless this would cause unreasonable delay.

3 Confrontation may take place either in a normal room or one equipped with a screen permitting a witness to see the suspect without being seen. In both cases the procedures are the same except that a room equipped with a screen may be used only when the suspect's solicitor, friend or appropriate adult is present or the confrontation is recorded on video.

Annex C

Showing of Photographs

2 Only one witness shall be shown photographs at any one time. He shall be given as much privacy as practicable and shall not be allowed to communicate with or overhear any other witness in the case.

3 The witness shall be shown not less than twelve photographs at a time. These photographs shall either be in an album or loose photographs mounted in a frame and shall, as far as possible, all be of a similar type. If the photographs include that of a person suspected by the police of the offence concerned, the other photographs shall resemble the suspect as closely as possible.

4 When the witness is shown the photographs, he shall be told that the photograph of the person he saw may or may not be amongst them. He shall not be prompted or guided in any way but shall be left to make any selection without help.

5 If a witness makes a positive identification from photographs, then, unless the person identified is otherwise eliminated from enquiries, other witnesses shall not be shown photographs. But both they and the witness who has made the identification shall be asked to attend an identification parade or group identification if practicable unless there is no dispute about the identification of the suspect.

6 Where the use of a photofit, identikit or similar picture has led

Appendix 5

to there being a suspect available who can be asked to appear on a parade, or participate in a group identification the picture shall not be shown to other potential witnesses.

7 Where a witness attending an identification parade has previously been shown photographs or photofit, identikit or similar pictures then the suspect and his solicitor must be informed of this fact before any committal proceedings or summary trial.

8 Any photographs used shall be retained for production in court if necessary, whether or not an identification is made.

9 Whether or not an identification is made, a record shall be kept of the showing of photographs and of any comment made by the witness.

INDEX

ABUSE OF PROCESS, 333
ACCOMPLICES,
   corroboration of, 169
ACCUSATION,
   silence in face of, 180
   statements made on, 107
ACCUSED,
   character,
      bad, of, 205–236
      cross-examination as to, 221–236
      good, of, 204
   competent witness in own defence, 131
   failure,
      to give evidence, by,
         comment on, 187
      to mention defence, by, 184
ADMISSIBILITY,
   definition of, 10
   weight, distinguished from, 13
ADMISSIONS,
   agent, by, 279
   circumstances of, may be proved, 275
   denial, by, 183
   documents, as to contents of, 274, 347
   formal, 28
   hearsay, founded on, 275
   nature of, 273
   privies, by, 278
   silence, by, 181
   "whole statement" rule, 106, 276
   "without prejudice", 276
AFFIDAVIT,
   former suit, in, admission by, 281
   trial upon, 95
AGE,
   court's own estimation of, 27
   opinion evidence of, 21
AGENT,
   admissions by, 279
AGENT PROVOCATEUR,
   accomplice, not, 170
AGREED WRITTEN STATEMENTS,
   criminal cases, in, 295
ALIBI,
   evidence of, 185

AMBIGUITY,
   extrinsic, evidence to solve, 360
APPEAL,
   fresh evidence on, 127
   power to dismiss, if no miscarriage of justice, 40, 128
ARRANGEMENT OF SUBJECT, , 6
AUTREFOIS ACQUIT, 330
AUTREFOIS CONVICT, 336

BANKERS' BOOKS,
   statements in, 283
BEST EVIDENCE RULE, 12
BIAS OF WITNESS,
   credit affecting, 122
BIBLE,
   entries in family, to prove matters of pedigree, 287
BURDEN OF PROOF,
   accused, when on, 67—60
   evidential, 61–65
   exceptions, as to, 56–57, 67–70
   meanings of, 53
   persuasive, 54–61
      civil cases, in, 54–60
      criminal cases, in, 60–61

CAUTIONS, 182, 404
CHARACTER,
   accused, of, 205–236
   co-accused of, attacks on, 234
   in issue, 205, 226
   party, of, in issue, 18
   prosecution witnesses, of, attacks on, 228
   prosecutrix, of, in rape cases, 120
CHILD,
   sworn evidence of, corroboration of, 174
   unsworn evidence of, corroboration required, 166
   when need not swear or affirm, 130
CIVIL EVIDENCE ACT 1968
   common law exceptions to hearsay rule preserved by, 271
   judgments made evidence by, 338
   statements admissible under, 259–268

417

CO-ACCUSED,
    attacks on, 234
    competence of, as witness, 131
CODES OF PRACTICE, 404–415
    admissibility of, 199
    identification, on, 111, 410
    questioning suspects, on, 202,
        404–409
COLLATERAL MATTERS,
    finality of answers on, 118
COMPELLABILITY OF WITNESSES, 133
COMPETENCY OF WITNESSES. *See*
    INCOMPETENCY.
COMPLAINTS IN SEXUAL CASES, 108
COMPUTER,
    statements produced by, 247, 267,
        294
CONDUCT,
    hearsay evidence, as, 252
    similar. *See* SIMILAR FACT EVIDENCE.
CONFESSIONS,
    admissible,
        common law, at, 192
        Police and Criminal Evidence Act,
            under, 195
    burden of proof, as to, 196
    Code of Practice, 199, App. 4
    discretion, as to, 201
    facts discovered, in consequence of
        inadmissible, 200
    hearsay rule, exception to, 299
    oppression, 197
    rationale of doctrine, as to, 192
    unreliability, 199
    voir dire on, 196
    what are, 199
    whole confession must be proved,
        106, 276
CONSTRUCTION OF WORDS, 37
COPIES OF DOCUMENTS, 349
CORROBORATION,
    accomplices, by, 169
    children, evidence of, 166, 174
    common law rules on, 166
    failure to give evidence is not,
        161
    identification evidence, of, 175
    judge and jury, functions of, as to,
        165
    lies, by, 161
    nature of, 160, 173
    sexual offences, in, 172
    similar fact evidence, by, 218
    statute, required by, 165

COUNSEL,
    admissions by, 280
CREDIBILITY,
    weight, distinguished from, 13
CREDIT,
    bias, affected by, 122
    cross-examination as to, 118
    discrediting own witness, 112
    finality of answers, as to, 118
    physical or mental disability,
        affected by, 123
    previous contradictory statements,
        affected by, 114
    previous convictions, affected by,
        121
    reputation for untruthfulness,
        affected by, 122
CROSS-EXAMINATION, 116–123
    accused, of, character, as to,
        221–236
    credit, as to, 118
    liability to, 116
    objects of, 117

DEATH,
    presumption of, 85
DECEASED PERSONS, DECLARATIONS BY,
    duty, in course of, 297
    homicide, as to, 298
    interest, against, 297
    pedigree, as to, 285
    public rights, as to, 288
DEED,
    estoppel by, 315
    sealing and delivery, proof of, 344
DEFINITIONS, 8 *et seq.*
DEPOSITIONS, 296
DISCOVERY, 140
DISCRETION,
    confessions, as to, 201
    cross-examination of accused as to
        character, as to, 231
    Crown evidence to reject,
        unfairly got, where, 44
        unfairly used, where, 43
    discovery, as to, 141
    generally, 41
    insufficiently relevant evidence, as
        to, 18
    prosecutrix, attacks on, as to, 120
    statements under Civil Evidence Act
        1968, to admit, 270
    stay proceedings which are an abuse
        of process, to, 333

Index

DISCRETION—*cont.*
  warnings on corroboration, as to, 167
  witnesses, to call, 124
DOCUMENTS,
  ancient, 345
  attestation of, proof of, 344
  contents of, proof of, 347–351
  execution of private, proof of, 343–347
  execution of public and judicial, proof of, 343
  extrinsic evidence in relation to. *See* EXTRINSIC EVIDENCE.
  presumptions as to execution of, 346
  primary evidence of contents, 347
  secondary evidence of contents,
    kinds of, 349
    when allowed, 348
DUTY,
  declarations in course of, by deceased persons, 297
DYING DECLARATIONS AS TO HOMICIDE, 298

ESTOPPEL,
  agreement, by, 314
  conduct, by, 311
  deed, by, 315
  issue, 324
  per rem judicatam. *See* RES JUDICATA.
  positive rules of law, cannot override, 308
  promissory, 312
  proprietory, 313
  record, by. *See* RES JUDICATA.
  representation, by, 311
EVIDENCE,
  appeal, on, 126–128
  alibi, 185
  circumstantial, 11, 16
  definitions of, 9
  direct, 11
  extrinsic. *See* EXTRINSIC EVIDENCE.
  generally, contrasted with judicial, 3–6
  identification, 110, 175
  illegally obtained, 44
  parol, 351
  previous trial, at, exception to hearsay rule, when, 295
  primary, as to contents of documents, 347
  real, 26

EVIDENCE—*cont.*
  rebuttal, in, 99
  similar facts, of, 207–221
  sufficiency of, 39
  testimonial, 26
EXAMINATION-IN-CHIEF, 100–116
  discrediting own witness, 112
  leading questions, 101
  object of, 100
  refreshing memory, 101
EXAMINATION OF WITNESSES, 100–125
  judge and jury, by, 124
EXCEPTIONS,
  burden of proof, as to, 56–59, 67–70
EXPERT WITNESS,
  competency of, 122
  opinion of,
    scope of, 22–25
    foundation of, 22
EXTRINSIC EVIDENCE,
  ambiguity, to solve, 360
  capacity of parties, of, 357
  collateral agreements or warranties, of, 356
  consideration, of, 357
  custom or usage, of, 355
  equivocations, to solve, 362
  fraud, of, 357
  interpretation, in aid of, 358
  invalidity of transaction, of, 357
  omitted terms, of, 355
  subsequent modification or rescission, of, 358
  substitute for document, as, 352
  true nature of transaction, of, 356
  vary or contradict a document, to, 354

FACTS,
  collateral, 25
  judge decides, 47
  discovered as result of inadmissible confession, 200
  in issue,
    definition of, 10
    determinable by the pleadings, 15
  punishment, bearing on, 48
  relevant to the issue, 16 *et seq.*
    character, 18
    conduct of others, 19
    habit, 17
    opinion, 20
    similar conduct, 19
    standards of comparison, 17

FACTS—*cont.*
  relevant to the issue—*cont.*
    state of mind, 17
FOREIGN LAW,
  expert evidence on, 22
  judge decides, 47
FRAUD,
  allegations of, standard of proof, 75
  extrinsic evidence of, 357

HANDWRITING,
  evidence of, 22
  proof of, 344
HEARING,
  must be in open court, 95
HEARSAY,
  civil cases, in, 259–290
  criminal cases, in, 291–303
  defined, 239
  exceptions to rule, 255
  grounds of exclusion, 240
  original evidence, contrasted with, 243
  scope of rule, 242–255

IDENTIFICATION,
  evidence, guidelines as to, 177
  opinion evidence of, 21
  parade, 110, 410
  photographs, from, 111, 414
  previous statements of, 110
INCOMPETENCY,
  child, of, 129
  criminal proceedings, in, 131–133
  defective intellect, from, 129
INCRIMINATING QUESTIONS,
  privilege, *re*, 151
INNOCENCE,
  presumption of, 72, 77
INTEREST,
  declarations against, by deceased persons, 297
INTERROGATORIES, 95
INTOXICATION,
  opinion evidence, proof by, 21

JOINDER OF OFFENCES, 218
JOURNALISTS,
  privilege, *re*, 150
JUDGE,
  control of jury by, 37–47
  directed verdicts by, 46
  discretion of. *See* DISCRETION.

JUDGE—*cont.*
  functions of, with regard to evidence, 35–49
  must not act on personal knowledge, 30
  summing up by, 45
JUDGMENTS,
  binding force of, 321
  evidence, as, 337–340
  foreign, 319
  in personam, 321
  in rem, 321
JUDGE'S RULES,
  confessions, as to, 194
JUDICIAL DISCRETION. *See* DISCRETION.
JUDICIAL NOTICE, 29–35
  legally binding, when, 35
  notorious facts, of, 32
JURY,
  functions of, with regard to evidence, 37

LEADING QUESTIONS,
  examination-in-chief, in, 101
LEGITIMACY,
  presumption of, 83

MAPS, 284
MARRIAGE,
  presumption of, 82
MERGER,
  cause of action, of, 335

NO CASE TO ANSWER,
  submission of, 97
NOTICE TO ADMIT, 28
NOTICE TO PRODUCE DOCUMENT,
  when excused, 350

OATHS AND AFFIRMATIONS, 129
OMNIA PRAESUMUNTUR RITE ESSE ACTA, 87
OPINION,
  expert witness, of, 23 *et seq.*
  foundation of, 22
  "ultimate" question, on, 24
  ordinary witnesses, of, 20
  usually irrelevant, 20
ORDER OF PROCEEDINGS, 97

PAROL EVIDENCE, 351
PEDIGREE,
  statements as to, 285
PERSONAL KNOWLEDGE OF TRIBUNAL, 30

Index

PHOTOGRAPHS,
  identification, used in, 111, App. 5
POLICE AND CRIMINAL EVIDENCE ACT 1984,
  confessions admissible under, 195 *et seq.*
  judgments, made evidence by, 339
  statements admissible under, 291 *et seq.*
POSSESSION,
  presumed to follow legal title, 89
  stolen goods, of, 89, 108
PRESUMPTIONS, 77–91
  continuance, of, 90
  death, of, 85
  documents, as to execution of, 345
  fact, of, 89–91
  guilt, of, from conviction, 81, 338
  innocence, of, 72, 77
  intention, of, 90
  law, of, 78–89
    basic fact of, function of, 81
  legitimacy, of, 83
  marriage, of, 82
  regularity, of, 87
PREVIOUS STATEMENTS,
  consistent, 103–111
  inconsistent, 114
PRIVILEGE, 144–155
  confidential communications, 148
  incriminating questions, 151
  journalists, 150
  professional confidences, 144
  public interest protection, compared with, 136
PRIVITY,
  admissions, in relation to, 272
  estoppel by representation, in relation to, 311
  res judicata, in relation to, 327
PRODUCTION OF DOCUMENTS, 347
PROOF,
  burden of, 53 *et seq.*
  definition of, 9
  standard of, 71 *et seq.*
PROSECUTRIX,
  character of, attacks on, 231
PUBLIC OR OFFICIAL DOCUMENTS,
  contents, provable by copy, 351
  statements in, 281
    bankers' books, 283
    registers, 281
    returns, 283
    works of reference, 284

PUBLIC INTEREST PROTECTION, 137–144
  information for the detection of crime, 142
  judicial disclosures, 143
  ministerial certificates, 139
  national security and public functions, 137
  privilege, compared with, 136
PUBLIC RIGHTS,
  statements as to, 288

RAPE,
  cross-examination of prosecutrix, 119
REAL EVIDENCE, 26
REASONABLE DOUBT, 71–73
REBUTTAL,
  evidence in, 99
REBUTTING AFTERTHOUGHT, 107
REBUTTING EVIDENCE, 99
RECORD,
  estoppel by. *See* RES JUDICATA.
  evidence in,
    civil cases, in, 264
    criminal cases, in, 291
RE-EXAMINATION, 123
REFORM,
  proposals for,
    caution, as to, 190
    confessions, as to, 194
    hearsay in criminal cases, as to, 291
    identification of evidence, as to, 176
    right of silence, as to, 189
REFRESHING MEMORY,
  expert, of, 23
  judge, of, 33
  witness, of, 101
RELEVANCE,
  definition of, 10
  matter of degree, 17
REPLY,
  right of, 97
REPUTATION,
  witness for untruthfulness, of, 122
RES GESTAE, 109
  bad character, evidence of, as, 206
  definition of, 15
  statements as part of, exceptions to hearsay rule, 300
RES JUDICATA, 317–336
  cause of action estoppel, 322
  criminal proceedings, in, 330

RES JUDICATA—cont.
  estoppel *per rem judicatam*, 320
  final judgment of competent court, 318
  issue estoppel, 324
  matrimonial proceedings, in, 327
  merger, 335
RIGHT OF SILENCE,
  in court, 187
  out of court, 180
  proposals for reform of, 189

SELF-SERVING STATEMENTS,
  rule against, 104
SEXUAL OFFENCES,
  corroboration, in, 172
SIMILAR FACT EVIDENCE, 207–221
  categories, of, 215
  corroboration, as, 218
  criminal propensity, to prove, 214
  cross-examination of accused, when allowing, 225
  discretion to exclude, 217
  joinder of offences, 218
  principle of admission, of, 209
SOLICITOR,
  admissions by, 280
SPOUSE,
  accused of, competence as witness, 133
  compellability, 134
STAMPS, 346
STANDARD OF PROOF,
  civil cases, in, 74
  criminal cases, in, 71
STATEMENTS,
  agreed written, criminal cases in, 295
  bankers' books, in, 283
  deceased persons, by. *See* DECEASED PERSONS, DECLARATIONS BY.

STATEMENTS—cont.
  party's hearing, in, 181
  public or official documents, in. *See* PUBLIC DOCUMENTS.
  records, in. *See* RECORD.
  spontaneous, by participants in event, 301
SUMMING UP, 45

TESTIMONY, 26

VERDICT,
  directed, 46
  perverse, 41
  unsafe or unsatisfactory, 40
VOIR DIRE, 47, 196

WEIGHT OF EVIDENCE,
  credibility, distinguished from, 13
  definition of, 13
  jury, to decide on, 37
"WITHOUT PREJUDICE", 276
WITNESSES,
  adverse, 112
  compellability of, 133
  competence of, 129
  examination of, 100–126
  expert, 21 *et seq.*
  hostile, 113
  judge, called by, 125
  previous statements, by,
    admissible under Civil Evidence Act 1968. . .261
    evidence under s. 3, Civil Evidence Act 1968 . . . 268
  unfavourable, 112
WORDS,
  ordinary, in statute, meaning of, 38
WORKS OF REFERENCE, 284